THE SOVIET
NATIONALITY READER

Published in cooperation with the
Nationalities and Siberian Studies Program,
W. Averell Harriman Institute
for Advanced Study of the Soviet Union,
Columbia University

THE SOVIET NATIONALITY READER

The Disintegration in Context

EDITED BY

RACHEL DENBER

WESTVIEW PRESS

Boulder • San Francisco • Oxford

Copyright © 1992 by Westview Press, Inc.

Published in 1992 in the United States of America by Westview Press, Inc., 5500 Central Avenue, Boulder, Colorado 80301-2847, and in the United Kingdom by Westview Press, 36 Lonsdale Road, Summertown, Oxford OX2 7EW

Library of Congress Cataloging-in Publication Data
The Soviet nationality reader : the disintegration in context / [edited by]
    Rachel Denber.
        p.   cm.
    ISBN 0-8133-1026-1 (hc.)   ISBN 0-8133-1027-X (pbk.)
    1. Federal government—Soviet Union.   2. Soviet Union—Politics
and government—1985–   3. Nationalism—Soviet Union.   4. Soviet
Union—Ethnic relations.   5. Soviet Union—Economic policy—1986–
I. Denber, Rachel.
JN6520.S8S7   1992
321.02′0947—dc20   91-23167
                                                                                          CIP

Printed and bound in the United States of America

The paper used in this publication meets the requirements
of the American National Standard for Permanence of Paper
for Printed Library Materials Z39.48-1984.

10   9   8   7   6   5   4   3   2   1

CONTENTS

PART IV
Economy

PART V
Language

PART VI
Nationalism and Nationalist Movements

PART VII
Coping with the Nationalities Crisis

ACKNOWLEDGMENTS

The Program on Nationalities and Siberian Studies at the Harriman Institute for Advanced Study of the Soviet Union provided funding for this volume. My warmest thanks to Professor Alexander Motyl for his encouragement, to Colin Barraclough, Thomas Christenfeld, and Joan Lofgren for tireless technical support, and to Tim Christenfeld for everything else.

Rachel Denber

EDITOR'S NOTE

The selections in this volume appear in the form in which they were first published. They retain their original style, spelling, and footnote format. However, tables and figures have been omitted (except in Chapter 15), and some articles have been condensed; otherwise this book would be far too fat to fit between the covers.

R.D.

THE FORMER SOVIET REPUBLICS

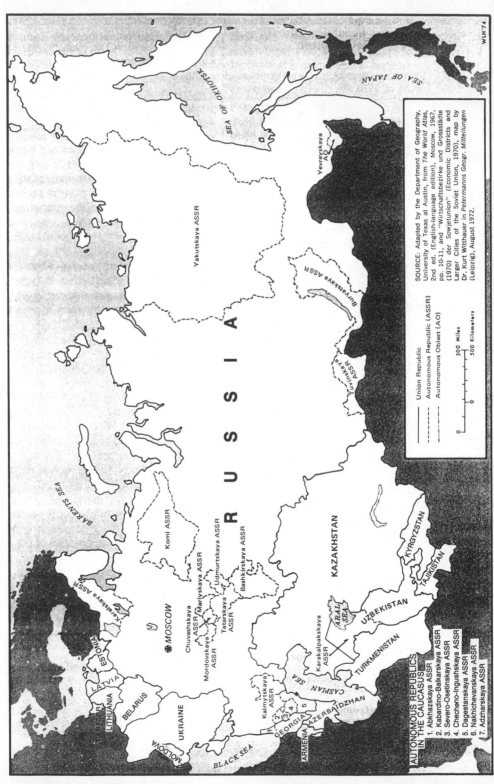

SOURCE: Adapted by the Department of Geography, University of Texas at Austin, from *The World Atlas*, 2nd ed. (English-language edition), Moscow, 1967, pp. 10–11, and "Wirtschaftsbezirke und Grossstädte (1970) der Sowjetunion" (Economic Districts and Larger Cities of the Soviet Union, 1970), map by Dr. Kurt Witthauer in *Petermanns Geogr. Mitteilungen* (Leipzig), August 1972.

Union Republic
Autonomous Republic (ASSR)
Autonomous Oblast (AO)

0   500 Miles
0   500 Kilometers

 AUTONOMOUS REPUBLICS
IN THE CAUCASUS:
1. Abkhazskaya ASSR
2. Kabardino-Balkarskaya ASSR
3. Severo-Osetinskaya ASSR
4. Checheno-Ingushskaya ASSR
5. Dagestanskaya ASSR
6. Nakhichevanskaya ASSR
7. Adzharskaya ASSR

GENERAL INTRODUCTION

The Soviet government, presiding over more than a hundred nationalities, always sought to discourage nationalism, to maintain a firm grip on centralized power, and to avoid the interethnic violence that racked other multiethnic states. At the same time, however, it ruled a federation structured along ethnic lines. Thus, despite their totalitarian-authoritarian nature, past Soviet regimes had to choose whether and how to accommodate the economic and political claims of the nationalities.

While these issues long produced tensions in the USSR, after Mikhail Gorbachev began reforming the Soviet political and economic systems, radically breaking with the legacies of Leonid Brezhnev and Joseph Stalin, they developed into a full-blown crisis. As an unintended result of Gorbachev's programs, the central government proved unable to prevent bids from republics for sovereignty or outright independence from the Soviet Union.

In 1988, nationalist movements in various republics began demanding more republic autonomy; several republics later formed governments (in most cases competitively elected) that rejected Moscow's authority to rule. Beginning in 1989, six republics declared their intention to secede from the Soviet Union,[1] and nearly all republics insisted on the preeminence of republic laws over USSR (Union) laws. These developments threatened the Soviet Union's very integrity, and, consequently, Moscow lost not only its capacity to dictate policy to the republics but virtually all control over events in most non-Russian republics and in even the Russian Soviet Federated Republic (RSFSR). Gorbachev could no longer rely on the precepts of "socialist internationalism" to justify Moscow's domination of the republics, and the use of violence and coercion to punish breakaway republics grew increasingly unsuccessful. The failed coup in August 1991 caused the final collapse of Moscow's authority, leaving power in the hands of republic governments.

This crisis, though devastating, should not eclipse the importance of how pre-Gorbachev regimes managed for seventy years to prevent the Soviet nationalities problem from seriously threatening the USSR's political stability. This is no mean feat in a country as ethnically diverse as the Soviet Union. Russians, Ukrainians, Uzbeks, Belorussians, Kazakhs, Azerbaijanis, Armenians, Georgians, Moldavians, Tadzhiks, Latvians, Lithuanians, Turkmens, Kirghiz,

1

and Estonians are among the most numerous nationalities, but the Soviet Union is also home to more than ninety other nationalities— from the numerous Tatars, Chuvash, and Bashkirs to the dozen or so smaller nationalities that count fewer than 2,000 members each.[2] The major nationalities have fifteen union republics bearing their names. These are the main components of the Soviet federation, endowed by the USSR Constitution with a broad array of formal rights to self-determination and self-rule. Within these fifteen union republics lie twenty autonomous republics, eight autonomous provinces, and ten autonomous areas, which are the homelands of some of the smaller nationalities.

Soviet regimes have historically tolerated only limited expressions of national diversity, yet the peoples of the Soviet Union embrace diverse cultural traditions. They practice a variety of religions (including Eastern Orthodox, Islam, Roman Catholicism, Protestantism, and Judaism) and speak a wide array of languages from different language families. Russian is spoken primarily in the Russian Republic but is considered by Moscow as the lingua franca throughout the Union. The languages in the western part are Ukrainian and Belorussian (also belonging to the Slavic family), Estonian (of the Finno-Ugric language family), Moldavian (a Romance language close to Romanian), Lithuanian, and Latvian. To the south of Moscow but west of the Urals, Udmurt, Mari, and Mordvin are spoken. The peoples of the Caucasus speak Georgian, Armenian, and a few languages of the Turkic and Iranian families, including Ossete and Kurdish. Many other Turkic languages are spoken in Central Asia, southern Siberia, and in the Urals, including Uzbek, Kirghiz, Kazakh, Azerbaijani, Karakalpak, Tatar, Meskhitian, Chuvash, Yakut, and Gagauz (which is also spoken by the Gagauz minority in Moldavia).

In spite of this national and linguistic diversity, the USSR was hierarchically ruled until the Gorbachev era by a single entity—the Communist Party of the Soviet Union (CPSU). The philosophical foundation of the Party's rule was that the elimination of class divisions would lead to ethnic harmony, and the Soviet Union's federal structure expressed this idea in constitutional terms. The Party based its political domination of the republics on the principle of democratic centralism, or subordination to the highest unit of administration, i.e., Moscow.

The philosophical, constitutional, and political approaches of the pre-Gorbachev regimes to national diversity generated serious tensions but did not necessarily lead directly to the disintegration of the superpower. *The Soviet Nationality Reader* is intended to help the student understand how past Soviet regimes dealt with the nationalities question and how their legacy contributed to the present nationalities crisis. The book also assesses the effect that Gorbachev's reforms had on the unraveling of this system of rule and his government's attempts to cope with the crisis it unwittingly unleashed.

This volume offers material on many aspects of the nationalities question, aims to include diverse scholarly views that have enduring relevance, and seeks to impart a sense of the major issues and conflicts in academic debates concerning the Soviet nationalities. Part I provides a historical overview of the emergence of the Soviet Union and introduces the main concepts of Leninist and Stalinist ideology that guided later policy. The material in Part II outlines the development of Soviet federalism and suggests the particular problems federalism faces in a multinational socialist state.

The remainder of the anthology assesses particular policy problems, all of them affected by the important problem of control. The Marxist-Leninist approach to politics and the economy called for a strict centralization of control through Party and government institutions in Moscow, but both the country's federal structure and its national diversity inhibited the efficacy of such central control. Finding suitable elites and political cadres to administer the republics, then, was imperative (Part III). Likewise, the centralized, Stalinist command economy served Moscow's interest in industrialization, but it aggravated interethnic tensions and did not eliminate conflicts between the republics and Moscow over the distribution of resources, regional development, and local economic autonomy (Part IV). To prevent a Tower of Babel of more than a hundred languages, Moscow implemented a language policy that encouraged the use of Russian in order to provide an effective means of communication throughout the country. This policy, however, clearly clashed with the interests of non-Russians, for whom language is a sensitive matter, involving strong emotional and historical ties (Part V).

All Soviet leaders since Lenin proclaimed the goal of eliminating nationalism; many Western academics argue that the final goal of many of the country's nationalities polices was to prevent national consciousness from becoming a force that could be marshaled into an oppositionist movement. Part VI evaluates the extent to which nationalism threatened the stability of the Soviet regimes prior to Gorbachev and discusses the nationalist movements that brought about the Soviet Union's federal crisis. Finally, Part VII assesses Gorbachev's reform program, how it contributed to the federal crisis, and the measures Gorbachev took to resolve that crisis.

II.

The Soviet nationalities question refers to ethnopolitics and the issue of self-determination. "Ethnopolitics" generally describes the political activities—mobilization, use of resources, planning, stratagems, and the like—of elites and masses of different nationalities who make specific claims vis-à-vis other national groups and Moscow and who may or may not seek independence. It also encompasses a set of regime strategies—in addition to coercion—to prevent national groups from seeking independence, to respond to national claims, and to solve the problems generated by the Soviet Union's widely diverse ethnonational composition and federal structure.

Combined, the problems impinge upon Moscow's capacity to rule with complete independence. Moscow had to implement policies concerning the recruitment of political leaders in the republics, the promotion of republic elites into the central government and Party bureaucracies, which languages would be spoken in the republics, which languages would be taught in schools, and how to make regional economic development more equal. These policies, and the responses to them, often pitted the major nationalities, represented by the union republics, against the "center." The nationalities question also encompasses the issue of how the Soviet nationalities have historically tried to gain more control over their destinies and emphasizes Moscow's interest in eliminating nationalism, or at least in minimizing its effect on politics.

At the time of the formation of the Soviet Union, many nationalities wanted to form independent states, but the Bolsheviks employed tactics ranging from enticement to coercion to convince them to join the Soviet Union (see Chapter 2). Stalin's policies halted quests for national autonomy and cultural independence, but after his death the republics once again sought greater autonomy in policy-making (see Chapter 3). Nikita Khrushchev and Brezhnev had to deal with increasingly bold expressions of nationalism from the minorities and with more demanding political claims from the republic elites. This situation continued throughout the early part of the Gorbachev reform period; after 1988, however, the relaxation of coercion permitted the emergence of radical demands for independence. The Khrushchev and Brezhnev periods witnessed rising national tensions, but the Gorbachev period gave rise to a real nationalities crisis.

Most of the chapters in this volume are devoted to pre-Gorbachev nationalities problems in order to define the context in which the USSR's nationalities crisis has unfolded. A rich and useful scholarly literature is now appearing on the evolution of this crisis.[3] Some parts of this literature are represented here (mainly in Parts VI and VII, which deal most directly with the current crisis), but the material in this book is by no means a comprehensive sampling. All the literature included here should encourage the student to understand the origins of the Soviet Union's federal crisis not only as the "unintended consequence"[4] of Gorbachev's reforms but also in terms of what he inherited from the Brezhnev era.[5]

III.

Since the fundamental crisis of governability confronted Gorbachev's government with problems that differed significantly from those of the Brezhnev era, his response to the nationalities problem also differed from that of his predecessors.[6] During the Brezhnev era, the regime had firm faith in Marxist-Leninist ideology, which subjected the understanding of nation and nationalism to class analysis. The nations was viewed as an epiphenomenon of bourgeois society, and the victory of socialism in the USSR meant that national differences would gradually disappear. Members of the USSR's diverse nationalities were proclaimed to be embracing class rather than national identity and to have a stronger sense of Soviet patriotism than of loyalty to their respective ethnonational groups. As part of the construction of a communist state, the effort to erase wide economic disparities across the USSR would supposedly provide the material basis necessary for members of national groups to abandon their national loyalties and emotional ties (see Chapter 10).

The formula "national in form—socialist in content," inherited from Lenin's approach to the Soviet federation, explains how national diversity in social life could supposedly persist under socialism. National republics and federal forms of economic and political organization could continue to exist because they helped to fulfill socialist goals and to implement policies conceived in Moscow; national cultures could flourish—primarily in the teaching of national languages, folk dances, and other harmless manifestations—so long as they carried the message of socialism (see Chapter 13). The national question—the problem of self-determination and autonomy—was therefore solved: National integration (internationalization) was taking place voluntarily, or so the regime claimed.

The quasi-totalitarian regimes of Brezhnev, Yuri Andropov, and Konstantin Chernenko were politically stable.[7] Coercion kept most expressions of nationalism underground and in the samizdat presses, and a network of loyal political cadres and elites could enforce Moscow's policy priorities in the republics. Yet, despite the fact that these regimes enjoyed order and stability, one should question their pronouncements that the nationality problem had been solved; indeed, much of the literature in this volume exposed these pronouncements as myths even as they were being perpetuated. Previously Moscow had at its disposal greater resources than Gorbachev had for curbing the expression of nationalism, limiting ethnic violence, and ensuring loyalty in the republics to Moscow. As the contents of this volume demonstrate, however, the repressive policies not only failed to achieve their stated goals but also contributed to national unrest in the pre-Gorbachev years and to a host of pent-up demands that were released under *perestroika*.

Teresa Rakowska-Harmstone, for example, argues that nationality policy aimed at modernizing the Soviet economy and integrating the nations of the USSR generally failed, spurred nationalist sentiment, and revived old ethnic antagonisms (see Chapter 16). In the area of language policy, John Dunlop's piece discusses the fierce Georgian and Estonian reactions to Moscow's attempts to make more non-Russians learn Russian (see Chapter 13). Soviet elites policy enjoyed some success in training political cadres in the republics and in imparting to them a sense of having a stake in the system. Moreover, Brezhnev found an equation for keeping republic elites in check so that they would administer republic politics and implement USSR policies (see Chapters 7 and

8 respectively). These policies, however, did not prevent the growth of regionalism or of entrenched, national "family circles" around the local elites (see Chapter 16). Similarly, the chapters on the economy in Part IV point out that though economic equalization did reallocate resources to needy regions, this policy did not expunge nationalism.

A more fundamental source of the nationality problems that the Brezhnev regime sought to resolve concerned the federal structure of the USSR. The conclusion to Richard Pipes' chapter on the establishment of the USSR (Chapter 2) recognizes that the federal structure may well be "historically one of the most consequential aspects of the formation of the Soviet Union." Academic debates among Western scholars (and recently, among Soviet scholars) address the degree to which this federation has been a hollow form for a unitary state and even for imperial rule.[8] No matter how history judges this question, the federal structure has had a tremendous impact on the way Moscow and the republics deal with each other. In 1980, Seweryn Bialer warned of the dangerous "dualism" of Soviet federalism: "In theory and practice it denies any but the slimmest margins of autonomy to the federated nationalities, but at the same time its symbolic institutions and administrative framework provide the base from which the struggle for national autonomy can be waged."[9] Philip Roeder's 1991 article (Chapter 6) revives this debate by examining how post-Stalinist policies created republic elites that would later give these symbolic institutions new meaning, and why these institutions became "vehicles of protest."

Many specialists recognized that the nationality "factor" was potentially the greatest danger to the stability of the Soviet regimes of Brezhnev and his successors;[10] others argued that it would not be a destabilizing factor, at least not during the Brezhnev era. Gail Lapidus, for example, maintained in 1984 (see Chapter 17) that a combination of factors prevented the realization of this destablilizing potential. While Soviet citizens indeed did not abandon their ethnonational identities, there was no imminent threat of the rise of nationalist movements. Nationalist "incidents" occurred sporadically in Lithuania, Estonia, Georgia, and elsewhere, but generally the state kept a lid on ethnic violence and eliminated the possibilities for collective action on the part of dissident nationalists.

The articles by Roeder, Stanley Vardys, Paul Goble, and Alexander Motyl (Chapters 6, 18, 21, and 22, respectively) explain how Gorbachev's reforms—*glasnost, perestroika,* and democratization—permitted the unleashing of ethnic grievances and the formation of nationalist movements. The freedom of expression enshrined in *glasnost* led the Soviet regime to tolerate new forms of ethnopolitics and expressions of previously illegal nationalist sentiment—for example, the open demands of the Baltic republics for wider use of native languages, exposition of the tragic consequences of the Stalin era for particular nationalities, and the hoisting of the flag of pre-Soviet Estonia. In the struggle to revive the disaster-stricken Soviet economy, *perestroika* entailed economic decentralization, which promised more power over economic decision making to the republics.

Democratization, including relatively open elections to the USSR Congress of People's Deputies and elections for republic leaders in 1989, made republic elites more accountable to their constituencies. Significantly, this policy also sanctioned the organization of unofficial political groups and called for the rule of law, the end of arbitrary domination by the Communist Party, and the end of extensive use of coercion and violence as means of social control.[11] With *glasnost'*, Gorbachev questioned the infallibility of the Party and Marxist-Leninist ideology, but the republics were the first to openly and completely reject communism as a form of social and political organization, a position Moscow slowly came to accept. Thus, Moscow lost ideology as a moral adhesive to help hold the Soviet federation together.

It is baffling that the Soviet leaders could not foresee the dramatic consequences the new policies would have on Moscow's control over the republics. Nationalist movements and popular front organizations in the Baltic republics and Armenia (then later in nearly every republic of the USSR) forced republic elites to take up nationalist postures, to make demands for autonomy from Moscow, and to have reversed many of the nationality policies pursued by the previous Soviet regimes. Vardys's account of the genesis of the Lithuanian popular front and Ronald Suny's narrative of the Armenian movement for the transfer of control over Nagorno-Karabakh (Chapters 18 and 19 respectively) illustrate these processes.

Under the leadership of elites beholden to their respective constituencies, the union republics—and autonomous republics and even autonomous regions—became, in Roeder's words, "vehicles of protest."[12] The lines of authority and divisions of jurisdiction between Moscow and the republics have dissolved, which has allowed federal institutions to revive and to serve the interests of the republics. This new life for federal institutions is most apparent in the activities of republic Supreme Soviets. Throughout 1990 and 1991, these republic parliaments reversed the nationality policies implemented in the pre-Gorbachev era, and legislation and government decrees often advanced the interests of the titular nationality to the perceived detriment of residents of other ethnonational origins in a republic. Thus, the Baltic republics, Georgia, and Moldavia sought to end what they saw as a conscious Soviet policy of russification (see Part VI) and adopted language laws that require all citizens to use the language of the republic in public life and in education. Some republics have enacted citizenship legislation that excludes residents who are not citizens of the republic from benefits such as access to scarce goods and the right to run in competitive elections.

Moreover, the republics—including the RSFSR—adopted laws on banking, taxation, enterprise activity, privatization, customs, and other areas of economic and political life that contradicted all-Union legislation. The "war of laws" was waged with a vengeance, as nearly all republic supreme soviets enacted declarations of sovereignty, claiming that republic law takes precedence over all-Union law. Moscow responded frequently by issuing decrees that declared certain republic laws illegal and that call for the enforcement of all-Union laws, but these salvos proved ineffective.

The Republics have asserted themselves in other ways. The RSFSR, for example, has refused to contribute to the federal budget the amount Moscow prescribed. Since the USSR relies on the RSFSR for the lion's share of the federal budget, this bold move has pushed the Soviet economy into deeper peril. In the Baltic republics, national guards have formed and young men have refused to serve in the USSR's armed forces. It is important to note that all of these actions and other assertions of independence derive from long-standing grievances against centralized rule from Moscow—and in the case of the non-Russian republics, against rule by Russians.

In addition to the reaction against Russification, the republics' determination to undo through legislation the long-standing policy of economic equalization was especially fierce. The RSFSR, for example, announced in January 1991 that its resources—including precious metals and petroleum—belong exclusively to the RSFSR and that the RSFSR alone has jurisdiction to adopt and implement economic policy. Most republics claimed that they gave more than they have received under the policy of equalization, and they were eager to reinstate local economic development to a position of high priority. These open calls by non-Russians for autonomy and independence weakened Moscow's already shaky position of political superiority in the Soviet federation. Moscow's position was further weakened when the RSFSR began in mid-1990 to behave as an injured party with claims against the all-Union government. The RSFSR legislative and political activities indeed effected the institutional separation of the RSFSR from the USSR, which non-Russians (according to Roman Szporluk in Chapter 18) suggest is a *sine qua non* for overcoming imperial thinking and practices in the Soviet Union.

All of these activities exposed the lack of agreement on the boundaries of authority between Moscow and the republics. And, as Stephan Kux argues, Moscow did not have authoritative, legitimate political institutions to resolve federal conflicts (see Chapter 23). Gorbachev's attempts to resolve the crisis were unsuccessful as long as he clung to the idea that a solution in the form of a new Union treaty could be imposed from above on the republics and that the interests of the center could continue unequivocally to be advanced over those of the republics. The Union treaty negotiations were, as Kux presciently notes, tarnished from the beginning.

Gorbachev turned sharply away from this centrist approach to the Union treaty in April 1991. The "nine-plus-one" talks (symbolizing the nine cooperating republics and Moscow) held out a vision of federal relations close to the Baltic republics' own vision advanced in early 1988: powers delegated from the republics to Moscow, republic jurisdiction over most government functions, and a single currency for the entire country (see Chapter 18). The chapters in Part VII demonstrate that Moscow's slowness to agree to republic politics proved costly. In later negotiations with the leaders of nine union republics, Gorbachev had to relinquish many powers that previous Union treaty drafts had preserved for Moscow, including Moscow's right to levy taxes in the republics and Union jurisdiction over many of the republics' natural resources. He also agreed that the republics can make direct contributions to the drafting of the Union treaty, an approach that demonstrated more respect for the authority of the republics and might have proved more fruitful than simply imposing Moscow's idea of a renovated federation upon the republics. A truncated Soviet Union might continue to cohere without socialism, without the newly independent Baltic states, and with a radically different political arrangement between Moscow and the republics. The collapse of the old Soviet federation may seem to vindicate those scholars who argued during the Brezhnev era that the Soviet nationalities problem would bring about the end of the Soviet Union,[13] but the works in this volume should shed light on why the Soviet system endured for as long as it did and help us understand why Gorbachev's centrist policies, aimed at containing the current crisis, failed so miserably.

Notes

1. Lithuania, Latvia, Estonia, Georgia, Moldavia, and Armenia.

2. A classic guide to the many Soviet nationalities is Zev Katz, ed., *The Handbook of Major Soviet Nationalities*.

3. See, for example, Lubomyr Hajda and Mark Beissinger, eds., The *Nationalities Factor in Soviet Politics and* Society (Boulder, Colo.: Westview Press, 1990); Alexander J. Motyl, *Sovietology, Rationality, Nationality: Coming to Grips with Nationalism in the USSR* (New York: Columbia University Press, 1990); Alexander J. Motyl, ed., Building Bridges: *From Soviet Studies to Post Soviet Studies* (forthcoming); Nahylo and Swoboda, *Soviet Disunion* (New York: Free Press, 1990); Viktor Zaslavsky, *Das Russische Imperium unter Gorbatschow* (Berlin: Wagenbach, 1991). *Soviet Nationalities Papers* has published transcripts of the Harriman Institute's annual conference on Soviet nationalities: see "The Soviet Nationalities and Gorbachev," "The Soviet Nationalities Against Gorbachev," and "The Soviet Nationalities Despite Gorbachev," in Spring 1989, Spring 1990, and Fall 1991 respectively. *The Journal of Soviet Nationalities*, which began publication in the spring of 1990, has had many excellent scholarly articles on the nationalities crisis. Finally, for an excellent scholarly work on the Soviet nationalities question generally, see Gerhard Simon, *Natisionalismus und Nationalitatenpolitik in der Sowetunion: von der totaltarien Diktatur zur nachtstalinshchen Gesellschaft* (Baden-Baden: Nomos, 1986), which has just been translated into English under the title *Nationalism and Policy toward the Nationalities in the Soviet Union* (Boulder: Westview

Press, 1991).

4. See especially Alexander Motyl's article in Chapter 22 for a treatment of the nationalities crisis in terms of the "unintended consequences" of Gorbachev's reforms. See also, Olcott, *infra*, note 9.

5. Phillip Roeder in particular favors this approach. See Chapter 6.

6. For a good, general analysis of how Brezhnev dealt with the nationalities question and how it affected state stability, see Seweryn Bialer, *Stalin's Successors* (New York: Cambridge University Press, 1980), pp. 207-225.

7. For an overview of the literature on stability and its particular application to the Soviet Union, see Bialer, *op. cit.*

8. Indeed, Pipes goes so far as to say that the Soviet Union in 1923 was "a unitary, centralized, totalitarian state such as the tsarist state had never been." See p. 80.

9. See Bialer, *op. cit.*, p. 210.

10. See Alexandre Bennigsen and Marie Broxup, *The Islamic Threat to the Soviet State* (London: Croom Helm, 1983), and Hélène Carrère d'Encausse, *Decline of an Empire, passim*.

11. This does not mean that Moscow renounced all use of coercion against nationalist, as the military interventions in Lithuania in 1991, in Azerbaijan in 1990 through the present, and in Georgia in 1989 demonstrate.

12. For an excellent summary of the actions undertaken by revived union republics in 1990-91, see Martha Brill Olcott, "The Soviet (Dis)Union," in *Foreign Policy*, no. 82 (Spring 1991), pp. 118-136.

13. Philip Roeder and Gail Lapidus (chapters 6 and 17 respectively) take issue with the assumptions common to this literature. Here is a convenient synopsis of the debate between the "disintegrationists," who believed during the Brezhnev era that the Soviet Union would collapse, and the non-disintegrationists. The Soviet policy of indigenization and affirmative action created leaders capable of administering their republics without Russians. Rising ethnic consciousness and the demographic vitality (in the case of the Central Asians) would lend popular support to leaders seeking greater autonomy from Moscow. The central Party-state, however, would be unwilling to change the power structure to permit greater competence to republic leaders, and would grow increasingly incapable of coopting them. Moscow would attempt to use traditional methods of coercion to contain the conflict, but this would only make matters worse: the country seemed to be set on an irreversible course towards disintegration.

Other scholars, however, argued that the Soviet Union was in no immediate danger of disintegrating and that the threat to stability the nationalities posed was manageable. Soviet nationality policies had enjoyed success in containing ethnic conflict, coopting elites, and imparting among the nationalities a sense of allegiance to the Soviet Union. The state enjoyed legitimacy, many nations prospered, and, moreover, limited amounts of coercion and control worked to prevent the development of potentially dangerous ethnonational movements. This was not to deny the gravity of the problems sketched out by the "disintegrationists." Some other factor—involvement in a major war, tremendous economic chaos, etc.—might exacerbate tensions between the nationalities and Moscow and indeed bring the system to the brink; unlike the disintegrationists, however, they held that the nationalities problem on its own would not.

PART I

HISTORY AND IDEOLOGY

The Soviet Union was built on what remained of the crumbling Russian Empire after World War I and the 1917 Revolution. The Bolsheviks rapidly had to create a framework for governing the territory they had inherited, which meant they had to reconcile ideology with the need to consolidate power. But under what form of government would power be consolidated—centralist or federated? Would the former "inmates" of the "prison of peoples" have the rights to self-determination and to secede from Bolshevik political arrangements? Pre-1917 debates within the Russian Social Democratic Labor Party had conceded that the nationalities should enjoy cultural autonomy, but rejected federalism, which it considered to be a reactionary form of government that created barriers to class solidarity.

The formation of the Soviet Union, and of the Soviet system of governing a multinational state, was thus driven both by ideas about nations and nationality and by power imperatives. The chapters in this section describe how this process took place and explain some of the key ideas that helped inform Soviet nationality policy—the concepts of nation and nationality, national self-determination, federalism, and internationalism. The authors discuss various periods and have different foci, but they all raise questions about how ideology is used to justify policy and about whether institutions embody their proclaimed goals, especially the goal of internationalism.

Walker Connor suggests how Soviet regimes used the idea of self-determination in forming domestic and foreign policy strategies. The Soviet goals of winning the civil war, advancing the communist movement abroad, and gaining political leverage over bordering states determined the Soviet conception of national independence movements, at the expense of Marxist theory. According to Connor, ideology was used as a tool, and Lenin—an expedient but nearsighted politician—did not foresee the unintended consequences of granting nations of the former Russian Empire the rights of self-determination and secession.

Like Connor, Richard Pipes argues that Lenin underestimated the origins and depth of nationalism in the USSR, but Pipes draws conclusions that go beyond Connor: A naive Lenin did not recognize that political concessions to nationalists needed to be made, and he relied perilously on the goodwill of Russian bureaucrats not to provoke nationalist impulses. Pipes addresses the questions of how the Bolsheviks established control over the disintegrating Russian Empire and how they came to divide power and jurisdiction between the center and the republics. If the Bolsheviks departed from their ideological hostility to federalism, their concession to federalism was minimal, for, according to Pipes, without a federated Party (which the Bolsheviks staunchly refused to allow) there could be no distribution of power. Pipes focuses on institutions (the Council of Peoples' Commissars, the Russian Communist Party, and the Commissariat of Nationality Affairs) and shows how they carried out the Bolsheviks' bald aim of consolidating and expanding power, despite the opposition of the national communists.

Pipes then turns to the question of how the reconquered territories were to be administered, with the Bolsheviks seeking tighter political control over the borderlands than previous bi-lateral treaties between the RSFSR and the outlying regions had called for. They drafted and adopted a Union agreement in 1922 and adopted a new constitution in 1924, and together, these documents set out the divisions of power and jurisdictions between the center and the other territorial units. Pipes details the intense personal and political struggles between Lenin and Stalin that accompanied the drafting of these documents.

Connor rejects a conventional wisdom that Stalin perverted Leninist policy on self-determination and claims that Lenin had all along intended to reabsorb nations that had declared independence after the Revolution. After self-determination became a "dead letter," however, the task remained of dividing power between the center and the republics. Pipes traces the deep political and ideological differences that separated Lenin and Stalin on this issue and concludes that, had Lenin not fallen ill, he might have stemmed the encroaching centralism. Be that as it may, the Bolsheviks, in Pipes's view, were still "perhaps the least qualified of all the Russian parties . . . to solve the national problem."

During the Stalin era centralism prevailed and—according to Hélène Carrère d'Encausse—"empire" was consolidated. The Russian people benefited from this arrangement, which was justified by the myth of the "friendship of peoples" and executed by the imposition of Cyrillic alphabets on non-Russian languages, the rewriting of non-Russian histories, and the creation of new elites. The elevation of the Russian people to the status of primus inter pares among Soviet peoples occurred at the expense of the idea of egalitarianism and led to the bleakest period in Soviet history for some non-Russian nationalities. D'Encausse's chapter ends with the Khrushchev era, the return to egalitarianism, and the turn toward rapid "internationalization" and the "fusion" of peoples. Because Khrushchev, like his predecessors, mistakenly believed that nationalism was the residual outcome of class oppression, the attempt to form a "Soviet people" seemed off to a shaky beginning.

Throughout the years, Soviet regimes based their approach to the nationality question on Bolshevik notions about class, nationality, and centralized power. The constitutional structure the Bolsheviks established, which in Pipes's estimation is "historically one of the most consequential aspects of the formation of the Soviet Union," has endured despite its apparent incompatibility with centralization, a problem that is dealt with in Part II.

1

The Soviet Prototype

Walker Connor

Holding out the vision of independence for non-Russian peoples proved very instrumental in the Bolsheviks' acquisition of power. The lengthy and demoralizing war, the overthrow of tsarism, and the general air of indecision and powerlessness that hung over the provisional government had understandably led many non-Russians to contemplate a severing of the Russian tie; and Lenin and Stalin did not pass up the opportunity to contrast, in the sharpest possible relief, their own commitment to independence movements with the vacillating and temporizing stance of the provisional government. During the hectic events of 1917, repeated statements of support emanated from the Petrograd Soviet, materially aiding the undermining of Kerensky's government. Thus at the Seventh All Russian Socialist Democratic Labor Party Conference of May 12, 1917, both Lenin and Stalin made speeches excoriating the government for not immediately extending the right of secession to the Finns and Ukrainians.[1] And in a resolution drafted by Lenin, the conference unequivocally endorsed "the right of all of the nations forming part of Russian freely to secede and form independent states."[2] Similarly, at the first All Russian Congress of Soviets in June 1917, the Bolshevik faction criticized the congress's decision to place a series of qualifications upon its demands that the provisional government issue a formal edict recognizing the right of secession.

The party's debt to this strategy was later acknowledged in a resolution which characterized it as a "decisive" factor:

Our party took these circumstances into consideration when it made the basis of its

Published in Connor, W., *The National Question in Marxist-Leninist Theory and Strategy*. Copyright © 1984 Princeton University Press. Excerpt, pp. 212-222 reprinted with permission of Princeton University Press.

policy in the national question the right of nations to self-determination, the right of peoples to lead an independent political existence. . . Our Party in its work never tired of advancing this programme of national emancipation in opposition to both the frankly coercive policy of tsarism and the half-hearted, semi-imperialist policy of the Mensheviks and Socialist-Revolutionaries. Whereas the tsarist Russification policy created an abyss between tsarism and the nationalities of old Russia, and whereas the semi-imperialist policy of the Mensheviks and Social Revolutionaries led the best elements among these nationalities to desert Kerenskyism, the policy of emancipation pursued by our Party won for it the sympathy and support of the broad masses of these nationalities in the struggle it waged against tsarism and the imperialist Russian bourgeoisie. There can be little doubt that this sympathy and support was one of the decisive factors that determined the triumph of our Party in the October Revolution.[3]

The Bolsheviks' formal support for the right to secede did not end with their assumption of power on November 7. The following day, in its first official pronouncement, the Soviet government reaffirmed its support for self-determination:

> If any nation whatsoever is forcibly retained within the boundaries of a given state, if, in spite of its expressed desire—no matter whether that desire is expressed in the press, at popular meetings, in party decisions, or in the protests and revolts against national oppression—it is not permitted the right to decide the forms of its state existence by a free vote . . ., [then] such incorporation is annexation, i.e., seizure and coercion.[4]

A week later, an official document signed by the chairman of the Council of People's Commissars (Lenin) and the People's Commissar on Nationality Affairs (Stalin) specifically committed the new Soviet state to supporting "the right of the peoples of Russia to free self-determination, even to the point of separation and the formation of an independent state."[5]

For a time it appeared that this commitment would be honored. In the interval between the Soviet takeover and the end of 1918, at least thirteen new states came into being within what was formerly the Russian Empire.[6] And the new Soviet government did in fact extend recognition to many of these new entities.

Several factors helped to account for the Soviet leadership's early willingness to preside over the dissolution of the Russian Empire. It is important to remember that the seizure of governmental power did not guarantee political control of Russia. There remained the need to consolidate power against the armed forces of the counterrevolutionaries and foreign states. In this situation, the Bolsheviks' stance on self-determination had the advantage of permitting the new government to concentrate upon the more serious threat to its survival. Moreover, in the struggle with the Whites, the Soviet leaders, by identifying themselves with national aspirations of the minorities, could expect to gain the passive support, and perhaps the positive sympathy, of the non-Russian peoples.

This support was a matter of the greatest strategic import, for the White forces were almost totally located in the non-Russian regions. Aided in their courtship of the minorities by the Whites' refusal to countenance any secessionist tendencies, the Bolsheviks' continued willingness to promise self-determination unquestionably paid handsome dividends. Indeed, we have Stalin's word that it was *the* critical factor in the war's outcome:

> Do not forget that if in the rear of Kolchak, Denikin, Wrangle, and Yudenich we had not had the so-called "aliens," if we had not had the former oppressed peoples who undermined the rear of these generals by their silent sympathies with the Russian proletariat—and this comrades, is a special factor in our growth, this silent sympathy; nobody sees or hears it, but it decides everything—if it had not been for this sympathy, we should not have beaten one of these generals. While we were marching against them, the collapse began in their rear. Why? Because these generals relied on the "colonizing" element among the Cossacks, they offered to the oppressed peoples a prospect of further oppression, and the oppressed peoples were obliged to come forward and embrace us, seeing that we unfurled the banner of the liberation of these oppressed peoples.[7]

At its twelfth Congress (April 1923), the party also went on record as recognizing the absolute essentiality of the support provided by the non-Russian peoples during the Red-White struggle. Referring to "the confidence of its brothers of other nationalities," the party resolution added that "it need hardly be shown that if it had not enjoyed this confidence the Russian proletariat could not have defeated Kolchak and Denikin, Yudenich and Wrangle."[8]

Quite aside from such strategic considerations, the Bolshevik leadership could also defend its endorsement of secession by noting that its action was, in any case, only a recognition of the existing state of things. Since most of the territories populated by the peoples who had defected were either in the hands of the Whites or of foreign occupation forces, recognition of their independence was only recognition of what could not be immediately rectified. Moreover, quite apart from these war-related considerations, there remained Lenin's thesis that Soviet support of self-determination was the best guarantee against secession and for the speedy return of those who did secede.

Despite these strategic and presumptive considerations, growing nervousness about actual developments became manifest almost immediately after the revolution, in the form of hedging on what had hitherto been the unqualified acknowledgement of the right of secession. In an article dealing with the Ukraine, which was published less than five weeks after the revolution, Stalin reaffirmed the willingness of the Soviet authorities to support secession, but he now added the proviso "if the toiling population of the region desires its."[9] The following month he made clear that this qualification was not to be construed as empty rhetoric: "All this points to the necessity of interpreting the principle of self-determination, not of the bourgeoisie, but of the toiling masses of the given nation.   The principle of self-determination must be subordinated to the principles of socialism."[10]

Here indeed was an unheralded shift of major consequence in the meaning that Marxists attached to self-determination.   No longer a right adhering to the nation, it had been transformed into self-determination of the proletariat.   And since the Communist party was the sole group qualified to speak for the proletariat, Stalin's alteration would in practice mean that all decisions concerning self-determination would henceforth fall within the exclusive domain of the highest reaches of the party.

Marx, Engels, and Lenin, as we have documented, had often maintained that support for specific self-determination movements should be highly selective. But they had never contended that the right was concentrated in a single class of the nation, rather than in the nation as a whole.[11]   Nor had Stalin.   Indeed, as recently as May 1917, he had indicated that even the most reactionary of secessionist movements would not be resisted.   After noting that "recognition of the right of secession must not be confused with the expediency of secession in any given circumstances," Stalin had added, by way of illustration, that he "personally would be opposed to the secession of Transcaucasia, bearing in mind the general level of development in Transcaucasia and in Russia, the conditions of the struggle of the proletariat, and so forth."   His opposition, however, would not take precedence over his commitment to the right of secession: "But if, nevertheless, the peoples of Transcaucasia were to demand secession, they would, of course, secede, and would not encounter opposition on our part."[12]

The view from inside the palace was remarkably different, however.   Lenin's strategy of championing independence had always been thought suspect by a number of Bolsheviks, and the growing number of secessionist movements reinforced these reservations.   Lenin was himself troubled by these developments, as indicated by the following passage which was written in January 1918:

> There is not a single Marxist who, without making a total break with the foundations of Marxism and Socialism, could deny that the interests of Socialism are above the interests of the right of nations to self-determination. Our Socialist Republic has done and is continuing to do everything possible for implementing the right of self-determination for Finland, Ukraine, etc. But if the concrete position that has arisen is such that the existence of the Socialist Republic is endangered at a given moment in respect of an infringement of the right to self-determination of a few nations (Poland, Lithuania, Courland, etc.) then it stands to reason that the interests of the preservation of the Socialist Republic must take preference.[13]

There is, to be sure, no hint in this passage of a desire to restrict self-determination to the "toiling masses."   And Lenin did, in fact, resist Stalin's narrower definition as an acceptable postulation for all situations.   However, a statement drafted by Lenin, which became official party policy following its adoption in March 1919, gave to the party the right to view self-determination from this narrower perspective when such a limitation appeared appropriate:

> The All-Russian Communist Party regards the question as to which class expresses the desire of a nation for separation from a historical point of view, taking into consideration the level of historical development of the nation, i.e., whether the nation is passing from medievalism toward bourgeois democracy or from bourgeois democracy toward Soviet or proletarian democracy, etc.[14]

It would be difficult to offer a better illustration of Lenin's ability to keep policy flexible so that the strategic value to the Marxist movement that could be derived from any situation could be maximized. In reserving to the party the power to determine who is entitled to speak for the nation, Lenin designed a formula that would permit the Soviet government to remain the foremost champion of independence of colonies and specified nations,[15] while concurrently denying the propriety of the self-determination doctrine to any case in which it might be detrimental to the Soviet state. In the latter situation, the party need only proclaim that separation was not in the best interests of the toiling masses, in order to brand any move in that direction as counterrevolutionary.[16] Thus, Stalin writing in *Pravda* during 1920 in relation to the rights of the non-Russian peoples to secede, simply averred that "the interests of the masses of the people render the demand for secession of the border regions at the present stage of the revolution a profoundly counter-revolutionary one."[17]

It is sometimes implicitly suggested that the subsequent fortunes of the non-Russian peoples would have been qualitatively different had Lenin lived long enough to have his national policies firmly entrenched. To holders of this view, Stalin is the villain who broke faith with non-Russians. The evidence usually advanced for this thesis revolves about the displeasure which Lenin expressed in late 1922 concerning Stalin's harsh treatment of the Georgians following their reannexation by Moscow. Lenin's displeasure was quite consistent with his conviction that minority nationalism, the product of past oppression, must be eradicated by a period of overindulgent behavior on the part of the Soviet authorities. Anything which was apt to provoke the sensibilities of the minorities must be studiously avoided. It is therefore likely that the treatment accorded to non-Russian peoples, once back in the fold, would indeed have been less coercive and high-handed had Lenin lived another decade or two. But it does not follow that Lenin was any less intent than Stalin on reabsorbing, with whatever force was required, the recently seceded peoples. On this there was no disagreement. One biographer maintains that Lenin personally directed the campaigns to reacquire the various territories and their peoples.[18] Moreover, regarding the Georgians whose harsh treatment he would later protest, an earlier directive by Lenin rather cynically expressed his awareness that their militarily achieved reannexation was not justifiable in terms of the popular will. Rather than recommending a defense on the merits, he therefore instructed the propaganda apparatus to pitch its defense solely in sarcastic references to the sins of others:

> Some caustic journalists should be instructed at once to prepare the draft of a note in reply to the British Labour Party in the politest terms. In this note it should be made thoroughly clear that the proposal to evacuate Georgia and to conduct a referendum there might be a reasonable suggestion coming from sensible people who have not been bribed by the Entente, providing the same measure were applied to all nations of the globe. More particularly, in order to suggest to the leaders of the British Labour Party the great importance of modern imperialist relationships in international politics, we respectfully propose that the British Labour Party favorably consider the following measures:
>
>   First, to evacuate Ireland and conduct a popular referendum there; second, to take the same steps in India; third, to apply the same measures in Korea; fourth, to take the same action in all countries where armies of any of the great imperialist powers are kept.
>
>   The note should emphasize in the politest terms possible that those willing to reflect on our proposals on the system of imperialist relations existing in international politics will also be capable of appreciating the implications of the suggestions made to us by the British Labour Party. The purpose of the note, extremely polite in form and popular style (so as to appeal to the intelligence of ten-year-old children) should be to ridicule the idiotic leaders of the British Labour Party.[19]

Sarcasm aside, Lenin's comments constituted an admission that, faced with the rash of unanticipated secessions, the Soviets had resorted to aping the imperialists.[20]

By the combined use of the Red Army and local Communist elements, the Soviet government succeeded in returning most of the minority areas to Soviet control by 1922;[21] and, with the end of World War II, it regained control over the remaining peoples of the of Russian Empire, with the exception of the Finns.[22] As described in the constitutions of 1924, 1936, and 1977 (the last is still in effect), the state is a federation of union republics. Today totalling fifteen, each of the republics bears the name of one of the country's major national groups. Of particular interest to a discussion of self-determination is that all three constitutions declare the union republics to be sovereign and possessed of the right to secede at will from the Soviet Union.[23] Moreover, one of the prerequisites for a people to gain their own union republic is that their territory touch one of the Soviet Union's external borders, in order that the right of secession be meaningful. And yet, as we have note, the abbreviated period of meaningful self-determination had certainly ended by 1922. The emptiness of constitutional phraseology on this point is illustrated, *inter alia*, by the many political prisoners who have been found guilty over the years of separatist, "antistate" activities, despite invoking in their defence the constitutional guarantee of a union republic's right to secede.[24]

But since in fact the right to secession is not meaningful, what purpose is served by its constitutional assertion? A number of overlapping possibilities suggest themselves:

1. *For internal propaganda purposes.* Perpetuating the myth of a right of secession would be quite consonant with Lenin's view of nationalism as the product of past discrimination which is to be exorcised by a period of "national in form." One consistent element in this psychological campaign has been the attempt to convince the fourteen minorities, whose ethnic name adorns one of the union republics and who *in toto* account for approximately 75 percent of the country's non-Russian population, that they each possess their own sovereign state and that their national aspirations have therefore already been perfectly fulfilled within the union. The official claim that the republics enjoy sovereignty is supported by several attributes, theoretically enjoyed by the republics, which are customarily associated with independent states. Among them are the right to exchange diplomatic personnel with foreign states, to enter into treaty obligations, and, of course, to secede from the union. Here again, however, one encounters the Leninist distinction between the right to a right and the right to exercise that right. The attempt to sublimate the contradiction between constitutionally guaranteed right to secession and the government's unrelenting hostility to the least hint of exercise of that right can be seen in the following passage by a Soviet scholar:

> Experience shows that there may be different forms of statehood. Under a socialist democracy the substance of national sovereignty lies not in the mandatory secession of one nation from another but in the freedom of choosing any desired form of state organization. From their own experience Soviet nations know that sovereignty is best achieved and guaranteed in a fraternal multinational family and they bend every effort to develop and strengthen the Union state.[25]

2. *For general external propaganda purposes, particularly with regard to the colonial and former colonial areas.* We have noted the great emphasis that Lenin placed upon the need to convince the peoples of the Third World that the Soviets were the principal bearers of the banner of national self-determination. In order to maintain that image, it would also be necessary to maintain the illusion of full independence for the nations under Moscow's direct supervision. As Stalin noted in 1921: "And inasmuch as we are concerned with colonies which are in the clutches of Great Britain, France, America and Japan, inasmuch as we are concerned with such subject countries as Arabia, Mesopotamia, Turkey, Hindustan. . . the slogan of the right of peoples to secession is a revolutionary slogan, and to abandon it would be playing into the

hands of the Entente."[26]   Writing in *Pravda* during the same year, Stalin colorfully added:

> If Europe and America may be called the front the scene of the main engagements between socialism and imperialism, the nonsovereign nations and colonies, with their raw materials, fuel, food and vast store of human material, should be regarded as the rear, the reserve of imperialism. In order to win a war one must not only triumph at the front but also revolutionize the enemy's rear, his reserves. Hence the victory of the world proletarian revolution may be regarded as assured only if the proletariat is able to combine its own revolutionary struggle with the movement for emancipation of the toiling masses of the nonsovereign nations and the colonies against the power of the imperialists and for a dictatorship of the proletariat. This "trifle" was overlooked by the moving spirit of the Second and Two-and-a-Half Internationals when they divorced the national and colonial questions from the question of power in the period of growing proletarian revolution in the West.[27]

Two years later, Stalin added, "We must here, in Russia, in our federation, solve the national problem in a correct, *a model way*, in order to set an example to the East, which represents the heavy reserves of our revolution."[28]   The strategic importance which the Soviet leadership ascribes to their role as the foremost champion of political independence has not perceptibly waned with the dying of colonialism. The thesis that the former colonies have acquired only the form but not the content of independence, due to the fact that the imperialists have developed more indirect techniques for perpetuating their exploitation of the Third World (that is, "neo-colonialism"), has struck a broadly popular chord.[29]   By thus insisting that political self-determination remains a sham in the presence of neocolonialism, the Soviets have projected the strategic advantage of being identified as the champion of independence into the postcolonial era. One manifestation of this persevering interest in their image as the sentinel of self-determination was offered by Khrushchev in his famous denunciation of Stalin at the Twentieth Party Congress in 1956. Stalin's maltreatment of various national groups within the Soviet Union was attacked in part because of its negative impact upon the "justly considered" image of the socialist fatherland "as a model of a multinational state."[30]   But while the image of the Soviet Union held by outsiders is therefore of keen interest to the authorities, there are two more specific situations in which that image is particularly consequential.

3. *In order to increase the appeal of a union republic to people of the same ethnic stock immediately across the Soviet Union's borders.*   From the very outset, the Soviet authorities were aware that their borders would be strengthened and perhaps advanced if neighboring peoples perceived the national situation of their kin within the Soviet Union as vastly superior to their own. Thus Stalin commented in 1930:

We must bear in mind another circumstance which affects a number of nationalities of the USSR. There is a Ukraine in the USSR. But there is another Ukraine in other states. . . Take, further, the nationalities of the USSR situated along the Southern frontier from Azerbaijan to Kazakhstan and Buryat-Mongolia. They are all in the same position as the Ukraine.[31]

Following World War II, the Soviets extended their territory in a manner which caused their European borders generally to coincide with ethnic distributions, thus eliminating irredentist questions in this area.[32] However, the Asiatic land borders of the Soviet Union still bisect peoples throughout their length, enabling the Soviets to make propagandistic usage of the image of an independent Armenian, Azerbaijan, Turkmen, Uzbek, Tadzhik, Kirgiz, or Kazakh state existing just across the Soviet border. In recent years, the Soviets have not pressed this advantage except with regard to the Chinese People's Republic, but the knowledge of the governments of neighboring states that the Soviets may at any time elect to take advantage of the possibilities offered by the ethnic map in and by itself furnishes the Soviet Union with a powerful lever in any negotiations with states to the south.[33] The myth that national groups within the Soviet Union enjoy full sovereign status, including the right of secession, therefore still exerts an important influence upon neighbors.

4. *In order to aid the Communist parties of multinational states, by permitting them to point to the motherland of socialism as self-determination in practice.* If Lenin's first injunction on the national question (i.e., prior to the assumption of power, promise minorities the right of self-determination, specifically including the right of secession) was to be applied outside of the first Marxist-Leninist state, then it was essential that the Soviet Union maintain an impeccable demeanor with regard to the honoring of that principle at home. If the non-Communist leaders of foreign states were enabled to illustrate convincingly that national groups were being forcibly retained within the Soviet Union despite earlier promises of independence, Lenin's first stratagem with regard to the national question would quite assuredly prove ineffective. But in being able to point to a constitutional guarantee of the right of secession, the Soviets could project a faithfulness to principle which would do honor to a Caesar's wife, for no non-Marxist state could boast of a similar constitutional guarantee. Maintaining such an image would be essential if the Communist parties in prerevolutionary states were to adopt successfully Lenin's stratagem of promising independence to all national groups. The fact that the Soviet authorities did in fact continue to place much store in this stratagem as a means of furthering the world revolution is heavily documented by resolutions and directives that emanated from the Third International (the Comintern) throughout its existence from 1919 to 1943.

The Comintern was created to coordinate the activities of all Communist parties. Article 16 of the "Conditions of Admission" mandated that "all the decisions of the Congresses of the Communist International, as well as the decisions of its Executive Committee [which was located in Moscow], *are binding* on all parties belonging to the Communist International."[34] A major preoccupation of the organization was the national question, for, steeped in its own internal experience, the Soviet leadership was particularly cognizant of the powers of ethnonationalism as a potential Trojan horse within the enemy camp. The opportunism that came to characterize the Comintern's approach to the national question was captured in a speech by Bukharin, made shortly after the organization's formation: "If we propound the solution of the right of self-determination for the colonies. . . we lose nothing by it. On the contrary, we gain. . . The most outright nationalist movement in only water for our mill.[35]

Armed with this vision of nothing to lose and everything to gain, the Soviet authorities embarked on a program to convince other Communist parties of the necessity to conform to Soviet strategy on the matter. The Manifesto passed at the first conference of the Comintern (March 1919) outlined the official Communist view of the issue.

> While oppressing and coercing the small and weak peoples, condemning them to hunger and degradation, the allied imperialists, like the imperialists of the Central Powers a short while ago, do not stop talking about the right of national self-determination, which is today trampled underfoot in Europe as in all other parts of the world.[36]

The Manifesto was addressed to the world's proletariat and therefore did not lay down the course of action to be followed by Communist parties with regard to the national issue. Such a blueprint for concerted action first appeared in Lenin's "Theses on the National and the Colonial Question," which were adopted by the Comintern at it Second Party Congress in July 1920. Lenin insisted that all parties ". . . render direct aid to the revolutionary movements among the dependent and underprivileged nations (for example, Ireland, the American Negroes, etc.) and in the colonies." Otherwise, he noted, "the struggle against the oppression of dependent nations . . . as well as recognition of their right to secede, are but a false signboard."[37] Consonant with this policy, "particularly explicit and clear attitude on the question of the colonies and the oppressed peoples" was made a prerequisite of membership.

> Every party which wishes to join the Communist International is obliged to expose the tricks and dodges of its imperialists in the colonies, to support every colonial liberation movement not merely in words but in deeds, to demand the expulsion of their own imperialists from these colonies, to inculcate among the workers of their country a genuinely fraternal attitude to the working people of the colonies and the oppressed nations, and to carry on systematic agitation among the troops of their country against any oppression of the colonial peoples.[38]

Over the next few years, the Communist parties of other countries were bombarded with reminders of the need to honor this pledge. One of the more broadly aimed statements on the matter can be found in the resolutions of the Fifth Comintern Congress of 1924:

> On the nationality question the Executive has ample cause to remind many sections, for which this question is of the utmost importance, of their inadequate execution of the decisions of the second congress. One of the basic principles of Leninism, *requiring the resolute and constant advocacy by communist of the right of national self-determination* (secession and the formation of an independent State), has not yet been applied by all sections of the Comintern as it should be.[39]

In a document dealing with tactics, the same congress further pressed this theme:

5. Correct Policy in the National Question

In a number of countries, as a result of the re-division of the world after the first imperialist war, there is greater national oppression and dismemberment. In a number of European countries, and still more in colonial and semi-colonial countries, a mass of inflammable material has been heaped up which may blow bourgeois rule sky-high. Correct communist policy on the national question, which was thoroughly analyzed in theses of the second world congress, forms one of the most important constituents in the policy of winning the masses and preparing a victorious revolution. Nihilism and opportunist deviations in the national question, which still prevail in a number of communist parties, are the weakest side of these parties, which will never be able to accomplish their historical mission, if they do not overcome these weaknesses.[40]

The following year, the Comintern had occasion to berate the parties for not heeding such directives, noting that "communists have again and again made the mistake of underestimating the national question, a mistake which deprives them of the opportunity of winning over substantial, at times decisive strata of the population."[41]

In adopting this posture on the national question, the Comintern was in effect requiring that party members agitate against the territorial integrity of their respective states and/or overseas empires. This policy could remain constant only so long as it harmonized with the foreign policy objectives of the Soviet Union, for, as laid down in Lenin's "Theses on the National and the Colonial Question," "a policy must be pursued that will achieve the closest alliance, with Soviet Russia, of all the national and colonial liberation movements."[42] In time, therefore, the directives of the Comintern concerning the national question necessarily came to mirror each major vicissitude in Soviet foreign policy.

Between the October Revolution and the end of World War II, that foreign policy underwent three major shifts, each accompanied by a correspond change in the policies that the Communist parties were ordered to take on the national question. In the immediate aftermath of the revolution, when the authorities tended to perceive the Soviet Union as alone in a sea of equally hostile capitalist states, a policy which indiscriminately aimed at the weakening of all multinational states and empires blended well with Soviet objectives. But as the threat of fascism became increasingly ominous, the Soviets correspondingly came to appreciate that non-Fascist states might be essential allies against this more immediate danger. Strategy therefore dictated a change of course, and Communists were instructed to enter into united fronts with, and lend support to, all anti-Fascist forces. Propaganda aimed at dismemberment of non-Fascist states and their empires was shelved. This period of the united front against Fascism began in 1935 and ended in August 1939 with the signing of the Nazi-Soviet Non-Aggression Pact. During the period of the pact, Moscow insisted that any course of action which might provoke Hitler was to be avoided. United fronts with anti-Fascist forces were therefore out, and mobilization efforts on the part of non-Fascist states were not to be supported. The final phase, which commenced with the Nazi attack on the Soviet Union in June 1941, was one in which no action was to be taken which would impede the prosecution of the anti-Fascist war by the Allied countries. As one means of assuring its allies that it intended no threat to their political and territorial integrity, Moscow ordered the Comintern dissolved in 1943.

These shifts in Soviet perceptions concerning the utilitarian value of one or another group of states were accompanied by intriguing alterations in Soviet propaganda concerning the proper focus for the political loyalty of the working classes. Prior to 1935, the Comintern's position was that unlike 1848, when Marx and Engels had drawn up the Communist Manifesto, the working men of the world now had a country. Loyalty of working men everywhere was owed not to their state but to "the Worker's Fatherland," that is, the Soviet Union. As ringingly proclaimed on the fourteenth anniversary of the revolution:

Working people of the World!
Defend with your lives the Soviet Union, the only fatherland of the workers of all countries. Use every means at your command to protect the victorious construction of socialism.[43]

However, with the need for allies who would resist Fascist expansionism, the working classes were told in 1935 that if their state's independence were threatened by Fascist invaders, resistance to such a threat would "assume the character of a war of liberation" in which the proletariat must be "in the front ranks of the fighters for [their country's] independence and fight the war of liberation to a finish, without allowing 'their' bourgeoisie to strike a bargain with the attacking powers to the prejudice of the interests of their country. "[44] By 1938, with an attack upon the Soviet Union by Germany an imminent possibility, the working class, nation, and defense of state were identified as a single trinity in a rousing call to the colors.

> The nation is the many millions of workers, peasants, and working peoples generally—the people that is devoted to its country, cherishes its liberty, and defends its independence. . . . In all countries menaced by fascist invasion from without, only the working class can rally, rouse, and lead the people to a victorious struggle for national liberation. The working class is the backbone of the nation, the bulwark of its liberty, dignity, and independence.[45]

In sharpest contrast was the exhortation to the same workers, only one year later, in the period of the German-Soviet Non-Aggression Pact. In a stunning about-face, workers were now told not to rally to defense of country:

> Workers! Don't believe those who wave the flag of national unity. What can there be in common between you and those who profit by war? What unity can there be between exploited and exploiters"
> Don't believe those who are calling upon you to support the war under the false pretext of the defense of democracy.[46]

Yet less than two years later, in still another complete turnabout, the French Communist Party could report: "For us there is no division into communists, socialists, radicals, catholics or de Gaulle followers. For us there are only Frenchmen fighting Hitler and his agents. "[47] Other parties behaved in corresponding fashion, for in the interim the Nazis had attacked the Soviet Union, and the Comintern had given instructions to give total support to the anti-Fascist effort. For most parties this meant unswerving loyalty to their own state apparatus. As set forth in the document of intention to dissolve itself, the Comintern's parting message to the workers was to continue this support. The concluding paragraph read as follows:

> The Presidium of the Executive Committee of the Communist International calls on all supporters of the Communist International to concentrate their energies on whole-hearted support of and active participation in the war of liberation of the peoples *and States* of the anti-Hitlerite coalition for the speediest defeat of the deadly enemy of the working class and toilers—German fascism and its associates and vassals.[48]

Though the Soviets therefore often stressed state unity at the expense of a right of separation during the decade from 1935 to 1945, they never formally repudiated their commitment to the right of self-determination, including secession. Similarly, with regard to their domestic scene, we have noted that the myth of a right of secession, unlike its reality, was never terminated. In the postwar years, with the Fascist threat eradicated, their forbearance would permit the Soviets to regain the pose of the consistent champion of national self-determination. But as a survey of Soviet practice reveals, the ostensible commitment with regard to both the internal and external application of self-determination rested on opportunism and pretense. Candid acknowledgement was offered by the president of the Comintern, Zinoviev, while furnishing advice in 1923 to Communist parties outside of the Soviet Union: "What we ask is that those of our parties in countries where the national question is important should learn to make use of the nationalist element against the bourgeois regime. Our parties must try to set in movement against the government those elements which are naturally discontented," just as the Bolsheviks exploited Ukrainian discontent against Kerensky "for the good of the proletarian revolution." He added that the Ukrainians had been told that they would be independent, not that Karl Marx had said that the proletariat had no fatherland.[49]

Soviet experience has vindicated Lenin's assessment of the serviceability of national self-determination as a key lever for gaining power in a multinational environment. But it has also exposed the fallacy of presuming that peoples, upon being offered independence, would not take it. Nations had chosen separation, and force and artifice had been necessary to bring about their return. Official Soviet history would later attempt to mask Lenin's miscalculation, maintaining that all the member peoples of the Soviet Union had acceded voluntarily.[50] Thus Article 70 of the 1977 constitution proclaims: "The Union of the Soviet Socialist Republics is an integral federal, multinational state formed on the principle of socialist federalism as a result of the free self-determination of nations and the voluntary association of equal Soviet Socialist Republics."[51] This official myth has permitted the Soviet Union to pose as the champion of self-determination abroad. But it is doubtful that it has exerted much influence upon popular perceptions within those nations who, consonant with Lenin's promises, elected to secede at the time of the revolution. Thus in 1979, more that one-half century after Lenin's death, forty-five notables living within Estonia, Latvia, and Lithuania set forth in an open letter to the United Nations their case for independence from Moscow. The letter noted that in 1920, the Soviet authorities had solemnly ceded independence to the three republics "for all time" and had relinquished "all sovereign rights" over them.[52] Lenin's stratagem for taking power thus continues to have consequences far beyond what he had anticipated.

Notes

1. See Lenin, *Right of Nations*, particularly p. 125; and Stalin, *Marxism: Selected Writings*, 70-71. See also in Pipes, *Formation*, 68, the reference to Lenin's newspaper article which had been written to embarrass the provisional government for its failure to respond to Ukrainian aspirations.

2. Cited in Groshev, *Fraternal Family*, 36.

3. "National Factors in Party and State Development," Resolution Adopted by the Twelfth Congress of the Russian Communist Party, April 1923, in appendix to Stalin, *Marxism and National, Colonial Questions*, 279-287.

4. The entire text is reproduced in Christman, *Communism*, 2-6.

5. Entitled, "Declaration of the Rights of the Peoples of Russia" (November 18, 1917), in ibid., 11-12.

6. See Farmer, "Theory," 253. For a listing of most of these states by date of secession, see Kristian, *Right to Self-Determination*, 21.

7. Cited in Carr, *Bolshevik Revolution* 1:263, who concludes (p. 264) that "the Bolshevik doctrine of nationalism proved a vital contribution to the Soviet victory in the civil war." For a few details on non-Russian forces who fought against the Whites, see Salov, "Soviet Nationality Policy," 89.

8. "National Factors in Party and State Development," in Stalin, *Marxism and National, Colonial Questions*, 281.

9. Clarkson, *History of Russia*, 636. This article was published on December 12, 1917.

10. Ibid.

11. As noted in chapter 2, on the occasion when Lenin was publicly queried about the specific course of actions he would recommend in the event that a nation dominated by reactionaries sought to secede, he elected to be evasive rather than to take on the opportunity to restrict the right of secession to progressive movements.

12. Stalin, *Marxism: Selected Writings*, 71.

13. Cited in Conquest, *Nation Killers*, 118-119. Lenin never publicly acknowledged that his assumption that the promise of secession would in fact deter secession was erroneous. In a *Pravda* article, he placed the blame for the spate of secessions on "capitalists" who had played upon "the national distrust of the Great Russians felt by Polish, Latvian, Estonian and Finnish peasants and small owners." This development, however, would prove temporary. By recognizing the independence of the new states, "we are . . . winning the confidence of the laboring masses of the neighboring small states. It is the surest way of wresting them from the influence of 'their' national capitalists, and leading them to full confidence, to the future united international Soviet republic." See "Letter to Workers and Peasants of the Ukraine," December 28, 1919, in Lenin, *Selected Works* 3:260-261. On the other hand, some nine months earlier, Lenin had suggested his embarrassment concerning developments by playing down the significance of self-determination and its consequences: "Our criticism [of self-determination and secession] has served to exaggerate the importance of this question. The defect in our criticism was that it attached special significance to this question, which, in substance, is of less than secondary importance to the programme's general structure, in the sum total of programme demands." See "Speech Closing the Debate on

the Party Programme," March 19, 1919, in Lenin, *Selected Works* 3:136.

14. "The Program of the All-Russian Communist Party" (March 1919), in Christman, *Communism*, 14-46. The cited section is on p. 27.

15. In the same 1919 party program, it was termed "necessary" that the party "recognize the rights of colonies and oppressed nations to political separation."

16. The following year (1920), Lenin restated his renunciation of the "abstract" principle of self-determination in the following terms: "The Communist Party . . . must base its policy on the national question too, not on abstract and formal principles but, first, on a precise appraisal of the specific historical situation and, primarily, of economic conditions; second, on a clear distinction between the interests of the oppressed classes, of working and exploited peoples, and the general concept of the national interests as a whole, *which implies the interests of the ruling class*; third, on an equally clear distinction between the oppressed, dependent and subject nations and the oppressing, exploiting and sovereign nations." "Preliminary Draft Theses on the National and Colonial Question (For the Second Congress of the Communist International)," in Lenin, *Selected Works* 3:373 (Emphasis added.)

17. *Pravda*, October 10, 1920.

18. Shub, *Lenin*, 402.

19. Ibid., 402-403.

20. There is evidence that Lenin never accepted any of the secessions as permanent. For data indicating that Lenin tried to reverse the Finnish separation as early as January 15, 1918, see M. Fol, "L'Accession de la Finlande à l'Indépendance," unpublished paper (Paris: 1976), cited in Hélène Carrère d'Encausse, "Determinants of Parameters," in Azrael, *Soviet Nationality Policies*, 40. Shortly after Lenin's death, party units for the western Ukraine and western Belorussia (then parts of Poland) were established within the Soviet Union. Both parties demanded reunification with the Soviet republics. Burks, *Dynamics of Communism*, 81. We will recall that the Finns and Ukrainians were the two peoples most favored for independence by Lenin in his prerevolutionary writings. For an interesting article maintaining that Lenin had never, even prior to the revolution, intended to permit any secession whatsoever, see Israel Kleiner, "On Lenin's Attitude toward the Right of Nations to Self-Determination," *Crossroads* 5 (Winter 1980): 177-197. The article's conclusion is based on Lenin's refusal to permit the Ukrainians a separate party. But Lenin has always adamantly maintained the need for a single party incorporating all national groups. When analyzing Lenin's position on a right of separation, one must therefore distinguish between party and nations and, with regard to the latter, between his pre- and postrevolutionary positions.

21. For detailed accounts of the various ways in which nations were reabsorbed, see Conquest, *Soviet Nationalities*, 21-35 and Farmer, "Theory," 197-281.

22. Soviet determination to reannex all the territories of the Russian Empire was indicated in 1939, when the Soviet-Nazi Non-Aggression Pact was signed. Secret protocols of the agreement gave the Soviet Union control over western Poland, Bessarabia, Estonia, Latvia, and Lithuania. Combined with the fruits of the Soviet war against Finland, these concessions would have made the western border of the Soviet Union correspond closely with that of pre-World War I tsarist Russia. Although the areas acquired under the secret protocols were lost during World War II and reacquired only with the expulsion of German forces, voices both from within and outside the

regions continued to embarrass the Soviet authorities by drawing attention to the fact that it was the secret protocols with the Nazis that in effect ripped up the Soviet Union's earlier treaties that had recognized the independence of these peoples. For example, in 1920 the Soviets had entered treaties renouncing "all sovereign rights" over the Baltic republics and had recognized their independence "for all time." It is obviously embarrassing for the Soviet Union to have the Nazi-Soviet Pact re-aired and to have it pointed out that "for all time" was reduced to nineteen years. See later parts of this chapter.

23. Chapter 3, Article 4 of the 1924 constitution reads, "Each one of the member Republics retains the right to freely withdraw from the Union." Article 17 of the 1936 constitution and Article 72 of the current (1977) constitution acknowledge the same right.

24. See, for example, the plea addressed to the Supreme Soviet of the Ukrainian Republic by the incarcerated V. Moroz in *Problems in Communism* 17 (July-August 1968): 85-86: "My colleagues and I were convicted for 'propaganda directed at the separation of the Ukraine from the USSR.' But Article 17 of the Constitution of the USSR clearly states that each republic has the right to leave the Union."

25. Lebedinskaya, "Nationality Question," 15.

26. Stalin, *Marxism: Selected Writings*, 106.

27. *Pravda*, May 8, 1921. Reprinted in Stalin, *Marxism and National, Colonial Questions*, 115. Both the wording and the thrust of this passage anticipate Mao Tse-tung's later claim to originality in advancing a global strategy involving the city-states (the industrial states) being surrounded by and dependent upon the country-states (the Third World). Both in turn owe an intellectual debt to Lenin's *Imperialism: The Highest Stage of Capitalism*.

28. Stalin, *Marxism: Selected Writings*, 156. Emphasis added.

29. With his usual aptitude for locating the jugular, and with amazing foresight, Lenin outlined this strategy before the decolonizing period was much underway. Writing in 1920, he noted "the need constantly to explain and expose among the broadest masses of the toilers of all countries, and particularly of the backward countries, the deception systematically practiced by the imperialist powers, which, under the guise of politically independent states, set up states that are wholly dependent upon them economically, financially and militarily." "Preliminary Draft Theses on the National and the Colonial Question (for the Second Congress of the Communist International)," in Lenin, *Selected Works* 3:377.

30. The text of Khrushchev's address is reprinted in Christman, *Communism*, 158-228. The citation is from p. 202.

31. Stalin, *Marxism: Selected Writings*, 214.

32. The major exception involved Moscow's absorption of the Bessarabian area, which left the Rumanian nation divided. However, the official Soviet position is that the people of Bessarabia are not Rumanians but Moldavians, who have their own Moldavian Soviet Socialist Republic within the Soviet Union.

33. The possibility that the Soviets might revert to the use of such propaganda at any time was driven home in 1981-1982, when the radio and press of the Azerbaijan Soviet Socialist Republic began publicizing the ardent aspirations for the unity of "Southern Azerbaijan" (that is, the Iranian sector) with Soviet Azerbaijan, which was allegedly broadly shared throughout Southern Azerbaijan. For several examples, see JPRS 80829

(May 17, 1982): 2-4.

34. "Conditions of Admission to the Communist International," August 1920, in Christman, *Communism*, 62-70. Emphasis added.

35. Degras, *Documents* 1:138.

36. "Manifesto of the Communist International to the Proletariat of the Entire World," March 1919, in Christman, *Communism*, 46-61.

37. "Preliminary Draft Theses on the National and the Colonial Question," in Lenin, *Selected Works* 3:375. Interestingly, what the Soviets translate as a "false signboard," the Chinese translate as "a deceitful pretense." See *Lenin on the National and Colonial Questions: Three Articles* (Peking: Foreign Language Press, 1967): 25.

38. "Conditions for Admission to the Communist International," August 1920, in Christman, *Communism*, 66-67.

39. "Extracts from the Resolution of the Fifth Comintern Congress on the Report of the Executive Committee of the Communist International," June 26, 1924, in Degras, *Documents* 2:106. Emphasis added.

40. "Extracts from the Theses on Tactics Adopted by the Fifth Comintern Congress," July 1924, in ibid. 2:142-156.

41. "Extracts from the Theses on the Bolshevization of Communist Parties Adopted at the Fifth Executive Plenum," April 1925, in ibid. 2:188-200.

42. "Theses on the National and Colonial Questions," in Lenin, *Selected Works* 3:374.

43. "Extracts from a Comintern Executive Committee Manifesto on the Fourteenth Anniversary of the Russian Revolution," November 1931, in Degras, *Documents* 3:179-180.

44. "Extracts from a Resolution of the Seventh Comintern Congress on the Danger of a New World War," August 1935, in ibid., 427-433.

45. "Extracts from a Comintern Executive Committee Manifesto on the Anniversary of the Russian Revolution," November 1938, in ibid., 427-433.

46. "Extract from the Comintern Executive Committee Manifesto on the 22nd Anniversary of the Russian Revolution," November 1939, in ibid., 439-448. An article published during the same month by the secretary of the Executive Committee warned the parties against "slipping into the position of 'defending the Fatherland,' in support of the fairy-tale about the anti-fascist character of the war." Ibid., 459. This, of course, was precisely the "fairy-tale" that the Comintern had been propagating between 1935 and August 1939.

47. Ibid., 471.

48. "Resolution of the Comintern Executive Committee Presidium Recommending the Dissolution of the Communist International," May 1943, in ibid., 476-479. Emphasis added.

49. Ibid. 2:157-158.

50. See, for example, the 1982 article by the editor-in-chief of the leading party journal, *Kommunist* (Kosolapov, "Class and National Relations" in JPRS 82852, February 11, 1983, p. 12):

"The freer Russia is and the more resolutely our republic recognizes the freedom of secession on the non-Great Russian nations," Lenin emphasized, "the more strongly other nations *will strive* for an alliance with us, the fewer clashes there will be, the rarer the instances of actual secession will be." Splendid words! And we had the honor today to confirm for certain that history has completely justified this prediction, without making any amendment to it.

51. While the constitutions of 1924 and 1936 spoke of voluntary union, the constitution of 1977 was the first to contain a reference to "free self-determination." It is probable that Yugoslav practice was the inspiration for this inclusion.

52. See the article by Peter Reddaway in *The Observer* (London), January 11, 1981.

2

The Establishment of the Union of Soviet Socialist Republics

Richard Pipes

The CONSOLIDATION OF THE PARTY
AND STATE APPARATUS

The belief that the socialist state required a centralized administration was common to both wings of the Russian Social Democratic Labor Party, as indeed it was to European Marxism in general. The Marxists viewed the government as an instrument of class warfare and a weapon by means of which the class in power asserted its will, destroyed its opponents, and enacted socioeconomic and political legislation which best served its interests. Only a government which had at its disposal complete political and economic authority could accomplish these tasks. The pre-1917 opposition of the Mensheviks and Bolsheviks to federalism, as well as the specific interpretation given by Lenin to the right of national self-determination, were largely inspired by a desire to avoid the evils of a system which permitted hostile elements to find escape from the socialist regime by utilizing the privileges inherent in states' rights.

The Bolsheviks' adoption of the principle of federalism upon their accession to power in no way signified an abandonment of the traditional Marxist hostility to the decentralized state. In the first place, under the circumstances in which it had been adopted, federalism was a step in the direction of centralization, since it gave an opportunity of bringing together once more borderland areas which during the Revolution had acquired the status of independent republics.

In the second place, the existence of the Communist Party, with its unique internal organization and extraordinary rights with regard to the institutions of the state, made it possible for the rulers of the Soviet republic to retain all the important features of a unitary state in a state which was formally decentralized.

In Communist political theory the supreme legislative authority belonged to the soviets. "Russia is declared a republic of Soviets of workers', soldiers' and peasants' deputies," stated the Declaration of Rights of the Toiling and Exploited People, issued in January 1918; "All power in the center and locally belongs to these Soviets."[1] According to the Russian-Soviet constitution, local soviets delegated their representatives to the All-Russian Congress of Soviets, which in turn appointed an All-Russian Central Executive Committee (VTsIK). The Council of People's Commissars, the supreme executive organ of the state, was in theory responsible to the VTsIK and to the All-Russian Congress of Soviets. In practice, however, the Council of People's Commissars early in the revolution made itself independent of the VTsIK, which did little more than give formal approval to measures promulgated by the Council of People's Commissars.

Side by side with the soviets, the Communists recognized another sovereign institution, the Russian Communist Party. The Bolshevik leaders conceived of the Communist Party as the vanguard of the proletarian revolution and as an organization which provided the soviets with intellectual and political leadership. They drew no clear-cut division of authority between the soviets and the party, on the assumption that the interests of the two were in full harmony, but they admitted openly that the chain of command descended from the party to the soviets, and not vice versa. In March 1919, when they drew up their first party program (superseding the general Russian Social Democratic program of 1903), the Bolsheviks stated the relationship between these two institutions with the following words:

> The Communist Party assigns itself the task of winning influence and complete leadership in all organizations of the laboring class: the trade unions, the coöperatives, the village communes, etc. The Communist Party strives particularly for the realization of its program and for the full mastery of contemporary political organizations such as the Soviets . . .
>
> The Russian Communist Party must win for itself undivided political mastery in the Soviets and *de facto* control of all their work, through practical, daily, dedicated work in the Soviets, [and] the advancement of its most stalwart and devoted members to all Soviet positions.[2]

The sovereign legislative powers, theoretically vested in the soviets, were, therefore, absorbed not only by the Council of People's Commissars, which operated on the highest level, but also by the Communist Party, which operated on all levels, down to the smallest town soviets.

The leaders of both the Council of People's Commissars and the Communist Party were in fact the same persons. The intertwining of the personnel and activities of the state and party institutions was so intimate that the process of the integration of the Soviet territory occurred not on one, but on two levels. The evolution of Soviet federalism, therefore, cannot be studied merely from the point of view of the changing relations between the central and provincial institutions of the *state*; it must be approached, first of all, from the point of view of the relations between the central and provincial institutions of the Communist *Party*.

One of the characteristic features of the Bolshevik party organization, the feature which perhaps most distinguished it from the other political organizations of twentieth-century Russia, was its internal discipline. In contrast to the Mensheviks, who thought of the party in terms of a loose association of persons holding similar views, Lenin felt that only an organization which was highly centralized and uncompromising on all matters of party activity, practical as well as theoretical, could perform effective political work. Indeed, the issue of party discipline had been the main cause of the split of Russian Social Democracy into two factions, Menshevik and Bolshevik, at the 1903 Congress. After the Bolsheviks had come to power and assumed the responsibilities of government, their views on this matter were asserted with ever greater emphasis. They were thus enunciated in the program in 1919:

> The party finds itself in a situation in which the strictest centralism and the severest discipline are absolute necessities. All decisions of the higher instance are absolutely binding on the lower ones. Every decision must first of all be carried out, and only later can it be appealed to the proper party organ. In this sense, the party must display in the present epoch virtually a military discipline . . . [3]

The highest organ of the party was its Central Committee; after March 1919, this position was assumed by the Central Committee's Political Bureau (Politburo).

The power which the Communist Party enjoyed in regard to state institutions accounted for the fact that the decisive battles for political control in Soviet-held territories took place within the party organizations. The question of how much authority was to be in the hands of the central organs and how much in the provincial ones was in fact determined by the settlement of relations between the Central Committee and the regional organizations of the Communist Party.

Now, Lenin was firm in insisting that the principles of nationalism and federalism, introduced on his own initiative in the state apparatus, did not apply to the Communist Party. Throughout his life, he remained opposed to the ideas which the Jewish Bund had advocated at the beginning of the twentieth century. During all of 1918 Lenin suppressed repeated efforts of Communists in the republics to win some autonomy from the Central Committee of the RKP, even when such efforts did not go beyond the demand for the right to join the Third International.

His task was facilitated by the fact that nearly all the republican Communist parties were not indigenous, national political organizations, but merely regional branches of the Russian Communist Party. Thus, the Communist Party of the Ukraine was the product of a merger of the Southwestern and Donets-Krivoi Rog Regional Committees of the RKP; the Belorussian Communist Party was the old Northwestern Committee of the RKP under a new name; the Georgian, Armenian, and Azerbaijani Communist parties emerged from the organizational breakup of the Transcaucasian Regional Committee of the RKP; the Turkestan Communist Party came into being through the renaming of the Turkestan Committee of the RKP. Lenin, therefore, did not so much have to centralize the party organization as keep it from falling apart.

In the spring of 1918 the Central Committee of the Communist Party of the Ukraine was compelled to acknowledge the authority of the Central Committee of the RKP and to give up its claims of membership in the Communist International. Late in 1919 it was altogether dissolved. The plan of the Belorussians to institute a separate national Communist Party was vetoed by Lenin. The Moslem Communist Party was first subordinated to the Russian Communist Party and then done away with altogether. Similar steps were taken in the other borderland areas. Lenin had thus made it clear that if he had requested the various regional committees of the RKP to change their designations to correspond to the names of the republics in which they were operating, it was largely a concession to mass psychology; he had no intention of splitting party authority or even of introducing the ideas of nationality and federalism into the party organization. As the Communist Party program stated:

> The Ukraine, Latvia, Lithuania, and Belorussia exist at this time as separate Soviet republics. Thus is solved for the present the question of state structure.
>
> But this does not in the least mean that the Russian Communist Party should, in turn, reorganize itself as a federation of independent Communist parties.
>
> The Eighth Congress of the RKP resolves: there must exist a *single* centralized Communist Party with a single Central Committee leading all the party work in all sections of the RSFSR. All decisions of the RKP and its directing organs are unconditionally binding on all branches of the party, regardless of their national composition. The Central Committees of the Ukrainian, Latvian, Lithuanian Communists enjoy the rights of the regional committees of the party, and are entirely subordinated to the Central Committee of the RKP.[4]

If the soviets were to be the supreme legislative organs of the new state; if they, in turn, were to be subjected to *de facto* control by the Communist Party; and if, finally, the Communist Party itself in Russia as well as in the non-Russian Soviet republics, was to be completely subordinated to the Central Committee, then clearly actual sovereignty in all Soviet areas belonged to the

Central Committee of the Russian Communist Party. Soviet federalism did not involve a distribution of power between the center and the province; only a corresponding decentralization of the Communist Party would have made the establishment of genuine federal relations possible. If, in 1917, Lenin had accepted state federalism so readily, it was because he knew that the existence of a unified, centralized Communist Party with authority over political institutions throughout the Soviet territories made possible the retention of unalloyed centralized political power.

The Communist leaders, however, were concerned not only with unifying in their own hands the ultimate political authority over the entire Soviet domain, but also with extending the scope of this authority as widely and as deeply as possible. Partly for reasons of dogma (the conviction that in the period of revolution the total resources of society must be brought to bear on the class-enemy), partly for reasons of practical statesmanship (greater efficiency in governing the country and the opportunity for economic planning), they undertook to augment the ultimate policy-making authority—assured them by the party—by assuming control over the entire administrative apparatus of the state.

The integration into a single state of the borderlands conquered in the course of the Civil War began in 1918 and terminated in 1923 with the establishment of the Union of Soviet Socialist Republics (USSR). It was a complex process. Before the Revolution, the Bolsheviks had given little thought to the problems of federalism, and now had to proceed entirely by trial and error. The fundamental incompatibility between the division of powers inherent in federalism and the striving toward the centralization of Communism lent the evolution of the Soviet state a peculiar character. Most of the time it is impossible to tell whether an act involving the transfer of authority from one of the republics to the government of Soviet Russia represented a genuine shift in political power, or only a formal expression of a fact which had been accomplished quietly some time earlier by order of the Party or the Council of People's Commissars. The Communist adherence to democratic terminology in a social order which was authoritarian in the fullest sense of the word also does not contribute to a greater understanding of the growth of Soviet state structure.

For purposes of historical analysis, the territories of the Soviet state which were involved in the process of political consolidation may be divided into three categories: the autonomous regions and republics, the Union Republics, and the People's Republics. It must be borne in mind, however, that such a division is artificial. The centralization occurred in all those areas simultaneously and, even before the formal establishment of the USSR, they were (with the exception of the People's Republics) reduced to a status which was, for all practical purposes, identical.

THE RSFSR

The first Constitution of Soviet Russia (1918), while accepting the general principle of federalism, had made no provisions for the settlement of relations between the federal government and the individual states. Indeed, as one historian points out, the very word "federation" was not even mentioned in the body of the Constitution.[5] During 1918, it was not clear what, if any, difference in status there was between the autonomous regions, the autonomous republics, and the Soviet republics, and all those terms were used interchangeably. Wherever the Communists came into power they simply proclaimed the laws issued by the government of the RSFSR valid on their territory and announced the establishment of a "union" with the Russian Soviet republic.

The first attempt to put into practice the principles enunciated in the Constitution was made in the spring of 1918, when the government of the RSFSR (or, more precisely, its All-Russian Central Executive Committee) ordered the formation of the Tatar-Bashkir and Turkestan republics. As we have seen, these attempts were not successful. The Tatar-Bashkir state never came into being because the Russians evacuated the Volga-Ural region in the summer of 1918; while Turkestan, cut off from Moscow by the enemy, had, until the end of the Civil War, no administrative connection with the RSFSR.

It was only in February 1919, with the signing of the Soviet-Bashkir agreement, that the decentralization of the administrative apparatus along national lines began in earnest. Between 1920 and 1923, the government of the RSFSR established on its territory seventeen autonomous regions and republics. The autonomous regions (sometimes called "Toilers' Communes") had no distinguishing juridical features even in terms of Soviet law and were described by one Soviet authority as "national *gubernii*."[6] The antonomous republics, on the other hand, were regarded as endowed with a certain degree of political competence, although what the limits of this competence were posed a question that troubled the best legal minds of the time.[7]

The common feature of these autonomous units—regions and republics alike—was the fact that they came into being by decree of the All-Russian Central Executive Committee acting alone or in conjunction with the Council of People's Commissars of the RSFSR. The only exception to this rule was the Bashkir Republic founded, as we saw, in February 1919, by agreement between the government of the RSFSR and a group of Bashkir nationalists; but since the 1919 agreement was unilaterally abrogated fifteen months later with the introduction of the new Bashkir constitution on the orders of the Russian Soviet government, this exception cannot be said to have affected the general practice.

The origin of the autonomous states provided additional assurance that they would not infringe in any manner upon the centralized structure of Soviet political authority. "Autonomy means not separation," Stalin told the North Caucasians in 1920, "but a union of the self-ruling mountain peoples with the peoples of Russia."[8] Indeed, the main stress in the Communist interpretation of autonomy was on closer ties between the borderlands and Russia and on the enhancement of the authority and prestige of the Soviet regime in areas where nationalistic tendencies were deeply rooted. As Stalin's statement emphasized, autonomy was considered as an instrument of consolidation, not of decentralization.

As indicated in the sections dealing with the history of the borderlands during the Revolution and Civil War, the government of the RSFSR retained in the reconquered territories full control over the military, economic, financial, and foreign affairs of its autonomous states. These were granted competence only in such spheres of government activity as education, justice, public health, and social security; and even in these realms they were subject to the surveillance of the appropriate commissariats of the RSFSR as well as the local bureaus of the Russian Communist Party. The governments of the autonomous regions and republics, as one Soviet jurist correctly remarked, had more in common, from the point of view of authority and function, with the prerevolutionary Russian organs of self-rule, the so-called Provincial *zemstva,* than with the governments of genuine federal states.[9]   There can be little doubt that the tradition of those institutions, introduced during the Great Reforms of the 1860's, had much to do with the evolution of Soviet concepts of autonomy.

The first attempt to consolidate the state apparatus of all the autonomous regions and republics was made in the early 1920's by the Commissariat of Nationality Affairs (Narkomnats or NKN). This commissariat, originally established to serve as an intermediary between the central Soviet organs and the minorities and to assist the government in dealing with problems of a purely "national" nature (which could not be too numerous, in view of the Communist attitude toward the entire problem of nationality and nationalism), had displayed little activity in 1919 and the first half of 1920. Stalin, its chairman, was absent; its vice-chairmen and higher functionaries were called in by the Soviet authorities to fill various posts in the reconquered borderlands; and the remaining borderland areas were largely in the zone of combat or under enemy occupation. As a result, the commissariat led only a nominal existence, publishing a weekly newspaper and occasionally engaging in propaganda activity.

In the spring of 1920 Stalin resumed the active chairmanship of the Commissariat of Nationality Affairs and began to transform it into a miniature federal government of the RSFSR. A decree issued on May 10, 1920, instructed all the national minority groups on the territory of the RSFSR to elect deputies to the Narkomnats.[10] This was intended to give the Commissariat a representative character and, in a sense, was the first step in the abandonment of the purely executive aspect of the Commissariat. On November 6, 1920, the Narkomnats decreed that it would assume jurisdiction over the agencies of the autonomous regions and republics which had been attached to the Central

Executive Committee of the All-Russian Congress of Soviets.[11]   In December 1920 the government of the RSFSR decreed that the Narkomnats was to open provincial branches and attach them to the Central Executive Committees of the autonomous regions and republics of the RSFSR.[12]

In April 1921 the executive officers of the Narkomnats, and the chairmen of the delegations from the autonomous regions and republics, were constituted into a new body, called the Council of Nationalities *(Sovet Natsional'nostei)*.[13]

While undergoing all those important structural changes, the Commissariat of Nationality Affairs claimed for itself ever broader and greater powers.   The November 1920 decree stated that no economic and political measures of the Soviet government applicable to the borderlands could become law unless approved by the Narkomnats, and that all the political organizations of the minorities were to deal with the central Soviet government only through their agencies at Narkomnats.[14]   When, a month later, the Commissariat established its branch offices in the autonomous states, it gave them authority to participate in the activities of the Central Executive Committees of the autonomous regions and republics.[15] In the summer of 1922, the Narkomnats claimed that it had the right to supervise the other commissariats of the Soviet Russian government insofar as their activities affected the national minorities, that it represented the autonomous republics in all budgetary matters, and that it alone directed the education of the non-Russian party and state cadres.[16]   In 1923, the forthcoming dissolution of the Narkomnats was justified by the fact that "it had completed its fundamental task of preparing the formation of the national republics and regions, and uniting them into a union of republics."[17]

Through such measures the Narkomnats was transformed from one of the minor ministries of the RSFSR into a federal government of the autonomous regions and republics of the RSFSR.[18]   At least, so it was in theory.   In reality, the role of the Narkomnats in the integration of the Soviet state was considerably smaller than its claims implied.   The autonomous regions and republics had so little self-rule left that their formal merger in a federal institution had virtually no practical consequences.   It was a measure of primarily bureaucratic significance.   In 1924 the Commissariat was dissolved and its Council of Nationalities became, through the addition of representatives of the full-fledged Soviet republics, the second chamber of the legislative branch of the government of the USSR.

RELATIONS BETWEEN THE RSFSR
AND THE OTHER SOVIET REPUBLICS

One of the main reasons why the Communists found it necessary to differentiate constitutionally between the various conquered borderlands, forming some into autonomous regions or republics and others into Soviet or Union republics, was the fact that some of the borderlands which had separated themselves from Russia in 1917 and 1918 had entered during the period of their independence into diplomatic or military relations with foreign powers. Thus, the Ukraine had participated in the Brest Litovsk negotiations; Belorussia had dealt with Germany and with Poland; the Transcaucasian republics had signed treaties with Turkey, had maintained diplomatic missions abroad, and had been recognized *de facto* and *de jure* by the most important Western powers. In order to replace the diplomatic representatives of the overthrown borderland republics and to take over their foreign commitments, it was necessary to create the impression that the subjugated lands retained their independence even after Soviet conquest. Hence, a certain distinction was made in Soviet political theory and constitutional law between the non-Russian areas situated inland, out of contact with foreign powers, and those located on the fringes. The inland areas were formed into autonomous regions and republics, while the outlying ones were made into so-called Union republics. Constitutionally, the cardinal difference between the two types of political organization lay in the fact that the Union republics were recognized as sovereign and independent states, with a right to separate from the RSFSR, whereas the autonomous regions and republics were not. But inasmuch as the right to separation was acknowledged by Soviet leaders to apply primarily to nations living in the "capitalist" part of the world, and the mere mention of this right in connection with areas under Soviet control was regarded as *prima facie* evidence of counterrevolutionary activity, this constitutional distinction had no practical consequences whatsoever, although it did have some psychological ones.

Having been conquered from without, the borderland areas in the Union category presented specific problems of integration. In the first flush of the Revolution (1917-18), the Communist regimes which had arisen in the borderland areas such as the Ukraine, Belorussia, and the Baltic states, had assumed all the prerogatives of the governments which they had overthrown. The first Communist government of the Ukraine, for example, had had a Council of People's Commissars composed of thirteen members, including the Commissars of War, Labor, Means of Communication, and Finance.[19] A similar situation had prevailed in the other borderland areas occupied by the Communists at this time. These governments had, therefore, to be absorbed gradually. The spread of authority of the RSFSR over the republics in this category began in the autumn of 1918 and continued virtually without interruption until 1923.

The first move to integrate the administration of the Soviet republics lying outside the RSFSR with that of the RSFSR was taken in connection with the centralization of the Soviet military apparatus. On September 30, 1918, the VTsIK created a Revolutionary-Military Committee, (*Revvoensovet*) of the Republic, under the chairmanship of Trotsky, to direct and coördinate the entire Soviet war effort against the White forces. The Revvoensovet was granted extraordinary authority in the combat zones and was empowered, somewhat ambiguously, to utilize all the resources of the Soviet state for the defense of the regime.[20] Its headquarters were in the railroad train which Trotsky used on his rapid inspections of various sectors of the front endangered by the enemy. From there, Trotsky made requests for manpower and supplies to the vice-chairman of the Revvoensovet, who resided in Moscow and served as a liaison between him and the pertinent government agencies.[21]

To overcome the delays and other difficulties which such an informal arrangement between the military and civil authorities' entailed, the Soviet government established on November 30, 1918, an organ which united all the agencies directly concerned with the prosecution of the war: the Council of Workers' and Peasants' Defense (*Sovet Rabochei i Krest'ianskoi Oborony*). This supreme administering body of war mobilization consisted of Lenin, Trotsky, Stalin, and representatives of the Commissariats of Communication (Commissar V.I. Nevskii), Provisions (Deputy Commissar N.P. Briukhanov), and the Extraordinary Commission for the Supply of the Red Army (Chairman L.B. Krasin). The decree establishing the Council instructed all the provincial Soviet institutions to obey the Council's directives.[22] From the point of view of the integration of the Soviet state, the importance of the Council lay in the fact that it exercised authority not only in the RSFSR, but also in Lithuania, Latvia, Belorussia, and the Ukraine; that is, in all those borderland areas where the Communists were in power at that time. The authority of the Council grew rapidly, especially in the Ukraine, which was for the major part of the Civil War an arena of military operations.

The question of formal relations between the government of the Soviet Ukraine and that of the RSFSR was raised in the early part of 1919, shortly after the Communists had dispersed the Directory at the Third Congress of the KP(b)U, held in March 1919 in Kharkov. The majority of the delegates agreed that the Ukraine and Russia should establish as close economic and administrative ties as possible. They also agreed that the Constitution of Soviet Ukraine should in all essential respects resemble that of Soviet Russia (adopted in 1918), with minor alterations to suit local conditions. However, Sverdlov, the representative of the Central Committee of the Russian Communist Party at the Congress, refused to approve even such a moderate view, insisting that the Constitution of the RSFSR was not merely a Russian one, but an international one, and therefore should be adopted by the Ukrainian Soviet Republic without any changes whatsoever.[23]

The relationships between the two governments were actually settled by a decree of the Central Committee of the Russian Communist Party, which was conveyed to the Ukrainian Communists by a directive dated April 24, 1919. According to this directive, the Ukrainian Commissariats of War and of the Means of Communication were to subordinate themselves fully to the corresponding ministries of the RSFSR; the Ukrainian Commissariats of National Economy and Food Supply were to be transferred from Kiev to Kharkov, where they could work under the direct supervision of Moscow and receive necessary funds directly, without requiring the services of the Ukrainian Soviet government; the Commissariat of State Control of the RSFSR was to extend its authority throughout the entire Ukraine; and finally, the Ukrainian railroads were to be directed by the Commissariat of Roads in Moscow.[24]

In May 1919 Trotsky arrived in the Ukraine and took over the government. He did away with the separate Ukrainian Red regiments, merging them with units of the Russian Red Army, and liquidated altogether the Ukrainian Commissariats of National Economy, Finance, and Means of Communications, transferring their functions to the local bureaus of the corresponding Russian commissariats.[25] In place of the Ukrainian Council of People's Commissars, which was, in effect, deprived of its *raison d'être* by the removal of its principal organs, Trotsky formed a local branch of the Russian Council of Workers' and Peasants' Defense. The Ukrainian Council had as chairman Rakovskii, and as deputy chairmen G.I. Petrovskii and A.A. Ioffe—persons unconnected with the Ukrainian Communist movement.[26] The measures put into practice in the Ukraine in the spring of 1919 were given broader validity in a decree of the Central Committee of the RKP of May 1919, which ordered the unification of all the Red Armies and railroad networks on the territories of the Ukraine, Latvia, Lithuania, Belorussia, and the RSFSR under the Council of Workers' and Peasants' Defense.[27]

A further step in the amalgamation of the RSFSR with the conquered borderlands was a decree of the VTsIK of June 1, 1919, called "On the Unification of the Soviet Republics of Russia, the Ukraine, Latvia, Lithuania, and Belorussia for the Struggle against World Imperialism." This decree deprived the enumerated non-Russian republics of their commissariats of War, National Economy, Railroads, Finance, and Labor, in favor of the corresponding commissariats of the RSFSR.[28] The decree broadened the authority which the RSFSR had enjoyed through the Council of Defense and embodied in the Soviet constitution legislation originally introduced as wartime emergency measures. The foundations of the state which eventually became the Union of Soviet Socialist Republics were thus laid not by agreement between the RSFSR and the individual, theoretically independent republics, but by decree of the Russian government. In this respect, therefore, there was little difference in the origins of the RSFSR and the USSR.

Another important similarity between the position of the autonomous states and the Soviet republics *vis-à-vis* the RSFSR was that in both instances the functions of federal government were vested not in a third power, separate and superior to the federating units, but in one of the states which itself was involved in the act of federation. The government of the RSFSR served as the highest state authority not only on its own territory, but also on the territories of the Ukraine, Belorussia, the Baltic states, Transcaucasia, and whatever other lands were conquered by Soviet troops.[29]

When, in 1920, the Communists conquered Azerbaijan, an area which, save for a brief period in the spring of 1918, had not been previously under their control, they found it desirable to establish interrepublican relations in a more formal manner. The discussions which ultimately led to the signing of a treaty between RSFSR and Azerbaijan were carried on between Lenin, Chicherin, and N.N. Krestinskii on the one side, and M.D. Guseinov and B. Shakhtakhtinskii on the other.[30] The treaty, signed on September 30, 1920, provided for the government of the RSFSR taking over the commissariats of War, Supply, Finance, Means of Transportation, and Communications, as well as all the organs regulating foreign trade and the internal economy. Significantly, it left Azerbaijan the right to retain its own commissariat of Foreign Affairs.[31] The treaty with Azerbaijan thus followed the pattern set by the decree of June 1, 1919.

On December 28, 1920, and January 16, 1921, the government of the RSFSR signed identical treaties with the governments of Soviet Ukraine and Belorussia. The divisions of authority between the government of the RSFSR and the republican governments was substantially the same as that provided for by the treaty with Azerbaijan. In addition, it stipulated that the two republics would appoint representatives to the commissariats taken over by the RSFSR, and that the exact relationships between the government agencies of the contracting parties would be determined by separate agreements. The two republics were allowed to retain their commissariats of Foreign Affairs and were declared in the preamble to be "independent and sovereign" states. The signatory for the Ukrainian side was Khristian Rakovskii, who two years earlier had served as a representative of the Russian Soviet government in its negotiations with the Ukrainian Rada.[32]

In 1921 and 1922 the republics certainly did not treat the right to the maintenance of diplomatic relations as a formality. Azerbaijan, to mention one example, established full relations with six foreign countries, dispatched its representatives to Turkey and Persia, and accredited diplomatic representatives of Germany and Finland.[33] The other republics also maintained at that time active diplomatic relations and participated in international negotiations either jointly with Soviet Russia or, on occasion, separately.

Such was the situation on the eve of the Soviet conquest of Georgia, which rounded out Communist possessions in Transcaucasia. The integration of Georgia, however, proved a much more difficult task than had been the case with the other borderland areas. The patriotic fervor of the Georgians, as well as the existence in Georgia of a relatively strong and rooted Bolshevik organization, precluded a simple incorporation of that area into Soviet Russia. The Soviet government preferred to accomplish the integration of Georgia and the other Transcaucasian republics in two phases: first, it made them surrender political power to a newly created Transcaucasian Federation and then it made the Federation cede these powers to Moscow. This procedure was in part dictated by economic considerations (Transcaucasia having traditionally functioned as an economic unit) and in part by political ones, namely, the desire to neutralize potential national opposition to "Russification."

In fact, the device of incorporating the republics by means of a federation engendered such bitter resistance, especially in Georgia, that the story of the relations between the Transcaucasian republics and the RSFSR after February 1921 belongs more properly in that part of our narrative which deals with the opposition to centralization.

THE PEOPLE'S REPUBLICS

The only political formations under Communist control which, for a time at least, enjoyed self-rule in practice as well as in theory were the so-called People's Republics, of which there were three in 1922: Bukhara, Khorezm (Khiva), and the Far East. The agreement between Soviet Russia and the Khorezmian Soviet People's Republic—which was signed on September 13, 1920, and established the pattern for this type of relationship—granted the RSFSR on the territory of Khorezm certain economic privileges, such as the right to exploit natural resources, to import and export without the payment of tariffs, and to use Russian currency.[34] In all other respects, Khorezm remained an independent republic. A similar agreement was signed on March 4, 1921, with the Bukharan People's Soviet Republic,[35] and on February 17, 1922, with the Far Eastern Republic.[36] In all three of these states the rights of the RSFSR were limited to economic matters.

The self-rule acquired by the Khorezmian, Bukharan, and Far Eastern Republics by virtue of treaties with the RSFSR was not left intact for long. In the case of Khorezm and Bukhara, their autonomy under the Communists was not intended as a permanent deviation from the pattern established in other parts of the country, but rather as a temporary *de facto* recognition of the unique status which these principalities had enjoyed under tsarist rule. The Far Eastern Republic, on the other, was quite frankly established as a buffer state intended to keep out the Japanese. Its government was not formally Communistic, but represented an alliance of various "democratic" groups under Communist control. As soon as the Red Army entered Vladivostok in the wake of the evacuating Japanese, the Far Eastern Republic was abolished and its territory incorporated into that of the RSFSR (October-November, 1922).[37] In Khorezm and Bukhara, the Communists gradually increased their authority throughout 1922 and 1923. In 1924, the Soviet government abolished these two People's Republics and later distributed their land among the five new republics created in place of those of Turkestan and Kirkhiz: Uzbek, Turkmen, Tajik, Kazakh, and Kirghiz.

THE OPPOSITION TO CENTRALIZATION

The process of integration of the state apparatus encountered serious opposition in the borderlands from groups both inside and outside the Communist Party. This "nationalist deviation" of the early 1920's constituted a stormy chapter in the history of the formation of the Soviet Union. The opposition can be divided into two principal types. There was the resistance of groups which, having collaborated with the Communists for the sake of essentially nationalistic aims, became eventually disillusioned with Communism and turned against it. There was also the opposition of those who had taken seriously the slogans of national self-determination and federalism and, seeing them violated by Stalin and his associates, became defenders of decentralization and states' rights. The former fought for nationalism, the latter for Communism. No collaboration between these two groups was possible, and hence opposition to centralization proved in the end ineffectual.

NATIONALIST OPPOSITION:
ENVER PASHA AND THE BASMACHIS

The Soviet conquest of Bukhara (September 1920) reinvigorated the Basmachi movement, which had begun to subside somewhat with the introduction by the Communists of a policy of economic and religious concessions in the first half of 1920. At first the Red Armies had little difficulty in conquering the mountainous sectors of the Bukharan principality, where the population, dissatisfied with the regime of the deposed Emir, was willing to accept a change in rule. But as soon as the Reds began to evacuate Eastern Bukhara, entrusting authority to native militias, various Basmachi chieftains appeared and took those territories back from the Communists. In the fall of 1921 most of Eastern Bukhara was in the hands of rebels. They were supplied with arms and personnel by the deposed Emir, who had fled to Afghanistan to continue from there the struggle for his throne.

Before long the Soviet regime also suffered setbacks in Western Bukhara. The two groups with whose assistance the Communists had come to power and to whom they entrusted the reins of government in the republic—the Young Bukharans and Young Bukharan Communists—disagreed sharply over the relations of the Bukharan Republic with Soviet Russia. The Young Bukharans, composed largely of liberals associated with pre-1917 jadidism, resented Communist penetration into Bukharan institutions and their meddling in local affairs. They complained that the new regime had brought "seven emirs" in the place of one—a reference to the seven commissars (*nazirs*) who comprised the all-powerful government of the Bukharan Republic.[38] The Young Bukharan Communists, on the other hand, among whom the younger, more radical elements predominated, cooperated fully with the Communists and strove for a closer integration of Bukhara with the Soviet system.

In the fall of 1921, when such internal difficulties threatened to upset Soviet authority in the Bukharan Republic, Enver Pasha, one of the leaders of the defunct Young Turkish government of Turkey, appeared in Turkestan.

Enver, who had acquired great fame throughout the Moslem world for his victories over the Italians in the African War of 1911-12, escaped at the end of World War I from Turkey to Germany. An ambitious man, endowed with a vivid imagination and undaunted personal courage (though quarrelsome and politically unskilled), Enver had little taste for the life of an émigré which the Turkish defeat had imposed on him. After a brief stay in Berlin, he decided to join his one-time associates Nuri Pasha, Dzhemal Pasha, and Halil Pasha, who had gone into the Soviet service. Hostile to England, he found in the anti-British policy pursued by the Soviet regime in 1920 an opportunity to play once more an active part in Middle Eastern politics. Enver arrived in Moscow in the fall of 1920, following a forced plane landing and brief detention in Riga. In September he attended the Baku Congress of Eastern Peoples sponsored by the Third International, where he presented a memorandum denouncing his own role in the First World War and pledging the Communists his support in the struggle against "Western imperialism."[39]

Enver spent most of 1921 in Transcaucasia, first in Baku and then, after the Communists had conquered Georgia, in Batum. Apparently he desired to reside as near the Turkish frontier as possible, to be in a position to assume leadership in Turkey. In the fall of that year the Soviet government decided to exploit his popularity among Moslems and to send him to Central Asia to help fight the Basmachis. Experience had shown that much success could be achieved by employing one-time Turkish officers to win the sympathies of natives for the Soviet cause.[40] At the same time, Dzhemal Pasha, who had resided in Tashkent since August 1920, was sent on a diplomatic mission to Afghanistan, probably to prevail on the Afghan authorities to stop the Emir of Bukhara and other Turkestani refugees from using that country as a supply base for the Basmachis.

Enver arrived in Bukhara at the beginning of November 1921. It did not take him long to perceive that he could achieve greater glory by joining the native dissidents than by continuing his ambivalent and uncertain role as a Communist agent. The Basmachi movement was as divided as ever after the failure of an attempt made earlier in the year to unite all the rebel groups under one leader.[41] The Khivan Basmachis were led by Dzhunaid Khan; those of the Samarkand district by Akhil Bek, Karakul Bek, and several other *kurbachis*; a chieftain named Hamdan ruled the district around Khodzhent; the Ferghana Basmachis were quarreling with each other, and so bitter were the rivalries there that, in some cases, partisan leaders resorted to assassination or went over to the Communists to help destroy their opponents. Even in Eastern Bukhara, where the Emir and his chief lieutenant, Ibrahim Bek, claimed full authority, there were numerous independent partisan leaders, who looked with disfavor upon the deposed monarch.[42]   Another source of weakness of the Basmachi rebellion, in addition to the rivalry of individual chieftains, was tribal feuding. Basmachi units of different ethnic origin were at times as busy warring with each other as they were fighting the Communists. Especially bitter was the hostility between the Kirghiz and the Uzbeks, and between the Turkmens and Uzbeks.[43]

It seemed to Enver that all that was needed to transform the genuine and deep-seated dissatisfaction, evident in all parts of Central Asia, into a vast and successful movement for the liberation of all of Turkestan, was the appearance of a personality able to overcome the disunity of Basmachestvo.   Enver apparently counted on his personal popularity with the Moslem population and on the appeal of his Pan-Turanian ideology, of which he had long been an avid exponent, to unite the rebel leaders and to stop the intertribal rivalries. With the boldness characteristic of his entire career, he decided, shortly after his arrival in Turkestan, to desert the Communist regime and to defect to the Basmachis. Sometime in November 1921, he left Bukhara with a small retinue, ostensibly to take part in a hunt.   In reality he made straight for the headquarters of Ibrahim Bek. With him deserted some of the most prominent members of the Bukharan government, including its chairman, Osman Khodzha, and the Commissars of Interior and of War.[44]

The Basmachis at first received Enver coolly, fearing a Communist snare and suspicious of the jadidist group which accompanied him.   But the Emir of Bukhara, with whom Enver had entered into a correspondence, instructed Ibrahim Bek to utilize Enver's military skills and to place him in command of the rebel armies fighting in Eastern Bukhara.[45] Establishing his headquarters in the mountains of Bukhara, Enver began to gather around himself some of the independent chieftains operating in that area.   His greatest success occurred early in 1922 when he captured Diushambe. From there he was able to impose his authority on the adjoining towns and villages. In the spring, having built up his force to an army of several thousand men, he began to attack Baisun, which obstructed the road to Western Bukhara and prevented him from spreading to the plains of Turkestan, but despite numerous charges he could not capture it.

Notwithstanding his initial triumphs, Enver failed to rally the bulk of the Basmachi forces to his leadership. He was merely another war lord, ruling a small territory and engaging in fights with neighboring chiefs. Of the sixteen thousand rebels active in Eastern Bukhara no more than three thousand owed him allegiance.[46] Great damage to Enver's cause resulted from his disagreements with the Emir and Ibrahim Bek. Enver was too ambitious to be content with mere partisan warfare, and so he interfered as well with the political life of non-Communist Bukhara. He tried to establish control over all the Basmachi units operating in Eastern Bukhara and incited the native population to expel all the Europeans from Central Asia.[47]   In May 1922, he sent an "ultimatum" to the government of Soviet Russia (through Nariman Narimanov, chairman of the government of Soviet Azerbaijan), in which he demanded the immediate withdrawal of all Russian troops from Turkestan, offering in return to assist the Communists in their Middle Eastern activities.[48] Before long he completely lost all political judgment and, when issuing decrees affecting the civil life of Eastern Bukhara without the consent of the Emir, he signed himself "Commander in Chief of all the Islamic troops, son-in-law of the Caliph, and representative of the Prophet."

Such behavior aroused the suspicions of the Emir, who was altogether none too pleased with the association between the Turkish general and the jadidist defectors from Soviet rule, such as Osman Khodzha, who only recently had been his worst enemies. In the summer of 1922, relations between the headquarters of Enver, located near Diushambe, and those of Ibrahim Bek, situated among the Lakai (a Turkic group, settled among the Iranian Tajiks), came near the breaking point. Soon, the Emir began to withhold support from Enver. On at least one occasion when Enver was hard pressed in combat, Ibrahim Bek refused to come to his assistance.[49] Later in the summer of 1922, the Afghan tribesmen who had been sent to his aid were ordered back to their homeland. Without the wholehearted support of the Emir, Enver was doomed. It is difficult to determine which played a larger part in his failure: his unwise handling of the Emir, or the struggle between the conservatives, represented by the Emir, and the progressive jadidists, of which he had become an unwitting victim. In August 1922, Enver was killed in combat with Red troops, who had surprised him and his small detachment in the mountains. His death ended all hope of a consolidation of the Basmachi forces.

To the Communist authorities the defection of Enver and the spread of the Basmachi revolt to Bukhara demonstrated conclusively that neither the policy of mere military suppression, tried between 1917 and 1920 and in 1921-22, nor the palliative measures tried in 1920-21 were sufficient to bring order to Central Asia. It was necessary to reverse completely the basic economic and political policies of the regime. Consequently, while undertaking a general military offensive against the Basmachis in Bukhara and other parts of Central Asia, the *Turkbiuro* of the Central Committee of the RKP and the *Turkomissia* introduced, in 1922, a series of far-reaching reforms. The most unpopular legislation of the previous rule was abrogated: the *vakuf* lands, previously confiscated for the benefit of the state, were returned to the Moslems; the religious schools, *medresse* and *mektebe*, were reopened; the *shariat* courts were brought back.[50] After these religious concessions, economic concessions were also granted. The New Economic Policy permitted the return of private trade and put an end to the forcible requisitions of food and cotton which had played a considerable part in arousing popular ire against the Communists.[51]

All these concessions had a pacifying effect on Central Asia. The natives, having suffered from the Civil War longer than the other inhabitants of the Soviet state, were eager for peace. As soon as the Communist regime had made it possible for them to return to their traditional ways of life, the Central Asian

Moslems gave up the struggle. The entire resistance movement known as Basmachestvo had been not so much an embodiment of a positive political or social philosophy as a desperate reaction to ill-treatment and abuse of authority, and it collapsed as soon as these irritants were removed.

The economic and religious concessions of the Communists deprived the Basmachi movement of its popular support and permitted the authorities first to localize and then to suppress it entirely. In the fall of 1922 the Ferghana rebels were wiped out. Although Ibrahim Bek continued to resist until 1926, when he fled to Afghanistan, the backbone of resistance in Bukhara was also broken by 1923. In Samarkand, however, the Red Army had to fight regular campaigns, supported by airplanes and tanks, as late as 1924.[52] Cut off from the population, the Basmachis reverted once more to brigandage, losing entirely the socioeconomic and political character which they had acquired temporarily in the course of the Civil War.

NATIONALIST-COMMUNIST OPPOSITION: SULTAN-GALIEV

Another form of nationalistic opposition occurred within the ranks of the Communist Party itself. Prominent in it were non-Russians of radical views who had joined the Communist movement in the course of the Revolution because of their conviction that the establishment of a socialist economy would more or less automatically lead to the destruction of all national oppression. Their nationalism, though tempered and molded by social radicalism, was not entirely dominated by it. When their faith in the ability of the new order to eliminate national inequalities had been shattered by the experiences of the Civil War period, Communists of this type sought redress in nationalism and independence from Moscow. The most important exponent of this tendency was the Tatar Communist, Sultan-Galiev. His quarrel with the party in 1922-23 became a *cause célèbre,* a test case which opened a heated discussion of the entire national question in the Soviet Union.

Sultan-Galiev had had much opportunity in his capacity as a high official in the Commissariat of Nationality Affairs to observe the effects of Soviet rule on the Moslem population. He was in contact with the Tatar Republic, where, as the leader of the right-wing Communist faction, he enjoyed considerable personal following; he had been sent to inspect and report on the situation of the Moslem population in the Crimea; and he had had many opportunities to meet and confer with important Moslem Communists and nationalists from Central Asia and other borderland areas. The total impression was so discouraging that Sultan-Galiev began to doubt whether the assumptions which had originally led him to embrace Communism had been sound. As early as 1919, in conversation with his Volga Tatar colleagues, he had expressed doubt whether the world-wide class struggle which the Russian Revolution had unleashed would really improve the lot of the colonial and semi-colonial peoples of the East. The industrial proletariat, he now suspected, was interested less in liberating the exploited colonial peoples from imperialism than in taking over for its own benefit the entire colonial system. From the point of view of the nonindustrial, colonial peoples, the proletariat's seizure of power would signify a mere change of masters. The English or French proletariats would find it advantageous to retain their country's colonial possessions and to continue the previous exploitation.[53]

Sultan-Galiev did not at first apply those ideas to Soviet Russia and coöperated with the Communist regime for at least two more years after he had first begun to question the inherent ability of the proletariat to solve the national question in the East. It was apparently under the impact of the New Economic Policy that he finally lost all hope in Communism. The NEP, which improved the material situation of the native population, also returned to positions of power the classes which he and other Moslem Communists had identified with the old colonial regime: Russian merchants and officials, as well as Moslem tradesmen and clergymen. Sultan-Galiev viewed the establishment of the NEP as the first formal step in a return to pre-1917 conditions and as the beginning of the liquidation of the socialist revolution in Russia; it increased his skepticism concerning the industrial proletariat's ability to liberate the world's oppressed nations.

He now began to draw broader theoretical conclusions from the evidence provided by four years of Communist rule. The economic inequalities of the world, he argued, could be eradicated not by a victory of the proletariat over the bourgeoisie but by the establishment of the hegemony of the backward areas over the industrialized ones. The war against the imperialism of industrialized societies, not the war against the bourgeoisie: this was the real conflict for universal liberation.

> We maintain that the formula which offers the replacement of the world-wide dictatorship of one class of European society (the bourgeoisie) by its antipode (the proletariat), i.e., by another of its classes, will not bring about a major change in the social life of the oppressed segment of humanity. At any rate, such a change, even if it were to occur, would be not for the better but for the worse . . . In contradistinction to this we advance another thesis: the idea that the material premises for a social transformation of humanity can be created only through the establishment of the dictatorship of the colonies and semi-colonies over the metropolitan areas.[54]

Such views struck at the very heart of the Marxist doctrine, but as long as Sultan-Galiev spread them only among his close associates, the Central Committee, which could not have been unaware of the trend of his thought, did not interfere. In the summer of 1921, as a matter of fact, the left-wing faction that had controlled the Volga Tatar Communist party and state apparatus was ousted, and the rightists took over. The chairmanship of the Tatar Council of People's Commissars was assumed by Keshshaf Mukhtarov, a friend and follower of Sultan-Galiev.[55] Soon, however, Sultan-Galiev began to make political demands as well. He advocated the creation of a Colonial International which would unite all the victims of colonial exploitation and would counterbalance the Third International, dominated by Western elements. He also desired the establishment of a Soviet Moslem (or Turkic) republic and the revival of the Moslem Communist Party, destroyed in 1918 by the Central Committee of the RKP.[56]   At this point the heavy hand of party discipline fell on his shoulder.

Sultan-Galiev was arrested in April or May 1923 on the order of Stalin, his immediate superior and former protector.[57]   His case was discussed at a special conference of representatives of minorities which gathered in Moscow in June 1923.   The charges against him were presented by Stalin who stated that whereas the shortage of adequate party cadres had compelled the Communists to cooperate with Moslem nationalists in the borderlands, the Soviet regime would not tolerate treason.   Stalin specifically accused Sultan-Galiev of collaboration with the Basmachis, with Validov, and with other Moslem nationalists fighting against the Soviet regime.   Sultan-Galiev, according to Stalin, "confessed his guilt fully, without concealment, and having confessed, repented."[58]

Despite his repentance, Sultan-Galiev was expelled from the Communist Party. According to Lev Kamenev, he was the first prominent party member purged on orders from Stalin.

COMMUNIST OPPOSITION: THE UKRAINE

The characteristic quality of the opposition to centralization in the Ukraine as well as in Georgia derived from the fact that nationalism in both these areas was not so much a cause as a consequence. The leaders of the opposition here were old and tried Bolsheviks, often with a record of outspoken hostility to nationalism in any form. If in 1922 and 1923 they became identified with the ideals of states' rights, it is largely because they perceived behind the process of centralization the growth of a new Russian bureaucracy and the personal ascendancy of Stalin and his coterie. The tenuous guarantees secured by the republics by decree and treaty became for them now bulwarks against the encroachments of a new breed of official whom the Revolution was supposed to have destroyed once and for all. While an Enver Pasha or even a Sultan-Galiev collaborated with Communism because Communism seemed best to further their national goals, men like Mykola Skrypnik, Rakovskii, Mdivani, or Makharadze turned nationalist in order to safeguard Communism.

The "nationalist deviation" in the Ukraine arose principally because of the failure of Moscow to adhere to the terms of the treaty of December 28, 1920. That treaty, it will be recalled, established an economic and military union between the RSFSR and the Soviet Ukraine. The Ukraine surrendered to the RSFSR certain commissariats (Army and Navy, Foreign Trade, Finance, Labor, Means of Communication, Post and Telegraphs, and the Higher Economic

Council), but was recognized, in return, as a sovereign and independent republic. The commissariats of the RSFSR had no right to issue directives to their Ukrainian counterparts without the sanction of the Ukrainian Sovnarkom (*Sovet Narodnykh Komissarov* or Council of People's Commissars); nor could they interfere at all with the commissariats left within the competence of the republic. The Ukrainian republic also retained the right to maintain its own commissariat of Foreign Affairs and to enter into diplomatic relations with foreign powers.[59]

It takes no expertise in the theory of federalism to realize that such an arrangement could not work. A country formally recognized as sovereign and independent, and engaged in foreign relations, could hardly allow another power to direct its internal affairs. Conversely, the officials of the government of the RSFSR, accustomed to treating all the territories of the old empire as one, had neither the experience nor the mental habits required to show respect for the intricacies of federal relations. As a result, the elaborate provisions of the 1920 treaty—which at least some officials in the Ukraine interpreted in good faith—remained a dead letter.

The clauses of the treaty, calling for mixed commissions to work out in detail the relations between the Russian and Ukrainian commissariats, were never actually carried out.[60] Throughout 1921 and the first half of 1922, the Sovnarkom and VTsIK of the RSFSR treated the Ukraine as if it were an intrinsic part of the RSFSR. It neither admitted Ukrainian representatives to the commissariats, as provided by the treaty, nor submitted to the Ukrainian Sovnarkom for approval directives to the Ukrainian commissariats.[61] Indeed, in most cases the Russian commissariats did not even trouble to consult their Ukrainian counterparts. The Ukrainians, naturally, protested against such violations of the treaty, but without effect. Their anger increased on occasions when Moscow issued directives to organs which the treaty left fully within the competence of the republic, such as the commissariats of agriculture and justice.[62] And when in May 1922 the Russian Commissariat of Foreign Affairs (probably in connection with the conferences at Genoa or Rapallo) infringed on the international status of the Ukrainian republic, the Ukrainian government sent to Moscow a formal protest, in which it objected to the presumption of the Russian government to speak in its name.[63]

In response to this note, the Central Committee of the Russian Communist Party appointed on May 11, 1922, a mixed commission, headed by Frunze, to investigate the Ukrainian complaint. The commission held two meetings in the course of the month. The main result of its deliberations was a resolution whose lengthy title conveys its contents: "On the inadmissibility of any measures which would lead in practice to the liquidation of the Ukrainian Soviet Socialist Republic, and to the reduction of the powers of its Central Committee, Council of People's Commissars, and central organs."[64] The commission condemned the Russian Commissariat of Foreign Affairs for having violated Ukrainian sovereignty and drafted several agreements between the commissariats of the two republics.[65] But it did not solve the more fundamental problems affecting Russo-Ukrainian relations.   Violations of Ukrainian constitutional rights continued. In September 1922, for example, the Commissariat of Education of the RSFSR issued an order applicable to the Ukraine, even though education was entirely within the competence of the latter.[66]

The chief spokesman of the Ukrainian grievances was M. Skrypnik. Little in his background pointed to his becoming the leader of the nationalist opposition in the Ukrainian Communist movement. Although born in the Ukraine, he had moved in 1900, at the age of 28, to St. Petersburg to attend the Technological Institute, and from then until 1917 he had resided in Russia or Siberia. He was an old Marxist, having joined the movement in 1897. After the split in the party in 1903 he had associated himself with the Bolsheviks and had worked for Lenin on various important assignments, including for a time as editor of *Pravda*. In October 1917, he had served on the Revolutionary Committee which directed the Bolshevik *coup d'état* in St. Petersburg. During 1918 and 1919, as a high Soviet official in the Ukraine, he had taken a "centrist" position between the pro-Ukrainian and pro-Moscow factions. The fact that in 1919 he had been appointed head of the department of the Cheka charged with fighting "counter-revolutionary movements," and in 1920 had been made Commissar of the Interior of the Ukraine, testifies to Lenin's having complete confidence in him.[67]

Skrypnik watched with apprehension and anger the utter disrespect which the Russian party and state apparatus showed for the Ukrainian republic. The violations of the 1920 treaty, related above, convinced him that a powerful faction in the Russian apparatus actually wanted to liquidate his republic and, being an outspoken man, he did not hesitate to make his views known. During the discussion of the nationality question at the Eleventh Party Congress, which met in March 1922, he delivered a brief but very pointed criticism of the party's Ukrainian policy. Referring to Lenin's statement that the Communists would emancipate the oppressed peoples of the whole world, Skrypnik said that they would achieve this aim only if they began to do so at home. The Communist party apparatus, in his opinion, was infiltrated with adherents of *Smena vekh*, ready to violate the party's solemn pledge proclaiming the Ukraine independent. "The one and indivisible Russia is not our slogan," he exclaimed—at which point a voice from the audience, however, shouted back ominously: "The one and indivisible Communist Party!"[68]

Skrypnik had occasion to make his views heard both at the Twelfth Party Congress (of which later) and at the special party conference which discussed the case of Sultan-Galiev. At this latter meeting, he took issue with Stalin's analysis of what came to be known as "sultangalievshchina." Sultan-Galiev's actions, he said, were a symptom of a grave disease affecting Communism, a disease caused by the failure of the Communists to carry out their national program, and particularly by their inability or unwillingness to check the growth of Great Russian chauvinism in the party and state apparatus. Sultan-Galiev was merely a scapegoat for the failures of others. The proper way to prevent the emergence of nationalist deviations, according to Skrypnik, was to destroy the national inequalities and injustices present in the Soviet system.

It is not possible to discover in Skrypnik's speeches or writings anything like a concrete ideology. His opposition was that of a convinced Communist who saw nationalism as a legacy of capitalism and, dismayed by its persistence under Communism, fought as best he could for Ukrainian autonomy. His uncompromising position made him many enemies in Moscow. In 1933, threatened with expulsion from the party, he committed suicide.[69]

COMMUNIST OPPOSITION: GEORGIA

The bitter conflict which broke out in Georgia almost immediately upon the establishment of Soviet rule there, and which lasted until the death of Lenin three years later, involved questions of both policy and personality. On the level of policy the main issue was one of authority: What was the power of the Kavbiuro, as an agency of the Russian Central Committee, over the Central Committees of the republican Communist parties? The leaders of these parties, especially those of the most powerful of them, the Communist Party of Georgia, were quite prepared to subordinate themselves to the directives of Moscow; but they were not willing to do the bidding of the Caucasian Bureau of the Central Committee, headed by the high-handed Ordzhonikidze. Their differences with the Kavbiuro came to a head over the establishment of a Transcaucasian federation, conceived in Moscow and executed by Ordzhonikidze, which threatened to deprive the three Transcaucasian republics of their independence and to transform them into something like the autonomous republics of the RSFSR. It was not long before a dispute over matters of policy transformed itself into a vicious personal feud between two groups of Georgian Communists: the Moscow group, represented by Ordzhonikidze and his supporter, Stalin, and the local, Tiflis group, headed by Mdivani. Lenin at first backed the former, but with time, as we shall see, changed his mind and became so angered by Stalin's and Ordzhonikidze's Caucasian activities that he contemplated taking disciplinary action against them.

On May 21, 1921, the RSFSR and the Georgián Soviet Republic signed a formal treaty modeled on the treaty with Azerbaijan, which recognized Georgia's "sovereignty and independence." The treaty established a military and economic union (but not a political one) between the two republics and provided that the exact arrangements on the merger of commissariats would be worked out by separate agreements. Implicitly, Georgia was allowed to retain its foreign representations, armed forces, and currency.[70]

Yet even before the treaty had been signed, the authorities in Moscow indicated that they were not prepared to respect the sovereignty of the

Transcaucasian republics, so solemnly proclaimed on various occasions. Lenin was anxious to achieve quickly the economic unification of Transcaucasia and particularly to integrate the Georgian transport facilities with those of Azerbaijan and Armenia with which they had been traditionally linked. He accordingly instructed Ordzhonikidze on April 9, 1921, to establish a single economic organization for all of Transcaucasia.[71] Ordzhonikidze began by merging the railroad network, the postal and telegraphic services, and the organs of foreign trade. In so doing, he did not consult the Central Committees of the republican parties, causing the Georgian Communists to protest to Moscow.[72]

In the summer of 1921, having concluded that economic integration was not possible without a political one, the Kavbiuro proceeded to lay the foundations for a Transcaucasian federation. To prepare the ground for what promised to be a delicate undertaking, Stalin was dispatched in early July to Tiflis. He was present at the meeting of the Kavbiuro which passed a resolution approving the federation. He also delivered a rather mild, reasonably worded speech in which he pointed out all the reasons for establishing a "certain degree of unity" between the RSFSR and Transcaucasia, but at the same time hastened to assure his audience that there was no intention of depriving the republics of their independence. In his talk he did say a few words, clearly directed at the Georgians, about the dangers of nationalism, but even they were quite conciliatory in tenor; and when some Communists from Baku accused Mdivani and Kote Tsintsadze, members of the Georgian Central Committee, of "nationalist deviationism" Stalin denied that this was the case.[73]

The Georgian Communists were unimpressed by the conciliatory tone of Stalin's words. Convinced that Stalin and Ordzhonikidze, with the support of some Armenian and Azerbaijani Communists, were in fact encroaching upon Georgian sovereignty, they openly disregarded the various measures which the Kavbiuro took to integrate their republic with the rest of the country. On at least one occasion Mdivani and his group sent a personal protest to the TsK (Central Committee) in Moscow.[74]

In view of this situation, it is not surprising that when on November 3, 1921, on instructions from Moscow, the Kavbiuro passed a formal resolution proclaiming the necessity of establishing a Transcaucasian federation, the Georgians protested most violently. The Kavbiuro took its decision without prior consultation of the republican Central Committees—a procedure which was improper as well as tactless. For the federation envisaged by the Kavbiuro was not only a military and economic one, but also a political one. It meant that the three republics surrendered the "independence and sovereignty" guaranteed them by their treaties with the RSFSR, and became in effect transformed into autonomous republics of a federation whose own relations with the RSFSR were not spelled out.[75]

The response was swift. Mdivani, speaking for a growing faction of the Georgian Communists, sent Lenin a personal message in which he predicted that if Ordzhonikidze persisted in forcing through the federation, Transcaucasia would rise in rebellion.[76] This time the opposition was not confined to the Georgians, however. Two young members of the Azerbaijani party, R. Akhundov and M.D. Guseinov, also advised Lenin against carrying out the federation at that time; [77] and so did M. Frunze, who could not be accused of any local interests.[78] The strength of the opposition was such that Lenin decided to reverse himself. On November 28, 1921, he issued a directive stating that while the Transcaucasian federation was necessary, it seemed premature; and that before being put into effect, it ought to be widely popularized in the Caucasus.[79]

The failure of the projected federation, on which Ordzhonikidze had pinned his hopes of smothering his Georgian opponents, certainly did not improve relations between the Georgian Central Committee and the Kavbiuro. The numerous political intrigues in which the two bodies engaged in their bitter rivalry need not detain us. Suffice it to say that the Kavbiuro, enjoying the support of Moscow, always had the upper hand, and the Georgians had to confine themselves to dilatory tactics.

In line with Lenin's instructions the Kavbiuro undertook in the winter of 1921-22 a propaganda campaign to persuade the population of the advantages of the projected federation. At the very same time, the Georgian government and Central Committee did everything in their power to keep the Kavbiuro from interfering in internal Georgian affairs. Early in January 1922, the Revolutionary-Military Committee of the Georgian Republic issued a decree proclaiming that, until the convocation of the First Congress of Soviets of the Republic, it claimed full and exclusive authority on the territory of the republic.[80] And the First Congress of Soviets of Georgia, meeting toward the end of February, approved a constitution of the republic which stated that "the Socialist Soviet Republic of Georgia was a sovereign state which did not permit any foreign power whatever to exercise equal authority on its territory." On the subject of the relations between Georgia and the other Soviet republics it was pointedly ambiguous. The constitution stated that when the "conditions for its creation came about" Georgia would join the International Socialist Soviet Republic; until then it expected to maintain "close" political and economic relations with the existing Soviet republics.[81]

Notwithstanding Georgian opposition, the Kavbiuro (renamed in February the Transcaucasian Regional Committee, or *Zakraikom*) proclaimed on March 12, 1922, the establishment of the Federal Union of the Soviet Socialist Republics of Transcaucasia *(Federativnyi Soiuz Sovetskikh Sotsialisticheskikh Respublik Zakavkaz'ia,* or *FSSSRZ).* The constitution of the federation provided that a Plenipotentiary Conference of representatives of the three federating republics elect as its supreme executive organ a Union Council *(Soiuznyi Sovet).* The Union Council had competence over the following spheres of governmental activity: military, financial, foreign affairs, foreign trade, transport, communications, organized combat against the counterrevolution (i.e., Cheka), and direction of the economy. Absolute control of the economy rested in a Higher Economic Council (*Vysshyi Ekonomicheskii Sovet*), which was to function as a permanent committee of the Union Council. The republics were allowed to retain their foreign legations and certain privileges in matters of tariffs and currency. They also were recognized as remaining legally independent and sovereign. The important matter of relations between the new federation and the RSFSR was to be left to be regulated by a separate agreement.[82]

The proclamation of the Transcaucasian union left little doubt in anyone's mind that the days of Georgian "independence and sovereignty" were numbered. The Central Committee of the Communist Party of Georgia commissioned, in December 1921, its most respected member, Makharadze, to address a memorandum to the Central Committee of the RKP expressing its principal grievances. In it Makharadze charged that the Georgian Communists had not been informed of the intention of Moscow to invade Georgia in February 1921, and for that reason had not been able to stage an internal uprising which would have prevented the entire coup against the Mensheviks from acquiring the character of a foreign invasion. Furthermore he alleged that the Kavbiuro had ignored the Georgian Central Committee and Revkom and thus had failed to win the sympathies of the Georgian population for the Soviet cause; that Ordzhonikidze had disobeyed Lenin's directives concerning the gentle treatment of the population, the creation of a Georgian Red Army, and a moderate economic policy; and that he had refused to take the Georgian Central Committee into his confidence in the matter of the proposed federation. Makharadze urged in conclusion that the process of federating the three Transcaucasian republics be considerably slowed down.

FORMULATION OF CONSTITUTIONAL PRINCIPLES OF THE UNION

The opposition in the Communist apparatus of the Ukraine and Georgia, particularly intense in the spring of 1922, induced the Central Committee to review the system of relations between the RSFSR and the other Soviet republics. This system had so far evolved haphazardly, by means of bilateral treaties. It not only failed to define with the necessary precision the division of authority between the Russian and republican governments, but confused matters by assigning to the government of the RSFSR functions involving at one and the same time the RSFSR and the federation as a whole. Soviet Russia's entrance on the international diplomatic scene in the spring of 1922 made the need for normalizing relations between the center and the borderlands more urgent than ever. Clearly, Moscow's international position was not strengthened by its recognition of Ukrainian, Belorussian, and Transcaucasian independence. The time had come to supplement the economic and military unions of 1920-21 with a tighter political one.

Which precise event caused the Central Committee on August 10, 1922, to appoint a constitutional commission is a matter of controversy. Frunze hinted that it was the dispute with the Ukraine over foreign policy.[83] Ordzhonikidze, on the other hand, claimed that the commission was convened on the initiative of Stalin and himself in connection with the Georgian affair.[84] Georgian matters seem to have had something to do with initiating the procedures which eventually led to the formation of the union, for the commission was appointed immediately after the Central Committee had heard a report on Georgia.[85] The commission, whose assignment it was to draft for the Plenum a statement defining the relations between the RSFSR and the republics, was headed by Stalin, and included representatives of both the RKP and the republican parties; but the final report was drafted by a four-man subcommittee consisting of Stalin, Ordzhonikidze, Molotov, and A.F. Miasnikov—all reputed "centralists."[86]

Stalin had never been much impressed either by Lenin's fine distinction between "autonomous republics" and "Soviet republics," or by his high regard for diplomatic niceties in the matter of independence of the republics. This much he had made clear in 1920 in a private letter to Lenin. Commenting on the theses on the national and colonial questions which Lenin had drafted for the Second Congress of the Comintern, Stalin denied that there was a meaningful difference between "autonomous" and "Soviet" republics. "In your theses," he wrote, "you draw a distinction between Bashkir and Ukrainian types of federal union, but in fact there is no such difference, or it is so small as to equal zero."[87] Since by 1921 the position of the Soviet republics had declined as compared to 1920, Stalin had no reason to change his mind; and in drafting his project he proceeded from the same assumption.

In the project Stalin strove to give a straightforward and realistic expression to the constitutional practice that had evolved in the preceding five years under Lenin's personal tutelage. That is to say, he treated the Soviet domain as a unified, centralized state and the government of the RSFSR as the *de facto* government of all the six Soviet republics. In this manner he hoped to eliminate all those difficulties which the legal fiction of "independence" of the republics had made for those who were running the country.

His draft, called "Project of a Resolution Concerning the Relations between the RSFSR and the Independent Republics," first revealed in 1956, has not yet been published in its entirety, but its main points can be readily reconstructed. The key clause was the first one, calling for the entrance of the five border republics into the RSFSR on the basis of autonomy.[88] If carried out, this clause would have transformed the Ukraine, Belorussia, Georgia, Azerbaijan, and Armenia into autonomous republics of the RSFSR, on a par with the Iakut or the Crimean republics, and would have swept aside the whole elaborate system of relations established by the treaties. The second article provided for the organs of the RSFSR—its Central Executive Committee, Council of People's Commissars, and Council of Labor and Defence—to assume the functions of the federal government for all the six republics. The remaining three articles specified which commissariats were to be taken over by the Russian government, which were to be left to the republics but to function under the control of the corresponding agencies of the RSFSR, and which were to be entrusted entirely to the autonomous republics.[89]

Stalin completed his project at the end of August and dispatched it to the Central Committees of the republics for discussion and approval. It is important to note, however, that even before the republics had reacted, Stalin, on August 29, 1922, sent a wire to Mdivani announcing the extension of the authority of the Russian government: the Sovnarkom VTsIK, and STO (*Sovet Truda i Oborony*, or Council of Labor and Defence), over the governments of all the republics.[90] The Georgians were so enraged by this unilateral abrogation of the 1921 treaty that they dispatched to Moscow a three-man delegation, which was later joined by Mdivani.[91]

As may be expected, Stalin's draft had no difficulty securing the approval of the Azerbaijani Communist Party, which was under Ordzhonikidze's firm control.[92] But no other republican Central Committee (with the possible exception of the Armenian) followed suit. The first vocal opposition came from the Georgians. On September 15, 1922, the Georgian Central Committee flatly turned down Stalin's theses, voting unanimously, with one dissent (Eliava) "to consider premature the unification of the independent republics on the basis of autonomization, proposed by Comrade Stalin's theses. We regard the unification of economic endeavor and of general policy indispensable, but with the retention of all the attributes of independence."[93] Ordzhonikidze, who with Kirov attended these proceedings, then decided to overrule the Georgians. On the following day he convened the Presidium of the Zakraikom, which he headed, and had it pass a resolution approving Stalin's project. The Presidium also ordered the Georgian Central Committee, on its personal responsibility, not to inform the rank and file of its negative decision and to carry out faithfully Stalin's instructions.[94]

The Belorussians responded (on September 16) evasively. First, they asked for territory to be added to their republic; then they stated that as far as relations with the RSFSR were concerned, they would be satisfied with the same arrangement as that made by the Ukraine.[95] The Ukrainians, having procrastinated until October 3, finally passed a resolution which categorically demanded the preservation of Ukrainian independence and the establishment of relations with the RSFSR on the basis of principles formulated by Frunze's commission the previous May.[96]

Stalin's commission reconvened on September 23. It had little to show by way of republican approval, but the lack of enthusiasm in the borderlands apparently did not much trouble either Stalin or his colleagues. There was more discussion of the draft, during which some clauses were criticized and possibly even changed. No one, however, challenged the fundamental premise of "autonomization."[97] Having secured the approval of the commission, Stalin forwarded to Lenin the minutes of its meetings, as well as the favorable resolutions of the Azerbaijani Communist Party and the Zakraikom.[98]

Lenin apparently had not been kept well informed of the commission's work, for the data which Stalin supplied dismayed and angered him. From Lenin's point of view, the project undid the pseudofederal edifice which he had so carefully constructed over the past five years. Worst of all, it threatened to upset the whole fiction of national equality which Lenin counted on to mollify and neutralize the nationalist sentiments of the minorities. He saw no practical advantages to be derived from incorporation of the five independent republics into the RSFSR. Its only consequence would have been to reveal, with brutal frankness, the dependence of all the Communist republics on Russia and to make it very difficult in the future to win nationalist movements for Bolshevism in the so-called colonial and semi-colonial areas.

As soon as he had become acquainted with the commission's materials, Lenin summoned Stalin. He severely criticized his project and exerted on him strong pressure to modify all those points which formalized the hegemony of the RSFSR over the other republics. He wished for an arrangement whereby all the republics, the RSFSR included, constituted a new federation, with a separate government, called the Union of Soviet Socialist Republics of Europe and Asia. Stalin yielded to Lenin on this and agreed to abandon the idea of "autonomization" advocated in the first article of his project in favor of a federal union of equal states. But he refused to concede on the second article. Lenin's demand for the creation of new federal central organs—an All-Union Central Executive Committee, Sovnarkom, and Council of Labor and Defence—to supersede those of the RSFSR seemed to him administratively cumbersome and superfluous. Stalin thought that Lenin's purpose could be achieved as well by the simpler device of renaming the organs of the RSFSR as all-Union ones. But Lenin disagreed and criticized Stalin for being impatient and excessively addicted to administrative procedures. On the conclusion of their interview, both men put down their views in a memorandum which they forwarded to Lev Kamenev, then acting chairman of the Sovnarkom.[99] Stalin's note was surprisingly insolent in tone.

In the end, Stalin had to yield all along the line and, on the basis of Lenin's criticism, to revise his entire project. The project was discussed at a meeting of the Plenum on October 6, 1922. Lenin, suffering from a severe toothache, had to absent himself from this session, but he made his views unmistakably clear in a note which he sent to his colleagues on that day: "I declare war on Great Russian chauvinism; a war not for life but for death. As soon as I get rid of that accursed tooth of mine, I shall devour it with all my healthy ones."[100] He also repeated his insistence that Stalin modify article two of his project. The Plenum accepted Lenin's suggestions, and voted in favor of a new draft calling for the establishment of a Union of Soviet Socialist Republics governed by a newly created Union Central Executive Committee of representatives of the republican Central Executive Committees. The Plenum also appointed a commission of eleven members to translate these principles into a constitutional project.[101] It may be noted that Mdivani participated as a guest in these deliberations and, however reluctantly, gave his approval in the name of the Georgian party, but only after having insisted that the Georgian republic enter the Union directly, as a full-fledged member.[102]

After its approval by the Plenum, the new draft of constitutional principles was sent to the Central Committees of the non-Russian republics. In Transcaucasia, the Azerbaijani and Armenian parties gave their approval promptly, but the Georgians once more made difficulties. From one point of view, the new statement was preferable to the previous one, which they had so unceremoniously rejected on September 15: the federating republics now entered the Union as formally independent states, equal to the RSFSR. But the new project also had one very serious drawback. Whereas Stalin's old project envisaged the three Transcaucasian republics as entering the RSFSR directly, the new one provided for their joining the Union through the intermediacy of the Transcaucasian Federation. To the Georgian Communists this provision seemed ludicrous and insulting. Why, for instance, should Belorussia have the right to become a full-fledged member of the Union, and not Georgia? And what was the point of creating a federation if the proposed Union would absorb most of the republican commissariats anyway? A double political union—once with the Transcaucasian Federation, and then, through the Federation, with the Union—simply made no sense to them. The Georgians, therefore, protested to Moscow, demanding the abandonment of the projected federation.[103] To this request Stalin replied on October 16 in the name of the Central Committee, stating that it was unanimously rejected.[104]

Tempers in Georgia now reached the point of explosion. Dissident Communist leaders held secret meetings at which they complained of the violation of their rights and criticized the policies of Moscow.[105] They secured at this time the support of the most distinguished Georgian Communist, Makharadze, who on October 19 made a speech in Tiflis pleading for Georgia's direct entrance into the Union.[106] Makharadze was not only the oldest Georgian Bolshevik (like Zhordania he had become a Marxist while attending the university in Warsaw in 1891-92), but he had a well-earned reputation of being an irreconcilable enemy of nationalism. Before the Revolution he had opposed Lenin's slogan of national self-determination from a position which Lenin called "nihilistic"; during the Revolution (at the April 1917 Bolshevik Congress) he had led the faction which demanded the removal of that slogan from the party's program; and in 1921-22, despite some misgivings, he had collaborated with Ordzhonikidze's centralistic measures. That a Communist of such background should have joined the opposition provides evidence of the near unanimity which existed in Georgia at this time.

On October 20, the three members of the Georgian delegation returned from the mission to Moscow on which they had been dispatched at the end of August and reported to the Central Committee. Having heard them, the Committee voted (twelve to three) to appeal to Moscow once more for reconsideration. Accepting now as binding the decision to establish a Transcaucasian federation, it nevertheless requested the abolition of the Union Council and Georgia's direct entrance into the Union, on the same terms as the Ukraine.[107] Simultaneously, Makharadze and Tsintsadze sent strong personal letters to Kamenev and Bukharin complaining about Ordzhonikidze.[108]

Lenin by this time had had his fill of the Georgians. He interpreted their actions as a breach of party discipline as well as a failure to adhere to a decision taken with the concurrence of their representative. On October 21 he dispatched to Tiflis a sharply worded wire in which he rejected their request and stated that he was turning the whole matter over to the Secretariat, that is, to Stalin.[109] Kamenev and Bukharin sent separate wires to Makharadze and Mdivani accusing them of nationalism and insisting that they coöperate in the establishment of the federation.[110] Upon receipt of these dispatches the Central Committee of the Georgian Communist Party on October 22 took the unprecedented step of tendering the Central Committee of the Russian Communist Party its resignation.[111] The resignation was accepted, and a new Georgian Central Committee was promptly appointed by the Zakraikom. It consisted mostly of young converts to Communism who lacked both experience and reputation, and whom Mdivani contemptuously dismissed as "Komsomoltsy."[112] With their support, Ordzhonikidze had no difficulty securing full cooperation and approval of the new constitutional project.[113]

The Georgian affair delayed by several weeks the drafting of the Union agreement. The constitutional committee reassembled again only on November 21, without having accomplished anything in the interval. It now appointed a subcommittee, chaired by the Commissar of Foreign Affairs, G.V. Chicherin, to prepare the draft of a constitution.[114] Chicherin had his draft ready within a week's time.[115] It was at once approved by the constitutional committee and by the Central Committee (Lenin included) and, in the course of December, by the Congresses of Soviets of the four federating republics (Transcaucasia being treated now as a single federal republic).[116] On December 29, 1922, representatives of the republics attended a conference in the Kremlin at which Stalin read the articles of the Union. After some protests, most likely from some Georgians, the majority of those present voted in favor of the act.[117] Next day a joint session of the Tenth Congress of Soviets of the RSFSR and the deputies of the congresses of soviets of the Ukraine, Belorussia, and Transcaucasia took place in Moscow's Bolshoi Theatre. This joint session called itself the First Congress of Soviets of the Union of Soviet Socialist Republics.[118]

Its main order of business was to ratify the agreement establishing the Soviet Union—a task which it was confidently expected to fulfill, since 95 per cent of all the deputies were members of the Communist Party and as such were required by party discipline to vote for resolutions passed by the Central Committee.[119] The Congress did not disappoint those expectations.

The agreement stipulated that the supreme legislative organ of the new state was the Congress of Soviets of the USSR and that during intervals between its sessions, the role passed to the Central Executive Committee of the Congress of Soviets. The sessions of the Congress of Soviets were to be held by rotation in the capitals of each of the four republics. The highest executive organ of the Union was to be the Council of People's Commissars of the USSR (*Sovnarkom Soiuza*), elected by the Central Executive Committee and composed of the following officials: a chairman, a deputy chairman; the Commissars of Foreign Affairs, War and Navy, Foreign Trade, Means of Communications, Post and Telegraphs, Workers' and Peasants' Inspection, Labor, Supply, Finance; the Chairman of the Higher Council of National Economy; and in an advisory capacity, the head of the Secret Police (OGPU). The Union republics were to have their own councils of people's commissars composed of the Commissars for Agriculture, Supply, Finance, Labor, Interior, Justice, Workers' and Peasants' Inspection, Education, Health, Social Security; the Chairman of the Higher Council of National Economy; and as consultants, representatives of the federal commissariats. The Commissariats of Supply, Finance, Labor Workers' and Peasants' Inspection, and the Higher Council of National Economy of each of the republican governments were to be directly subordinated to the corresponding agencies of the federal government. The agreement thus distinguished three types of commissariats: federal, republican, and joint. Strictly within the competence of the republican governments were only the Commissariats of Agriculture, Interior, Justice, Education, Health, and Social Security. The final article of the agreement guaranteed every republic the right of secession from the Union, despite the fact that, according to the preceding article, only the federal government could effect changes in the Union Agreement—such as, presumably, matters of entering and leaving the Union.[120]

The Presidium of the Central Executive Committee, appointed by the First Congress of Soviets of the USSR, formed on January 10, 1923, six separate commissions to prepare the draft of a constitution based on the articles of the Union Agreement.[121]

LENIN'S CHANGE OF MIND

The Georgian opposition, whose history since early 1921 we have traced, was of importance not only for its role in shaping the constitution, but also for its impact on Lenin's attitude toward the nationality question. It provided overwhelming evidence against the basic premise of Lenin's nationality policy: that nationalism was a transitional, historical phenomenon associated with the era of capitalism and bound to dissolve in the heat of intense class struggle. Lenin observed with obvious dismay a new kind of nationalism emerging in the

Russian as well as in the minority Communist apparatus—that very apparatus on which he depended to eradicate national animosities. As this evidence accumulated in the winter of 1922-23, Lenin went through a reappraisal of Soviet nationality policy which bore all the marks of a true intellectual crisis. It is likely that had he not suffered a nearly fatal stroke in March 1923 the final structure of the Soviet Union would have been quite different from that which Stalin ultimately gave it.

To understand Lenin's change of mind one must bear in mind the effect which both internal and external events since 1917 had had on his nationality policy. Self-determination interpreted as the right to secession was in fact a dead letter. So was federalism, since the military and economic exigencies of the Soviet state, requiring the merger of the conquered borderlands with the RSFSR, had vitiated the very essence of the federal system which Lenin had been forced to adopt as a substitute for self-determination. The minorities were thus left without any effective guarantees against the encroachment of the central authorities; and yet they needed these more than ever in view of the unlimited authority enjoyed by the Communist party over the citizenry. In the end, Lenin's national program reduced itself to a matter of personal behavior: it depended for the solution of the complex problems of a multinational empire upon the tact and good will of Communist officials. To Lenin such a solution seemed perfectly feasible, in part because he himself was a stranger to national prejudices, and in part because he believed that the establishment of Communism destroyed the soil in which nationalism could flourish.

In fact, however, Lenin's expectations were quite unfounded. Like every staunch realist, he mistook that segment of reality of which he happened to be aware for reality as a whole, and in the end displayed no little naïveté. Nationalism may well have been rooted in psychology, in the memory of wrongs done or in sensitivity to slights; but surely it was more than that. It reflected also specific interests and striving that could not be satisfied merely by tact but required real political and other concessions. Nor could the groups on which Lenin counted to carry out what was left of his nationality program display that reasonableness this program demanded. Before as well as after 1917 even the closest of his followers had rejected his concessions to the nationalities as impractical and incompatible with the Bolshevik ideology. If the Soviet Constitution of 1918 and the Communist program of 1919 had included his formulae calling for a federation based on the national principle and the retention of the slogan of national self-determination (although in a highly qualified form), it was only because of Lenin's tremendous prestige with the Party. The majority of the Bolshevik leaders remained unconvinced, and the numerous new rank and file who had joined the Communists since the Revolution (in 1922 they constituted 97.3 per cent of the active party membership)[122] were even less prepared to assimilate the subtle reasoning which lay behind his national program. To the overwhelming majority of Communists and Communist sympathizers, the goals of the movement—the "dictatorship of the proletariat," the "unity of the anticapitalist front," or the "destruction of counterrevolutionary forces"—were synonymous with the establishment of Great Russian hegemony. The Soviet Russian republic alone had the industrial and military might necessary to accomplish these ends. After the failure of the Communist revolutions in Central Europe, it became the arsenal and fortress of world Communism. The Communist movements in the Russian borderlands had proved themselves weak and incapable of survival without the military assistance of Soviet Russia. The bulk of the membership of the Communist Party came from the urban and industrial centers of the country and hence was predominantly Russian ethnically and culturally. In 1922, 72 per cent of all the members of the Communist Party (including its regional organizations in the Ukraine, Transcaucasia, and the other borderlands) were Russian by origin, and at least another 10 per cent were Russian by language . . .. The administrative personnel of Soviet republics, drawn largely from the bureaucracy of the *ancien régime*, was probably even more heavily dominated by Russian and Russified elements.

The preponderance of Great Russians in the political apparatus was not in any sense due to a peculiar affinity of members of that nationality for the Communist movement, since, as statistics indicate, the proportion of Communists among the entire Russian population was only slightly higher than the country-wide average, and there were several national groups whose ratio of Communists was considerably larger. It was rather due to the fact that the industrial and urban population in the country was predominantly of Russian stock, and that a large proportion of the non-Russians likely to engage in political activity were assimilated. In a democratic state such a one-sided ethnic composition of a party would not necessarily have had great practical consequences; it was different in a totalitarian country, where the party was in full control. Already in the course of the Revolution the equation *Communism = Russia* had been made in many of the borderlands by both Russians and non-Russians, especially in the eastern regions. As I indicated in the discussion of the 1917-20 period, many elements that had nothing in common with Communist ideology had sided with the Communists because they felt that the regime was essentially devoted to Great Russian interests. This identification of the Communist movement with the Russian cause had inspired much of the opposition in the borderlands to the Soviet government. But it was only after 1920, after the end of the Civil War, that the growth of Great Russian nationalism in the Communist movement became unmistakably evident. At the Tenth Party Congress, held in 1921, a number of speakers called attention to it:

> The fact that Russia had first entered on the road of the revolution, that Russia had transformed itself from a colony—an actual colony of Western Europe—into the center of the world movement, this fact has filled with pride the hearts of those who

had been connected with the Russian Revolution and engendered a peculiar Red Russian patriotism. And we now see how our comrades consider themselves with pride, and not without reason, as Russians, and at times even look upon themselves above all as Russians.[123]

Communist writers acquainted with the Soviet Moslem region pointed to the prevalence of Great Russian nationalism in the eastern borderlands:

It is necessary to acknowledge the fact that not only the officialdom in the borderlands, which consists largely of officials of the old regime, but also the proletariat inhabiting those areas which actively supports the revolution, consists in its majority of persons of Russian nationality. In Turkestan, for example, Russian workers thought that once the dictatorship of the proletariat had been established, it should work only for *their* benefit as workers, and that they could fully ignore the interests of the backward agricultural and nomadic population, which had not yet reached their "proletarian" level of consciousness. The same thing had occurred in Azerbaijan, Bashkiriia, and elsewhere. This situation had caused the broad masses of the native population to think that, when you come right down to it, nothing has changed, and that the *Russian* official has been replaced by a *Russian* proletarian, who, although he talks of equality, in reality, like the previous *Russian* official, takes care only of himself, ignoring the interests of the local population.[124]

The Tenth Congress was the first to take cognizance of the emergence of Great Russian nationalism in the Communist apparatus by including in its resolutions a strongly worded condemnation of what it called "the danger of Great Russian chauvinism."[125]

In view of this development, was Lenin realistic in entrusting the ultimate authority in the controversial matter of relations between the Great Russian majority of the population and its non-Russian minority to the Communist Party? It was psychologically as well as administratively contradictory to strive for the supremacy of the proletariat, and at the same time to demand that this proletariat, which was largely Russian, place itself in a morally defensive position regarding the minorities; to have an all-powerful party, a fully centralized state, and also genuine self-rule in the borderlands; to have the political apparatus suppress ruthlessly all opposition to the regime in Russia proper and adopt a conciliatory attitude toward dissident nationalism in the republics.

Yet if, despite all these factors, Lenin stood fast by his solution of the nationality question, it is because of its bearing on the long-range prospects of Communism. The failure of the revolution in Germany, which he had regarded as essential for the eventual triumph of the Communist Revolution, made Lenin pay even greater attention to the so-called colonial peoples of the East. Hence the possibilities of a successful revolution seemed much greater than in Europe. And even though such a revolution would not immediately bring down the capitalist powers, it was expected so to weaken their economic position as to make an ultimate collapse inevitable. But a revolution in Asia and Africa required the use of nationalist slogans, which the Communists could employ only if they proved to be effective champions of national independence. It is for this reason that Lenin considered it of vital importance to dissociate Communism from Great Russian nationalism, with which it had tended to fuse since the end of the Civil War.

Of the three outstanding Communist leaders in the early 1920's, Stalin seems to have realized most clearly the contradictions inherent in the Communist nationality program. The nationalist opposition was divided and ineffective; Lenin approved all the measures giving priority to the Russian apparatus, though he winced at their inevitable consequences; while Trotsky showed little interest in the whole national question. Stalin, however, placed himself squarely on the side of the central apparatus and identified himself with the Great Russian core of the Party and state bureaucracy. He thus stood in the center of Communism's last, and perhaps bitterest, struggle over the national question.

The demoted Georgian Communists kept on sending Lenin telegrams and letters in which they complained of their treatment at the hands of Ordzhonikidze, and requested an impartial inquiry. One such letter particularly attracted Lenin's attention. Written by a prominent figure of the opposition, M. Okudzhava, it accused Ordzhonikidze of personally insulting and threatening Georgian Communists.[126] Lenin turned this letter and other documents over to the Secretariat of the Central Committee, which on November 24 appointed a three-man commission to investigate on the spot the whole Georgian party crisis and in particular the circumstances surrounding the resignation of the old Central Committee. The commission was headed by Dzerzhinskii, and included V. S. Mitskevich-Kapsukas and Manuilskii.[127] Although technically all three were non-Russians, they could hardly have been regarded as representatives of the minority point of view. Manuilskii in particular was known as an outspoken centralist: only three months before he had welcomed enthusiastically Stalin's plan of "autonomization."[128] Dzerzhinskii's ties with Stalin also did not augur well for the opposition. Lenin must have had some misgivings of this kind, for a few days after the departure of the Dzerzhinskii commission, he asked Rykov to follow it to Tiflis to make an independent inquiry.[129] According to the log of Lenin's secretary, he awaited the return of the emissaries with great impatience.[130]

Rykov came back first and reported to Lenin at Gorki on December 9.[131] What he said we do not know. But how anxious Lenin was to learn all he could is seen from the fact that the instant Dzerzhinskii returned to Moscow (December 12) he departed in haste from Gorki, where he was convalescing, for the Kremlin, and there met with Dzerzhinskii the very same day.[132] Although Dzerzhinskii completely exonerated Ordzhonikidze and Stalin in their dealing with the Georgians,[133] some of the evidence he brought back greatly disturbed

Lenin—so much so that from then on he could hardly get the Georgian affair out of his mind. He was troubled most of all by a rather minor incident, to which, for some reason he attached great importance. It involved a quarrel between Ordzhonikidze and a Georgian Communist named A. Kabakhidze, which ended with Ordzhonikidze giving his opponent a beating.[134] Lenin was infuriated both by Ordzhonikidze's use of physical violence and by Dzerzhinskii's casual treatment of it. He instructed Dzerzhinskii to return to Tiflis to gather more information on this incident, and in the meantime called in Stalin, with whom he had an interview lasting for over two hours.[135] The facts which began to come in from Georgia confirmed his worst suspicions, and he became acutely depressed.[136] Having returned to Gorki, he intended the following day (December 15) to write Kamenev a substantial letter on the nationality question,[137] but before he had a chance to do so he suffered another stroke.

While Lenin lay incapacitated, Ordzhonikidze, with Stalin's support, proceeded further to whittle down the powers left the Transcaucasian federation. The new federation, established in December 1922 as the Transcaucasian Soviet Federative Socialist Republic (*Zakavkazskaia Sovetskaia Federativnaia Sotsialisticheskaia Respublika,* or *ZSFSR*), was much more centralist than that envisaged in the constitution of the previous March. It also said nothing about the independence of the constituent republics.[138] To reduce anticipated Georgian resistance, the Central Committee of the RKP on December 21 ordered the leaders of the opposition, Mdivani, Makharadze, Tsintsadze, and Kavtaradze, to leave Georgia, justifying its decision by the information which it said Dzerzhinskii's commission had supplied.[139] How powerful Ordzhonikidze's hold on his area was by now may be gleaned from the fact that in December 1922, at the First Congress of Soviets of Transcaucasia, he was hailed by someone as "the leader of the toiling masses of Transcaucasia."[140]

Lenin, having toward the end of December recovered from his stroke, tried at all costs to resume work. He had difficulty with the doctors who did not permit him to do so, until, by threatening to ignore medical advice altogether, he won from them the right to dictate every day, for ten or fifteen minutes, a personal diary.[141] He immediately took advantage of this right to dictate several important memoranda, including one on the nationality question. . . . This memorandum, Lenin's last theoretical contribution on the subject of the national problem, was originally not intended for publication, inasmuch as it contained derogatory remarks about three members of the Central Committee. It became known only because of its involvement in the rivalry between Trotsky and Stalin. . . .

Lenin's analysis of the Georgian incident suffered from all the limitations imposed on him by the Communist dogma. He was unable to perceive that the failures of the Soviet national policy were due to a fundamental misinterpretation of the entire national problem and followed naturally from the dictatorial system of government which he had established. His mind operated only in terms of class enemies.   Seeking scapegoats, he blamed all national friction on the "bourgeois" elements in the state apparatus, disregarding the fact that in the Georgian crisis the guilty ones, by his own admission, were top members of the Communist Party.   His remedies consisted only of reversion to party control of the political apparatus, linguistic measures, and the introduction of "codes of behavior" for Communist officials working in the borderlands—methods which had proved themselves unequal to the task in the previous years of Soviet rule. Nothing illustrated better the confusion which by now pervaded his thoughts on the subject than his contradictory recommendation that the union of republics be both "retained and strengthened" and in effect weakened by restoring to the republics full independence in all but military and diplomatic affairs.[142]

Lenin, hoping to recover from his illness, kept the memorandum to himself, with the intention of basing on it a major policy statement at the forthcoming Twelfth Party Congress.   In the meantime he busily gathered evidence against Stalin and Ordzhonikidze.   He probably did not realize, however, how quickly power was slipping from his hands.   When, on January 27, 1923, Dzerzhinskii had returned from his second Caucasian mission and Lenin, through his secretary, demanded to see the materials he had brought back, Dzerzhinskii replied that he had turned all materials over to Stalin.   A search for Stalin revealed that he was out of town and unreachable.   Upon his return two days later, Stalin flatly refused to surrender the materials and did so only when Lenin threatened to put up a fight for them.[143]   There can be little doubt that, although Stalin pretended to be concerned with Lenin's health, in fact he was personally interested in keeping Lenin as much as possible out of the Georgian feud.

Lenin by now could rely only on a few devoted women from his private secretariat.   He turned over to them all the materials brought back by Dzerzhinskii and prepared a questionnaire which they were to use in analyzing them.   The questionnaire contained the following seven questions: What was the deviation with which the Georgian Central Committee was charged?   In what respect did it violate party discipline?   In what ways was it oppressed by the Zakraikom?   What instances were there of physical violence used against the Georgians?   What was the policy of the Central Committee of the RKP when Lenin was present compared to when he was absent?   Did Dzerzhinskii on his second trip also investigate the charges against Ordzhonikidze?   What was the present situation in Georgia?[144]   While the secretaries were busy at work preparing the report, Lenin constantly inquired about their progress.   According to the diary of his personal secretary, in February 1923 the Georgian question was then uppermost in his mind.[145]

In the meantime, the formation of the Soviet Union was forging ahead.   In February 1923 the Plenum of the Central Committee (from which Lenin was also absent) decided to add a second chamber to the Union legislature to represent the national groups.   Originally, the Communists had been hostile to the idea of a bicameral legislature, considering it a feature of a "class society" and unnecessary in the "proletarian" state. In November 1922 Stalin had stated that, although some Communists were advocating the creation of a second, upper chamber to provide representation for the nationalities as such, he felt that this view "will undoubtedly find no sympathy in the national republics, if only because the two-chamber system, with the existence of an upper chamber, is not compatible with the Soviet government, at any rate, at the present stage of its development."[146] By February, however, Stalin changed his mind in favor of a bicameral legislature, largely, in all likelihood, because it enabled him to increase his personal control over the Soviet legislature. The Council of Nationalities (*Sovet natsional'nostei*), which was approved by the party and incorporated into the Constitution, was the same Council of Nationalities that Stalin had formed as part of the Commissariat of Nationality Affairs in April 1921, with the addition of deputies from the three Union republics. The second chamber was, therefore, staffed with people who had Stalin's personal approval.[147]

Lenin finally received the report on March 3. It must have infuriated him, because he now switched his support completely to the side of the Georgian opposition. His first impulse was to form a new and impartial investigating commission;[148] the second, to entrust the handling of the whole Georgian affair to Trotsky. On March 5, he addressed to Trotsky the following letter:[149]

> Respected Comrade Trotsky! I would very much like to ask you to take upon yourself the defence of the Georgian case in the Central Committee of the Party. The matter is now being "prosecuted" by Stalin and Dzerzhinskii, on whose objectivity I cannot rely. Quite on the contrary. If you agree to assume responsibility for the defence, I shall be at ease. If for some reason you do not agree to do so, please return the materials to me. I shall consider this a sign of your refusal. With best comradely greetings,
> Lenin

With this letter, Lenin forwarded to Trotsky his memorandum on the nationality question.[150]

The following day Lenin sent a brief but significant message to the leaders of the Georgian opposition:[151]

> To Comrades Mdivani, Makharadze, and others: copies to comrades Trotsky and Kamenev. Respected Comrades! I follow your case with all my heart. I am appalled by the coarseness of Ordzhonikidze, and the connivances of Stalin and Dzerzhinskii. I am preparing for you notes and a speech.
> Respectfully,
> Lenin

Simultaneously, Lenin dispatched to Georgia a new investigating commission, consisting of Kamenev and Kuibyshev.

Decidedly, events were taking a dangerous course for Stalin and Ordzhonikidze. They were saved from a public chastisement by sheer good fortune. On the day when he had dictated his letter to Mdivani and Makharadze, Lenin suffered his third stroke, which paralyzed him completely and removed him for good from all political activity.

THE LAST DISCUSSION OF THE NATIONALITY QUESTION

Lenin's third attack deprived the Georgian opposition, and all those who for one reason or another wanted to slow down the inexorable advance of centralization, of their main means of support. It soon became evident that Trotsky neither could nor would assume the task which Lenin had entrusted to him. Instead of taking the issue to the party leadership, he tried first to obtain permission from the entire Central Committee to make public Lenin's memorandum on the nationality question.[152] Whether he failed to secure it, or whether courage deserted him, is not certain. At any rate, Trotsky did not take charge of the anti-Stalinist opposition among the minorities; and thus he failed to take advantage of an excellent opportunity to embarrass his principal rival at a critical phase in their struggle for power. Lenin's note, having passed through the hands of the entire Central Committee, became widely known to the deputies to the Twelfth Party Congress which assembled in Moscow in April 1923. It was behind all the acrimonious debates on the nationality question which took place there.

The nationality question broke into the open at one of the early sessions of the Congress, during the discussions of the report on the party's Central Committee. Mdivani, unable to control his anger, launched a bitter tirade against the policies pursued by the Central Committee and its Caucasian Bureau in Georgia. Makharadze supported him, charging that much of the responsibility for the interparty quarrels in Georgia rested on Ordzhonikidze, who had ignored the old Georgian Bolsheviks in favor of newcomers. He emphatically denied the charge that the Georgian Communists had hindered the unification of Transcaucasia, asserting that they had objected only to the methods and the tempo with which this unification was being accomplished. Ordzhonikidze and Orakhelashvili, speaking for the Stalinist faction, pointed to numerous examples of "nationalist deviations" on the part of the Georgian Central Committee and Georgian government. They also taunted Makharadze with his record as a "nihilist" in the national question and as an opponent of Lenin's national program.[153] Stalin took no pains to conceal his utter contempt for the Georgian oppositions. "I think that some of the comrades, working on a certain piece of Soviet territory, called Georgia," he said, "have apparently something wrong with their marbles."[154]

The discussion on the national question, temporarily shelved after this premature explosion, was resumed at a later session. The principal report was delivered by Stalin. In his report, Stalin skillfully maneuvered between the two extreme views on the problem, stressing simultaneously the danger of Great Russian nationalism under the New Economic Policy and the need for the unification of the Soviet state.[155] But in the course of the discussions, in which he answered criticism leveled at the Soviet treatment of the minorities, Stalin made it unmistakably plain that he was not prepared to go along with Lenin's thesis on the relationship of the Russians toward the minorities:

> For us, as Communists, it is clear that the basis of all our work is the work for the strengthening of the rule of the workers, and only after this comes the second question—an important question, but subordinated to the first—the national question. We are told that one should not offend the nationalities. This is entirely correct, I agree with this—they should not be offended. But to create from this ideal a new theory, that it is necessary to place the Great Russian proletariat in a position of inferiority in regard to the once oppressed nations, is an absurdity. That which Comrade Lenin uses as a metaphor in his well-known article, Bukharin transforms into a whole slogan. It is clear, however, that the political basis of the proletarian dictatorship is in the first place and above all in the central, industrial regions, and not in the borderlands, which represent peasant countries. If we should lean too far in the direction of the peasant borderlands at the expense of the proletarian region, then a crack may develop in the system of proletarian dictatorship. This, comrades, is dangerous. In politics it is not good to stretch too far, just as it is not good to stretch too little.[156]

Next, Stalin proceeded to quote from Lenin's previously published works to the effect that the class principle had priority over the national one, and that the Communists from the minority areas were obliged to strive for a close union with the Communists of the nation which had oppressed them. It did not take great subtlety to realize that "the proletarian region," whose hegemony Stalin advocated, meant Russia, and that his references to Lenin's works were inspired by a desire to offset the damage which Lenin's memorandum had done to Stalin's prestige, by indicating the inconsistencies inherent in Lenin's national theory. To Lenin's statement that "it is better to stretch too far in the direction of complaisance and softness toward the national minorities, than too little," Stalin replied that it was not advisable to stretch too far, either.

The case for the opposition was hopeless. Not only was the Congress packed with Stalinists,[157] but the opposition was also severely handicapped in its choice of arguments. The basic Communist assumptions worked to the advantage of Stalin. The unity, centralization, and omnipotence of the Communist Party, the hegemony of the industrial proletariat over the peasantry, the subordination of the national principle to the class principle—all those Communist doctrines which were in fact responsible for the plight of the minorities—were axiomatic and beyond dispute.   By challenging them, the opposition would have placed itself outside the party.   The opposition, therefore, had to limit itself to criticism of the practical execution of the Communist national program.   One speaker after another of the opposition pointed out the injustices and failures of the Communist regime in the borderlands: the discrimination against non-Russians in the Red Army ("The army still remains a weapon of Russification of the Ukrainian population and of all the minority peoples," Skrypnik stated),[158] in schools, and in the treatment of the natives by officials.   But such charges, damning as they were, did not affect the fundamental premises of Stalin's case and were easily brushed aside as exaggerations or minor infractions.

The only attempt to analyze the deeper causes of the crisis in the national policy was made by Rakovskii, who rested his argument on Lenin's thesis of the defective apparatus:

> Comrades, this [national question] is one of those questions which is pregnant with very serious complications for Soviet Russia and the Party. This is one of those questions which—this must be said openly and honestly at a Party Congress—threaten civil war, if we fail to show the necessary sensitivity, the necessary understanding, with regard to it. It is the question of the bond of the revolutionary Russian proletariat with the sixty million non-Russian peasants, who under the national banner raise their demands for a share in the economic and political life of the Soviet Union.[159]

Stalin, Rakovskii continued, was oversimplifying the danger of Great Russian nationalism in the party and state apparatus when he called it, in the course of his report, a mere by-product of the New Economic Policy. The real cause of the crisis lay deeper: "[It is] the fundamental divergence which occurs from day to day and becomes ever greater and greater: [the divergence] between our Party, our program on the one hand, and our political apparatus on the other." The state apparatus was, as Lenin said in his memorandum, an aristocratic and bourgeois remnant, anointed with the Communist chrism." Rakovskii cited a number of instances of the organs of the RSFSR having issued decrees and laws for the other three Soviet republics even before the Union had been formally ratified and the authority of the federal government constitutionally ascertained, and he charged that since December 1922 the Union commissariats had actually governed the entire country, leaving the republics no self-rule whatsoever. To implement Stalin's suggestions on the means for combating the mounting wave of Russian nationalism, Rakovskii concluded, it was necessary to strip the government of the Union of Soviet Socialist Republics of nine tenths of its commissariats.[160]

How weak the opposition really was became painfully evident when Rakovskii placed before the Congress formal resolutions to reduce the preponderance of the Russian republic in the Union government. He had occupied himself much during the previous several months with constitutional questions and even had drafted a constitutional project which vested much more authority in the republics than did the one formulated in Moscow.[161] That Rakovskii should have become a defender of states' rights seemed rather strange in view of his whole record as a "nihilist" on the nationality question. But he was a close and loyal friend of Trotsky, and, armed with Lenin's memorandum, he must have felt on solid ground. He now pointed out that, under the existing system, the RSFSR had three times as many representatives in the Soviet of Nationalities as the remaining three republics put together, and suggested a constitutional arrangement which would prevent any one republic from having more than two fifths of the total representation. Stalin, however, brushed aside this motion as "administrative fetishism." It was subsequently voted down.[162] The inability of the opposition to secure acceptance of even such a watered-down version of Rakovskii's project (his original idea of granting the republics nine tenths of the commissariats which the articles of Union had given the federal government was whittled down in committee during the discussion of the constitutional question) indicated the extent to which Stalin and the central party apparatus had gained mastery of the situation.

The Twelfth Congress thus rejected all the suggestions which Lenin had made in his article in the hope of healing the breach in the party caused by the national question: it refused to diminish the centralization of the state apparatus of the USSR by granting the republics more organs of self-rule; it vindicated Stalin and Ordzhonikidze; and most important of all, it turned down, through Stalin, the fundamental principle of Lenin's approach, namely the necessity of having the Russians place themselves in a morally defensive position in regard to the minorities. The Twelfth Congress, the last at which the national question was discussed in an atmosphere of relatively free expression, ended in the complete triumph of Stalin. The issue of self-rule versus centralism on the administrative level was decided in favor of the latter. Henceforth nothing could prevent the process of amalgamation of the state apparatus from being brought to its conclusion—the more so, since Lenin, the only person capable of altering its course, was entirely eliminated from active participation in politics.

On July 6, 1923, the Central Executive Committee of the USSR formally approved the Constitution of the USSR, and on January 31, 1924—ten days after Lenin's death—the Second All-Union Congress of Soviets ratified it. The process of formation of the Soviet Union was thus brought to an end.

CONCLUSION

Although the roots of the national movements which emerged in the course of the Russian Revolution have to be sought in the tsarist period, their anti-Russian and separatist aspects were a direct result of the political and social upheaval which followed the breakdown of the *ancien régime*. Before 1917 the political activities of the minorities were closely integrated with the socialist and liberal tendencies of Russian society itself and represented regional variants of developments which were occurring at the same time on an all-Russian scale. These activities were limited to relatively small groups of intellectuals, who sought to secure for the minorities a greater degree of participation in the government of the Empire through democratization and autonomy. After 1917 the national movements assumed a somewhat different character. The disintegration of political authority and the eruption of violent agrarian revolutions throughout the Russian Empire had severed the bonds between the borderlands and the center and had left the responsibility for the solution of the most urgent social and political problems to the population itself. Those groups came to power which were most capable of adjusting themselves to the rapid vacillations of public opinion. In Russia proper and in other areas inhabited by Great Russians, it was the Bolshevik Party which, with its slogans of peace, division of land, and all power to the soviets, temporarily won considerable public support. In most of the borderlands, power was won by the nationalist intelligentsia, which pledged an independent solution of the agrarian problem, the redress of injustices committed by the tsarist regime, and neutrality in the Russian Civil War. In Russia, as well as in some of the borderlands, political authority was seized by extremists who had attained mass following only after the outbreak of the Revolution, when the spread of anarchy, confusion, and fear favored groups advocating radical solutions.

But whereas the Bolsheviks had long prepared for a revolution and knew what to do with power once they had attained it, the nationalists did not. They had lacked the opportunities to evolve an ideology or to secure disciplined party cadres. The nationalist movements after 1917 suffered from profound cleavages among conservative, liberal, and radical tendencies, which prevented them from attaining the unity necessary for effective action. In critical moments, the national governments which had sprung up in the borderlands were weakened from within, torn by dissensions among the divergent groups combined under the banners of nationalism. Another weakness of the nationalists was their inability, and, in some instances, their unwillingness, to win over the predominantly Russian and Russified urban population of the borderlands. They were also far too dependent on the politically immature and ineffective rural population. When in the winter of 1917-18 the Bolsheviks and their followers in the armed forces struck for power in the borderland territories, most of the national governments collapsed without offering serious resistance. The only notable exception was Transcaucasia, where the existence of strong indigenous parties, especially the Georgian Social Democrats, and the fear of foreign invasion which united the Russian and most of the non-Russian population, gave the local governments a certain degree of cohesion and strength. The circumstances under which the national republics of what became the Soviet

Union emerged were too exceptional and their life span too short for the record to be used as evidence either for or against their viability.

The conflict between the Bolsheviks and the nationalists which broke out in all the borderland areas after the October Revolution, as a result of the Bolshevik suppression of nationalist political institutions, would probably have led to a lasting rupture between them, had it not been for the leaders of the White movement who virtually drove the nationalists into the arms of the Bolsheviks. The White generals proved incapable of grasping either the significance of the national movements or the assistance which they could offer in fighting the Communists. They rejected outright the political claims of the minorities and postponed the solution of the national question to the time when the Bolshevik usurpers should be overthrown and a legitimate Russian government established. In some instances, the White leaders antagonized the minorities inhabiting the theater of combat or their own rear lines to the point where armed conflicts broke out.

The Bolsheviks, on the other hand, made determined efforts, throughout the Civil War, to exploit minority nationalism. The entire Bolshevik national program was designed to win nationalist sympathies through generous offers of national self-determination. Whenever expedient, they made alliances with even the most reactionary groups among the minorities, who, fearful of losing the freedom which the collapse of all government authority had given them, lent a willing ear to Bolshevik promises. Though there were some exceptions—notably in Central Asia—the Communists generally succeeded in winning nationalist support at a time when the struggle for power in Russia was at critical stages. In the campaigns against Kolchak in the Urals and against Denikin in the Northern Caucasus, the alliance between the Reds and the nationalists helped tip the scales in favor of the Soviet regime.

The Bolshevik approach, however, although it had brought immediate advantages, also had its shortcomings. It was more useful as a means of fighting for power than as a program for a party which had acquired power. It was one thing to exploit the mistakes of the opponent by means of promises, and another to make those promises good after the enemy had been overcome. Their entire approach to the national idea, moreover, made the Bolsheviks perhaps the least qualified of all the Russian parties (save for those of the extreme right) to solve the national problem. Not only was their political system based on the dictatorship of a single party, on strict centralism, and on the superiority of the urban, industrial elements over the remainder of the population—doctrines which in themselves precluded an equitable solution of the minority problem—but they also underestimated the viability of nationalism. They were inclined to view it as a mere relic of the bourgeois era, which was bound to disappear once the proletarian class struggle and the world revolution got under way, and they ignored the fact that nationalist movements represented in many cases genuine social, economic, and cultural aspirations. All manifestations of nationalism appearing after the establishment of Soviet power Lenin considered to be due either to the aftereffects of the old regime, or to the alleged influence of functionaries of the tsarist bureaucracy on the Soviet political apparatus. To destroy it once and for all, in Lenin's opinion, it was necessary only to adopt a friendly, conciliatory attitude toward the non-Russian subjects. That nationalism itself represented an aspect of the economic struggle, the Bolsheviks neither could nor would admit. Lenin, the chief architect of Soviet national policy, thus fell victim to his own doctrinairism. The crisis which shook the Communist Party over the national question in the early 1920's, and the Communist confusion over the persistence of national antagonisms in the Soviet Union and even in the party itself, were due largely to the inability of the Communists to recognize the flaw in their monistic class interpretation of world events.

The Soviet Union, as it emerged in 1923, was a compromise between doctrine and reality: an attempt to reconcile the Bolshevik strivings for absolute unity and centralization of all power in the hands of the party, with the recognition of the empirical fact that nationalism did survive the collapse of the old order. It was viewed as a temporary solution only, as a transitional stage to a completely centralized and supra-national world-wide soviet state. From the point of view of self-rule the Communist government was even less generous to the minorities than its tsarist predecessor had been: it destroyed independent parties, tribal self-rule, religious and cultural institutions. It was a unitary, centralized, totalitarian state such as the tsarist state had never been. On the other hand, by granting the minorities extensive linguistic autonomy and by placing the national-territorial principle at the base of the state's political administration, the Communists gave constitutional recognition to the multinational structure of the Soviet population. In view of the importance which language and territory have for the development of national consciousness—particularly for people who, like the Russian minorities during the Revolution, have had some experience of self-rule—this purely formal feature of the Soviet Constitution may well prove to have been historically one of the most consequential aspects of the formation of the Soviet Union.

Notes

1. Quoted in E. H. Carr, *The Bolshevik Revolution, 1917-1923*, I (New York, 1951), 117.

2. Program of the Russian Communist party (1919), in TsK, RKP(b), *Rossiskaia Kommunisticheskaia Partiia (bol'shevikov) v rezoliutsiiakh ee s"ezdov i konferentsii* (1898-1922 gg.) (Moscow-Petrograd, 1923), 255-56.

3. *Ibid.*, 254.

4. *Ibid.*, 253-54.

5. Carr, *The Bolshevik Revolution*, I, 139.

6. D. Magerovskii, "Soiuz Sovetskikh Sotsialisticheskikh Respublikh," *SP,* no. 1/4 (1923), 30-33.

7. *Ibid.* 10; V. Durdenevskii, "Na putiakh k russkomu federal'nomu pravu," *SP*, no. 1/4 (1923), 30-33.

8. *Stalin*, IV, 402.

9. B.D. Pletnev, "Gosudarstvennaia struktura RSFSR," *Pravo i zhizn'* (Moscow), no. 1 (1922), 29-30. See also the opinions of D.A. Magerovskii, *Soiuz Sovetskikh Sotsialistichestikh Respublik (obzor i materialy)* (Moscow, 1923), 20; G.S. Gurvich, *Osnovy sovetskoi konstitutsii* (Moscow, 1926), 149ff; N.N. Alekseev, "Sovetskii federalizm," *Evraziiskii vremennik* (Paris), V (1927), 255, and M.Langhans, "Die staatsrechtliche Entwicklung der auf Russischen boden lebenden kleineren Nationalitaeten," *Archiv fuer Oeffentliches Recht, Neue Folge*, IV (1925), 195.

10. *Izvestiia*, 22 May 1920.

11. *Ibid.*, 6 November 1920.

12. *Ibid.*, 21 December 1920.

13. *Ibid.*, 27 April 1921.

14. *Ibid.,* 6 November 1920.

15. *Ibid.*, 21 December 1920.

16. *Revue du Monde Musulman*, LI (1922), 26-33.

17. G.K. Klinger, ed., *Sovetskaia politika za 10 let po natsional'nomu voprosu v RSFSR* (Moscow-Leningrad, 1928), 24; cf. I. Trainin, "K likvidatsii Narkomnatsa," *ZHN*, no 1/6 (1924), 19-30.

18. P. Miliukov, *Rossiia na perelome*, II (Paris, 1927), 249.

19. KP(b)U, Institut Istorii Partii, *Istoriia KP(b)U* (Kiev, 1933), II, 264-65.

20. *Sistematicheskii sbornik vazhneishikh dekretov, 1917-1920* (Moscow, 1921), 63.

21. L. Trotsky, *My Life* (New York, 1931), 411-22.

22. *LS,* XVIII (1931), 243; *Lenin*, XXVI, 619-20.

23. M. Ravich-Cherkasskii, *Istoriia Kommunisticheskoi Partii Ukrainy* [Kharkov], 1923), 111.

24. E.G. Bosh, *God bor'by* (1917) (Moscow, 1925), 92.

25. B.D. Wolfe, "The Influence of Early Military Decisions upon the National Structure of the Soviet Union," *"The American Slavic and East European Review*, IX (1950), 1969-79; Ravich-Cherkasskii, *Istoriia*, 131-32.

26. Ravich-Cherkasskii, *Istoriia*, 131-132.

27. *LS,* XXXIV (1942), 120-21.

28. Magerovskii, *Soiuz,*, 68-69.

29. S.I. Iakubovskaia, *Stroitel'stvo Soiuznogo Sovetskogo Sotsialisticheskogo gosudarstva, 1922-1925 gg.* (Moscow, 1960), 123.

30. The background of the Russian-Azerbaijani treaty is discussed by M.S. Iskenderov, *Iz istorii bor'by Kommunisticheskoi partii Azerbaidzhana za pobedu Sovetskoi vlasti* (Baku, 1958), 515-17, and E. A. Tokarzhevskii, *Ocherki istorii Sovetskogo Azerbaidzhana v period perekhoda na mirnuiu rabotu po vosstanovleniiu narodnogo khoziastva (1921-1925 gg.)* (Baku, 1956), 88-90.

31. RSFSR, Narodnyi komissariat po inostrannym delam, *Sbornik deistvuiushchikh dogovorov, soglashenii i konventsii, zakliuchennykh RSFSR s inostrannymi stranami* (Moscow-Peterburg, 1921-22), I, 1-9; henceforth referred to as NKID, *Sbornik*.

32. *Ibid.*, 15-17 and 13-15; cf. above, 137-38.

33. Tokarzhevskii, *Ocherki*, 89.

34. NKID, *Sbornik*, I, 17-27.

35. *Ibid.*, II, 7ff.

36. Iu. V. Kliuchnikov and A. Sabanin, *Mezhdunarodnaia politika noveishego vremeni v dogovorakh, notakh i deklaratsiiakh* (Moscow, 1925-29), III, 167ff.

37. "Dalnevostochnaia Respublika (DVR)," *Bol'shaia Sovetskaia Entsiklopedia*, 1st ed., XX (Moscow, 1930), 216-21.

38. *Revue du Monde Musulman*, LI, 224-25.

39. Kommunisticheskii Internatsional i osvobozhdenie Vostoka, *Pervyi s "ezd narodov Vostoka--stenograficheskie otchety* (Petrograd, 1920), 108-12 (NN).

40. D. Soloveichik, "Revoliutsionnaia Bukhara," NV, no. 2 (1922), 277.

41. M. Chokaev, "The Basmaji Movement in Turkestan," *The Asiatic Review* (London), XXIV, no. 78 (1928), 284-85.

42. K. Okay, *Enver Pascha, der grosse Freund Deutschlands* (Berlin, [1935]), 387-88.

43. Soloveichik, "Revoliutsionnaia Bukhara," *passim*.

44. *Ibid.*, *Revue du Monde Musulman*, LI, 229.

45. Soloveichik, "Revoliutsionnaia Bukhara," 283; Saïd Alim Khan (Emir of Bukhara), *La Voix de la Boukharie opprimée* (Paris, 1929), 37.

46.[K.] Vasilevskii, "Fazy basmacheskogo dvizheniia v Srednei Azii," NV, no. 29 (1930), 134.

47. Soloveichik, "Revoliutsionnaia Bukhara," 283.

48. *Revue du Monde Musulman*, LI, 229-30, cites text of the ultimatum.

49. Soloveichik, "Revoliutsionnaia Bukhara," 284, has Enver's letter to the Emir; cf. Vasilevksii, "Fazy," 134.

50. Vasilevskii, "Fazy," 135; Chokaev, "The Basmaji Movement," 282; J. Castagne, *Les Basmatchis* (Paris, 1925), 34.

51. Vasilevskii, "Fazy," 135.

52. I. Kutiakov, *Krasnaia konnitsa i vozdushynyi flot v pustyniakh--1924 god* (Moscow-Leningrad, 1930).

53. VKP(b), Tatarskii Oblastnoi Komitet, *Stenograficheskii otchet IX obslastnoi konferentsii tatarskoi organizatsii R.K.P. (b)* (Kazan, 1924), 130.

54. Sultan-Galiev, quoted in A. Arsharuni and Kh. Gabidullin, *Ocherki panislamizma i pantiurkizma v Rossii* [Moscow], 1931), 78-79; see also A. Arsharuni, "Ideologii Sultangalievshchiny," *Antireligioznik* (Moscow), no. 5 (1930), 22-29, and M. Kobetskii, "Sultan-Galievshchina kak apologiia Islama," *Antireligioznik*, no. 1 (1930), 12-16, (NN).

55. L. Rubenstein, *V bor'be za leninskuiu natsional'nuiu politiku* (Kazan, 1930), 75ff.

56. Arsharuni and Gabidullin, *Ocherki*, 78-86; G. von Mende, *Der nationale Kampf der Russlandtuerken* (Berlin, 1936), 158.

57. L. Trotsky, *Stalin* (New York, [1941]), 417.

58. *Stalin*, V, 305.

59. NKID, *Sbornik*, I, 15-16.

60. Magerovskii, *Soiuz*, 24.

61. Iakubovskaia, *Stroitel'stvo,* 130.

62. V.M. Kurtisyn, *Gosudarstvennoe sotrudnichestvo mezhdu Ukrainskoi SSR i RSFSR v 1917-1922 gg.* (Moscow, 1957), 141, 144.

63. S. Gililov, *V.I. Lenin—Organizator Sovetskogo mnogonatsional'nogo gosudarstva* (Moscow, 1960), 145-46.

64. V.V. Pentkovskaia, "Rol' V.I. Lenina v obrazovanii SSSR," *VI,* no. 3 (1956), 14-15; Iakubovskaia, *Stroitel'stvo,* 139-40.

65. Iakubovskia, *Stroitel'stvo,* 140-41; Pentkovksia, "Rol' V. I. Lenina," 15; V. Chirko, *Ob"iednavchyi rukh na Ukraini za stvorennia Soiuzu RSR* (Kiev, 1954), 120.

66. Iakubovskaia, *Stroitel'stvo,* 130, 141-42.

67. See his autobiographical sketch in *Entsiklopedicheskii slovar' . . . Granat',* XLI, pt. 3, supplement, 47-59.

68. Institut Marksizma-Leninizma pri TsK KPSS, *Odinadtsatyi s"ezd RKP(b)—stenograficheskii otchet* (Moscow, 1961), 72-75.

69. R.S. Sullivant, *Soviet Politics and the Ukraine, 1917-1957* (New York, 1962), *passim.*

70. NKID, *Sbornik,* III, 18-19.

71. *Lenin,* XXVI, 191; *LS,* XX (1932), 178.

72. NKID, *Sbornik,*III, 9-13; Akademiia Nauk Gruzinskoi SSR, *Bor'ba za uprochenie Sovetskoi vlasti v Gruzii* (Tiflis, 1959), 347-48; Gililov, *V.I. Lenin,* 157-58; FKP(b), *Dvenadtsatyi s"ezd—stenograficheskii otchet* (Moscow, 1923), 152.

73. *Bor'ba za uprochenie,* 59-61; Gililov, *V.I. Lenin,* 151; Iakubovskaia, *Stroitel'stvo,* 131; *Dvenadtsatyi s"ez,* 558; *Stalin,* V, 48.

74. Gililov, *V.I. Lenin,* 159; V.S. Kirillov and A. Ia. Sverdlov, *Grigorii Konstantinovich Ordzhonikidze (Sergo)—Biografiia* (Moscow, 1962), 158-59; henceforth referred to as *Ordzhonikidze.*

75. *Bor'ba za uprochenie,* 65; Gililov, *V.I. Lenin,* 161.

76. Iakubovskaia, *Stroitel'stvo,* 48-49; Gililov, *V.I. Lenin,* 160; *Ordzhonikidze,* 162-63.

77. Gililov, *V.I. Lenin,* 160.

78. *Ibid.,* 161.

79. Lenin, *Sochineniia,* 4th ed., XXXIII (1953), 103; Gililov, *V.I. Lenin,* 161.

80. *Bor'ba za uprochenie,* 38.

81. *Ibid.,* 89.

82. Text, *ibid.,* 108-10.

83. *Kommunist* (Kharkov), no. 238 (17 October 1923) in M.V. Frunze, *Sobranie sochinenii* (Moscow-Leningrad, 1926), I, 476-78.

84. Speech cited in *Zaria vostoka,* no. 228, 21 March 1923, reported by E.B. Genkina, *Obrazovanie SSSR,* 2nd ed. (Moscow, 1947), 101; Gililov, *V.I. Lenin,* 151.

85. Gililov, *V.I. Lenin,* 151-52.

86. *Ordzhonikidze,* 171; *Bor'ba za uprochenie,* 117.

87. *Lenin,* XXV, 624; this letter is not reproduced in Stalin's Collected Works.

88. Pentkovskaia, "Rol' V. I. Lenina," 117.

89. My reconstruction rests partly on Iakubovskaia, *Stroitel'stvo,* 144, 148, and Pentkovskaia, "Rol' V. I. Lenina," 17, and partly on Lenin's and Stalin's letters of 27 September 1922, referred to below (see note 99).

90. S.S. Gililov, "Razrabotka V. I. Leninym printsipov stroitel'stva mnogonatsional' nogo Sovetskogo gosudarstva," Akademiia Obshchestvennykh Nauk pri TsK KPSS, *O deiatael'nosti V. I. Lenina v 1917-1922 gody—Sbornik Statei* (Moscow, 1958), 76; Gililov, *V.I. Lenin,* 165-66; *Ordzhonikidze,* 171.

91. *Bor'ba za uprochenie,* 117.

92. Iakubovskaia, *Stroitel'stvo,* 145.

93. First published in *Sotsialisticheskii vestnik,* no. 2/48 (17 January 1923), 19; reprinted, with a record of the vote, in *Bor'ba za uprochenie,* 116-17.

94. Pentkovskaia, "Rol' V. I. Lenin," 17; Iakubovskaia, *Stroitel'stvo,* 148-49; Gililov, *V. I. Lenin,* 169.

95. Gililov, *V.I. Lenin,* 67; Iakubovskaia, *Stroitel'stvo,* 146.

96. Iakubovskaia, *Stroitel'stvo,* 151-52.

97. Pentkovskaia, "Rol' V. I. Lenina," 17; Iakubovskaia, *Stroitel'stvo,* 148-49; Gililov, *V.I. Lenin,* 169.

98. Iakubovskaia, *Stroitel'stvo,* 149.

99. Lenin's memorandum is reproduced in *LS, XXXVI* (1959), 496-98; Stalin's has not been published in full, but can be found in the Trotsky Archive, T-755. Both documents are dated 27 September 1922.

100. Lenin, *Sochineniia,* 4th ed., XXXIII, 335.

101. The revised project, accepted by the Plenum on 6 October, is reproduced in *Bor'ba za uprochenie,* 117-18.

102. *Ordzhonikidze,* 172; Gililov, *V.I. Lenin,* 175.

103. *Dvenadtsatyi s"ezd,* 536; *Stalin,* V, 433.

104. *Sotsialisticheskii vestnik,* 17 January 1923; cf. L. Beriia, *K voprosu ob istorii Bol'shevistskikh organizatsii v Zakavkaz'e,* 7th ed. (Moscow), 1948), 245.

105. *Dvenadtsatyi s"ezd,* 464.

106. Gililov, *V.I. Lenin,* 175-76.

107. Beriia, *K voprosu,* 243-44; Gililov, *V.I. Lenin,* 174-76; Iakubovskaia, *Stroitel'stvo,* 154; *Ordzho0nikidze,* 172-73.

108. *Sotsialisticheskii vestnik,* 17 January 1923, 19; Gililov, *V.I. Lenin,* 176.

109. *Sotsialisticheskii vestnik,* 17 January 1923, 19; Beriia, *K voprosu,* 245-46. L. Schapiro observes (*The Communist Party of the Soviet Union,* London, 1960, 227) that this letter is not reprinted in Lenin's Collected Works; but it should be noted that it is listed in the complete catalogue of Lenin's published writings, Institut Marksimza-Leninizma, *Khronologicheskii ukazatel' proizvedenii V. I. Lenina* (Moscow, 1959-62), II, no. 10,276. See also L. Trotsky, *Stalin* (New York, [1941]), 357.

110. *Sotsialisticheskii vestnik* (17 January 1923), 19.

111. *Ibid.; Dvenadtsatyi s"ezd,* 156-57; Iakubovskaia, *Stroitel'stvo,* 154; *Gililov,* V.I. Lenin, 178-79.

112. *Sotsialisticheskii vestnik,* 17 January 1923, 19; *Dvenadtsatyi s"ezd,* 158; Gililov, *V.I. Lenin,* 178-79.

113. *Bor'ba za uprochenie,* 118-20.

114. Iakubovskaia, *Stroitel'stvo,* 160.

115. *Ibid.*

116. Carr, *The Bolshevik Revolution,* I, 397.

117. *Pravda*, 30 December 1922; S.I. Iakubovskaia, *Ob"edinitel'noe dvizhenie za obrazovanie SSSR* (Moscow, 1947), 194.

118. TsIK, SSSR, *I s"ezd sovetov Soiuza Sovetskikh Sotsialisticheskikh Respublik—stenograficheskii otchet* (Moscow, 1923).

119. *Ibid.*, 19.

120. *Ibid.*, 8-11.

121. Genkina, *Obrazovanie SSSR*, 123; Iakubovskaia, *Stroitel'stvo, 193*.

122. Based on figures supplied in RKP(b), TsK, Statisticheskii otdel, *RKP(b) v tsifrakh* (Moscow, 1923).

123. VKP(b), *Desiatyi s"ezd RKP(b)* (Moscow, 1933), 206-07; speech of Zatonskii.

124. I.P. Trainin, "K postanovke natsional'nogo voprosa," *VS*, no. 5 (1923), 29.

125. TsK, RKP(b), *Rossiiskaia Kommunisticheskaia* Partiia (bol'shevikov), 330-31; *Stalin*, V, 40.

126. *Ordzhonikidze*, 174-77.

127. *Dvenadtsatyi s"ezd*, 157; L.A. Fotieva, "Iz vospominanii o V.I. Lenine," *Voprosy istorii KPSS*, no. 4 (1957), 159; "Novyi dokument o zhizhni i deiatel'nosti V.I. Lenina," *ibid.*, no. 2 (1963), 71.

128. *Izvestiia*, 17 November 1922; Fotieva, "Iz vospominanii," 158-59; "Novyi dokument," 71.

129. "Novyi dokument," 69.

130. *Ibid.*, 74.

131. *Ibid.*, 76.

132. *Ibid.*, 77; Fotieva, "Iz vospominanii," 150.

133. *Ordzhonikidze*, 177-78.

134. The incident is described in *Ordzhonikidze*, 175-76.

135. "Novyi dokument," 77.

136. Fotieva, "Iz vospominanii," 159.

137. "Novyi dokument," 69, 77.

138. Magerovskii, *Soiuz*, 56-57.

139. *Dvenadtsatyi s"ezd*, 150, 159; *Bor'ba za uprochenie*, 146.

140. G.K. Ordzhonikidze, *Stati'i i rechi* (Moscow, 1956-57), I, 266.

141. Fotieva, "Iz vospominanii," 156-158.

142. See [this book], pp. 285-86.

143. Fotieva, "Iz vospominanii," 161-62.

144. "Novyi dokument," 90-91.

145. *Ibid.*, 84, 91; Fotieva, "Iz vospominanii," 162-63.

146. *Stalin,* V, 143. Cf. Genkina, *Obrazovanie SSSR*, 125ff and V.I. Ignat'ev, *Sovet National'nostei TsIK SSSR* (Moscow-Leningrad), 1926).

147. Cf. J. Stalin, *Marxim and the National Question* (New York, 1942), 134,142; Iakubovskaia, *Stroitel'stvo*, 198-99.

148. "Novyi dokument," 91.

149. *Sotsialisticheskii vestnik*, no. 23/24 (69/70) (17 March 1923), 15. Copy in Trotsky Archive, T-787. Trotsky's reply is in *Stalin School of Falsification* (New York, 1937), 71.

150. Trotsky Archive, T-794.

151. *Sotsialisticheskii vestnik*, no. 23/24 (69/70), 17 March 1923, 15.   Trotsky Archive, T-788.

152. See his circular to the members of the Central Committee of 16 April 1923 in the Trotsky Archive, T-794.

153. *Dvenadtsatyi s"ezd*, 150-159.

154. *Ibid.*, 185-86.

155. Stalin, *Marxism*, 137-57.

156. *Stalin*, V, 264-65.

157. Trotsky, *Stalin*, 357.

158. *Dvenadtsatyi s"ezd*, 523; cf. *ibid.*, 548.

159. *Ibid.*, 529.

160. *Ibid.*, 531-32.

161. See his constitutional project in V.I. Ignat'ev, *Sovetskii stroi*, Vyp. I (Moscow-Leningrad, 1928), 115-19, and his theoretical analysis in *Soiuz Sotsialisticheskikh Sovetskikh Respublik—Novyi etap v Sovetskom soiuznom stroitel'stve* (Kharkov, 1923). The latter contains a critique of the Union constitution.

162. *Dvenadtsatyi s"ezd*, 532-34.

3

When the "Prison of Peoples" Was Opened

Hélène Carrère d'Encausse

STALINIST FEDERALISM: CONTROL WITHOUT EQUALITY

The equality of peoples, the basis of federal equilibrium in the 1920s, was intended to build the "friendship of peoples" living together. This equality was also to lead to the creation of a new elite which, like its culture, would be national in form, but which would be the same from one republic to another: it would be a Soviet elite devoted to the system which had promoted it, and serving as a bridge between different traditions and a common future.

By 1930, however, it became apparent that the results of this cultural revolution within the USSR were more ambiguous than its promoters had expected. On all sides, new elites were springing up, gradually replacing the old ones steeped in nationalism. But at the same time, these new elites, pushed forward by the Communist Party, became imbued with the very nationalism which they were to have stamped out. The most flagrant case was that of the Belorussian elite.

To bind the people of Belorussia to their language, the regime had been forced to demonstrate real tenacity. Notwithstanding this, the 1926 census showed that, out of four million Belorussians, a quarter still considered the Russian language as their mother tongue.[1]

Here, where the penetration of Russian culture was strong, the elite affirmed that there was no room for the class struggle. They maintained that the characteristic feature of the Belorussian nation was the absence of any bourgeoisie. Here, Westernized ideas were developing and, along with them, the refusal to belong to the Eastern Slavic world.

Published in *Decline of an Empire: The Soviet Socialist Republics in Revolt* (New York: Harper Colophon Books, 1979), excerpted from ch. 1, pp. 13–36. Copyright © 1978 by Flammarion et Cie. English translation copyright © 1979 by Newsweek, Inc.

In the early 1930s Moscow discovered that the Belorussian elite had formed
a national center whose aim was to get Belorussia out of the federation.[2]
Whether or not this center carried on activities dangerous to Soviet unity was
incidental. The mere fact that it existed was important. It showed the elite's
deep attachment to traditional values—ones foreign to Soviet society. This
situation was all the more disquieting because, in other regions, too, the Soviets
could see the drawbacks involved in salvaging national elites that had played a
role before the revolution.

In Central Asia a former leader of the local nationalist movement, Faizullah
Hodjaev, promoted to the summit of the Communist hierarchy, was doing his
best to hinder the region's economic integration into the Soviet Union, while
acting the part of a national leader won over to Communism. In that same
region the Soviet regime was bogged down in the insidious war waged by the
Basmachis, Moslem guerrillas who resisted for nearly ten years with the tacit
support of the population.[3]

By the early 1930s Stalin, having rid himself of all his adversaries, could
finally impose his own thinking on the national problem. His approach was
multi-faceted. From previous experience he retained the cultural compromise
and the federalism that he was to improve.

Unlike the Fundamental Law of 1924, the 1936 Constitution was truly federal.
National formations were increasing in those days, and the hierarchy of nations
and nationalities, with their inherent theoretical rights and jurisdictions, had been
clearly established.[4] But alongside of this theoretical respect for the federal
structure, Stalin plunged into a cataclysmic operation aimed at transforming
society. In so doing, he believed that nationalism would lose all reason for
being.

The nations in the Union were essentially peasant nations, and some were still
nomadic. Collectivization for all and "sedentarization" for nomads would have
a twofold effect on the country as a whole: first, it would eliminate the peasant
and his individualism, his system of values so foreign to the new society; and
secondly, for the non-Russians it would eliminate all roots of traditions peculiar
to each people, traditions which rural life tends to foster. At the national level
this attachment to typically non-Russian values had given desperate strength to
the people's resistance to collectivization.

Everywhere in the USSR, social change—one aim of which was the eradication
of all national peculiarities and particular ways of living—went hand in hand
with violence, a violence which was characteristic of the Stalinist approach to
the problem. Lenin's confidence in the teaching of internationalism never
tempted Stalin. In the early 1930s he replaced education with naked violence.
After destroying the traditional conditions of life for society as a whole, he went
on to purge all the national elites of the 1920s. Their unpardonable crime:
returning to the springs of national fidelity. While Stalin's purges seemed to
strike blindly throughout the USSR, they had a deliberate purpose in the

borderlands, making possible the systematic destruction of both the old elites and the new ones established in the 1920s.

On the eve of the Second World War, the consequences of the purges were clear: Stalin had made room for a new elite that would embody a new concept of relations between nations of the USSR, a concept that was patently unegalitarian, borrowed from the imperial past. This concept of a federation of unequals did not emerge officially until 1945. But by the end of the 1930s, harbingers had announced its coming. First of all, the Cyrillic alphabet was universally imposed. In the 1920s many of the Soviet languages using different alphabets such as Arabic and Mongolian, or those lacking any alphabet at all, had been provided with the Latin alphabet.[5] The demands of a rapid method of universal education coupled with Soviet poverty justified this step. The Latin alphabet, which was not used in Russia itself, offered the additional advantage of not giving this change of intellectual traditions an imperial stamp. At the end of the 1930s the very rapid replacement of the Latin alphabet by the Cyrillic alphabet[6] revealed an effort to bring diverse languages closer to Russian—at least as regards the written language. It also suggests that a general process of cultural Russification had begun.

In like manner, toward the end of the 1930s, the history of the Russian Empire began to be revised in a direction that stressed the persistent inequality of the nations. Immediately after the Revolution the Bolsheviks had proclaimed the hateful nature of imperial domination, condemning everything connected with it. They maintained that the resistance of the conquered nations to the Russian invader had been a "progressive" historical act, regardless of whether the leaders had been religious chiefs like the Imam Chamil in the Caucasus, or tribal chiefs like Khan Kennesary Kasymov who had been the implacable foe of the Russians on the Kazakh plains a century before. On the eve of the Second World War, the cleavage between the Imperial Russian domination and legitimate movements for national independence no longer seemed quite so pronounced in the interpretation of history.[7]

The 1936 Constitution already revealed this change of attitude. The Soviet State implicitly declared itself the heir, territorially and historically, of the Empire.[8] Under Stalin's orders, the historians rediscovered the positive historical role played by the "land-gathering" princes, by the Orthodox church, by monasticism, that bearer of Byzantine civilization.

While deploring the authoritarian character of the Empire of the czars, historians in the 1930s began to uncover the good side of that Empire. For them the first of these positive traits was the power of the state which had enabled Russia to become the rampart of Europe against the invasions from the east. Little by little, Russian history was vindicated,[9] not only that of the people, but also that of the sovereigns who had forged the nation against the foreign enemy. The cinema lent assistance to this new awareness of history, glorifying Peter the Great and especially Alexander Nevsky. Along with the rulers, the military leaders were celebrated—especially those who had fought against Napoleon, and could be evoked in the commemoration of the Battle of Borodino. Thus the Russian people began to regain a past which they had become accustomed to repudiate since 1917.

But this rehabilitation of Russian history raised a serious problem as regards the histories of the other peoples of the Soviet Union. Here, too, the view of history accepted since the Revolution would gradually be reversed. The revolutionary egalitarianism led to glorifying all movements of national resistance to oppression, which was considered as an "absolute evil." In the mid-1930s the historians began to wonder. Undoubtedly the czarist oppression had been condemnable; but hadn't its effects been beneficial? Thanks to colonial domination, the peoples of the Empire had rallied to the Revolution at the same time as the Russian people, leaping over that painful historical phase—capitalism. Hadn't the ultimate benefits of colonialism been at least as great as the drawbacks? Thus colonialism, regarded as an "absolute evil" up until then, was toned down by post-revolutionary history and became a "relative evil."

Gradually the reasoning developed still further. Soviet historians found that, for many peoples subjugated by Russia, the choice had not been between colonization or liberty, but between two colonizations. For instance, Georgia had been threatened on the one hand by Turkey, which would have destroyed its culture; and on the other by Russia, which had preserved the culture and opened the way to socialism. Consequently, colonization became the "lesser evil."[10] Seen in this light, the national movements of resistance to colonization seemed to foster outmoded sentiments rather than to further the national interest of the peoples concerned. The history books were full of new heroes. To the wise rulers of Russia—who certainly had been autocrats, but who had been forced by history into their roles—were added the heroes of the national histories who had understood the need for union with Russia, the need to accept that "lesser evil." Actually, there was only a handful of them. On the eve of the Second World War the only historical figure of any real stature meeting these conditions was Bohdan Khmelnitskii,[11] who in the sixteenth century had signed the agreement uniting the Ukraine with Russia.

These changes were still unclear until 1941. Soviet society, as it emerged from the nightmare of collectivization and purges, could not yet see the implications of this new history of the peoples forming the USSR. It was the Second World War which would give a definitive meaning to the Stalinist version of "the friendship of peoples." What the war showed, first of all, was the precariousness of the multinational structure. The lightning speed with which the German armies rolled across Soviet soil stems, in part, from the fact that those armies were crossing territory that was not inhabited by Russians, but by peoples who grudgingly accepted incorporation in the Soviet state; some only a short time before, such as the Baltic states. The Ukrainian attitude to the advancing German troops revealed the depth of this national bitterness which was fostered to some extent by German policy in the Soviet territory.[12]

. . . The war had also proved to the central government that the borderlands were vulnerable, and that this vulnerability, in a tense international situation, might threaten the entire system with death. Also, Stalin had observed the weak response to appeals for international solidarity and decided it was necessary to replace them with an appeal for another kind of solidarity, one involving history, the nation, religion.[13] In so doing, he introduced new elements into Soviet ideology, elements which would profoundly modify it.

THE REHABILITATION OF THE "ELDER BROTHER": A NEW IMPERIAL SYSTEM

Victory revealed the extent of the change that war had brought to the USSR, and the lessons that Stalin drew from it. In this country of exacerbated nationalisms he would completely renounce prewar egalitarianism, establish levels of priority for local nationalist sentiments, and raise the Russian nation to the top rank, exalting its traditions and culture. The war had provided him with an excellent pretext.

As soon as the German armies retreated from the national territories in which autonomist tendencies had appeared, Stalin moved in ruthlessly. Between October 1943 and June 1944, the peoples of six small nations were accused of treason, ripped from their native soil, and deported to Central Asia or Siberia. They suffered the same fate as the Volga Germans who had been deported in 1941. At least a million people—in 1939 there were 407,690 Chechens, 92,074 Ingush, 75,737 Karachays, 42,666 Balkars, 134,271 Kalmyks, more than 200,000 Crimean Tatars, and 380,000 Volga Germans—were accused of a collective crime, one that was attributed to entire nations.[14] In 1946 a decree would specify that these measures called for the dissolution of the national territories of the Chechens, the Ingush and the Tatars. And for ten years these national groups would have no legal existence, no representative to the Soviet of Nationalities, and no mention anywhere.

By attacking entire nations in this way—and not simply individuals—Stalin was doubtless trying to make examples of them. But mainly he was following a clear-cut program, trying to assign different levels to national responsibilities in Soviet life. There were bad nations; there were also some exemplary ones; but of them all, the most exemplary was the Russian nation. The message was clear.

When he celebrated victory on May 24, 1945, Stalin toasted the *Russian people*—not the Soviet people. He declared that "Russia is the leading nation of the USSR," and that "in this war she had won the right to be recognized as the guide for the whole Union." He defined her dominant traits as "intelligence, perseverance and patience." In contrast to the other peoples that had shown their weaknesses in the war, the Russian people had demonstrated where it belonged—in first place. Thus the officially professed egalitarianism vanished, yielding to a community of nations that would be organized around an "elder brother," the Russian people, in charge of all and a guide for all.[15]

The light of the present now illuminated the past. Russia had succeeded in its Revolution in 1917 because everything in its past had predestined it for this vanguard role. As early as the Kievan era in the ninth century, Russia was as developed as the Carolingian State and exerted a real influence on Western Europe.

In the nineteenth century—and here Stalin corrected Engels—far from being a bastion of reaction, Russia was moving toward revolution. Consequently, for the conquered peoples, Russian domination—once an "absolute evil," then a "relative evil," then the "lesser evil,"—now became an "absolute good."[16]

The position was clearly expressed by the main Communist leader of Azerbaidzhan, Baghirov, who wrote in 1952: "Without underestimating in any way the reactionary nature of czarist colonial policy, it must be borne in mind . . . that Russia's annexation of the peoples was the only answer for them and had a highly favorable effect on their future."

Since conquest was an "absolute good," those who had fought against it no longer possessed any claim to fame. Accordingly, all national heroes who had led movements of resistance to colonialism were damned by history. Despite the love of national elites for their heroes—such as Imam Chamil—such resistance was condemned as a display of feudal obscurantism. The non-Russians were urged to recall from their national histories only those events which had brought them closer to Russia. Thus stripped of their own past, they had only to identify historically with the Russian people, just as Baghirov urged them to do: "The leading force that unites, cements and guides the people of our country is our big brother, the great Russian people . . . Its virtues deserve the trust, respect and love of all the other peoples."

In 1918, the *de facto* inequality of the Soviet federation stemmed from the numerical weight of the Russian people, from its central position, from its head start on most of the peoples around it. After the Second World War, this inequality, justified by ancient and modern history, was set up as a basic principle for relations between the nations. The federation, like the Empire before it, grouped many peoples around one guiding people.

Coupled with the historical legitimization of the leading role henceforth assigned to the Russian nation was an attempt at cultural assimilation in the same period. This move marked a complete break with the earlier cultural compromise.[17] National cultures were suddenly denounced, both because they divided the various points of view instead of bringing them closer together, and because they represented for Stalin symbols of a reactionary past.

All the monuments of national cultures—sagas, ballads, legends—were subjected to merciless attack and were banned. But Stalin did not stop at the literary monuments of the past. He attacked and suppressed any expression—even the most modern—of national culture. Literature everywhere was accused of transmitting antiquated words and concepts. Singing the praises of roses in imitation of the medieval Persian poet Saadi, even in a Soviet novel, became an intolerable display of nationalism. The minority languages were intended to elucidate the world of socialist realism—the technology of tractors and milking machines. Under no circumstances were those languages to be used to convey traditions peculiar to a given people. What this cultural revision forced the nationalities to do was copy a single cultural model, retaining only words as a national form. If the national languages lacked technical words, they had only to borrow them from Russian. If their grammatical and syntactical forms were ill-suited to such rigidity, they could pattern themselves after Russian.

While minority cultures were thus reduced to a mere shell of words, Russian culture flourished and prepared to replace the doomed cultures. In contrast to minority epics—such as the Azeris' *Dede Korkut* or the Uzbeks' *Alpamysh*, such monuments of Russian culture as the *byliny* (long narrative poems) and *The Song of Igor's Campaign* were elevated to the level of a legacy intended for the whole human race. Non-Russian peoples were urged to adopt this heritage and use it to inspire their future creations.

Lenin had imagined that some day the non-Russian peoples would voluntarily adopt the Russian language for the sake of ease and because they had been left free to develop their own cultures. But in 1952 the community of Soviet nations had to turn to Russian culture, for it no longer had any other choice.

Often indifferent to its minorities, the czarist Empire had never tried to carry out such a systematic Russification of its subjects. Nor did it ever have a clear imperial doctrine applicable for the entire area that it covered. The Soviet federation of 1952 was a real empire, one in which the preeminence of the Russian people was justified—as in the colonial empires of the past—by a superior civilization and the progress toward which it led its subjects. The "prison of the peoples" no longer existed. But the federation was a perfectly unegalitarian community, where the "elder brother" dominated and sought to assimilate others. Stalin responded to the outburst of nationalism in the war years by imposing a brutal solution on the nations: rapid Russification.

AFTER STALIN: A RETURN TO UTOPIA

Stalin's legacy is without ambiguity. He always believed in the permanence of nations. To reduce national antagonisms within his country, he could imagine no other solution than the domination of one nation over the others. This was also his view at the international level. That is why after the war, whenever he could foment revolutions outside the USSR, he transferred his solutions to the new socialist states of Eastern Europe—notably, Soviet control and the systematic elimination of local national leadership. The East European bloc is an almost exact copy of the Soviet monolith.

But Stalin's death marked a radical break for the nations. His successors were unable to follow the course he had charted. They sensed their country's weariness, the need to find new answers; they perceived outside the USSR a changed world, one to which they would have to adapt. By 1953 the trail had been blazed for a total revision which was actually begun in 1955, and became definitive at the Twentieth Congress. . . .

In 1955 Khrushchev went to Belgrade to put an end to the conflict which, since 1948, had separated two great socialist states, the USSR and Yugoslavia. He thought that making this obvious peace gesture of going to his adversary's country would be enough to settle all problems. But what was to have been a pardon generously granted by Moscow turned into humiliation.

So that his trip might bear fruit, Khrushchev acknowledged that the USSR had abused its power and had confused socialist solidarity with a striving for domination. He had to admit that each socialist nation was free to choose its own path. Thus, National Communism—so long opposed in the Soviet Union—had received startling approval. No doubt, Yugoslavia had always been independent of the USSR, and the principles henceforth governing its relations with Moscow were not transferable to the Soviet domestic situation. But the meaning of this change was perceived in the USSR.

The message was clear. It meant the rehabilitation of nations and of equal relations between nations—even at the stage of socialism. It was also Moscow's tacit renunciation of the thesis of its own infallibility and primacy. But while the full consequences of Khrushchev's trip to Belgrade were not immediately apparent, they were present—latent forces in a fantastic upset of the socialist world.

Internal change would also come for reasons outside the socialist world. In 1955 Stalin's foreign policy—one of withdrawal and distrust—had led the Soviet Union into a true state of siege. At its borders or at the frontiers of the socialist domain, the United States, which was becoming increasingly powerful, had set up a network of alliances aimed at containing the USSR.

By 1952 Stalin had sensed the changes wrought in the world, the stabilization of capitalism and the need for his country to adapt by moving into a policy of peaceful competition. While Stalin had been unable to make this perception a concrete reality, Khrushchev intended to do just that. He sensed that the prime targets for Soviet intrusion could be neighboring areas, namely India and the Middle East. He also perceived that such intrusion might find allies in the nationalist movements springing up everywhere. On this point, Khrushchev's thinking coincided with that of Lenin in 1916. The latter had considered nationalist forces in the nonindustrial world to be historical forces at work. But, like Lenin, Khrushchev knew that a policy banking on national forces abroad cannot accommodate itself to crushing nations at home without facing domestic crises of unforeseeable dimensions.

These ideas were developed and presented at the Twentieth Congress. The USSR, which officially professed its support of Third World national movements, declared itself a model of national emancipation at home. Khrushchev denounced all the crimes Stalin had committed against the non-Russian nations: the liquidation of minority leadership; excessive centralization; the striving for Russification; the rehabilitation of colonialism; and the setting up of new, unequal relations.

In place of Stalin's imperialistic policy, Khrushchev urged the nations to resume their cultural rights and enjoy once more their own traditions. The provisions making it possible to gauge the extent of the change then increased by leaps and bounds. The classification of the nations at the end of World War II, according to their respective degrees of adherence to the Soviet Union, was largely abolished by the official rehabilitation (in the decree of the Supreme Soviet of January 9, 1957) of five nations deported for treason after the war, and by the restitution of their territories.

While the Chechens, Ingush, Karachays, Balkars and Kalmyks thus gained the right to return to their homes, two other nations which had shared the same fate, the Volga Germans and the Tatars, were excluded from this rehabilitation.

The nations of the USSR also regained possession of their pasts. The Communist Party of the Soviet Union was doubtless very cautious when it came to specifying Stalin's crimes. In a general way, while the Party admitted the destruction of national elites, it tried not to stir up the memory of particular national leaders, probably in order to forestall any serious discussion of centralizing options vs. national options. It also sought to avoid giving the nations models for national Communist heroes. This explains the fact that so few individuals were rehabilitated and that the privilege was reserved for those who had not defended subversive ideas.

It was chiefly the distant, colonial past that regained its right to a place in history. Once more, Soviet historians were asked to rewrite history, but now rather more subtly shaded than in the 1920s, thereby breaking with Stalinist history. This of course meant breaking with the justification for Russian domination, which became an evil once more. It also meant assigning a place in history to those who had defended national independence, and the symbol of this revision would be the Imam Chamil, who became the focal point for all the great debates of the 1950s.[18] This choice sheds light on the meaning of the revision and its limitations. The Imam Chamil epitomized the struggle of Islam against the infidel. Here, nationality and religion were closely intertwined. This explains why a debate on the Chamil movement was opened after the Twentieth Congress, pitting local national historians against the Soviet academic community. It also explains why this debate, which the minority elites followed closely, took place in an intellectual climate that alternated between openmindedness and withdrawal.

While the intelligentsia in the Caucasus hoped for a recognition of the absolute legitimacy of the Imam Chamil's resistance to Russia, the Party's theoretical organs attempted to solve the problem by a partial rehabilitation. It was said that national resistance was undoubtedly legitimate in its time, but that this legitimacy should not conceal the fact that the Imam Chamil was head of a politically reactionary movement whose victory would have cut the Caucasus off from historical progress.

This quarrel gave rise to an ambiguous theory.[19] The colonial evil at least had been mitigated, if not actually offset, by post-revolutionary history. While restoring history and honor to the nations, the USSR's new leaders refused to let the past serve to fire a new nationalism. Nearly forty years of communal life under the banner of socialism had to be recognized in bringing into being a new human community, a Soviet people.

In this respect, Khrushchev—like Lenin—showed some optimism. He believed in the pedagogical value of concessions, which, in his time, came under the heading of a break with Stalinist policy. But he refused to give up what he regarded as part of a long history in common—one not limited to what had happened since 1917. He believed that there was consciousness of a common destiny in the Soviet nations, and for that reason he would not accept a pure and simple condemnation of unification with Russia. For Khrushchev historical continuity was a factor in improving ways of thinking.

After the rehabilitation of peoples, history, and culture, there came a revision of the practice of federalism. To give new life to the Soviet system, to make it rational, Khrushchev strove to decentralize the Soviet economy, thereby linking all territorial and national communities in a new organization. The reform of the *Sovnarkhozes* (regional economic councils) stemmed from this desire to decentralize powers.[20]

On May 30, 1956 the process began with a joint decision of the Party's Central Committee and the USSR's Council of Ministers. By this decision a number of enterprises which until then had been subordinated to federal ministries were transferred to the federal republics. In February 1957 the republic's powers with regard to judicial organization and legislation were considerably bolstered. Finally, the USSR Council of Ministers, on August 29, 1957 and June 22, 1959, issued decrees enhancing the powers of the councils of ministers of the federal republics.[21]

Here, too, Khrushchev was following in Lenin's footsteps. To make reform meaningful, a real place had to be given to the national cadres—hence, a return to the policy of "indigenization" practiced in the 1920s. At every level, in every sphere, the late 1950s were marked by an increased number of indigenous cadres and by a decline in the representatives of the central government.

A few signs nevertheless suggest that de-Stalinization was encouraging local nationalist demands rather than leading to internationalist progress. On August 21, 1956, for instance, the Supreme Soviet of Azerbaidzhan proclaimed that, henceforth, Azeri would be the only official language of the republic. The coexistence of local national cultures with Russian culture seemed in jeopardy once more.

In the economic sphere as well, limited conflicts revealed that the local national authorities wanted more than the concessions they had been granted. At the Twenty-first Congress in 1959, Khrushchev pointed to these demonstrations of what he termed "local chauvinism" and was disturbed by them.[22] De-Stalinization was to have promoted a common consciousness. This resurgence of local nationalistic feeling, encouraged by Soviet concessions and a foreign policy that supported nationalist movements, prompted Khrushchev to disrupt the evolution of Soviet society and return to the idea of the internationalist utopia.

The Twenty-second Congress, held in 1961, gave him the opportunity he needed. He announced a new Soviet society for all the nations, namely Communism.[23] Could Communism still adapt to a society divided into local national groups faithful to traditions that belonged to the past? Khrushchev's response to this question was clear. Soviet society, which was striding toward what Marx had described as the kingdom where need would no longer exist, had nothing in common with the multi-ethnic society of 1917. The Soviets had profoundly changed and the changes served to unify rather than differentiate them.

New developments had been brought about by cultural and economic progress. The people of Soviet society in the 1960s were highly educated, having mastered two languages: their own national one, learned in childhood, and Russian. This language, henceforth common to all and spoken so fluently that it resembled a second mother tongue, was a powerful cement for unity.

The second factor in the qualitatively changed status of the non-Russian nations was economic progress. It had unified Soviet territory, creating migratory currents by making jobs accessible to everyone. As a result of educational progress and the mastery of the common language, everyone could fill these jobs. Seen in this new light, the national territorial divisions had only nostalgic value; population mobility and fusion represented the trend of the future.[24]

Khrushchev outlined the history of the Soviet nations and the work accomplished by the regime in three points: (1) The egalitarian course charted by Lenin had led to the "flowering" of national consciousness and national cultures; (2) economic and cultural progress, as well as the trust generated by Lenin's policy, had produced the "rapprochement" of the nations; and (3) this stage of the march toward Communism would also lead toward the "fusion" of those nations, creating a new type of community in which the memories of past inequality or injustice would disappear.[25]

Just what the legal framework for this new community would be Khrushchev did not explain; but his plan as a whole suggested that the framework itself would be new. From 1961 on he was asserting that the nature of the Soviet

State had changed and that it had become the "State of the Entire People." Furthermore, he announced that a new constitution was being drafted, one which would reflect the profound changes of society.

Clearly, this constitution would also reflect the USSR's transition from a multi-ethnic society attached to its national characteristics to a society undergoing ethnic fusion. Cultural differences would fade behind the unity of political culture, a common language, and increasingly loose ties between the individual and his native soil.

In 1961 all of Khrushchev's pronouncements suggested that Lenin's belief in the primacy of social solidarity over national loyalties was being realized. Everything pointed to the national policy proposed by Lenin in 1922, namely that the development of the nations and egalitarianism had created the conditions necessary to transcend prejudice and strong nationalist feelings. At least that was Khrushchev's conviction, and one that would be shared by his successors.

* * *

Between 1917 and 1964 the national policy of the USSR did not follow a uniform course. Circumstances and leaders dictated so many shifts and ruptures that it is hard to fathom Soviet aims. Yet, by examining this complex period, which historians generally forget is a decisive part of overall Soviet history, several constants can be found. First of all, every policy after 1917 was marked by an underestimation of the national problem and an inadequate knowledge of the facts involved. Lenin, so close to the events and so aware of the weapon that the freedom-hungry nations offered him, was nevertheless optimistic enough to think that he could master "the chaotic forces" he had unleashed against the czarist regime. Indeed, he had seriously underestimated the autonomous strength of the national movements, not to speak of the strength of Russian nationalism, which would not allow Russia to be reduced to the rank of a state like the ones she had dominated until then.

This underestimation can be ascribed mainly to Lenin's lack of real concern for the nations. He was only interested in the nation as a tool to be added to his arsenal of revolutionary means, and not at all for its own sake. He knew nothing of the realities in the Russian borderlands, of the actual conditions of coexistence between different communities. In many cases, this ignorance explains the errors of judgement and tactics committed by the Bolsheviks.

Stalin, unlike Lenin and the others, was keenly aware of the overwhelming difficulty of the national problem, but he had only a limited understanding of it. Looking at it in terms of force, Stalin thought that the power of the central government would prevail; and, if the problem were not actually solved, at least it would cease to hang as a threat over Soviet political life. Here, too, the facts refuted this approach. When war broke out, the national borderlands would prove to be the weakest link in the Soviet system.

Trying to return to a more egalitarian concept of national problems, Khrushchev—like Lenin—would find that, while national feelings were invariably stirred up by injustice and violence, they were also fostered by concessions. Thus, after trying to respond to national tensions by returning to the egalitarianism of the 1920s, Khrushchev turned to a utopian solution—to transform the whole Communist society in a very short time—without taking into account the realities of life.

Thus, we see what has been common to the Soviet leaders since 1917. Primarily, they have all seen the national problem as a legacy from the past or the result of political errors. They all turned to solutions they believed would enable them to eliminate this problem for good. Then they realized its real dimensions and the lasting threat that it posed for the whole Soviet system.

Another trait shared by all the Soviet leaders has been the belief that the only solution to the national problem lies in eliminating national differences. Only the methods have changed. Lenin relied on education to reach this goal; Stalin on violence; Khrushchev on breaking with Stalinist methods and seeking political and economic rationality. But the passage of time had brought about one important difference: Lenin and Stalin realized that they had done nothing to ease inter-ethnic relations, that the difficulties persisted, threatening the whole system. On the other hand, Khrushchev—ousted from power—was to leave his successors facing a situation apparently simpler than the one Lenin and Stalin had confronted. The fruits of the Revolution seemed to have ripened at last. Nearly a half century had elapsed since 1917, almost two generations that had known nothing but the Soviet system, its ideology and institutions. This explains why Khrushchev said that nothing remained in the past. The federation had finally taken on its full meaning and had accomplished the historic task assigned to it, i.e., of erasing every trace of the unegalitarian relations inherent in the "prison of peoples," which the Bolsheviks had opened. It was up to Khrushchev's successors to do their utmost so that the new community of people, the socialist community, might develop in place of dispersed and divided ethnic groups. The era of a *Soviet people* had begun.[26]

Notes

1. S.L. Guthier, "The Bielorussians: National Identification and Assimilation—1897-1970," *Soviet Studies* 24, no. 1 (January 1977): p. 27.

2. *Bol'shevik* 4 (1935): 24-26, regarding the national crisis in Belorussia in 1933.

3. For further information on the Basmachis, cf. J. Castagné, *Les Basmachis—le mouvement national des indigènes d'Asie centrale*, (Paris, 1925), 88 pp.; in addition, cf. Jeyoun B.H.B, Observer, in *The Asiatic Review* 27 (92) (London, 1931): 682-692. With regard to F.K. Hodjaev, cf. H. Carrère d'Encausse, *Central Asia, A Century of Russian Rule*, (New York: Columbia University Press, 1967), p. 252.

4. This hierarchy is covered by chapters VIII and IX of the 1936 Constitution; cf., in particular, Articles 70, 84-86.

5. Khansuvarov, *Latinizatsiia, orudie Leninskoi natsional'noi politiki* (Moscow, 1932), 38 pp. The contradictions involved in Latinization should be noted; i.e., before the revolution, the Kalmyks, who had a highly complex Mongol alphabet, were in the process of adopting the Cyrillic alphabet, which held sway until 1929 when authorities replaced it with the Latin one; Khansuvarov, p. 26.

6. L. Zak and M. Isaev, "Problemy pismennosti narodov v kul'turnoi revoliutsii," *Voprosy Istorii* 2 (1966): 13, concerning the shift to Cyrillization.

7. Cf. Lowell Tillet, *The Great Friendship* (Chapel Hill: University of North Carolina Press, 1969), 322 pp.

8. With regard to this trend, cf. Pachukanis, "Mezhdunarodnoe Pravo" in *Entsiklopedia i prava* (Moscow, 1925), vol. 2, p. 857 ff; Pachukanis, *Ocherki po mezhdunarodnomu pravu* (Moscow, 1935), pp. 14-15, 20, 78; and Kozhevnikov, *Sovetskoe gosudarstvo i mezhdunarodnoe pravo, 1917-1947* (Moscow, 1948), p. 32 (continuity of the State) and p. 180 (territory).

9. K.F. Shteppa, *Russian Historians and the Soviet State*, (New Brunswick, 1962), p. 133 ff.; A. Popov in *Protiv antimarksistkoi kontseptsii M.N. Pokrovskogo* (Moscow, 1940), vol. 2, p. 320 ff.

10. Curiously enough, this theory was revived in 1977 by E. Chevarnadzé in "Internatsionalistkoe vospitanie mass," *Kommunist*, no. 13 (Sept. 1977): 46-47. Chevarnadzé even rejects the idea of a lesser evil, writing on p. 46, "Evil is evil, regardless of whether it is lesser or greater. In the final analysis, the term *lesser* alters nothing. It would therefore be fairer for us to give up this term."

11. R. Portal, in *Russes et Ukrainiens* (Paris, 1970), pp. 118-126, discusses the scope of the agreement and the part played by B. Khmelnitski.

12. On this policy, cf. H. Carrère d'Encausse, *L'Union soviétique de Lénine à Staline* (Paris, 1972), pp. 309-328.

13. Ibid., pp. 329-351.

14. R. Conquest, *The Nation Killers—Soviet Deportation of Nationalities* (London, 1970), 222 pp.; and A.M. Nekrich, *The Punished Peoples* (New York, 1978), 244 pp.

15. Speech by Stalin in *Pravda* (25 May 1945); and F. Barghoorn, "Stalinism and the Russian Cultural Heritage," *Review of Politics* 14, no. 2 (April 1952): 178-203.

16. *Bakinskii Rabochii*, 8 July 1950.

17. A. Bennigsen, "The Crisis of the Turkic National Epic, 1951-1952: Local Nationalism or Internationalism?," *Canadian Slavonic Papers* 17, nos. 2 and 3 (1975): 463-475.

18. Beginning with the 20th Congress, the history review *Voprosy Istorii* set up a conference at which six hundred historians revised the "chauvinist concepts" that had prevailed until then.

19. Cf. in *Voprosy Istorii*, December 1956, the entire November 1956 debate.

20. M. Lavigne, *Les Economies socialistes soviétiques et européenes* (Paris, 1970), pp. 54-58.

21. On the development of republican rights, *Sovetskii narod, novaia istoricheskaia obschchnost' lyudei: stanovlenie i razvitie* (Moscow, 1975), pp. 349-350, is remarkable for its brevity.

22. This anxiety would be expressed in plainer language by leaders of Moslem republics in the Party's theoretical review; cf. *Kommunist*, October 1959, pp. 39-53 (the article by Rachidov), and ibid., December 1959, pp. 30-44 (the article by Djandildin.)

23. *Programma kommunisticheskoi partii sovetskogo soyuza* (Proekt) (Moscow, 1961), proclaims from the first page the withering away of social classes.

24. *XXII s'ezd kommunisticheskoi partii sovetskogo soyuza* (Moscow, 1961), pp. 362, 402.

25. Ibid., and Kaltchakian, "O natsii," *Voprosy Istorii*, June 1966, pp. 24, 43.

26. On this concept, see two recent works: *Natsional'nye otnocheniia v razvitom sotsialisticheskom obshchestve* (Moscow, 1977), 385 pp.; and *Sovetskii narod...* (op. cit.), 520 pp.

PART II

FEDERALISM

The selections in Part II examine the main ideological and political problems that federalism has posed for the Soviet Union. Since 1989 the Soviet republics sought greater legal, political, and economic autonomy from Moscow, provoking a federal crisis that has crippled Moscow's power. This crisis sharpened the question of the division of power in the administration of the multi-ethnic Soviet state and raised the question of whether the USSR was administered as an empire, as a unitary state, or as a peculiar kind of federation.[1]

Federal arrangements allow for power sharing between a central government and constituent units—states, republics, and the like—and they grant autonomy and jurisdiction over certain subject matters to these units, which often have their own political institutions to administer those areas. A constitution or other agreement (in the Soviet case, the Union Treaty of 1922) delimits power between the center and the units and establishes institutions and practices to settle conflicts that may arise. Federalism usually makes for dynamic, tense relations between the center and periphery, as states (or republics) make claims for autonomy or for resources from the center.[2] The authors represented in Part II discuss these aspects of federalism in the USSR and the political consequences of multinationality for Soviet federalism.

Federalist principles contradict the essential ideas of Leninism upon which the Soviet state was founded—strong, centralized party and state agencies and the eventual withering away of the state. The Pipes excerpt in Part I focuses on this contradiction and shows how federalism was used in consolidating and centralizing Soviet power. In Part II, Gregory Gleason's chapter explains the development of federalism in Soviet constitutions and the evolution of centralism. In 1918 the first Soviet constitution set out a unitary state structure, but the fight to regain control over the borderlands forced the Bolsheviks to grant those territories political concessions, reflected in the 1924 Constitution. Republics then gained many new rights—including the right of secession—in the 1936, or "Stalin," constitution, but those rights were fictional; any attempt to exercise these rights incurred the threat of severe repression.

Gleason recognizes the gap between the autonomy that these constitutions granted republics in theory and the reality of centralized power. To explain this gap, Gleason emphasizes the "branch principle," a notion dating to the beginning of the Soviet state, which posits that the socialist economy is best administered through functional branches that have special expertise in specific fields (e.g., agriculture or heavy industry) rather than through regional administration. It was this branch principle, as opposed to Stalinism per se, that determined the centralized nature of Soviet federalism.

Despite fierce debates in the 1960s and 1970s over the future of federalism in the USSR, the 1977 constitution did not alter the federal arrangements instituted in the Stalin constitution. Grey Hodnett's 1966 article, "The Debate Over Soviet Federalism," captures the debate at one of its sharpest moments, when the Party forecast the imminent merging of peoples in the USSR, a merging that would make union republics superfluous as territorial divisions.

The adversaries in the debate—the liquidationists and the pro-federalists —reopened the contradictions discussed in the Pipes selection in Part I: the incompatibility of federalism and communism, the fate of nations in a classless society, and self-determination pitted against a centralized Party. Different interpretations of Lenin's federal compromise justified the arguments of both adversaries, and thus the debate gives us a more balanced image of Lenin's views on federalism than Pipes allows. The pro-federalists found various ways to demonstrate Lenin's commitment to federalism, from deducing that a federal formula follows necessarily from his desire for a voluntary union of nationalities to claiming that Lenin believed the transformation of nations "required a diversity of state forms," i.e., federalism. Similarly, the liquidationists had no trouble finding aspects in Leninism to support their arguments. They insisted that Lenin saw federalism as a necessary evil, a transitional step on the road to democratic centralism.

Predictably, the pro- and antifederalists have different conceptions of the Soviet nationality problem. Liquidationists adopt an assimilationist stance that puts the concept of class at the center of its understanding of nationality. Pro-federalists, in contrast, accept the historical continuity of nations and, unlike their adversaries, accept that conflicting interests are inevitable in a multiethnic state; they believe, though, that Soviet federal institutions are capable of resolving the conflicts. For the radical liquidationists, the national-territorial system of administration had "outlived its usefulness" because developed socialism surmounted these conflicting interests. Indeed, the withering away of the state, a concept that Khrushchev revived, required first and foremost the elimination of these divisions.

According to Hodnett's interpretation of Soviet federalism, Soviet republics "have access to the levers of state power" and, moreover, a legitimate claim to authority over their jurisdictions.[3] In the Soviet Union, national homelands coincide with federal units (e.g., union republics), which adds an ethnonational dimension to legitimacy and the kinds of claims republics might seek. Power relations between Moscow and the republics (center-periphery relations) are therefore often recast as interethnic relations and raise the issue of who rules in the center and in the republics—Russians or non-Russians.

Philip Roeder argues that this coincidence of national homelands with federal units gave rise to ethnofederalism, which he describes as demands for increasing autonomy and control over policy that has specific bearing on the homelands. Roeder emphasizes the pre-*perestroika* sources of the current Soviet federal crisis. Ethnofederalism, he maintains, derives from the federal structure of the Soviet Union and the country's national elites policy, and began with the post-Khrushchev thaw. Pipes's claim that the Soviet federation was conjured cynically only to expand power, and was a thin guise for the reality of Party rule, may be valid. Roeder indeed recognizes that federal institutions were designed to expand control over ethnic groups, but he places more importance on the fact that these institutions that "were thought to be moribund have taken on a new life."

Republic national elites revived these federal institutions. Although these elites owed their political existence to Moscow, they had the power to decide when and how to mobilize ethnic groups in the republics. According to Roeder, before 1990 the republic elites' dependence on Moscow constrained their choices for when, how, and for what purposes they could mobilize ethnic and national groups. In Roeder's account, these elites were limited to socio-economic demands until 1990; after 1990 republic elites could mobilize for more purely nationalist demands. Roeder also explains the pressures that lead republic elites to pursue particular combinations of demands.

Notes

1. Alexander J. Motyl has used the notions "empire" and "imperial decay" to explain the collapse of the Communist Party's rule in the USSR (see "Imperial Collapse and Revolutionary Change: Austria-Hungary, Tsarist Russia, and the Soviet Empire in Theoretical Perspective" [unpublished manuscript prepared for the Symposium Wiener Moderne, Universität Kässel, July, 1991]).

2. Stephan Kux's chapter in Part VII discusses the difficulties Gorbachev has faced in crafting new federal relations in the USSR. It is placed in Part VII rather than here because Kux focuses as much on how Gorbachev attempted to cope with the nationalities crisis as on the elements of Soviet federalism.

3. This is a different picture than the one of empire d'Encausse suggests in Chapter 3.

4

The Evolution of
the Soviet Federal System

Gregory Gleason

*Soviet autonomy is not a rigid thing fixed once and for all time; it permits of
the most varied forms and degrees of development.*

—Stalin

The first document adopted by the first official organ of Soviet power, the
Second All-Russian Congress of Soviets, meeting on November 7, 1917,
promised to guarantee "all nations inhabiting Russia" the "complete right of self-
determination."[1] A week later Lenin's "Declaration of Rights of the Peoples
of Russia" was announced by the Soviet government. The Declaration offered
an array of promises. It declared: (1) equality and sovereignty of the peoples
of Russia; (2) the right of self-determination extending to secession and the
formation of an independent government; (3) the rejection of all national and
national-religious privileges; and (4) the free development of all national
minorities and ethnographic groups inhabiting the territory of Russia.[2] This
document was quickly followed by the "Appeal to All Laboring Muslims of
Russia and the East," promising to defend the rights of Muslims and urging their
support for the Soviet regime.[3] So began the process that Soviet sources refer
somewhat ambiguously as *"natsional'noe stroitel'stvo"* (national construction).
It was a process complicated by territorial concessions resulting from the
separate peace of Brest-Litovsk, the travail of the ongoing civil war, the lack of

---

Published in *Federalism and Nationalism: The Struggle for Republican Rights in the
USSR* (Boulder, Colo.: Westview Press, 1990), ch. 3, pp. 41-59. Reprinted with
permission from the publisher.

administrative experience on the part of the new rulers, and by the extreme variations in political styles among regions with differing languages, cultures, and political traditions.

In the struggle for ascendancy after the seizure of power, the Bolsheviks, with promises of peace, land, food, and power to the Soviets, won popular support in the Russian heartland. But even as they gained the support of the Russian core, the Bolsheviks' initial bids for popular support in the borderlands of the Empire were not successful. In the Baltics, in the Western provinces and Ukraine, in the Caucasus, and in Central Asia popular support initially swung behind the national intelligentsia. Internally divided, poorly organized, and not driven by the millennial zeal of a revolutionary ideology, however, the members of the local political elite lacked the political resources, organizational capability, and the political appeal necessary to counter the Communists' promises. The Bolsheviks possessed an ardor inspired by a vision of a revolutionary future and a shrewd pragmatism inspired by years of experience as political underdogs. The Bolsheviks held forth the offer of a "new society" beyond the divisiveness and national enmity of Tsarist colonialism. At the same time, the Bolsheviks were ready to exploit local political cleavages by making alliances with even the most reactionary groups when it served their purposes.

Out of pride and a lingering Great Russian Chauvinism, the White armies of Denikin and Kolchak were unwilling to forge alliances with local political figures. Discredited by the humiliating defeat of World War I, the forces of the status quo and monarchist restoration could excite few political imaginations among those who had been subject to Tsarist colonialism. The prospect of change offered by the Bolsheviks eventually proved magnetic. In this atmosphere, the nascent political organizations in the borderlands proved unable to rival the Bolsheviks. Even as the principles of local autonomy were elevated in Bolshevik theory, the economic and political subordination of the borderlands to the center proceeded in practice. . . .

THE SOVIET CONSTITUTIONS AND FEDERALISM

. . . In January 1918, the Third Congress of Soviets undertook to embody the changes that were taking place in the USSR in constitutional form. The congress passed a resolution declaring the existence of "a federation of Soviet republics founded on the principle of a free union of the peoples of Russia." The following July, the first socialist constitution came into force, a federal constitution.[4] This "1918 Constitution" was followed by a Treaty of Union in 1922. This treaty later served as the basis for the second Soviet Constitution, adopted in 1924. Twelve years later a new constitution, the 1936 "Stalin" Constitution, was adopted. In the 1960s Khrushchev made reference to the need for yet a new constitution, and appointed himself chairman of a committee charged with drafting it. Fifteen years later, in 1977, the committee's product, the "Brezhnev Constitution," was unveiled. The recent constitutional amendments of November 1988 stand out as more important than any of the preceding constitutional revisions. The following pages survey the evolution of Soviet Constitutions. No description of Soviet constitutionalism would be complete without reference to the party. The Party Program and the Party Statute are arguably more "fundamental" than the fundamental law. Practice indicates that they are indeed more difficult to revise than the constitution.

The first Soviet Constitution was adopted in July 1918. It announced the legal creation of the Russian Soviet Federated Socialist Republic (RSFSR).[5] The first "fundamental law" of socialism was distinguished from more traditional constitutions by both its tone and context. It was both programmatic and ideological in its complexion.[6] The organization of state-party-society relations described in the document set the stage for the historical evolution of Soviet political institutions. It recognized the institutional "triad" which continues to exist in the USSR, dividing power among the: (1) party; (2) government (commissariats and, later, ministries) and (3) soviets (legislative bodies). The first Soviet Constitution does not explicitly mention the party as an instrument of Soviet government. It does, nevertheless, implicitly grant a role to the party by acknowledging the ideological and teleological goals of Soviet society. In this way it provides an implicit rationale for the party acting as a shadow government.

The constitution vested control of the means of production in the government. The land, natural resources, and banking system were nationalized and the factories, mines, and other means of production and transport were placed under the direction of the Supreme Soviet of the Public Economy (VSNKh). The constitution provided for a legislature by creating an All-Russian Congress of Soviets. For reasons of both ideology and politics, suffrage was intentionally restricted by this constitution. Tradesmen, clergy, tsarist police officials, and those living on unearned income were excluded from voting. The procedures and principles of representation were designed to exclude the "exploiters" of the early period.

The RSFSR was called "federated" because it contained within it smaller politico-administrative units, eight so-called "autonomous republics" and thirteen "autonomous regions." But the real departure from the concept of a unitary form of government came with the discussions preceding the adoption of the Treaty on the Formation of the USSR late in 1922. A commission had been set up in August 1922 for the purpose of drafting a new constitution. The commission, in which Stalin played a central role, produced a draft which extended the centralized government machinery into the borderland peripheries under the rubric of "autonomization." Lenin joined the advocates of minority rights in opposing the draft plan. The Commission relented and produced a revised, less centralized version of a political compact. Even as the discussions of the constitution continued, practical steps were being taken to adopt a "Treaty of Union" which would draw the border republics into closer association with

Moscow. An October CPSU Central Committee resolution called for the creation of a union; plenary meetings of the party central committees in the republics followed. Congresses of the soviets of the republics "unanimously" voted in favor of the plan. Despite criticism from Georgia and Ukraine, a new Declaration on the Formation of the USSR was adopted. Finally, a Treaty of Union, incorporating the RSFSR, the Ukrainian SSR, the Belorussian SSR, and the Federal Republic of Transcaucasia into a Union of Soviet Socialist Republics was concluded on December 30, 1922, by the First Congress of Soviets.

In the Treaty, the principle of federation was expressed in a separation of functions between the all-union and republican organs of government. All-union organs were in charge of foreign relations, military affairs, transport, and communications. Such functions as financial affairs, food production, labor, and transport were to be dually administered by center and republic. Justice, education, health, social welfare, and internal affairs, however, were to be left in the hands of the republican commissariats.

The materials of the Twelfth Party Congress of the Russian Communist Party (Bolsheviks) held in April 1923 made clear the continuing tension between the center and peripheries. A resolution of the congress referred in critical terms to "a significant proportion of Soviet functionaries" who regarded the USSR not as a union of equal republics, but as a step toward the liquidation of the republics, as "the beginning of a so-called indivisible whole."[7] Lenin, who did not attend the congress for reasons of health, sent a letter, dated December 22, 1922, to be read to the delegates. (On the Question of Nationalization and Autonomization). The letter expressed his changing notion of a voluntary union.[8] As control was being re-extended over the colonized areas, the varied multinational composition of the state was held out as a rationale for a new formulation of federal relations. It was this formula which resulted, on January 31, 1924, in the adoption of the second Soviet Constitution.

Like its predecessor, the 1924 Constitution distinguished between the government, state, and party functions. Its legislative provisions described an all-union Congress of Soviets which was to meet annually until 1927 and, afterwards, every two years. The membership of the congress ranged from 1540 to more than 2000. Elections were held for each congress. When the congress was not in session, power was exercised through the all-union Central Executive Committee (TsIK). . . . The TsIK was bicameral, including a Soviet of the Union and a Soviet of Nationalities. The Soviet of the Union was elected by the congress delegates from among their numbers on the basis of the population of each republic. The Soviet of the Nationalities was elected by the Congress of Soviets of the union republics, autonomous republics, and autonomous oblasts on the basis of a fixed formula. The TsIK was to hold at least three sessions during each of its convocations between the all-union congresses of Soviets. On paper this arrangement gave a good deal of representation to the republics.

The third Soviet Constitution, or as it is often called, the "Stalin" Constitution, identified the USSR as a "federal state formed on the basis of a voluntary association of equal Soviet socialist republics" (Article 13). The Stalin Constitution, adopted by the extraordinary Eighth Congress of Soviets on December 5, 1936, was said to introduce the victory of socialism. . . .

In many respects the rights of the republics appeared to be enhanced in the Stalin Constitution. Each republic had a right to its own constitution (Article 16), was guaranteed the "right to freely secede from the USSR" (Article 17), and was offered the right to exercise residual powers (Article 15). The new constitution nominally expanded the representation of the republics by boosting their deputies in the Soviet of Nationalities from five to twenty-five. The autonomous republics, under the old arrangement, enjoyed equal representation with the republics. The new arrangement altered this equivalence by leaving the autonomous republics with eleven deputies. Moreover, Stalin took the opportunity to define three conditions under which a national group was entitled to republican status. He pointed out that the republic "must be a border republic . . . because, since the union republics have a right to secede from the USSR, a republic . . . must be in a position logically and actually to raise the question of secession from the USSR."[9] Second, the national group must constitute a compact majority within the republic. Third, the group should have a substantial population, which Stalin, apparently arbitrarily, fixed at one million. A group of this size, it was reasoned, would be capable of standing alone and thus would have, "in principle," a chance of succeeding as a separate state. . . . The Stalin Constitution also introduced a new nomenclature, identifying the territorial units of *krai* and *oblast*. The prerogatives of the republics were nominally extended by two amendments in the 1940s. On February 1, 1944 the Law on the Creation of Military Forces of Republics was passed. At the same time a law permitting the republics to conduct foreign affairs was also passed.[10] On March 15, 1946, an amendment provided for the Chairman of the Presidium of the Supreme Soviets of each of the republics to become a vice-chairman of the USSR Supreme Soviet. Meanwhile, the number of republics had increased. The original treaty forming the USSR had united four republics. The number later increased to six and, with the promulgation of the Stalin Constitution, to eleven. At the close of the post-war territorial consolidations, the number stood at sixteen. The Karelian republic was reduced to autonomous republic status in 1956, bringing the number of republics to its present fifteen.

A mood of decentralization set in during de-Stalinization. Khrushchev announced publicly that changed conditions called for a revision of the 1936 Constitution. In April 1962 a constitutional commission was established to produce a new draft. No doubt in part because of the resentment amid the mid-elite provoked by Khrushchev through his administrative changes, Khrushchev was removed from power before the commission could make public its product. A political consensus for a new constitutional draft did not emerge for another fifteen years. But by this time, under Brezhnev's leadership, the mood was decidedly centralist. This was reflected in the draft constitution unveiled on May 27, 1977, which proclaimed itself the constitution of "developed, mature socialism." The final form of the Brezhnev Constitution, enacted into law on October 7, 1977, adopted a slightly new nomenclature, championed some new political slogans, and changed the formulas of representation somewhat. But the overall delineation of powers between the central government and the constituent republics was unchanged.

THE STALIN REVOLUTION AND PARTY SUPREMACY

The shape of the federal structure of the USSR today cannot be understood without reference to three factors: Marxist-Leninist ideology; the crucible of the revolutionary situation; and the centralizing pressures exerted upon the Soviet Union as it passed through the revolution of Stalinism. . . .[T]he impact of Stalinism, is, both within and outside the USSR, the most provocative and often disputed factor.

Since glasnost has expanded the domain of political discourse in the USSR, the prevailing tendency is to attribute the rapid centralization of the Soviet polity to the forced modernization under Stalin. As a recent commentary noted:

> the years of the "great change" . . . saw the beginning of forced collectivization. Economic accountability in industry was done away with. The scientifically-based and balanced plan of the first 5-year period was replaced by a race to attain arbitrarily set targets. Thus the bureaucratism of the center vanquished federalism in the organization of national life.[11]

To what extent is the "abandonment" of federalism attributable to Stalin alone?

The gradualism of the period of the New Economic Period (NEP) brought the USSR to what Stalin and his entourage saw plainly as a historical turning point. Stalin saw that a transformation was taking place as members of the peasantry, unschooled in the ways of the world, unmoved by Marxist philosophizing, and unsteeled by participation in pre-revolutionary clandestine politics, were increasingly joining the ranks of the party. Many peasants had reached an accommodation with the provisions of New Economic Policy. They were beginning to respond not to the development of socialism but, rather, to marketplace incentives the NEP created. Industry was increasingly in the hands of technical specialists, "experts" who were often politically neutral. The sharp class cleavage between workers and exploiters that was anticipated by Marxist doctrine was diffused by the heterogeneity of social, cultural, and national conflicts. The oligarchy that ruled over a coalition of peasants, workers, intelligentsia and specialists—Kirov, Ordzhonikidze, Kaganovich, Voroshilov, Molotov, Kuibyshev, with Stalin at their head—could prevision the entire demise of the regime unless a new direction was launched. Yet the country was not prepared for the new direction and, as some presciently observed, would not be able to support it. . . .

Against the backdrop of the social changes unleashed by the war, the Revolution, modernization, and greater access to the West made possible through NEP, Stalin sought to use the new political currents for mobilizing political support against his opponents. For Stalin, federalism was useful because it was associated with his mentor's name. Lenin's influence loomed ever larger as his memory was eulogized during the socialist hagiography of the 1930s. Stalin deliberately encouraged this mythification of Lenin; it allowed him to bask in Lenin's reflected glow.

The federal structure was rationalized by Stalin as a basis for maintaining the Leninist line of nationality policy. The Lenin-Stalin formula operated at first to guide nationality questions. Later, it also served to guide interrepublican and federal relations. It was based partially on Stalin's idiosyncratic interpretation of Marx and partially in calculations of political expediency. From Marxism, Stalin appropriated the ideas that: (1) No nation can be free which suppresses another nation; (2) The nationality question should be considered in terms of the historical stage and the class conflicts prevailing at the time; and (3) Working class solidarity requires the unification of all workers regardless of national origin. From Lenin and political expediency, Stalin acquired the principles that: (a) The national question and the colonial question were closely connected; (b) The national question played a role in the proletarian revolution; (c) Nations required a right to "self-determination," the right of secession, and the right to "independent national statehood"; and (d) The solution to national conflicts required not only legal but factual equality. This in turn implied the fraternal help of the proletariat to all "backward" peoples.[12]

Stalin, like Lenin, regarded federalism as transitional. He explained that:

> in all existing federative organizations—the most characteristic of the bourgeois-democratic type are the American and Swiss federations. Historically they have been formed from independent governments, from a confederation to a federation, but in fact they have transformed to a unitary government, maintaining only the form of federalism.[13]

Moreover, Stalin turned the use of the purported federal structure of the state to his benefit by using it as a political weapon against his foes. His discussion of nationality policy during the late 1920s and the 1930s was invariably tied to the assertions of "deviations" in nationality policy by his opponents or by nationalist apologists in the localities. Stalin sought to identify assimilationism with Great Russian Chauvinism, thereby branding his opponents with the onus of association with Tsarist policies. Ironically, his own policies were indistinguishable from those that he ridiculed. The "essence of the deviation towards Great Russian chauvinism," he explained, is an effort to ignore national differences of language, culture and mode of life; an effort to prepare the way for the liquidation of the national republics and regions; an effort to undermine the principle of national equality and bring into disrepute the party policy of nativizing the administrative apparatus, and of nativizing the press, schools and other state and public organizations.[14]

He claimed that deviation towards nationalism was an attempt to identify the interests of the party with those of the bourgeois exploiters.[15]

Stalin's accusations of deviation found a certain resonance among the minority borderland populations, of course, because Stalin, by way of contrast with his straw men "deviationist" opponents, appeared to champion a color-blind policy of national equality. At the same time, Stalin's accusations appeared to be consistent with Marxist and Leninist thought. He thus could claim to be a defender of the "autonomy" of the national populations. He argued against "those who sought to do away with the boundaries" of the national republics as following a "most subtle and therefore the most dangerous form of Great-Russian nationalism."[16] But his definition of autonomy was, to use his own term, "elastic." "Soviet autonomy," he noted, "is not a rigid thing fixed once and for all time; it permits of the most varied forms and degrees of development. It ranges from narrow administrative autonomy . . . to the supreme form of autonomy—contractual relations."[17] He went on to add that the "elasticity of Soviet autonomy constitutes one of its prime merits."[18]

In his early, theoretical writings, Stalin had argued against cultural autonomy in favor of regional autonomy. He made the familiar Leninist argument that cultural autonomy must be rejected because it was "artificial and impractical." Claiming that it attempted to draw people into a single nation who are being dispersed by the "march of events," he argued that cultural autonomy stimulates nationalism by cultivating "national peculiarities."[19] He argued in favor of regional autonomy because it specified a relationship with "a definite population inhabiting a definite territory" and did not "serve to strengthen partitions, but unites the population."[20]

Even while cloaking his arguments in the language of the protection of minorities, Stalin developed the most "Sovietizing," centralizing policies. At the forefront was the centralizing impetus of the equalization policy. As Stalin told the Tenth Party Congress,

> the essence of the national question in the Soviet [Union] is to liquidate the backwardness (economic, political, and cultural) of the nationalities. We inherited this backwardness from the past. This is in order to give the possibility to the backward peoples to catch up with central Russia in government, cultural, and economic relations.[21]

Stalin's approach to educational policy in the borderlands, for instance, superficially supported the minorities by defending the right to native languages.

The thrust of this policy was to give concessions to the minorities in order that they would understand the importance of building the central government. He claimed that the "development of national cultures is bound to proceed with a new impetus when universal compulsory elementary education has taken root."[22] His detractors, labeled nationalists or Great Russian chauvinists, failed "to realize that only if the national cultures develop will it be possible to secure the real participation of the backward nationalities in the work of socialist construction." He explained that his detractors did not realize that this is the "very basis of the Leninist policy of assisting and supporting the development of the national cultures of the peoples of the USSR."[23]

A suggestion of the importance that Stalin attributed, probably only subconsciously, to nationalism can be gathered from his remarks concerning the irredentist threat posed by the division of ethnic Ukrainians between east and west. Stalin explained that:

> There is a Ukraine in the USSR. But there is another Ukraine in other states. [sic] There is a White Russia in the USSR. But there is a White Russia in other states. [sic] Do you imagine that the question of the Ukrainian and White-Russian languages can be settled without taking these peculiar conditions into account?[24]

The opportunity to alter this situation arose with the Molotov-Ribbentrop Agreement. The pact provided for the westward extension of Soviet borders to those most closely approximating the borders of the Tsarist period, thus initiating the third wave of border changes. During this period the Karelian ASSR was transformed into a Karelo-Finnish Soviet Socialist Republic. In October 1939, the Ukrainian and Belorussian Republics added parts of Poland. In June 1940 Northern Bukhovina was taken from Romania and added to the Ukrainian Republic. This area was incorporated into the Moldavian Soviet Socialist Republic. In the same year the three Baltic Republics, Estonia, Latvia, and Lithuania, were re-incorporated into the USSR.

Stalin took the opportunity offered by the war to bring boundaries into ethnographic balance to the advantage of the USSR. This was celebrated in a eulogy to the Ukrainian nation in *Pravda*, which noted that the power of the USSR made it possible to "realize the yearning for national reunion which the Ukrainian people have carried through the centuries."[25]

Stalin's policies limited the appeal of irredentist claims. They also suggest the weight that national consciousness continued to have on Soviet practice during the Stalin period.

THE FEDERAL STRUCTURE AND THE CENTRAL ECONOMIC MINISTRIES

How great then was Stalinism's contribution to determining the actual functioning of the federal structures of the socialist state? One point to note is

that during Lenin's time the federal structure was *potentially* more important than it later became. Lenin's power was first exercised not through the party, but through the government. To be sure, government authority was quickly centered in the executive rather than legislative bodies of the government. In November 1917, the Central Executive Committee (TsIK) of the All-Russian Congress of Soviets granted the Council of People's Commissars (SNK) the "right to issue decrees of immediate necessity." The legislative wing of the Soviet system never regained full operation oversight, veto power, or directive control over the administrative wing.[26] The exigencies of War Communism established the paradigm for a centralized socialist economy. When the situation returned to normal, there was no bureaucratic structure to which to revert; the standard operation procedures of an earlier period were thoroughly discredited as remnants of the Tsarist administration. Specific administrators and methods were rehabilitated, but the paradigm of administration had undergone a revolutionary change. The results of centralization were an absence of: (1) constitutional guarantees, (2) institutional countervailing forces, and (3) an effective political opposition. Policy opposition that did arise exhausted itself in disputes between local secessionist nationalists and pro-communist opposition.
. . .

Despite administrative centralization, the authorities in Moscow were forced to rely upon the compliance of local officials. Therefore, the critical contest for political control in the borderlands came not with centralization as such—much of this was essentially "on paper"—but with the issue of the staffing of the local apparatus. In this respect the Bolsheviks again proved to be very pragmatic. By adopting a policy of "nativization" (*korenizatsiia*) of the indigenous administrative and party and managerial apparatus—that is, advancing individuals from a local ethnic minority within the apparatus of the region—the Bolshevik officials assured themselves of having friendly forces in positions of authority and power and, at the same time, satisfying local yearnings for local control. The Bolsheviks were no doubt assisted in this matter by the fact that the central government neither had the capacity nor, at the early stages, the intention of determining the *nomenklatura* of the borderlands. Nevertheless, during the process of nativization, the central authorities practiced a studied refusal to adopt a principle of proportional representation, reserving to the party the right to use judgment in appointments. As power flowed to the center after political consolidation, and as central government and party capacity increased, the *nomenklatura* formula gradually changed to the benefit of the center.

By the late 1920s the major battles over the "principles" of the organization of the socialist political and economic system had been fought and won. As we have seen, principles of "autonomy," "national statehood," and "rights to independence extending to secession" had triumphed in the political rhetoric. Political reality was quite different. Given the limited capacity of the central government, the national republics wielded certain *de facto* powers by virtue of the fact that policy was implemented through the various branches of the administrative apparatus in the localities. Whether these branches of the apparatus were more responsive to local or central interests often depended on the political acumen of local leaders as much as the formal designation of authority.

In the earliest days of Soviet power the administration was defined in terms of functional branches or groupings of enterprises and management offices divided in terms of their function or product line specialization. To the economic philosophers whose chief shibboleth was "production for use," the organization of the economy seemed naturally to flow from the nature of the production process itself. In this idealized, socialist economy the functional lines of demarcation were quite straightforward. Each sector of the economy required a functionally differentiated structure. Each sector, then, had associated with it a commissariat, or as it later came to be known, a ministry. In such a framework, agriculture was one sector, "public entertainment" was yet another, and so on until all the goods and services were represented in the hierarchical organization.

The original administrative structure identified three tiers of commissariats: one level at the center; one shared central-republican level; and one level under the complete control of the republic. The Commissariats of Foreign Trade, War and Navy, Foreign Affairs, and Communication were positioned at the center. The Commissariats of Finance, National Economy, Food, Labor, and Inspection were to be jointly operated according to shared direction. Internal Affairs, Justice, Education, and commissariats relating to the "mode of life" were to be reserved to the republics. One additional commissariat, the Peoples Commissariat for Nationalities, was explicitly charged with protection of nationality rights, although, under Stalin's guidance as Commissar, it acted to promote central interests. The Narkomnats, as it was called, passed out of existence in July 1923. By 1929 the Commissariat of Agriculture was transformed into a joint commissariat in preparation for the intense period of agricultural collectivization. Shortly thereafter Internal Affairs was centralized, becoming an all-union commissariat in 1930. With the introduction of the Stalin Constitution, Health and Justice became joint commissariats. At the same time, a number of transitions from local identity to central identity were introduced. A number of autonomous regions became autonomous republics, autonomous republics in some cases became union republics, and republican commissariats became union republic commissariats.

In Soviet parlance this functional division was known as the "*otraslevoi*," or "branch" principle of organization. The "branch" principle was first adopted when the organizational structure of the commissariats was established in November 1923, with the formation of the Narkomnats of the USSR.[27] The branch principle guided the organization of the commissariats throughout the 1920s and 1930s and, after March 15, 1946, their successors, the ministries.[28]

According to the principle of branch organization, decisions radiate from the center to all parts of the economy of the USSR.

The question arises, then, of the day-to-day control over economic and material affairs that is in the hands of the territorially-defined (republican) federal structures. To the extent that the republican-level structures have authority over economic decision making, they are practicing, again, in Soviet parlance, the "territorial" (*territorial'nyi*) principle of organization.

In addition to the question of the competition between these two principles of management, there is also the competition between the vertical levels of the administrative process. This is the first question of jurisdiction or, to use the Soviet expression, the issue of "competence" in a given area. The standard historical explanation for the division of authority among the three principal rungs of the ministries (all-union, union republic, and republic) is that the all-union and union republic ministries administer functions requiring higher levels of centralization.[29] But the historical record does not bear out this explanation as an actual rationale. Until 1936 there were only a few commissariats of strictly economic purpose; most were concerned with utilities, services, or public works. For instance, Heavy Industry was an all-union commissariat while Light Industry was a union republic commissariat. Defense and Foreign Affairs were all-union commissariats until 1944, when, strangely, they were grouped with the Justice, Finance, and Health union republic commissariats. The Ministry of Defense was returned to an all-union ministry only in 1978.

The tension between the centrally-oriented branch principle of organization and the republican-oriented territorial principle could only result in a continuing source of conflict. The political extremes of Stalinism could keep this conflict in check, but modernization and technocratic adaptation of the economy would eventually require a resolution of this tension either in favor of the republics or in favor of the center.

Notes

1. V.I. Lenin, *Polnoe sobranie sochinenii* Vol. 35, p. 11. The offices and structures of the Soviet state and Communist Party have changed names frequently over the years. A good source for identifying the various iterations of these structures is Edward L. Crowley, *et al.*, eds. *Party and Government Officials of the Soviet Union, 1917-1967* (Metuchen, NJ: Scarecrow Press, 1969).

2. *Dekrety Sovetskoi vlasti* Vol. 1 (Moscow: Politizdat, 1957), p. 40.

3. *Dekrety*, p. 114.

4. One of the first and still most lucid discussions of the relationship between nationality and the federal structures may be found in Julian Towster, *Political Power in the USSR* (New York: Oxford University Press, 1948), pp. 50-92.

5. The committee designated to draft the constitution had Sverdlov at its head, but Stalin played a major role. The outcome of the committee's disputes was to grant recognition along national-territorial lines rather than to corporatist organizations, and to situate the urban proletariat as the principal pillar of regime rather than to constitutionally recognize a workers-peasants alliance.

6. It is interesting to note that Soviet "politologs" have long regarded the Soviet Constitutions as more important for their educational than for their legal qualities. An authoritative Soviet history source, for instance, describes the 1918 Constitution briefly, but points out as one of its more important facets the fact that it was translated into many languages and had a "wide foreign response." B.N. Ponomarev, ed., *Istoriia Kommunisticheskoi partii Sovetskogo soiuza* (Moscow: Izpollit, 1973), p. 258.

7. See V.V. Koroteeva, *et al.* "Ot biurokraticheskogo tsentralizma k ekonomicheskoi integratsii suverennykh respublik," *Kommunist* 15 (1988): p. 23.

8. See *Dvenadtsatyi s"ezd RKP(b): Stenograficheskii otchet* (Moscow: Politizdat, 1968).

9. Joseph V. Stalin, "Report on the Constitution," in *Leninism* (New York: International Publishers, 1942), pp. 399-400. Some authorities on Soviet constitutionalism have asserted that Stalin's formula is no longer taken seriously by Soviet constitutional scholars. See Donald Barry and Carol Barner-Barry, *Contemporary Soviet Politics*, 2d ed. (Englewood Cliffs, NJ: Prentice Hall, 1982), p. 108, ft. 23.

10. While some observers initially interpreted this as a decentralizing move, most have seen it in terms of the objectives of Soviet foreign policy. A discussion of the rationale for these laws may be found in Vernon V. Aspaturian, "The Union Republics and Soviet Nationalities as Instruments of Soviet Territorial Expansion," reprinted in Vernon V. Aspaturian, ed., *Process and Power in Soviet Foreign Policy* (Boston: Little, Brown and Company, 1971), pp. 452-490.

11. Korotaeva, p. 24.

12. The discussion of the principles of Soviet nationality policy are a regular and familiar feature of the political discourse in the USSR. For a recent scholarly treatment see, for instance, M.I. Kulichenko, ed., *Rastsvet i sblizhenie natsii* (Moscow: Politizdat, 1981).

13. I. Stalin, *Sochineniia* Vol. 4, p. 66.17. I. Stalin, "Extract from a Report Delivered at the Sixteenth Congress of the CPSU, June 27, 1930," reprinted in *Marxism and the National and Colonial Question* (London: Lawrence and Wishart, 1936), p. 256.

14. Stalin, "Extract."

15. Stalin, "Extract," p. 267.

16. Stalin, "Extract," p. 257..

17. Stalin, "Extract," p. 81.

18. Stalin, "Extract," p. 81.

19. Stalin, "Extract," p. 57.

20. Stalin, "Extract," p. 57.

21. Stalin, "Extract," p. 103.

22. Stalin, "Extract," p. 261.

23. Stalin, "Extract," p. 261.

24. Stalin, "Extract," p. 266.

25. *Pravda* (12 January 1954).

26. Peter Vanneman, *The Supreme Soviet* (Durham: Duke University Press, 1977), pp. 30-32.

27. See *Vestnik rabochego i krest'ianskogo Pravitel'stva Soiuza SSR* No. 10 (1923): Article 299.

28. For the observation that the branch principle has always guided the organization of the ministries see V.M. Manokhin, ". . . S uchetom otraslevogo i territorial'nogo printsipov . . .," *Sovetskoe gosudarstvo i pravo* No. 10 (1978): p. 22. "It is correct, obviously, to recognize that the strengthening in the 1936 Constitution of the first Narkomat [Narodnyi komissariat] was the affirmation of the branch principle of government administration, although that principle was not actually articulated there." Manokhin contrasts this with the 1977 Constitution which does not explicitly proclaim the branch principle.

29. N.A. Volkov, *Vysshie i tsentral'nye organy gosudarstvennogo upravleniia SSR i soiuznykh respublik v sovremennyi period* (Kazan: Izdatelstvo Kazanskogo Universiteta, 1971), p. 111.

5

The Debate Over Soviet Federalism

Grey Hodnett

BACKGROUND OF THE DEBATE

In the decade since the XX Congress of the Communist Party, the problem of dealing with the non-Russian nationalities has been a major preoccupation of the Soviet leadership. The future of the national-territorial federative structure of the Soviet state has consequently been a focal point of particular concern. At the XX Congress, in February 1956, the relatively liberal nationality policy that was approved held out hopes for the development of national statehood. A year later, in the spring of 1957, the establishment of *sovnarkhozy* (regional economic councils) as a means of decentralizing economic management increased the power of local leaders, including those in union and autonomous republics. The 1957 re-organization was opposed by some members of the "anti-Party Group" among other reasons precisely because it increased the likelihood of nationalist deviation. Experience soon tended to confirm these fears. Purges of indigenous leaders in Azerbaydzhan (1959), Latvia (1959), Uzbekistan (1959), Kirgizia (1961), Tadzhikistan (1962) and Turkmenistan (1963) brought to the surface a number of troublesome issues which had significant nationality overtones. These included disputes over such economic matters as the budgetary autonomy of the republics; long-range patterns of industrial growth; crop structures and procurement targets; the level of consumer goods production and consumption; fairness in inter-republic economic relations; and immigration or emigration policies that threatened individual republics with denationalization. Cultural disputes centered on school affairs, linguistic policy, and the interpretation of symbolically important persons and events in the history of individual nationalities. The most overtly political issue was the balance that should be

Published in *Soviet Studies*, 28: 4 (April 1967), pp. 458-81. Reprinted with permission from the publisher.

maintained between local nationals and non-nationals in top leadership positions in the republics.

This turbulence in the élite stratum of the nationalities stemmed in part from the post-Stalin relaxation and Khrushchev's destalinization campaign. But it was also a response to a fundamental shift in the party's position on the nationality question that occurred in the late 1950's. By the summer of 1958 a new theme was being emphasized in Soviet nationality policy—the hastening of "coming together" (*sblizhenie*) of the nations in the USSR.[1] The new trend coincided with the preliminary discussion of the seven-year plan, which, in its stress on regional economic specialization, inter regional cooperation and priority development of the eastern areas of the Soviet Union, had profound implications for each of the national republics.

The ultimate goal of merging the nationalities into a homogeneous whole was elaborated at the XXI (1959) and XXII (1961) Party Congresses. Subsequently, following the November 1962 plenum of the Central Committee, a Central Asian *sovnarkhoz* was set up and bureaus for Transcaucasia and Central Asia were established in the Central Committee apparatus. Although they were liquidated in 1964 and 1965 after Khrushchev's expulsion from the leadership, his departure was followed by no immediate change in the broad formulation of long-range objectives of Soviet nationality policy.[2] The abolition of the *sovnarkhozy* and restoration of the ministerial system in September 1965 signified a further erosion of local autonomy in the economic realm. However, the controversial formulae of the XXII Congress and the Party Programme were abandoned at the XXIII Congress in favour of mild references to the "coming together" of nations.

Under the Soviet system state bureaucratic organs at one level or another necessarily play a central role in the formulation and execution of policy in most areas in which issues of a nationality nature arise. By controlling these organs it is possible to exert a substantial degree of control over policy, just as to lose them means to suffer a serious loss of influence. Soviet federalism, potentially and to some extent in practice, implies that local nationals have greater ease of access to the levers of state power than they probably would under other organizational arrangements. A union republic is not an ordinary territorial administrative division, however much it may resemble, let us say, an oblast. Union republics are organized along ethnic lines and their "sovereignty," Constitution, "right of free secession from the USSR," territory, right to enter into diplomatic relations with foreign states and "military formations" are formally guaranteed by the Soviet Constitution. Thus the major nationalities have a strong legitimate claim that substantial legislative and administrative authority should be lodged in their "own" state bodies and that their own nationals should be given preference in assignments to leading positions. During Stalin's lifetime Soviet federalism provided a legitimized cover for rule over the borderlands by Moscow, facilitated the recruitment of local nationals to administer the centre's policies and may have permitted these policies to be applied with greater deftness than would otherwise have been the case. These advantages of a federative state structure remain relevant today. Yet various factors have sharply increased the dangers inherent in Soviet federalism. One might merely note the relaxation of terror; the actual decentralization of some authority in the post-Stalin period; the growth in size and awareness of the native intelligentsia in several republics; the Afro-Asian example and the regime's own policy of encouraging comparisons between the Soviet republics and the ex-colonial nations; the use of native Communist leaders for special diplomatic tasks; the fissiparous forces released by the Sino-Soviet schism; the spread of racialist notions; and the opportunity for freer communications within and among the national elites. This shift in the balance between benefits and possible costs of the federative system confronts the Soviet leadership with a profound dilemma. A prolonged, bitter and unresolved debate over what should be done has been taking place in the USSR.

The current debate must be viewed against the backdrop of Stalinist ideas about Soviet federalism. The essence of this outlook is contained in the following much-quoted passage from Stalin's writings:

> In Lenin's book *The State and Revolution* (August 1917), the Party, in the person of Lenin, made the first serious step towards recognition of the permissibility of federation, as a transitional form "to a centralized republic," this recognition, however, being accompanied by a number of substantial reservations.[3]

From this sentence was drawn the official, if in part implicit, dogma of many years that Lenin was "in principle" unqualifiedly in favor of the unitary state; that he accepted federalism grudgingly and very late in the course of events; that his acceptance of it was a matter of tactical expediency; and that he saw it merely as a "transitional form."

Stalin's theoretical views on federalism were not publicly questioned until after the XX Party Congress. In March 1956 V.V. Pentkovskaya's article, "The Role of V.I. Lenin in the Formation of the USSR," critically examined many of the received notions concerning Soviet federalism.[4] The publication three months later of Lenin's hitherto suppressed letter (of December 1922) "On the Question of Nationalities or 'Autonomizing'"[5] had a lasting impact on the debate over federalism. The letter cast Lenin's views in a much more positive light. Editorial comment[6] and articles[7] which appeared soon after publication of this document provided further details of Lenin's dispute with Stalin over the nature of the future federative structure of the Soviet Union, indicating that Lenin was the "real inspirer and creator of the USSR," that previous accounts of the formation of the USSR had falsified Stalin's role and that in bringing the USSR into being Lenin had been deeply concerned with combating "great power chauvinism."

Reaction against this one-sidedly pro-federative view was unquestionably reflected in the new Party Programme adopted in October 1961 at the XXII Congress. Yet the Programme's passages on the nationality question and Khrushchev's comments at the congress on them were marked by a fundamental ambivalence. According to the Programme:

Under socialism nations flourish and their sovereignty is strengthened. . . . Full-scale communist construction signifies a new stage in the development of national relations in the USSR in which the nations will draw still closer together and their unity will be achieved. . . .

The Programme spoke of the need to achieve

the utmost strengthening of the Union of Soviet Socialist Republics; to make full use of and improve the forms of the national state system of the peoples of the USSR. . . .

It also contained an ominous assertion:

The borders between the union republics within the USSR are increasingly losing their former significance, since all the nations are equal, their life is organized on a single socialist foundation, the material and spiritual needs of each people are satisfied to the same extent, and they are united into one family by common vital interests and are advancing together towards a single goal—communism.[8]

The notion of the replacement of the "dictatorship of the proletariat" by a "state of all the people," which had been launched in 1959 and was developed elsewhere in the Programme, had a direct—if ambivalent—bearing on the nationality problem, since to some extent nationality affairs had traditionally been subsumed under the category of relationships between the proletariat (Russian) and the peasantry (non-Russian).[9] On the one hand the doctrinal change implied the possibility of less tutelage by Russians over non-Russians. On the other, it could be interpreted to imply homogenization of the nationalities when linked with the idea that a new and higher form of community, the "Soviet people," was beginning to supplant the nation as the focus of ethnic identification.

Khrushchev's Report on the Party Programme included the following passages which were later to be frequently quoted in support of the pro-federalist position:

Under socialism two interconnected, *progressive* tendencies operate in the national question. In the first place, each nation is undergoing a tempestuous all-round development and the rights of the union and autonomous republics are expanding.

In the second place, under the banner of proletarian internationalism the socialist nations are drawing ever close together. . . .

The development of the socialist nations also finds expression in the improvement of the national state system of the USSR. The Party will continue to respond to the needs that arise in this sphere. Full advantage must be taken of all the potentialities of federation and autonomy. Life already indicates the need for setting up several inter-republic zonal agencies to improve the coordination of the republics' efforts in carrying out the plans for communist construction.[10]

Mikoyan's speech contained a forthright defence of Soviet federalism that has since been repeatedly cited by pro-federalist writers.[11]

In comparison with the position of 1956, the Programme was much less accommodating to federalism, implying but not formally declaring the long-term goal of doing away with ethnic administrative divisions. While russifying *apparatchiki* were free to draw their own operational conclusions from it, the Programme could also be taken to suggest, if "dialectically" understood, a quite contrary path to ultimate "complete unity." It seems evident that the formulations of the Programme reflected a basic divergence of views over the prospects of Soviet federalism. . . .

II
FOR OR AGAINST FEDERALISM

The debate over Soviet federalism has touched directly upon the issue of whether the time has come—or is near at hand—to eliminate national-territorial divisions. A liquidationist view, attributed to a certain "comrade" from Ufa, the capital of the Bashkir Autonomous Republic, reads that "all these national [autonomous] state superstructures have today, in essence, only decorative value." "I think," he is quoted as saying, "that all our national state structures, union and autonomous republics, oblasts and okrugs, should follow this path [i.e., be done a way with]. Then still another hindrance would disappear in our movement to the communist, proletarian tomorrow."[12] No Soviet leader has publicly expressed such frank opinions. Yet, it might be argued that the position taken by the important writer P.G. Semenov is close to this extreme,[13] as is the position implicit in the plea that territorial divisions should be based on the "economic principle."[14] The de-federalization notion is also present in the argument that national territorial divisions are anachronistic where the nationality after which the division is named composes less than a majority of its population.[15]

A variation of the latter argument is that nationalities which come to form a majority in particular oblasts of a national republic should be allowed to form their own "autonomous republics." Such a proposal, if adopted, could lead to the formation of Russian autonomous republics and the eventual annexation of at least some of them (e.g., those in the Northern Kazakhstan) by the RSFSR.[16]

The overall issue of de-federalization is raised more frequently, however, in conflicting evaluations of the degree to which Stalin's position on federalism deviated from Lenin's. If Stalin agreed with Lenin then Stalinism equals Leninism, and Stalinism's opposition to federalism is "Leninist." Conversely, if Stalin diverged fundamentally from Lenin then the Stalinist attitude towards federalism "has nothing in common with Leninism." When posed in this manner three distinct positions on the question can be seen: (1) Stalin's role in dealing with the nationalities and in the formation of the USSR was more or less in harmony with Lenin's views;[17] (2) Stalin was wrong on such matters as the question of "autonomizing," but recognized his errors and took a firm "Leninist stand (for example: "I.V. Stalin, under the influence of V.I. Lenin's criticism, quickly rejected it [the "autonomizing" idea] and then consistently implemented [Lenin's] plan for the formation of the USSR"[18]; (3) Stalin not only took a position diametrically opposed to Lenin's on federalism and the nationality problem as a whole, but stuck to it after he had been corrected by Lenin and did so in a deliberately deceitful way. According to this last interpretation Stalin was both wrong and disloyal. Thus:

> Facts exist which show that Stalin, persisting with the idea of "autonomizing " attempted in one way or another to realize it. Thus, on 4 February 1923 he sent a letter to all members and candidate members of the TsK of the RKP(b) in which—albeit in a diplomatic form this time—he quite clearly raised the question of converting the independent republic peoples' commissariats . . . into unified peoples' commissariats subordinate to union organs. . . . It should be stressed that this was done more than a month after V.I. Lenin's letter "on the question of nationalities or 'autonomizing'" . . .[19]

> The assertion by M.I. Kulichenko that Stalin purportedly *quickly* rejected the idea of "autonomizing" and *consistently* implemented the plan for the formation of the USSR also does not correspond to reality.[20]

Nature of the Nationality Problem

The question of the nature of the nationality problem forms one of the principle battlegrounds in the dispute over federalism and is in turn closely linked to the question of proper therapy. The argument begins at the most basic, "methodological" (cognitive-explanatory) level: how should one set about analysing and describing the nationality problem? The anti-federalist writers say in effect that the nationality problem should be perceived in terms of (a) the general (abstract) Marxist doctrine of the class derivation of nationalism and (b) Lenin's subordination of the problem to the broader task of establishing the "dictatorship of the proletariat."[21] Those who are sympathetic to federalism strongly emphasize the need to look at the nationality problem empirically, with a sense of historical perspective. They reject the anti-federalist "methodology" as "dogmatic." E.V. Tadevosyan, who steers a middle course, has spoken most about the "methodological" issue. He states:

> The most important methodological principle of the Marxist-Leninist solution of the problem of national-state forms is the concrete-historical, dialectical-materialist, and proletarian-class approach to the evaluation of these forms.[22]

This is a formulation that would probably be supported by most pro-federalists.[23] The "concrete-historical" component is aimed at blunting, rendering irrelevant, or in effect refuting the Stalinist charge that Lenin was "in principle" opposed to federalism. It thus supports a more benevolent approach towards federalism today. The "proletarian-class" feature provides a vehicle, it would seem, for insinuating that Stalin's approach to federalism was a manifestation of bourgeois nationalism and cosmopolitanism.[24] Writers who oppose anti-federalism insist that "great-power chauvinism" and "local nationalism" are sociologically identical. The main thrust of Tadevosyan's argument, however, turns on the demand for a "dialectical-materialist" approach—the quintessence of the pro-federalist "methodology." He builds his argument upon the Leninist idea that in the modern world "two tendencies" exist: a tendency towards the development of individual nationhood and a tendency for nations to come together. Under imperialism these two tendencies clash, whereas under socialism they reinforce one another. Historically, Lenin took a "dialectical-materialist" approach because he perceived that with the overthrow of capitalism in Russia social relations had changed, the interests of national development of non-Russians ran in tandem with the interests of supra-national political and economic integration, and thus federalism was no longer anathema as a form of state organization. Likewise, in the present stage of "developed construction of communism," the two tendencies for nations to "flourish" and to "come together" should not be juxtaposed since further progress towards "unity" depends upon their continued dialectical interaction. A theoretical outlook that focuses only on "coming together" will lead to self-defeating practices.

Disagreement at the cognitive level is mirrored in a lack of consensus concerning the seriousness and meaning of national differences and tensions. Unlike other aspects of the debate over the nationality problem, this one is not easily verbalized. The anti-federalist's "methodology" tell him that nationalism ought to cease to exist with the demise of capitalism, while his emotions tell him that nationalist sentiments—which are basically the work of "hostile elements"—flourish in a permissive atmosphere and are best treated by repression. The pro-federalist's "methodology," on the contrary, tells him that nationalism is deeply rooted and that it is therefore delusory to believe—or assert—that it should have disappeared along with capitalism. Nationalist sentiments are a response to repression and are best treated by removing the stimuli that produced them.

Both positions are deviant in certain respects, but the pro-federalist is more awkward to defend in public. It involves arguing explicitly that mass nationalist sentiments were and are a significant factor that must be taken into consideration, while arguing implicitly that the nationalities can be trusted. The dilemma for the pro-federalist is thus partly an intellectual one of reconciling the logical incompatibility of these notions, but more a political one of handling the retort: "What do you mean when you talk about the existence of a 'nationality problem?'" To lean too far in asserting the seriousness of national differences in the early years of Soviet rule is to risk being charged with deviating from the Marxist class analysis of nationalism, underestimating the popular support of the Bolsheviks and denying the efficacy of Lenin's nationality policy—including its federative element. Similarly, to stress the continued seriousness of the nationality problem in the Soviet Union makes one vulnerable to the charge of denying the successes of past Soviet policy, contradicting the programmatic documents which enshrine these successes, or—even worse—of attempting to stir up nationalist sentiments.

Among writers on federalism the most articulate exponent of the pro-federalist view on the nature of nationalist feelings has been A.E. Kaikhanidi. Kaikhanidi sharply criticizes Stalin's time perspective on the nationality problem, pointing out that ever since the sixteenth century "national relations have been an integral part of the world historical process." He completely rejects Stalin's formulation: "The national question is part of the general question of the dictatorship of the proletariat." In its place he offers the following:

> The national question is part of the general question of the development of society, of its revolutionary transformation, an integral part of the general struggle of the working class and its allies for democracy, the socialist revolution and dictatorship of the proletariat, for the building of socialism and communism.[25]

The implication is that the national problem did not cease to be a problem with the advent of the "dictatorship of the proletariat" and will not cease to be a problem during the "building of communism."[26] The opposite point of view concerning the base of support of local nationalism in 1917-22 is defended by P.G. Semenov[27] and M.I. Kulichenko. Kulichenko in particular emphasizes the class solidarity of the "toilers" in the national regions with their Russian brothers and the broad support among the masses of these regions for the Bolsheviks and for union with Russia.[28]

The same individuals fall into the same groups when the issue of contemporary national emotions is raised less obliquely. Those who imply that the nationality question was not entirely "solved" by Lenin imply that much still remains to be done with regard to the "further strengthening of the friendship of peoples, of fraternal cooperation and mutual aid among socialist nations in the construction of communism, of the education of the toilers of all nations in the spirit of internationalism and of overcoming all nationalist survivals."[29] A Central Asian writes, for example:

> Taking as our point of departure the concrete-historical posing of the nationality question at each stage of social development, we may say that the nationality question—in that sense in which it was posed historically—has been fully and decisively solved in our country. However, this does not mean that in general a nationality question does not exist for us. To deny the existence of a nationality question at the present time would be fundamentally incorrect and extremely harmful.[30]

Not surprisingly, those favorably inclined towards federalism stress the enormous damage that the "cult of personality" inflicted on national relations in the USSR and on Soviet federalism.[31] This argument performs the double function of drawing opponents into an incriminating denial of the injustices of the Stalin era while explaining why national relations require "further perfection." Those, on the contrary, who take a "no conflict" position simply assert that the nationality problem has been "solved" and that the effects of Stalinism have already been eradicated. They attempt to trump the "cult" charge by stressing (especially in anti-"communist" writings) that bourgeois falsifiers' reduce "the entire essence, the entire content of the Soviet practice of regulating national relations to the negative phenomena in this area in the 1930's and 1940's.[32]

Trends in National Relations

"Methodology" and an evaluation of the seriousness of the nationality problem contribute to an estimate of the direction in which national relations are developing and the speed with which they are doing so; in other words, to an estimate of the *zakonomernosti* (laws of development) of national relations in the USSR. This question will be treated below with specific reference to Soviet federalism. Here it should be noted that there are three main positions on this broad issue, each with its historical analogues: (1) the current phase of national relations is one involving the "flourishing" as well as the "coming together (*sblizhenie*), but not of the "effacing" (stiranie) of national distinctions, much less the "merging" (sliyanie) of nations; (2) the current phase is one involving the "flourishing" and "coming together" of nations, and the partial "effacing" of national distinctions, but not the "merging" of nations; (3) the current phase is one involving the "emerging" of nations as well as their "coming together.'[33] The first position makes the achievement of "unity" a matter of utopian speculation; the last schedules it for the relatively near future.

III
TASKS AND FUTURE OF FEDERALISM

At the heart of the debate over federalism lie two questions: What tasks should federalism perform? What future does it have? The kinds of answers to these questions which Soviet writers give are suggested by the positions they take on the functions Lenin assigned to federalism in the USSR. These functions are inferred partly by determining the precise time at which Lenin accepted a federative structure as "permissible" or "expedient" for Russia, and partly by direct examination of Lenin's motives. The extreme pro-federalist position has been defended by three writers: A.E. Kaikhanidi, G.V. Aleksandrenko (a Ukrainian) and A. Spasov (a Russian?). Kaikhanidi asserted categorically in 1958 that "the basic works of Marxism-Leninism have always regarded the slogan of state federation to be one of the demands of democracy in the nationality question."[34] Aleksandrenko took a similar stand in 1960: "In those cases in which a multinational state is erected on the basis of unequal right, on national oppression and force, V.I. Lenin assigns preference not to the unitary, but to the federative form as one of the means of a democratic solution to the nationality problem."[35] He concluded in the same vein that Lenin had already decided by the late spring of 1917 that federalism was "necessary," not simply "permissible" in the future Soviet Russia. Two years later he argued that Marx and Engels offered two evaluations of federalism—a "negative" and a "positive," while

> V.I. Lenin showed that the classics of Marxism treated the problem of federalism *not as a variant of decentralization*, but as a means to unification, as a form of political and economic concentration on the basis of proletarian democratism, which draws the concept of federation closer to democratic centralism.[36]

Spasov states that "long before October V.I. Lenin also preferred federation (a union of sovereign and autonomous socialist states—A.S.) as the sole path to full democratic centralism";[37] "the right of nations to self-determination . . . did not exclude, but presupposed the establishment of federative relations in the future proletarian state." All three writers assert in effect that Lenin had always been in favor of a federative state for post-revolutionary Russia. Lenin, they seem to say, argued that if a voluntary unification of the nationalities were to be achieved, the latter would have to be allowed the right of self-determination, which—under the circumstances—necessarily implied a federative state. Federation, by facilitating self-determination, was "democratic." Those who interpret Lenin in this way imply that a federative state based on national-territorial divisions is unqualifiedly desirable today and in the future—a conclusion that, as will be shown below, Kaikhanidi explicitly defends. This view, publicly expressed by these three writers before or shortly after the adoption of the Party Programme in 1961, has been rejected as historically inaccurate even by those whose sympathies lie with the federative state.[38]

At the other extreme is the Stalinist view, according to which Lenin began to accept the "permissibility" of federalism only in August 1917, and merely as a "transitional form." In recent literature on Soviet federalism the late S.B. Batyrov, formerly First Secretary of the Turkmen C.C. and more recently President of the Turkmen Academy of Sciences, appeared as the most outspoken defender of this interpretation; and he alone of all the writers did imply that in 1922 Lenin wanted the national republics to become part of the RSFSR rather than of a federative government to which the RSFSR would also be subordinate—in other words, attributes Stalin's views to Lenin.[39] However, a recent textbook, *Foundations of Soviet State Construction and Law*, issued by the Higher Party School's Department of State and Law and the Soviet Constitution, tacitly reaffirms Stalin's periodization of the evolution of Lenin's views.[40]

The prevailing view today is that before 1917 Lenin, while opposed to federalism "in principle," had commended its application in several specific historical instances and that in the spring or early summer of 1917 he came to accept its "permissibility" in what was to become the Soviet Union. Some writers (in addition to those already mentioned) go further to assert that Lenin accepted the "necessity" of federation at this time.[41] Others say that this moment came only in the wake of the October revolution. The date at which Lenin conceived of the final form of the Union is also disputed. Regardless of which date is offered for Lenin's conversion to federalism, the key question is, why did Lenin change his views? Why was the federative state structure established? And here a basic conflict of opinion can be discerned.

One answer to the question is that Lenin's acceptance of a federative state did not entail a fundamental change in his perspective on federalism. Revolutionary Russia was a partial and temporary exception to the general rule; the exigencies of war and diplomacy called for special measures. The writings of M.I. Kulichenko offer the most sophisticated version of this interpretation. Kulichenko's argument stresses, on the one hand, the strong desire of the non-Russian "toilers" and party leaders to unite with the RSFSR at the very outset of the Soviet regime, and, on the other, the practical economic and security reasons for firm ties between the RSFSR and the national republics. Neither Lenin nor anyone else *imposed* such ties on the republics (or granted them as a concession to local pressures) either before the Civil War, when a federative state encompassing the Ukraine existed (that is, the RSFSR), or afterwards when fully independent republics once again gathered themselves together. Nor, most important, was there any conflict *within* the party over federalism. "It is untrue . . . that V.I. Lenin developed the idea of the USSR as the highest form of Soviet federation 'in a struggle against manifestations of chauvinist and nationalist attitudes within our Party.' The Leninist idea arose in the first place

out of objective economic and political factors of the life of the country."[42]
Lenin's criticism of Stalin's "autonomizing" plan was based on a fear that it
would "play into the hands of great-power chauvinism and local bourgeois
nationalism" *outside* the party—as indeed proved to be the case, Kulichenko
argues, in the "conflict that arose between the Georgian national-deviators and
the communist-Leninists in Transcaucasia" and in the retrogressive position
temporarily adopted by the Ukrainian Central Committee "under the influence
of the Trotskyist Rakovsky." Lenin established the Union of Soviet Socialist
Republics rather than a unitary state—so Kulichenko seems to argue—as a form
of insurance against bourgeois nationalist subversion from without during the
period of "final liquidation of enmity and distrust among peoples, their education
in the spirit of proletarian internationalism." Federalism was thus a transitional
step *to* "democratic centralism."[43]

Semenov offers a modified version of the same argument. Lenin's position on
federalism never changed *fundamentally*; to say that it did would be to claim that
Lenin's views before the revolution proved to have been wrong. Rather, Russia
at the time of the revolution was merely one of the exceptional cases Lenin had
long recognized.[44] Because of Lenin's foresight the nationalities did not wish
to secede from their original incorporation within the RSFSR. The Ukrainians,
for example, left the RSFSR only in order to be free to fight "the bourgeois-
nationalist governments of the Ukraine and the German-Kaiser armies which had
occupied the country."[45] Lenin supported a federative state composed of
"sovereign" and "equal" republics not because this had any connection in
principle with the party's acceptance of the right of nations to self-determination
or with "democratic centralism" but because it was the best way to eradicate
resentments generated by inequality of treatment under Tsarist rule and to
overcome the economic and cultural backwardness of the non-Russian
nationalities. The implication of Semenov's interpretation—as of
Kulichenko's—is that Lenin saw only a limited future for Soviet federalism.

. . .

The basic pro-federalist answer to the question of why Lenin came to support
a federative state structure is that his shifting stand was grounded in a consistent
application of the party's fundamental nationality policy, including the right of
self-determination. Proponents of this view would agree with Akhmedov's
criticism of Kulichenko that "the creation of the Soviet republics was brought
about not by circumstantial considerations [*kon"yunkturnymi soobrazheniyami*],
however important they may have been, but was the result of an objective and
progressive process that Lenin's party led."[46] Tadevosyan provides the most
elaborate defence of this portion. Lenin's view on federalism *did* change,
Tadevosyan says, but as a response to the first experience of the "dictatorship
of the proletariat" in a multinational state. As indicated above, Tadevosyan
relies heavily on the argument that Lenin quickly grasped the theoretical key to
the "permissibility" of federalism—the altered relationship between the "two

tendencies" brought about by the revolution. Tadevosyan's position leads him to attempt to qualify Lenin's pre-1917 hostility to federalism in such a way as to hint, perhaps, that Lenin may even then have seen a connection *in principle* between self-determination and federalism in a multinational state. Tadevosyan does state unequivocally that "after October it would be incorrect to characterize the attitude of Marxist-Leninists towards federation as in principle negative, as allowing the use of this form of state only in special exceptional cases."[47] Semenov accuses Tadevosyan of interpreting Lenin in such a way as to draw the conclusion that the sovereignty of the nationalities in the Soviet Union must, as a matter of right, be expressed through a federative state.[48]

However, Tadevosyan and others who disagree with Kulichenko and Semenov cannot and do not base their explanation of why Lenin *wanted* a federative state primarily on abstract notions of self-determination and democracy. A number of more concrete arguments are advanced. The first is the implicit assertion that Lenin regarded a federative state as a long-term commitment which had to be made to rally the distrustful non-Russian masses to the side of the Bolsheviks. The second is that Lenin believed that the effective revolutionary transformation of different nations at different stages of development inevitably required a diversity of state forms, i.e. a federative state.[49] The third—only hinted at—is that Lenin saw the adoption and maintenance of a federative system as one of the means of containing and resolving then-existing and future political conflict between the central leadership in Moscow and the national elites. It may be relevant that those writers who stress the depth of Lenin's commitment to the federative state also stress the existence of conflicting attitudes towards the rights of the national republics within the party and the extent to which Lenin was responding to the situation within the party in 1922 when he proposed establishing the USSR.[50]

The positions of Soviet writers on the present role of the national-territorial structure quite naturally correspond to their views on Lenin's approach to federalism. The key question to which they must address themselves is: to what extent has the national-territorial system already fulfilled its tasks (and therefore become unnecessary)? Semenov most openly minimizes the role left for the system. His argument is that the Soviet national state structures have had three functions to perform, determined by the three historical goals of Soviet nationality policy: the *democratic* goal of "establishing full [legal] national equality and eradicating national privileges"; the *socialist* goal of developing factual equality in "all areas of social, political and cultural life"; and the *communist* goal of achieving "all-round unity of the Soviet nations with the ultimate perspective of their full merger."[51] The first goal was achieved with the October revolution; the second has already been "basically" achieved; and the third remains to be accomplished during the new historical phase of "developed construction of communism." By assuming that the "socialist" goal has been achieved Semenov can assert:

If formerly the degree of federativeness, the character of national statehood, the juridical content of national-state borders had significance as a guarantee of national freedom, then now essentially they no longer have such a meaning. . . .

Under conditions of full, friendly, fraternal relations among all nations *it is not national borders, not national statehood*, but the really democratic of the Soviet state that is ever more becoming—in the eyes of the toiling masses themselves of the national republics—the basic, decisive guarantee of national rights and freedoms.
. . .

One may now already state with assurance that *from this standpoint national statehood and federation as a whole have fulfilled their historical mission.*[52]

He therefore draws the conclusion that

The existence of a federation, as well as the Programme's provisions for full utilization during the period of building communism of the principles of federation and national-territorial autonomy and for the further perfection of all forms of Soviet national statehood, are now conditioned *exclusively by the tasks of economic and cultural development* of the nations and peoples of the Soviet Union.[53]

He then proceeds to answer the question: will the national-territorial state structure "wither away" before or concurrently with the general "withering away of the state?" His view is that the disappearance of national-territorial state divisions is a *precondition* for the withering of the state as a whole and that it will occur relatively rapidly:

The mutual assimilation of nations in essence denationalizes national-territorial autonomous divisions and even union republics, bringing Soviet society even from this standpoint closer to the point at which the full state-legal merger (*sliyanie*) of nations will become a matter of the foreseeable future.[54]

The position taken by Semenov represents a minority view,[55] yet it has found support among a number of prominent people—including E.M. Zhukov, the academic secretary of the Division of Historical Sciences of the Academy of Sciences of the USSR, and V.I. Kozlov, Chairman of the Belorussian Supreme Soviet.[56] Most writers assume, however, that Soviet federalism still has a political role to perform. The standard argument is that Soviet federalism *has* successfully filled its mission in the past, but that its possibilities are still far from exhausted." A disputatious tone hints that in the private discussion of Soviet federalism some people have claimed that federalism has not "fulfilled its mission" and has not promoted the "coming together" of the nationalities, but has led to their separation from one another. Tadevosyan, who flatly rejects Semenov's conclusions, states unequivocally:

Soviet federation and Soviet autonomy have played an *outstanding* role in strengthening the friendship of peoples of our country, in bringing them closer together. . . . However, the possibilities inherent in Soviet federation and Soviet autonomy are still far from exhausted. *And those possibilities are not limited exclusively merely to the realm of solving tasks of the further economic and cultural development of nations.* . . . Soviet federation is even now one of the most important *political forms* of further solidifying the friendship of peoples.[57]

"Deliberately or not," Tadevosyan continues, Semenov fails to understand that "the all-around development and perfection of national forms of Soviet statehood in combination with a strengthening of their international unity is an objective law of the present stage of development of the Soviet multinational state. . . ." The root of Semenov's error—Tadevosyan implies—lies in believing that if national forms of Soviet statehood are preserved and perfected, this will "retard the process of the coming together of nations and effacing of national differences." On the contrary, Tadevosyan asserts:

The deeply dialectical development of this process consists precisely in the fact that only an attentive consideration of the conditions of each nation (including questions of state structure as well) will be able to ease and hasten their coming together and ever mote complete unity. In the realm of national state structure an artificial acceleration of the withering away of forms of socialist national statehood, just as the rejection of their further perfection and development, can only harm matters.[58]

The controversy over federalism turns ultimately around the concrete means through which federative relationships are realized. Semenov's position is that institutional forms are now a matter of secondary significance; that the factual *equality* of nations in all areas of life is the most important index of sovereignty; and that the increased administrative and legislative rights ("competence") of the union republics in the post-Stalin period should be interpreted as a response to the demands of "democratic centralism," not as a concession to the right to sovereignty of the nationalities. To conceive otherwise is to open the way for "false notions concerning the character of relationships between nations and peoples—truly friendly—which have grown up in our country."[59] Semenov has strongly urged that the new Soviet Constitution under consideration since 1962 should not include a specific guarantee of the "sovereign" rights of the national republics.[60] There has undoubtedly been a heated controversy over this issue. Semenov has recently reiterated: "National sovereignty under the conditions of the Soviet socialist state is provided for by the necessary guarantees; the state organizes the effective increase in the economic and spiritual forces of all nations and peoples, it equalizes the level of their economic and cultural development."[61] The stress he places on the lack of any need for constitutional guarantees of equal economic development points to a major source of tension.[62]

Each of Semenov's assertions is denied by his opponents. The latter are unwilling to concede either that equality and institutional forms, or "democracy" and federalism are functionally unrelated. The danger of an accusation of "administrative-bureaucratic" measures of control over the republics is a theme constantly emphasize in their writings. Those who frame their case in legal terms argue that while sovereignty is in principle distinct from "competence" (meaning among other things that a decision to reduce the powers of the republics cannot juridically alter their full "sovereignty"), the exercise of "competence" is still a necessary attribute of national sovereignty.[63] They are supported in this instance by the regime's own claim that the post-1953 devolution of administrative authority "strengthened" the sovereignty of the republics. Some persons argue that the *only* way the sovereignty of the republics can be "strengthened" is to expand their competence.[64] All who favor the federative structure insist that the sovereignty of the republics must be upheld.

The jurisprudential contribution to the literature on federalism is especially attuned to the drafting of the new all-union and republic constitutions. As noted above, an argument has apparently taken place over whether the Constitution should include what would amount to a "bill of rights" for the republics. At a meeting on 18 May 1959 in the Institute of Law in the USSR Academy of Sciences, D.A. Gaidukov and I.D. Levin proposed that the new Constitution explicitly recognize the sovereignty of the republics.[65] Several years later D.L. Zlatopol'sky also supported the idea that the Constitution should specify the rights of the central and republic governments, but as a means of limiting the power of the latter.[66] In 1962 Manelis stressed Lenin's remark that "a detailed code is required" to secure the sovereign rights of the republics.[67] Three years later in an article published in Uzbekistan he repeated this plea and specified not only what the new Constitution should include, but what it should exclude.[68] Those provisions of the Constitution dealing with the sovereign rights of the republics were to be entrenched:

> It would be expedient to specify more precisely the system for changing the norms of the Constitution of the USSR which strengthen the guarantees of sovereignty of the union republics (the right of secession from the USSR, the right of adopting their own constitutions, the right of republic legislation, etc.). It seems to us that . . . a preliminary juridical expression of consent of all the union republics to a change in these norms, and in individual cases the holding of a referendum, ought to be provided for.

Manelis's proposals amounted to a demand for substantial republic autonomy. More recently it has been urged—in the context of an attack on Semenov's views—that the new Constitution contain guarantees of the sovereignty of the union republics reflecting the expansion of their rights in state, economic, and cultural affairs.[69]

The reference in the Programme to borders "losing their former significance" is a serious threat to the pro-federalist position. It is obviously hard to conceive of a union republic without borders. Some writers choose to ignore the dilemma. Others in effect reject this section of the Programme.[70] Still others will admit that borders are no longer needed as a guarantee of national independence, but argue that the concept of "national borders" is not identical with the concept of "national statehood."[71] And Manelis, as indicated in footnote 69, shifts the entire frame of reference to propose that since borders have "lost their former significance," jurisdiction over border changes should be entrusted completely to the republics themselves.[72] The most spirited pro-federalist arguments on this question are offered by an Armenian, A.M. Egiazaryn, who sharply attacks Zhukov's notion that community of territory no longer applies as a defining characteristic of Soviet nations, and also anti-federalist interpretations of the passage on borders in the Programme. Egiazaryn equates his opponents with the Polish Social-Democrats, who—he quotes Lenin—ignored the "will and "sympathies" of the population" and insisted that "borders be determined "exclusively" on the basis of production requirements."[73] The Polish case showed that

> V.I. Lenin did not reduce to naught the significance of borders for socialist nations, did not reduce to naught the territorial community of the nation, which—without such territory—is altogether unthinkable, cannot exist as a nation. . . .[74]

Citing recent evidence to prove that the party did recognize nationality factors in making border changes, Egiazaryn proceeds to reject the assertions that Lenin was speaking only of the first phase of communism, i.e., socialism, and that because the territory of a union republic is an indivisible part of the USSR it thus cannot belong simultaneously to "the given socialist nation."

In attacking "bureaucratic centralism," the pro-federalists stress alternative processes for harmonizing the interests of the republics and the state as a whole. They accept as a matter of course the existence of conflicting interests. Thus Lepeshkin asserts that unity of the republics is achieved

> not by means of the centralization of operative-managerial functions of branch economic-administrative administration and the concentration of almost all powers of leadership of the economy and culture in the hands of all-federal organs, but by means of strengthening centralization in the realm of planning and decentralization in the realm of operative administration of industry and construction. . . .

He adds that

> the role of the union republics in the decisions of affairs [*v reshenii del*] of the all-union state is growing by means of the strengthening of national-republic representation in the all-federal organs of power and administration.[75]

Manelis repeats these points in arguing that an expansion of the rights of the republics "should not be viewed as a weakening of the sovereignty of the USSR and of centralized leadership by union organs." He emphasizes in particular the increasingly overlapping "competence" of all-union and republic bodies and approvingly notes that

> in practice at the present time things are arranged in such a way that questions touching the mutual interests of the USSR and the union republics, regardless of whose competence they fall within, are decided on the basis of mutual consultations and agreement.[76]

While stressing the importance of representation of the nationalities in all-union and inter-republic agencies, Manelis would also assign greater power to local soviets and allow more scope for various forms of direct mass participation in government. Not surprisingly, pro-federalists tend to be relatively vocal supporters of "Soviet democracy."[77] I.P. Tsameryan poses the question somewhat differently by arguing in his writings that the objective factors which necessitated a high degree of centralization in the past have been superseded by new factors (a sufficient pool of qualified local cadres, the growing complexity of the economy, etc.) which make possible and desirable an increase in the functions performed by the union republics.[78]

Manelis most openly expresses an important notion that appears in articles by other writers of the same general persuasion—that the role of settling conflicts and coordinating central and local activities is one that should be assigned to the Communist Party.[79] References to the role of the party appear when pro-federalists attempt to answer the question put to them: how is unity to be assured if state (i.e. bureaucratic) ties between the centre and republics are weakened? Pro-federalists seem to imply—although they do not openly assert—that the coordinating and integrating function is thoroughly political in nature, and therefore must be performed by a body authoritative yet flexible enough to make the concessions, compromises and local adjustments required if the "coming together" of the nationalities is to occur voluntarily. Consistent with this fear of bureaucratic rigidity and receptivity to a political process more open to influences from below is the pro-federalist emphasis that main reliance should be placed on such "natural" social processes as population migration and increasing economic interdependence to bring about the "coming together" of nations in the Soviet Union.

All pro-federalists thus assert that political, economic and cultural functions which must be performed assure the national-territorial structure a lengthy continued existence. Among those who have explicitly declared themselves, some suggest that the national republics will last for the entire period of the transition to "full communism"—that is, until the state in general withers away (Lepeshkin, Dzhunusov, Tsameryan, Tadevosyan and Abaeva); one asserts that a federation will be preserved after the withering away of the state, although "no longer as a state unification (*gosudarstvennoe ob'edinenie*) of nations" (Mnatsakanyan);[80] several imply that national state differences will remain after the worldwide achievement of the "dictatorship of the proletariat" (Radzhabov and Urazaev); and still another hints that the nationalities will retain their statehood until the attainment of "full communism" on a world-wide scale (Kaikhandi).

IV
THE MEANING OF THE DEBATE

What does the debate over federalism among Soviet academics reveal? It shows, first, that there has been no firm party "line" on the future of federalism for the better part of a decade. The Party Programme can be and has been quoted to justify mutually contradictory courses of action. Secondly, the debate provides some insight into the various perceptions of federalism which exist and the kinds of arguments being used to justify different courses of action. Thirdly, the debate indicates something about the underlying alignment of forces among the academicians. Although non-Russians are prominently among the pro-federalists, there are Russians as well. Less significantly, perhaps, there are non-Russians among the anti-federalists. Nor does the debate pit institution against institution. The Institute of State and Law, for example, speaks with a divided voice, as do the Institute of History and the Institute of Marxism-Leninism. Fourthly, it may be argued that the debate reflects the existence of indecision—and perhaps serious conflict—over the future of federalism within the top Soviet leadership both before and after Khrushchev's fall. This hypothesis depends upon several assumptions which cannot be argued within the scope of this present article. One may simply observe that changing the nation-territorial structure of the Soviet state is an extraordinarily sensitive matter, and that it is therefore unlikely that such highly controversial views could have been expressed on this matter for so long a time had unanimity of opinion prevailed among the leaders.

Notes

1. B. Gafurov, "Uspekhi natsional'noi politiki KPSS i nekotoroye internatsional'nogo vospitaniya," *Kommunist*, 1958, no. 11, p. 16. Also Sh. R. Rashidov, "Leninskaya natsional'naya politika v deistvii," *Voprosy istorii KPSS*, 1959, no. 1, p. 41.

2. "Edinaya bratskaya sem'ya narodov SSSR," *Kommunist*, 1964, no. 16, p. 15 .

3. J. Stalin, *Works* (English ed.), vol. 3, p. 31.

4. V.V. Pentkovskaya, "Rol' V.I. Lenina v obrazovanii SSSR," *Voprosy istorii*, 1956, no. 3.

5. *Kommunist*, 1956, no. 9, translated in Leo Gruliow (ed.), Current Soviet Policies—II (N.Y. 1957), pp. 214-16.

6. *Ibid.* p. 211.

7. Z. Levina and A. Romanova, "Velikaya rol' V.I. Lenina v organizatsii Soyuza Sovetskikh Respublik," *Pravda*, 11 July 1956; S. Yakubovskaya, "Rol' V.I. Lenina v sozdanii Soyuza Sovetskikh Sotsialisticheskikh Respublik," *Kommunist*, 1956, no. 10.

8. Leo Gruliow and Charlotte Saikowski (eds.), *Current Soviet Policies—IV* (N.Y. 1962), p. 26.

9. See A. Ya. Vyshinsky, *Voprosii teorii gosudarstvo i pravo*, 2nd ed. (M. 1949), p. 303. Also S.I. Yakubovskaya, *Stroitel'stvo soyuznogo sovetskogo sotsialisticheskogo gosudarstva 1922-1925 gg.* (M. 1960), pp. 8-10, 24, 26-27, 35.

10. *Current Soviet Policies—IV*, p. 103 (emphasis added).

11. *Ibid.* p. 141.

12. Quoted critically by M.S. Dzhunusov, "O sovetskoi avtonomii i perezhitkakh natsionalizma," *Istoriya SSSR*, 1963, no. 1, p. 3.

13. See especially "Programma KPSS o razvitii sovetskikh natsional'no-gosudarstvennykh otnoshenii," *Sovetskoe gosudarstvo i pravo*, no. 12. E.V. Tadevosyan accuses Semenov of misinterpreting Lenin's view "that the national composition of the population is not the sole nor even the main factor" in determining internal boundaries within the RSFSR in such a way as to leave the reader with the impression that Semenov would apply this principle to the national republics as well. See E.V. Tadevosyan, "Leninskii etap v marksistskom uchenii o federatsii, *ibid.*, 1962, no. 12, p. 40n."

14. For a refutation by Dzhunusov of this view see "O sovetskoi avtonomii . . .," pp. 6-7. Dzhunusov rejects the following arguments: economic efficiency demands adherence to the "economic principle"; the nationality principle infringes the interests of the "proletariat"; and the nationality principle has the effect of artificially exacerbating nationalist passions. He points out, referring to the debate over the formation of the Tatar-Bashkir republic, that Lenin considered persons who propounded such views to be "Great Russian chauvinists."

15. Dzhunusov refutes the view that such an arrangement creates "unjustifiable privileges for the minority" involved and discriminates against the rest (i.e. Slavs and others) by quoting Lenin to the effect that small nations as well as large have a right to their own national-state units; by pointing out that the only practical way this right can be realized is by creating these units where the largest concentration of the given nationality is located; and by citing statistical data to prove that a nationality group like the Bashkirs can be a minority within their own republic but still be far from "privileged" in terms of union-wide comparisons with other nationalities (*ibid.*, pp. 3 ff.). Other pro-

federalist writers are also sensitive to the charge that the national-territorial system leads to discrimination against Russians. For example, see S. Radzhabov and Sh. Urazaev, "Obshchee i osobennoe v natsional'no-gosudarstvennom stroitel'stve," *Sovetskoe gosudarstvo i pravo,* 1966, no. 2, p. 26. Stalin's argument that a union republic is defined, among other criteria, by "the presence of a more or less compact majority of that nationality which has given [the republic] its name" is attacked by one writer as especially inapplicable "under contemporary conditions" when mass population migration has reduced some nationalities to minorities within their own republics. See N.P. Farberov, "Nekotorye voprosy sovetskogo federalizma", in *Torzhestvo leninskoi natsional'noi politiki* (M. 1963), p. 237. Also see A.V. Radvogin, "O ponyatii sovetskoi natsional'noi gosudarstvennosti," *Sovetskoe gosudarstvo i pravo,* 1966, no. 7, pp. 129-32.

16. For an attack on this proposal see E.V. Tadevosyan, "Dal'neishee sblizenie sotsialisticheskikh natsii v SSSR," *Voprosii filosofii,* 1963, no. 6, pp. 8-9. Tadevosyan argues, having cited Kazakhstan as a place in which the issue had been raised, that the national republics do provide equal rights for non-national inhabitants. He also states in effect that the institutional form of national "autonomy" was designed to protect the "free and independent development" of small nations against encroachment by the large, not vice-versa.

17. Sh. B. Batyrov, *Formirovanie i razvitie sotsialisticheskikh natsii v SSSR* (M. 1962), pp. 29-30, 46, 70, 83; also 86-88 and bibliography.

18. M.I. Kulichenko, "V.I. Lenin o federatsii i ee roli v stroitel'stve sovetskogo mnogonatsional'nogo gosudarstva," *Voprosy istorii KPSS,* 1961, no. 5, p. 72. This passage has drawn the fire of D.A. Chugaev and M.S. Akhmedov (see footnotes 19 and 20).

19. M.S. Akhmedov, "V.I. Lenin i obrazovanie Soyuza SSR," *ibid.,* 1962, no. 6, p. 33. Akhmedov cites as his source for these "facts" the Central Party Archives of the Institute of Marxism-Leninism.

20. D.A. Chugaev, "Obrazovanie Soyuza SSR," *ibid.* 1962, no. 6, p. 180.

21. Yakubovskaya, *Stroitel'stvo* . . . (see footnote 9), p. 9. The use of the labels anti-federalist and pro-federalist is intended merely to indicate a relatively lesser or greater attachment to the federative state. Within each category there is a diversity of views. Thus, for example, Yakubovskaya does not take as extreme a position on all issues as some of her anti-federalist colleagues.

22. E.V. Tadevosyan, "V.I. Lenin o gosudarstvennykh formakh sotsialisticheskogo razresheniya natsional'nogo voprosa," *Voprosy filosofii,* 19, no. 4, p. 28.

23. A.I. Lepeshkin, "Nekotorye voprosy leninskoi teorii sovetskogo federalizma v svete novoi programmy KPSS," *Sovetskoe gosudarstvo i pravo,* 1963, no. 5, p. 67; B.L. Manelis, "Razvitie V.I. Leninym vzglyadov marksizma na federatsiyu," *ibid.,* 1962, no. 4, pp. 20, 25, 27; Akhmedov, *op. cit.* (see footnote 19), pp. 30-31.

24. See the Stalinist Batyrov's rejection of these accusations, which he attributes to "the ideology of 'national communism'" and "revisionists" (*op. cit.*—see footnote 17—pp. 29-30, 48).

25. A.E. Kaikhanidi, *Leninskaya teoriya i programma po natsional'nomu voprosu* (Minsk, 1962), p. 26.

26. For essentially similar positions on the Civil War period see A.I. Lepeshkin (General Editor), A.I. Kim, N.G. Mishin, P.I. Romanov, *Kurs sovetskogo gosudarstvennogo prava, tom vtoroi* (M. 1962), p. 31; Chugaev, *op. cit.* (see footnote 20), p. 181; Tadevosyan, "V.I. Lenin o gosudarstvennykh formakh . . ." (see footnote 22), p. 33.

27. P.G. Semenov, "Suverenitet sovetskikh natsii," *Voprosy istorii*, 1965, no. 12, p. 32.

28. M.I. Kulichenko, "Reshnie natsional'nogo voprosa v SSSR v iskazhennom svete burzhuaznoi istoriografii," *Voprosy istorii KPSS*, 1966, no. 1, pp. 62-78, as well as his other works cited in this article.

29. I.P. Tsameryan, "Razvitie sovetsogo mnogonatsional'nogo gosudarstva," *Voprosy filosofii*, 1962, no. 11, p. 47.

30. M.M. Abaeva, "Nekotorye voprosy razvitiya sotsialisticheskikh natsii v period razvernutogo stroitel'stva kommunizma," *Izvestiya Akademii nauk Turkmenskoi SSR: seriya obshchestvennykh nauk*, 1963, no. 6, p. 40.

31. Chugaev, *op. cit.* (see footnote 20), pp. 176-7; Tadevosyan, "V.I. Lenin o gosudarstvennykh formakh . . ." (see footnote 22), pp. 27, 36; Kaikhanidi, *op. cit.* (see footnote 25), p. 65; Lepeshkin, "Nekotorye voprosy . . ." (see footnote 23), p. 61; Akhmedov, *op. cit.* (see footnote 19), p. 34; A.G. Lashin, *Vozniknovenie i razvitie form sotsialisticheskogo gosudarstva* (M. 1965), p. 309.

32. Semenov. "Suverenitet . . . (see footnote 27), p. 22. Also see Semenov's article "Natsiya i natsional'naya gosudarstvennost' v SSSR," *Voprosy istorii*, 1966, no. 7, pp. 80-81.

33. For a discussion of these differences see Tadevosyan, "Dal'neishee sblizhenie . . . ." (see footnote 16), pp. 11-12. Tadevosyan himself takes the middle position.

34. *Sbornik nauchnykh rabot Belorusskogo gosudarstvennogo universiteta imeni V.I. Lenina*, vyp. I(40), Kafedra istorii KPSS (Minsk, 1958), p. 81 (quoted critically by Tadevosyan, "V.I. Lenin o gosudarstvennoi federatsii," *Voprosy istorii KPSS*, 1961, no. 2, p. 49).

35. G.V. Aleksandrenko, *Marksizm-leninizm pro derzhavnu federatsiyu* (Kiev, 1960), p. 61 (quoted critically by Tadevosyan, "V.I. Lenin o gosudarstvennykh federtsii" (see footnote 34), p. 48).

36. G.V. Aleksandrenko, *Burzhuaznyi federalizm* (Kiev, 1962), p. 12 (emphasis added).

37. *Uchenye zapiski Leningradskogo gosudarstvennogo pedagogicheskogo instituta*, Kafedra dialekticheskogo i istoricheskogo materializma, t. 31, vyp. 1 (Leningrad, 1957), pp. 172,173 (quoted critically by Tadevosyan, "V.I. Lenin o gosudarstvennoi federatsii" (see footnote 34), p. 57).

38. e.g. Chugaev, *op. cit.* (see footnote 20), p. 179; Manelis, *op. cit.* (see footnote 23), p. 18.

39. Batyrov, *op. cit.* (see footnote 17), pp. 53-54, 87. See also Tadevosyan's criticism of Batyrov in "V.I. Lenin o gosudarstvennykh formakh . . ." (see footnote 22), pp. 33, 36n.

40. *Osnovy sovetsogo gosudarstvennogo stroitel'stva i prava* (1st ed. M. 1961), p. 140; (2nd ed. 1965), p. 161.

41. e.g. Lepeshkin, *op. cit.* (see footnote 23), p. 62; A. Agzamkhodzhaev, *Sovetskoe mnogonatsional'noe gosudarstvo* (Tashkent, 1962), pp. 36-37 (referred to approvingly in a review by M. Kh. Khakimov and R.K. Kayumov in *Obshchestvennye nauki v Uzbekistane*, 1963, no. 10, p. 59).

42. Kulichenko, "V.I. Lenin o sovetskoi federatsii . . ." (see footnote 18), p. 70.

43. For a thorough pro-federalist critique of Kulichenko's position see M.S. Akhmedov's view of the former book, *Bor'ba Kommunisticheskoi partii za reshenie natsional'nogo voprosa v 1918-20 godakh* (Khar'kov, 1963), in *Voprosy istorii KPSS*, 1964, no. 7, pp. 115-20.

44. Tadevosyan has sharply attacked this assertion. See "Leninskii etap . . ." (see footnote 13), pp. 38-39. Cf. P.G. Semenov and E.L. Rozin, "Formy sotsialisticheskogo gosudarstvo," in K.A. Mokichev (ed.), *Teoriya gosudarstvo i prava* (M. 1965), p. 225.

45. Semenov, "Suverenitet..." (see footnote 27), p. 31.

46. *Voprosy istorii KPSS*, 1964, no. 7, p. 118. For a similar statement see Lashin, *op. cit.* (see footnote 31), p. 298.

47. "Leninskii etap . . ." (see footnote 13), p. 45.

48. "Suverenitet . . ." (see footnote 27), pp. 28-29. This position is certainly implied in the writings of Lepeshkin and Dzhunusov. The author of a recent article in the theoretical journal of the Ukrainian Communist Party has observed: ". . . V.I. Lenin decisively and consistently upheld the right of the Ukrainian people to self-determination and the creation of their own sovereign state." Lenin recognized "the right of the Ukraine to such a state." The quotation from Lenin then continues: "We respect this right, we do not support privileges for Great Russia over the Ukrainians, we are educating the masses in the spirit of accepting this right, in the spirit of denying state privileges for any nation whatsoever" (A. Likholat, "V.I. Lenin i obrazovanie ukrainskogo sovetskogo gosudarstva," *Kommunist Ukrainy*, 1966, no. 1, p. 41.)

49. See especially Tadevosyan, "V.I. Lenin o gosudarstvennykh formakh . . ." (see footnote 22), pp. 33-34; also A.I. Lepeshkin, *Kurs sovetskogo gosudarstvennogo prava, tom pervyi* (M. 1961), p. 292. The argument here unmistakably borrows from the discussion in relation to foreign countries of multiple paths to socialism. This blurring of the distinction between foreign and domestic in national relations has probably been stimulated by the officially sponsored campaign to draw a parallel between the more backward republics of the Soviet Union and the underdeveloped nations of the world, and to picture these republics as models for "bypassing capitalism." However, the casual shift in frame of reference from domestic to foreign and then back again has always been a characteristic feature of discussions of the nationality problem.

50. Tadevosyan, "V.I. Lenin o gosudarstvennykh formakh . . ." (see footnote 22), pp. 34-35; Chugaev, *op. cit.* (see footnote 20), p. 178; B.L Manelis, V.I. Lenin—organiztor Soyuza SSR," *Sovetskoe gosudarstvo i pravo*, 1962, no. 12, p. 21n; Akhmedov, "V.I. Lenin i obrazovanie . . ." (see footnote 19), pp. 27-29, 34; Pentkovskaya, *op. cit.* (see footnote 13), p. 15.

51. Semenov, "Programma KPSS . . ." (see footnote 13), p. 15.

52. *Ibid.* p. 23 (emphasis added). In this passage Semenov equates "national borders" with "national statehood," thus making it possible to argue that the passage in the Programme about borders "losing their former significance" applies to national statehood in general.

53. *Ibid.* pp. 23-24 (emphasis added).

54. *Ibid.* p. 25. Kulichenko hints that federation may preserve its *raison d'etre* only "for the period of socialism" ("Voprosy obrazovaniya SSSR v novykh trudakh sovetskikh istorikov," *Voprosy istorii,* 1962, no. 1, p. 136.)

55. At the All-Union Coordinating Meeting of 1963 in the discussion section on "Problems of the Development of Soviet National Statehood" Semenov's portion "to a certain degree was also echoed in the speeches . . .; it did not, however, receive the support of a majority of those who spoke" (E.V. Tadevosyan, "Pervyi opyt vsesoyuznoi koordinatsii nauchnykh issledovanii v oblasti natsional'nykh otnoshenii," *Voprosy filosofii,* 1964, no. 2, p. 160). Semenov's ideas were attacked on this occasion by I.P. Tsameryan (G.O. Zimanas, "O sushchnosti protsessa sblizheniya sotsialisticheskikh natsii," *ibid.* 1966, no. 7, p. 7).

56. In an important leading article in *Voprosy istorii,* Zhukov argued that territorial and economic community—two of Stalin's four criteria of nationhood—had "almost completely lost their former significance" and were "dying away," but that nations would continue to exist in the USSR ("XVII s"ezd KPSS i zadachi sovetskikh istorikov," *ibid.* 1961, no. 12, p. 9). Semenov's contribution to the recent discussion of the "concept of the nation" in the same journal similarly asserts that "nations will remain, but national statehood in the USSR will whither away" ("Natsiya i natsional'naya gosudarstvennost v SSSR," *ibid.* 1966, no. 7, p. 81). By separating statehood from nationhood Semenov reduces the opportunity for counter-attack provided by his earlier references to "assimilation" and "denationalization," although he increases his vulnerability to charges of advocating "national-cultural autonomy." Kozlov published an article in March 1963 that clearly echoed the ideas about national statehood expressed by Semenov in 1961 ("V semernoe ukreplenie soyuza SSR i sovershenstvovanie natsional'noi gosudarstvennosti narodov SSSR v svete istoricheskikh reshenii XXII s"ezda KPSS," *Sovetskoe gosudarstvo i prava,* 1963, no. 4, pp. 40-42).

57. Tadevosyan, "V.I. Lenin o gosudarstvennykh formakh . . ." (see footnote 22), p. 36 (emphasis added).

58. *Ibid.,* p. 37. For a more recent statement of this position, see Radzhabov and Urazaev, *op. cit.* (see footnote 15), p. 26.

59. Semenov, "Suverenitet . . ." (See footnote 27), p. 33.

60. Semenov, "Programma KPSS . . ." (see footnote 52), p. 25.

61. Semenov, "Suverenitet . . ." (see footnote 27), p. 24.

62. In May 1965 Tadevosyan expressed his argument with a proposal that a discussion of the "theory of the nation" should be opened in the pages of *Voprosy istorii* as follows; "I am for a discussion of national relations. There are many problems whose elaboration might provide the basis for subsequent general conclusions. For example, the principle of just distribution of goods [*blag*] among nations; the achievement of communist equality of nations. . . ." (R.F. Vinokurova, "Obsuzhdenie stat'i P.M. Rogacheva i M.A. Sverdlina 'o ponyatii natsii'" *ibid.* 1966, no. 2, p. 170).

63. See B.L. Manelis, "Edinstvo suvereniteta soyuza SSR i suvereniteta soyuznykh respublik v period razvernutogo stroitel'stva kommunizma," *Sovetskoe gosudarstvo i pravo,* 1964, no. 7, pp. 20-21; M.Kh. Khakimov, "O nekotorykh voprosakh razvitiya natsional'noi Sovetskoi gosudarstvennosti v sovremennyi period," *Obshchestvennye nauki v Uzbekistane,* 1964, no. 6, pp. 19-20 (Khakimov defends the position that the creation

of the Central Asian inter-republic agencies in no way affected the sovereignty of the republics and quotes a speech by Khrushchev in Tashkent to prove his point); A.I.Peleshkin, "O razmezhevanii kompetentsii mezhdu organami soyuza SSR i soyuznykh respublik v oblasti rukovodstva narodnym khozyaistvom," *Sovetskoe gosudarstvo i pravo*, 1966, no. 6, pp. 4-5.

One of the questions touched upon in the technical literature on sovereignty is the "subject" of sovereignty. Pro-federalists on the whole are not inclined to deny that the bearer of sovereignty in a republic is the entire population, not just the ethnic national group after which the republic is named. For example: "The bearer of the sovereignty of the USSR is the Soviet people, while the bearer of the sovereignty of union republic is the nation after which it is named, its population as a whole" (Khakimov, "O nekotorykh voprosakh . . .," p. 19).

64. On this point see, for example, the moderate Khakimov's criticism of the dissertation by L.M. Strel'tsov dealing with the Ukraine, "Rasshirenie prav soyuznykh respublik na sovremennom etape kommunisticheskogo stroitel'stva" (Khar'kov, 1963) (Khakimov, *op. cit.* (see footnote 63), p. 17). For a refutation of "the opinion that the expansion of the rights of union republics is nothing more or less than a law . . . of development of soviet federalism," see D.L. Zlatopol'sky, "Sovetskaya federatsiya na novom etape razvitiya natsional'nykh vzaimootnoshenii," *Vestnik Moskovskogo universiteta*, 1962, no. 2, pp. 21-22. This opinion appears to be held by I.P. Tsameryan, one of the most prominent Soviet spokesmen on nationality affairs. (See his *Sovetskoe mnogonatsional'noe gosudarstvo, ego osobennosti i puti razvitiya* (M. 1958), p. 192).

65. G. Aleksandrov, "O razvitii konstitutsii SSSR v svete reshenii XXI s"ezda KPSS," *Sovetskoe gosudarstvo i pravo*, 1959, no. 9, pp. 113-15.

66. Zlatopol'sky, *op. cit.* (see footnote 64), pp. 22-23.

67. "V.I. Lenin—organizator . . ." (see footnote 51), p. 23.

68. The Constitution of the USSR should not fix the rights of supreme soviets of union republics, nor determine the composition of the presidiums of supreme soviets of republics, nor determine questions related to the election of the chairman and deputy chairmen of supreme soviets, nor fix the composition of the council of ministers of republics, nor determine the rights of ministers of republics, nor contain detailed regulation concerning local government. These matters should be dealt with in the republic constitutions. Republic constitutions in general need not and should not be carbon copies of the all-union constitution. They should continue to reflect the specific character of each republic. The new Constitution should contain detailed clauses stipulating: (1) those constitutional principles common to all republics (sovereignty, principles of public and state structure, nationality policy, domestic and foreign policy, economic structure, basic rights and duties of citizens, electoral system, role of the Communist Party and mass public organizations); (2) the sovereign rights of the USSR and of the union republics, and their legislative and executive powers; (3) the structure, manner of formation and powers of all-union organs; (4) the membership of the USSR and the basic forms of organization and activity of republic and local state organs. Jurisdiction over internal border changes should be completely shifted to the republics. Interested republics should be given the right to express their "will" concerning changes in the external borders of the USSR (B.L. Manelis, "Sootnoshenie konstitutsionnogo zakonodatel'stva Soyuza SSR i soyuznykh respublik," *Obshchestvennye nauki v*

Uzbekistane, 1965, no. 1, pp. 24-26). Cf. A.I. Lepeshkin, "Nazrevshie voprosy razvitiya nauki sovetskogo gosudarstvennogo prava," *Sovetskoe gosudarstvo i pravo*, 1965, no. 2, p. 8.

69. D.S. Kiselev, "O roli perspektivakh natsional'no-sovetskoi gosudarstvennosti v protesse kommunisticheskogo stroitel'stva," *Izvestiya Akademii nauk Turkmenskoi SSR, seriya obshchestvennykh nauk*, 1966, no. 2, p. 16.

70. "Individual authors assert that the preservation of national sovereignty and guarding [*okhrana*] of the borders established between union and autonomous republics is supposedly one of the main domestic tasks of the Soviet state . . ." (Khakimov, *op. cit.* (see footnote 63), p. 17). Khakimov cites as an example G.L. Furmanov, *V.I. Lenin o vysshem tipe gosudarstva* (M. 1962), p. 42.

71. See Lashin's criticism of Semenov on this point, *op. cit.* (see footnote 31), pp. 313-14n.

72. Manelis, "Sootnoshenie . . ." (see footnote 68), p. 26. If implemented, this proposal would create a bulwark of sorts against sweeping border revisions or creeping changes that alter the ethnic balance as well as the territorial size of individual republics (e.g. the transfer of about a million hectares of territory with a largely Kazakh population from Kazakhstan to Uzbekistan in January 1963, which "denationalized" Kazakhstan and "internationalized" Uzbekistan).

73. A.M. Egiazaryan, *Ob osnovnykh tendentsiyakh razvitiya sotsialisticheskikh natsii SSSR* (Yerevan, 1965), p. 100.

74. *Ibid.*

75. Lepeshkin, "Nekotorye voprosy . . ." (see footnote 23), p. 67. Cf. Lashin, *op. cit.* (see footnote 31), p. 313. G.O. Zimanas, who supports national statehood and sovereignty in principle, suggests that the development of the sovereignty of socialist nations is conceivable also along lines of strengthening the role of representatives of republics in the federal organs" (*op. cit.* (see footnote 63), p. 7).

76. Manelis, "Edinstvo suvereniteta soyuza SSR . . ." (see footnote 63), p. 22.

77. In addition to his various articles, see the review by manelis of V.F. Kotok's *S"ezdy i nauki v Uzbekistane*, 1965, no. 12, pp. 58-59. Lepeshkin in early 1965 supported the proposal that more than one man should be placed on the ballot in elections to soviets. See "Nazrevshie voprosy . . ." (see footnote 68), p. 12.

78. For example, see "Razvitie natsional'noi gosudarstvennosti narodov SSSR," *Voprosy filosofii*, 1956, no. 3, p. 25; *Sovetskoe mnogonatsional'noe gosudarstvo* . . . (see footnote 64), p. 179.

79. Cf. Manelis, "Sootnoshenie . . ." (see footnote 68), pp. 20, 27-28; Khakimov, *op. cit.* (see footnote 63), p. 18; Radzhabov and Urazaev, *op. cit.* (see footnote 15), p. 28.

80. M.O. Mnatsakanyan, "Deyatel'nost KPSS po rasshireniyu prav soyuznykh respublik," *Voprosy istorii KPSS*, 1963, no. 10, p. 9. Mnatsakanyan is the author of one of the articles in the *Voprosy istorii* symposium on the "concept of the nation." In it he attacks Semenov's views while arguing that national statehood should be regarded as one of the defining characteristics of a nation. (See "Natsiya i natsional'naya gosudarstvennost," *Voprosy istorii*, 1966, no. 9, pp. 27-36).

6

Soviet Federalism
and Ethnic Mobilization

Philip G. Roeder[1]

A central element of the Soviet developmental strategy was the creation of political institutions that expanded the control of the regime over the processes of social mobilization associated with modernization. This strategy was noteworthy for providing a considerable measure of interethnic peace as the Soviet regime began the process of industrialization. And yet seven decades after the Soviet regime assumed power, with the industrialization of the economy and urbanization of society well under way, this developmental strategy instead fuels a divisive and destructive ethnopolitics.

The Soviet developmental strategy seems to turn around a pattern familiar in the Western developmental experience. As Ernest Gellner notes: "The age of transition to industrialism was bound" also to be "an age of nationalism."[1] But the Soviet strategy delayed the political reckoning with the "age of nationalism" to a much later stage of industrialization. In the short term this was a prudent means to avoid the simultaneous crises that can overtax the capabilities of a new polity: the Soviet regime did not confront a crisis of identity as it sought to build the foundations of Soviet power and initiate the economic transformation of society.[2] This strategy nonetheless contained the roots of its own longer-term dysfunction and in the past three and a half decades has given rise to new ethnic assertiveness and protest.[3]

The Western experience with peripheral nationalism has differed more significantly from the Soviet pattern in a second respect. In the West—regardless of macroeconomic conditions that occasion the rise of peripheral nationalisms—it has been most pronounced among the less

Published in *World Politics*, 23: 2 (January 1991), pp. 196-233. Reprinted with permission from Johns Hopkins University Press.

advantaged.   In nineteenth-century Western Europe, according to Joseph
Rudolph and Robert Thompson, "the most common causal element giving rise
to the urge for autonomy" was the aggravation of a peripheral ethnic group's
"marginality in, or exploitation by, the state system to which it belongs."[4]
During periods of economic prosperity in the more recent rise of peripheral
nationalisms, Peter Gourevitch has found that those most likely to support ethnic
political movements are disadvantaged ethnic groups drawn by the opportunity
or promise of expanded resources.[5]

   In the Soviet Union the rise of ethnopolitics has been most significant in the
Caucasian and Baltic republics.   It is there that local leaders have pressed the
most ambitious legislative agendas for change and that citizens have mounted the
largest and most frequent demonstrations.   Yet, these nationalities—particularly
the Armenians, Georgians, and Estonians—are among the most successful ethnic
groups in terms of educational and occupational attainment, in many instances
reporting rates even higher than those for the numerically predominant Russian
population.   Even in the area of Party membership, Georgians report far higher
rates among the adult population than do the Russians, and the Armenians report
rates above the average for all nationalities.   Far less inclined to mount this form
of political action in recent years have been the least advantaged nationalities,
such as those in Central Asia.   Thus, it is the nationalities with the highest levels
of educational, occupational, and often political attainment, rather than the
disadvantaged or marginal ones, that have advanced the most ambitious agendas
for change and engaged in the most extensive protest.

   The new Soviet ethnopolitics is structured by the federalism of nominally
autonomous ethnic homelands.   Appreciating the strategic value of organizational
weapons, political entrepreneurship, and mobilizational resources, the architects
of the Soviet regime came to understand that federal institutions could expand
their control over the politicization of ethnicity.   Within each homeland the
regime created a cadre of party and state officials drawn from the indigenous
ethnic group but dependent upon Moscow for its members' positions.   As this
cadre was assigned a monopoly over the mobilizational resources within the
ethnic community, it determined when the ethnic group would be mobilized to
action.   It was a strategy that achieved interethnic peace not so much by
removing the root causes of ethnic grievances as by eliminating mobilizational
opportunities for independent ethnic protest.

   It is therefore an ironic twist that after the transition to industrialism these
federal institutions and indigenous cadres became instruments of the new ethnic
assertiveness.   Institutions that were designed to expand Moscow's control over
ethnic groups (and that were generally thought in the West to be moribund as
federal guarantees of ethnic rights) have taken on a new life.   Autonomous
homelands provide essential resources for the collective mobilization of ethnic
communities, and both federal institutions and indigenous cadres shape ethnic
agendas.

Central to what we have witnessed in the Soviet Union is an expanding and increasingly public politics of *ethnofederalism*. This is not a new phenomenon initiated by the policies of Mikhail Gorbachev but the continuation of a trend that began to unfold as early as the rule of Nikita Khrushchev. As examples below will show, demands for expanded autonomy, protests over language policy, pressures to reduce Russian migration, and intercommunal violence have surfaced in every decade since the mid-1950s. Gorbachev's policies are clearly not sufficient explanation for a pattern that predates Gorbachev and the introduction of his reforms.

The key to three questions raised by the present ethnic crisis lies within the Soviet developmental strategy that created those homelands and cadres. First, *origins*: Why have institutions that fostered interethnic peace during the transition to industrialization later become the vehicles of protest? Second, *incidence*: Why have the relatively advantaged ethnic groups been the most assertive, whereas ethnic groups near the lower end of most comparative measures of socioeconomic and political success have been relatively quiescent? And third, *agendas*: Why have the most important issues of contention between center and periphery focused to such a large degree upon the details of the Soviet developmental strategy and upon federalism in particular? As is argued in the conclusion, the answers to these questions point up the centrality of Soviet political institutions to the politicization of ethnicity.

THE SOVIET DEVELOPMENTAL STRATEGY AND ETHNICITY

Political entrepreneurs play a critical role in the mobilization of protest, the politicization of ethnicity, and in many cases even the creation of ethnic identities.[6] In the European experience, for example, regional intellectuals who felt their aspirations to elite status frustrated by the status quo were often the pioneers of ethnic revival. Anthony Smith contends that these intellectuals sought to create a separate, ethnically distinct system of stratification within which the "professional and bureaucratic apparatus would naturally satisfy the career aspirations of a multitude of hitherto excluded diploma-holders."[7] These regionally oriented intellectuals were a necessary, although not sufficient, ingredient in the rise of peripheral nationalisms.

Political entrepreneurs in ethnic communities have available to them two mobilizational strategies: *primordial* and *instrumental*. The primordial strategy focuses on ethnic revival—in Smith's words, "communal regeneration through self-discovery and self-realization."[8] The mobilization of the ethnic community for political action often centers on an assertion of the ethnic group's identity, usually in the context of issues of culture, identity, or belief and in reaction to threats to the identity from assimilative policies. The instrumental strategy focuses on the pursuit of social and economic interests. The mobilization of ethnicity, according to Rothschild, is "a highly conscious, political, and new mode of interest articulation."[9] The ethnic group itself, in the words of Nathan

Glazer and Daniel Moynihan, is "defined in terms of interest, *as* an interest group."[10] Political entrepreneurs may also seek to mix these strategies.

The Soviet developmental strategy sought to control ethnopolitics by prohibiting all but sanctioned political entrepreneurs from mobilizing their communities and by deterring these entrepreneurs from pursuing any but the regime's instrumental strategies of plan fulfillment and social transformation. The Soviet strategy achieved this control through a threefold policy of (1) creating within each ethnic homeland an indigenous cadre assigned a monopoly over the mobilizational resources of the community, (2) constraining the behavior of this new ethnic cadre by creating an incentive structure that deterred the expression of unsanctioned, particularly primordial ethnic agendas, and (3) assigning the cadre the responsibility for creating an ethnically distinct stratification system within official institutions and for impeding the emergence of alternative ethnic entrepreneurs outside these institutions. Let us examine each in turn.

Creating an Ethnic Cadre

The Soviets have labeled the structural foundations of their "nationalities policies" socialist federalism and indigenization (*korenizatsiia*). The socialist federation, in the formulation of the Great Soviet Encyclopedia, "differs radically from the bourgeois federation," for the former is "the state form for solving the *national questions* . . . [and] is based on the national-territorial principle."[11] Thus, at present fifty-three of the territorial administrations of the Soviet Union are based on designated ethnic homelands—fifteen as union republics, twenty as autonomous republics, eight as autonomous oblasts, and ten as autonomous *okrugs*.[12] Indigenization has sought to tie the minorities to the Soviet regime by drawing national cadres into the political and administrative posts of Party and state in these territories. In 1920 then People's Commissar of Nationality Affairs Joseph Stalin explained that to make Soviet power "near and dear" to the minorities would require:

> that all Soviet organs in the border regions . . . should as far as possible be recruited from the local people acquainted with the manner of life, habits, customs, and language of the native population; [and] that all the best people from the local masses should be drawn into these institutions.[13]

Federalism and indigenization came at the expense of simple economic rationality and assimilation. The national-territorial principle has not always led to optimal administrative units. In some instances, particularly among less modernized groups, it perpetuated or strengthened ethnic differences that might otherwise have disappeared. In the case of the Ukraine, Alexander Motyl can ask, "Why . . . did the Soviet state . . .discourage Little Russianization [i.e., assimilation] by pursuing *korenizatsiia?*"[14] The answer would appear to be the primacy the Soviet regime placed on checking the mobilizational sources of ethnopolitics and the critical role it assigned the ethnic cadres in this strategy. These policies provided opportunities for nationalities representing over 93 percent of the non-Russian population to create ethnically distinct political elites within formally autonomous homelands. Grey Hodnett's extensive data show that by the early post-Stalinist period (1955-72), indigenization in eleven of the fourteen non-Russian republics led to proportionate overrepresentation of the titular nationality in Party and state leadership posts at the republic level. By the 1980s indigenization extended well beyond the most visible posts, such as each republic's Party first secretary, chairmen of its Presidium and Council of Ministers, first secretary of its Union of Writers, president of its Academy of Sciences, rectors of its principal universities, and chair of its council of trade unions. The data compiled by Ellen Jones and Fred W. Grupp show that it also reached such sensitive and less visible areas as internal security, including each republic's Ministry of Internal Affairs, Committee on State Security, and the Party's Administrative Organs Department. It also touched lower levels of administration. In 1988, for example, in each union republic with oblasts the indigenous nationality held a greater proportion of oblast Party committee first secretaryships than its proportion of the republic's population.[15]

The indigenous cadre was given an institutional monopoly on the public expression of ethnic identity, that is, it defined the ethnic markers that distinguish the nationality. These markers were then central to communicating the socialist message in national cultural forms and propagandizing populations being brought into the modern sector. For many Soviet citizens undergoing social mobilization the first sustained contact with the great traditions of their own ethnic group was in the form of this national-Soviet hybrid. In the extreme, the markers identified by these elites defined new ethnic groups, such as the Tadjiks, that had not previously been communities with which elites and the masses had identified. Yet, as the recent political activism by Tadjiks attests, even these markers became the basis for the mobilization of the population in political action.[16]

More importantly, within each republic this cadre was assigned the role of gatekeeper, to determine when the ethnic group would be mobilized politically. Insofar as anyone within the homeland had access, this cadre monopolized the mobilizational resources essential to sustained, large-scale political action. The means of communication, particularly the indigenous-language press and broadcast media, were monopolized through the republican institutions controlled by this cadre.[17] Access to meeting places, such as auditoriums and public squares within the public, was at the discretion of this cadre. And republic protests could avoid violent suppression only with the cadre's approval.

The Deterrence of Primordial Strategies

These cadres were encouraged to pursue the regime's instrumental strategies and deterred from primordial strategies by the offer of material rewards and status, which were tightly tied to the regime's goals.[18] Particularly after Stalin's purge of traditional native elites and the sovietization of indigenous institutions, the cadres enjoyed access to these rewards only by virtue of Soviet institutions. Their privileged positions would not be improved in alternative (even independent) institutions. Indeed, the collapse of Soviet power within their homeland would mean their own fall from power—or perhaps worse. Cadres thus had a strong incentive to resist the articulation of agendas that might be subversive of existing federal institutions.

Rewards were tightly tied to the norms and goals of the Soviet developmental strategy. Soviet federalism embedded these cadres within the all-union Soviet administrative hierarchy. Cadres could only succeed within an incentive system that defined individual and collective success in instrumental terms of quota fulfillment and socioeconomic growth. By integrating the cadres into Party and state hierarchies, Soviet federalism made the "normal" politics of competitive appeals for resources the norm among ethnic elites as well. Much of the politics between Moscow and the nationality-based territorial units came to involve the petitioning for funds from above; beginning with the last years under Khrushchev speeches by leaders of the republics appealing for funds and projects to benefit their people came to be an increasingly prominent feature of meetings of the Party Congress, the Central Committee, and the Supreme Soviet.[19]

Those who engaged in unsanctioned mobilizational strategies could be punished with total deprivation of these rewards by being removed from their positions of authority. The monopoly of official institutions meant that a purge at the very least threatened one's access to these rewards; cadres could not return to a prosperous private life. Purges of ethnic leaders charged with articulating particularistic, primordial agendas also deterred others from making such appeals. Since 1960 over a dozen first secretaries of union republics have been removed under circumstances that suggest the cause was either their own endorsement of primordial agendas or their unwillingness to silence others who articulated such agendas. For example, after an official reception in 1962 the chairman of the Council of Ministers of the Kazakh Republic was apparently removed for making unguarded comments while intoxicated—comments that were just too nationalistic. In 1966 the first secretary of the Armenian Party was removed for failure to curb anti-Turkic protests on the fiftieth anniversary of the massacre of the Armenians. And in 1972 the Ukrainian and Georgian secretaries were both removed for "national narrow-mindedness" and overzealous promotion of local interests.[20]

Creating an Official Indigenous Elite

A major responsibility assigned this new cadre by Moscow's all-union authorities was to block the emergence within the ethnic community of counterelites that might challenge Soviet institutions. Within their autonomous homelands the cadres implemented policies that extended the institutional and personnel strategies of the center. These policies sought to (1) create a new, open indigenous elite of professionals and intelligentsia within official institutions, (2) tie professional and material rewards to membership in this elite, while denying these rewards to those outside the elite, and (3) limit access to the mobilizational resources of the community to these official institutions.

The ethnic cadres enacted affirmative action policies during a period of rapid economic growth and modernization in order to expand opportunities for mobility for those aspiring to positions within the professional strata and intelligentsia. Extension of the policy of indigenization opened career opportunities throughout the administrative apparatus of the homeland. Programs of collectivization and industrialization offered opportunities for mobility in management. And the creation of universities and academies of sciences in the republics dramatically expanded the number of professional positions reserved for the minorities.

These affirmative action policies in the institutional context of Soviet federalism elevated titular nationalities to privileged positions in higher education and professional employment within their homelands. For example, whereas Georgians constituted 67 percent of their republic's population in 1970 (and approximately the same proportion of the college-age cohort), they constituted 83 percent of the student body of the republic's institutions of higher education.[21] Similarly, although Moldavians constituted under two-thirds of the total population of their republic in the mid-1980s, they were at least 80 percent of the student body in the law and business schools of Kishinev State University, the republic's leading educational institution. Commenting on the rapid upward mobility of the Uzbek population within their republic, Nancy Lubin contends that the Central Asians "tend to hire 'their own' first."[22]

It is probably true—as critics have charged—that these opportunities have been opened by crudely implemented quota systems. These have apparently lowered standards in higher education and employment and discriminated against "minority" ethnic groups living within the homelands of other ethnic groups. Mark Popovksy alleges that in the universities of Uzbekistan, for example,

young men and women from primitive villages with scarcely any education. . . are given scholarships and free lodging, and are assured passing marks whether they study or not. The philosophy behind this strange proceeding is that all nations in the brotherly family of the USSR are equal, and that all of them therefore can and must have their own intelligentsia, their own doctors, engineers, writers, and scholars.[23]

And Soviet officials themselves have warned that favoritism in appointments toward the titular nationality of a republic often discriminates against other nationalities. In 1986, for example, the all-union Party leadership chastised Kirgiz leaders for favoring Kirgiz candidates among new recruits to the republic's Party organizations and for discriminating against other nationalities (notably Uzbeks) residing within the republic.[24]

Nonetheless, these policies, to expand the opportunity for mobility, represent a particularly astute accommodation with ethnicity. From 1950 to 1975, for example, among the fourteen titular nationalities of union republics (other than Russians) the annual growth in scientific workers with either a candidate of science or a doctor of science degree was 9.6 percent—a rate 54 percent higher than among Russians.[25] While demanding political loyalty to the Soviet regime, the mobility opportunities did not require denial of ethnic identities. Indeed, ethnicity became a condition for success, since the positions of status within homelands were often reserved for specific minorities. Soviet federalism offered minorities the opportunity to realize their aspirations to create separate stratification systems—but within the Soviet Union.

To block the emergence of counterelites *within* this official elite, the cadres presided over a dense network of parallel institutions that controlled all aspects of professional life.[26] Research of significance to the ethnic group and its homeland was controlled by indigenous academies of sciences and universities. Creative professionals such as writers, artists, or architects who sought to disseminate their work under the cultural monopoly of the regime were required to join the official unions of the homeland for their respective professions. Members of the new scientific and creative elite were dependent upon the official institutions, and most could not hope to improve their lot in an alternative ethnic elite created outside and in opposition to these institutions. This was particularly true for those in positions of power such as leaders of professional unions, those with academic positions in fields heavily encumbered by ideology, and creative artists who depended upon the hegemony of socialist realism for their success. The purge threatened deprivation of both rewards and the means to practice one's profession.

To block the emergence of counterelites *outside* the new professional elite and intelligentsia, the cadre denied those outside official institutions access to mobilizational resources. The ethnic cadre prohibited independent association, severed unofficial lines of communication between the intelligentsia and the populace, and deprived incipient dissident movements of their leadership by "decapitating" them—that is, threatening, imprisoning, or executing exemplary figures. Those outside were limited to the inefficient means of illegal associations, samizdat, and underground dissemination. Muslims opposed to the official religious hierarchy in the mid-1980s, for example, still had to rely upon religious tracts—many of them handwritten—smuggled across the borders from Afghan resistance groups. And Muslims of the Sufi underground borrowed a technique from dissidents in the European parts of the Soviet Union: they distributed their religious texts by chain letters.[27] Soviet policies punished severely those who attempted to articulate primordial agendas outside the official institutions. For example, in an attack on what *Kommunist Ukrainy* labeled the "belching of debilitated nationalism," the KGB in August-September 1965 arrested over twenty intellectuals who had attempted to lead a Ukrainian cultural renaissance.[28] In order to crack down on nonofficial Muslim preaching, a 1982 decree of the Turkmen Supreme Soviet Presidium authorized sentences of up to two years imprisonment and corrective labor for the crime of "social vagabondage."[29] And in Armenia arrests in late 1988 and early 1989 sought to decapitate the protest movement by targeting its leaders (such as the Karabakh Committee).[30]

Consequences for Ethnic Political Action

As a consequence of the monopoly over mobilizational resources held by the official institutions, in most circumstances only instrumental political action behind the objectives of the cadre could muster the mobilizational requisites for sustained large-scale action. There were, of course, spontaneous incidents of primordial ethnic protest. In Tashkent in September 1969, for example, an Uzbek crowd assaulted Russian bystanders after a match between the local "Pakhtar" soccer team and visitors from the Russian Republic.[31] And many individual participants in officially sponsored political action harbored private primordial agendas. Nevertheless, aspiring counterelites were handicapped in their attempts to form and mobilize effective political action in support of primordial agendas; and when it occurred, primordial protest was more likely to be expressed in isolated, ineffective, small-scale events.

Even in the period of perestroika, in republics where these cadres exercise decisive control over mobilizational resources, they can determine whether protest will be on a sustained large scale or simply sporadic. This is illustrated by the differing fortunes of popular fronts in the Ukraine and the Baltic republics during 1988 and 1989. In the Ukraine, according to an American corespondent, "the hard line of the [union-republic] Communist leadership here is one reason the rise of Ukrainian self-consciousness has been slower than the surge of nationalism in the Baltic republics."[32] In the Baltic republics, by contrast, the cadre made available to the popular fronts the mobilizational resources of the Party and state. Thus, the founding of the Latvian Popular Front was attended by the republic's Party leadership, which applauded its call for autonomy. Statements by the national fronts were published by the official press. Their newspapers were printed by the official publishing houses. Their programs appeared on state-run television, including two full days of live coverage of the Sajudis Conference in 1988. Their meetings were sanctioned, including the assembly of the three Baltic popular fronts held at the Estonian Central Committee's House of Political Enlightenment. Their demonstrations received permits.   As the chairman of the Sajudis Assembly, Vytautus Landesbergis, stressed in a 1989 interview with *Tygodnik Powszechny*, the ability of his movement to conduct its activities depended upon its close relationship with the republic's Party authorities.[33]   The importance of these cadres is further illustrated by the republic's elections in 1990: the cadres in the Baltic republics permitted a choice among candidates with alternative ethnic agendas, whereas in other republics, such as Belorussia, cadres blocked this.[34]

The ethnic cadres have actually instigated many of the protests of the past few years. In the Baltic republics demonstrations have been orchestrated to support legislative initiatives on state languages and republican sovereignty.   In November 1988 the Estonian Party leadership reportedly pressed members of the republic's Supreme Soviet for a unanimous vote and then orchestrated demonstrations on behalf of legislation to grant itself the power of nullification over all-union legislation.   Similarly, in May 1989 Lithuanian Party leaders mobilized demonstrations in Vilnius to support legislation giving the republic power of nullification and then claiming exemption from the new all-union highway tax.[35] In Nagornyi Karabakh and Armenia demonstrations on behalf of Armenian annexation of the Karabakh began in early 1988 with the support of the local Party and state leadership—including formal legislative endorsement of their cause by local soviets. And apparently even much of the violence to force Azeris from Armenia (and Armenians from Azerbaidjan) that began in late November 1988 took place with the support of local Party and state officials.[36] Where leaders of a republic take decisive action to block protests (as in the Ukraine until mid-1989) or to silence them (as in Georgia after five days of protest in April 1989), future political action is usually sporadic and small-scale.

The ability of different ethnic groups to mount large-scale, sustained political action has thus been closely tied to the resources controlled by their cadres. The mobilizational opportunities are greatest among those cadres in control of a union republic or even an autonomous republic or oblast. At the other extreme, ethnic groups without an autonomous homeland or living outside it suffer a major handicap, though they may still find local mobilizing cadres and elites, as the Gagauz found among town and village authorities in southern Moldavia. "Exclave" Russians in Estonia and Moldavia have found these cadres among factory managers and subordinate Party officials in those republics.[37] Nationalities lacking even these resources suffer the greatest handicap in attempting to express their protest in any sort of sustained large-scale manner. Thus, the protests by Jews have been sporadic and small-scale: in 1988 and 1989, for example, the largest demonstrations by Jews drew only several hundred, and most demonstrations, only two to three dozen.[38]

ORIGINS: THE RISE OF ETHNOFEDERALISM

Over the past three decades three changes have transformed the Soviet developmental strategy into a source of ethnofederalism.   First, with the trimming of the terror apparatus under Khrushchev and the policy of "respect for cadres" under Brezhnev, that is, the relaxation of Moscow's deterrent threat, these cadres had greater leeway in pressing their particularistic agendas.[39] Second, as the cadres built institutional and even popular support within their ethnic communities, their dependence upon the center declined. These new power bases enabled the cadres to take more assertive policy stands against Moscow. Third, these cadres encountered mounting difficulties in securing resources to continue the expansion of mobility opportunities within their homelands. In response, they often resorted to a strategy of mobilizing their elites behind legislative agendas and their populations in ethnic protest in order to secure additional resources from Moscow and to maintain their hegemony within their homelands. Ironically, the last two of these factors are natural consequences of the very means by which these cadres had previously controlled their ethnic communities on behalf of the center.

Policies of affirmative action permitted these cadres to build more secure political bases within their ethnic communities, for these policies created a loyal clientele. The creation of this clientele was also fostered by the post-Stalinist decentralization. As many administrative tasks were transferred from all-union to union-republic or republican ministries and as the cadres' discretion in personnel matters was expanded, the cadres' control of patronage opportunities was enlarged. Efforts to cement loyalties with the indigenous elite were aided—particularly during the Brezhnev years—by the lengthening term of office of these elites and by the reduction in the amount of rotation of personnel among homelands.[40] These power bases blunted the deterrent threat of the purge, for they made removal of a republic's first secretary more costly for Moscow. The removal of Dinmukhamed Kunaev brought two days of riots to Kazakhstan, for example. The ethnic constituencies developed by these ethnic elites became resources in showdowns with the all-union leadership over key policy choices.[41]

The cadres' motivation to mobilize their ethnic constituencies rose in recent decades as their monopolistic leadership within the ethnic community came under increasing threat. One threat has been the indigenous professional elite and the intelligentsia itself. The very success of previous affirmative action policies created a large group with the skills to constitute themselves as independent political entrepreneurs. A second threat has come from the disparity between the increasing demands for reward and mobility opportunities and the diminished capacity to meet those demands. Given the large size of this elite and its already high levels of material rewards, it has become more difficult to provide the still larger material rewards necessary to ensure their continuing loyalty. And a third threat has resulted from the increasing difficulty encountered in further expanding the ethnic elite to accommodate new aspirants to this elite. The rapid growth of a large professional elite and intelligentsia has virtually saturated some ethnic communities with elite positions. Declining economic growth has compounded these problems over the past two decades.

This threatened, first, the cadres' capacity to continue expanding the rewards of the elite and the mobility opportunities for new aspirants to elite positions and, second, their ability to offer the improved living standards necessary to keep the population tied to themselves rather than to alternative leaders. In short, the last three decades brought increasing threats to some of the very means by which the cadre had previously blocked the growth of counterelites and prevented the mobilization of the population behind primordial agendas. It is an irony of the Soviet developmental strategy that some of these threats are products of the very success of the means previously used to control ethnic assertiveness.

A crisis developed over the past decade as the number of ethnic groups experiencing this threat increased. Ethnic cadres were forced to intensify their pressure on Moscow to gain additional resources, and consequently, competition for the same scarce resources grew among ethnic communities. But declining growth rates left Moscow with even fewer resources to respond to rising demands. Faced with this crisis, ethnic cadres have found they must press Moscow still harder for investments and must devise strategies that are more clever yet to underscore the urgency of their agendas. For example, in pressing Moscow for expanded autonomy, Baltic Party leaders have turned to legislative showdowns and have mobilized popular demonstrations to support the position of the republics' elites.[42] Ethnic cadres have found enthusiastic allies in these strategies among their dependent elites and among aspirants to elite positions. Even aspiring independent political entrepreneurs pursuing primordial strategies often joined the political action mobilized by the cadres, viewing it as the best or only vehicle to press their own agendas in public. The cadres often have a strong incentive to make common cause with members of potential counterelites such as popular fronts in order to increase the pressure on Moscow. Thus, the late 1980s witnessed both dominant elites and potential counterelites making common cause to mobilize the ethnic community.

INCIDENCE: FLASH POINTS OF ETHNOFEDERALISM

The pattern of ethnofederalism in the Soviet Union contains yet a further ironic twist: the incentive to mobilize their ethnic constituency is greatest for those ethnic cadres that have previously been most successful at the Soviet developmental strategy—notably in the Caucasus and the Baltic republics. The pressure of potential counterelites, the difficulties of further expanding elite positions and material rewards, and so the threat to their positions are greatest for those cadres that were previously most successful at engineering affirmative action and creating an indigenous elite.

This pressure on the cadres of the more developed ethnic communities has been piqued by the redistributive consequences of these affirmative action policies. With declining growth rates, the redistributive consequences of these policies have been transformed: policies that had once involved transfers between titular nationalities and minorities within ethnic homelands came to involve instead transfers between the principal titular nationalities of union republics. These transfers are now adversely affecting the more modernized ethnic communities.

In building an indigenous cadre and intelligentsia within each ethnic group, the Soviet developmental strategy had a powerful leveling impact on ethnic groups. The growth of mobility opportunities has been highest among the nationalities with the lowest levels of socioeconomic attainment.[43] Thus, as Figure 2 shows, in the post-Stalinist years differences among nationalities in levels of elite occupational status (measured by per capita employment as specialists with higher education) narrowed.[44]

This redistribution has in part been a consequence of Moscow's allocation of resources among republics. For example, the Unified State Budget, which includes the budgets for each union republic, transfers funds from more developed to less developed republics. In the 1989 budget only the five Central Asian republics were permitted to retain 100 percent of both turnover and income taxes collected within their borders; they were to receive, in addition, subsidies ranging from 321 million rubles for the Tadjik Republic to 2.7 billion rubles for the Kazakh Republic. Conversely, the Latvian Republic was to retain the lowest proportion of its turnover tax (56.8 percent), and both the Armenian Republic (with 76.7 percent) and the Estonian Republic (with 79.4 percent) were to retain only slightly over three-quarters.[45] Although these official statistics appear to overstate the extent of this phenomenon, less developed republics have received higher rates of investment than their level of economic development would predict. And per capita expenditures on health and educational programs have been relatively equal among republics even though revenues have been far lower in the less developed republics.[46]

It is, indeed, inherent to a policy of promoting the growth of indigenous elites and engineering equality under circumstances of tighter constraints on resources that some previously advantaged groups will suffer relative stagnation in their life chances. One of the most visible examples of this restriction on life chances for a previously advantaged group has been the imposition of quotas on Jewish admissions to Soviet universities. Although in 1970 Jews represented 2.3 percent of the students in institutions of higher education (a proportion that is above their official proportion of the population—0.89 percent in 1970), this, nonetheless, represents a significant decline since 1935, when the figure stood at 13.3 percent of these students. Against the general trend toward higher rates of educational attainment in the Soviet population, the proportion of Soviet Jews aged eighteen to twenty-three who attend college full-time remained constant at 30 percent or at most increased only marginally to 36 percent between 1935 and 1965. Thus, many have been blocked in their aspirations for higher education and the elite employment it would make possible.[47] And as economic growth has slowed, more ethnic groups have felt this pinch in life chances. In Central Asia, according to Lubin, "Russians are beginning to sense they are being denied access to jobs for which they are equally if not more qualified than their Asian counterparts."[48] And Popovsky complains that in Uzbekistan "it is almost impossible for non-Uzbeks with a higher education to get jobs."[49]

In the geographically segmented multiethnic society of Soviet federalism the redistributive consequences of these policies remained a less contentious issue in federal politics as long as economic growth permitted the continued expansion of mobility opportunities for all titular nationalities within their homelands. With their high growth rates the titular nationalities of union republics could escape the consequence of interrepublic transfers by shifting the brunt of their impact to their minority populations—that is, by discriminating against them. Under these circumstances the minorities within the homelands of other nationalities (including the "exclave" minorities, such as Jews or Russians) were the greatest losers from interrepublic redistribution. The economic slowdown, however, made it more difficult for the titular nationalities to escape the effects of interrepublic transfers, which made redistribution a highly contentious issue among the cadres. The effect of the Soviet developmental strategy in a period of tight constraints on resources has been to limit the growth of mobility opportunities in the more developed ethnic communities in order to permit continued expansion in those that are less developed.

As a consequence, cadres of ethnic communities with higher levels of socioeconomic attainment (particularly in the Baltic and Caucasus) have led the way in pressing their ethnic legislative agendas, while cadres in less advanced communities (notably in Central Asia) have been less inclined to do so. As continuing beneficiaries of the developmental strategy enforced by the center, the latter cadres have often been harsh critics of the decentralization proposed by their peers in the more developed communities; for example, at the meeting of the all-union Supreme Presidium to veto Estonia's act of nullification, the chairmen of the Presidia of Uzbekistan (Khabibullaev) and Tadjikistan (Palaev) voiced strong criticism of the Estonian move and support for centrist policies.[50] Also as a consequence, protest has been more common in the more developed communities. The rank-order correlation between number of demonstrations and levels of educational attainment is 0.67.[51]

AGENDAS: THE FEDERAL POLITICS OF
RESOURCES AND LIFE CHANCES

The policy concerns of the ethnic cadres shape the public agendas of ethnofederalism by controlling the way dominant themes will be framed in legislation and by determining which issues are to be supported by sustained large-scale political pressure. Cadres must define the agendas of ethnopolitics so as to permit as many as possible in their ethnic communities to join the "official" ethnic bandwagon. Often this requires redefining the dominant popular concerns, particularly where they are primordial. The cadres must deny these constituents and issues to potential counterelites, even as they use them to put pressure on Moscow. A test of the success of the entrepreneurship of the cadres is the extent to which they can insert the most important material and symbolic concerns of their constituents into the public agendas in ways that protect or promote their own power base. The dominant themes on the cadres' agendas reflect the threats that confront them within their own communities: these themes concern resources and life chances. Specifically, this politics of mobility opportunities is expressed in a number of recurring policy issues that go to the very foundations of the Soviet developmental strategy that created and sustain these cadres: federalism, indigenization, language, economic development, and migration.

Federalism

The most volatile issue of federalism has been the balance of power between center and periphery, since at stake are the resources controlled by the cadres and the mobility opportunities within their communities. Party leaders have used this issue to co-opt primordial concerns for independence to instrumental demands for expanded republic autonomy within Soviet federalism.[52] Expanded autonomy is one way for ethnic cadres to enlarge the resources within their control. Autonomy increases their discretion in the allocation of positions of power within the republic and in the administration of educational and occupational policies. And for cadres within the more developed republics that have felt most severely pinched by affirmative action, autonomy is a way to retain resources at home.

The cadres in the more developed union republics have been particularly quick to raise the banners of autonomy and sovereignty in order to blunt the redistributive consequences of all-union policies. Thus, for example, in 1989 Lithuanian leaders sought exemption from the all-union highway tax since the tax was levied on vehicles (which are more common in the relatively wealthy Baltic region) but spent disproportionately to build and repair roads in the less developed republics.[53] In all three Baltic republics calls for "regional economic accountability," "territorial cost accounting," and "self-financing" have supported the attempts on the part of republican cadres to wrest control of industries from the centralized ministries. These plans envision the isolation of their markets from the larger economy of scarcity by such mechanisms as *export* barriers to other union republics, identity cards to limit purchases by visitors from other republics, prices determined at the republic level to improve the terms of exchange among republics, and even separate currencies for some republics.[54]

For ethnic cadres of "minorities" subordinate to the union republic of another nationality, the issue of autonomy has often taken the form of demands over the "status" of their homelands within the federal hierarchy—that is, whether a homeland is a union republic, an autonomous republic, an oblast, or an *okrug*. The control of resources by the cadres of a nationality increases with this hierarchy. Thus, in a 1988 report on the mounting pressure and public rallies on behalf of the elevation of the Tatar Autonomous Republic to union-republic status, the writer Rafail Mustafin asked in the pages of *Pravda*:

> After all, what prompted the proposals for the creation of a new union republic? The existing inequality in social, political, and economic rights between union and autonomous formations. Tataria surpasses some union republics in both population and industrial potential. Yet we don't have a feature-film studio of our own, we have only one publishing house (which is not very big), and there is an acute shortage of paper for publishing books, newspapers, and magazines.[55]

With similar objectives the Party leadership in Abkhazia has sought elevation of their autonomous republic to union-republic status, leaders of Moldavia's Gagauz minority have demanded creation of their own autonomous republic, and Polish leaders in the Shalchinin district of Lithuania have asked for autonomous status. In the last case, according to *Izvestiia*, "perhaps the sorest point was the impossibility for Poles to obtain higher education in their native language" within Lithuania.[56]

Taking a different tack, the cadres of other "subordinate" minorities have mobilized their populations to demand changes in the lines of authority among homelands. A nationality subordinate to the republic of a different titular nationality may find its resources and life chances limited. In Nagornyi Karabakh, Armenians protested that even though their autonomous oblast had the second-highest industrial production per capita within the republic, the leadership of the Azerbaidjan Republic allocated it lower than average per capita investments. G.A. Pogosyan, the first secretary of the autonomous oblast, is reported to have told the all-union Supreme Soviet Presidium that as a consequence, "even today, the Nagorno-Karabakh Autonomous Oblast does not have its own flour mill, nor its own concentrate-feed plant, nor its own reinforced-concrete structures plant, nor its own housing-construction combine." These investments lagged particularly in the social sphere. The Nagorno-Karabakh Armenians complained that inadequate investment in institutions of higher education within the oblast and Baku's opposition to letting Armenians attend institutions in the Armenian Republic meant that the Armenians within the oblast were denied access to higher education and career advancement.[57] Reassigning the Nagorno-Karabakh Autonomous Oblast to the Armenian Republic would put an end to the discrimination by Azeris and also open up union-republic mobility opportunities to its Armenian majority.[58] (Similar complaints and demands for removal from the jurisdiction of the Georgian

Republic have come from the leaders of the Adzhar Autonomous Republic and the South Osetian Autonomous Oblast.)[59]

Indigenization

Cadres of titular nationalities have also mobilized political action in order to preserve the results of indigenization. Cadres have found that this issue harnesses both the instrumental interests of those in their ethnic community who aspire to elite positions and the primordial sentiments of those who see ethnic similarity as a requisite of legitimate authority. At stake for union-republic cadres are the very means by which they have built their supporting clientele and popular constituencies. In Kazakhstan the removal of First Secretary Kunaev and the purge of the republic party apparatus in 1986 threatened the clientele network drawn disproportionately from the first secretary's own tribal group; it threatened the career prospects of the indigenous nationals who had tied their careers to the local leadership; and it brought a wave of violent protest.[60] More recently, Georgian leaders have mobilized protesters to challenge Moscow's intrusion in the republic's personnel policy—particularly the efforts to challenge discrimination by the Georgians against minorities.

"Minority" cadres within the national territories of others have mobilized their constituencies for the opposite end—to criticize abuses of indigenization by the titular nationalities and to call for Moscow's intervention against the practice. The creation of an ethnic elite and intelligentsia by the titular nationality often denies minorities within its national territory comparable opportunities. In a recent roundtable held under the auspices of the Research Council on Nationality Problems of the Academy of Science, E.V. Tadevosian complained that indigenization in some national republics has "often led to an artificial overrepresentation of the indigenous nationalities at the expense of other nationalities residing in those areas in the state organs, the administrative apparatus, the students and faculties of higher educational institutions, etc."[61] Gagauz in Moldavia and Nagorno-Karabakh Armenians in Azerbaidjan have demonstrated to protest discrimination in political appointments and career opportunities. The chairman of the presidium of the Abkhaz Supreme Soviet claims that such grievances led to violent disturbances in his republic not only in 1989, but also in 1957, 1967, and 1978.[62]

Language

To preserve the foundation on which ethnic affirmative action was built, cadres have mobilized political action to raise or preserve the status of the language of their respective communities. Mobility opportunities are inextricably tied up with the status of indigenous languages. At stake for the constituents is their instrumental interest in privileged access to economic, social, and political power. For example, the language used in universities influences admissions as well as later career opportunities of different ethnic groups within a republic.

But language is also one of the most important primordial markers defining an ethnic community.

Through legislation that their languages supplant Russian as the language of communication within their republics, ethnic leaders in the union republics have sought to strengthen indigenous control over political and economic institutions. An article declaring the language of the titular nationality to be the state language of the republic was included in the 1978 constitutions of Armenia, Azerbaidjan, and Georgia. On April 14, 1978, an estimated five thousand Georgian demonstrators took to the streets to protest Moscow's attempt to amend this article in their republic's constitution. Indigenous cultural, educational, and scientific elites were particularly eager to maintain Georgian as the language of discourse in their professions. Georgian students joined the protests, as Ronald Suny notes, since the language clause ensured that "higher education in Georgia had become the prerogative of Georgians, and other nationalities found it difficult to enter schools of higher learning."[63] In 1988 and 1989 six other republics adopted legislation establishing a state language.

Minority cadres within national territories of others have mobilized political action to protest exactly this form of preference for the language of the titular nationality. At stake for the leaders of these minority communities is often the control of mobility opportunities, the future of the constituency on which they have built their power, or even their own positions. Protests against new language laws that would place them at a disadvantage have come from the Abkhazians in Georgia, "exclave" Russians and Poles in Lithuania, and both the Turkic Gagauz and the "exclave" Russians in Moldavia. Non-Estonian cadres in Estonia have called strikes to protest a law requiring that those who do not learn the language of the republic within four years be dismissed from their jobs: on March 14, 1989, as many as sixty thousand Russians and other "minorities" (according to *Izvestiia's* count) took to the streets of Tallinn to protest "creeping counterrevolution endangering socialism in Estonia." Russian Party officials and factory managers within the republic reportedly mobilized their constituencies because they feared that the law of January 18, 1989, would cost them their positions.[64]

Development and Migration

To preserve the ethnically exclusive institutions on which their power rests, ethnic cadres have mobilized political action to oppose all-union economic development and migration policies. Although two different issues, they have become closely connected in public discussions since rapid industrialization has become the principal magnet for workers of other nationalities. For the population this threatens dissolution of the ethnic community, heightened competition for the leading political and economic positions in the republic, and loss of their affirmative action advantage in life chances. For the cadres this migration threatens the ethnic community on which their political power is based. It increases the pressure on the cadres to incorporate these other ethnic groups into the elite of the republic—pressure, that is, to dilute the ethnic homogeneity of the elites on which the cadres base their power. Failure of a titular nationality to maintain its numerical predominance within a republic might lead to the replacement of ethnically exclusive cadre by one of more diverse ethnic composition; it might bring demotion to the status of an autonomous republic (as happened to the Karelo-Finnish Republic) or even outright dissolution of its autonomous homeland. Thus, in the early 1960s Georgian and Latvian officials opposed Khrushchev's plans for further expansion of heavy industry in the republics precisely because they feared it would bring still more Russian workers.[65] Armenian officials reportedly excluded Russian workers from permanent housing during the construction of the Erevan subway in order to prevent them from remaining. In the late 1980s protesters in the Baltic republics and Armenia demanded that their republics be given control of industrial and agricultural policy in order to slow the influx of outsiders. And Estonian cadres have attempted to blunt the effect of migration on their ethnic constituencies in future elections: legislation of the Estonian Republic disenfranchised those not resident in a district for two years (or in the republic for five years) and barred from office those not resident in a district for five years (or in the republic for ten years).[66]

THE RISKS OF ASSERTIVE FEDERALISM UNDER PERESTROIKA

With perestroika the homeland cadres press their agendas of ethnofederalism in a more complex environment. Within their homelands they are increasingly called upon to control and balance three very different forms of political action that draw together different sets of actors behind three often diverging agendas. Alongside the assertive federalism of the cadres is a second arena—the organizing activity and popular demonstrations of the popular fronts. Drawing particularly upon students, the intelligentsia, and the professional elite, the programs of the fronts often give expression to many of the primordial concerns of these ethnic communities. In a third arena communal violence draws heavily from the unemployed and from displaced refugees. Intercommunal violence has pitted Armenians against Azeris, Georgians against Abkhazians, and Georgians against Osetians in the Caucasus; young Uzbeks have attacked Meskhetis in the Fergana region, and Kazakh youths have attacked immigrants in the Novyi Uzen region of Central Asia.[67] The ethnic cadres in a number of republics have sought to use the political pressure of the second set of actors to support its showdowns with Moscow. Even without endorsing all the particulars of the fronts' agendas, the cadres have found that the fronts strengthen their own hands in negotiations with Moscow by permitting them to argue convincingly that their hands are tied at home. In some instances cadres have even encouraged the third form of political action in order to solidify their hold within the homeland and to press Moscow. In Azerbaidjan, for example, local Party leaders reportedly encouraged the growth of the popular front and helped found the more militant and violence-prone National Defense Committee.[68]

The ethnic cadres run immense risks, for these strategies may undermine their positions or even unleash forces they cannot control. Moscow, for example, could respond with coercion, as it did in 1988 and 1989, when the all-union leadership removed over twenty-five hundred officials (including the union-republic first secretaries) accused of abetting the intercommunal violence in Armenia and Azerbaidjan.[69]   Cadres with strong ethnic constituencies may gamble that Moscow will be unable to remove them or will hesitate to pay the costs associated with such actions. The extensive power base of Vladimir Shcherbitskii in the Ukraine made his removal in 1989 a slow and complicated process requiring elaborate institutional maneuvering by Gorbachev. The protests in Kazakhstan were the costly consequence of Kunaev's removal. Nonetheless, Moscow has been willing to pay these costs in many instances; in 1988 and 1989 the first secretaries in ten of the fourteen union-republic parties were replaced. And in at least eight of these instances the secretaries were removed because of displeasure with republic policies.[70]

The cadres run a second risk: that those threatened by assertive federalism will initiate counteraction. Indeed, it was Moldavian pressures for new language legislation that ignited protests by the republic's Gagauz minority; but the agenda of the Gagauz went beyond language to include complaints of discrimination in economics and politics. The mobilization of Estonians, Latvians, Lithuanians, and Moldavians brought the countermobilization of their "exclave" Russians behind *Interdvizhenie*, the Committee for Defense of Soviet Power in Lithuania, and *Edinstvo* (Unity). In the future, similar counterprotests may be mobilized by cadres of the less developed republics of Central Asia in order to blunt the political impact of mass demonstrations in the Baltic and Caucasus against the allocation decisions made in Moscow.[71]

A third risk to cadres is that political action mobilized by them may actually facilitate the creation of counterelites and their mobilizational activities. Much of the apparent "bandwagoning" the cadres seek to promote may actually be used as opportunities for "piggybacking" by potential counterelites; that is, aspiring independent political entrepreneurs maintain their particular agendas while using "official" political action as a cover for their own mobilizational activities and as an opportunity to publicize their agendas.[72]   Rather than depriving these potential counterelites of support, the cadres' gambit may provide their opponents with the opportunity to expand it. In some republics the political action mobilized by cadres has become self-sustaining and has slipped from their control, only then to provide counterelites with a ready-made movement. In Armenia the cadres appear to have lost control over the Karabakh protest by the late summer of 1988. According to a TASS report: "Taking advantage of the fact that the former leaders of the central committee of the Communist Party of Armenia let the initiative slip from their hands and retreated step-by-step, members of the Karabkh committee created ramified organizational and political structures."[73]   In 1989 the initiative in Azeri protests over the status of Nagornyi Karabakh apparently passed from the cadres to counterelites within the popular front. By early 1990 the Azeri popular front was complaining that the initiative in the communal violence had even slipped from its control and passed to radicals in the National Defense Committee.[74] In Lithuania, Party First Secretary Algirdas Brazauskas was reportedly surprised when Sajudis deputies he had helped elect to the republic's Supreme Soviet rejected him as the republic's chief of state and elected their own leader, Landsbergis.[75]

Finally, the cadres' gambit may encourage unwanted primordial violence. The mass demonstrations in Erevan and Baku in 1988, 1989, and 1990 were catalysts for waves of violence across the republics. Small groups of Armenians and Azeris attacked minorities in their republics by intimidating many into emigration and by simply killing others.

POLITICAL INSTITUTIONS AND POLITICIZED ETHNICITY

The rise of assertive ethnofederalism in the Soviet Union since the mid-1950s points up how political institutions shape the mobilization of ethnic communities. On the one hand, Soviet federalism delayed the *origins* of politicized ethnicity, but on the other hand, it distributed mobilizational resources such as entrepreneurial skills and means of communications in a manner that eventually shaped its *incidence* and *agendas*.

This emphasis on institutions offers an amendment to those studies that explain the rise of politicized ethnicity by emphasizing attitudes rather than resources needed to mobilize an ethnic community. These studies have introduced at least two alternative paradigms for the study of ethnopolitics, which are distinguished from one another by alternative views of the nature of ethnic identity, the sources of cohesion, and the objectives of politicized ethnicity and protest. The *primordialist* paradigm sees ethnic identities as one of the givens of social existence, shaped by historic memory, language, religion, and geographic compactness.   The politicization of ethnicity is communal self-discovery; protest, often an expressive act affirming communal solidarity.[76]   The *instrumentalist* paradigm sees ethnic identities as contingent and changing self-ascribed roles.   The politicization of ethnicity and protest are goal-oriented behaviors—often focused on the pursuit of socioeconomic gain. According to the instrumentalist paradigm, an ethnic identity becomes a basis for collective action when there are comparative advantages to be gained from that specific ethnic identity over alternative ethnic, class, or other identities.[77]

The prevailing paradigm in Sovietology has been primordialist. In explaining the *origins* of Soviet ethnopolitics, it focuses our attention on attitudes such as assimilation rather than on incentives and constraints on action.[78]   Certainly these attitudes are important ingredients of the current crisis. Yet there is little indication that these alone can account for the rise of ethnopolitics—little indication that assimilation has become any less advanced, assimilative pressures any more intense, or national consciousness any higher in the decades since 1955 than in those before.   The failure of Soviet policies of ethnic fusion (*sblizhenie*) to reduce cultural barriers among ethnic groups and to bring about the merger (*sliianie*) of nations cannot account for the *rise* of ethnic assertiveness over the past three decades.

In predicting the *incidence* of ethnic assertiveness, the primordial paradigm argued that the most extensive resistance to the policies of the Soviet regime would be mounted by those minorities that were culturally remote from the Russian majority.[79]   In particular, it focused our attention on Islam, arguing that this provides a cultural bond among Soviet Muslims and, in the words of Kemal Karpat, "creates an invisible barrier separating them from the ruling Slavs."[80]   Moreover, as Alexandre Bennigsen and S. Enders Wimbush argue, "the critical issue determining the extent and degree of long-term commitment of Soviet Muslims to the Soviet Russian state is not 'socio-economics' but identity."[81]   Contrary to these expectations, however, those nationalities most remote in culture from the Slavs have been among the most quiescent.   There is little evidence to suggest that it is the relative strength of their primordial sentiments that distinguishes the minorities that have engaged in sustained, effective political action from the more quiescent minorities.   The primordial paradigm had not predicted the pattern of *flash points*.[82]

The primordial paradigm had also predicted that protest would mobilize behind *agendas* of cultural expression.   Yet Soviet ethnofederalism has raised many issues that are poorly explained by this paradigm.   For example, the recommendation by leaders of the Nagorno-Karabakh Armenians, Abkhazians, and South Osetians to transfer jurisdiction over their homelands to the Russian Republic evinces an acceptance rather than rejection of Soviet federalism and of its institutional protections for minority interests.   The terms in which they have cast their legislative agendas concerning autonomy, indigenization, language, development, and migration suggest that the public agenda for most ethnic cadres is less a primordial assertion of cultural identity than an instrumental pursuit of other interests.   Thus, the predictions of the prevailing paradigm concerning the *agendas* of ethnopolitics were inaccurate.

Alternatively, an analysis that draws solely upon the instrumentalist paradigm would lead to significant misprediction as well.   It would miss the constraint of primordialist sentiments in the population that must be co-opted into the agendas of Soviet ethnic entrepreneurs.   It would dismiss the possibility that cadres might switch to primordial agendas as incentives and institutional constraints change. It would be unable to explain the willingness of some counterelites such as Landsbergis to sacrifice socioeconomic benefits for symbolic issues of self-expression.

These mispredictions point up the narrow or incomplete nature of a paradigm, such as the primordialist or instrumentalist, that focuses on attitudes. These paradigms fail to take two facts into consideration. First, the attitudes that sustain either primordial or instrumental agendas exist side by side in many Soviet ethnic communities and often within the same individual.[83] They coexist among Soviet cadres as well as in the general population. Second, the politicization of either primordial sentiments or instrumental interests and the mobilization of ethnic communities in sustained, large-scale action has required the conjunction of these attitudes with resources that can mobilize an ethnic community. The attitudes cited by one or the other paradigm are necessary, but not sufficient, for the explanation of ethnopolitics.

Political institutions like Soviet federalism play a critical role in this conjunction and so in shaping ethnic communities, politicizing ethnicity, and mobilizing protest. They empower entrepreneurs and constrain their choice of either primordial or instrumental strategies.[84] The politicization of ethnicity has been the work of political entrepreneurs created by Soviet federalism.[85] In the three decades before 1990 the most significant pressure on Moscow for ethnic interests was orchestrated by the Party and state leadership of ethnic homelands. By assigning a monopoly over mobilizational resources, Soviet federalism delayed the rise of ethnofederalism but at the same time made it likely and possible that ethnic cadres of more developed ethnic communities would later mobilize their constituents. By constraining their choice of strategies, Soviet federalism made it likely that cadres would mobilize their constituents behind instrumental rather than primordial agendas. Since January 1990 the magnitude, patterns, and agendas of ethnic assertiveness have evolved most in those areas in which institutional changes have transformed the incentive structures of cadres or empowered new elites (notably in the Baltic republics).[86]

Where political institutions neither establish monopolistic ethnic entrepreneurs nor constrain their choice of strategies in this way, political institutions distribute mobilizational resources and shape ethnic strategies differently.[87] This is illustrated poignantly by the changes in Soviet political institutions. In some republics the cadres' control over their communities has been weakened by the loss of their monopoly over the mobilizational resources of the ethnic community. The policies of *demokratizatsiia* and *glasnost* have undermined the ability of cadres to contain the protest they have mobilized as well as to suppress autonomous ethnopolitics. Where threats to their control have grown, their strategies have often changed. Cadres in some republics now engage in competitive efforts to mobilize different segments of elite and popular constituencies behind competing agendas reflecting different balances of primordial and instrumental concerns.[88] By early 1990 competition had led to an outright split in the Communist parties of the republics of Latvia and Lithuania. Alternative leaderships have articulated competing ethnic agendas, and Party assets including buildings have been divided.[89]

Lithuania before and after January 1990 provides an excellent diachronic study of how changes in the Soviet electoral system can empower new political entrepreneurs in the homeland and shift the emphasis in ethnic agendas from instrumental to primordial issues. The pragmatic leadership of Brazauskas was replaced by that of Landsbergis, which immediately emphasized symbolic issues of sovereignty even if they did not impart real autonomy. Pressed by Moscow, the new leadership quickly agreed that all instrumental issues were negotiable but not the primordial ones—that is, the symbolic declaration of independence.[90] Because Soviet institutions have not changed evenly in all republics, the contrast between Lithuania and certain other union republics after January 1990 offers a cross-sectional comparison of the consequences of changed institutions. In Belorussia, for example, the elections of early 1990 did not offer an open contest of elites and failed to empower alternative political entrepreneurs. The Belorussian political agenda remained much more instrumental and supportive of Moscow, so that in Moscow's confrontation with the Sajudis government, the Belorussian leadership announced it would demand the renegotiation of its borders with Lithuania should the latter secede from the Soviet Union.[91]

The Soviet experience with ethnofederalism illustrates the importance of bringing institutions back into the analysis of ethnopolitics—for Sovietology, for comparisons of Leninist with non-Leninist polities, and possibly for comparisons of Soviet politics before and after 1990. Within the institutions of Soviet federalism may be keys to the future of the Soviet system. In particular, the direction the Soviet Union takes will depend on the ability of ethnic cadres to adapt to the role of entrepreneurs in a competitive arena as well as the ability of Soviet institutions to constrain the cadres' choice of strategies to those that do not threaten the unity of the Soviet polity.

Notes

For their comments on earlier drafts, I thank my colleagues and good friends—Deborah Avant, Anthony Brunello, Ellen Comisso, Patrick Drinan, Arend Lijphart, Richard Little, Debra Rosenthal, Gershon Shafir, Susan Shirk, Tracy Strong, and Michael Tierney.

1. Gellner, Nations and Nationalism (Ithaca, N.Y.: Cornell University Press, 1983), 40.

2. Sidney Verba, "Sequences and Development," in Leonard Binder et. al., Crises and Sequences in Political Development (Princeton: Princeton University Press, 1971), 283-316; Dankwart A. Rustow, *A World of Nations* (Washington, D.C.: Brookings, 1967), 120-32.

3. I make a parallel argument concerning the relationship between the Soviet developmental strategy and political participation; see Philip G. Roeder, "Modernization and Participation in the Leninist Developmental Strategy," *American Political Science Review* 83 (September 1989), 859-84.

4. Rudolph and Thompson, "Ethnoterritorial Movements and the Policy Process: Accommodating Nationalist Demands in the Developed World," *Comparative Politics* 17 (April 1985), 292. See also Ernest Gellner, *Thought and Change* (Chicago: University of Chicago Press, 1969), 147-78; Michael Hechter, *Internal Colonialism: The Celtic Fringe in British National Development, 1536-1966* (London: Routledge and Kegan Paul, 1975).

5. Gourevitch, "The Reemergence of 'Peripheral Nationalisms': Some Comparative Speculations on the Spatial Distribution of Political Leadership and Economic Growth," *Comparative Studies in Society and History* 21 (July 1979), 303-22, at 319-21. See also Donald L. Horowitz, "Patterns of Ethnic Separatism," *Comparative Studies in Society and History* 23 (1981), 1965-95.

6. William Bernard, "New Directions in Integration and Ethnicity," *International Migration Review* 5 (Winter 1971), 464-73; Michael Hechter, Debra Friedman, and Malka Appelbaum, "A Theory of Ethnic Collective Action," *International Migration Review* 16 (Summer 1982), 412-34; Phillip M. Rawkins, "An Approach to the Political Sociology of the Welsh Nationalist Movement," *Political Studies* 27 (September 1979), 440-57; Joseph Rothschild, *Ethnopolitics: A Conceptual Framework* (New York: Columbia University Press, 1981), 27.

7. Smith, *The Ethnic Revival* (Cambridge: Cambridge University Press, 1981), 87, 126.

8. Ibid., 105; James McKay, "An Exploratory Synthesis of Primordial and Mobilizational Approaches to Ethnic Phenomena," *Ethnic and Racial Studies* 5 (October 1982), 395-420, at 399.

9. Rothschild (fn. 6), 30.

10. Glazer and Moynihan, *Ethnicity: Theory and Experience* (Cambridge: Harvard University Press, 1975), 7.

11. *Bol'shaia Sovetskaia Entsiklopediia* (Moscow: Sovetskaia entsiklopediia, 1977), 27:255.

12. A new (eleventh) autonomous *okrug* was created for the Even-Batagai district in Yakutia in October 1989; *Pravda*, October 30, 1989. Other changes are likely to follow.

13. Stalin, "The Policy of the Soviet Government on the National Question in Russia," in *Works* (Moscow: Foreign Languages Publishing House, 1953), 4:370-71.

14. Motyl, *Will the Non-Russians Rebel?* (Ithaca, N.Y.:Cornell University Press, 1987), 104. See also Grey Hodnett, "The Debate over Soviet Federalism," *Soviet Studies* 18 (April 1967), 458-81; Daniel C. Matuszewski, "Nationalities in the Soviet Future: Trends under Gorbachev," in Lawrence C. Lerner and Donald W. Treadgold, eds., *Gorbachev and the Soviet Future* (Boulder, Colo.: Westview Press, 1988), 95-96.

15. Hodnett, *Leadership in the Soviet National Republics* (Oakville, Ontario: Mosaic Press, 1978), 101-3, 377-78; Jones and Grupp, "Modernisation and Ethnic Equalization in the USSR," *Soviet Studies* 36 (April 1984), 159-84, at 174; *Deputaty verkhovnogo soveta SSSR, odinadtsatyi sozyv* [Deputies of the Supreme Soviet of the USSR, eleventh convocation] (Moscow: Izvestiia, 1984); Gavin Helf, comp., *A Biographical Directory*

of Soviet Regional Party Leaders, 2d ed. (Munich: Radio Free Europe/Radio Liberty, 1988). For long-term trends in indigenization within specific republics, see John A. Armstrong, *The Soviet Bureaucratic Elite: A Case Study of the Ukrainian Apparatus* (New York: Praeger, 1959), 15-17; Ronald Grigor Suny, *The Making of the Georgian Nation* (Bloomington: Indiana University Press, 1988), 209-318; Martha Brill Olcott, *The Kazakhs* (Stanford, Calif.: Hoover Institution Press, 1987), 199-246. See also Steven L. Burg, "Russians, Natives, and Jews in the Soviet Scientific Elite: Cadre Competition in Central Asia," *Cahiers du Monde Russe et Soviétique* 20 (January-March 1979), 43-59; Nancy Lubin, "Assimilation and Retention of Ethnic Identity in Uzbekistan," *Asian Affairs* 12 (October 1981), 277-85, at 283; J.W.R. Parsons, "National Integration in Soviet Georgia," *Soviet Studies* 34 (October 1982), 547-69, at 554.

16. Teresa Rakowska-Harmstone, *Russia and Nationalism in Central Asia* (Baltimore, Md.: Johns Hopkins University Press), 1970, 76; *Izvestiia*, July 14, 1989; *Kommunist Tadzhikistana*, June 28, 1989; *Pravda*, June 25, 1988.

17. Alex Inkeles, *Public Opinion in Soviet Russia: A Study in Mass Persuasion* (Cambridge: Harvard University Press, 1950); Peter Kenez, *The Birth of the Propaganda State: Soviet Methods of Mass Mobilization, 1917-29* (Cambridge: Cambridge University Press, 1985).

18. Seweryn Bialer, *Stalin's Successors* (Cambridge: Cambridge University Press, 1980), 216. See also Motyl (fn. 14), 104-5, 119-22.

19. Donna Bahry, *Outside Moscow: Power, Politics, and Budgetary Policy in Soviet Republics* (New York: Columbia University Press, 1987), 1-5; Jerry F. Hough and Merle Fainsod, *How the Soviet Union is Governed* (Cambridge: Harvard University Press), 510-17.

20. Robert Conquest, *Soviet Nationalities Policy in Practice* (New York: Praeger, 1967); Teresa Rakowska-Harmstone, "The Dialectics of Nationalism in the USSR," *Problems of Communism* 23 (May-June 1974), 1-22, at 13.

21. Parsons (fn. 15), 558-59.

22. Lubin (fn. 15), 283.

23. Mark Popovsky, *Manipulated Science* (Garden City, N.Y.: Doubleday, 1979), 118.

24. John Soper, "Nationality Issues Under Review in Kirgizia," *Radio Liberty Research Bulletin* RL 49/88 (January 29, 1988).

25. USSR Tsentral'noe Statisticheskoe Upravlenie, *Narodnoe obrazovanie, nauka i kul'tura v SSSR* [Popular education, science, and culture in the USSR] (Moscow: Statistika, 1977), 308-39.

26. See, for example, Dietrich A. Loeber, "Administration of Culture in Soviet Latvia," in Adolf Sprudz and Armin Rusis, eds., *Res Baltica* (Leiden: A.W. Sijthoff, 1968), 133-145; Nicholas P. Vakar, *Belorussia: The Making of a Nation* (Cambridge: Harvard University Press, 1956), 150-51.

27. Timur Kocaoglu, "Muslim Chain Letters in Central Asia," *Radio Liberty Research Bulletin* RL 313/83 (August 18, 1983); Alexandre Bennigsen, "Mullahs, Mujahidin, and Soviet Muslims," *Problems of Communism* 33 (November-December 1984), 28-41, at 36-37.

28. Ludmilla Alexeyeva, *Soviet Dissent* (Middletown, Conn.: Wesleyan University Press, 1985), 31.

29. Bennigsen (fn. 27), 40.

30. *New York Times*, November 25, 1988, November 26, 1988, December 22, 1988, January 2, 1989. See also *Pravda*, January 26, 1990.

31. Michael Rywkin, *Moscow's Muslim Challenge* (Armonk, N.Y.: M.E. Sharpe, 1982), 121; B. Brown, "Kazakhstan in 1987: The Year after Alma Ata," *Radio Liberty Research Bulletin* RL 5/88 (December 23, 1987), 2. See also Ronald Grigor Suny, *Armenia in the Twentieth Century* (Chico, Calif.: Scholars Press, 1983), 78-80.

32. *New York Times*, March 9, 1989; see also June 20, 1988, August 24, 1988, August 25, 1988, October 10, 1988, November 30, 1988, December 2, 1988, December 7, 1988, February 5, 1989, April 9, 1989, April 14, 1989, April 22, 1989; Bohdan Nahaylo, "Baltic Echoes in the Ukraine," *Report on the USSR* 1 (January 13, 1989), 18-20; idem, "Confrontation over Creation of Ukrainian 'Popular Front,'" *Report on the USSR* 1 (March 3, 1989), 13-17.

33. *Tygodnik Powszechny*, February 5, 1989. See also *Izvestiia*, May 15, 1989; Saulius Girnius, "Unofficial Groups in the Baltic Republics and Access to the Mass Media," *Report on the USSR* 1 (May 5, 1989), 16-19.

34. *New York Times*, March 5, 1990, March 6, 1990, March 31, 1990.

35. Moscow TASS, November 20, 1988, reported in FBIS, *Daily Report: Soviet Union*, November 21, 1988, pp. 42-43; *New York Times*, November 17, 1988, November 27, 1988, December 8, 1988, May 19, 1989, May 25, 1989.

36. *Kommunist* (Baku), October 14, 1988; *Izvestiia*, January 5, 1989.

37. *New York Times*, March 15, 1989; Vladimir Socor, "Politics of the Language Question Heating Up in Soviet Moldavia," *Report on the USSR* 1 (September 8, 1989), 33-36; *Pravda* July 29, 1989.

38. See, for example, *Radio Liberty Research Bulletin* RL 43/88 (January 29, 1988), 5, RL 167/88 (April 15, 1988), 9, RL 177/88 (April 22, 1988), 10, RL 258/88 (June 17, 1988), 7; *Report on the USSR* 1 (May 19, 1989), 33.

39. H. Gordon Skilling, "Group Conflict in Soviet Politics: Some Conclusions," in H. Gordon Skilling and Franklin Griffiths, eds., *Interest Groups in Soviet Politics* (Princeton: Princeton University Press, 1971), 399-405; Robert E. Blackwell, Jr., "Cadres Policy in the Brezhnev Era," *Problems of Communism* 28 (March-April 1979), 29-42.

40. For example, the average term of union-republic first secretaries nearly doubled from 4.5 years on January 1, 1960 to 8.7 years ten years later, it then rose again to 12.0 years ten years after that. Grey Hodnett, *Leaders of the Soviet Republics 1955-1972* (Canberra: Australian National University, 1973); Central Intelligence Agency, *Directory of Soviet Officials: Republic Organizations* (Washington, D.C.: Central Intelligence Agency, 1980); Hodnett (fn. 15), 63-65.

41. Mark Beissinger, "Ethnicity, The Personnel Weapon, and Neo-Imperial Integration: Ukrainian and R.S.F.S.R. Provincial Party Officials Compared," *Studies in Comparative Communism* 21 (Spring 1988), 71-85; Patrick Cockburn, "Dateline USSR: Ethnic Tremors," *Foreign Policy* 74 (Spring 1989), 174-75; Suny (fn. 15), 301-5; Suny (fn. 31), 73-75; Joel Moses, "Regionalism in Soviet Politics: Continuity as a Source of Change, 1953-82," *Soviet Studies* 37 (April 1985), 184-211; Martha Brill Olcott,

"Gorbachev's Nationalities Policy and Soviet Central Asia," in Rajan Menon and Daniel N. Nelson, eds., *Limits to Soviet Power* (Lexington, Mass.: Lexington Books, 1989), 77-81.

42. See Bahry (fn. 19), 2-3, 25-31, 77-85; Steven L. Burg, "Muslim Cadres and Soviet Political Development: Reflections from a Comparative Perspective," *World Politics* 37 (October 1984), 24-47, at 33, 36.

43. USSR (fn. 25), 308-9.

44. Ellen Jones and Fred W. Grupp, "Measuring Nationality Trends in the Soviet Union: A Research Note," *Slavic Review* 41 (Spring 1982), 112-22. This is not to say that equalization has brought equality or status reversal, see Rakowska-Harmstone (fn. 20), 12; Peter R. Zwick, "Soviet Nationality Policy: Social, Economic, and Political Aspects," in Gordon B. Smith, ed., *Public Policy and Administration in the Soviet Union* (New York: Praeger, 1980), 159. Moreover, as Figure 2 shows, the slowdown in economic growth has slowed (but not stopped) this leveling process.

45. *Pravda*, October 29, 1988.

46. Martin Spechler, "Regional Development in the USSR, 1958-1978," in *Soviet Economy in a Time of Change*, U.S. Congress Joint Economic Committee (Washington, D.C.: Government Printing Office, 1979), 145. See also Donna Bahry and Carol Nechemias, "Half Full or Half Empty? The Debate over Soviet Regional Inequality," *Slavic Review* 40 (Fall 1981), 96; Elizabeth Clayton, "Regional Consumption Expenditure in the Soviet Union," *ACES Bulletin* 17 (Winter 1975), 35-43; James W. Gillula, "The Economic Interdependence of Soviet Republics," in *Soviet Economy in a Time of Change*, 629; Gertrude Schroeder, "Soviet Regional Policies in Perspective," in *The USSR in the 1980's* (Brussels: NATO Directorate of Economic Affairs, 1978), 131; Brian Silver, "Levels of Sociocultural Development among Soviet Nationalities: A Partial Test of the Equalization Hypothesis," *American Political Science Review* 68 (December 1974), 1637.

47. William Korey, "The Legal Position of Soviet Jewry: A Historical Enquiry," in Lionel Kochan, ed., *The Jews in Soviet Russia since 1917* (London: Oxford University Press, 1972), 94-95; Alec Nove and J.A. Newth, "The Jewish Population: Demographic Trends and Occupational Patterns," in Kochan, 147.

48. Lubin (fn. 15), 228, 283-84.

49. Popovsky (fn. 23), 138.

50. Moscow Television, November 26, 1988, reported in FBIS, *Daily Report: Soviet Union* November 28, 1988, p. 50. See also James Critchlow, "How Solid is Uzbekistan's Support for Moscow?" *Report on the USSR* 1 (February 10, 1989), 7.

51. See also Philip G. Roeder, "Electoral Avoidance in the Soviet Union," *Soviet Studies* 41 (July 1989), 478-80.

52. *New York Times*, September 24, 1989; see also March 25, 1988; *Pravda*, November 2, 1988; *Sovetskaia Estoniia*, November 29, 1988.

53. Moscow TASS, November 20, 1988, reported in FBIS, *Daily Report: Soviet Union*, November 21, 1988, pp. 42-43; *New York Times*, November 17, 1988, November 27, 1988, December 8, 1988, May 19, 1989, May 25, 1989.

54. *Izvestiia*, September 11, 1988, August 3, 1989, August 15, 1989; *Sovetskaia Industriia*, March 2, 1989; *Sovetskaia Litva*, October 7, 1988. See also *Izvestiia*, May 19, 1989; *Sovetskaia Litva*, May 19, 1989; *Pravda*, July 30, 1989; Dzintra Bungs, "A Comparison of the Baltic Declarations of Sovereignty," *Report on the USSR* 1

(September 15, 1989), 13-16; Kestutis Girnius, "The Lithuanian Communist Party and Calls for Sovereignty," *Report on the USSR* 1 (February 17, 1989), 18-20.

55. *Pravda*, January 25, 1989.

56. *Izvestiia*, September 7, 1989, November 14, 1989; *Literaturnaia Gazeta*, March 9, 1988. See also *New York Times*, April 8, 1989, April 9, 1989, April 16, 1989, August 7, 1989; and the interview with G.A. Pogosyan of the Nagornyi Karabakh, ArmenPress International Service, August 16, 1988, reported in FBIS, *Daily Report: Soviet Union*, August 23, 1988, p. 43.

57. *Pravda*, July 20, 1988.

58. On December 1, 1989, the Supreme Soviet of the Armenian Republic and the National Council of Nagornyi Karabakh jointly passed a resolution annexing the autonomous oblast to Armenia; *Kommunist* [Erevan], December 3, 1989.

59. *Bakinskii Rabochii,* March 11, 1988; *Izvestiia*, March 25, 1988; *Krasnaia Zvezda*, February 28, 1989; *Moskovskie Novosti*, March 20, 1988; Roman Solchanyk and Ann Sheehy, "Kapitonov on Nationality Problems in Georgia," *Radio Liberty Research Bulletin* RL 125/78 (June 1, 1978), 1-5; Elizabeth Fuller, "How Serious are Inter-Nationality Tensions in Georgia?" *Radio Liberty Research Bulletin* RL 444/83 (November 25, 1983), 1-9; idem, "Abkhaz-Georgian Relations Remain Strained," *Report on the USSR* I (March 10, 1989), 25-27; Rasma Karklins, "Ethnic Politics and Access to Higher Education: The Soviet Case," *Comparative Politics* 16 (April 1984), 277-94, at 278.

60. Brown (fn. 31), 1-4.

61. I.D. Koval'chenko et. al., "Natsional'nye protsessy v SSSR—itogi, tendentsii, problemy" [National processes in the USSR: Results, tendencies, problems], *Istoriia SSSR* (November-December 1987), 5-120, at 63, 73, 74, 79-80. See also Erwin H. Epstein, "Ideological Factors in Soviet Educational Policy towards Jews," *Education and Urban Society* 10 (February 1978), 227-28; Rasma Karklins, *Ethnic Relations in the USSR* (Boston: Allen and Unwin, 1986), 142, 146, 219.

62. V. Kobakhia, Pis'mo [Letter], *Argumenty i fakty* (October 7-13, 1989), 8.

63. Suny, "Georgia and Soviet Nationality Policy," in Stephen F. Cohen, Alexander Rabinowitz, and Robert Sharlet, eds., *The Soviet Union since Stalin* (Bloomington: Indiana University Press, 1980), 213, 219. See also *Izvestiia*, February 25, 1989; Charles E. Ziegler, "Nationalism, Religion and Equality among Ethnic Minorities: Some Observations on the Soviet Case," *Journal of Ethnic Studies* 13 (Summer 1985), 9-32, at 27.

64. *Izvestiia*, March 17, 1989. See also *Izvestiia*, March 10, 1989, August 31, 1989; *Pravda*, August 17, 1989; *Sovetskaia Litva*, February 14, 1989; Karklins (fn. 59), 290-91; Roman Solchanyk, "Russian Language and Soviet Politics," *Soviet Studies* 34 (January 1982), 23-42; *New York Times*, June 21, 1988, June 22, 1988, July 23, 1988, September 2, 1988, January 19, 1989, July 27, 1989, July 28, 1989, August 7, 1989.

65. Suny (fn. 63), 213; Juris Dreifelds, "Latvian National Demands and Group Consciousness since 1959," in George Simmonds, ed., *Nationalism in the USSR and Eastern Europe in the Era of Brezhnev and Kosygin* (Detroit: University of Detroit Press, 1977), 136-56; Jaan Pennar, "Nationalism in the Soviet Baltics," in Erich Goldhagen, ed., *Ethnic Minorities in the Soviet Union* (New York: Praeger, 1968), 206. See also *Pravda*, March 1, 1989.

66. *Pravda,* July 29, 1989, August 10, 1989. See also *New York Times*, June 21, 1988, June 22, 1988, June 23, 1988. After this was nullified by the All-Union Supreme Soviet Presidium, Estonia adopted new legislation requiring that candidates for republic positions must have been residents of Estonia for at least ten years; *Pravda,* November 18, 1989.

67. *Izvestiia*, June 9, 1989, June 10, 1989, June 20, 1989, June 23, 1989, December 1, 1989; *Pravda,* June 5, 1989, June 6, 1989, June 7, 1989, June 10, 1989, June 12, 1989, June 20, 1989, June 25, 1989, January 17, 1990; Annette Bohr, "Violence Erupts in Uzbekistan," *Report on the USSR* I (June 16, 1989), 23-25; Ann Sheehy, "Interethnic Disturbances in Western Kazakhstan," *Report on the USSR* I (July 7, 1989), 11-14.

68. This is not to say, as some have alleged, that the motive of the Party leaders was to instigate violence as a pretext for a military crackdown; *New York Times*, February 19, 1990. See also *Izvestiia*, January 15, 1990, January 16, 1990.

69. *Report on the USSR* I (January 27, 1989), 29.

70. *Pravda*, January 13, 1988, May 21, 1988, June 17, 1988, October 5, 1988, October 21, 1988, April 15, 1989, June 23, 1989, June 24, 1989, September 29, 1989, November 17, 1989.

71. *Izvestiia*, March 17, 1989, May 25, 1989, August 23, 1989; *Pravda,* July 29, 1989, August 10, 1989, August 11, 1989, August 23, 1989, August 25, 1989, September 5, 1989; *Sovetskaia Estoniia*, March 1, 1989, March 7, 1989.

72. *Izvestiia*, July 13, 1989; *Komsomol'skaia Pravda*, March 3, 1989; *Sovetskaia Litva*, February 25, 1989.

73. Quoted in Cockburn (fn. 41), 178.

74. See *Pravda*, April 9, 1989, August 23, 1989, August 24, 1989, September 10, 1989, February 2, 1990; *Zaria Vostoka*, April 12, 1989, April 14, 1989; *New York Times*, August 28, 1989, August 29, 1989, August 30, 1989, September 1, 1989, September 17, 1989; Saulius Girnius, "Sajudis' Parliament Statement on Independence," *Report on the USSR* 1 (September 15, 1989), 17-18.

75. *New York Times,,* March 13, 1990.

76. Smith (fn. 7), 105. See also Walker Connor, "Nation-Building or Nation-Destroying?" *World Politics* 24 (April 1972), 319-55; Milton Esman, ed., *Ethnic Conflict in the Western World* (Ithaca, N.Y.: Cornell University Press, 1977); Clifford Geertz, "The Integrative Revolution: Primordial Sentiments and Civil Politics in the New States," in *Old Societies and New States* (New York: Free Press, 1963), 105-57; Edward Shils, "Primordial, Personal, Sacred, and Civil Ties," *British Journal of Sociology* 8 (June 1957), 130-145.

77. Crawford Young, *The Politics of Cultural Pluralism* (Madison: University of Wisconsin Press, 1976), 43. See also Frederick Barth, ed., *Ethnic Groups and Boundaries* (Boston: Little, Brown, 1969); Glazer and Moynihan (fn. 10); Robert Melson and Howard Wolpe, *Nigeria: Modernisation and the Politics of Communalism* (East Lansing: Michigan State University, 1971); Ronald Rogowski, "Causes and Varieties of Nationalism: A Rationalist Account," in Edward A. Tiryakian and Ronald Rogowski, eds., *New Nationalisms of the Developed West* (Boston: Allen and Unwin, 1985), 87-108.

78. Arend Lijphart, "Political Theories and the Explanation of Ethnic Conflict in the Western World," in Esman (fn. 76), 46-64.

79. Teresa Rakowska-Harmstone, "The Soviet Union," in Robert G. Wirsing, ed., *Protection of Ethnic Minorities: Comparative Perspectives* (New York: Pergamon Press, 1981), 127. For a fine critical discussion of this approach, see Gail Warshofsky Lapidus, "Ethnonationalism and Political Stability: The Soviet Case," *World Politics* 36 (July 1984), 555-80.

80. Karpat, "Moscow and the 'Muslim Question,'" *Problems of Communism* 32 (November-December 1983), 79.

81. Bennigsen and Wimbush, *Muslims of the Soviet Empire* (London: C. Hurst, 1985), 3, 31.

82. The paradigm might be "saved" by claiming that assertiveness of ethnic leaders in the Baltic, followed by such assertiveness in the Caucasus, is evidence of the relative levels of ethnic awareness in these lands. But in this sense the concept of relative levels of national consciousness is not a predictor of politicized ethnicity or part of a causal relationship; it is, rather, a description or definition.

83. Suny (fn. 63), 220. This may also be true in many Western societies; see Anthony Mughan, "Modernization and Ethnic Conflict in Belgium," *Political Studies* 27 (March 1979), 21-37; Rogowski, "Conclusion," in Tiryakian and Rogowski (fn. 77), 374-76.

84. Karl W. Deutsch has noted that political systems also differ in the degree to which their institutions influence ethnic attitudes (particularly assimilation); see Deutsch, *Political Community at the International Level: Problems of Definition and Measurement* (Garden City, N.Y.: Doubleday, 1954), 33, 39-40. The "new institutionalism" argues a more general case for the "endogeneity" of preferences; for example, James P. March and Johan P. Olsen argue that traditionally "political theory has treated political institutions as determining, ordering, or modifying individual motives"; see March and Olsen, *Rediscovering Institutions: The Organizational Basis of Politics* (New York: Free Press, 1989), 4-7, 154-56. For additional motives that incline ethnic elites toward intercommunity conflict regulation, see Eric A. Nordlinger, *Conflict Regulation in Divided Societies* (Cambridge: Harvard University Center for International Affairs, 1972).

85. Illustrations of this approach include Edward Allworth, "Restating the Soviet Nationality Question," in Allworth, ed., *Soviet Nationality Problems* (New York: Columbia University Press, 1971); Helene Carrere d'Encausse, *Decline of an Empire* (New York: Newsweek Books, 1978); Rakowska-Harmstone (fn. 79).

86. Gorbachev's initial response to new elites such as Landsbergis and his Sajudis government has been consistent with the Soviet ethnic strategy that has emphasized institutional constraints to shape ethnic agendas. Using deterrent and compellent constraints, he has sought to induce the Lithuanian government to abandon its primordial agenda and pursue the instrumental objectives of *perestroika* within the context of Soviet federalism.

87. Sidney Tarrow described how in democratic systems as well the strategies of regional leaders acting as brokers between center and periphery are shaped by bureaucratic institutions; see Tarrow, *Between Center and Periphery: Grassroots Politics in Italy and France* (New Haven: Yale University Press, 1977), 7-8, 43-44.

88. *Sovetskaia Latviia*, March 19, 1989.

89. *Pravda*, February 8, 1990, February 9, 1990; *New York Times*, March 24, 1990. In Lithuania, sensing the consequences of these institutional changes for their power, members of the republic Politburo, such as the prime minister of the Sajudis government, have also begun to resign from the Communist Party.

90. *New York Times*, March 30, 1990.

91. *New York Times*, March 5, 1990, March 6, 1990, March 31, 1990.

PART III

ELITES AND ETHNIC STRATIFICATION

The chapters in Part II suggested ways in which the federal structure and federal institutions might encourage the pursuit of local interests in the republics and impede central control over politics and the economy in the Soviet Union. The works in Part III continue the discussion of how republic elites balance republic and all-Union interests in the implementation of central policies. Specifically, the authors discuss how Soviet personnel—or cadres—policy sought to assure the primacy of Moscow's priorities in republic administration.

Collectively, the authors identify four key priorities of Moscow's personnel policies: maintaining the cohesion of the Soviet federation, guaranteeing the stability of the Soviet system of rule, preempting the formation of nationalist movements, and ensuring the implementation of the central economic plan. The authors share the assumption that republic-based nationalist movements constitute the most serious threat to the cohesion and stability of the Soviet Union, and because such movements could operate successfully without elites, central policy at the most basic level had to prevent republic elites from shifting their loyalties and from sanctioning nationalist agendas.

The elites literature represented here focuses on central recruitment policies to staff republic elite positions, and on efforts aimed at ensuring the loyalty of republic and regional elites to Moscow. Since the 1920s, Soviet regimes (except Stalin's) actively sought authentic, or indigenous, leaders in the republics. The process of *korenizatsiia*, or indigenization, involved seeking out and training suitable local people to staff visible administrative posts and attempting to build trust between the local populations and political personnel. This process attempted to impart local authority to the execution of central polices (thereby deflecting charges that the Bolsheviks were merely replicating Russian imperial rule), but the process frequently backfired as local leaders adopted national communism to the detriment of central economic and political priorities. The emphasis on control in cadres policy—a recurring theme in these chapters— demonstrates that the lesson of national communism was not lost on Moscow and continues to provoke debate about whether Soviet rule over the republics may be characterized as imperial.

179

John Miller's article pieces together a Soviet formula for control over the republics through "dyarchy" in the republic's top Party administrative posts. Focusing on the careers of first and second secretaries of republic Party organizations, Miller argues that a specific division of responsibilities between these two positions and a specific pattern of ethnic recruiting to staff them began to evolve in the 1950s. In the tradition of *korenizatsiia*, dyarchy means that the first secretary typically is recruited from the titular republic, performs general functions, and receives public exposure; he is supposed to enjoy the trust of the local nationality as the representative of their interests. The second secretary—recruited from the central Party apparatus—is frequently Russian or Slavic and acts as a watchdog or viceroy over the republic. Assuming the position of what Miller calls a "nationalities administrator," this secretary is charged with the sensitive task of organizing republic personnel. This formula suggests Moscow's continued appreciation of local sentiment toward republic leaders. Even more important, the ethnicity, career, and education patterns of the people who served as second secretaries led Miller to conclude that Moscow was concerned more with federal cohesion than the economy when it appointed republic administrators; Russians with experience on the Central Committee can be trusted more than any other group to preserve this cohesion.

Miller believes that the dyarchy formula for control was pursued at the expense of encouraging loyalty through granting local autonomy, and that it was developed in a differentiated manner, depending on the reliability of the population in a given republic. He does not, however, address specifically the debate about how to characterize Soviet rule over the republics (leaving the reader to determine how literally one is to understand the term "viceroy," which he uses to describe second secretaries); federal cohesion is quite a different thing from imperial domination. Mark Beissinger's article on the recruitment of provincial Party secretaries also points to a cadres policy that is differentiated according to the loyalty of the local population. Unlike Miller, however, Beissinger has no qualms about drawing on colonial models of rule.

Concentrating on trends in educational and technical experience, Beissinger's research comparing the Ukraine and the RSFSR shows that Brezhnev's policy of fostering stability among administrative personnel (or "trust-in-cadres") varied with the regime's perception of rising nationalism and with shifts in other nationality policies. Trust-in-cadres was meant to improve the implementation of the all-Union economic plan; but this policy incurred high political costs, as it fostered nationalism and entrenched localism, which made local personnel unreliable and threw into question their loyalty to Moscow. After Moscow's unsettling experience with Petro Shelest, a Ukrainian Party first secretary, political recruitment was carefully controlled from Moscow; the relationship between the local secretary and Moscow took precedence over the relationship of trust between the Party secretary and the local population. "Informal" imperial rule thus gave way to more formal imperial rule in the late 1970s as Moscow's priorities regarding nationalities shifted from concern for the economy to alarm over rising nationalism.

John Armstrong was the first observer of Soviet politics to recognize Moscow's differentiated approach to nationalities, an approach tradition that Beissinger and Miller follow. According to Armstrong, Soviet nationalities may be placed into different categories according the functions they serve in helping preserve Russian control over decision-making power. Four functional groups, however, also generate dysfunctions. The highly educated, "mobilized diaspora" (e.g. Armenians) serve as model achievers to less mobilized groups but become dysfunctional when the latter gain suitable qualifications and seek jobs that the mobilized diaspora continue to fill. "Younger brothers" (e.g., Ukrainians) are easily assimilated into the dominant culture and can be used to help rule the "colonials." This process strengthens Russian rule, but it could easily backfire if it stimulates ethnic resentment among other ethnic groups or taps (in this case) Ukrainian anti-Russian sentiment. The prototypical "state nations" are the Baltic republics, whose nationalities serve important territorial security interests. But these people also happen to be highly unreliable because they enjoyed independence as recently as the interwar period. Finally, the "colonials" (Central Asians) provide the Soviet regime with a plentiful source of labor power. The Soviet regime promotes modernization among the colonials in order, among other things, to enhance its image in the Third World, but in doing so the regime risks arousing ethnic resentment among the least advantaged peoples of the Soviet Union toward those who are better off.

Armstrong's interpretive framework for this functional analysis is not colonialism or neo-imperialism but totalitarianism. The Soviet regime needs to maximize central control and external expansion; it therefore adopts this segmented policy, which paradoxically blocks solutions that could reverse the policy's dysfunctional aspects.

7

Cadres Policy in Nationality Areas: Recruitment of CPSU First and Second Secretaries in Non-Russian Republics of the USSR

John H. Miller

I. INTRODUCTION AND AIMS[1]

Multi-ethnic polities have opted usually for one of two strategies to maintain their cohesion. One has been the promotion of loyalty to the multiethnic system by encouraging the autonomy of local communities or elites, or their specific contribution to the 'commonwealth,' or both.[2] The other has been the control or suppression of centrifugal tendencies often accompanied by a policy of assimilation to the 'central' culture. This has been particularly common in situations where either one ethnic group (whether through numerical majority or for other reasons) is acknowledged as, or claims to be, the dominant one, or where the political leadership sets goals for the polity that may not be shared by all the ethnic groups. A predictable feature of such control would be strict supervision from the center over the selection of administrative personnel in ethnic minority or ethnically mixed areas.

The USSR must certainly be classified among the polities inclining more towards the latter strategy. Its ethnic balance, whereby about half the citizens belong to one nationality and the other half is divided among scores of major ethnic groups, seems to be unique in history. There have certainly been periods in Soviet history (not to speak of attitudes inherited from pre-revolutionary times) when the Russians have overtly claimed primacy among the ethnic groups of the Union. It is also a state whose leadership is determined to implement the

Published in *Soviet Studies*, 29: 1 (January 1977), pp. 3-36. Reprinted with permission from the publisher.

goal of centrally-planned economic development. This may not always be entirely welcome to ethnic minorities,[3] and its centralized nature is incompatible with local autonomy. Not surprisingly, therefore, a systematic and highly centralized policy on personnel deployment (the *nomenklatura* system) has developed into one of the keystones of Soviet government.[4] At the same time, as has been noted, we know remarkably little about the details of this policy.[5]

Foremost among the centrally appointed administrators in the Soviet system, including its ethnic minority areas, are the party secretaries, and it has been remarked several times that in non-Russian areas the chief party secretary is conventionally from the titular nationality and his deputy an ethnic Russian.[6] The present study is an attempt to probe this and other possible *nomenklatura* policies governing the appointment of party secretaries in ethnic minority areas, and, if possible, to suggest conclusions about the Soviet approach to governing a multi-ethnic polity. I shall make the assumption that *nomenklatura* principles and policies do exist and work, i.e., that by and large personnel are selected for their suitability or qualifications for a job, though what constitutes "suitability" or "qualifications" may at times be something unfamiliar or complex.[7]

The party secretaries I wish to examine are the *first and second secretaries of Union Republics* (SSRs) and *Autonomous Republics* (ASSRs),[8] and I have tried to assemble as many political biographies as I could of officials holding one of these four posts between March 1954 and March 1976.[9] Altogether, 259 such tenures have been registered, held by 236 persons (some held more than one of the posts under consideration); 125 were held by Russians and 134 by non-Russians; 44 were tenures of the post of SSR first secretary, 73 of SSR second secretary, 66 of ASSR first secretary and 76 of ASSR second secretary.

What these tenures have in common is that they were all held in a "designated" national minority area. But, it may be argued, there are other ways in which the posts selected are anything but comparable. First, some of the areas are nationality areas in name, but majority in Russian population: the Buryat, Karelian, Mordovian, Udmurt and Komi ASSRs. In such areas considerations of ethnic cohesion may arguably be only a minor component in policy. However, in singling out the designated nationality areas we are in fact dealing with virtually all the areas in which the non-Russian presence is most sizable, and hence where ethnic considerations *may* affect policy. Of the other RSFSR oblasts not designated as nationality areas, only Orenburg is comparable with Buryatia or Karelia in the size of its non-Russian population.

The second objection is more forceful. The first secretary for the Ukraine and the second secretary for Nakhichevan', it will be said, have no more in common with each other than have a Cabinet Minister and a county councillor. Far more care will be taken over personnel deployment in, say, Karaganda oblast, or Kiev or Tashkent cities, than in Nakhichevan' or Abkhazia, whether on economic, strategic or ethnic grounds, and the comparison should be between areas of comparable importance: all the oblasts in the Ukraine or Uzbekistan for instance.

The reason I have opted with reluctance against such a sample is that I wished to obtain one in which fairly complete career details would be available for Russians and non-Russians alike, so as to compare the two. In this, as will be seen, I have been moderately successful. The trouble with a study of party careers at oblast levels is that we know a good deal about *first* secretaries; they are usually *ex-officio* in the Supreme Soviet, and the Central Committee or Central Auditing Commission, and hence earn a published biography.[10] We tend to know very little about obkom second secretaries. Since the former are frequently non-Russians and the latter Russians, this would give rise to a sample in which data on non-Russians were relatively full and on Russians relatively fragmentary.

This sample, therefore, consists of tenures of first and second secretaryships in all the Union and Autonomous Republics, however great or small. It is a sample of *tenures*, and not of persons; thus if a man is successively *second* secretary in Tataria and Bashkiria and *first* secretary in the Mari ASSR his career appears in the sample three times as if he were three separate officials.
. . .

II. FUNCTIONS OF FIRST AND SECOND SECRETARIES

What is known about the functions of first and second secretaries? For the first secretary we can answer immediately that he has general powers of leadership, supervision and coordination in his obkom or Central Committee, and, by extension, throughout his region;[11] he is given a good deal of local publicity. For *second* secretaries the answer is not so simple—for two reasons. First, "second" secretary is not yet (or only just) a firmly established title (he may be given that title in the press, or he may be called plain "secretary"[12]), and is not yet firmly associated with a particular function. Thus in the period under review second secretaries have been responsible about three-quarters of the time for organizational and personnel matters, and this function appears to have become regular from the early 1960s,[13] but in some republics, particularly in the Khrushchev period, the man with the title of second secretary has had special responsibilities for some other sector, most commonly agriculture,[14] and organizational matters have sometimes been the preserve of the *first* secretary.[15] So, though it would be fair to assume that a post "second secretary in charge of organization and cadres" has now evolved,[16] it must be kept in mind that the sample of second secretaries since 1954 includes some who did not exercise that function.

The second reason why the function (and careers) of second secretaries is easy to define is that, by contrast with the publicity surrounding first secretaries, second secretaries seem to be kept deliberately out of the limelight; they rarely speak, for instance, at Republican or oblast party congresses or conferences, though people of (one would have thought) less "weight" do.[17] I shall note below how cadres work tends to be kept deliberately inconspicuous.

To have charge over the *nomenklatura* of a republic is a position of some power. The second secretary with this portfolio can presumably veto any suggestions on personnel that the first secretary might put forward, and thus prevent him from assembling any faction or entourage about himself. He will have considerable influence over the non-Russian cadres pool from which future local leaders (including first secretaries) will be drawn. It has even been claimed that a second secretary can recommend the dismissal of a first secretary, but not vice versa.[18] All this makes of the second secretary something rather more than a mere deputy to the first secretary; whether he is more of a partner, or watchdog, or fellow-consul, he functions as an institutionalized check on the first secretary. To be sure, the latter, if he is native, knows the local language and culture, and will have a wide array of local contacts. How these two sources of strength, one formal, the other informal, balance out in practice must vary from place to place and time to time. One suspects that they are *meant* to balance out.[19]

Thus, in dealing with first and second secretaries, we are dealing with a leadership dyarchy, consisting of a publicly identified chief official, but one whose powers are limited, and his deputy, an independent appointment who exercises perhaps the most important of these limiting functions—control of personnel. Something of the roles expected of each is conveyed by the report of the spectacular dismissals among the Tadzhik leadership in April 1961.[20] The first secretary, the Chairman of the Council of Ministers and a large number of other native Tadzhik officials are sacked (and in some cases expelled from the party) for falsification of the cotton crop returns. The Russian second secretary, P. S. Obnosov, suffers the same penalties—but on a somewhat different charge: "lack of political principle" and "connivance" (*prisposoblenchestro*).

III. REQUIREMENTS OF NATIONALIST ADMINISTRATIONS

In his discussion cited above[21] Hough argues that, when a whole region and all its population can be affected by fulfillment or nonfulfillment of the plan, "rational-technical" qualifications for the job will probably be decisive in the selection of economic administrative personnel; but "electoral appeal," i.e., the ability to maintain smooth industrial relations and work harmoniously with colleagues, will also be taken into consideration; as will "being known to the appointments board," which is, for all the offices under consideration here, the CPSU Central Committee Department for Organizational-Party Work (Cadres' Department). One will tend to be known by the staff of this department if one is or has been based in Moscow, or if one has worked with its members elsewhere at an earlier stage of one's career.

I would suggest that the administration of ethnically mixed or minority areas is also treated as a highly serious matter;[22] things could go badly wrong[23] and officials need to be selected who are qualified for and efficient at the job. One *prima facie* reason for believing this is the presence of so many Russians in leading positions in non-Russian parts of the Union. In the 1930s this might have been explained by the skills that only the Russians could offer to the industrialization drive, but this can scarcely be the case now. If economic performance or ideological rectitude were the only consideration to be borne in mind in appointing people in Tadzhikistan, there would surely be sufficient trained native Tadzhiks to fill the posts.

But what exactly is the job of a nationalities administrator—the analogue of plan-fulfillment in industrial administrations—and what are the qualifications for it? I would advance the following, on common-sense grounds and as a working hypothesis.

The job is to strike the best compromise between a number of conflicting claims on policy. First, government in Moscow is interested above all in maintenance of federal cohesion, and hence in the loyalty or at least social tranquility of local populations. But at the same time it is interested in rapid economic development, something that may upset that tranquility.[24] The good nationalities administrator must be able to promote both these interests, and minimize the contradictions between them.

Second, government in Moscow intends that its policies shall at all times have priority; but the localities will wish their interests to be represented too. This may be a relatively inarticulate pressure, it may be a pressure merely to see one's own people in certain jobs (rather than one in favor of specific policies), and it may be a pressure that can be satisfied with the semblance rather than the substance of influence. But it has to be reckoned with.

The nationalities administrator, then, must be able to implement (and, therefore, "sell") federal policy without intolerably offending local tradition or pride. If he is a Russian he must know something about the local tradition, even if he has to be firm with it. If he is non-Russian he must place his knowledge of local culture and interests at the service of the federation. His prime loyalty must be seen to be unreservedly federal, not local. Yet he must enjoy at least some respect from the non-Russian communities, or his value as a communications link between them and the federal administration would be lost. To preserve this respect, he must be felt to be some sort of a spokesman for non-Russian interests—but only in such a way or over such issues as never to cast in doubt his overriding loyalty to the federation.[25]

Third, ethnic minority areas in the USSR are rarely homogeneous; they often have large Russian populations and often the non-Russian population is very mixed. Administration, then, is not merely a matter of striking an acceptable balance *between* central priorities and local interests, but of adjudicating *between* local interests so as to preserve local harmony. So the non-Russian official, necessary though he may be as spokesman for the non-Russian community, must not be allowed to turn this role into one of favoring his own community to the disadvantage of others. And the Russian official will have to be a watchdog, not just for federal interests, but for those of the local Russian community.

There are further complications, reminiscent of current Irish politics. The non-Russian population of a given area may regard themselves as a minority—within the Union as a whole. The local Russian population of the same area may also look upon itself as a minority—within that area. Each group may therefore consider itself threatened with encroachment (cultural, political or economic) and officials drawn from either group might be under temptation to try to ward off such encroachment and defend what they consider to be the minority. The reaction of the central authorities might well be to cut back on, or supervise carefully, *locally* recruited personnel of *any* nationality.[26]

The bargaining and diplomatic skills suggested by the above discussion might well be too many to expect in one man. Arguably, what is required is a judicious combination of Russians and non-Russians acting in check on each other, and a judicious combination of personnel with local ties and knowledge and personnel imported from outside. The distinction between "rational-technical qualifications" and "electoral appeal" or "being known to the appointments board" seems to be a good deal more blurred than in the case of the selection of industrial administrators.

IV. THE TOP TWO SECRETARIES—
RECRUITMENT AND LENGTH OF SERVICE

The sample comprises 236 persons, all male,[27] who between them have occupied 259 first or second secretaryships since March 1954. Of them, 21 held two such tenures, and one other, three;[28] 119 of the tenures where held be persons of Russian nationality and 123 by non-Russians.[29]

An obvious question arising here concerns the appropriate classification for Ukrainians, who are often appointed to high office in non-Slavonic areas of the USSR. I have classified Ukrainians working inside the Ukraine as "non-Russians" and outside the Ukraine as "Russians."[30] This is not just a piece of classificatory convenience, but reflects, I believe, a substantial point about the emergence of multi-ethnic systems: that it is perfectly possible to combine loyalty to one's nation with loyalty to a cause in which several nations share. The role of the Scots and the Irish in the spread of the London-based Empire would be a useful analogy to the role of Ukrainians and Belorussians in the Moscow-based Soviet Union.

The nationality of 17 persons (all second secretaries in ASSRs) is uncertain, but with moderate confidence I have apportioned six of them to the Russian and 11 to the non-Russian categories,[31] and in what follows I shall redistribute them accordingly.

1. *Nationality of the Top Leadership Team*

Thus the cliché that the first secretary is normally a native and the second secretary a Russian looks at first sight as if it were over-simplified. Nearly a third of first secretaries have been Russian, and nearly two-fifths of second secretaries have been non-Russian. Nevertheless, on closer examination, there is more to be said for the cliché than might appear, but with significant exceptions as to both time and place. To argue this, we shall divide the 34 republics into six groups, according to the way they have treated the nationality of the top leadership dyarchy.[32]

a) First and second secretaries both native. A small group of republics have fairly consistently had *both* first and second secretaries native. These are the Ukraine (until March 1973), Belorussia (since July 1956), Armenia (until March 1973), Estonia (until February 1971), and the small Georgian republics of Abkhazia and Adzharia.[33] If one had to name the major non-Russian nationalities that for historical reasons might be most amenable to Moscow-centered federation (even though they might retain their local national feelings side by side with this) one would probably place Ukrainians, Belorussians and Armenians at the top of the list: the first two because they are fellow slavs, the last because, after the 1916 massacres, Soviet Armenians were prepared to offer a wide measure of loyalty to Moscow in return for protection. These three nationalities have been offered a share in the joint Moscow-based enterprise not given to others; they are, for instance, the only non-Russians who serve as officials to any substantial extent outside their home republics.[34] The presumption is that a team of native first *and* second secretaries has been permitted here because of the relative reliability of the native population.

Why, then, have Russian second secretaries been introduced in Armenia and the Ukraine in the last three years? As will emerge, it is in line with the trend that has been in evidence since the early 1960s. In the case of Armenia, Moscow's dissatisfaction with the local party's conduct of affairs may well be a factor, as it undoubtedly has been in the other two Transcaucasian republics recently; also improved relations with Turkey probably entail the show of a firmer hand in Armenia. Regarding I. Z. Sokolov, the new second secretary for the Ukraine, his passport nationality may not be of much political significance. He seems to have spent all his career since 1950 in Khar'kov, and might be from the substantial Russian community in that city. And anyway, does the distinction between Russian and non-Russian mean much in official circles in Kiev, as it might, say, in Ashkhabad or Dushanbe?

On paper, Estonia also looks as if it belonged to the group having native first and second secretaries, but there is an important difference between party leaders here and in the Ukraine, Belorussia or Armenia. Its first secretary ever since 1950 has been I. G. Kebin; Estonian second secretaries have been L. N. Lentsman (1953-64) and A. P. Vader (1964-70). Kebin and Lentsman certainly, and Vader probably, spent the inter-war years in the USSR, presumably as communist emigrés or the children of communist emigrés. (Lentsman in fact was born in the Crimea and may never have visited Estonia before 1944). The same thing can be observed elsewhere; in Latvia and Lithuania, also, a disproportionate number of leading non-Russians in public life were inter-war emigrés in the USSR; in Moldavia a disproportionate number come from the left (Tiraspol') bank of the Denstr, that is, from the tiny Moldavian Autonomous Oblast that was within the Ukraine before the war; hardly any leading Moldavians were Rumanian citizens at an age when it mattered. For these areas, it would be fair to assume, *nomenklatura* officials distinguish between communists who have experienced the pre-war political systems, and those who do not, and give preference to the latter.[35]

The small ASSRs within Georgia, Abkhazia and Adzharia also fall into this group; with one exception[36] they have had native first and second secretaries throughout the period. It may be argued that this is unimportant, provided personnel in Tbilisi is reliable. The only oddity is that the other two ASSRs outside the RSFSR, namely Nakhichevan' and Karakalpak ASSR, have regularly had a Russian second secretary. One might have expected these four regions to conform to a single rule, or else that Adzharia, which, like Nakhichevan', is a frontier area (even if demographically insignificant) would show evidence of the stricter policy.

b) *First and second secretaries both native: phased out.* Four Union Republics, Latvia, Lithuania, Georgia and Azerbaidzhan, began the post-Stalin period adhering to the same pattern as Group a). The native first secretaries were, respectively, Ya. E. Kalnberzin, A. Yu. Snechkus, V. P. Mzhavanadze and I. D. Mustafaev. For short periods in the 1950s they had native second secretaries as well: in Latvia, V. K. Krumin'sh (1954-56 and 1958-60), in Lithuania, M. Yu. Shumauskas (1954-56), in Georgia, M. P. Georgadze (1954-56) and in Azerbaidzhan, V. Yu. Samedov (1952-55). This has not since been repeated, and it looks very much as if the Group a) pattern was deliberately phased out, to be replaced by the pattern of native first secretary and Russian second secretary (see Group c) below). Snechkus and Kalnberzin were both inter-war emigrés in the USSR, whereas Krumin'sh and Shumauskas seem not to have been; so that the situation here seems to have been halfway towards that of Estonia before 1971. As regards to two Transcaucasian republics, it may have been thought inadvisable to drop too abruptly the policy of favor towards Transcaucasian personnel characteristic of the late Stalin period. (Even so, Mzhavanadze was brought in from nearly 30 years' service as an army officer, *inter alia*, one might guess, because he was unconnected with any Georgian factions).

c) *First secretary native, second secretary Russian.* This pattern, the "archetypal" one, has been consistently true of only a quarter of the republics, the four Union Republics of Central Asia proper, Uzbekistan, Kirgizia,

Tadzhikistan and Turkmenistan; the Karakalpak, Nakhichevan', North Ossetian and Dagestan ASSRs, socially similar to Central Asia in many ways; and probably, but not certainly, Buryatia and Yakutia. But it is a pattern to which other regions (those in Groups b), d) and e)) have come round in the post-Stalin period.

d) First and second secretaries both Russian. In two Union Republics for a short time both first and second secretaries were Russian; these were Kazakhstan (1954-57) and Moldavia (1954-59).[37] In both cases this pattern was replaced, first by that of a Russian first secretary and native second secretary, until 1960-61, and since by native first secretary and Russian second secretary. I do not know of any features specific to Kazakhstan and Moldavia which might have prompted this unusual arrangement in the mid-1950s. More likely, it is an example of the comparatively unsystematic procedures of that time—viewed from the vantage point of the mid-1970s.

e) First secretary Russian, second secretary native—temporarily. Some republics have had a pattern the reverse of the archetype, that is, Russians have been first secretaries and natives second. In some cases this has been a regular policy, and in others (the present group) it was a feature only of the 1950s. In addition to Kazakhstan (1957-60) and Moldavia (1959-61), mentioned above, it was true of Bashkiria (1953-57), Tataria (1957-60) and Karelia (1950-58); also of the Kalmyk ASSR at the time (1957-61) of the resettlement of the deported native population, and of the Kabardinian ASSR before the return of the deported Balkar population. In all these cases, the pattern that replaced Russian first and native second secretary was the reverse, that is, the archetypal Group c) pattern.

f) First secretary Russian, second secretary native—consistently. The final group consists of the republics where a Russian has consistently been the first secretary, and a native second secretary throughout the period. These are i) the three Finnish-speaking ASSRs of the Middle Volga region—the Udmurt, Mordva and Mari ASSRs—plus the Komi ASSR until 1965, and ii) the Chechen-Ingush ASSR in North Caucasus.

Regarding the four Finnish-speaking republics, they have a substantial Russian population, sometimes a majority, sometimes just under,[38] and the settlement is centuries old. The local non-Russians are arguably so russified that no local pride will be hurt by having ethnic Russians in the first secretaryship. This is probably the correct explanation. It is true that there are other regions—Karelia, Buryatia and Yakutia, for example[39]—which have a comparable proportion of Russians in the population and which have native first secretaries. But, in the case of Karelia and Buryatia, public relations (both at home and abroad) may account for the retention of the native first secretary; each borders on a foreign state (Finland and Mongolia) to which it feels ethnically akin.

The case of the Chechen-Ingush ASSR is most illuminating (even if it concerns a population of only a million) and merits detailed discussion. As is well known, the native population was deported in 1944 and allowed to resettle from 1957 onwards. The careers of its Russian first secretaries (so far as I have been able to piece them together) are as follows:

A.I. Yakovlev
 b. 1911
1940-"in party work"
1955- or 1956-59
 First secretary, Grozny/Chechen-Ingush obkom
1959-
 Inspector CC CPSU

A.S. Trofinov
 b. 1903
1937-39
 Secretary, second secretary, Saratov gorkom
1939-46
 Official of the Committee of Party Control, inter alia its plenipotentiary in Chita, Krasnodar and Azerbaidzhan
1946-52 Second secretary, Lithuania
1952-54 ?
1954-57
 First secretary, Balashov obkom
1957-59
 in CC apparat
1959-63
 First secretary, Chechen-Ingush obkom
1963
 retires?

F.E. Titov
 b. 1910
  -1944
 Head of department, Yaroslavl' obkom; instructor CC CPSU
1944-52
 Secretary, second secretary, Latvia
1952-59
 First secretary, Ivanov obkom
1959-62
 Second secretary, Uzbekistan
1963-65
 First secretary, Chechen-Ingush obkom
1966-71

Ambassador in Budapest
1971-
Minister of Foreign Affairs, RSFSR

S.S. Apryatkin
b. 1911
1934-40
Succession of engineering and administrative posts in oil industry in Baku
1940-?42
Oil administrator in Maikop
?1942-45
Oil administrator in Kokand
1945-57
Oil administrator in Grozny (joins CPSU 1948)
1957-58
First deputy chairman, Chechen-Ingush sovnarkhoz
1958-66
Secretary, Chechen-Ingush obkom
1966-76
First secretary, Chechen-Ingush obkom

Yakovlev's career is too obscure to evaluate. What is striking about the other three is the strength of their experience in nationalities administration. All three had been in two or more other nationality areas before posting to the Chechen-Ingush ASSR. Trofimov and Titov were both in the Baltic in the tough post-war years. Apryatkin had 20 years' experience of North- and Transcaucasia before moving into party office there. It looks like a succession of highly experienced professionals.

Now Conquest[40] proffers quite separate evidence that the resettlement of the Chechen and Ingush was more trouble, over a long period, than the other resettlements of deportees. Further, party membership among the Chechen and the Ingush has been very low. In recent years statistics concerning nationalities of Autonomous Oblast status and above, they appear to have the lowest party membership rate (per head of population) of any of the nationalities named.[41] The retention of Russian first secretaries in the area, and their high calibre, could well be seen as a consequence of their unreliability.

There would be an interesting objection to this line of argument. That is that the Chechen-Ingush ASSR is of minor importance in demographic and economic terms, and a posting there constitutes a demotion, a penalty for poor performance. Of the four careers above, only that of Titov offers relevant evidence, and it is against this hypothesis; some diplomatic postings probably do amount to a "kick upstairs" but surely not the embassy in Budapest? In fact, the Chechen-Ingush episode in Titov's career does not look like a setback, but more as if a high-calibre man had been moved in because the area or situation was felt to warrant it. If this is so, then considerations of control outweighed factors such as size or economic importance when this appointment was made.

Well-known attempts have been made[42] to draw up a rank-order of oblasts such as might be used by the Cadres Department when moving people from job to job; clearly some oblasts are more important than others and would have first claim on the most experienced or gifted administrators. Typically the basis for such rank order has been sought in quantifiable social indices such as population, party membership or contribution to the GNP. The Chechen-Ingush ASSR seems to me to stand higher in the notional rank-order than its social indices would warrant—simply because of the restlessness of its population. In other words, if we are to draw up a realistic rank-order of oblasts, we must include some factor such as "difficulty to control" along with the others—however hard it may be to measure!

Two conclusions emerge from this survey of the leading party dyarchy in nationality areas. First, it is a matter of policy to have one Russian among the two top party officials in non-Russian areas. This can hardly be dictated—as it might once have been—by lack of non-Russian expertise, technical or ideological. If economic and ideological considerations are excluded, political cohesion of the Moscow-centered Union seems the most plausible reason for this policy. Areas where this Russian presence has not been required (and they are a declining number) are areas that Moscow has best reason to trust.

Second, over the years the pattern of native first secretary and Russian second secretary has spread and become considerably more regular, replacing a wide variety of patterns that were in use in the mid-1950s. It now applies to at least 25 of the 34 republics under review, compared with ten in the 1950s. The exceptions are areas of heavy Russian settlement, or where Moscow has reason for particular trust or distrust of the non-Russian population. This regularization has coincided with increased identification of the second secretaryship with cadres work. Overall arrangements are more systematic and predictable now than they have even been.

L. I. Brezhnev in his report to the XXIV Congress in 1971 drew attention to a closely related issue:

> Many new comrades with good political and specialist qualifications have been promoted to the leadership of local party and Soviet organs, including the post of first secretary of republican, krai and oblast party committees. Moreover, the Central Committee has pursued a consistent policy of promoting local personnel; the people have been promoted to these posts from the center only in exceptional circumstances.[43]

The fact that this topic was singled out for mention at all, and that the sentences above were repeated verbatim in a subsequent article in *Kommunist*,[44] suggests that it had been a matter of concern and debate among the political leadership. If the General Secretary's words are taken to refer strictly to first secretaries (the text is ambiguous), then the present study confirms the announced change of policy. But side by side with the regularization of local recruitment of first secretaries has gone a regularization of external recruitment of second secretaries, at any rate in nationality areas—something Brezhnev glosses over in the above speech.

Further, he treats this regularization as a praiseworthy feature of his own, post-1964 administration. The process has in fact been a continuous one, but with an odd watershed in the late 1950s, ending in 1961.[45] In general, Western scholars have accepted Brezhnev's claims that 1964 was the important turning point in cadres policy, for instance, regarding security in office.[46] But the decision to cut down on native second secretaries and standardize the position of Russian second secretaries in charge of cadres policy in nationality areas seems to have been a decision of the middle Khrushchev period. A possibly related factor could be the sovnarkhoz reforms begun in 1957. These devolved some economic power to the regions and, conceivably, the Department of Party Organs (like some Western scholars) may have thought that this could lead on to pressures for *political* devolution. So they set about strengthening the institutional checks in this.

2. Age and Length of Service

The average first or second secretary in this sample joined the CPSU aged 24 and entered the office in question 21 years latter aged 45. These figures vary remarkably little over the period, or comparing Russians with non-Russians or first with second secretaries. They also agree with the data for obkom first secretaries calculated by Hough and Frank;[47] obkom first secretaries would seem to be the group of officials most nearly comparable in rank with the present sample. In 1955 non-Russians were being hired on average nearly five years younger than Russians, but this difference has now dwindled almost to nothing. Arguably, as the pool of trained non-Russians increases, so their career mobility slows.

Length of time in office, however, and consequently, age of office-holders, presents a different picture. Two conclusions emerge clearly from these data. First, the average length of tenure has been rising steadily for the past two decades and is now, for all the posts under consideration, more than twice what it was in 1955. Correspondingly (though there is not table to illustrate this) the average age of an incumbent has risen from 46 to 54. This is in line with other studies,[48] and has usually been associated with the bargain struck between Brezhnev and Kosygin on the one hand, and the Central Committee members who agreed to support them in the deposition of Khrushchev.

Second, the expectation of tenure of a native or of a first secretary has consistently been much higher than that of a Russian or second secretary:

between 50% and 100% higher. This prompts modification of the judgment made by Bilinsky (in the seminal article on this subject) concerning "the high political casualty rate among native first secretaries."[49] This might be taken to imply that it is Russians who have the longer tenures; it is probably not what Bilinsky meant but it deserves clarification. Turnover rates are quite definitely higher for Russians than for natives, but that is not the same thing as demotion or dismissal with ignominy. . . . The sample does not suggest that the high turnover rate for Russians is equivalent to a high rate of demotion. On the contrary, it suggests that Russians in nationalities postings are doing a tour of duty which both they and the Cadres Department expect to be fixed in term; their career opportunities in the All-Union stage are much more extensive and they expect to utilize them. Natives by contrast tend to make their whole career in their native area (both by preference and because that is where their expertise is needed) which may have the effect of slowing their personnel turnover.

Furthermore, it has already been suggested that the first secretary is a public official, one of whose roles is the promotion of public confidence; the second secretary is by contrast deliberately inconspicuous. It would be conductive to public confidence and the communications role of the first secretary if he stayed relatively long in office; the public image of local government would be relatively unaffected by frequent changes of second secretary.[50]

V. Previous Careers of First and Second Secretaries

The background, qualifications and careers of the officials in this sample are the next object of scrutiny.

1. *Place of Origin*

Non-Russian first and second secretaries come, with one exception, from the titular nationality of the republic in which they hold office. Overwhelmingly, they were born and brought up there.[51]

As for Russians, about 23% of all Soviet Russians live in the 34 designated nationality areas, and the question immediately arises whether the Central Committee seeks to draw on the first-hand experience of such Russians for the administration of nationality areas. They must, after all, possess among themselves a fund of knowledge and expertise about non-Russian cultures, ways of doing business, pet susceptibilities, etc., which might be put to good use by appointing say, Russians from Bashkiria, Kirgizia or Latvia to posts in those republics.

In fact, the reverse would seem to be the case. Of the 113 Russian persons in the sample, I have confirmed only *one* who was born in a nationality area and worked in the same and nearby ones. This is P. V. Uraev. . . . In addition, S. S. Apryatkin, mentioned above, spent more than 20 years in the Caucasian area before becoming first secretary in the Chechen-Ingush ASSR; he was not a career party official and extensive local knowledge seems to have been one of his qualifications for this post. So far, this is tenuous evidence; place of birth is conventionally only given in obituaries in Soviet sources, and I know it only in 20 cases. For about twice that a number plausible—but by no means certain—guess may be hazarded from a person's place of education or first employment, and, of these, eight [went] on to relevant party office in the same or a nearby area. . . . The paucity of this evidence underlines my point. If Russian settler communities are being drawn in for administrative personnel, one would have expected more substantial evidence . . . As it is, I would argue, at least tentatively, that Russian settlers are at a *disadvantage* regarding promotion to high office in their own areas. If so, the reason would be that advanced hypothetically in Section II above: Moscow subjects the top non-Russian officials to the check of a Russian second secretary, but it is just as wary of potential localism or lordliness on the part of Russian settler communities. The resident Russian official must watch over their interests to be sure, but must not be the sort of person who might identify too easily with them. Hence a preference for officials from ethnic Great Russia.

2. *Tertiary Qualifications*

The educational qualifications of 198 of the sample are known. Fourteen had only secondary or unfinished tertiary education. Of the other 184 with tertiary qualifications (*vysshee obrazovanie*) about half have a single vocational qualification (most commonly in engineering, agriculture or teaching), about a quarter a qualification from on of the Higher Party Schools,[52] and about a quarter have both.

Two conclusions can be drawn. First, the quarter who have two qualifications is disproportionately non-Russian. Such people require, in fact, more training before proceeding to a post of Union importance. Russians, by contrast, are more likely to be appointed simply on the basis of their vocational qualifications.

Second, Russian officials are much more likely to have technical or agricultural ("production-oriented") qualifications, whereas non-Russians are more likely to proceed from teaching or ideological ("communications-oriented"?) training. This could be a preference on the part of the Cadres Department in the selection of officials, but this is unlikely. Alternatively, it reflects the qualifications typical of the different nationalities, as a result either of the sort of education they seek, or have available to them. The latter seems the more plausible explanation. If one surveys the data on students in different types of higher education in the Union Republics,[53] it is clear that even now in the RSFSR a higher proportion of students are in "production-oriented" *vuzy* (particularly engineering), and in other republics, particularly the southern ones, a higher proportion are in teacher-training and related subjects. The educational bias of officials in fact reflects the educational opportunities open to them in the region from which they came.

Might there also be an element of preference in this? For instance, one against heavy industry on the part of the Muslims and Transcaucasians? After all, the type and size of *vuzy* set up was a matter of someone's decision with both central and local interests being at least voiced. Probably modernizers of all ideological persuasions or nationalities would agree that, in a place like Tadzhikistan, teacher-training should precede the establishment of heavy industry. But there are other oddities about the distribution of *vuzy* that make on wonder whether local preference did not play a role. It is, for instance, three times easier to enter courses in "art and cinematography" in Transcaucasia than in the RSFSR.[54]

3. *Place of Previous Employment*

. . . [N]on-Russians spend their careers overwhelmingly in their home republic. Transfers of non-Russian personnel between different Central Asian or Caucasian republics occur, but very "infrequently."[55] A slightly larger proportion of non-Russians have had work experience in the RSFSR, but this figure consists mainly of inter-war emigré Balts, career officers (like V. P. Mzhavanadze) and Ukrainians and Belorussians who move into RSFSR employment more easily that other non-Russians; otherwise one is left with four names.[56] That they spend their careers almost exclusively in their native republics, does not, however, entail lack of acquaintance with Russian ways and values; virtually all of them either had some education in the RSFSR (typically at the Higher Party School in Moscow) or were in the Soviet army during the Second World War.

Russians have geographically much more versatile careers. Two-thirds have previous experience in the same or another non-Russian region, two-thirds experience in an ethnic Russian province and more than half experience of All-Union work in Moscow, principally in the Central Committee *apparat*. Taking the first and last of these categories, only ten out of 103 do *not* have previous nationalities experience, or experience in Moscow, or both.[57] There are strong indications, discussed below, that the period in Moscow includes specific preparation for future nationalities postings. If so, then 90% of these Russians come to their first or second secretaryship "not unprepared" in training or past experience. It would be going too far to claim that they are all specialists in nationalities administration, though such careers do exist,[58] but officials are not usually posted to the nationality areas without prior experience, for instance, they do not proceed fresh from a career exclusively in the ethnic Russian oblasts.

Yet I have argued above that the authorities are willing to forego the useful experience of Russian *settlers* in making these postings, because of the risk of too great identification with local Russian communities. So the previous experience in question here is something gained *en poste* rather than during upbringing. Are there any further indications as to the nature of this experience? Is there any suggestion, for instance, of "area of specialization"—in such areas as Muslim or Transcaucasian or Baltic affairs? One might argue that specialist knowledge of cultures that are often very foreign to the Russian one would be very useful to the Central Committee; on the other hand, many diplomatic and colonial services have deliberately discouraged this sort of specialization, because of the risk of over-identification warping judgement.

The evidence from this sample is ambiguous. There certainly are cases of Russians who spend long periods, either in a succession of posts in the same republic, or in several culturally similar republics. The careers of P. V. Uraev in the Middle Volga region, and of S. S. Apryatkin in Caucasia are examples. More impressive, to my mind, is the list of Russians transferred, gratuitously it might seem, across vast cultural gaps. The most conspicuous examples are worth noting:

F. E. Titov ASSR   Latvia (1944-52); Uzbekistan (1959-62); Chechen Ingush (1963-65)

B. V. Popov   Uzbekistan (1949-57); Lithuania (1961-67)*

A. S. Trofimov Ingush ASSR   Azerbaidzhan (?-1946); Lithuania (1946-52); Chechen- (1959-63)*

P. M. Elistratov (1968-71)   Ukraine (1946-61); Azerbaidzhan (1961-68); Mordovia

V. N. Churkin   North Ossetia (1938-50); Kirgizia (1951-72)*

D. S. Zemlyansky   Kazakhstan (1941-? and 1955-61); Georgia (1962-63)*

F. I. Kashnikov   Moldavia (?-1951; Latvia (1956-58)

N. A. Voronovsky   Dagestan (1957-61); Chuvash ASSR (1968-73)*

V. I. Kharazov   Kazakhstan (1954-61); Lithuania (1967-)*

A. V. Vlasov   Yakutia (c.1966-71); Chechen-Ingush ASSR (1976-)

* Some or all of the intervening periods spent in the Central Committee apparat

Deliberate culture shock-treatment? These cases certainly suggest a policy of promoting experience in non-Russian administration as a whole, and of discouraging area of specialization.

4. *Previous Office Held*

. . .[There are] some prominent "take-off" positions from which to move to the first or second secretaryship. For non-Russian these are an ordinary secretaryship in the same republic, or, still more important, the Chairmanship of the local Council of Ministers. This is in line with the late Dr. J. Cleary's argument[59] that there is easy interchange between party posts and a Council of Ministers Chairmanship, but not between party and ministerial posts; in fact, that—in so far as there exist two distinct career hierarchies, a party one and a government one—the Council of Ministers Chairmanship is treated as part of the former, not the latter. What is more, in non-Russian areas it tends to be reserved for non-Russians.The comparatively large fraction of non-Russians promoted from miscellaneous "other" posts is noteworthy. About a third of these are from party offices junior to the secretaryship (such as department head) in the same locality, but the others are drawn from varied sources. Most of these appointments were made during the 1950s and reflect what I have already referred to as the unsystematic state of appointments policy then as compared with now.

For *Russians* the key "take-off" position, overshadowing all others, is the Central Committee apparat in Moscow. The majority of postings from the *apparat* are into the office of second secretary in a Union Republic, and in fact this is perhaps the most predictable promotion step encountered in this study. The men in question tend to come from the "upper middle" ranks of the CC apparat . . .

One would like to know more about the precise nature of this specialist preparation. For instance, does K. V. Lebedev (who had been in the CC apparat for 20 years) speak or understand Estonian? Come to that, what language is *used* in the *apparat* in Estonia—or, more pointedly, in Armenia or Georgia?

This is evidence, tenuous, but, I think, strongly suggestive, for the existence of area specialists within the Central Committee Cadres Department. Unfortunately, some other cases provide clear evidence for the discouragement of such specialization. A neat example is that of Yu. N. Pugachev who between 1972 and 1974 seemed to hold a Georgian portfolio within the CC apparat;[60] 12 days after his last appearance at a meeting in Georgia, his appointment as second secretary in Kirgizia was announced.[61] If Pugachev knows Georgian, is not his expertise rather wasted in Kirgizia? In other words, the suggestion emerges again that the Central Committee is not wholeheartedly committed to area specialization, but rather to promoting the variety of specialist expertise.

The argument above has been based on the scanty evidence we have about people's rank and function within the CC *apparat*. There are plenty of other careers where we know nothing beyond the fact that the man was a CC *apparatchik*, and even that knowledge depends on his emergence from the obscurity of the apparat to the prominence of a second secretaryship.[62] Presumably, we might not have heard of them at all if they had not become second secretaries—until their deaths, that is.[63] It is a warning against drawing conclusions about "the Soviet elite" simply from a study of *known* office-holders. There exists a "para-élite" of "non-public" officials or posts whose existence we hear of, if at all, by accident, and which are often just as influential as the "public" officials and posts that merit biographies—if not more so.[64]

5. *Main Thrust of Previous Career*

Finally, in this section an attempt has been made to classify the "main thrust" or "areas of substantial experience" of the careers in the sample, and to compare them with another sample of officials not engaged in nationalities work. The method employed was as follows:

Nine "areas of substantial experience" were defined, namely:

1) State: meaning Council of Ministers or ispolkom work, where a career showed more than one such post.

2) Agriculture: more than one post in agricultural administration, at any level.

3) Youth: komsomol posts, if the incumbent was aged 28 or over.

4) Ideology: any connection with teaching, journalism, departments of propaganda and agitation, etc.

5) Industry: more than one post in industry, from engineering to management.

6) Control: any work as a career officer in the peace-time army, for the KGB or MVD, the procuracy or the Committee of People's Control.

7) Cadres: any connection with departments of organizational-party work.

8) Finance: economic planning, sovnarkhoz administration.

9) Miscellaneous: diplomacy, the Academies, the trade unions, underground or emigré work in the case of Balts.

Each career was examined for its area of substantial experience. If, in my judgement, it showed substantial experience in one of the above nine areas, a mark was awarded to that area. (The average number of marks awarded per career was about one and two-thirds.) The marks allotted to each specialization were then added up and reduced to a percentage of all the specializations noted. This distribution of substantialspecializations is what forms [group A]. The percentages are based on the total of specializations observed, not on the total careers examined. . . .

[For group B] the same [is] operation carried out on a random sample of obkom first and second secretaries in the 55 ethnic Russian oblasts of the RSFSR areas where ethnicity would not be an important concern when making appointments. If there are types of experience that are thought to be qualifications for nationalities work, or the reverse, they should show up in the comparison between group A and group B. A word of caution about the comparability of the two groups should be mentioned, however. Much more work (with republican newspapers, etc.) went into the career data for group A than for group B. There are sectors of employment—cadres and control, for example—where Soviet sources are coy and reticent,[65] but where, nevertheless, facts can be unearthed if one digs deep enough. So some of the discrepancies between group A and group B may simply be a consequence of putting more work into one than the other.

The discrepancies within group A, that is, between Russians and non-Russians, are not surprising, and reinforce conclusions that have already been suggested. Russians are more likely to have had industrial experience, and non-Russians ideological experience. Russians are far less likely to have had "State" (that is, Council of Ministers or ispolkom) experience, but, as we have seen, the chairmanship of these bodies tends to be reserved for non-Russians in nationality areas. Most conspicuously, there is a very great discrepancy between Russian and non-Russian experience in cadres work, and the conclusion is unavoidable: where nationalities postings are concerned, the CC has kept a near-monopoly of cadres experience in the hands of Russians. Perhaps surprisingly, this discrepancy is not repeated in the field of "control," where equal proportions of Russians and non-Russians have past experience in the field. Perhaps, indeed, having been a career officer, like V. P. Mzhavanadze, or a security chief, like G. A. Aliev, counts as a qualification in the selection of non-Russian party officials. The discrimination shown in favor of Russians in the field "cadres" and the lack of any such discrimination either way in the field "control" offers, I suggest, an interesting glimpse of real Moscow priorities.[66]

Comparison between group A, officials in nationality areas, and group B, officials in ethnically homogeneous Russian areas, reveals a simple and clear-cut contrast. Group B shows a much higher incidence of experience in the economy—industry and agriculture—and a much lower incidence of experience in control and cadres. It is in the latter fields that experience is sought when appointing nationalities administrators. Considerations of federal cohesion and communal harmony must weigh very heavily indeed with the Cadres Department.

VII. CONCLUSIONS

1. The top party leadership in nationality areas is a carefully designed system in which Russian and native officials act as a check on each other. The Russian presence is built in for political reasons and is no longer a consequence of lack of non-Russian expertise. It does, however, seek to avoid drawing on Russian settle communities. The key to its power is control of cadres. The turnover of these officials is fairly rapid; they are doing a tour of duty.

2. The conventions of this system have been considerably regularized and strengthened since Stalin died. The dyarchy of native first secretary and Russian second secretary in charge of cadres is now the norm. This is not the same as strengthening of Russian control, but represents rather the strengthening of institutional procedures, in an area where, before 1953, equivalent functions would have been performed by the security police.

3. Russians in education and experience tend to be more production-oriented, non-Russians more "communications-oriented" with experience in teaching, ideology and journalism. This began as a function of education opportunities available, but one wonders if it may not become a habitual pattern.

4. Non-Russian party officials are employed overwhelmingly in their home areas. Russians move from place to place with considerable versatility. There

is obscure, but none the less strong evidence for a profession of nationality affairs specialist based on the Central Committee Cadres Department.

APPENDIX

Main sources have been: 1) *Deputaty Verkhovnogo Soveta SSSR* for 1958, 1962, 1966, 1970 and 1974; 2) *BSE Ezhegodnik,* "Biograficheskie spravki," particularly for the years 1958, 1962, 1966, 1971; 3) Election results to the RSFSR Supreme Soviet—most conveniently in *Pravda,* 22 February 1951, *Ivzestiia,* 3 March 1955, *Sovetskaya Rossiya,* 6 March 1959, *Vedmosti Verkhovnogo Soveta RSFSR,* 1963, no. 9, 1967, no. 12, 1971, no. 25, 1975, no. 26; 4) Selective but not comprehensive coverage of *Pravda, Sovetskaya Rossiya, Pravda Vostoka, Zarya Vostoka, Bakinskii rabochii* and other republican newspapers; 5) The series produced by the Institute for the Study of the USSR, Munich: *Biographic Directory of the USSR* (New York, 1958), *Who's Who in the USSR, 1961/62* (Montreal, 1962), *Who's Who in the USSR, 1965/66* (New York, 1966), *Prominent Personalities in the USSR* (Metuchen, N.J., 1968), *Who Was Who in the USSR* (Metuchen, N.J., 1972); these contain inaccuracies but supplement newspaper reading, particularly for the 1950s; 6) G. Hodnett and V. Ogareff, *Leaders of the Soviet Republics* (Canberra, ANU, 1973).

The 22 persons at footnote 29 are:

1) *Three tenures*

	Republic	Nationality
P. V. Uraev	Tataria, Bashkiria, Mari ASSR	Russian

2) *Two tenures in the same republic*

L. I. Brezhnev	Kazakhstan	Russian
I. D. Yakovlev	Kazakhstan	Russian
A. I. Berezin	Mordovia	Russian
N. V. Podgorny	Ukraine	Ukrainian
D. A. Kunaev	Kazakhstan	Kazakh
P. M. Masherov	Belorussia	Belorussian
F. A. Surganov	Belorussia	Belorussian
I. I. Bodyul	Moldavia	Moldavian
V. K. Krumin'sh	Latvia	Latvian
Ya. N. Zarobyan	Armenia	Armenian
Z. N. Nuriev	Bashkiria	Bashkir
I. P. Morozov	Komi ASSR	Komi
I. I. Sen'kin	Karelia	Karelian
B. B. Gorodovikov	Kalmyk ASSR	Kalmyk

3) *Two tenures in different republics*

F. E. Titov	Uzbekistan and Chechen-Ingush ASSR	Russian
P. M. Elistratov	Azerbaidzhan and Mordovia	Russian
S. D. Ignat'ev	Bashkiria and Tataria	Ukrainian
V. P. Nikonov	Tataria and Mari ASSR	Russian
N. A. Voronovsk	Dagestan and Chuvash ASSR	Russian
G. I. Osipov	Komi ASSR and Mordovia	Russian
A. V. Vlasov	Yakutia and Chechen-Ingush ASSR	Russian (?)

If account is taken of tenures held by officials in this sample but before the terminus post quem of March 1954, then four others (L. I. Brezhnev, F. E. Titov, S. D. Ignat'ev and G. I. Osipov) have held three tenures, and eight persons may be added to the list of those with two tenures: A. I. Kirichenko, S. K. Kamalov, P. K. Ponomarenko, A. S. Trofimov, D. S. Gladky, V. N. churkin, B. G. Gafurov, T. K. Mal'bakhov.

Notes

1. I should like to express my gratitude to Professor T. H. Rigby of the Australian National University and the Social Sciences Research Committee, La Trobe University, for help in compiling the data for this study.

2. Switzerland, Canada, the United Kingdom might be cited as examples; but at the time of writing the long-term future of the UK experiment is open to doubt. In our own time Yugoslavia and Lebanon have experimented in different ways with a similar strategy; their experience highlights its extreme difficulty; unless conditions are very favorable, leadership will be under the constant temptation to move in a centralizing direction.

3. In different ways: in high-productivity areas such as the Baltic the policy entails redistribution of profits away from where they were earned; in areas such as Central Asia, though it has improved social welfare beyond recognition, it may entail a worrying erosion of traditional values, authority and identity—particularly if it is associated with Russian immigration.

4. A. H. Brown, *Soviet Politics and Political Science* (London, 1974), p. 69 and footnotes 190-8 collects references to this; in addition F. C. Barghoorn, *Politics in the USSR* (Boston, 1972), p. 182, and David Lane, *Politics and Society in the USSR (London, 1970), p. 219.*

5. B. Harasymiw, "Nomenklatura: the Soviet Communist Party's Leadership Recruitment System," *Canadian Journal of Political Science*, vol. 11, no. 4 (December 1969), p. 493; G. Ionescu, *The Politics of the European Communist State* (London, 1967), pp. 60-61; Barghoorn, *op cit*, p. 180.

6. For instance, Y. Bilinsky, "The Rulers and the Ruled," *Problems of Communism*, vol. 16 (September-October 1967), pp. 20-21, quoted by several authors such as David Lane and R. J. Osborn since then; A. Nove and J. A. Newth, *The Soviet Middle East* (London, 1967), p. 116; R. Conquest, *Soviet Nationalities Policy in Practice* (London, 1967), p. 129; M. Rywkin, *Russia in Central Asia* (New York, 1963), p. 121.

7. Appointments on merit may merge imperceptibly with satisfying an "electorate" or promoting one's trusted personal adherents. It would be misleading to counterpoise appointments on merit with "patronage" as if they were mutually exclusive alternatives. Here and below I follow the useful discussion of J. F. Hough, *The Soviet Prefects* (Cambridge, Mass., 1969), pp. 173-7.

8. There are 14 of the former (discounting the RSFSR, which does not have a separate party organization) and 20 of the latter, all but four of them within the RSFSR. I have opted to include officials from the Karakalpak, Nakhichevan', Abhkazian and Adzharian ASSRs even though these lie within other republics which are also included in the study.

9. See Appendix.

10. In the first two sources named in the Appendix.

11. See, for instance, Hough, *op cit*, p. 15; G. Hodnett and V. Ogareff, *Leaders of the Soviet Republics 1955-72* (Canberra, ANU, 1973), p. ix; Brown, *op cit*, pp. 66 and footnote 175.

12. Thus L. I. Naidek is attested as second secretary of the Ukrainian party in *Pravda Ukrainy*, 27 December 1957, yet *Deputaty Verkhovnogo Soveta SSSR* for 1958 (and subsequently) refers to him merely as "secretary." B. A. Novitsky is described as second secretary for the Karakalpak obkom in *Pravda Vostoka*, 26 January 1971 and 6 February 1974, but merely as "secretary" in *Pravda* 22 December 1973. In the period 1959-62 the Nakhichevan' obkom organization seems to have deliberately avoided naming anyone publicly as second secretary; compare *Bakinskii rabochii*, 5 February 1960 and 27 August 1961 with similar reports of oblast party conferences elsewhere in the Republican press.

13. Reckoned from Hodnett and Ogareff, *op cit.*, *passim* (data concerning Union and Republics only).

14. For instance, in Belorussia for three periods between 1955 and 1968, in Georgia until the end of 1962, in Lithuania until September 1961 (*ibid*, pp. 65, 123, 239).

15. For instance, in Georgia (until 1964), in Estonia, Kirgizia and Tadzhikistan (until 1959), in Turkmenistan (until 1958) (*ibid*, pp. 123, 95, 183, 293, 319).

16. It deserves more emphasis how much the Soviet system of offices, ranks and spheres of duties is not yet firmly established and still in the process of crystallization. Students of the Roman Empire are taught initially about an "Imperial System" with its *cursus honorum*; but these did not begin to operate in anything like a predictable manner until at least the time of the Flavian emperors; that is, a hundred years after the nominal inauguration of the Empire. Before that, the titles and status of offices were fluid, and power did not necessarily go with office, but rather with one's access to (favor with) the Princeps. The parallels with Stalin's court and the subsequent regularization of

administrative structures need no amplification.

17. Compare, for example, the reports of oblast conferences and Republican Congresses in *Pravda* and the Republican newspapers between mid-January and mid-March 1971. Republican newspapers (unlike *Pravda* and *Sovetskaya Rossiya*) do name the second secretary. It may be, of course, that the second secretary is absent from conferences because someone has to be minding the office whilst the first secretary, with his more public duties, is "on stage!"

18. In an interview conducted by Mervyn Matthews, "Inside the CPSU Central Committee," *Survey*, vol. 20, no. 4 (1974), pp. 100-1.

19. One is reminded of the uneasy balance between a military commander and his *zampolitruk*.

20. *Kommunist Tadzhikistana*, 14 April 1961.

21. Hough, *op cit*, pp. 173-7.

22. I wonder what the Cadres Department think in private of S. P. Huntington's assertion that "during the past decade communal conflict, in contrast, for instance, to social revolution, has emerged as the dominant form of social strife in both modernizing and modern societies" (Foreword to E. A. Nordinger, *Conflict Regulation in Divided Societies*, Occasional Papers in International Affairs, no. 29, January 1972, Center for International Affairs, Harvard University). Certainly, if there has been any Soviet argument (in private) about cadres policy in nationality areas, events in Yugoslavia in and around 1971 must have strengthened the hand of the traditionalists.

23. First, if there were to be strong local objections to central policy; second, if inter-communal frictions rose. Allegations of discriminatory conduct by officials, unequal job opportunities in towns, the language of schooling, pressure for or resentment against migration are all examples of issues that might be the basis of this. John Besemeres, "Population Politics in the USSR," *Soviet Union* (University of Pittsburgh), vol. 2, part I (1975), pp. 70-76, surveys some of these possibilities in greater detail.

24. See previous note, and also note 3 above.

25. This is the most difficult tightrope for a non-Russian party official. When such officials are dismissed, the charge of nationalism is often made, but it is not always clear whether it is to be taken as seriously as some of their other alleged misdeeds; but for what seems like a clear instance of speaking out too boldly for non-Russian interests, see Y. Bilinsky, "The Educations Laws of 1958-59 and Nationalities Policy," *Soviet Studies*, vol. XIV, no. 2 (October 1962), pp. 146-7.

26. Akin to Whitehall's imposition of direct rule in Ulster.

27. This absence of women is normal for the upper reaches of Soviet administration and policy-making.

28. See Appendix.

29. Of the 123 non-Russian, all but one belong to the titular nationality of the republic in which they served. Hence, the use of the word "native" henceforward in this study. The exception is I. Yusupov, first secretary for Kazakhstan 1962-64, who is an Uigur not a Kazakh.

30. The list of known Ukrainians classified as "Russian" under this rule is: N. A. Belukha, D. S. Gladky (?), S. D. Ignat'ev, I. G. Koval', N. A. Shchelokov, V. E. Semichastny, Z. T. Serdyuk, B. S. Sharkov, V. N. Titov. It is an impressive list; five have also held important all-Union posts in Moscow.

31. The surest grounds for doing this are other posts held by the person: for instance, it seems to be extremely rare for the Chairman of the Presidium of the Supreme Soviet not to be of the titular nationality. A more dubious method is to work backwards from my conclusions below, that where possible cadres officials aim to have a team of one Russian and one native and to avoid two simultaneous natives in the top party positions. Almost all the difficult cases stem from the Autonomous Republics of the Middle Volga, or Eastern Siberia. The Russian presence here is centuries-old, and non-Russians (inconveniently for the pedantic ethnographer) often bear pure Russian names.

32. Two—the Chuvash and Tuvinian ASSRs—have had to be excluded for lack of firm data. . . .

33. Until 1956 Belorussia had a Russian first secretary, N. S. Patolichev. In the Ukraine, Armenia and Estonia, Russian second secretaries have been introduced in the 1970s, respectively, I. Z. Sokolov, P. P. Anisimov and K. V. Lebedev.

34. In the days of Stalin and Beria, the Georgians could have been added to this list; but their presence on the all-Union stage seems to have been much reduced since then. In fairness also, a distinction should be drawn between the Ukraine as a whole, and the eight West Ukrainian oblasts which came to the USSR in the course of the Second World War; attitudes to the Union in the latter (often Uniate Catholic) areas are likely to be much cooler than elsewhere in the Ukraine.

35. This is, of course, similar to the widespread use of emigré personnel in Eastern Europe after the war.

36. A. I. Bondarev, attested second secretary in Abkhazia in *Varya Vostoka*, 29 January 1955.

37. Z. T. Serdyuk and D. S. Gladky in Moldavia were, of course, Ukrainian and not Russian in the strict sense. There seems to be a preponderance on Ukrainians among the non-native officials in Moldavia.

38. In the Udmurt ASSR, 57%, Mordva 59%, Mari 47%, Komi 53%.

39. Percentage of Russians in the population: Karelia 68%, Buryatia 73%, Yakutia 47%.

40. R. Conquest, *The Nation Killers* (London, 1970), pp. 155-8.

41. *Partiinaya zhizn'*, 1976, no. 10, p. 16.

42. Summarized and evaluated by M. McAuley, "The Hunting of the Hierarchy," *Soviet Studies*, vol. XXVI, no. 4 (October 1974), pp. 437-501. I am here adding another small item to the impressive case she marshals for caution with the hierarchy concept (though I believe that, in broad terms, the hierarchy does exist).

43. XXIV *S"ezd, stenograficheskii otchet*, vol. I, p. 124.

44. P. A. Leonov in *Kommunist*, 1971, no. 18. p. 51.

45. With the transfer of I. I. Bodyul from second to first secretary in Moldavia.

46. For the claim to have reduced unnecessary turnover of staff, see XXIII *S"ezd, stenograficheskii otchet*, vol. I, p. 90, or *Pravda*, 25 February 1976, and the data of Hough and Frank cited below.

47. Hough, *op cit*, ch. III *passim*; P. Frank in A. H. Brown and M. Kaser (eds.), *The Soviet Union since the Fall of Khrushchev* (London, 1975), p. 115.

48. Hough, *op. cit.*, p. 71; Frank, *loc. cit.*

49. Bilinsky, "The Rulers and the Ruled," pp. 21-22, followed by R. J. Osborn, *The Evolution of Soviet Politics* (Dorsey, Ill., 1974), p. 436.

50. It is perhaps not irrelevant to remark that of the officials in this sample who stayed in office between 1952 and 1955 (a period of unusual turnover) more that three-quarters were first secretaries.

51. F. K. Karibzhanov, second secretary of Kazakhstan 1957-60 and a Kazakh, was in fact born and brought up in Omsk oblast. Ya. N. Zarobyan, second, then first secretary for Armenia 1960-66 may well, in the light of his early career data, come from an Armenian family resident in the Ukraine.

52. Principally from one of the Higher Party Schools in Moscow, but occasionally from one in a Union-Republican capital. Just over a quarter of the Moscow qualifications are from the Correspondence Higher Party School (*Zaochnaya vysshaya partiinaya shkola*), obtained while the student is in provincial employment, usually in a party post.

53. *Narodnoe obrazovanie, nauka i kul'tura v SSSR* (M., 1971), pp. 169-76.

54. *Ibid.*

55. I. R. Razzakov and A. I. Niyazov both worked in two Central Asian republics, B. E. Kabaloev and T. K. Mal'bakhov in two Caucasian ones. In addition, A. Ya. Pel'she worked in Kazakhstan before the war, and the second secretary of the Chechen-Ingush ASSR from 1957, O. A. Chakhkiev was a factory director, presumably somewhere in Central Asia or Kazakhstan, before that. A sprinkling of Armenians and Georgians appear in official posts in Central Asian republics, though none at the first or second secretary level.

56. Two Armenians (Ya. N. Zarobyan and K. S. Demirchyan), one Georgian (O. D. Gotsiridze) and one Karelian (I. I. Sen'kin).

57. And, of these ten, five are persons whose careers show conspicuous gaps; see note 11 above.

58. Five Russians in this sample have worked in three different designated nationality areas (A. S. Trofimov, F. E. Titov, P. M. Elistratov, D. S. Zemlyansky, V. I. Cherny). Two (P. V. Uraev, S. S. Apryatkin) have worked in four, and one (S. D. Ignat'ev) in five. Eight others have worked for more than 15 years in a succession of posts in the same republic.

59. "Elite Career Patterns in a Soviet Republic," *British Journal of Political Science*, vol. 4, no. 3 (1974), pp. 323-44, particularly pp. 328, 338.

60. Because of his presence at meetings in Georgia; *Zaraya Vostoka*, 15 March 1972, 29 July 1973, 6 February 1974, 15 April 1975.

61. *Sovetskaya Kirgiziya*, 26 April 1975. Similarly, S. V. Kozlov appeared repeatedly in Kazakhstan (*Kazalhstanskaya pravda* 22 February 1966, 11 March 1966, 5 May 1967, 7 February 1968, 10 February 1968) and was then transferred to Azerbaidzhan in May 1968.

62. Thus D. N. Yakovlev (Azerbaidzhan 1955-590), B. S. Sharkov (Lithuania 1956-61), M. A. Pimenov (Turkmenistan 1960-63). Their previous job was "*v apparate Ts.K. KPSS*," and that is all we know.

63. *Pravda*, 4 February 1960 and 9 January 1965, prints the obituaries of G. I. Chernov and V. N. Chernukha who had been in the CC apparat respectively 34 and 40 years, apparently without interruption. It would be valuable to know whether their names had appeared in print before this (and also what are the qualifications for a *Pravda* obituary).

64. McAuley, *op. cit.*, pp. 477-8, makes the same point.

65. Compare, for example, the careers of F. I. Kolomiets (*Deputaty Verkhovnogo Soveta SSSR, Bol'shaya Sovetskaya Entsiklopediya*, 1966), V. K. Marisove or V. I. Stepakov (*ibid* 1966). In all three cases, *Deputaty Verkhovnogo Soveta SSSR* glosses over periods of security work which *Bol'shaya Sovetskaya Entsiklopediya* reveals.

66. KGB Chairmen in the Republics are not exclusively Russian either. . . .

8

Ethnicity, the Personnel Weapon, and Neo-imperial Integration: Ukrainian and RSFSR Provincial Party Officials Compared

Mark Beissinger

Perhaps the two key developments in Soviet politics during the Brezhnev era were an increasing awareness of the need for technical expertise in political decision-making and the growing tenure of officials throughout the political hierarchy. Symbolized in the slogans of "scientific-technical revolution" and "trust-in-cadres," the policies have been viewed as the essence of Brezhnev's conservative, consultative, and consensual style of decision-making. They also had their reflection in the personnel policies of the regime. This article argues that within the multinational context of the Soviet Union the cooptation of specialists, high levels of personnel stability, and the local recruitment of personnel represent specific dangers to Russian dominance over the political process, for they aid the penetration of local nationalism into the party apparatus. A comparison of recruitment patterns among the RSFSR and Ukrainian provincial party secretaries over the past two decades demonstrates an implicit ethnic component to the personnel weapon that has previously been overlooked. Patterns of cooptation, patronage, and local recruitment in the Ukraine have corresponded to shifting policies towards the national question. One can observe a growing differentiation along ethnic lines over time in personnel policies both between the Ukraine and the RSFSR and within the Ukraine itself. These findings in turn point to the need to pay close attention

Published in *Studies in Comparative Communism*, vol. XXVI, no. 1 (Spring 1988), 71-85. Reprinted with permission of the publisher.

to what I have chosen to call the "neoimperial" dimension of Soviet personnel policies.

ETHNICITY AND MODELS OF ELITE RECRUITMENT

Studies of personnel decision-making in Soviet politics tend to resolve around three approaches: rational-technical, patronage, and authority-building models. The rational-technical approach focuses on the technical and managerial skills which officials bring with them to the office. It is based on the assumption, derived from convergence theory, that ruling a modern industrial society requires the recruitment of personnel who possess increasing technical skill levels. Within a communist context, this has usually been interpreted to mean a trend towards the cooptation of specialist elites into political positions within the hierarchy.[1] The result of this absorption of the intelligentsia has been envisioned as a "creeping rationalism" within the party apparatus (i.e., the penetration of rational-technical values) and ultimately its transformation into a technocracy.

Cooptation was a growing phenomenon in the Soviet Union in the early and mid-1960s. But, at least among RSFSR obkom first secretaries, trends towards cooptation were arrested during the Brezhnev period. Studies found that the number of RSFSR obkom first secretaries lacking professional training declined sharply. But simultaneously a significant drop took place in the number of years in which officials had worked outside the party apparatus. Although a large proportion of RSFSR party officials continued to have significant specialist experience before embarking on a full-time party career, a trend towards early recruitment into the party apparatus occurred.[2]

The patronage model focuses on the personalistic ties which bind members of the hierarchy into factional entities and which are used by leaders to consolidate their power. Clientelistic relationships can vary in intensity, ranging from pure nepotism to a loose alliance based on mutual personal interest. In all cases, they involve an exchange of services between patron and client (in this case, an exchange of tenure in office or upward mobility for personal loyalty).[3] By contrast, an authority-building approach assumes leaders take personnel largely as given and seek to weave together a policy platform capable of building support within existing elites. Brezhnev's trust-in-cadres policy fit well within this pattern. Studies of the RSFSR party apparatus during the Brezhnev era found that turnover among RSFSR obkom first secretaries fell and that a concomitant rise took place in their tenure in office. A distinctive feature of trust-in-cadres in the RSFSR was the extent to which it was linked with the growth of localism and regionalism, phenomena which were expressed in the career experiences of officials. A growing proportion of Russian provincial party officials during the Brezhnev period were recruited locally rather than appointed from outside. At the all-union and republican levels, clientelistic ties were loosened, as factions were transformed from personalistic followings into loose confederations of officials. At the provincial level, however, trust-in-cadres led to a burgeoning of clientelism. Within the RSFSR, trust-in-cadres did not mean the elimination of clientelism, but rather its localization and its debasement as an instrument of power-building at the national and republican levels.

This article explores the association of patterns of political-cooptive recruitment and centralization-localization in personnel decision-making with policies towards ethnic nationalism in the Soviet Union. Anthony Smith has defined nationalism as "an ideological movement" aimed at attaining or maintaining "self-government and independence" for a specific group which claims the status of a nation. Smith argued that ethnic nationalism as an ideological movement is born within and led by the intelligentsia. The failure of portions of the intelligentsia either to fully assimilate or to reform their situation results in the rejection of assimilation and a revival of ethnic identity.[4] In terms of the cooptation of a national technical intelligentsia into the Soviet political elite, the danger this poses outside of the RSFSR is not so much that rational-technical outlooks might penetrate into the party apparatus, but rather that as a by-product of cooptation *nationalist* outlooks might penetrate into the party apparatus as unassimilated or frustrated technical elites move into positions of authority.

Nationalism can run counter to localism, for whereas the former aims for greater autonomy from central decision-making, the latter seeks to gain greater allocations of resources from central authorities in pursuit of centrally approved tasks.[5] But a policy of trust-in-cadres pursued in the nonRussian republics on the same scale as in the RSFSR, with its associated patterns of local recruitment and personnel tenure, can encourage the development of nationalist outlooks within local elites. The attenuation of clientelistic networks at the all-union and republican levels that accompanies trust-in-cadres *de facto* insulates local politics from effective penetration by all-union and republican elites. Moreover, a fullscale policy of trust-in-cadres would encourage authority-building (as opposed to power-building) strategies within republican leadership, rasing the likelihood that republican elites might seek to bring ethnic issues onto the political agenda in order to gain legitimacy.

A considerable body of literature has pointed to distinctive patterns of personnel appointments in the nonRussian republics of the Soviet Union. These studies have noted that key positions within the hierarchy have traditionally been reserved for ethnic Russians, that nonRussian cadres have been promoted to all-union positions of prominence with less frequency than Russians, and that patterns of cooptation and tenure among nonRussian cadres differ from those of Russians.[6] Less attention, however, has been paid to the connection between policies towards ethnonationalism and patterns of specialist cooptation, patronage, and authority-building in the union republics. To the extent that the threat of nationalism has been a factor in personnel decision-making, one would expect patterns of ethnic representation, cooptation, patronage, and local recruitment in the nonRussian republics to deviate considerably from those found within the RSFSR and to vary largely according to shifts in nationality policiesrather than according to the simple logic of economic development, political succession, or authority-building.

The case of the Ukraine offers an interesting opportunity to explore these issues. For one thing, the Ukraine is the most strategic of the 14 nonRussian union republics economically, accounting for approximately a fifth of the USSR's population, its industrial output, and its agricultural production. One would expect that personnel decision-makers in such a situation would come under strong pressures to coopt specialist elites for the sake of achieving national economic priorities. Moreover, in the late 1960s and early 1970s, under the leadership of Ukrainian Party First Secretary Petr Shelest', the Ukraine underwent an unusual national ferment which penetrated deeply into the Ukrainian party elite. In the early 1970s, the Shelest' heresy came under attack from Moscow, leading to the replacement of Shelest' in 1972 by Brezhnev protege Vladimir Shcherbitskii. Shcherbitskii's assignment coincided with a concerted effort to root out nationalist deviations from the political, cultural, and economic spheres of Ukrainian life.[7] An examination of the Ukraine allows one to compare patterns of personnel recruitment during sharply delineated periods of rising and waning nationalist influence on republican politics. Finally, the Ukraine has been renowned for its role as a breeding ground for clientelistic factions.   Several national leaders, including Nikita Khrushchev, Leonid Brezhnev, Andrei Kirilenko, and Nikolai Podgornyi, used their career experiences in the Ukraine as the subsequent basis for building national patronage networks.

For purposes of analysis and comparison, I gathered biographical data for all obkom first secretaries of the 25 oblasty of the Ukraine and of 40 out of the 55 oblasty and krai of the RSFSR (excluding autonomous republics and oblasty) who occupied these posts from December 1966 to August 1985. For the Ukraine sample, this included 64 officials, for whom biographic and career data were found for all but one. The RSFSR sample consisted of 98 officials, for whom biographical and career data were found for all but six.[8] The breadth and depth of these samples allowed for significant comparisons of the changing composition of these two groups of officials over a period of almost 19 years.

FORMAL AND INFORMAL EMPIRE:
ETHNIC BACKGROUND

The Soviet empire has sometimes been likened to a form of "internal colonialism," described in some sources as a "cultural division of labor" in which a dominant ethnic group defines and regulates political roles in such a way as to exclude members of the peripheral community from meaningful participation in politics and in which the development of the periphery is centrally controlled towards the purposes of the imperial center.[9] The forms in which such systems of domination have manifested themselves, however, have varied. In his study of empires Michael Doyle distinguished between formal and informal modes of imperial rule. Formal rule has corresponded with annexation and governance by direct representatives of the metropole, often with the collaboration of local elites. Informal rule, by contrast, has been accomplished through local elites who are politically dependent on the metropole, but who are formally part of an independent political entity.[10] The period of Stalin's rule, with its successive annexations, its purges, its ideology of Russian nationalism, and its influx of Russians into governing republican elites, represents an approximation of the formal mode of imperial domination. The visible presence of the symbols and structures of Russian domination were akin to modes of colonial occupation.

The post-Stalin period, by contrast, can be envisaged as movement in the direction of a more informal mode of empire. Obviously republican elites in the Soviet Union are not part of an independent political entity and continue to be subject to hierarchical and political discipline, like all Soviet officials. But trends towards the nativization of republican elites and the granting of a modicum of independent administrative authority in comparison with the past indicate an effort to exercise political determination in a less overt fashion. For instance, in terms of ethnic composition, the Ukrainian party elite over the past 20 years has not been skewed towards excessive Russian representation. Rather, the Ukrainian and RSFSR party elites have ethnically been mirror images of one another. Whereas 14 percent of all obkom officials in the Ukraine from 1966 to 1985 were ethnic Russians, 12 percent of all RSFSR obkom officials during this period were ethnic Ukrainians. In this way, the Ukraine system typifies a form of "neoimperial" domination, a system of external control exercised increasingly through local elites rather than through a visible external presence.

The trend towards informal modes of rule in the post-Stalin period has not been pursued uniformly over time. When one examines the ethnic composition of Ukrainian and RSFSR party organizations over the past 20 years, one discovers some interesting variations which, at first glance, appear to have been only weakly connected with the vicissitudes of nationality politics. The number of Ukrainians in the RSFSR party apparatus reached its height in the early 1970s, largely due to the impact of patronage politics at the all-union level—i.e., an influx of ethnic Ukrainians with career ties to Brezhnev and Kirilenko. At the same time, Russian ethnic representation in the provincial party elite of the Ukraine had declined slightly while Shelest' was at the peak of his powers. Immediately after Shelest's removal, the number of ethnic Russians in the Ukrainian provincial party apparatus rebounded to previous levels. But Shcherbitskii's consolidation of power over the Ukrainian party organization was not accompanied by a major influx of Russians into the Ukrainian party apparatus and a movement back towards formal modes of rule. Instead, a marked trend towards nativization of the Ukrainian party organization took place. By 1980, in fact, ethnic Russians comprised only four percent of the Ukrainian provincial party elite. Moreover, the proportion of Ukrainians within the RSFSR party apparatus remained at high levels. Immediately after Brezhnev's death, this situation began to reverse itself, as a new influx of Russians into the Ukrainian regional party apparatus took place. In the years following Brezhnev's death, Russian representation in the Ukrainian party apparatus rebounded to levels akin to the early 1960s, while the number of Ukrainians in the RSFSR party apparatus declined significantly.[11] Thus, while nativization (in the sense of growing Russian representation) was pursued vigorously in the RSFSR in the post-Brezhnev period, trends towards nativization in the Ukraine were arrested and even reversed.

In sum, nativization in the Ukraine over the past 20 years can roughly be divided into three periods. Under Shelest', a modest policy of nativization was pursued inside the Ukraine, and all-union patronage networks favored the assignment of Ukrainians outside the republic. Under Shcherbitskii, a slight trend away from nativization was soon followed by a major effort towards nativization within the Ukraine. Shcherbitskii's crackdown on Ukrainian nationalist deviations paradoxically was executed by a party apparatus that was staffed by the highest proportion of ethnic Ukrainians ever. In this sense, Shcherbitskii effectively reconstituted a Ukrainian elite capable of maintaining political integration of the periphery into the prevailing system of domination. Finally, although the number of cases is small, the death of Brezhnev appears to have been accompanied by a drop in Ukrainian representation outside the Ukraine due to the breakup of Brezhnev's patronage network, as well as by trends away from nativization within the Ukraine itself. This is in accord with developments in other union republics in recent years, where the Russian presence has become increasingly visible, particularly in Central Asia. Gorbachev himself endorsed this shift in the January 1987 Central Committee Plenum, condemning "the mechanical distribution of places and posts according to national criteria" as a "vulgarization of the very idea of internationalism."[12] While the Brezhnev years as a whole were characterized by the further development of modes of informal domination within the Ukraine, simply in terms of ethnic representation the post-Brezhnev period witnesses some movement towards a more formal system of empire.

CO-OPTATION: THE NATIONAL FACTOR

As with ethnic background, the educational experiences of obkom first secretaries in the Ukraine and the RSFSR have varied considerably over time. In 1966, the educational profiles of the two party organizations were roughly similar. Over the past 20 years both underwent a profound change in the educational backgrounds of their members. In 1966, nearly a quarter of Ukrainian obkom first secretaries had a higher party education only and less than two-thirds had *vuz* degrees in either industrially related or agricultural specializations; by 1985, only one Ukrainian provincial party official had no higher education other than having attended a higher party school, and 90 percent had received industrial or agricultural vuz degrees. Similarly, almost a quarter of the RSFSR party apparatus in 1966 either had no higher education or a party education only; by 1985, that proportion had dropped to three percent.

This trend has obviously been a response to the need for greater technical expertise in a rapidly changing economic environment. It hides, however, some significant differences between the educational backgrounds of the two groups. For one thing, although both groups by 1985 consisted overwhelmingly of *vuz* graduates, the pace of change in the RSFSR throughout the late 1960s and 1970s was significantly greater than in the Ukraine. In the mid-1960s the educational qualifications of Ukrainian party secretaries were approximately the same as those of RSFSR party officials. But while the educational qualifications of RSFSR party officials were constantly increasing during these years, those of Ukrainian party secretaries at the height of the Shelest' heresy (1970) remained constant. Third, the fall of Shelest' actually corresponded with a drop in the number of industrial specialists coopted into the provincial party apparatus. While in the RSFSR the number of industrial specialists increased sharply, in the Ukraine under Shelest' those industrial specialists already in office tended to remain in office, while no new industrial specialists were coopted into the apparatus. After Shelest's fall the proportion of officials with a higher industrial education in the Ukraine actually dropped from 32 percent to 28 percent, while the proportion of RSFSR officials with a higher industrial education during these same years rose precipitously to 50 percent. Only in the early 1980s did the industrial qualifications of Ukrainian obkom first secretaries begin to catch up with those of their Russian counterparts.

Shelest's fall from power was accompanied by a significant increase in the agricultural educational qualifications of the Ukrainian party apparatus. The Shcherbitskii cohort among Ukrainian obkom first secretaries tended to be drawn from among agricultural specialists rather than from among industrial intelligentsia. The impact of this policy could still be seen in 1985 in the relative differences in the educational backgrounds of officials in the two party organizations. Whereas a third of Ukrainian officials had higher agricultural degrees in 1985, only 18 percent of RSFSR officials did. Moreover, the two party organizations demonstrated divergent trends towards the recruitment of officials with degrees in noneconomic fields connected with the supervision of ideology and cultural affairs (specifically, pedagogy and law). At the height of the Shelest' heresy, this group represented a significant proportion of the Ukrainian party apparatus (16 percent). By 1985 it had declined to four percent of the Ukrainian provincial party elite. By contrast, in the RSFSR the proportion of this group within the party apparatus rose to significant levels by the early 1980s (17 percent) and subsequently levelled off at 12 percent by the mid-1980s. Thus, it would appear that the fall of Shelest' was accompanied by a growing recruitment of agricultural specialists into the Ukrainian party apparatus at the expense of both industrial and ideological specialists, whereas the RSFSR party apparatus developed in precisely the opposite direction.[13]

In terms of the second element of cooptation (the number of years of managerial and technical experience before embarking on a full-time party career), the two party organizations also demonstrated diverging trends. A comparison of the average age at which Ukrainian and RSFSR provincial party secretaries embarked on full-time party, komsomol, or soviet careers shows that while the average age for RSFSR officials remained constant over the past 20 years, hovering around 31, the average age for Ukrainian officials dropped almost consistently, falling from 30 in 1966 to 28 in 1985. While on the average RSFSR officials had eight and a half years of work experience in technical or managerial posts before embarking on a political career, Ukrainian officials had on the average only five and a half years such experience. A large proportion of Ukrainian officials recruited since Shcherbitskii's rise to power began their careers in full-time komsomol work at a relatively young age and embarked on full-time party careers immediately afterwards, thereby foregoing any meaningful professional managerial or technical experience. In this regard, specialist cooptation, in the sense of hiring officials with significant professional managerial experiences, was on a much sharper decline in the Ukraine that it was in the RSFSR over the past two decades, and the pace of professionalization of party work in the Ukraine significantly exceeded the pace of professionalization in the RSFSR.

It is interesting to note that of the eight officials (all ethnic Ukrainians) who were demoted or transferred from 1970 to 1973 and who have been regarded by Western experts as Shelest' supporters, five (Sinitsa, Kutsevol, Grigorenko, Golovchenko, and Bubnovskii) had at least seven years of technical or managerial work experience before embarking on their party careers, a proportion which was significantly higher than for the Ukrainian apparatus as a whole. Shelest' himself qualified as a coopted specialist, having spent a large proportion of his career in industrial managerial posts in the 1930s, 1940s, and 1950s before embarking on a full-time party career. On the other hand, the other three officials associated with Shelest' who were removed from office (Kochubei, Muzhitskii, and Shevchenko) had no economic training or experience whatsoever, either in agriculture or industry, working largely as cultural or ideological specialists. The Shelest' coalition within the Ukrainian party apparatus was an alliance of ethnic Ukrainians drawn from both coopted industrial specialists and professional party ideologists. The turn away from the cooptation of industrial specialists under Shcherbitskii appears to have been in part a reaction to the ethnic dangers represented by the penetration of the Ukrainian technical intelligentsia into the party apparatus and the implications which this may have had for policies of Ukrainian cultural and economic autonomy under Shelest'. In the Ukrainian case, specialist cooptation and the penetration of nationalism into the party apparatus were viewed by Shelest's successors as parallel phenomena.

These distinctive patterns of cooptation are not likely to change in the near future as a new generation of officials moves into the provincial party elites of the RSFSR and the Ukraine. Data comparing the average age at which Ukrainian and RSFSR obkom first secretaries began full-time political work according to generation and on the number of years of professional experience according to generation indicate that generational change is likely to have a minimal impact on the differences between the RSFSR the Ukrainian recruitment patterns. The younger generation (born after 1925) in both groups is more likely to begin party work at an earlier age than the older generation. It is also likely to have slightly less managerial and technical experience in industry and agriculture before embarking on a party career than the older generation. This has been due to an increase in the number of officials in both groups who have been pulled into full-time Party work from lower-level managerial and technical posts at a young age—a pattern noted by Rigby for the RSFSR as early as the mid-1970s.[14] Nevertheless, the careers patterns of Ukrainian provincial officials regardless of generation more closely resemble each other than do the career patterns of the younger generations from the Ukraine and the RSFSR. Ukrainian officials, irrespective of generation, continue to have significantly less managerial or technical experience than RSFSR officials, and a much larger proportion of Ukrainian officials of both generations undertakes full-time party, komsomol, or soviet work before the age of 28 that RSFSR officials of both generations. The data point to an enduring distinctiveness between the early career patterns of Ukrainian and RSFSR first obkom secretaries irrespective of generational change—a pattern which emerged first in the early and mid-1970s in response to the dangers which cooptation posed for the maintenance of ethnic domination.

AUTHORITY-BUILDING, PATRONAGE, AND ETHNICITY: TRUST AND MISTRUST IN CADRES

Viewed in the context of "neoimperial" rule, the Shelest' heresy, with its aims of greater cultural and economic autonomy within the context of the existing system of domination, was not unlike other nationalisms commonly found throughout the post-colonial world. In many such cases, local demands for the nativization of institutions and for cultural and economic autonomy have been put forth precisely by native elites whose function has been, according to theory, the mediation of imperial domination and the integration of the periphery into the prevailing system of dominant relationships. In the post-colonial world, such developments have usually been associated with the rise of "populist" movements within local ruling coalitions that aim to build legitimacy through the extension of participation to sectors of the elite, the intelligentsia, and the population which were formerly excluded from meaningful roles in local politics. Within this context nationalism has been associated with policies of authority-building and the extension of participation in imperial peripheries.

Perhaps the most striking difference between the Ukrainian and RSFSR provincial party elites over the past 20 years has been their varying patterns of patronage and authority-building. In this respect the Ukrainian and RSFSR party bureaucracies developed in totally opposite directions over the past 20 years. In 1966, a larger proportion of Ukrainian provincial party officials were locally recruited than was the case in the RSFSR. Local recruitment continued to grow more common on the late 1960s and early 1970s under Shelest', but declined sharply in the late 1970s and early 1980s. By contrast, in the RSFSR there was an enormous expansion of local recruitment of obkom first secretaries connected with Brezhnev's trust-in-cadres policy. Thus, by the early 1980s RSFSR provincial party officials were more than twice as likely to have been recruited locally than Ukrainian provincial party officials.

While in the RSFSR clientelistic ties between Moscow and the provinces attenuated, patronage was localized, and factions were transformed into looser alliances, in the Ukraine, beginning with the fall of Shelest', clientelistic ties between the republican center and the provinces were reconstituted, patronage was recentralized, and personalistic factions were strengthened at the expense of authority-building. This recentralization of patronage at the republican level involved two processes: a shift in the geographical locus of clientelism; and a growing pattern of outside appointments to provinces with above-average Ukrainian populations. During the Shelest' period, the proportion of Ukrainian obkom first secretaries with some career experience in Kiev and Khar'kov provinces (known for their close ties with Shelest') had risen to 16 and 12 percent respectively. By 1975 this proportion had dropped to eight percent for both party organizations. The proportion of officials with some career experience in Dnepropetrovsk province (Shcherbitskii's bailiwick) in 1966 was only eight percent. It rose precipitously in the late 1970s and early 1980s, reaching 21 percent by 1985.

There is nothing surprising about this shift; its occurrence would be clearly predicted by a patronage model. But a patronage model cannot explain why patronage was localized in the RSFSR over the past 20 years, while during these same years in the Ukraine patronage grew increasingly centralized at the republican level. A closer examination reveals that in the Ukraine the centralization of patronage was used not only as an instrument of power-building, but also as an instrument of consolidating the center's hold over the nonRussian periphery. It is well known that the Ukraine has traditionally been divided into "right bank" and "left bank" regions, the former being characterized by significant Russian populations and having experienced high rates of Russification among Ukrainians residing there. Under Shelest' the local recruitment of cadres began to take place largely without regard for the ethnic composition of a province, the proportion of provinces with locally recruited officials being roughly the same for the two groups. But the fall of Shelest' and the consolidation of Shcherbitskii's power coincided with a marked drop in the proportion of provinces with locally recruited officials among provinces with above-average Ukrainian populations, while those with below-average Ukrainian populations continued to recruit their officials locally in approximately the same proportions as in the past. Thus, within the Ukraine itself trust-in-cadres was a prize reserved predominantly for officials of the more Russian provinces. Significantly enough, ethnic Russians within the Ukrainian regional party apparatus tended to be assigned to regions with above-average Russian populations. In fact, among the nine Russians who held positions in the Ukrainian regional party apparatus from 1966 to 1985, six were appointed to regions with above-average Russian populations, and five of these were locally recruited. Thus, in a number of cases, local recruitment, when it was carried out, meant the local recruitment of ethnic Russians in oblasty with above-average Russian populations.

Increasingly in the late 1970s and early 1980s, the more Russified provinces of the Ukraine served as a reservoir for cadres for the rest of the republic. In 1966, 56 percent of the Ukrainian provincial party elite had some work experience in one of the nine oblasty of the Ukraine with above average Russian populations. By 1980 that proportion had risen to 68 percent, and by 1985—to 75 percent. Out of a total of 31 personnel shifts over the 1966 to 1985 period among obkom first secretaries from provinces with above-average Ukrainian populations, only 12 (39 percent) involved promotions or transfers, while 19 (61 percent) involved demotions or retirements. By contrast, out of a total of 15 personnel shifts over the 1966 to 1985 period among obkom first secretaries from regions with above-average Russian populations, nine (60 percent) involved promotions or transfers while six (40 percent) involved demotions or retirements. Irrespective of the nationality of an official, career prospects for officials from more Russified provinces were significantly better than for officials from less Russified provinces. Apparently, work in more Russified provinces bred trust.[15]

Similar trends emerge when one compares tenure in office of Ukrainian and RSFSR obkom first secretaries over the past two decades. In both 1975 and 1980, 35 percent of the RSFSR provincial party elite had held their posts for more than ten years. In the Ukraine only eight percent of the Ukrainian provincial elite in 1975 and 12 percent in 1980 enjoyed a similar tenure in office. In 1975, 57 percent of RSFSR obkom officials had held their post for more than five years, and in 1980, 73 percent had. By contrast, only 36 percent of Ukrainian obkom officials in 1975 and 48 percent in 1980 had held their posts for more than five years. Total turnover among Ukrainian obkom first secretaries from 1966 to 1985 was significantly higher than for RSFSR obkom first secretaries. If for the RSFSR there were on the average 2.45 occupants for these posts for each province from 1966 to 1985, in the Ukraine that figure remained 2.95. (For the 12 provinces of Uzbekistan during the same period, the corresponding figure was 3.08.) When one looks at the ethnic composition of a province, however, one finds that Ukrainian provinces with an above-average Ukrainian population had on the average 3.00 obkom first secretaries from 1966 to 1985, while those with a below-average Ukrainian population had only 2.78 occupants. In other words, the response to the penetration of nationalism into the Ukrainian party under Shelest' was a sharp ethnic differentiation, both between the RSFSR and the Ukraine and within the Ukraine itself, in the treatment accorded cadres.

ETHNICITY AND PERSONNEL RECRUITMENT:
TOWARDS A NEOIMPERIAL MODEL

Political recruitment in the Ukraine over the past two decades can be understood in terms of two contending approaches to the dilemmas posed by Russian political domination. A "populist" policy of ethnic integration by means of authority-building under Shelest' was followed by a turn towards ethnic differentiation under Shcherbitskii through centralization and patronage. Under Shelest' an effort was made to recruit provincial party officials locally and to integrate elements of the Ukrainian cultural and technical intelligentsia into party politics. These trends were brought to an abrupt halt in 1972 with Shelest's removal for nationalist deviations. What followed was a clear movement away from local recruitment and specialist cooptation and towards the centralization of patronage at the republican level, which Shcherbitskii used for asserting control over the ethnic periphery. Both localism and cooptation were treated by the Ukraine's new rulers as dangerous phenomena not because they threatened a technocratic counterrevolution or gave rise to excessive demands on the center by local patron-client groups, but because they implicitly undermined ethnic domination by aiding the penetration of nationalist outlooks into the party apparatus.

Trust-in-cadres never materialized in the Ukraine to the same extent as it did in the RSFSR, for authority-building in a situation of Russian political domination encouraged the rise of Ukrainian nationalist sentiments in the Ukrainian party apparatus, as took place under Shelest'. Instead, trust-in-cadres was reserved for the more Russified provinces of the Ukraine, which served as a reservoir for outside political appointments to the ethnic periphery of the republic. The result was a process of differentiation within local elites in which those local nationals who were closely integrated into the dominant ethnic system through their career ties and experiences in the more Russified provinces of the Ukraine were used to mediate Russian political dominance over outlying areas.

This approach differed significantly from Stalinist patterns of direct Russian domination over local affairs. In fact, during the late 1970s and early 1980s a marked trend towards nativization took place within the Ukrainian party apparatus at the same time as policies of centralization, patronage, and the rooting out of Ukrainian nationalist deviations were perused. Ethnic Ukrainians were thus pressed into the task of exorcising Ukrainian separatist nationalism. Such an arrangement was directed against the more populist localization and integration of native elements into the political process that was pursued under Shelest' through a strategy of authority-building. It represented instead an attempt, under conditions of political stress, to reconstitute the peripheral center, to remake a coalition of local elites to act as a linkage and mediator between the imperial metropole and its periphery through patronage and a subtle ethnic division of labor. What is striking about elite recruitment in the Ukraine over the previous two decades has been the extent to which processes of cooptation, patronage, and authority-building have been shaped not by secular socioeconomic trends or by the logic of succession, but rather by the regime's attitudes towards ethnonationalism and perceptions of the dangers it posed for Russian political domination.

Viewed through the prism of the Ukrainian experience, the personnel policies of the Brezhnev regime should be interpreted in a new light. Trust-in-cadres was not pursued with equal vigor throughout the Soviet Union, but was rather a segmented policy whose associated benefits were reserved primarily for officials in the RSFSR, and secondly for native elites in the union republics who, in Moscow's judgment, had proven capable of demonstrating their loyalty and their "Russianness." Trust (in the sense of stability) was highly differentiated and varied, depending on the extent to which a hierarchical level was integrated into the dominant system of ethnic relations. Ultimately, the danger in this policy was that native elites in the republics, having solidified their dominance through extensive patronage networks and having been granted some of the benefits of trust-in-cadres, might eventually lose touch with the demands of the center and come to identify their personal interests with those of their regions. The problems associated with post-populist elites in the union republics have been excessive personal aggrandizement, burgeoning localism, and aggressive lobbying for centrally distributed resources, not ideologically nationalist demands for greater economic and cultural autonomy, as were put forth under Shelest'. National separatism is a disease of native elites pursuing an authority-building strategy; a decline in discipline is a disease of local elites who are integrated into the dominant system of ethnic relations and who rely on patronage and resource distribution as their basic approach to mediating center-periphery relations.

Ironically, although trust-in-cadres was perused less vigorously in the union republics than in Russia proper, in recent years the main thrust of efforts to rein in on what Central Committee Secretary Ligachev has called the "unchecked trustfulness and. . . lack of control" associated with trust-in-cadres[16] has fallen not on the RSFSR, but rather disproportionately on nonRussian republic elites—i.e., on precisely those whose primary role has been to mediate ethnic dominance in the Soviet multinational empire. The "interregional [i.e., interrepublic] exchange of cadres" and a trend away from nativization in the union republics (including the Ukraine) have now become Moscow's instruments for breaking through the insulation of the very patronage groups which Moscow's segmented policy of trust-in-cadres produced and which post-populist republican elites used for building power. Johan Galtung observed that an empire which is in need of exercising direct control over its periphery is an inefficient empire.[17] It is precisely the inefficiencies associated with informal modes of imperial domination which have led the Soviets on the path back to more formal mode of rule, as the Russian presence in the union republics becomes increasingly more visible.

Notes

1. On the concept of cooptation, see Frederic J. Fleron, Jr., "Cooptation as a Mechanism of Adaptation to Change: The Soviet Political Leadership System," in Roger E. Kanet (ed), *The Behavioral Revolution and Communist Studies* (New York: The Free Press, 1971), pp. 125-50.

2. See T. H. Rigby, "The Soviet Regional Leadership: The Brezhnev Generation," *Slavic Review*, vol. 37, no. 1 (March 1978), pp. 1-24.

3. For examples of the patronage model, see J. P. Willerton, Jr., "Clientelism in the Soviet Union: An Initial Examination," *Studies in Comparative Communism*, vol. 12 (Summer/Autumn 1979), pp. 159-83; Joel C. Moses, "Regional Cohorts and Political Mobility in the USSR: The Case of Dnepropetrovsk," *Soviet Union*, vol. 3, part 1 (1976), pp. 63-89; and T. H. Rigby and Bohdan Harasymiw (eds.), *Leadership Selection and Patron-Client Relations in the USSR and Yugoslavia* (London: George Allen and Unwin, 1983).

4. Anthony D. Smith, *Theories of Nationalism* (New York: Harper and Row, 1971), pp. 171, 230-54.

5. See Mark R. Beissinger, "Nationalism, Localism, and Cadres," in Martha Olcott and Lubomyr Hajda (eds.), *The Soviet Multinational Empire* (Armonk, NY: M. E. Sharp, 1988).

6. Teresa Rakowska-Harmstone, *Russia and Nationalism in Central Asia: The Case of Tadzhikistan* (Baltimore: Johns Hopkins Press, 1970); John H. Miller, "Cadres Policy in Nationality Areas: Recruitment of CPSU First and Second Secretaries in Non-Russian Republics of the USSR," *Soviet Studies*, vol. 29, no. 1 (January 1977), pp. 3-36; and Grey Hodnett, *Leadership in the Soviet National Republics* (Oakville: Mosaic Press, 1978).

7. On the background of the Shelest' period and the political reaction it evoked, see Yaroslav Bilinsky, "The Communist Party of the Ukraine After 1966," in Peter J. Potichnyi (ed.), *Ukraine in the Seventies* (Oakville, Ontario: Mosaic Press, 1975), pp. 239-55.

8. These missing cadres were recent appointments, all of which took place after Gorbachev's accession to power: Nivalov of Chernovets oblast'; Bakatin of Kirov; Kniazuk of Ivanov; Kuptsov of Vologda; Litvintsev of Tula; Petrov of Sverdlovsk; and Plekhanov of Kurgan.

9. Michael Hechter, *Internal Colonialism: The Celtic Fringe in British National Development, 1536-1966* (Berkeley: University of California Press, 1978); Michael Hechter, "Internal Colonialism Revisited," in Edward A. Tiryakian and Ronald Rogowski (eds.), *New Nationalisms of the Developed West: Toward Explanation* (Boston: Allen and Unwin, 1985), pp. 17-26; and Anthony Birch, "Minority Nationalist Movements and Theories of Political Integration," *World Politics* vol. 30, no. 3 (April 1978), pp. 325-44.

10. Michael W. Doyle, *Empires* (Ithaca, New York: Cornell University Press, 1986).

11. Among the ethnic Russians who were brought into the Ukrainian party apparatus at the time were first secretary of Donetsk obkom V. P. Mironov, first secretary of Ivano-Franko obkom I.A. Liakhov, and first secretary of Odessa obkom A. P. Novchekin. In all of these cases Russians replaced ethnic Ukrainians. The author realizes that these numbers are small. However, it is often the case that in an ethnically heterogeneous and politically charged environment, even small shifts in the representation of ethnic groups in elite positions are perceived as significant by the community at large. One assumes that the ethnic background of the first secretary of a Ukrainian province would be perceived as an important matter by the local Ukrainian and Russian populations of that province.

12. *Pravda*, 28 January 1987, p. 3.

13. The considerable fluctuations in levels of expertise in agriculture and industry within the Ukrainian party apparatus cannot be explained by long-term secular trends in the economy of the Ukraine, unless one argues that in the late 1970s the economic priorities of the government suddenly shifted from a primary concern with agriculture to a primary concern with industry. There is little to suggest that this was the case. Regardless of leadership shifts and the changing composition of the elite, throughout these years Ukrainian industry grew at approximately the same rate as Russian industry, while Ukrainian agriculture expanded at a faster pace than Russian agriculture.

14. Rigby, op. cit., note 4, pp. 20-22.

15. These findings are not affected when one controls for the economic performance of a province during an official's tenure in office. [T]he extent to which officials in the Ukraine were held responsible for the economic performance of the provinces was tempered by ethnic factors, with those from provinces with above-average Ukrainian populations being held to much stricter standards of performance than those from provinces with above-average Russian populations.

16. *Izvestiia*, 28 February 1986, pp. 3-4.

17. Johan Galtung, "A Structural Theory of Imperialism," *Journal of Peace Research*, vol. 13, no. 2 (1971), pp. 81-117.

9

The Ethnic Scene in the Soviet Union: The View of the Dictatorship

John A. Armstrong

It has been customary to regard Soviet nationality policy, and, indeed, the entire ethnic problem in the USSR, as a single, homogeneous phenomenon. A major reason for this approach is the influence of the early writings of Lenin (and his protégé Stalin), which treated the nationality problem in the Czarist empire as a single facet of the revolutionary program. This tradition has been perpetuated by the Soviet Communist Party Program.[1] Although this prolix manifesto devotes 3,500 words to the nationality question, it manages to avoid mention of a single specific ethnic group other than the Russian. In his Twenty-second Congress commentary on the Program, Khruschev devoted nearly a thousand words to the nationalities question, but apart from a passing reference to Ukrainians and Kazakhs, he mentioned no nationality other than the Russian.[2] Because of the complexity of the Soviet nationality picture, with its more than one hundred diverse ethnic groups, many non-Soviet commentators, accepting the facile generalization that it is impossible to deal with specific nationalities, embrace the basic Soviet framework by confining themselves to abstract, one might almost say philosophical, criticism of the avowed Soviet nationality position.

A failure to examine the general features of Soviet policy would be almost as wrong, however, as accepting these general features as the entire policy. Fortunately, the evolution of these general features since Stalin's death can be summarized in a brief examination of the Party Program and the speeches and publications associated with it.[3] The basic element is the stress on the development in the USSR of a Communist culture common to all its member

Reprinted by permission of Greenwood Publishing Group, Inc., Westport, CT, from *Ethnic Minorities in the Soviet Union* edited by Erich Goldhagen. Copyright © by Praeger Publishers.

nations. Eventually, sometime in the indefinite future, this process, the Program states, will bring about an effacement of national distinctions. Khrushchev described this process in a dialectic framework: After an initial period in which the culture of each nation develops rapidly, the "socialist" nations in the USSR will begin to merge. But, the Program emphasizes, a distinctive language is a persistent national characteristic. The dialectic of national merging will not lead to a composite language within a single multinational "socialist" state like the USSR, but to the adoption of the most appropriate existing national language as the "inter-national" (*mezhnatsional'nyi*) language of the socialist state. Much later, when such multinational socialist states predominate throughout the world, a world language will develop, but it is too early to predict what form it will take.[4] In one respect this argument is more moderate than the extreme views dominant in Stalin's later years, when Russian was regarded as the future world language. Still, the Program and its commentators stress the dominant position of Russian within the USSR. Individuals (or, in the case of minors, their parents) are free to choose their languages, but the "voluntary" study of Russian is warmly praised by the Program. A commentator called the increase (between the 1926 and 1959 censuses) in the proportion of non-Russians using Russian as their native language a progressive step, and noted with approval that non-Russian parents in the autonomous republics are demanding that Russian replace the local languages as the medium of secondary-school instruction.[5]

The reasons given for the increased use of Russian between the 1926 and 1959 censuses were, of course, derived from historical materialism. The rapid economic development of the USSR necessitates, it was stated, a common medium of communication. Since Russian was the most advanced language, the language of science and technology, as well as the language of the country's majority, it would seem essential for all Soviet citizens to learn Russian, at least as a second language. The predominance of Russian publications in scientific and technical fields is advanced as evidence.[6]

Another major point of the Party Program is that Communist construction requires the continuous exchange of trained personnel. Any attitude of "national exclusiveness" is, therefore, abhorrent. Khrushchev expressed satisfaction that the population of the republics was becoming more mixed.[7] Evidently—though neither the Program nor its commentators draw the conclusion—individual members of smaller nations increasingly will find themselves in situations where they cannot effectively use their own languages or train their children in them.

In proceeding from the generalities of the Program to a consideration of the operational features of Soviet nationality policy, an analytic framework is essential. A comparative approach to the complex problem is suggested by a functional theory. Usually, sociological discussions of functional relationships treat the society as an "equilibrium system"—i.e., one in which subsystems perform latent or overt functions in maintaining the system as a whole. Such an approach to Soviet nationalities would introduce two difficulties: (1) the equilibrium model is essentially static, while it is precisely the rapidly changing nature of the Soviet nationality situation which interests the analyst; (2) while functional theory generally assumes that elements of a social system tend automatically to maintain the system or to further its unconscious goals, the direction of change in the Soviet system is clearly due, at least in part, to conscious manipulation. Consequently, the functional framework employed here will depart from the usual model. It will be assumed that the fundamental objectives of the ruling Soviet elite are to maintain control of the decision-making process in the present Soviet Union and to expand the power of the USSR as widely as possible. It is further assumed that the elite believes (and is factually correct in its belief) that maximum centralized control and expansion of Soviet power require a unified national culture; that given the numerical and historical predominance of Russians, this culture must be Russian; but that, except in special cases, the elite is not primarily motivated by Russian ethnocentrism as such. Given these assumptions, the function of each element of the present Soviet system can be viewed not as the maintenance of the society in an equilibrium state, but as a contribution toward maximum centralization of control in the system and its maximum external expansion. Obviously such an approach neglects many aspects of the nationalities and their cultures, which are inherently interesting and (by any usual scale of values) important. But the functional approach appears the best available to bring out the relation of the nationalities and nationality policy to the dynamics of the Soviet system. There is some evidence that the regime understands the function of a nationality, but it is of course possible that in some cases the functional basis of nationality policies rests on tacit understandings.

Most available evidence on the nationality situation in the USSR is qualitative, consisting of literary and historical interpretations, ideological exegesis, and observations (frequently intuitive in nature) by qualified observers. Although the amount available has grown immensely in the past decade, quantitative information is limited and unsatisfactory in many respects. Nevertheless it seems useful to employ certain available quantitative data as *indicators* of basic trends and policies. Since the relationship of each nationality to the Russians is the prime consideration, the Russians (or Russian culture) will generally be taken as the standard of reference. Indicators will be divided into three classes:

1. *Indicators of the extent of social mobilization (change from traditional to modernized ways of life) of the ethnic groups.* As will be shown, social mobilization is a category directly related to the function of the group. It is also indirectly related to the group's function through the impact on secondary phenomena, such as the extent of Russification. Important indicators of social mobilization are the degree of urbanization; the level of education, particularly higher education of a technical or scientific nature, and the relative education level of women; geographical mobility; and access to media of communication.[8]

2. *Indicators of the specific objectives and tactics of Soviet policy.* These indicators include the proportion of schools providing instruction in non-Russian languages and of students enrolled in them; Communist Party enrollment; publication in national languages;[9] employment of members of the national group in official posts.

3. *Indicators of the degree of Russification achieved.* The principal indicator available is the extent to which individuals of another nationality claim Russian as the language that they customarily speak. Since the available census data frequently make it possible to distinguish age groups, urban and rural inhabitants, and inhabitants of territorial divisions, this indicator is especially flexible. Where available, intermarriage rates constitute a highly significant indicator.

It should be evident that the above classification of indicators, while analytically useful, is not definitive. Particular aspects of social mobilization (e.g., level of higher education) have undoubtedly been manipulated by the regime in many instances to attain its objectives, and therefore might be considered in Class 2. For many groups use of Russian is, as the official program claims, actually a significant vehicle of social mobilization, and therefore should be considered as a Class 1 indicator. These overlapping considerations, of course, merely serve to re-emphasize the importance of considering quantitative indicators within the broader framework of qualitative evidence. In order to do this, one must turn to more concrete examination of the nationality situation.

THE INTERNAL PROLETARIAT

Among the major functional types of ethnic groups, one stands out because of its frequency in modern industrial societies and the problems arising in connection with it. This type consists of groups that have low indexes of education, political participation, and income, but are socially mobilized in respect to geographical mobility and, to a considerable extent, exposure to mass media. An essential characteristic of such ethnic groups is that their members are easily uprooted by job (and presumably living standard) attractions in distant places, usually urban, though sometimes agricultural. Members of these groups perform the "dirty work" of society. In nearly all cases their work is unskilled and undesirable. Their material rewards are low and many show little concern for occupational advancement. Their housing is inferior, they are usually segregated by income even if they do not encounter ethnic prejudice, and their children's chances for education and occupational advancement are inferior. Obvious examples are Negroes, Puerto Ricans, and Mexican-Americans in the United States; East and West Indians in Great Britain; and Algerians and Portuguese in France. Borrowing a term (though applied somewhat differently) from Arnold Toynbee, I have designated these ethnic groups the "internal proletariat."

It is one of the great accomplishments of the Soviet system that an internal proletariat in this sense scarcely exists in the USSR. It is, of course, true that very low-skilled ethnic groups do exist there, but on the whole they remain in their own national areas, rather than following the crop cycle or doing the dirty work in the territories of the dominant ethnic group. In a few areas, it is true, there has been a slight tendency to develop internal proletariats. The rapid expansion of industry in the Urals and the Kuzbass during the early Five Year Plans and World War II brought considerable numbers of unskilled workers from the nearby Moslem tribal societies and from as far off as Central Asia into basically Russian cities. During the war, Central Asians alone constituted 18 per cent of the workers in Cheliabinsk *oblast*. They generally replaced Russians mobilized by the army.[10] But, as any visitor to the great cities of European Russia knows, the street sweepers, ditch diggers, and washroom attendants are Russians, members of that very disadvantaged group in Soviet society—the female sex. Possibly reliance on an unskilled work force drawn from the dominant ethnic group is a feature of a modernized society in its early stages. At a similar stage, England and the northern United States used their own poor for dirty work or drew on the Irish or other closely related groups rather than on racially distinct minorities.

MOBILIZED DIASPORAS

While internal proletariats appear to be a feature of late stages of modern industrialized societies, "mobilized diasporas" clearly accompany early stages of modernization. By definition, a diaspora is a geographic dispersion of a small minority of the total population. But few diasporas exhibit a degree of social mobilization sufficient to enable them to occupy a special functional position in a modernizing society. Those that do qualify as mobilized diasporas are highly urban, have high relative educational levels, have access to mass media, and are geographically mobile. While mobilized diasporas are distinct in culture (frequently because of religious distinctiveness), their attachment to their own language is usually not too deep. They readily employ the dominant language in their homes as well as at their work. Partly as a consequence of this linguistic ability, members of this group are especially skilled in trade, communication, human relations, and other white-collar occupations. Members of mobilized diasporas have a very high achievement orientation, and women as well as men are mobilized. Therefore mobilized diasporas may be extraordinarily useful in a modernizing society where these characteristics are rare. On the whole, members of mobilized diasporas fill attractive jobs. As the society becomes more fully modernized, members of other ethnic groups seek to obtain these positions, frequently before their skills make them competitively equal to mobilized diaspora members. The result is resentment and, frequently, discrimination against the mobilized diasporas. The classic example of the mobilized diaspora in Western civilization is the Jews, but the Parsees in India, the Chinese in Southeast Asia, and the Lebanese in West Africa also fit the model.

Considering the complexity of the ethnic structure in the territories historically dominated by Russians, it is not surprising that more than one mobilized diaspora has existed there. The overlapping and succession of mobilized diasporas have been increased by the long transitional period that has characterized Russia's modernization. In many respects the Czarist empire was modernized fairly early in the nineteenth century. But the USSR has not yet achieved a high degree of modernization in consumer goods, personal services, and rural transportation. Consequently, the functional need for mobilized diasporas has existed for more than a century. Given the occupational and education mobility of various ethnic groups and the absence of a strong ethic of minority protection, it is not surprising that no single mobilized diaspora has been able to fill this functional need continuously.

1. In many respects the most important mobilized diaspora in the nineteenth century consisted of Germans. While most Russian Germans were sedentary farmers, a smaller but significant portion were tradesmen, engineers, physicians, teachers, and agricultural specialists scattered throughout the empire. The Baltic nobility in particular (and some bourgeois) played an almost indispensable role in the imperial bureaucracy. They readily learned Russian and many converted to the Orthodox faith. The Russian nationalist views sponsored by Alexander III encouraged exclusivist attitudes jeopardizing the Balts' position. World War I eliminated them as a significant mobilized diaspora even before the Revolution and collapse of Russian rule on the Baltic. There are still over 1.6 million Germans in the USSR, who, since the deportations of World War II, constitute a diaspora, but not a mobilized diaspora. Less than 40 per cent of the Soviet Germans are urban. It is unlikely that the regime trusts Germans enough to allow them to resume the function of a mobilized diaspora. The recent formal admission that the wholesale wartime deportations were not justified, together with minor concessions on schooling and other cultural activity, seem designed for propaganda in East Germany rather than as a major policy shift.

2. In some respects the Jews acted as a mobilized diaspora even in the nineteenth century, but the sharply restrictive policies of the Czars prevented them from fully occupying this functional role. When the Revolution temporarily reversed these policies, Jewish qualities of education, skill in human relations, achievement orientation, and personal mobility made them very useful in Soviet society. Jews rapidly acquired important positions not only in trade, the professions, and management, but in political affairs as well. By the late 1930's, however, the position of the Jews was again in jeopardy.

Today the Jews have all the social characteristics of a mobilized diaspora. In terms of the indicators of social mobilization, they rank far higher than any other Soviet ethnic group. Ninety-five per cent are urban. Their geographical dispersion is very wide, and it is very probable that individual change of residence is frequent. Women are as socially mobilized as men; proportions educated beyond the elementary level (in the R.S.F.S.R.) are virtually identical (695 and 686 per 1,000). Largely as a result of the Nazi massacres, the number of Jews, according to the official census of 1959, has declined to some 2.3 million, or 1.1 per cent of the total Soviet population. Yet as recently as about 1950, they constituted one—tenth of the nonmanual workers, one-tenth of the students in higher education, one-tenth of the writers, one-ninth of the scientific workers, and one-sixth of the physicians.[11]

Unfortunately (Soviet sources are extraordinarily reticent concerning the Jews), data to construct other indicators are sparse, but all evidence suggests that even today the Jews perform the function of a mobilized diaspora to such an extent that the Soviet system could dispense with their services only with great difficulty. In view of the general shortage of skills in the USSR, the country could ill afford the loss of roughly one-tenth of its skilled professionals. The presence of the Jewish group has another functional aspect. It serves to demonstrate the alleged ethnic equality and well—being of all nations in the USSR. On the other hand, two sets of factors prevent the Jews from fully playing their functional role. Under Stalin, informal factors probably predominated. Stalin's anti-Semitic prejudices resulted in a secret purge of Jewish leaders in all aspects of Soviet life and, but for his timely death, might well have led to violent mass persecution. Other Soviet leaders shared these prejudices. According to Ilya Ehrenburg, Aleksander Shcherbakov was one of these, and other sources indicate that T.A. Strokach, a prominent MVD chieftain, even criticized Khrushchev for being too lenient toward Jews.[12] Very probably, irrational prejudice *among the elite* is still responsible for anti-Semitic policies. Mass anti-Semitism, on the other hand, induces official calculation that it is functionally useful to minimize the role of Jews. Khrushchev has argued that, as the level of education among non-Russian and non—Jewish ethnic groups rises, non-Russians inevitably demand a larger share of desirable posts held by Jews.[13] It is probably true that this pressure really exists. However, a regime that on the one hand does not wish to deprive the dominant ethnic group of desirable positions, but that on the other hand has no scruples about treating minority group members as just that rather than as individuals, will tend to discriminate against members of a mobilized diaspora. Moreover (according to a totalitarian ethic), Jews, particularly in consumer-goods distribution, provide convenient scapegoats for the notorious failures and inefficiencies of the regime. The liberal ethos and international associations of the Jews seem to present a threat to centralized control of totalitarian regimes.

The combination of a continued functional role for the Jews, dysfunctional aspects (from the regime's standpoint), and irrational prejudice among the leadership has led to the following basic policies in the post-Stalin period: (1) refusal to permit Jews to emigrate; (2) avoidance of overt persecution, but large—scale intimidation; (3) severe restrictions on elements contributing to Jewish identity including (a) prohibition of Zionism or other foreign organizational contacts, (b) unusually severe restrictions on religious practices, (c) almost complete prohibition of Yiddish cultural activities, combined with strong pressures to Russify Jews linguistically. The proportion of Yiddish-speaking Jews is now the lowest of any major ethnic group in the USSR—about 20 per cent. Away from the former "Pale of Settlement" cities, the proportion is much lower. The lack of Yiddish-language schools (justified by the "impractibility" of providing schools for dispersed groups) is a major factor in limiting any transmission of concepts of national identity; (4) discrimination against individuals identified as Jews. There is strong evidence to suggest that during the war quotas (of about 10 per cent) were set for Jews in higher education or certain professions,[14] regardless of whether the individuals wished to identify with the Jewish ethnic group or not. Apparently steps have been taken to reduce the proportion of Jews still further; (5) continued, though reduced, utilization of Jews, especially in areas where other trained and reliable personnel is scarce. Though there are very few prominent Jewish officials, minor Jewish officials in Belorussia immediately after the war constituted 6.1 per cent of the total (as compared to 1.9 per cent of the population). Even in 1962, Jews constituted 6.4 per cent of the Party membership there, and probably a similar proportion of the Party in the Ukraine.[15]

3. Although the regime has to a considerable degree prevented the Jews from functioning as a mobilized diaspora, the role of the Armenians suggests that such a function is still important in Soviet society. On a world-wide basis, Armenians have constituted a diaspora since the Turkish massacres of 1915. Within the USSR, the Armenian situation as a diaspora is not wholly clear from census data alone. Fifty-five per cent live in the small Armenian S.S.R. No other nationality assigned a Union Republic has such a small proportion of its members living in it, yet, compared to the Jews, the Armenians are highly concentrated. The 45 per cent of Armenians living outside the republic is largely limited to the Transcaucasus, North Caucasus, and Transcaspian areas, and shows no signs of expanding greatly numerically relative to the total Armenian population. However, the proportion of highly trained Armenians leaving the republic is extraordinarily high (19 per cent of the scientific workers and 13 per cent of the students go to the R.S.F.S.R.). Fifty-seven per cent of all Armenians are urban. This is a high proportion compared to most Soviet nationalities, but it is almost exactly the same as the Russian proportion. If one looks at the Armenian S.S.R. and the dispersed Armenians separately, however, the picture is different: only 52 per cent in the republic is urban, while 62 per cent in the diaspora is urban. The urban percentage of the diaspora would be even higher were it not for concentrations of rural Armenian populations just outside the borders of the Armenian S.S.R.

The extent of social mobilization is also different for the two groups of Armenians, but unfortunately there are few data on this difference. Certainly the Armenian population as a whole has a relatively high degree of social mobilization in terms of education and occupation. Out of every 10,000 Armenians, 94 are full-time students in higher education (as compared to 90 Russians); 430 per 100,000 are scientific workers (compared to 327 Russians); 30 per 1,000 are specialists with higher educations (compared to 21 Russians).[16] In the cities, indexes of basic education are almost as high for women as for men (391 and 394, respectively, for the entire group, 398 and 387 within the republic). Yet the birth rate remains relatively high.

Armenians are, then, in a position to act as a mobilized diaspora at least in limited areas of the USSR. Armenians seem to occupy a wide range of posts (although in relatively small numbers) throughout the USSR concerned with consumer-goods distribution, finance, and (to a lesser extent) industrial management.

Armenians also play a functional role in Soviet foreign policy. Apparently they constitute as high a proportion of senior diplomatic officers as any non-Russian nationality, including the far more numerous Ukrainians.[17] More important, the nation's remaining homeland and headquarters of the distinctive Armenian Christian church are located in the USSR. As a result, from the regime's standpoint, Armenians constitute a far more useful diaspora than Germans or Jews, whose areas of compact national settlement lie beyond Soviet control. Whereas Jews and Germans have been regarded as subject to outside attraction, the Soviet regime to some extent can manipulate developments in the Armenian homeland so as to make it attractive to diaspora Armenians. For a time this even held true for Armenians in the United States, and it is still a factor of some importance in Soviet Middle Eastern politics. There some elements in the numerous, wealthy, and socially mobilized Armenian communities have provided bases for local Communist parties; even non-Communist Armenians have at times shown a certain sympathy for Soviet policies. Recently the USSR appears to have been exploiting Armenian ability to get along in the Middle East by sending technical assistance to Iraq from the Armenian SSR.[18]

The linguistic capabilities of the Armenians make them functionally useful in Soviet society as well as abroad. Their attachment to their language is fairly high. Even in cities outside Armenia, among a heavily Russian population, the proportion speaking Russian as the native language rarely rises over two-fifths, though it has greatly increased under Soviet rule. On the other hand, Armenians readily learn Russian and Asian languages. From the regime's standpoint, however, the position of the Armenians is not without its dysfunctions. In the first place, there is a strong current of anti—Soviet feeling among Armenians, fostered by the nationalist Dashnak organization. Secondly, like all mobilized diasporas, the Armenians arouse resentment. Among the Russians this resentment seems to be mild, mainly expressed in jokes like calling rumors "Armenian broadcasts" or saying that the British Ambassador, Sir Humphrey Trevelyan, "is one of the two most important Armenians in Moscow." But the Azerbaidzhanis and some other Turkic groups have a tradition of bitter animosity to Armenians. It is probably significant that in spite of the large-scale experimentation in multinational schools in the Azerbaidzhan republic, none is reported as encompassing only Armenians and Azerbaidzhani children.[19]

Soviet policies appear to take these functions and dysfunctions into account:

1. Apparently no limit is placed on Armenians in higher education or highly skilled occupations. While Armenians still constitute a far smaller proportion of highly skilled professionals than do Jews, the Armenian proportion has remained virtually constant.

2. Publicized Armenian cultural activities are largely confined to the Armenian SSR. Publicized symbols of Armenian activity in the Azerbaidzhan and Georgian SSR's are few, probably fewer than the actual extent of Armenian cultural activity there. For example, of 973 books published in Armenian in 1963, 939 were published in the Armenian SSR; none were explicitly identified as published in Georgia or Azerbaidzhan. There were four Armenian-language newspapers with an annual printing of 12 million in Azerbaidzhan, but these constituted 12 per cent of the Azerbaidzhan SSR's population (corresponding figures for Georgia: two newspapers, 1.5 per cent of total circulation, 11 per cent Armenians in population).[20] At the more symbolic level, in spite of the large number of Armenian writers (thirty-six, or 5 per cent of the total) at the Second Writers' Congress in 1954, only two identifiable Armenians were included in the large Georgian and Azerbaidzhani delegations.[21] Armenian representation in Party and state bodies in those republics is also very low.

3. A relatively wide range of tolerance is accorded to Armenian national organizations within the Armenian SSR——particularly to the Church.[22]

4. At the all-Union level, prominent Armenians are given great recognition, and, in fact, occupy a considerable number of major posts——the ubiquitous Mikoian was long the most obvious example. Party membership (67 per 1,000 population) is slightly higher than for Russians (64).[23]

5. Armenian-language schools exist outside the Armenian SSR, even in urban areas.

6. Since 1953, published references to the Transcaucasus occasionally appear to favor Armenians over Georgians. Several reports have identified Georgians as black marketeers in a context suggesting they may be the scapegoats for other Caucasians.

YOUNGER BROTHERS

The presence of mobile diasporas in the USSR indicates incomplete modernization of the society. Similarly, the presence of large ethnic groups, which I shall designate the "younger brothers," is characteristic of a transitional society. Younger brothers are nationalities low in social mobilization, yet close to the dominant ethnic group in major cultural aspects. In terms of relative social mobilization, the younger brothers are rural, low in education and access to skilled occupations and mass media, and low in geographical mobility except when transplanted by the dominant nationality. Women are somewhat less mobilized than men. The cities in the younger-brother areas are relatively small, but contain large majorities of members of the dominant group, mobilized diaspora members linguistically assimilated to it, and younger brothers themselves, who gradually, over a long period of time, have been linguistically assimilated by the dominant nationality. The cities are, therefore, fortresses from which dominant ethnic forces sally forth to control the countryside economically and politically, and (through control of rural socialization and communication processes) to effect a measure of assimilation even there. As the initial stages of modernization are succeeded by rapid industrialization, however, the picture changes rapidly. Large numbers of the younger-brother peasants pour into the cities, mainly as unskilled labor, but with a growing educated stratum as opinion leaders. At this point, as Karl Deutsch has pointed out, two divergent developments are possible.[24] If the erstwhile dominant ethnic group in cities in the younger-brother territory is cut off from areas where large numbers of the dominant group predominate in the rural as well as the urban population, the dominant group may be swamped by the influx of younger brothers, and the assimilative process may gradually reverse itself. If, on the other hand, the dominant ethnic group in the younger-brother cities can draw massive reinforcements from its own compact ethnic areas, it may successfully assimilate the enlarged influx of younger brothers. Then, as urbanization proceeds, assimilation of increasing proportions of the younger brother group will eventually reduce it to insignificance as a distinct nationality.

One need not subscribe completely to Deutsch's analysis, which may well overemphasize the purely demographic side of the interaction. (Deutsch does not restrict the model to culturally close nationalities.) The power and skill of the central government, its policies, and the extent of organized expression of national identity among the younger brothers is also highly important. Nevertheless, in broad outline the type of interaction described here is easily recognizable. In some such fashion the French have largely assimilated the Provencals and the Alsations; the German the Plattdeutsch and the Bavarians; and the English the Lowland Scots. The importance of factors other than social mobilization and cultural affinity is shown by the Irish and Luxembourgers' resistance to assimilation. A relatively small proportion of the Soviet younger brothers—4 million—consists of the Finnic or semi-Finnic ethnic groups of the upper Volga region.[25] These groups are linguistically quite distinct from the Russians. But their low degree of social mobilization, the primitiveness of their original culture, and centuries of acculturization by Russian Orthodox missionaries have evidently made the Finnic groups, once they are drawn to the cities, highly susceptible to assimilation. The rate of linguistic Russification among the urban portions of these groups is high, especially among adolescents, even in their own autonomous republics, and very high in the adjacent Russian *oblasts*.

Far more important numerically are the Ukrainians and the Belorussians; the latter number 8 million, the former more than 37 million, making them by far the largest minority in the USSR. Both groups are similar to the Russians in their predominantly Orthodox culture and in their East Slav languages. Soviet theorists rely heavily upon this linguistic affinity to strengthen Russian influence.[26]

Ukrainians and Belorussians are far behind the Russians in higher education, with indexes running from less than one-half to three-quarters of the Russians'. The urbanization indicator is similar: 40 per cent for the Ukrainians and 33 per cent for the Belorussians, as compared to 57 per cent for the Russians. Given the vast extent of the RSFSR, there is no easy way to compute indicators of East Slav relative geographical mobility, but they would appear to be much closer together. To a large extent, movement of Ukrainians and Belorussian peasants outside their republics is the result of deliberate (often forced) transplantation by the regime. On the other hand, the extraordinarily large number of Ukrainian and Belorussian students (one-eighth in each case) who attend RSFSR institutions of higher education, and scientific workers who settle there (nearly one-fifth in each case), probably indicate voluntary personal mobility.

Furthermore, while the *degree* of urbanization is much lower for the smaller East Slav groups, their *rate* of urbanization has recently exceeded the Russian: 2.7 times as many Russians were urban in 1959 as in 1926; the corresponding rate for Ukrainians is 3.8, and for Belorussians, 3.2. In view of this rapid urbanization, the educational situation is puzzling. When urbanized, Ukrainians and Belorussians apparently acquire *basic* education more readily than Russians (however, even when the urban factor is constant, Ukrainian and Belorussian women, in contrast to Russian women, lag behind men). Educational attainment above the elementary level for Russian urban males is 363 per 1,000; for females, 375; the Ukrainian rates are 426 and 385, respectively; and the Belorussian are 411 and 399, respectively. But, considered over almost any interval and under any classification of highly skilled training, the proportion of Ukrainians or Belorussians has dropped, or at the most remained approximately constant compared to the Russian. The failure of these ratios to increase during the postwar as they did in the prewar years is largely due to the incorporation in the USSR of a large population of educationally depressed Ukrainians and Belorussians from Poland; but it is hard to understand why the smaller East Slav groups have not shown a higher educational gain since 1950 corresponding to their urbanization.

The proportion as well as the absolute number of Ukrainians in the cities of the Ukrainian SSR has increased enormously since 1939. The stage has therefore been set for the theoretical interaction described by Deutsch. Large majorities in all Ukrainian S.S.R. cities except those in the Black Sea, Donbas, and Kharkov areas now speak Ukrainian, whereas these same cities were Russian-language fortresses until the Five Year Plans.[27] Not only have the Russian-speaking majorities given way to Ukrainian-speaking majorities, but the proportion of Ukrainians giving their language as Russian has also greatly diminished. From this point of view, it would appear that the Ukrainian language has won out in the assimilation interaction. In fact, however, a large *absolute* number of Ukrainians coming to the cities adopts Russian as their language. The net loss to the Ukrainian—speaking group from urbanization is, therefore, well over a million persons. The loss as a result of emigration from the republic is even greater. Consequently (as one Soviet source notes complacently), in spite of the enormous annexations of Ukrainians during the war period, the proportion speaking Ukrainian increased scarcely at all between 1939 and 1959—from 87.6 to only 88.8 per cent.[28] Moreover, there is no general diminution in the use of the native language among younger age groups. While urban adolescents are somewhat less apt to use Ukrainian than other age groups, the tendency is very slight compared to Armenian and Asian adolescents. The Belorussians, though of course more Russified on the whole, exhibit an even smaller tendency toward progressive Russification. On the other hand, the rate of intermarriage between Ukrainians and non-Ukrainians (obviously mostly Russians) in the Ukrainian S.S.R. is now 18.5 per cent, an enormous increase over the 3.4 per cent (for males only) reported for 1927.[29]

The question of the ultimate assimilation of the younger brothers therefore hangs in the balance. If all could be completely assimilated, the Russian ethnic group would constitute 76 per cent of the total Soviet population. The proportion of the core ethnic group would not be much below that of such nationally stable societies as the United Kingdom or the United States. Members of the group would be assignable throughout the territory and range of positions of the USSR, thus making for greater flexibility, efficiency, and centralized control. Ukrainians and others could be used to support Russian control in Central Asia, an objective already accomplished to a considerable extent: Ukrainians in Kazakhstan constitute 8 per cent of the population, nearly one-fifth as many as Russians there; Ukrainians constitute 7 per cent of the Kirgizstan population (more than one-fifth as many as the Russians); and 1 per cent of the Uzbekistan population (one—twelfth as many as the Russians). Ukrainians have constituted an even larger proportion of the Party membership and apparatus in the Asian areas.[30] Because many early Ukrainian immigrants in these areas have become assimilated to the Russians, the contribution of the Ukrainian ethnic group to Soviet power in Asia is undoubtedly much higher. The Soviet commentator on nationality theory repeatedly cited estimates that about half of the European settlers in Siberia between 1896 and 1914 were from Ukrainian and Belorussian territories. He remarks that "in the eyes of the

Kazakh, the Tatar, the Kirgiz, the Turkmen, or the Uzbek, the Ukrainian or the Belorussian are to an equal degree Russian," and that before the Revolution, Uzbeks used to say, "among the Russians there are many *khokhols* [the somewhat derogatory term for Ukrainian peasants]."[31]

Though the functional importance of the younger brothers in general, and the Ukrainians in particular, is overwhelming for the Soviet system, the presence of these ethnic groups is dysfunctional in some respects. Alignment of East Slavs inevitably arouses resentment among the other ethnic groups. It also tends to undermine the consistent Soviet claim to be a true union of disparate nations on the road to a world Communist society. The younger brothers also have certain social weaknesses that limit their usefulness. Their relatively low rate of social mobilization and their seeming inability to increase their share of highly trained manpower have already been noted. One might expect a less socially mobilized group to have a high birth rate. In fact, however, the Ukrainian and the Belorussian birth rates are about the same as the Russian (i.e., about 21 per 1,000). There are proportionately fewer Ukrainians and Belorussians under twenty (33.5 per cent and 35.8 per cent, respectively) than Russians (37 per cent).[32]

Certain irrational prejudices on the part of the Russians also limit the usefulness of Ukrainians. Rank-and-file Russians often regard a Ukrainian somewhat contemptuously as a "country cousin" *(khokhols)* or kulak *(kurkul)*, terms which sometimes even find their way into print.[33] Khrushchev, when he headed the Party and state, was careful to stress that he was not a Ukrainian: "I can tell you that I know Ukrainian rather well, but when people speak it rapidly I also must ask them to speak slowly. Naturally it is easier to speak in one's native language."[34]

A far greater dysfunction, however, arises from the attitudes of the Ukrainians toward the Russians. A considerable portion of this antagonism has its source in pride in Ukrainian historical and cultural accomplishments made in opposition to, rather than in collaboration with, the Russian "elder brothers." Probably more significant, however, are events associated with the totalitarian policies of the Soviet regime. Collectivization is an especially traumatic memory for the Ukrainians. Rightly or wrongly, Ukrainians felt that this repression, carried out by Russian-speaking officials and coinciding with attacks on Ukrainian literature and a purge of Ukrainian Party officials, was a discriminatory national as well as a "class warfare" measure. As a result, Ukrainians, largely still peasants, are extraordinarily suspicious of Soviet measures affecting the agricultural population. The need to take this factor into account puts a severe burden upon the regime's economic policy-making as well as its nationality policy.

In view of the factors just discussed, it is understandable that Soviet policy toward the Ukraine has been unusually devious:

1. The injustices heaped on the Ukrainians during Stalin's rule are admitted. Many prominent Ukrainians have been publicly rehabilitated.

2. Symbolic recognition of Ukrainian importance has been accorded through the transfer of the Crimea to the Ukrainian SSR and the appointment (for the first time in Soviet history) of clearly identifiable Ukrainians such as A. A. Kirichenko and N. V. Podgornyi to high posts.

3. There has been a great increase in Party membership of Ukrainians and Belorussians. In 1952, Ukrainian Party membership, in proportion to population, was probably no more than 40 per cent of the Russian, and Belorussian scarcely more than 35 per cent. By 1961, each of the two East Slav groups had about 70 per cent as many members proportionately as the Russians, and, by 1965, 77 per cent (ratios per 1,000 population in that year were Russian, 64; Ukrainian, 49; Belorussian, 49). Whatever the increase in Party membership may mean in terms of political control, near equality of Ukrainians and Belorussians was an important symbol of the regime's desire to demonstrate that the opportunities of members of the three groups were equal.

4. In fact, Ukrainians (and to a lesser extent Belorussians) have been employed in key control and managerial positions throughout the USSR and abroad. This is concrete evidence that members of these groups are not discriminated against if they acquire the proper education and submit to Russification.

5. Considerable latitude of literary and historical expression has been granted to Ukrainians in the Ukrainian SSR. High praise may at times be heaped on Ukrainian cultural accomplishments, and even the purity of the language has been stressed, so long as hostility or overt aloofness toward things Russian is avoided.

While the above moves are designed to assuage Ukrainian feeling, they have been accompanied by these firm measures to promote assimilation:

1. Reiteration of the theme that the Russians are the elder brothers and teachers, and that the accomplishments of Ukrainian history have been achieved with Russian help. The anniversary of the 1654 "union" with Russia at Pereiaslav was elaborately celebrated as the beginning of Ukrainian liberty.

2. Continued emphasis on Russian in Ukrainian-language schools, and strong influence of Russian-language schools in urban areas in the Ukrainian SSR. Apparently, schools are set up in rough proportions to existing ratios of Ukrainian and Russian *speakers* rather than of members of the Ukrainian and Russian groups.[35] Consequently, if the schools do not serve on the balance as a Russifying agency, they can do little to draw Ukrainian children back into their native tongue. This is apparently in accord with the policy of encouraging parents "voluntarily" to choose Russian-language instruction.

3. Fierce repression of any organized manifestation of Ukrainian national distinctiveness, especially in the Catholic West Ukraine.

4. The transfer of hundreds of thousands of Ukrainians and Belorussians outside their republics, both to strengthen Russian influence in Asia and to promote assimilation of the dispersed Ukrainians and Belorussians. In striking contrast to the treatment of nationalities like the Armenians and Tatars, who are

not scheduled for immediate, complete Russification, virtually no Ukrainian and Belorussian publications are issued outside the home republics. No Ukrainian newspaper or periodical is published outside the Ukraine, and of the 3,321 books published in the Ukrainian language in 1963, only 4 were printed beyond the borders of the Ukrainian republic. Similarly, only 3 of 359 Belorussian books and no periodicals or newspapers appeared outside Belorussia.[36] Even if, according to the official assertion, only "compact" areas of minority settlement are to be served by a local native-language press, settlers outside the two republics were obviously being discriminated against, for in considerable rural areas their settlements constituted majorities. The picture is probably no better in education. While there may be some rural Ukrainian schools, there are almost none in the cities of Russia or Kazakhstan in which Ukrainians are numerous. Soviet ethnographical studies generally try to minimize the importance of older Ukrainian settlements in areas like the Kuban and Kursk *oblast*. Census returns have called the huge areas of Belorussian language (as a recent Soviet map indicates)[37] east of the present Belorussian SSR boundary purely Russian.

5. In addition to all the above measures, the regime has sponsored a very large influx of Russians into the Ukraine, especially into the newly acquired western territories. No doubt this influx is designed partly to increase assimilation through greater exposure of the Ukrainians to Russian influence, but it is probably also designed to provide a cadre of thoroughly reliable personnel in case the assimilation efforts are not successful.

STATE NATIONS

As compared to the mobilized diasporas and the younger brothers, the "state nations" are groups typical of the ethnic interaction patterns that have prevailed in modern Europe. This category consists of nationalities with strong traditions of national identity, including distinctive languages, well-developed cultures, and distinctive historical traditions. From the standpoint of their functional relationship to the aims of the dominant ethnic group's elite, however, both the degree of social mobilization and the ease of assimilation of the state nations are of secondary importance. The prime importance of the state nations lies in the strategic territory they occupy. The dominant elite (if it is pursuing an expansive policy in competition with other powers) must at least control this territory.

The ethnic groups in the USSR that most closely fit this model are the Baltic nations. While all were associated with the Russians for several centuries, they maintained distinctive languages and cultures which developed rapidly in the nineteenth century. During the two decades between the world wars, each possessed an apparently viable national state. The degree of social mobilization varies considerably among the three nationalities, but in no case is it very different from the Russian. Consequently, it is not surprising that an overwhelming majority of all groups, urban and rural, regardless of age level, use their native tongues. Moreover, children born after World War II tend to turn back to their native language at adolescence, probably in a spirit of national pride and defiance.

The Baltic nations occupy a position of extreme strategic importance for the Soviet regime, hence the regime is firmly determined to hold the territories. The Russians remain to guarantee strategic control (20 per cent of the population in Estonia, 27 per cent in Latvia, and 9 per cent in Lithuania, plus very large numbers of military personnel). On the other hand, there has been considerable improvement in the treatment of the native intellectuals, including permission for many to return from exile. Some relaxation of control of national cultural life has occurred, though any manifestation of "bourgeois nationalism" is rigidly repressed. Apparently the regime relies on the sheer weight of numbers and the pervasiveness of Russian culture to achieve a measure of assimilation, but is not overly sanguine on the matter.

The regime's view on the continuing unreliability of these groups (as well, possibly, as their aversion to the regime's agencies) is indicated by the low ratios of Party membership: 34 per 1,000 for Estonians; 32 for Latvians, and 26 for Lithuanians, as compared to 64 for Russians. Given the unreliability of the Baltic groups, the regime apparently does not try to use them for skilled manpower, except to a limited degree within the Baltic republics. On the other hand, there has been increasing public recognition of the superior ability of the Latvians and Estonians in orderly, efficient management of community affairs and goods distribution.[38]

In contrast to the Baltic nations, the Finns, Poles, and Moldavians are irredentas—fragments torn from historic state nations. The Soviet regime obviously considers the strategic territory occupied by these irredentas well worth the resentment aroused in the parent nations, which are in no position to react forcibly. As there are only 260,000 Finns and Karelians, the significance of this minority is minimal. The position of the Poles is only a little more significant than that of the Finns. The most compact and nationally conscious Polish minorities were transferred to Poland shortly after World War II. In the Ukraine, most of the remaining Poles (363,000) have never lived in a Polish state. Widely dispersed among the Ukrainian population, both urban and rural groups have for the most part adopted Ukrainian or Russian as their native language and apparently possess only vestigial national feeling. Both absolutely (539,000) and proportionately (6.7 per cent of the total population), the Poles are more important in Belorussia and in Lithuania (230,000, 8.5 per cent of the total). Until 1939, they had been the dominant ethnic group in most of these areas. The almost unrivaled low rate of Party membership among Poles in Belorussia (5 per 1,000) indicates their alienation from the regime. The Poles therefore are typical irredentists, but in view of their low degree of social mobilization, the weakness vis-a-vis the USSR of their parent state, and the fact that they are surrounded by East Slavs and Lithuanians, the Poles scarcely pose a significant problem for the regime.

The Moldavians live in a compact area on the border of the parent Romanian state, but apparently their national consciousness is lower than that of the Poles. The Moldavians' Orthodox religious background makes them closer culturally to the Russians, while their very low degree of social mobilization makes them somewhat susceptible to assimilation measures. Recently Romania has begun to refer to Moldavia as an irredenta region. It is hardly likely that this poses a real threat to Soviet control, though the extremely low Party membership (19 per 1,000) suggests political unreliability.

The Georgians have occupied a unique position among the state nations. Though the independent Georgian republic (1918-21) was consideraby more stable and successful than its counterparts in the Ukraine, Belorussia, Armenia, and the Moslem areas, it scarcely compares as an experience in national identification with the Baltic republics. The extraordinarily high sense of Georgian national identification probably rests more firmly on the unusual role of the Georgians under Stalin, when they shared the role of dominant Soviet ethnic group with the Russians. Attachment to the native language is high (although a decline has been noted in the very young age groups), and Georgian is employed to a high degree in publications and scholarly activity. According to educational indicators, the Georgians are very highly mobilized socially. On the other hand, their urban proportion is quite low, and they are strikingly immobile geographically. (Only 4 per cent of scientific workers and 7 per cent of students leave for the RSFSR.)

Like the other nation states, the Georgians occupy a strategic position. Also, they serve a functional purpose in the Soviet system by providing a considerable portion (2-3 per cent) of its highly skilled manpower. This manpower resource is not as valuable as it would be if it were mobile, but it can be utilized in the highly developed scientific and educational institutions within the republic. Georgians have a reputation of being personally pleasant, but the fact that some Georgians were secret police officials under Beria made the whole nation suspect throughout the USSR. In their own Caucasian area, Georgian officials displayed "imperialist" tendencies that tended to alienate neighboring ethnic groups. Occasionally, Georgians are blamed explicitly for what are probably general Transcaucasian tendencies toward petty speculation. Prompt measures to curb Georgian linguistic dominance within the republic, and retrocession of territory north of the Caucasus acquired by the Georgian SSR when Moslem groups were banished are signs that the Georgians are no longer privileged politically. While Georgian Party membership (72 per 1,000) is proportionately still very high, it has not grown rapidly in the past twelve years, probably because the regime wishes to eliminate the impression that Georgians are favored politically.

COLONIALS

Like the nation states, "colonials" are a common ethnic phenomenon in the contemporary world. By colonials I do not mean members of a dominant ethnic group living abroad, but a subject nationality sharply differentiated from the dominant group in cultural background, physical appearance, and degree of social mobilization. Typically, colonials are just entering the transition to modernized society. The traditional culture pattern of the colonials (frequently shaped by a religion very different from the dominant group's) is regarded by the dominant elite as a barrier to modernization. The colonial language is regarded as inadequate for modern communication. Since language, religion, and traditional cultural patterns are closely linked, the potential for conflict between colonials and dominants is great during the transitional period. The higher and more integrated the traditional culture, the greater the likelihood of friction. As social mobilization (especially urbanization and access to mass media) increases, resentment rises. Sometimes the dominant nation will try to stem resentment by symbolic incorporation of the colonial group in the dominant nation, by providing educational opportunities, and by assigning some desirable posts to colonials, but this tactic has rarely succeeded.

The relationship of the Russians to the ethnic groups of Moslem background in the Asian-European borderlands and in Central Asia closely fits the model just presented.[39] Failure to recognize this phenomenon in the USSR is due partly to Soviet propaganda, partly to the gradual way in which physical traits change from the Baltic to the Altai, and partly to the fact that the Soviet colonies are not overseas.

While groups of Moslem background constitute less than one-eighth of the Soviet population, they are largely scattered over about a third of its vast territory. It is not surprising, therefore, that the Islamic groups vary greatly in traditional culture and language. It is impossible to discuss these factors in detail here, but some of the salient contemporary characteristics of the major groups must be noted.

1. The second largest group numerically, the Tatars, have played an extraordinarily important role in the Russian-colonial relationship. The Tatars are very widely dispersed—more so, in fact, than any major Soviet ethnic groups except the Jews and Germans. The Tatar levels of education and urbanization are much below the Russian, and not much higher than those of the other Moslem groups, but in the years preceding and immediately following the Revolution, Tatar social mobilization was much higher than that of the Moslem groups. At the same time, the principal Tatar group, the Volga or Kazan Tatars, had developed a high degree of national consciousness. Partly out of resentment toward Orthodox missionary and Czarist Russifying activities, many Volga Tatars at first sided with the Bolsheviks. Though this honeymoon was brief, Tatar services in propagating Communism and raising educational levels among the Central Asian and steppe Moslem groups (most of whom speak

related Turkic languages) were very important, as Soviet sources recognize even today. In 1926, there were, for example, 26,000 Volga Tatars in Uzbekistan; in 1939, 159,000; and today, 400,000, including a very significant portion of the urban population.[40]

In view of their wide dispersion, it is not surprising that a considerable number of Tatars have become linguistically assimilated under Soviet rule (in 1926, the proportion of Russian-speaking Tatar was still negligible), especially when they live in thoroughly Russian ethnic environments. Tatar adolescents tend to abandon their native tongue. On the other hand, the Soviet press has frequently criticized "nationalist deviations" in the substantial Tatar literary and historiographical output. Separate religious headquarters have been maintained in Ufa for those Tatars (and related Bashkirs) who still practice Islam.[41] Furthermore, the Tatars in dispersion enjoy the extraordinary privilege of schools using their own language. Slightly less than half the Tatar-language schools are located in the Tatar ASSR (the proportion of these schools parallels the proportion of Tatars in the total ASSR population). There are 1,450 Tatar-language schools in Bashkiria, 120 in Orenburg *oblast,* 150 in Tiumen *oblast*, but none for the large Tatar population in Uzbekistan.[42]

2. Azerbaidzhanis, though far less mobile geographically, have much higher educational and urbanization indexes than the Tatars. The Azerbaidzhani position grew out of the rapid industrialization of their petroleum-rich country before the Revolution, and the native population's exposure to a large immigration of socially mobilized Russians and Armenians. Culturally, however, the Azerbaidzhanis (traditionally Shi'a Moslems) are not as close to other Turkic-speaking groups as are the Tatars. This factor, together with their low geographic mobility has apparently restricted their use as a vehicle of Russian influence. A relatively sedentary group, the Azerbaidzhanis have preserved use of their own language to a greater extent than the Tatars, though adolescents are somewhat prone to abandon it in favor of Russian.

3. The Turkic-speaking Bashkirs, Kazakhs, and Kirgizes were, until fairly recently, nomadic. Though these groups are less urban than the more sedentary Uzbeks and Turkmens, the Kazakhs and Kirgizes already have about as many scientists and specialists with higher education in proportion to their total populations, and a significantly higher proportion of students in higher education. In many cases, however, Central Asian students and scientific workers tend to an overwhelming extent to remain in their home territories. Part of this trend is undoubtedly due to the very large proportion of East Slavs living among the erstwhile nomads (46 per cent in Bashkiria, 37 per cent in Kirgizia, and 52 per cent in Kazakhstan). Quite possibly the regime has deliberately accelerated the educational progress of the former nomads (as it almost certainly has their entry into the Party). The fact remains that social mobilization appears now to be progressing somewhat faster and more smoothly

among the ex-nomads, with their relatively primitive cultural background, than among the sedentary peoples.

4. One possible reason for the sedentary peoples' relative lag is that Moslem culture in their cases developed in a stricter, more fanatical form than among the nomads. Tatar urban women have the same access to education as men, but in all other groups there are distinct differences. In addition, the oasis Moslems seem to have clung more closely to other forms of maintaining the inferior status of women, such as bride purchase and kidnapping. From the regime's standpoint, these practices and attitudes are undesirable not only because they have religious roots, but because they waste work time, prevent economic development, and above all, adversely affect the recruitment of women into the skilled labor market. For example, only seven Uzbek girls graduated from the Tashkent Textile Institute between 1943 and 1953.[43] The situation is especially interesting as far as marriages are concerned. In 1959, 5.4 per cent of the families in Tashkent (the most urbanized) were Russo-Uzbek, and the rate of intermarriage in 1958 was about the same. Only one—fourth of the brides in these mixed marriages were Uzbek. The Soviet commentator notes with satisfaction that the Russian wives exerted a strong cultural influence in the mixed families.[44]

5. The small Moslem groups in the North Caucasus are divided between those who were banished en masse by Stalin at the end of World War I and those who, more loyal to the Soviet regime, were allowed to remain. In the former category, the Chechens are most numerous; while the Kabardins are not the most numerous of the more loyal groups, they can be taken as fairly typical. The degree of social mobilization among the Chechens is very low. This is due partly to the frightful losses the Chechens suffered in their years of banishment (only 19 per cent of the present population is in the thirty to fifty-nine age group). But it is also due to the Chechens' very conservative, clannish traditions, which accentuate the attitudes toward women described above. These same national traditions, of course, have been instrumental in fostering the fierce resistance to Russification demonstrated by the Chechen adherence to the native language.

Some of the functional aspects of the colonial ethnic groups are peculiar to each of these varied nationalities. Nevertheless, some important over-all functions can be identified: (1) In terms of sheer manpower, the colonials are important to the Soviet system, since they constitute about 12 per cent of the population. Because of their high relative birth rates, their value as a source of labor will increase. This value will also be increased by the growing level of education, though at present the colonials are much less useful as skilled manpower than the Europeans. On the other hand, on farms in the warmer Central Asian oases and parts of Azerbaidzhan they are able to produce some products more efficiently than is the case in other parts of the USSR. (2) Strategically, the territories inhabited by the colonials provided a vast *glacis* vis-à-vis both China and the American CENTO allies. (3) The claim of the USSR of being a truly multinational and multiracial society rather than merely a European federation depends upon continued, and at least ostensibly happy, association of the colonials in the USSR.

There are, on the other hand, a number of important general dysfunctions the regime must take into account: (1) The effort to increase the colonials' level of social mobilization is expensive in proportion to their contribution to the Soviet gross national product. [45] (2) Almost all the groups present strong traditional barriers to the full utilization of their labor. Their treatment of women also is a standing defiance of one of the major tenets of Communist ideology—however much it may be covertly flouted in other parts of the USSR . . . . (3) While Russians (and other Soviet Europeans) do not exhibit much prejudice toward Asians, the two groups remain aloof, especially as far as intermarriage is concerned. (4) In view of the high relative birth rate of the Central Asians, it is questionable whether the regime can promote assimilation and control there (as it has in the past) by increasing the European portion of the population. A possible course (also advantageous in view of labor shortages in Europe resulting from low birth rates) would be to transfer Asians to the metropolitan areas—but this would create an internal proletariat, with all its disadvantages. [46]

The policies adopted by the regime to deal with the complex functional position of the colonials have been equally complex. Some of these policies are designed to conciliate the colonials and to modernize them in a way that will bring them material benefits as well to as to make them more productive. (1) Strong efforts have been made to achieve rapid social mobilization. Very likely this has often involved giving the colonials preferential treatment, at least in funds. (2) The impression that the regime offers equal chances to colonials is fostered by strong efforts to enroll them in the Party. The Azerbaidzhani, Kazakh, and Kirgiz membership rates (48, 50, and 36 per 1,000, respectively) are not much below the Russian (64). The sedentary Central Asian groups have lower rates (Uzbek, 32; Turkmen, 32; Tadzhik, 30), but this may be due in part to resistance of these groups to association with Russians. (3) The impression of equality of opportunity is enhanced by giving high posts to symbolic figures such as M.D. Bagirov and N.A. Mukhitdinov. At present no colonial occupies a truly major post, while many important positions in colonial areas are held by Europeans. One Soviet source, however, emphasizes the importance of Asians (60.5 percent) and Uzbeks in particular (43 per cent) in the Uzbekistan MVD. [47] (4) Stalin's injustice in expelling Moslem Caucasian groups was publicly admitted in 1957 and the survivors returned to their homelands, which were again given administrative recognition. The Crimean Tatars were not, however, returned to their more strategic homeland. (5) Policies in relation to language and culture are more ambiguous. Probably the assurance (often expressed by regime spokesmen of Moslem background) that national languages will persist and be further developed is sincere. The firm adherence of the colonial groups to their own languages has probably convinced the regime that outright Russification would be a very long and costly process. Furthermore, as Soviet writers point out, it is simply impracticable to educate children in a language other than their native one if that language is as dissimilar to Russian as the Turkic tongues are. In some areas a considerable proportion of colonial children are enrolled in Russian-language schools (27 per cent in Kazakhstan), [48] but the regime is disturbed by the virtually complete segregation of colonial and European school children (99 per cent of Uzbek children in Uzbekistan attend Uzbek-language classes in which there are practically no Europeans). Conversely, 90 per cent of the students in Uzbekistan with Russian as the language of instruction are of European background. In an effort to overcome this segregation, some Uzbek S.S.R. schools (with over half the enrollment in Tashkent *oblast* outside Tashkent City) have been converted into dual or multilanguage schools. Ordinarily the children receive their instruction in Russian or Uzbek (or occasionally in another Central Asian language) in accordance with their backgrounds, but, a Soviet commentator notes, "in the process of daily study, occupation, and play, the children get accustomed to Russian." By 1960 nearly 10 per cent of the schools in the Azerbaidzhan Republic had been reorganized on this basis. [49] The process is hardly likely to assimilate many Asians, but it may enable them to use Russian effectively. The fact that many colonials cannot now do so poses an additional barrier to their full utilization. In Asia, the regime's avowed aim of bilingualism has very concrete meaning. Since Stalin's death there has been a considerable relaxation of cultural controls. Sometimes even Russians urge colonials to exploit their rich literary lore and to write. [50] The requirement that historiography should unfailingly praise everything associated with Russia has been somewhat modified. It is now possible to point out that Czarist colonizers used deplorable methods, but the end result—attachment of colonial areas to Russia—must still be acclaimed. [51] Khrushchev himself emphasized that the "voluntary" incorporation of Kirgizia into the Russian Empire had been a "progressive" step. [52] The role of Russian as a transmitter of all the benefits of culture is constantly stressed and colonials are urged to borrow new terms from it rather than adapt old words from their own languages. [53] Conversely, the millennium-old ties of the colonials with the great Middle Eastern cultures are ignored or minimized. [54]

Some policies pursued by the regime are even more definitely aimed at breaking down elements of the colonial people's traditions which stand in the way of Soviet aims: (1) The attacks on Islam, while falling short of those directed at Judaism and the Ukrainian Catholic Church, are very sharp. As suggested earlier, they are especially directed against elements associated with Islam which have stood in the way of full social mobilization. (2) The policy of divide and conquer has been assiduously pursued by the regime ever since the Civil War. In the great oases of Central Asia, artificial divisions among republics were created on a linguistic basis, whereas historically (and sociologically), the division has been between the sedentary "Sarts" and the nomads. A similar multiplicity of divisions was created in the North Caucasus. The Bashkirs, who were well on the way to Tatarization, have been "revived" as a separate nation. Now, however, the regime considers it safe, and more efficient, to promote change and consolidation. Important irrigable districts of Kazakhstan have been transferred to the Uzbek SSR. This move is praised as being in accord with Lenin's statement that nationality is merely one, and not the most important, principle for territorial division.[55] Experimentation with a council of national economy and a Communist Party Bureau for Central Asia (not including Kazakhstan) is obviously in accord with that concept. (3) As in other areas, Russians (and other Europeans, mainly East Slav) have been poured into the territories of the colonial nationalities to further assimilation, to promote modernization, and to serve as a bulwark of Soviet control. (4) Beyond all these policies aimed at *securing* the colonial areas and *exploiting* their resources are the policies directed at using them as a springboard for influencing the Asian and African world. Yet the Soviet regime is obviously uneasy concerning this tactic. Up to 1959, only two Asians were employed at the diplomatic first secretary level or above, both in minor countries.[56] In his speech in Kirgizia, Khrushchev boasted that he and his audience were in the "very center of Asia," but he was careful to point out that the USSR also had a claim to be Asian because of the *Russian* settlement of Vladivostok. Obviously the quarrel with China lay behind these nuances, but long before this quarrel was avowed the Soviet regime hedged on its use of Asians to appeal to Asians. Most of the delegates to the October, 1958, "Conference of Writers of the Countries of Asia and Africa" in Tashkent, were from Asia and Africa, with a few European and white American guests. The Soviet contingent, on the other hand, included many delegates of European background (as well as Georgians and Armenians, who were only geographically "Asian"). An obscure Dagestani, very likely inspired by the regime, emphasized that this distinction between continents was insignificant:

> My people live at the foot of the Caucasian ridge that divides Europe and Asia. But this ridge cannot separate the culture of Europe and Asia, of East and West. Peoples do not oppose one another in their literature.

> Mankind would be a thousand times poorer spiritually if the great culture of the West and the East did not feed him with its two breasts, just as a mother feeds her children. Possibly there is a border between East and West, but there is no border between their culture and literature.[57]

While awaiting more precise studies, it is the hope of the author that the functional examination of Soviet nationalities has provided a perspective for analyzing the broad policy statements that have characterized the regime's over-all approach to the nationality question. The denial of a proximate intention to merge non-Russian groups with the Russians linguistically is meaningful as far as the colonials and the state nations go, but dubious for the mobilized diasporas and the younger brothers, who appear to be scheduled for Russification. The other nationalities probably would satisfy the regime, for the time being at least, if they could use Russian fluently and willingly in occupational and political activity, retaining their native languages for use in the home and limited cultural pursuits.[58] The opposition to national aloofness and stress on the mingling of populations, on the other hand, fit in with the effort to provide strong Russian or Russified cadres in all strategic regions. Intermingling of populations is also an essential aspect of the process of isolating and Russifying major elements of the younger-brother groups.

The analysis also suggests that the major thrust of Soviet nationality policy in the short run (the next decade or two) will be toward drawing the younger brothers (especially the Ukrainians) into indissoluble junior partnership with the Russians as the dominant ethnic group, but avoiding the dysfunctions that open avowal of this aim would entail. If this aim is accomplished, the relatively small state nations can be "contained" without undue effort, and the mobilized diasporas can be treated as pawns. The situation of the colonials is more critical, mainly because of their importance for the Soviet image in the outside world. Overreliance on Slavs in Asia will tarnish this image, yet all precedents, and many concrete features of the Soviet system, suggest that the relationship with colonials is explosive. Finally, as far as the younger brothers are concerned, the success of their absorption depends in considerable measure upon the regime's implementation of programs that will greatly enhance the dignity and well-being of submerged social strata, particularly the peasantry. But the totalitarian system has yet to demonstrate that it has the will to undertake this, or the capacity to accomplish it. In the final analysis, the totalitarian ethos of the Soviet elite not only provides the motivation for its handling of the nationalities problem but erects what may well be insurmountable barriers to its solution.

Notes

1. *XXII s"ezd Kommunisticheskoi Partii Sovetskogo Soiuza: Stenograficheskii otchet* (Moscow, 1962), III, 312-15 (translated in the *Current Digest of the Soviet Press* [hereafter cited as CDSP] XIII, No. 46, 14-15).

2. *XXII s"ezd KPSS*, I, 215-217 (translated in *CDSP*, XIII, No. 30, 19-20).

3. I have not made any attempt to present a chronological treatment of the development of Soviet policy since 1953. There is considerable reason to support Paul Urban's view ("Moskaus heutige Kulturpolitik gegenueber den nichtrussischen Boelkerschaften der Sowejtunion," *Osteuropa*, XI, [March, 1961], 213-26) that an initial "thaw" (approximately 1953-57) was followed by an intensified drive for Russification

after Khrushchev had consolidated his power. There are some faint signs that Khrushchev's successors may permit a second "thaw." (See the discussions translated in *CDSP*, XVII, Nos. 15 and 16, on national characteristics and folk are, mainly related to Russians; and the sharp polemic against "assimilators" in A.M. Egiazarian, *Ob osnovnykh tendentsiiakh razvitiia sotsialisticheskikh natsii SSSR* [Erevan, released to press January, 1965].) It seems safest, however, to view the official Program and its exegeses as the basic current position.

4. K. Kh. Khanazarov, *Sblizhenie natsii i natsional'nye iazyki v SSSR* (Tashkent, 1963), pp. 82, 83, 222-23. This monograph provides an unusually detailed and explicit exposition of Soviet views, as well as much interesting factual material. Many of its points apply primarily to Central Asian nationalities, but its general significance appears to be enhanced by the fact that an Asian wrote it, just as Stalin's early essay on the national question (suggested by Lenin) had greater impact because it was written by a non-Russian. Khanazarov's book is introduced by the prominent philosopher M.D. Kammari.

5. *Ibid.*, pp. 165, 203.

6. *Ibid.*, pp. 180, 189-90.

7. *XXII s" ezd KPSS*, I, 215-217 (translated in *CDSP*, XIII, No. 30, 19-20).

8. The discussion of social mobilization draws heavily upon Karl W. Deutsch, "Social Mobilization and Political Development," *American Political Science Review*, LV (September, 1961), 493-514. In addition to the four indicators I have listed, Deutsch proposes voter participation (meaningless for comparative purposes in the USSR, in view of the universal participation reported); "exposure to modernity," a concept which I find impossible to quantify, at least in Soviet conditions; the shift out of agriculture (which, insofar as it is determinable by nationality in Soviet statistics, is almost identical to rural-urban differences). It should be noted that Deutsch anticipates the fact that indicators of social mobilization will tend to be identical. In the four indicators that I use, divergence is more frequent, however, than his model would suggest. It is, therefore, especially important for me to employ as many indicators (especially of different kinds of education) as is feasible. Unfortunately, I have not often been able to use indicator 4, exposure to mass media. At first sight it would seem simple to utilize the easily available data on publications in the national languages as indicators of exposure to printed mass media. In fact, however, a member of a nationality may obtain most of this exposure through Russian-language publications imported from Moscow or other centers. For example, in 1940, out of 5 million books printed in the Azerbaidzhanian S.S.R., 3.9 million were in Azerbaidzhani, whereas in 1958, 6.5 out of 8.3 million were in that language. (Tsentral'noe statisticheskoe upravlenie, *Narodnoe khoziaistvo* SSSR [hereafter cited as *N.Kh.*] *1960* [Moscow, 1961], p. 811.) These books constituted only a very small portion of all the books sold in the republic, however: 14.4 million in 1940 and 47.0 million in 1958. (M. K. Kurbanov, *Kul'tura Sovetskogo Azerbaidzhana* [Baku, 1959], p. 32.) Since almost no books were printed in Azerbaidzhani outside the republic, evidently—in sharp contrast to the impression created by the first statistics—the predominance of non-Azerbaidzhani books has increased from 73 per cent in 1940 to 86 per cent in 1958. Unfortunately, there are very few instances in which readily available data permit such comparative language calculations, or even an estimate of the total exposure of nationalities to printed media, films, radio, or television. Very intensive

research in local publications might provide important additional data, but even Yaroslav Bilinsky's extremely detailed investigation has not turned up much for recent years. (*The Second Soviet Republic: The Ukraine after World War II* [New Brunswick, N.J.: Rutgers University Press, 1964], p. 180).

9. In fact, because of the difficulties discussed in note 8 above, I have been cautious in using, for example, the per capita newspaper circulation as an indication of the relative exposure of ethnic groups to their own language or culture. If one groups has a high index on this score, yet also (though the data do not inform us on the point) reads numerous Moscow newspapers, its relative exposure to its own language may be less than that of another group with a low per capita newspaper circulation in its own language but with a far lower circulation of Moscow and other Russian-language papers. I have not used employment of national cadres extensively because the subject is treated at length by Dr. Seweryn Bialer in a paper that will appear in a separate work now in progress. In general, I want to emphasize that my essay is by no means exhaustive; it is an effort at outlining the problem, presenting an approach to it, and applying this approach in an illustrative fashion.

10. *Formirovanie i razvitie sovetskogo rabochego klassa (1917-1961 gg.): Sbornik statei* (Moscow, 1964), pp. 264-65.

11. John A. Armstrong, *The Politics of Totalitarianism* (New York: Random House, 1961), p. 242. At least Jews were 10 per cent of the delegates to the Second Writer's Congress, which is very unlikely to have overrepresented Jewish writers. (*Vtoroi vsesoiuznoi s "ezd sovetskikh pisatelei: Stenograficheskii otchet* [Moscow, 1956], p. 79.)

12. Ilya Ehrenburg, *The War: 1941-1945* (Cleveland: World Publishing Co., 1965, p. 121; Cf. Armstrong, *The Politics of Totalitarianism*, p. 154; and John A. Armstrong (ed.), *Soviet Partisans in World War II* (Madison, Wis.: University of Wisconsin Press, 1964), p. 68.

13. From an interview quoted in "Jews in the Soviet Union," *The New Leader*, September 14, 1959.

14. Armstrong, *The Politics of Totalitarianism*, p. 154. Ehrenburg's treatment (*op. cit.*) of this period (particularly Shcherbakov's role) seems to substantiate this conclusion.

15. Armstrong, *The Politics of Totalitarianism*, p. 242; and *Kommunist Belorussii*, No. 5 (May, 1962), p. 57. The Ukrainian calculation is based on the fact that about 10 per cent of the members of the Ukraine are unaccounted for ethnically (see V.M. Churaev, "Kommunisticheskaia Partiia Ukrainy v tsifrakh," *Partiinaia zhizn'*, No. 12 [1958], pp. 57-59), and seem likely to be predominantly Jewish.

16. *N. Kh. 1962*, p. 573; and *N. Kh. 1963*, pp. 493, 591. In all instances in this and subsequent indexes for the postwar period the poulation base for calculation is taken from the 1959 census, *Itogi vsesoiuznoi perepisi naseleniia 1959 goda* (16 vols. [one for the USSR and one for each Union republic]; Moscow, 1962-63). This census is also the source of other quantitative data when the origin is not otherwise indicated. Using the 1959 base gives an upward bias to indexes for the 1960's, since the population has been growing rapidly, and an even heavier downward bias for the early 1950's and late 1940's. Since, however, there are no reliable estimates on nationalities for other years, and since the main use of the indexes is for comparison (though nationality population growth rates have differed, these differences introduce less bias than the over-all growth rate), it has seemed advisable to use the single base.

17. Judging by the biographies in *Diplomaticheskii slovar'* (3 vols.; Moscow, 1960-64), Armenians are readily identified by their names, which (in the USSR) almost always end in "ian."

18. M. Keresselidze, "Transkaukasien im Jahr 1962," *Osteuropa*, XIII (May, 1963), 319, 322-23.

19. See below, p. 30. Of course, this lack of Armenian-Azerbaidzhani schools may be partly due to the regime's desire to mix all of them with Russian children. In view of the very high proportion of Armenians in the republic, however, it is curious that there should be no cases where it is convenient to mix Armenians and Azerbaidzhanis alone.

20. *Pechat' SSSR v 1963 godu* (Moscow, 1964), pp. 24, 115, 119, 121, 125, 152.

21. *Vtoroi vsesoiuznoi s"ezd sovetskikh pisatelei*, pp. 79, 594-95.

22. M. Keresselidze, "Transkaukasien im Jahr 1963," *Osteuropa*, XIV (July-August, 1964), 540-41.

23. Armenian Party membership is about 30 per cent higher outside than inside the Armenian S.S.R., but this is largely accounted for by the higher proportion of adults in the diaspora. Except where otherwise indicated, current Party membership is based on data from *Partiinaia zhizn'*, No. 10 (1965), pp. 8-17 (translated in *CDSP*, XVII, No. 29, 14-18); 1961 data is from *Partiinaia zhizn'*, No. 1 (1961), pp. 44-54 (translated in *CDSP*, XIV, No. 3, 3-6).

24. Karl W. Deutsch, *Nationalism and Social Communication* (Cambridge, Mass.: The M.I.T. Press, 1953), chap. vi.

25. The Chuvash speak a basically Turkic language with a strong Finnic influence. Though predominantly Orthodox, they were also influenced by Islam. As Table V indicates, the Chuvash seem distinctly less susceptible to Russification than the other groups.

26. Khanazarov, *op. cit.*, pp. 137, 140, 203.

27. See also the table in John A. Armstrong, *Ukrainian Nationalism*, (2d ed.; New York: Columbia University Press, 1963), p. 324. The reduction of the proportion of Russian speakers was due partly to Nazi massacre of the large Jewish urban populations; but the influx of Russians has largely replaced the Russian-speaking Jews in the linguistic sense.

28. I.M. Bogdanov, *Gramotnost' i obrazovanie v dorevoliutsionnoi Rossii i v SSSR* (Moscow, 1964), p. 134.

29. V.I. Naulko, in *Narodna tvorchist' ta etnohrafiia* (May-June, 1964) (translated in *Digest of the Soviet Ukrainian Press*, VIII, No. 10, 13). Professor Bilinsky has suggested to me, however, that the 1959 figure (in contrast to the 1927 one) probably refers to *urban* Ukrainians only.

30. Armstrong, *The Politics of Totalitarianism*, p. 278. The ratio of Ukrainian Party membership to Ukrainian population has been significantly higher in some parts of Asia than in the Ukraine. See *Rost i regulirovanie sostava Kommunisticheskoi Partii Kirgizii* (Frunze, 1963), p. 254.

31. Khanzarov, *op. cit.*, pp. 145-46.

32. Karl-Eugen Waedekin, "Nationalitaetenpolitik und Lebenskraft der Voelker in der Sowjetunion heute und morgen," *Osteuropa*, XIV (November, 1964), 839, 844.

33. "Is Such Generosity Necessary?" *Izvestiia*, September 6, 1961 (translated in *CDSP*, XIII, No. 36, 26).

34. Interview with the British journalist I. McDonald, *Pravda*, February 16, 1958 (translated in *CDSP*, X, No. 7, 16).

35. This calculation is based on inferences from fragmentary data. In 1958 there were 25,464 Ukrainian-language schools and 4,355 Russian schools (Radians'ka Ukraina, February 1, 1959 [translated in *Digest of the Soviet Ukrainian Press*, II, No. 5, 17]). Since the proportion of Ukrainian speakers in the urban population was 53 per cent, and that of Russian speakers was 44 per cent, one can calculate (the total number of urban schools being available in *Narodne hospodarstvo Ukrains'koi RSR v 1960 rotsi* [Kiev, 1961], pp. 439-41) that there should have been (according to the criterion suggested above) 2,777 Ukrainian-language and 2,314 Russian-language urban schools; similarly, there should have been 22,736 Ukrainian-language and 2,021 Russian-language rural schools. The estimated total of 25,514 Ukrainian and 4,435 Russian schools is so close to the figures reported by the regime that one is led to feel that the calculation is sufficiently exact to enable one to proceed to the next step of inferring that Ukrainian and Russian-language schools in the same types of areas have on the average similar attendance figures, and that, therefore, rural Ukrainian pupils are overwhelmingly instructed in Ukrainian, but that a high proportion of urban Ukrainians are instructed in Russian.

36. *Pechat' SSSR v 1963 godu*, pp. 25, 55, 61, 90, 93, 96, 97, 100, 102.

37. F.T. Zhylko, *Narysy z dialektologii Ukrains'koi movy* (Kiev, 1955), facing p. 308.

38. "Street Lights in the Evening," *Pravda*, July 14, 1965 (translated in *CDSP*, XLII, No. 28, 37).

39. For the sake of brevity the present discussion will omit the groups of Buddhist background which are relatively insignificant numerically. Similarly, the primitive, northern tribal-culture groups will be omitted. It can be argued that they should be considered a distinctive class (like the Australian, Papuan, and other primitive groups) from the functional standpoint; but their significance for the future of the Soviet system scarcely warrants extended treatment.

40. Khanazarov, *op. cit.*, p. 106.

41. "L'Islam en URSS apres 1945," *La documentation francaise*, December 8, 1953 (translated in *Ost-Probleme*, VI [April 24, 1954], 657).

42. F. F. Sovetkin (ed.), *Natsional'nye shkoly RSFSR* (Moscow, 1958), p. 180; and Khanazarov, *op. cit.*, p. 176.

43. Kamil Faizulin, "Interrupted Wedding," *Literaturnaia gazeta*, December 10, 1953 (translated in *CDSP*, V, No. 50, 7).

44. A.G. Kharchev, *Braki i sem'ia v SSSR* (Moscow, 1964), pp. 193, 195.

45. Analysis of union republic budgets is very complicated, but might be revealing in this respect.

46. Waedekin, *op. cit.*, p. 849. A Soviet writer (Egiazarian, *op. cit.*, p. 94) sharply rejects the possibility of large-scale labor transfer.

47. Hamid Inoiatov, *Otvet fal'sifikatoram istorii Sovetskoi Srednei Azii i Kazakhstana* (Tashkent, 1962), p. 119.

48. Baymirza Hayit, "Turkestan in der Sowjetpolitik," *Osteuropa*, XII, (January-February, 1962), 120.

49. Khanazarov, *op. cit.*, pp. 176-78, 196-98. See also A.M. Afanas'ev, *Narodnoe obrazovanie v Uzbekistane* (Tashkent, 1962), pp. 16-17.

50. See the speech by S.P. Borodin, in *II s"ezd intelligentsii Uzbekistana, 11-12 dekabria 1959 goda: Stenograficheskii otchet* (Tashkent, 1960), pp. 169-71.

51. Report on a conference of historians in Leningrad in *Vestnik Akademii Nauk SSSR*, No. 1 (1962), pp. 138-40 (translated in *CDSP*, XIV, No. 15, 12).

52. Speech at Central Committee and Supreme Soviet meeting in Kirgizia, *Pravda*, August 17, 1964 (translated in *CDSP*, XVI, No. 35, 3).

53. Khanazarov, *op. cit.*, pp. 64, 211.

54. See especially Inoiatov, *op. cit.*; and the critical articles by Urban, *op. cit.*, and Baymirza Hayit, "Turkestan im Lichte der KP-Kongresse," *Osteuropa*, X (July-August, 1960), 523.

55. P. V. Presniakov (ed.), *Formirovanie kommunisticheskikh obshchestvennykh otnoshenii* (Alma-Ata, 1964), p. 170.

56. Hans Koch and Leo Bilas, "Slawen und Asiaten in der UdSSR," *Osteuropa*, IX (July-August, 1959), 437-38.

57. *Tashkentskaia konferentsiia pisatelei stran Azii i Afriki* (Tashkent, 1960), p. 215.

58. Cf. Khanazarov, *op. cit.*, p. 189.

PART IV

ECONOMY

Marxist-Leninist ideology holds that nations are artifacts of capitalism and would disappear under socialism. Accordingly the USSR's socialist economy was intended to be the main force in eliminating national differences. Some policies (e.g., regional equalization) were explicitly designed to reduce differences in republic development and were meant to remove the basis for ethnic resentments, but policies pursuing broader economic goals often had the opposite effect. The chapters in Part IV explore both the effects of Soviet economic policies on national and ethnic differences and the constraints that the federal structure imposes on broader economic goals.

The stability of the Soviet political order faced two specific economic threats: the distribution of resources and economic reform. In many political systems, elites fight for resources from a central government in order to develop their respective regions. Economic regionalism or localism creates conflict, but such conflict is a mainstay of political life and is not necessarily debilitating. In the Soviet Union, however, the scramble for resources can contribute to a nationalist agenda. Because the republics represent nations, "nationalism intersects with localism when interests of a particular nationality group come to be identified with those of the administrative unit. In the context of Soviet federalism this means that the distribution crisis is a nationalities crisis."[1]

The Soviet Union's federal structure creates even more serious problems in the area of economic reform. The tendency for republic elites to advance their respective republics'interests above those of the USSR is most focused in the field of economic administration. To improve efficiency in production Soviet policymakers decentralize economic decision making by making it the responsibility of the republics and lower levels of administration. This process expands the political autonomy of the republics, enhances the authority of regional elites, and thus erodes Moscow's political control over republics and encourages republic independence.[2]

Gertrude Schroeder's chapter develops these and other themes, pointing out the dilemma of equality versus efficiency (supplemented with recent data comparing the results of economic policies in the republics), the impact of demographic shifts on the supply of labor, the ways in which localism inhibits economic administration, and the threat that economic decentralization (which is supposed to further the goal of efficiency) poses to political control. She predicts that Gorbachev's attempt to continue central management of certain industries and to transfer control over others to republics will court disaster, for the devolution of power would take on a life of its own, threatening to undermine his program for economic renewal.

Schroeder finds no evidence of a concerted policy to allocate investment funds to compensate underdeveloped regions in the period 1961-1985. Donna Bahry and Carol Nechemias, on the other hand, believe that regional economic equalization has been reasonably successful, even if Western and Soviet scholars have come to widely disparate conclusions about the degree of this success. Their survey of the scholarly literature in Chapter 11 reveals the absence of a consensus on the definition of equality, mainly on whether it is to be measured in in terms of allocations or in terms of real results (i.e., more enterprises, schools, and the like for a given republic). The manifold ways researchers choose data and statistical techniques further increase the likelihood of disparate findings.

Promoting regional economic equality was supposed to keep economic grievances from fueling destructive nationalism, but Bahry and Nechemais argue that economic equality does not necessarily weaken the forces of nationalism. Nationalism can flourish in regions that do not experience underdevelopment; furthermore, assuming a necessary connection between economic demands and nationalist impulses is to underestimate the causes of nationalism.

In Chapter 12, Donna Bahry uses budget allocations and the process of revenue collection to examine trends in economic centralization and decentralization and in the concomitant role of the republics in the Soviet economy. When budget allocations and revenue collection were highly centralized (e.g., during the First Five-Year Plan and during and after the Second World War), republics had administrative jurisdiction in only limited areas, such as health and education. During the later Sovnarkhoz experiment, republics gained more control over how to use funds and more independence in economic administration. This reform allowed localism to rear its ugly head, compelling Khrushchev's successors to recentralize the economic ministries. The results of the Sovnarkhoz experiment substantiate the above arguments about economic decentralization and political control, for the resulting deviations from central objectives exposed Moscow to the risks of both losing control over republics and of having its economic priorities undermined.

In her discussion of tax collection Bahry describes the predicament that local governments find themselves in as they try to obtain revenues to fund programs to satisfy increasing public demands. Since the 1920s Moscow jealously guarded control over turnover taxes, the most lucrative source of tax income, which left local elites with the task of collecting more politically sensitive taxes, such as personal income taxes.[3]

Notes

1. Lubomyr Hajda and Mark Beissinger, "Nationalism and Reform in Soviet Politics," in Hajda and Beissinger, eds., *The Nationalities Factor in Soviet Politics and Society* (Boulder, Colo.: Westview Press, 1990), p. 310.

2. See Wlodzimierz Brus, "Political Pluralism and Markets in Socialist Systems," in Susan Gross Solomon, ed., *Political Pluralism in the Soviet Union* (New York: St. Martin's Press, 1982), pp. 108-130. Alexander J. Motyl imputes an inevitable connection between the two (ee *Sovietology, Rationality, Nationality: Coming to Grips with Nationalism in the USSR* [New York: Columbia University Press, 1990], pp. 92-93).

3. The dilemma of the local official grew more acute as a result of Gorbachev's reforms, which made local leaders more accountable to their constituencies (democratization) and compelled republics to be self-financing (*khozrashchet*). For a full account of this dilemma, see Donna Bahry, "Perestroika and the Debate over Territorial Economic Decentralization, " *Harriman Institute Forum*, vol. 2:5 (May 1989).

10

Nationalities and the Soviet Economy

Gertrude E. Schroeder

The multinational character of the Soviet state, especially the concentration of particular nationalities in historically defined geographic areas, has greatly complicated the formulation of economic policy, planning, and administration in the USSR from the beginning to the present. There are two main reasons for this. First, the central government has had to formulate a set of policies to deal with the fact that initially the constituent republics, each dominated by a distinct ethnic group, differed greatly in levels of economic development, as they did in other ways. Second, the government had to devise a system of economic administration that both took account of the political sensitivities of major nationalities and simultaneously ensured the fulfillment of centrally dictated priorities.

Lenin's much-touted "nationalities policy" has provided the ideological framework for coping with the large economic and cultural disparities among ethnic groups. In Soviet political rhetoric, this policy aimed to promote both the "flourishing" (*rastsvet*) of all national groups and their "convergence" (*sblizhenie*) in a variety of respects. In the economic area, the first aspect of policy—"flourishing"—has been defined to mean that each nationality both contributes to and benefits from the drive for rapid industrialization and modernization that has been a priority goal of the Soviet state from the beginning. The latter facet of policy—"convergence"—came to signify the objective of "equalization" (*vyravnivanie*) of the levels of economic development among the republics and the standards of living among ethnic groups. Initially, such a policy required resource transfers from the richer to the poorer republics, in order to upgrade the education and skills of the work force and to launch the

Published in Lubomyr Hajda and Mark Beissinger, eds., *The Nationalities Factor in Soviet Politics and Society* (Boulder, CO: Westview, 1990), pp. 43-72. Reprinted with permission from the publisher.

development process in relatively backward regions. The gradual equalization of levels of development among national groups was a stated objective in the directives for the successive five-year plans, including that for 1971-75. After Leonid Brezhnev, in his speech of December 1972 commemorating the fiftieth anniversary of the USSR, declared that "the problem of the equalization of development of the national republics has been resolved, on the whole,"[1] the word "equalization" disappeared from published plan documents. The directives for the Twelfth Five-Year Plan, for example, state merely that "the harmonious economic and social development of all republics is to be assured. . . . Their contribution to the consolidation of the country's unified national economic complex and to the solution of social tasks is to be increased."[2]

Since its formation, the Soviet Union has been organized administratively on the basis of union republics, each being the designated homeland of a particular indigenous nationality. Lower ranked administrative units—autonomous republics, oblasts, and districts—have been established within several union republics for other, usually smaller, ethnic groups. Like everything else, the economy is administered through this structure, which is thus largely organized on the basis of nationalities and national territories, some of which had formed independent states at one time or another. This momentous fact of political life has seriously complicated the task of economic planning and administration. Not only have the central planners had to take local preferences into account, but they also had to make sure that local interests did not subvert the purposes and priorities of the all-union, Russian-dominated political leadership. In addition, the central authorities have had to strive for a tolerable degree of efficiency in the economic-administrative process. These imperatives have posed a perennial dilemma: how to decentralize decision making without losing economic and/or political control.[3]

Dealing with the nationality factor in economic policy making and management—never an easy task—has become more difficult in recent years. The rate of economic growth has fallen dramatically in the past quarter century, making resource allocation decisions more difficult, particularly in view of the urgent need for a major breakthrough in economic efficiency if the growth slide is to be halted or reversed. Moreover, widely differing demographic trends among regions, while producing little growth in the labor force overall in the 1980s, have resulted in stagnation or decline in some republics and rapid expansion in others, notably in the Muslim republics of Central Asia and Azerbaidzhan. The large size and complexity of the present Soviet economy in itself immensely complicates the task of the central planners, irrespective of the nationality factor. Substantial economic and administrative decentralization would appear imperative, but the political dilemmas posed by decentralization, with their troublesome ethnic dimension, remain a major impediment.

TRENDS AND RELATIVE LEVELS
OF ECONOMIC DEVELOPMENT

The Data

Assessing the economic fortunes of ethnic groups in the USSR is complicated by the fact that the available data pertain not to nationalities but to administrative units—the union republics and their political subdivisions. Because the populations of all republics consist of diverse nationalities, the propriety of using data for the republics as a proxy for the absent data on nationality groups requires close examination. To what extent do economic progress and relative levels of economic development shown by the data for republics reflect the experience of their titular nationalities?

One primary indicator is the proportion of the titular nationality in the total population of each republic. According to the 1989 census, the titular nationality comprised approximately four-fifths or more of the total population in five republics, between roughly two-thirds and three-fourths of the total in five republics, and between one-half and two-thirds in four others. Only in Kazakhstan did the titular nationality comprise less than half of the population—39.7%. Central Asian nationalities not residing in their own republics tend to live in contiguous republics of Central Asia. With a few exceptions, these proportions did not change greatly between the censuses of 1959 and 1989. In general, the preponderance of the titular nationality has increased in the republics of Central Asia and Transcaucasia and decreased in Latvia and Estonia. On this criterion, the use of republican data to examine the fortunes of their titular nationalities would seem reasonable for all groups except the Kazakhs and possibly the Kirghiz and Latvians. This conclusion is reinforced by the strong proclivity of all nationalities to reside in their own republics; over three-fourths of the members of each group, except the Armenians, did so, according to the 1989 census. For the most part, these ethnic concentration ratios remained stable or increased between 1959 and 1989.

Other information derived from data for the republics helps clarify the experience of their titular nationalities, especially with regard to living standards. According to the 1979 census data, there is a strong tendency for the titular nationalities to reside in rural areas; except for the Russians and Armenians, the titular nationalities were substantially less urbanized than their republics' total population. The margins ranged from 4 percentage points for Lithuanians and Georgians to 23 percentage points for the Kazakhs.[4] Also important for estimating relative levels of income is the fact that titular nationalities tend to be less well educated than other residents of their republics, a condition that correlates with their more rural character. In class composition, moreover, the proportion of collective farmers among the titular nationalities tends to be higher than in the total population of their republics;[5] educational levels tend to be relatively low among the *kolkhozniki*. In 1970, the latest year for which a direct comparison can be made, the number of secondary school graduates per 1,000 persons aged 10 or over was markedly lower for the titular nationalities than for their republics as a whole; the only exceptions were Russians in the RSFSR, Georgians in Georgia, and Armenians in Armenia. Thus, relative to the rest of the population in each republic, titular nationalities are likely to be more concentrated in low wage sectors, such as agriculture, the light and food-processing industries, and the trade and services branches.

Economic Development

Having concluded that, for the most part, the data for the republics reflect reasonably well the overall experience of their respective titular nationalities (with the provisos noted), the evidence depicting trends and relative levels of economic development can now be examined. As statistical indicators, it is necessary, unfortunately, to use the official indexes of national income and industrial production published by the Soviet government. Western scholarship has found that these data seriously overstate real growth for the USSR as a whole.[6] Only one study has attempted to assess this issue for a republic.[7] The study, which developed a Western-type industrial production index for Ukraine, found that the degree of overstatement of industrial growth in the official index was the same as—or possibly a little greater than—that shown by similar studies for the USSR as a whole. Nonetheless, the long-term trends revealed by official and Western-type indexes are similar. Since identical definitions and statistical procedures are supposed to be employed union-wide, one might expect the degree of upward bias to be similar among the republics, if one could allow for the differing sectoral and branch composition of output.

All republics experienced rapid growth during the past quarter century. Growth rates of national income ranged from 4.2% in Turkmenia to 7.8% in Armenia, compared with 5.5% for the USSR as a whole. By way of perspective, Western measures of GNP show an average annual growth of 3.4% for the USSR during 1961-85.[8] Since population growth rates differed markedly among the republics, the increase in national income per capita averaged less than 3% annually in Azerbaidzhan, Kazakhstan, and Central Asia, taken together; per capita growth was 4.4% for the USSR as a whole. As official Soviet indexes show, industrial growth also was rapid everywhere during 1961-85, with growth rates ranging from 5.6% in Turkmenia to 9.2% in Belorussia, compared to 6.5% for the entire country. A Western measure shows a growth rate of 4.6% for the USSR during this period. Except for Azerbaidzhan, all republics experienced the marked slowdown in the growth of national income and industrial production characteristic of the Soviet economy during the past fifteen years. Even so, the patterns were quite diverse among the republics, probably reflecting their differing agricultural performance and industrial structures. Agricultural production increased in all republics, with average annual rates of growth ranging from 1.7% in the RSFSR to 4.7% in Azerbaidzhan and averaging 2.1% for the USSR as a whole. The highest rates were achieved in the Transcaucasian and Central Asian republics and in Moldavia.

Additional evidence for relative rates of development is provided by data on the extent of urbanization and the shares of the agricultural and industrial sectors in total employment. Although the proportion of urban dwellers in the total population increased everywhere, the rates of growth differed widely.[9] The urban share doubled between 1959 and 1985 in Belorussia and Moldavia, where industrial growth was very rapid. The Central Asian republics and Azerbaidzhan experienced the slowest rates of change; indeed, in Tadzhikistan and Turkmenia, the level of urbanization declined slightly between 1970 and 1985. In the latter year, the urban population was still less than half of the total in all of Central Asia and Moldavia. The rates at which labor was transferred from the agricultural sector also differed greatly among the republics. The data for 1961-85 depict this diversity. (I have attempted to measure employment in agricultural activity alone by removing estimated employment in nonagricultural activity on state and collective farms and by developing estimates of average annual employment on private plots by republic.) The fastest rates of labor transfer occurred in Belorussia and Lithuania, where the agricultural share fell by nearly half. In 1985, over 30% of the labor force was still engaged in agriculture in Central Asia, Azerbaidzhan, and Moldavia, and in only two republics was the share below one-fifth. For the USSR as a whole, nearly five million workers were released from agriculture during this twenty-five-year period, and the total number engaged in that sector fell in many republics. Agricultural employment rose substantially, however, in Central Asia, Kazakhstan, and Azerbaidzhan.

Although the share of the industrial sector in total employment rose significantly in most republics during this period, there was considerable diversity in the extent of industrial employment among republics. In 1985, industry's share was less than one-fifth in seven republics, and in Turkmenia it was only 10%. Data giving the distribution of industrial employment by branch have been largely unavailable since 1975. Data for earlier years show a tendency for republican specialization rather than substantial diversification, with the southern republics tending to specialize in the light and food industries, and the machinery and chemicals industries remaining largely the province of the RSFSR and Ukraine.[10] But Belorussia is an exception. Its fast-paced development in the postwar years has been accompanied by considerable diversification; in 1980, for example, the shares of the machinery and (most probably) the chemicals industries in total industrial employment exceeded those for the USSR as a whole, whereas they had been well below that level in 1960.[11]

In addition to the pace of economic growth in the republics, it would be important to establish the relative levels of development achieved. Although the data for this, reported in accordance with Soviet definitions, are not ideal, they probably are not grossly misleading for what they purport to measure—national income (net material product) per capita, extrapolated with official "constant price" indexes from current price values available for 1970.[12] They very likely are the kind of data that Soviet officials and planners use to judge such matters. National income per capita in 1985 ranged from less than half the all-union average in Tadzhikistan to more than one-third above that average in Latvia and Estonia, with Belorussia and the RSFSR next. These latter four republics, along with Lithuania, also ranked highest with regard to industrial output per capita, while the four Central Asian republics were lowest on both measures. Although differentials clearly have widened during the past twenty-five years, the relative ranking of the republics has hardly changed. The exceptions are Belorussia, with a greatly improved position, and Turkmenia, with a much lower ranking. If Brezhnev had looked at such measures when he declared in 1972 that equalization of levels of economic development had been achieved "on the whole," he evidently did not consider the rather sizable interrepublican differences to be a matter of concern. Disparities on these measures were greater in 1985 than in 1970.

Living Standards

Turning from the production side of the development process to the consumption side, it is necessary to consider trends and relative living standards among the republics. Again, data for republics must suffice, since none are available for nationalities per se. To assess progress in raising living standards, the Soviet government employs a measure termed "real per capita incomes of the population." This concept is supposed to measure the value of material goods and the material component of all services provided to the population, deflated by an index of prices of goods and services.[13] The price index has not been published; nor has the methodology for constructing it been described in any detail. Although the relative levels of real incomes per capita were not reported for the republics, republican statistical yearbooks regularly include temporal indexes. Since this measure has well-known conceptual flaws, and because the price index is believed to have a serious downward bias, I have attempted to develop an alternative measure for the republics, patterned as closely as possible after the measure of real per capita consumption that is a part of the Western effort to construct Gross National Product measures for the USSR in current and constant values.[14] The methodology for measuring real per capita consumption in the republics relies in part on the meticulous work of Alastair McAuley[15] and has been described elsewhere.[16] In essence, the procedure is to estimate per capita consumption (by Western definition) in current prices for the selected years (1960, 1970, 1980, 1985) for each republic and then to deflate these values by a uniform price index that is implicit in Western measures of nominal and real consumption for the USSR as a whole. Although this methodology is far from ideal and involves some assumptions whose validity cannot be determined for lack of data,[17] I believe that the results are plausible, providing a far better basis for assessing trends and relative living standards among the republics than do the official statistics on national income or retail sales per capita that are often used. The results, moreover, are largely consistent with a variety of relevant data that cannot be aggregated. For example, the ranking of republics with respect to per capita consumption in 1985 was quite similar to their ranking with respect to per capita retail sales; the rankings were the same for eight republics on both measures.

Living standards improved markedly in all republics during the past twenty-five years, but the pace of improvement varied considerably—from growth at an average rate of 2% annually in Tadzhikistan to almost double that rate in Moldavia. Rates of improvement in the Central Asian republics were consistently lower than the all-union average annual rate of 2.7%. Well above average gains were registered in Belorussia and Moldavia—republics that had also exhibited the most rapid rates of urbanization. All republics experienced markedly lower growth in real per capita consumption during 1971-85 than in the 1960s, a pattern that is more uniform than that derived from growth rates of production among the republics. In the first half of the 1980s, only two republics registered average annual growth rates in real per capita consumption as high as 2%, and by my measure per capita consumption actually fell in three republics. In this period, at least, the central government clearly did not try to stem a relative deterioration in living standards in Central Asia that resulted largely from rapid population growth.

Sizable differences in the relative levels of per capita consumption in the republics are apparent throughout the period. In 1985, per capita consumption in the Baltic republics exceeded the all-union average by 12% to 28%, whereas it was below the all-union average in Tadzhikistan by more than 40%. Differences widened over the twenty-five year period; the coefficient of variation rose from .10 in 1960 to .14 in 1985, the major increase apparently having occurred in the first half of the 1970s. Again, however, republican rankings have been remarkably stable, with the Baltic republics occupying the top position by sizable margins throughout the period and the Central Asian republics and Azerbaidzhan bringing up the rear. The relative position of the latter group has tended to deteriorate, while that of Moldavia and Belorussia (the republics urbanizing at the fastest rates) improved substantially. While these regional differentials in living standards are not especially large by international comparison (they are much narrower than in Yugoslavia, for instance), they are substantial nonetheless, and the differences certainly are not being reduced.[18]

While it has not proved possible to disaggregate consumption into its major components for the republics, as has been done for the USSR as a whole, a wide variety of officially published data indicate that all republics have made substantial progress in all major areas—food, soft goods and durables, housing, services, health care, and education.[19] The gains in these categories have been far from uniform among the republics, but the differences display a pattern that is quite similar to that revealed by overall measures of per capita consumption. The Baltic republics have relatively more of everything, and the Central Asians have less. Also, the quality of the goods and services provided no doubt differs among republics, probably being poorer in the rural regions.

It may be of interest to inquire how living standards in the various republics compare with those in nearby countries. Sweeping under a very large rug the many methodological and conceptual problems involved, one can venture such an assessment using studies of relative levels of GNP and purchasing power parities for a number of Western and some Communist countries in 1975, together with a reasonably comparable set of data on consumption in the USSR and the United States in 1976.[20] The above estimates of relative levels of per capita consumption for the republics allow for such an international perspective. Tenuous though it may be, the general picture that this comparison provides is not grossly misleading. It suggests that living standards in Central Asia and Azerbaidzhan in 1985 were roughly the same as those in Syria and Iran in 1975, that living standards in the Baltic republics were nearest those in Hungary, Poland, and Ireland, and that living standards in the USSR as a whole and in all its constituent republics are far below those prevailing in most of the rest of Europe, Japan, and the United States.

Finally, it remains to examine the extent to which the measures of relative living standards among republics reflect the situation of their titular nationalities. We know that titular nationalities tend overwhelmingly to reside in their own republics and that they comprise more than half the population in all republics but Kazakhstan. We know as well that the titular nationalities tend to reside in rural areas in their republics and that rural living standards, while improving relatively, are still well below those in urban areas—perhaps two-thirds to three-fourths of the urban level. We also know that the titular nationalities tend to be less well educated than the average for their republics and are therefore more likely to be found in relatively low wage sectors and occupations. It seems reasonable, then, to conclude that the living standards of the titular nationalities probably are appreciably below those measured here for their republics, although the precise data needed to substantiate this are not available.[21] Russians in the RSFSR, Armenians in Armenia, and Estonians in Estonia might prove to be the exceptions. Titular nationalities in the other republics, however, may have experienced a more rapid improvement in incomes than the aggregate populations of their respective republics, because rural living standards in the USSR and, apparently, in all republics have been rising faster than urban living standards.

INVESTMENT ALLOCATION AND PRODUCTIVITY

If the central government had been determined to equalize levels of development among nationality groups, this policy presumably would have been most apparent in the allocation of investment. Even if this were not the only objective, its systematic implementation, given the large development gaps already existing, would have required an extensive and persistent favoring of the less developed regions, especially if equalizing the levels of development were to be achieved on a per capita basis. Investment in the USSR as a whole tripled during this period and increased substantially in each successive five-year plan in all republics, although at differing rates. The most notable trends are the fairly steady rise in the share of investment allocated to the RSFSR and Belorussia and the fall in the shares of Ukraine and Kazakhstan. The relative priority of the RSFSR is associated with the decision to develop natural resources and energy in the eastern regions, and that of Belorussia with the rapid industrial development promoted there. The share given to Central Asia rose by nearly one percentage point during this period, and that of Transcaucasia also increased slightly, while the shares of the Baltic republics and Moldavia remained essentially stable. When relative rates of population growth are taken into account, we again observe a marked improvement in the relative positions of the RSFSR and Belorussia and the substantial deterioration in the relative positions of Ukraine and Kazakhstan over this period. The position of Central Asia also dropped markedly; per capita investment in those republics in 1981-85 was less than two-thirds of the all-union level, compared to about three-fourths in 1961-65. The positions of the Transcaucasian republics fluctuated considerably during the period, possibly reflecting political factors, but per capita investment remained well below the union-wide average. Patterns of gross fixed investment per capita in the Baltic republics and Moldavia have been quite diverse, though the consistent erosion of the position of Estonia should be noted. Although the trends remain similar, the differences among republics are reduced considerably when investment is expressed per worker rather than per capita. For example, in the period 1981-85, investment per worker ranged from 70% of the all-union average in Kirghizia to 119% of that average in Turkmenia. The relative positions of the Central Asian republics and Azerbaidzhan—republics with especially fast rates of population growth—appear to be significantly higher on this measure.

The distribution of investment among republics during this period does not reveal any systematic effort to use investment as a means of reducing development gaps, particularly when allowance is made for differential population growth. Rather, it seems that the central government, while providing an increment in investment to ensure some development in all republics, based its allocation decisions on a variety of other factors, such as resource development in Siberia (with its attendant high costs), consideration of relative rates of return of investment, and geo-political considerations. This general observation accords with the conclusions reached by other investigators who have analyzed Soviet regional development and investment policy.[22] Detailed investigations for individual republics might offer further insights—for example, the changing fortunes of Georgia and Azerbaidzhan in the past decade might have an important political dimension. In any event, in explaining shifts in investment allocations among republics over the past three five-year plans, the primacy of all-union considerations over considerations of equalization is quite evident—an outcome appropriate for a government that viewed equalization as "basically" achieved.[23]

Rapid growth in investment has produced rapid increases in the capital stock and in capital/labor ratios in all republics. According to calculations made by Gillula, capital stocks in the material sectors of production increased during 1961-75 at average annual rates ranging from 6.3% in Azerbaidzhan to 11.7% in Moldavia and Uzbekistan, with an average of 8.9% for the USSR as a whole.[24] During the same period, fixed capital per worker increased at average annual rates ranging from 4.1% in Azerbaidzhan to 8.7% in Moldavia, and averaging 7.0% for the USSR. While these measures cannot be extended to 1985 with available data, it is nonetheless evident that growth in total capital stock and capital per worker continued in all republics, though at slower rates. Increased capital/labor ratios, in turn, have contributed to increased productivity in all republics. Using official data, Ivan Koropeckyj has estimated that factor productivity (national income per unit of combined capital and labor) increased at widely varying average annual rates among republics during 1961-75—from a mere 0.1% in Turkmenia to 4.1% in Belorussia, with an all-union average of 2.7%.[25] Levels of productivity also differ greatly among republics. According to a Soviet source, the productivity of social labor (national income per worker in material production) ranged in 1970 from 72% of the union-wide average in Moldavia to 120% in Estonia.[26] Martin Spechler estimated the relative levels in 1978 to range from 65% in Kirghizia to 124% in Estonia, and concluded that the differentials widened between 1970 and 1978.[27]

When central planners appraise relative trends and levels of efficiency in resource use among the republics, they focus on labor productivity, often citing Lenin's dictum that its growth is "the main thing, the most important thing for the victory of socialism." The official data for the industrial sector show that all republics participated in the marked slowdown in the growth of labor productivity characteristic of the USSR as a whole over this period. This suggests that the causes usually identified to explain the pronounced general slowdown were probably present in each republic.[28] In the two most recent plan periods, the lowest rates of growth in labor productivity are to be found in Central Asia and Kazakhstan. The reasons for the relatively favorable performance by the Transcaucasian republics are not readily apparent; a detailed investigation of the kind that has been made for Belorussia would seem desirable.[29] The data giving relative levels of industrial labor productivity represent gross value of output (in 1966 prices) per worker in 1980; they appear consistent with similar calculations for 1971 based on a Soviet source and published growth rates for labor productivity.[30] By definition, the relative levels reflect the product mix produced in each republic and the relative prices set for those products by the government. If the central planners use such data, they might conclude that the Central Asian republics are not as much a drag on overall productivity as one might think, even though their rate of improvement is slower. For agriculture, however, both rates of growth and relative levels of labor productivity tend to be low there. In any event, the planners evidently have not allocated investment funds to their most productive uses, as is revealed by data such as these. Even if they had done so, the choices hardly could have been optimal, given the well-known deficiencies of Soviet prices.

ETHNIC DIMENSIONS OF THE MANPOWER PROBLEM

The USSR is in the midst of a manpower management problem of unprecedented scope, complicated by its ethnic dimension. The situation has been created by declining birth rates overall and by the large differences in birth rates among nationalities. During the Eleventh Five-Year Plan (1981-85), the total addition to the working-age population in the USSR was only 3.6 million, compared with 11.8 million in 1976-80. All of the increment in 1981-85 came from the non-Russian republics, principally Central Asia, Kazakhstan, and Azerbaidzhan. In the period of the Twelfth Five-Year Plan, the total increment will be a mere 2.3 million, and will rise to only 2.9 million in the following five-year period. During the decade 1986-95, the working-age population will increase by 4.7 million in Central Asia and decline by 1.7 million in the RSFSR. Even in the last quinquennium of this century the estimated addition to the population of working age in Central Asia (3.3 million) will be double that in the RSFSR.

The labor problems confronting the USSR in the last two decades of the century are the subject of a sizable literature.[31] Essentially, the government's options for dealing with the problems are: (1) to encourage or compel migration from labor-surplus regions (mainly the southern republics) to areas of labor deficit (mainly the RSFSR); (2) to reallocate investment and the location of new facilities toward labor-surplus areas; or (3) to adopt some combination of these two approaches. From experience in 1981-85 and from the published targets for the Twelfth Five-Year Plan, we can observe the approach that the government has elected to take—one of "muddling through" with a wide variety of policies intended to make the situation reasonably tolerable. Although Western scholars have debated the probability of substantial out-migration from Central Asia,[32] whose peoples have shown great reluctance to relocate, Soviet policy makers are not opting for such a solution. The government has not announced substantial new incentives to foster migration, other than touting examples of brigades of Central Asians that have gone to work on showcase projects in Siberia and elsewhere in the RSFSR. Indeed, there is evidence that such migrants have soon returned, and that many were, in fact, local Russians rather than members of indigenous Central Asian nationalities. One writer states: "Let us look at the example of population movement from the so-called labor-surplus areas to labor-deficit areas, from Uzbekistan to Ivanovo oblast, in particular. Who came here? Not Uzbeks, but mainly Russians, and even the latter usually left the area soon afterwards."[33]

Any projected large-scale program to redistribute population from the labor-surplus regions of the south to the labor-deficit regions of the north would be extremely costly. Moreover, it would encounter strong resistance, from both the sending regions and those that would have to absorb large numbers of new migrants with radically different ethnic and cultural characteristics. The government wisely has chosen, at least for the time being, not to take this approach. Although the evidence is fragmentary, it is clear that no significant population redistribution from the south to the north is taking place. Data on employment and productivity by republic in 1981-85 suggest that instead the rapidly growing working-age population in Central Asia is being absorbed mainly by continuing rising employment in agriculture and probably also in the private sector—leading to even greater underemployment of manpower, with an adverse effect on productivity.[34] In the relatively labor-short areas of the north, the government has actively promoted a variety of policies to force managers to cope with fewer workers, and these policies have had some success. During the 1981-85 period, increased labor productivity accounted for 91% of the growth of industrial production in the RSFSR compared with 79% in 1976-80; in agriculture, employment declined by 4% in 1981-85 while output rose by 8%, a marked improvement over the preceding five years. The Twelfth Five-Year Plan indicates that these trends are expected to continue.

The government could balance the regional disproportions in labor force growth through systematic efforts to expand industry and economic infrastructures in the regions of fastest population growth, especially Central Asia, but also southern Kazakhstan and Transcaucasia. The regional distribution of investment indicates that the government in fact has elected to pursue that option, but not with much vigor and with considerable differentiation among the republics. Transcaucasia's share of total investment increased from 3.5% in 1976-80 to 4.1% in 1981-85, a shift sufficient to improve its relative position on a per capita basis. By contrast, Central Asia's relative standing on a per capita basis deteriorated markedly, even though the region's share of total investment rose from 6.2% to 6.5% during this period. Regions with fast-growing populations, of course, require more investment—not only to provide new industrial jobs, but also to build more schools, hospitals, and other service facilities. They also need additional budget allocations to finance current operations of public services. Although budget data do not fully reflect the relative appropriations, these, together with investment allocations, have been sufficient to permit real per capita consumption to grow faster in Transcaucasia than in the RSFSR in the 1981-85 period. In Kazakhstan and Central Asia, however, improvements in living standards were less substantial than in the RSFSR; by our measures there was a decline in Uzbekistan and Turkmenia.

The directives for the Twelfth Five-Year Plan indicate that this policy of temporizing and hoping for the best was to continue over the 1986-90 period. The plan called for new facilities to be sited to make fuller use of the labor and natural resources in Central Asia, southern Kazakhstan, and Transcaucasia, while the European regions were to be developed primarily through retooling and reconstructing existing enterprises, with a reduction in the number of persons employed in material production.[35] The plan envisioned above-average growth in industrial production in most of the republics with a rapidly increasing population. Data on planned investment allocations for 1986-90 in all republics can be culled from the press, mainly from the speeches by republican leaders at the Twenty-seventh Party Congress. From this information we can conclude that past regional allocation policies were planned to continue. According to these data, Central Asia's share in total investment in 1986-90 would rise slightly from 1981-85, Kazakhstan's share was to drop slightly, and Transcaucasia's to remain about the same. Ukraine's investment share would continue to drop, and the RSFSR's share to rise, perhaps to as much as 64%. But the population of Central Asia will have increased by about 14% during 1986-90, and that of Kazakhstan and Transcaucasia by about 8%, compared with less than 2% in the RSFSR and 4% in the USSR as a whole. On a per capita basis, then, the relative position of the RSFSR would rise and that of most other republics, particularly in Central Asia, would fall. This was essentially the pattern that prevailed in 1986-87.[36]

THE NATIONALITIES FACTOR IN ECONOMIC ADMINISTRATION
From Stalin to Gorbachev

From the advent of central planning, the Soviet economy has been administered largely on the basis of the union republics, each the "homeland" of a distinct nationality that constitutes in most cases the majority population, with many of the symbolic trappings and constitutionally sanctioned, though unrealized, prerogatives characteristic of a nation-state. The nationalities factor, therefore, inescapably politicizes all decision making at the central government level with regard to economic planning and administration, and lends the process a definite—and potentially divisive—ethnic dimension. Any scheme for the decentralization of decision-making authority aimed at improving economic management has had to be appraised with that dimension in mind. Initially, Stalin resolved the issue by establishing a highly centralized form of economic administration, with ever more numerous central ministries organized along sectoral lines and with planning authority centered in Moscow in the USSR Gosplan. The union republican Councils of Ministers and the republican Gosplans played a minor role in this scheme. For reasons both political and economic, Nikita Khrushchev in 1957 jettisoned virtually all of the sectoral administrative structures in favor of a system based on regional (republican) authority. His stated objectives were to eliminate the "departmentalism," inefficient and duplicative supply arrangements, inattention to regional planning, and excessive bureaucratism and red tape stemming from the overburdening of higher echelons in Moscow. Under the new scheme, the chain of authority went from the USSR Gosplan to the Councils of Ministers of the union republics and their Gosplans, then to 105 regional economic councils (*sovnarkhozy*), largely coterminous with oblasts, and finally to production enterprises. This drastic restructuring of the economic administrative machinery was bitterly controversial, with the nationalities element looming large.[37]

Such a radical devolution of administrative responsibility to the republics and their subunits created difficulties even more serious than those the new system was designed to eliminate. Since the decentralization was administrative and not economic in nature, problems of coordination of supply and demand for materials among the regional units became endemic. Tendencies toward "localism" and regional autarky were much in evidence in the behavior of the new *sovnarkhozy*. Complaints were made about imbalances in and inattention to the development of particular industrial branches. To cope with the growing mess, the central government drastically reduced the number of *sovnarkhozy*, established one coordinating body after another in a growing pyramid, gave ever more power to the USSR Gosplan, and reestablished the former ministries in the guise of state committees. Accusations of localism and regional autarky, as well as perennial disputes over investment and budgetary allocations, often acquired a nationalist coloration. Several major shakeups of republican leaderships occurred during this period.[38]

Khrushchev's successors moved quickly to end the experiment in regional economic administration, which surely was regarded as one of the deposed leader's "hare-brained schemes." The former system of economic management through all-union, union-republican and republican ministries was restored in 1965, and consequently the authority of the union republics sharply curtailed. Nonetheless, the question of how much decision-making authority to vest in the union republics and their subordinate units remained on the agenda. Apparently in an effort to assuage the feelings of republican leaders, the central leadership had intimated when the ministerial system was restored that additional authority in economic affairs would be accorded the republics.[39] In his report to the Central Committee Plenum in September 1965, Premier Kosygin stated that the republican Gosplans were to prepare draft plans for developing their regions, including the activities of enterprises under all-union ministries.[40] This procedure was codified in a Methodological Instruction issued by the USSR Gosplan in 1969.[41] Presumably, the republican leaderships could lobby for resources to carry out those plans, which otherwise did not seem to be binding on anyone.

The new Soviet constitution, adopted in 1977, neither ended the federal system, as some centralizers had recommended, nor expanded the powers of the republics and their local soviets, as regional leaders had urged. However, a planning reform decree of July 1979 directed the ministries to coordinate their annual and five-year plans with the relevant republican Councils of Ministers, which then would draw up and supervise the implementation of specific plans for "production of local building materials and consumer goods" and for "construction of housing and municipal and cultural services."[42] A decree issued in 1981 aimed to expand the role of local soviets by (1) requiring enterprises to obtain concurrence by the local soviet for all plans relating to "land use, environmental protection, construction, labor utilization, and social-cultural services"; (2) recommending that enterprises producing primarily for local consumption be put under the local soviets; and (3) assigning, "as an experiment," to republican Councils of Ministers all funds designated for investment in housing and services.[43] The latter provision sought to end the perennial tug of war between local authorities and the branch ministries, which control a substantial part of the funds for construction of housing and many service facilities.

These attempts to shift more control over economic affairs to regional levels evidently had little impact on economic administration, which had become highly complex. In Donetsk oblast of the Ukrainian SSR, for example, there were 404 enterprises subordinate to 26 all-union ministries; 2,787 enterprises under 55 union-republican ministries; and 2,339 enterprises under 21 different republican, local, and other jurisdictions.[44] This situation created severe problems for republican Gosplans, which, as the penchant for "improving planning" through "complex programs" grew, had to undertake very difficult tasks.[45] From time to time, the suggestion had surfaced that the economy should be administered through the nineteen large regions delineated for long-range planning purposes. Under this scheme, the Baltic, Transcaucasia, and Central Asia are treated as single suprarepublican regions; Kazakhstan, Belorussia, and Moldavia each constitute a single region; Ukraine is divided into three regions and the RSFSR into ten. Possibly referring to such suggestions, the 1961 Party Program had mentioned the possible establishment of "interrepublican economic organs," arousing fears among the nationalities that the republics might be weakened. The 1986 Party Program contains no such reference. But in the pre-congress discussion of that program, *Pravda* again published an article proposing that the present economic regions serve as administrative units.[46] Another would-be reformer recommended that the country be divided into "territorial-production complexes" and administered regionally on that basis, but with the retention of the branch ministerial structure.[47]

Not only did the nationality factor constrain decisions about how best to organize the administration of the economy, but it also politicized and sharpened the inevitable conflicts over budget allocations for social services and investment.[48] When Ukrainian leaders argued for development of Donbas coal, they could be seen as trying to promote Ukrainian interests at the expense of other republics and the country as a whole. For years, a Central Asian "lobby" had sought funding for a mammoth project to divert water from Siberian rivers to the south in order to promote more diversified agricultural development there. Having failed in their attempt, the native Central Asians can allege discrimination and neglect of their vital interests by the central—easily construed as Russian—government.

Gorbachev's Initiative

Frustration over ethnically divisive issues such as these was evident in Gorbachev's speech to the Twenty-seventh Party Congress, in which he talked about "contradictions," inveighed against "parochialism" and "attitudes of living at the expense of others," and even suggested that "thought should be given about how to link more closely the volume of resources allocated for social needs with the efficiency of the regional economy." He spoke even more sharply:

> Strengthening of the territorial principle of management requires a rise in the level of economic management in every republic, oblast, city and district. Frequently proposals come in from local bodies that have not been studied properly, are dictated not by national-economic interests, but rather by parasitical or even selfish interests, and that involve the economy in capital-intensive and inefficient projects.[49]

Such sentiments, repeated in subsequent major speeches, found expression in those parts of Gorbachev's program of economic reform that impinge on the relations between the central government and the republics. In July 1986 the CPSU, the Supreme Soviet, and the USSR Council of Ministers adopted a decree that considerably broadened the responsibility and authority of the republican governments, especially their subordinate local soviets.[50] This decree, in its focus on the consumer sector, reiterated and expanded many of the provisions of the earlier 1981 decree, which evidently had had little effect. As part of the package of measures promulgated to implement the overall economic reforms adopted by the CPSU in late June 1987,[51] a decree dated 17 July 1987 extended the authority of the republican governments even further.[52] Although it contains much ambiguity, the decree apparently does the following: (1) vests the republican Councils of Ministers with near total authority to plan economic and social development and to allocate investment, although coordination with all-union ministries is mandatory; (2) requires republican organs to ensure that the allocation of funds for social development in their territories depends on economic performance there; (3) expands the budgetary authority of local soviets and prescribes additional sources of revenues; (4) makes all regional bodies assume responsibility for coordinating and monitoring the activities of all enterprises on their territory in matters affecting the welfare of the local populations; (5) requires regional bodies to reduce staffs and simplify organizational structures, but also specifies that new planning-economic departments are to be established in the local soviets; and (6) stipulates that heavy industry, for the most part, be managed through all-union ministries, while the consumer sector is to be managed largely by the republics. In the implementation of this last provision, seven union-republic ministries were converted to all-union status in 1987 and 1988.[53]

In the discussions that preceded the Nineteenth Party Conference in June 1988, there surfaced the idea of introducing economic accountability (*khozraschet*) for an entire republic. This is analogous to the principle of self-financing on which the operation of all Soviet enterprises will be based beginning in 1989—an arrangement under which they are required to finance all their activities from internally generated funds and are accorded wide latitude in making decisions about production, inputs and the use of profits. Delegates from a few republics supported the idea, while others urged greater regional autonomy in general. The Conference resolution on the nationalities issue stated that the "idea of republics and regions going over to *khozraschet* is worth considering, with a clear definition of what they are expected to contribute to Union-wide programmes."[54] Subsequently, the idea became a rallying cry for the newly formed "Popular Front" groups in the Baltic republics. Apparently with the tacit approval of Gorbachev, representatives of the government and academic communities in the three republics drafted a document specifying the basic features of the proposed new system of autonomy. With an obviously ethnic cast, they are quite radical: republican ownership of all productive property except defense installations; abolition of the subordination of local enterprises and organizations to all-union organs; republican control of all economic activity on its territory, including issuance of currency and conduct of foreign trade; payment of a tax to the all-union budget to finance defense and foreign policy expenditures; conduct of economic relations with other republics on the basis of voluntary contracts, reflecting "mutually equivalent terms of exchange."[55]

Perhaps in an effort to steal a march on the more radical reformers, the USSR Council of Ministers at about the same time sanctioned an experiment with the regional *khozraschet* to begin in 1989 in the three Baltic republics, Belorussia, Sverdlovsk oblast, the Tatar ASSR, and Moscow. In connection with the presentation of the 1989 plan and budget to the Supreme Soviet at the end of October 1988, both the chairman of the USSR Gosplan and the minister of finance referred to a document still in preparation to establish a new mechanism for the management of regional economies.[56] This document, which was published in March 1989 in the form of a draft law, is far less radical than that put forth by representatives of the Baltic republics.[57] Essentially, the document spells out in some detail the provisions for enhanced republican authority for managing their economies and new budgetary arrangements with Moscow as laid out in the overall program for economic reform. In September the Supreme Soviet remanded the draft to the Council of Ministers with instructions to bring it into conformity with other proposed new laws on property, land, and related matters. In the interim, the Baltic republics and Belorussia have been authorized to experiment with various models of economic autonomy, beginning on 1 January 1990. Along with all this, a divisive discussion has surfaced over the question of resource transfers among the republics—the question of "Who feeds whom?". The arbitrary nature of Soviet prices and budgetary policies precludes a definitive resolution of that issue, which would require a price reform that reveals the actual costs and values of products and resources.

Finally, Gorbachev has continued to insist on the primacy of state interests in the management of the periphery. In his speech to the Nineteenth Party Conference, for example, he warned that "those who believe that decentralization is opening up the floodgates for parochialism or national egoism will be making a grave mistake," and that "any obsession with national isolation can only lead to economic and cultural impoverishment."[58] This theme was emphasized once more in his address at the Central Committee Plenum on nationalities policy held in September 1989.[59] The new party platform that was adopted at this plenum stressed the need to retain a large role for the central government in managing the economy and setting economic policy, while simultaneously according the republics wide latitude for decision making within that framework.[60] Such has been the thrust of economic *perestroika* from the outset. The current slogan is: "strong center, strong republics."

CONCLUSIONS

Over the past two decades, the official rhetoric on the economic aspects of the nationalities problem has changed dramatically. Before Brezhnev's speech in 1972 on the fiftieth anniversary of the formation of the USSR, economic plans and party statements had routinely declared the goal of equalizing the levels of economic development and living standards among national groups. Since then, this objective has disappeared from official documents, replaced by an ever more forceful stress on developing the USSR as a "unified national-economic complex." The CPSU resolution adopted in early 1982 to commemorate the sixtieth anniversary of the establishment of the USSR stressed this theme, declaring the intent to "decide economic and social questions primarily from a general state approach," while resolutely combatting all manifestations of "parochialism" and "nationalism."[61] In the past three five-year plans, the goal of equalizing development rates has been replaced by a stated intent to ensure economic development in all republics. According to some Soviet scholars, the very success of past policies in equalizing development rates and educational and cultural levels among national groups now makes it possible, indeed imperative, for all peoples to contribute to economic progress in the country as a whole.[62] This theme was emphasized in Gorbachev's speech to the Twenty-seventh Party

Congress: "It is especially important to see to it that the contribution of all the republics to the development of the single national-economic complex corresponds to their increased economic and spiritual potential."[63]

The change in policy, or at least rhetoric, is revealed clearly in a comparison of statements in the new Party Program adopted in 1986 with those in its predecessor approved in 1961.[64] The 1961 Program enunciated a policy of ensuring "actual equality of all nations with full consideration for their interests and devoting special attention to those areas of the country that are in need of more rapid development." The 1986 Program declares that the "nationalities question inherited from the past has been successfully solved" and stresses the primacy of all-union interests and the promotion of division of labor among the republics. The new Program also states the intent to "struggle consistently against any manifestations of parochialism and national narrow-mindedness" while "showing constant concern for further increasing the role of the republics, autonomous oblasts and autonomous districts in carrying out countrywide tasks."

Another theme stressed in recent policy pronouncements is the critical importance of full integration of the republican economies into the all-union economy. Gorbachev stated in February 1986 that "the development of cooperative production arrangements, cooperation and mutual assistance among the republics is in the highest interests of our multinational state and of each republic."[65] Past Soviet regional development policies already have produced an intricate web of mutual economic dependencies among the republics. As revealed by regional input/output data, each republic is now both a major exporter and importer of goods to and from other republics. As would be expected, the small republics are much more trade-dependent than the larger ones: according to Gillula's estimates for 1966, the ratios of exports to total output were 23% to 29% in the Transcaucasian republics, Moldavia, Kirghizia, Tadzhikistan, Estonia, and Latvia, compared to 6% for the RSFSR. Import ratios were of similar magnitude.[66] Gillula also concluded that Soviet development policies have tended to foster regional specialization rather than diversification, notably in Kazakhstan and Central Asia, partly to develop their natural resources as rapidly as possible, and partly to increase their dependence on the rest of the country.[67] As Grey Hodnett has shown with regard to Central Asia, this strategy has been the subject of controversy for decades.[68]

Nonetheless, republican specialization has continued, and republican interdependence has increased. According to the Soviet economist Aleksandr G. Granberg, interrepublican trade rose faster than production during the 1970s.[69] In an unspecified year (possibly 1977), exports as a percent of production exceeded 30% in six of the eleven republics for which data were cited; the ratio of imports to total republican consumption exceeded 30% in nine of them. From input/output tables for the republics, he concludes that, in its relationship with the rest of the country, the RSFSR is basically an exporter of capital goods and an importer of consumer goods. Since production of the latter is more labor-intensive, the RSFSR indirectly imports labor and exports capital. Granberg sees this pattern as an indication of rational specialization and exchange—a trend which, in view of the differential rates of labor force growth between the RSFSR and the other republics, should be strongly promoted. Indeed, a principal theme of recent policy statements is the need to deepen interrepublican—and thus internationality—interdependence. The leadership, no doubt, regards the success achieved thus far as a great political benefit.

Despite repeated assertions that equalization in levels of development among the nationalities has been essentially achieved, a mass of evidence indicates the persistence of substantial development gaps and disparities in living standards among national groups, as we have seen. Even if the leadership had the will to do so, narrowing these gaps, or even keeping them from widening, will prove exceedingly difficult in the near term. Rates of economic growth have decreased markedly, particularly since 1975. Since labor force growth will necessarily be slow because of demographic trends, and since growth of the capital stock will continue to decelerate as a consequence of reduced growth of investment in the past, increasing the rate of economic growth will require a radical breakthrough in productivity. The sources of such a breakthrough are hard to discern. Although the Gorbachev leadership hopes to accelerate rates of growth of national income in each of the three five-year plans during 1986-2000, the Western consensus is that this goal is unrealistic and that the large-scale industrial modernization program envisioned in these plans is likely to require faster investment growth than scheduled. If this assessment is correct, the outlook for consumers is not good. In a period of such stringency, the conflicts over allocation of investment and budgetary resources are bound to be severe. This is already the implication of the current stress on renovating old plants rather than building new ones—a policy that favors the European USSR in the allocation of investment. The Russian-dominated government will be hard pressed to provide enough funds even to ensure some economic progress in all the republics; to support per capita growth in output sufficient to raise the relative position of the poorer republics with fast population growth would be even more difficult. In such an environment of austerity, resource allocation choices will take on even more of an ethnic coloration than usual.

Besides constraining resource allocation choices, the nationalities factor will inhibit the substantial decentralization and devolution of authority to regional and local bodies that constitute a key part of Gorbachev's economic reforms. Indeed, Gorbachev's self-styled "radical" economic reforms pose serious dilemmas. On the one hand, local initiative must be unleashed if productivity is to be raised and the local populations better served. But, as under the *sovnarkhoz* reforms, regional authorities can be expected to promote regional interests; charges of "localism" and counter-measures by the center could be the consequence. Moreover, real decentralization requires large reductions in the regional bureaucracies, where increasingly well-educated local elites have found suitable employment. Such cutbacks, coupled with those mandated for enterprises, will heighten the competition for white-collar jobs. This situation will create much potential for ethnic conflict, which also will be exacerbated by the widened regional income differentials inherent in the economic reforms and the stated investment policies. Republican populations may respond quite differently to newly provided opportunities to form cooperatives and engage in private economic activity. Enterprise autonomy and self-finance may work better in some republics than in others, thus generating more revenues for local budgets and higher worker incomes there. The declared intent to allocate investment and budgetary funds in accordance with a region's "contribution" to the total economy is likely to be seriously divisive, given the present price structure; certainly it would be detrimental to regions with fast-growing populations, whose relative positions have been deteriorating for some time. These regions will have to find jobs for growing numbers of young people. Should the central government decide to provide subsidies to the "have-nots" nonetheless, the "haves" can cry foul, arguing that such a policy inhibits their own development and violates the spirit of the reforms, which aim to achieve an efficient allocation of resources. Slow economic progress will add to these sources of potential ethnic tension.

Gorbachev's economic reforms put the wager on the efficacy of economic stimuli to induce workers to work harder and managers to manage their firms better and more innovatively in order to bring about the dramatic upsurge in productivity that is so urgently needed. That approach may elicit quite different responses among and within the republics as a consequence of differing preferences, values, and cultures. Finally, the declared intent to manage overall economic development, the direction of scientific-technical progress, and heavy industry from the center, and at the same time to vest the republics with broad authority in planning and managing their own development and to hold them responsible for the results is a contradiction in terms. Bitter wrangles, unavoidably with an ethnic coloration, will surely be the result of such inconsistency.

How all these potential consequences of Gorbachev's economic initiatives will play out in the peripheries remains to be seen. Persistent ethnic tensions could threaten his ability to carry out his policies, and ethnic factors could limit their effectiveness. Both relative economic deprivation and frustration of perceived potential for economic gains also could exacerbate ethnic tensions that arise from non-economic sources. Both the economic and the political reforms foster centrifugal forces. The policy of openness (*glasnost'*) and democratization at all levels provides the nationalities with forums in which to lobby for their perceived interests. Mikhail Gorbachev is gambling on his ability to prevent those forces from undermining his program to revitalize the Soviet economy. Thus, the nationalities dimension compounds that already gargantuan task.

Notes

1. *Pravda*, 22 December 1972.

2. *Pravda*, 9 March 1986.

3. Gregory Grossman has described this dilemma in terms of the planners having to face a "triangle of hazards"—localism, overcentralization, and loss of control. Gregory Grossman, "The Structure and Organization of the Soviet Economy," *Slavic Review*, vol. 21, no. 2 (June 1962), p. 219.

4. Iu. V. Arutiunian and Iu. V. Bromlei, eds., *Sotsial'no-kul'turnyi oblik sovetskikh natsii: Po rezul'tatam etnosotsiologicheskogo issledovaniia* (Moscow: Nauka, 1986), p. 38.

5. On this point, compare data for 1970 and 1979 given in *Narodnoe khoziaistvo SSSR 1922-1982* (Moscow: Finansy i statistika, 1982), pp. 32-33, and in Iu. V. Arutiunian, "Korennye izmeneniia v sotsial'nom sostave sovetskikh natsii," *Sotsiologicheskie issledovaniia*, 1982, no. 4, p. 23.

6. Abram Bergson, *The Real National Income of Soviet Russia since 1928* (Cambridge, MA: Harvard University Press, 1961); and Rush V. Greenslade, "Industrial Production Statistics in the USSR," in Vladimir G. Treml and John P. Hardt, eds., *Soviet Economic Statistics* (Durham, NC: Duke University Press, 1972), pp. 155-94.

7. Roman Senkiw, "The Growth of Industrial Production in Ukraine 1945-1971" (Ph.D. diss., University of Virginia, 1974).

8. As Western measures of growth of GNP and its components, I employ indexes calculated by the Central Intelligence Agency. These are described in detail in U.S. Congress, Joint Economic Committee, *USSR: Measures of Economic Growth and Development 1950-80* (Washington: U.S. Government Printing Office, 1982); and in Laurie Kurzweg, "Trends in Soviet Gross National Product," in U.S. Congress, Joint Economic Committee, *Gorbachev's Economic Plans* (Washington: U.S. Government Printing Office, 1987), vol. 1, pp. 126-65.

9. Although our data on urbanization pertain to republics, the rates of change for the titular nationality groups, regardless of residence, in the period 1959-79 were similar. For a detailed assessment of the urbanization process among individual ethnic groups, see Robert A. Lewis, Richard H. Rowland, and Ralph S. Clem, *Nationality and Population Change in Russia and the USSR: An Evaluation of Census Data, 1897-1970* (New York: Praeger, 1976), pp. 129-91.

10. This conclusion is based on employment data given in Stephen Rapawy, "Regional Employment Trends in the USSR: 1950 to 1975," in U.S. Congress, Joint Economic Committee, *Soviet Economy in a Time of Change* (Washington: U.S. Government Printing Office, 1979), vol. 1, pp. 608-11.

11. Matthew J. Sagers, "The Soviet Periphery: Economic Development of Belorussia," *Soviet Economy*, vol. 1, no. 3 (July-September 1985), p. 273.

12. Ruble values of national income for the republics are published in *Narodnoe khoziaistvo Latviiskoi SSSR v 1971 godu* (Riga: Latviiskoe otdelenie izdatel'stva "Statistika," 1972), p. 56. Ruble values of industrial production for the republics are available from their input/output tables for 1966. I am indebted to Blaine McCants for providing these data. Indexes of national income and industrial production, along with population data, are regularly published in *Narodnoe khoziaistvo SSSR*.

13. For a description and evaluation of this official measure, see Gertrude E. Schroeder, "Soviet Wage and Income Statistics," in Treml and Hardt, *Soviet Economic Statistics*, pp. 303-12.

14. The derivation of consumption values in current and constant prices is described in *USSR: Measures of Economic Growth*, pp. 317-401.

15. Alastair McAuley, *Economic Welfare in the Soviet Union: Poverty, Living Standards, and Inequality* (Madison: University of Wisconsin Press, 1979).

16. Gertrude E. Schroeder, "Regional Living Standards," in I.S. Koropeckyj and Gertrude E. Schroeder, eds., *Economics of Soviet Regions* (New York: Praeger, 1981), pp. 149-53.

17. The principal assumptions are that the official indexes of real per capita incomes are of essentially uniform quality among the republics and that uniform price trends prevail. Although neither may be correct, I believe that any disparities are not large enough seriously to distort the general picture.

18. These conclusions accord with those reached by McAuley, using a somewhat different approach. Alastair McAuley, *Economic Welfare*, pp. 99-173.

19. A variety of such data are included in Schroeder, "Regional Living Standards," pp. 131-43.

20. Irving B. Kravis, Alan Heston, and Robert Summers, *World Product and Income: International Comparisons of Real Gross Product*, United Nations International Comparison Project, Phase III (Baltimore: The Johns Hopkins University Press, 1982); and Gertrude E. Schroeder and Imogene Edwards, *Consumption in the USSR: An International Comparison*, U.S. Congress, Joint Economic Committee (Washington: U.S. Government Printing Office, 1981).

21. In a study of living standards in the six Muslim republics in 1975, McAuley concludes that personal per capita incomes of their Muslim populations were no more than 570-600 rubles per year, but that their "living standards were perhaps twice those of Muslims elsewhere in the region." Alastair McAuley, "The Soviet Muslim Population: Trends in Living Standards, 1960-75," in Yaacov Ro'i, ed., *The USSR and the Muslim World: Issues in Domestic and Foreign Policy* (London: George Allen & Unwin, 1984), pp. 95-114.

22. For example, I.S. Koropeckyj, "Growth and Productivity," in Koropeckyj and Schroeder, *Economics of Soviet Regions*, pp. 96-106.

23. There is a large and contentious literature assessing Soviet policies and achievements with regard to the equalization of levels of development among the nationalities. For a survey of this literature, see Donna Bahry and Carol Nechemias, "Half Full or Half Empty?: The Debate over Soviet Regional Equality," *Slavic Review*, vol. 40, no. 3 (Fall 1981), pp. 366-83.

24. James W. Gillula, "The Growth and Structure of Fixed Capital," in Koropeckyj and Schroeder, *Economics of Soviet Regions*, p. 167.

25. I.S. Koropeckyj, "Growth and Productivity," p. 109.

26. T.V. Checheleva and N.S. Kozlova, "Vyravnivanie urovnia ekonomicheskogo razvitiia soiuznykh respublik SSSR," in *Problemy ekonomiki razvitogo sotsializma v SSSR* (Alma-Ata: Nauka, 1974), p. 147.

27. Martin C. Spechler, "Regional Developments in the USSR, 1958-78," in *Soviet Economy in a Time of Change*, vol. 1, p. 151.

28. Gertrude E. Schroeder, "The Slowdown in Soviet Industry, 1976-82," *Soviet Economy*, vol. 1, no. 1 (January-March 1985), pp. 42-74.

29. Matthew J. Sagers, "The Soviet Periphery: Economic Development of Belorussia," *Soviet Economy*, vol. 1, no. 3 (July-September 1985), pp. 261-84.

30. Checheleva and Kozlova, "Vyravnivanie," p. 137.

31. For example, Ann Goodman and Geoffrey Schleifer, "The Soviet Labor Market in the 1980s," in U.S. Congress, Joint Economic Committee, *Soviet Economy in the 1980s: Problems and Prospects* (Washington: U.S. Government Printing Office, 1981), vol. 2, pp. 323-48; and Gertrude E. Schroeder, "Managing Labour Shortages in the Soviet Union," in Jan Adam, ed., *Employment Policies in the Soviet Union and Eastern Europe* (London: Macmillan, 1982), pp. 3-35.

32. Murray Feshbach, "Prospects for Outmigration from Central Asia and Kazakhstan in the Next Decade," in *Soviet Economy in a Time of Change*, vol. 1, pp. 656-709; Robert A. Lewis and Richard H. Rowland, *Population Redistribution in the USSR: Its Impact on Society, 1897-1977* (New York: Praeger, 1979), pp. 404-27; and Michael Rywkin, *Moscow's Muslim Challenge: Soviet Central Asia* (Armonk, NY: M.E. Sharpe, 1982), pp. 58-82.

33. Iu. V. Arutiunian, "Natsional'nye osobennosti sotsial'nogo razvitiia," *Sotsiologicheskie issledovaniia*, 1985, no. 3, p. 29.

34. For an excellent analysis of manpower problems in Central Asia, see Nancy Lubin, *Labour and Nationality in Soviet Central Asia: An Uneasy Compromise* (Princeton: Princeton University Press, 1984).

35. *Pravda*, 9 March 1986.

36. *Narodnoe khoziaistvo SSSR v 1987 g.* (Moscow: Finansy i statistika, 1988), p. 297.

37. For an account of this period, see Harry Schwartz, *The Soviet Economy since Stalin* (Philadelphia: J.B. Lippincott, 1965), pp. 87-89; S.A. Billon, "Centralization of Authority and Regional Management," in V.N. Bandera and Z.L. Melnyk, eds., *The Soviet Economy in Regional Perspective* (New York: Praeger, 1973), pp. 221-28; and Herbert S. Levine, "Recent Developments in Soviet Planning," in U.S. Congress, Joint Economic Committee, *Dimensions of Soviet Economic Power* (Washington: U.S. Government Printing Office, 1962), pp. 49-65.

38. Grey Hodnett, "The Debate over Soviet Federalism," *Soviet Studies*, vol. 18, no. 4 (April 1967), pp. 458-59.

39. See Robert Conquest, *Soviet Nationalities Policy in Practice* (New York: Praeger, 1967), p. 128.

40. *Pravda*, 28 September 1965.

41. Gosplan SSSR, *Metodicheskie ukazaniia k sostavleniiu gosudarstvennogo plana razvitiia narodnogo khoziaistva SSSR* (Moscow: Ekonomika, 1969), pp. 672-83.

42. *Pravda*, 29 July 1979.

43. *Izvestiia*, 29 March 1981.

44. V.M. Birenberg, "Sovershenstvovanie upravleniia promyshlennym proizvodstvom," in N.G. Chumachenko et. al., *Intensifikatsiia promyshlennogo proizvodstva* (Kiev: Naukova dumka, 1985), p. 94.

45. See, for example, V.M. Borodiuk et al., *Kompleksnye tselevye programmy v soiuznoi respublike* (Kiev: Naukova dumka, 1984), pp. 6, 43.

46. *Pravda*, 18 January 1986.

47. G. Kh. Popov, *Effektivnoe upravlenie* (Moscow: Ekonomika, 1985), pp. 235-41.

48. For an excellent analysis of the regional politics of budgetary allocations, see Donna Bahry, *Outside Moscow: Power Politics and Budgetary Policy in the Soviet Republics* (New York: New York University Press, 1987).

49. *Pravda*, 26 February 1986, translated in *Current Digest of the Soviet Press* (henceforth *CDSP*), vol. 38, no. 8 (26 March 1986), p. 17.

50. *Pravda*, 30 July 1986.

51. *Pravda*, 27 June 1987. The document is entitled "Basic Provisions for Radically Restructuring Economic Management."

52. *O korennoi perestroike upravleniia ekonomikoi: Sbornik dokumentov* (Moscow: Gospolitizdat, 1988), pp. 208-35.

53. In 1985-86, the share of industrial output managed by all-union ministries ranged from 29% to 40% in the seven republics for which data were available in their statistical handbooks.

54. *19th All-Union Conference of the CPSU: Documents and Materials* (Moscow: Novosti Press Agency Publishing House, 1988), p. 48.

55. *Sovetskaia Estoniia*, 27 September 1988, translated in U.S. Foreign Broadcast Information Service, *Daily Report: Soviet Union*, 27 October 1988, p. 56-57.

56. *Pravda*, 28 October 1988.

57. *Pravda*, 14 March 1989.

58. *19th All-Union Conference of the CPSU*, pp. 60, 64.

59. *Pravda*, 20 September 1989.

60. *Pravda*, 24 September 1989.

61. *Pravda*, 21 February 1982.

62. For example, M.P. Osad'ko, "Vyravnovanie urovnei ekonomicheskogo razvitiia soiuznykh respublik," in V.N. Cherkovets, ed., *Teoreticheskie problemy formirovaniia i razvitiia edinogo narodnokhoziaistvennogo kompleksa* (Moscow: Izdatel'stvo Moskovskogo universiteta, 1985), pp. 36-49.

63. *Pravda*, 26 February 1986, in *CDSP*, vol. 38, no. 8 (26 March 1986), p. 23.

64. The full text of the 1961 Party Program was published in *Pravda*, 2 November 1961, and in English translation as: *Programme of the Communist Party of the Soviet Union* (Moscow: Foreign Languages Publishing House, 1961), the section on national relations on pp. 93-97. The new Program was published in *Pravda*, 7 March 1986, and in translation: *The Programme of the Communist Party of the Soviet Union: A New Edition* (Moscow: Novosti Press Agency Publishing House, 1986), the section on national relations on pp. 61-63.

65. *Pravda*, 26 February 1986, in *CDSP*, vol. 38, no. 8 (26 March 1986), p. 23.

66. James W. Gillula, "The Economic Interdependence of Soviet Republics," in *Soviet Economy in a Time of Change*, vol. 1, p. 640.

67. Ibid., pp. 646-52.

68. Grey Hodnett, "Technology and Social Change in Soviet Central Asia: The Politics of Cotton Growing," in Henry W. Morton and Rudolph L. Tökés, eds., *Soviet Politics and Society in the 1970s* (New York: The Free Press, 1974), pp. 60-117.

69. A.G. Granberg, "Ekonomicheskoe vzaimodeistvie sovetskikh respublik," *Ekonomika i organizatsiia promyshlennogo proizvodstva*, 1982, no. 12, pp. 3-37.

11

Half Full or Half Empty?
The Debate Over
Soviet Regional Equality

Donna Bahry and Carol Nechemias[1]

Ever since the early days of Bolshevik rule, Soviet leaders have promised to equalize socioeconomic development among the union republics. Their reasons, as I.S. Koropeckyj notes, have ranged from the ideological to the purely political.[2] Equality is deemed an ideological necessity: every region must achieve a similarly advanced stage of development in order to pave the way for communism. Regional equality is also viewed as a way to defuse the nationality issue—in the short run by minimizing the socioeconomic disparities inherited from tsarist days and in the long run by creating a new climate in which local nationalism will disappear. The benefits of equalization should also spill over into the international arena, where the advances of traditionally underdeveloped Soviet regions highlight the "appeals of the Soviet development model for impatient revolutionary modernizers."[3]

The question, however, is whether the USSR has actually closed the gap between rich and poor regions. Leonid Brezhnev claimed success in 1972, arguing that Soviet policy had eliminated the most significant regional disparities.[4] But Western assessments of republic conditions are contradictory. With respect to industrial production, for example, Vsevolod Holubnychy demonstrated that the disparities between Russia and the non-Russian republics grew until 1958 and then decreased slightly, while Koropeckyj has shown that inequality among the republics lessened until 1968 and then began to grow.[5] For urban housing, Gertrude Schroeder has noted that the republics became

From *Slavic Review*, 40: 3 (Fall 1981), pp. 366-83. Reprinted by permission from the publisher.

slightly more equal during the 1960s, while Henry Morton has concluded the opposite.[6] For economic appropriations, John Echols and Jack Bielasiak have found little evidence of any consistent equalization policy, while Alec Nove and J.A. Newth, Martin Spechler, and James Gillula have found a pattern of redistribution from rich to poor republics.[7] For social welfare, Schroeder, Echols, and Bielasiak have demonstrated that government spending has become more equal over time, and Elizabeth Clayton has shown that government policy has transferred income from the more to the less developed regions.[8] In contrast, Peter Zwick has found no pattern of compensation for poorer republics and argues that, if anything, Soviet policy has exacerbated old inequities.[9]

Finally, Ellen Mickiewicz has suggested that there has been neither a decline nor an increase in regional inequality: there is little evidence that conditions in any of the republics have changed more or less rapidly than in others.[10]

In one sense, these contrasting views are easily explained: each author has relied on a slightly different conception of equality or different data, methods, or standards to evaluate regional conditions. Thus the controversy can be traced to different research strategies. Our aim here is to show how these strategies influence assessments of Soviet regions. To simplify the discussion, we will explore the way Western scholars approach four basic issues: one, how to define "equality"; two, how to select data to measure regional disparities; three, how to choose statistical procedures to evaluate regional data; and four, how to assign meaning or significance to the results. This last issue deserves special emphasis, since Western and Soviet authors alike tend to attach great political importance to regional inequalities and to their implications for interethnic relations. We devote the final part of the article to questions about the statistical as well as theoretical significance of regional differences.

Several authors have written about the problems of measuring Soviet regional development, and we draw heavily on their valuable contributions and caveats.[11] We also reanalyze their data, wherever possible, in order to compare their findings. To assure comparability, we use examples for the same years and rely on a single statistical method—a coefficient of variation (CV)—that measures the gap among regions relative to the USSR average.[12] A CV of zero means that there is no gap; each republic is equal to all others. A CV greater than zero reveals inequality, and the higher the value, the more unequal the republics. Demonstrating the differences among alternate statistical procedures is more complicated. Where possible, we take a single set of data, calculate different statistics for it, and contrast the results. We will be concentrating on the fifteen union republics, the major political units in the Soviet federation and the ones most heavily emphasized in Western research. Scholars generally have treated them as surrogate variables for national minorities, since there are more data available for republics than for ethnic groups. But disparities among the republics may not correspond to patterns of inequality among nationalities (or among local communities).[13] In many non-

Russian regions, Russians and other nonindigenous nationality groups are disproportionately located in urban areas, where socioeconomic development is most advanced. As a result, republic-level data underestimate the amount of variation across nationalities. Nonetheless, all studies of inequality must deal with the same problems of conceptualization and measurement, regardless of the units they compare. In this sense, our discussion of research strategies applies to comparisons across ethnic groups (and localities) as well as to the republics.

We have been necessarily selective in choosing examples, since no single article can do justice to all the definitions, data, methods, and standards currently in use. We concentrate on the most disparate cases to show that even slight differences in research strategies have a profound effect on conclusions about Soviet regional development. By reviewing the "state of the art" in research on republic inequalities, we hope to reconcile seemingly divergent results and to suggest future lines of inquiry.

One of the primary reasons for Western disagreement about Soviet regional equalization is that Soviet authors do not agree on the meaning of equality. Should each republic have the same configuration of industries or the same level of urbanization? Must every region have the same level of income, identical types and levels of public services, or the same standard of living? All of these conditions have been cited as proper goals of Soviet policy in a debate that began soon after the Revolution and still rages. In the course of the debate, Soviet regional policy has undergone several changes in emphasis and interpretation.

Early party congresses called for industrialization in underdeveloped regions and massive investment in social overhead to provide the appropriate urban, industrial environment for the "new Soviet man."[14] Yet the blanket endorsement of equalization was by no means a simple issue. Regions with widely varying natural conditions and cultures were unlikely to develop equal industrial complexes quickly, if ever. More important, the insistence on equality could sacrifice nationwide economic growth by diverting scarce resources from more to less productive areas. Massive redistribution threatened to be expensive for a nation intent on rapid development. Thus when national industrialization became the top priority, regional economic equality was, as F. Douglas Whitehouse observes, "overshadowed."[15]

There was less controversy over equalization in social investment. . . . The question of how much to spend in each region remained. Equalization could be interpreted to mean higher appropriations in poorer regions, a course advocated in the 1920s and 1930s, or to mean equal funding, as recommended by Nikita Khrushchev in 1956.[16] Soviet authors still disagree about these issues. One group calls for comparable levels of industrialization to guarantee the same standard of living across republics.[17] Others claim that obvious differences in natural resources among the republics and differences in the branch structure of each region's economy make it unrealistic to equalize industry.[18] Social welfare provokes similar disagreement. There is a consensus that conditions should be the same across regions, but it is unclear whether this is to be achieved through equal levels of public services or equal levels of expenditures.[19]

Western research shares the same disagreements. All studies of regional equality are ultimately concerned with the leveling of socioeconomic disparities among the republics, but some concentrate on equality of government spending, some on equality of government services (such as education and health care), and others on equality in the impact of government actions (on such things as levels of income, urbanization, industrialization, and mortality). And many deal with a combination of the three.

These three emphases have very different implications for regional development. Equal expenditures need not produce equal services, and equal services are not likely to have the same effects everywhere.[20] The impact of government action in both cases depends on local social, economic, and cultural conditions which can frustrate the most sincere commitment to equality. While Moscow may set itself the goal of urbanizing and industrializing less developed regions, its success depends on local efficiency in carrying out central directives and local residents' willingness to move to urban areas, things over which Moscow exerts only limited control. As the current dilemma in Central Asia attests, some local residents are far from willing to give up the countryside for the city, even if city jobs are more plentiful and more lucrative than employment in the village.[21] The pull of traditional culture can outweigh the standard inducements to "modernization," especially when modernization is linked to a different (Russian) culture.

Local differences in productivity also frustrate efforts to modernize less developed regions. Identical levels of industrial investment can easily lead to unequal industrial growth, because of differences in local efficiency.[22] The same is true for other types of public expenditures: equal spending for health care, for example, can result in unequal medical facilities, because planning and construction are more efficient in some regions than in others. Furthermore, all republics could be equally well provided with doctors and hospitals, but may experience significant differences in the "health" of their residents because of varying social and cultural conditions.[23] This "slippage" between policy and outcome means that inequalities sometimes persist in spite of Soviet efforts to close the gap among the republics.

If outcomes are an imperfect guide to policy commitments, how do we judge whether Moscow has truly made an effort to promote regional equality? Western scholars are divided over the best approach. Some look for evidence of "compensation"—a pattern of budgetary appropriations, capital investments, and other benefits that are higher in less developed republics than in more developed regions.[24] Backward areas, so the argument goes, need to spend more than their richer counterparts in order to catch up. Other authors look for evidence of equal funding in each republic, a policy that also would constitute an attempt to close the gap in regional development.[25]   Equal appropriations mean that poor regions have more and rich ones relatively less to spend than the economic gap between them would normally permit.   A third strategy is simply to look for redistribution.[26]   In this case, even though poor republics spend less than their richer neighbors, they spend more than local economic conditions alone would allow, and the subsidy can help gradually to reduce the disparities among republics.

Intuitively, it might seem that nothing short of compensation could actually eliminate regional inequalities.   But the three funding options differ only in degree: a compensatory pattern is simply a more extensive form of redistribution.   The other two patterns are certainly less dramatic and are likely to be slower in combating inequalities, but they can still help to equalize regional development.   This would explain how health care and education could grow more equal among the republics between 1940 and 1970, as Zwick has shown, even though social welfare spending was not compensatory.[27]   Poor regions did, however, receive a social welfare subsidy.[28]   They spent more relatively, if not absolutely, than their richer neighbors.   Clearly, by looking only for proof of compensation, we would overlook important but less obvious patterns of redistribution.

This is precisely what has led to contradictory Western views about the Soviet commitment to equality.   Studies that emphasize compensation fail to find much evidence of it, while those that look for equal funding or redistribution find that Moscow *has* subsidized less developed regions.   The results are basically products of different research objectives: authors who focus on equality or redistribution of funds ask whether Moscow offers preferential treatment to poor republics.   To emphasize compensation, on the other hand, is to ask whether Moscow's policy is *sufficient* to reduce inequality.   But sufficiency is very difficult to define, unless we can specify the degree of redistribution needed to alter regional disparities.   Since some inequalities have lessened even without a compensatory policy, the emphasis on compensation may impose an unnecessarily high standard for evaluating Soviet policy.   A more appropriate standard is likely to emerge only with more extensive research on what regional expenditures actually buy.

Different definitions of equality and effort have given rise to even more varied types of data to measure regional conditions.   Western studies have assessed inequalities in government budgets, capital investments, wages, incomes, housing space, schools, doctors, hospital beds, land devoted to agriculture, electric power generation, industrial output, gross domestic and net material product, employment, urbanization, and more.   It goes without saying that each of these offers a different insight into regional disparities.   It is less obvious that similar types of data yield different results.   Alastair McAuley has demonstrated this in his careful study of incomes, and Schroeder, Spechler and Koropeckyj have provided similar analyses of wage and national income and product data.[29] Other important indicators of regional conditions have received less attention, even though they figure just as prominently in measuring inequalities.

Data on "impacts" or social conditions are the most complex, and nothing illustrates this better than the various attempts to compare levels of urbanization among the republics. Since other regional disparities can be traced to the urban-rural gap, a measure of urban development is a standard item in studies of Soviet regions. The most common choice is the official data offered in Soviet statistical publications. The figures are ambiguous, however: the definition of urban and rural communities varies from republic to republic and from one census to another. In addition, there are arbitrary distinctions made within each republic. As the list of Soviet definitions reveals, all urban communities must be of a specified minimum size, and all must have a minimum number of "workers and employees"—a category that includes blue- and white-collar workers and state farmers, but excludes collective farmers. An agricultural area can thus be considered either urban or rural depending on its mix of state and collective farms. Two republics with equal numbers of farmers or equal levels of agricultural output can have different levels of "urbanization," simply because one has more laborers on state, rather than collective farms.

Regions are also likely to have different levels of urbanization because republics use different criteria in defining an urban area. In Turkmenia, for example, a "city" must have at least 5,000 people, while a "city" in the Ukraine must have 10,000. And even within a single republic, a town with as few as 500 residents (251 of them "workers and employees") can be counted as urban, while a community of 5,000 or more could be counted as rural if "workers and employees" are in the minority. Moreover, many of the numbers were different for earlier censuses, so data from one census to another are not strictly comparable.

The effect of these inconsistencies becomes clear when we contrast official Soviet urban statistics with other measures of urbanization. We chose two alternatives that clearly show how similar data can yield very different results. For one indicator, we chose a single number—5,000 or more residents—to define a community as urban and applied it to all the republics.[30] For the second, we chose "agricultural land density" (the ratio of each region's sown area to its total area), a measure used in one recent study to assess "rural-urban polarization."[31] The two produce widely disparate CVs: one is 27 percent lower than that yielded by official Soviet urban data, and the other is 300 percent higher. Are the republics much more or much less equal than the official statistics indicate?

At the high end of the scale, the CV for agricultural land density overstates the gap among regions for two reasons. First, the ratio of sown area to total area in each republic represents just a fraction of all agricultural land: sown area makes up 20 percent of land devoted to agriculture in the USSR, and the percentages for the republics vary.[32]   Second, natural conditions also vary among regions. There are vast differences in arable land from one republic to the next, and this too contributes to the high CV for agricultural land density.

In contrast, the use of a single numerical standard to define urban areas reveals far less inequality among regions.   It also reveals that some traditionally underdeveloped regions (Uzbekistan, Kazakhstan, Moldavia, and Kirgizia) are more urban than they appear to be in official Soviet statistics, and some of the more developed republics (the Ukraine, Belorussia, and Estonia) are less so. The results might be different, of course, if a different cutoff point were used. Raising the minimum to 50,000 residents, for example, would give a CV of 0.29.[33]   Nonetheless, any cutoff point applied to all the republics guarantees a consistency lacking in the other definitions of urbanization and thus promises an equivalent measure for each region. Even where there is a consensus on the appropriate data to use in regional comparisons, researchers still come to different conclusions about inequality because of the need to estimate missing data.   Statistics on republic industrial production offer a case in point.   Since Soviet publications provide only piecemeal evidence on the output of each region's industries, Western authors must estimate annual industrial production. The numbers can vary enormously. . . .

In many ways, rival definitions and incomplete data are far less of a problem in measuring public services than in measuring outcomes.   Data on the availability of doctors, hospitals, schools, housing, and day care, for example, are relatively simple to locate and compare across republics.   Yet seemingly modest differences in the choice of data can still produce different conclusions about regional equality.   Consider two possible ways of measuring disparities in access to primary and secondary education.   On the one hand, we can count the number of schools available to children in each republic.   The result would be a CV that was relatively large in 1970 (0.41) and on the increase from earlier years—a development that has been labeled a "slipping backward in the availability of educational facilities" among the republics.[34]   On the other hand, we could measure the percentage of all school-age children *enrolled* in primary and secondary schools, and this would lead us to the opposite conclusion: the CV was small in 1970 (0.04) and diminishing in comparison with earlier years.[35]   The reason for the divergence is simple.   Consolidation, especially in rural areas, leads to fewer, but larger schools.   Thus the number of schools can grow marginally or even decline in some regions, while the number of students served can increase substantially.   Concentrating on the number of students who are actually served by each republic's educational establishment offers a truer picture of the inequalities in access to education.

In comparison with data on outcomes and public services, budget and investment statistics are the most straightforward, if only because there are few alternatives for measuring public spending. Yet appropriations data demand the most careful interpretation, precisely because they seem so unambiguous.[36]

Republic budgets, for example, omit a major share of government spending in the republic. The only expenditures they include are the ones made directly by republic governments on programs under republic subordination. If factories or farms in a region happen to fall under the central government's jurisdiction, expenditures devoted to them are not included in the republic budget. As a result, the more economic administration is centralized, the less republic budgetary expenditures reveal about actual government spending in each region.

This special feature of Soviet fiscal federalism affects republic budgets in three ways. First, it means that republic budgetary data omit more than half of all expenditures for economic development in the republics.[37] It also guarantees unequal republic expenditures, since only a few branches of production (for example, coal, metallurgy, and oil refining) come under even partial republic jurisdiction, and these branches of the economy are found in only a few Soviet regions.[38] Third, Soviet practices guarantee fluctuations in republic spending from one year to the next—there is no clear trend toward or away from equality. Soviet authorities tinker constantly with the division of tasks between central and republic agencies, so administrative and budgetary responsibilities are frequently shifted from central to regional, or regional to central, management. The changes were most pronounced, of course, during the *Sovnarkhoz* experiment (1957-65), but they have continued on a less dramatic scale ever since. As a result, increases or decreases in republic budgets are often products of budgetary reorganization rather than changes in spending policies.

Regional investment data present fewer problems. They represent all the capital expenditures allocated to each republic and are not subject to the distortions that characterize budgetary data. This distinction is important because budgets and investments—along with the other data we have reanalyzed—provide different estimates of the regional gap. For example, the CV for per capita investment in 1970 equals 0.22, while per capita budgetary expenditures for economic development give a coefficient (0.39) that is 77 percent higher.[39]

Regional social welfare spending poses similar but less serious measurement problems. Administration of health, education, welfare, and culture is also divided between central and regional agencies, and Moscow's expenditures are not counted in republic budgets (even though the money is spent in the republics). But all of the republics do have similar social welfare institutions to administer. Budgetary organization is therefore far less of a complicating factor than it is in economic expenditures.

The budgetary system goes a long way toward explaining why Western scholars disagree about inequalities in economic funding among the republics: research on budgets has found no obvious pattern of equalization or redistribution, while studies of investment have come to the opposite conclusion.[40] Since budgetary organization exaggerates differences in funding among the republics, budgetary data appear to be less reliable as evidence of regional equality.

Given the relative abundance of data on Soviet regions, there are many more ways of measuring interrepublic differences than the ones we have outlined. We have reanalyzed a few examples simply to show that the choice of data alone can lead to contradictory conclusions about the progress of equalization, even when the data—as in the case of urbanization, education, or appropriations—presumably measure the same thing.

The choice of a statistical technique also affects the way we view regional conditions. The same data, analyzed different ways, can produce very different results. By calculating the ratio of the highest to the lowest ranking republic scores as a percentage of the national average, we would conclude that the regional gap lessened somewhat between 1960 and 1970.[41] By comparing changes in average housing space for developed versus underdeveloped regions, we would conclude the opposite: inequalities grew over the decade.[42] A third conclusion emerges from the CVs for 1960 and 1970—that there was no change, since we obtain the same value (0.16) for both years. Which method is most appropriate?

The answer depends on the aspect of inequality to be emphasized. It may be useful to look at the highest and lowest ranking republics if local *perceptions* of inequality are deemed to be important; the population in any given republic may judge their well-being by comparing local conditions with the richest or poorest republic. But to focus on the highest and lowest ranking areas indicates little about the relative position of the other thirteen regions. The middle republics could be far more equal than the ones at the top and bottom of the scale, or they could be highly polarized; the highest/lowest ratio cannot tell us which. Comparing average conditions in certain regions, on the other hand, can help to identify differences among particular groups of republics. Yet this approach poses a similar problem, since it reveals nothing about the degree of differentiation within each group. In contrast, a CV reflects the entire distribution and thus gives a more complete summary measure of inequalities among all fifteen republics.[43]

A CV, however, can only be used to analyze a single variable at a time; it cannot reveal the interrelationships among different dimensions of inequality. Analysis of joint relationships requires multivariate procedures; and these too can produce conflicting views of the regional gap.

The same is true of results based on correlation and regression analysis. Two or more measures of regional conditions can be highly correlated, but still produce very different views of the degree of inequality. To illustrate this point, we compared the results of correlation analysis with CVs for several key measures of republic economic conditions—for republic gross domestic product, net material product, retail trade, industrial output, and "total income" (personal income plus the value of public goods and services) for 1970. All of the variables are highly correlated (the lowest coefficient is 0.93), and every coefficient is statistically significant. But one must compare them with the CVs for republic economic conditions, where some variables are much more equally distributed than others. The gap in republics' gross domestic products is almost 50 percent greater than the inequality in regional total income. Personal incomes are thus more equal than would be predicted from local levels of economic development. This is something that correlation coefficients simply cannot show.

Other examples lead to the same conclusion. For instance, there is an extremely high correlation coefficient (0.99) between each republic's gross domestic product and its level of spending for education in 1970.[44] One might argue that spending on education is almost wholly determined by each republic's level of economic development: rich areas do well by their schools, and poor ones do not. The strong correlation would seemingly belie Moscow's commitment to equality. But here, too, the CVs tell a different story. The CV equals 0.30 for gross domestic product per capita, but only 0.09 for per capita educational expenditures. Again, there is far less inequality in funding than is predictable from the gap in republic economic development, and correlation (or regression) analysis does not reveal this difference.

Since the choice of a statistical method alone can determine whether an assessment of Soviet regions will be positive or negative, each method demands careful evaluation. If it omits information about some regions (as in the case of the ratio between the highest and lowest ranking republics) or if it does not directly measure the dispersion among regions (as in the case of correlation and regression analysis), it should be interpreted accordingly.

Whatever the statistical method used, it is important to specify the standard by which results are to be judged. What exactly is "serious" inequality? How little of a gap must there be among republics before Soviet policy is pronounced a success? There must always be some differentiation across regions, if only because local needs, preferences, and costs inevitably vary. Thus the variance, or CV, will never reach zero. Then how much of the remaining inequality is significant?

There is no accepted common standard in Western studies of Soviet regions. Instead, there are two strategies for evaluating *relative* degrees of inequality—one based on cross-national comparisons and the other based on changes within the USSR over time. In fact, even cross-national studies compare temporal changes within each nation, so the choice of a time frame is equally important in both cases. The issue of temporal change raises several questions. First, how should the "right" time period be defined? All years are obviously not the same for purposes of measuring regional differences. Where research concentrates on a period initially marked by little inequality, the pace of further equalization should be predictably modest.

By the same token, a study of Soviet regions might focus on an "abnormal" period. Spechler points out, for example, that some research has focused on years marked by economic disruptions and so may not capture the real trend among republics.[45] Similarly, research on regional trends may simply underestimate the number of years required to assess equalization. As every policy analyst knows, it can take several years for government to initiate, adopt, and implement policy and several more before the effects are realized. This is especially true for regional equalization, which, as Holubnychy noted, is ". . . possible only in the sufficiently long run. . . ."[46] Conclusions about the success or failure of Soviet policy thus hinge on the time frame employed. The shorter the period, the less the odds of a positive assessment.

Studies that concentrate on selected years confront a different problem—the trend may not always move in the same direction. If regions are more (or less) equal in 1970 than in 1960 or 1950, Moscow is typically presumed to be a success (failure) in its quest for equalization. But data in the intervening years may move in a different direction. Koropeckyj shows, for example, that the degree of equality in industrial development fluctuated in the mere ten years between 1958 and 1968.[47] And Brian Silver has found evidence that inequalities move in a U-shaped curve over time. He suggests that the very "dynamic of change" itself may be curvilinear.[48] Thus longitudinal studies might well prove contradictory, depending on the number of years analyzed and the specific years from which the data are taken.

Yet however long the period studied and however well chosen, the question remains as to the significance of the findings. What is serious inequality to one author can just as easily be negligible to another. This is especially important since disparities among the republics presumably hold major theoretical significance. Political payoffs are supposed to follow logically from regional equalization, and in fact most of the justification for our concern with equality lies in this assumption. Ann Sheehy summarizes the argument: "Where ethnic and religious differences exist and have a territorial base, economic grievances can and do fuel potentially destructive nationalisms."[49] Soviet thinking on this issue is strikingly similar: since Lenin's time, the solution to nationality problems has been sought primarily through the equalization of socioeconomic conditions among republics and their resident nationalities. The rationale focuses on the grievances of the have-nots: once they are brought up to the same level as the most advanced regions and nationalities, the causes for strife will presumably disappear. Yet there are serious questions about the relevance and validity of the presumed relationship between regional inequality and ethnic conflict.

One such reservation we noted earlier: disparities among republics do not match inequalities among national minorities. Even if they did, we would still question whether socioeconomic equalization has the predicted effect on ethnic nationalism. For one thing, as in the case of the Croatians in Yugoslavia or the

Basques and Catalans in Spain, local nationalism is hardly confined to poor regions. The Baltic republics on the average are reported to be highly nationalistic, despite their advanced industrial development and high standards of living.[50]   Rather than regarding themselves as free from economic grievances, the Baltic peoples may instead think that they would be better off with more autonomy or even outright independence.   They may consider themselves exploited, since they are subsidizing less developed regions in the USSR.   And they may compare their living standards not with other Soviet regions but with their Scandinavian neighbors.   Rather than generating the acceptance of new identities, new loyalties, and a sense of brotherhood among Soviet nationalities, these circumstances are likely to promote ethnic hostility.

Socioeconomic advances in less developed regions may likewise be no guarantee of national harmony.   Some evidence suggests, for instance, that socioeconomic modernization may reduce traditional varieties of nationalism—prejudices stemming from low levels of education, religious differences, and simple lack of inter-ethnic conflict—only to stimulate a new variety, based on heightened competition among ethnic elites for high-level jobs. Iu. V. Arutiunian has pointed to this phenomenon among Tatars; Juris Dreifelds has noted resistance by the republic's leadership, to large-scale immigration in Latvia; and Tõnu Parming has spoken of ethnic conflict ensuing from increased "competition for the urban middle ground" among well-educated groups of natives and immigrants.[51]   The importation of labor, often a concomitant of development in the USSR, may give rise to tensions and complaints, especially among the intelligentsia of a minority nationality group living in its own union or autonomous republic.

In addition, emphasis on socioeconomic conditions may overlook the fact that nonmaterial factors also have an important influence on levels of ethnic nationalism.   Perhaps we go even further than those Soviet who view the "mental lives" of nations as determined by economic life.   Much Western research relies on the work of Karl Deutsch, whose basic theories emphasize that modernization, in the form of increases in urbanization, schooling, and communications, leads to assimilation, to the transfer of primary allegiances from the ethnic group to the state.[52]   Both Soviet and Western researchers have challenged this assumption.[53]   Arutiunian, for example, notes in his study of Moldavia that economic development internationalizes some aspects of life—sociooccupational structure, concentration in particular occupations, social mobility, use of leisure, family and home life, and so on.[54]   But other ethnic features such as national self-awareness and use of the native tongue tend to persist.   This leads Arutiunian to argue that various types of ethnic phenomena "are not necessarily very closely related" nor easily influenced by such factors as urbanization and rising levels of education.[55]   In sum, "the fact is that, regardless of the social position or level of education of a Moldavian, and whatever the intensity of his cultural life, he remains a Moldavian, just as a

Russian remains a Russian, and this is manifested quite clearly among people who play different social roles."[56]

Silver, comparing ethnic identification across the major Soviet nationalities, suggests that socioeconomic advances do further the goals of Russification, but the impact is mediated by traditional religion and culture. Moslems, for example, have been less likely than Orthodox groups in similar socioeconomic conditions to shift ethnic identity.[57] Thus the leveling of socioeconomic differences may contribute to but does not guarantee a corresponding reduction in traditional ethnic loyalties. Economic inequality may increase ethnic hostility, but to treat equality in the distribution of benefits and services as the cardinal factor in resolving the nationality problem is to underestimate the power of traditional culture.

Our first concern in this article has been to show that strategies used to evaluate Soviet regional equality often determine the results. To emphasize this point, we concentrated on examples that produce widely differing estimates of the gap among republics. Judging from the examples we reviewed, the most pessimistic assessments of Soviet efforts and successes in promoting regional equality are too pessimistic. In the case of urbanization, industrial development, economic and educational appropriations, and educational access, the most negative findings overstate the degree of inequality, primarily because of the particular choice of definitions, data, and methods used to assess regional conditions.

This is not to proclaim the Soviet promise of equality an unquestioned success: there are still disparities in virtually every aspect of regional development. The problem is to determine which of them are significant and to decide what implications they hold for the Soviet system. Though we attach great theoretical meaning to socioeconomic differences, there is little agreement on the degree of inequality likely to pose serious problems for the political order. As a result, virtually any disparity among the republics can be—and often is—labeled significant, no matter what its magnitude. And the ambiguity over the meaning of tangible inequalities is heightened by contrasting evidence on the link between such disparities and the ethnic tensions they presumably feed. In sum, there is clear evidence that the subsidies help to improve the lot of less developed regions (albeit slowly). But there is far less proof that equalization always has the intended results.

Notes

1. This is a revised version of a paper presented at the annual meeting of the Southwestern Social Science Association, Fort Worth, Texas, March 1979. The authors would like to thank Philip Stewart, Brian Silver, and the anonymous referees for their suggestions.

2. I.S. Koropeckyj, "Equalization of Regional Development in Socialist Countries: An Empirical Study," *Economic Development and Cultural Change*, 21, no. 1 (October 1972): 68.

3. Gregory J. Massell, "Modernization and National Policy in Soviet Central Asia: Problems and Prospects," in Paul Cocks, Robert V. Daniels, and Nancy Whittier Heer, eds., *The Dynamics of Soviet Politics* (Cambridge, Mass, 1976), p. 265.

4. *Pravda*, December 22, 1972, p. 5.

5. Vsevolod Holubnychy, "Some Economic Aspects of Relations Among the Soviet Republics," in Erich Goldhagen, ed., *Ethnic Minorities in the Soviet Union* (New York, 1968), p. 72 and Koropeckyj, "Equalization of Regional Development," pp. 79-80.

6. Gertrude E. Schroeder, "Regional Differences in Incomes and Levels of Living in the USSR," in V.N. Bandera and Z.L. Melnyk, eds., *The Soviet Economy in Regional Perspective* (New York, 1973), p. 183 and Henry W. Morton, "What Have Soviet Leaders Done About the Housing Crisis?" in Henry W. Morton and Rudolf L. Tökés, eds., *Soviet Politics and Society in the 1970's* (New York, 1974), p. 170.

7. John M. Echols, "Politics, Budgets, and Regional Equality in Communist and Capitalist Systems," *Comparative Political Studies*, 8, no. 3 (October 1975): 271-73; Jack Bielasiak, "Policy Choices and Regional Equality among the Soviet Republics," *American Political Science Review*, 74, no. 2 (June 1980): 399; Alec Nove and J.A. Newth, *The Soviet Middle East: A Communist Model of Development* (New York, 1967), p. 46; Martin C. Spechler, "Regional Developments in the USSR, 1958-78," in U.S. Congress, Joint Economic Committee, *Soviet Economy in a Time of Change*, vol. 1 (Washington, D.C., 1979), p. 145; and James W. Gillula, "The Economic Interdependence of Soviet Republics," in *Soviet Economy in a Time of Change*, p. 620.

8. Gertrude E. Schroeder, "Soviet Regional Policies in Perspective," in *The USSR in the 1980s* (Brussels, 1978), p. 131; Echols, "Politics, Budgets and Regional Equality," p. 271; Bielasiak, "Policy Choices and Regional Equality," pp. 397-400; Elizabeth M. Clayton, "Regional Consumption Expenditures in the Soviet Union," *ACES Bulletin*, 17, no. 2-3 (Winter 1976): 35-43.

9. Peter Zwick, "Ethnoregional Socio-Economic Fragmentation and Soviet Budgetary Policy," *Soviet Studies*, 31, no. 3 (July 1979): 395.

10. Ellen Mickiewicz, *Handbook of Soviet Social Science Data* (New York, 1973), pp. 35-40.

11. Some of the most detailed analyses are offered by Alastair McAuley, *Economic Welfare in the Soviet Union* (Madison, Wis., 1979); Spechler, "Regional Developments in the USSR," pp. 141-63; Gillula, "Economic Interdependence," pp. 618-55; I.S. Koropeckyj, "National Income of the Union Republics in 1970: Revision and Some Applications," in Zbigniew M. Fallenbuchl, ed., *Economic Development in the Soviet Union and Eastern Europe*, 2 vols. (New York, 1974-76), 1:287-331; Schroeder, "Regional Differences," pp. 167-95; and Gertrude Schroeder, "Soviet Wage and Income Policies in Regional Perspective," *ACES Bulletin*, 16, no. 2 (Fall 1974): 1-20.

12. Unless otherwise noted, we use unweighted coefficients of variation. . . .

13. See Brian Silver, "Levels of Sociocultural Development Among Soviet Nationalities: A Partial Test of the Equalization Hypothesis," *American Political Science Review*, 68, no. 4 (December 1974): 1618-37 and Carol Nechemias, "Regional Differentiation of Living Standards in the Russian Republic: The Issue of Inequality,"

Soviet Studies, 32, no. 3 (July 1980): 366-78.

14. Resolutions adopted by the Tenth (1921) and Twelfth (1923) Communist Party Congresses called for industrial development and social investment in less developed regions as top priority (see *KPSS v resoliutsiiakh i resheniiakh s"ezdov, konferentsii, i plenumov TsK*, 7th ed., 2 vols. [Moscow, 1953], 1:559-60, 713-14).

15. F. Douglas Whitehouse, "Demographic Aspects of Regional Economic Development in the USSR," in Bandera and Melnyk, eds., *The Soviet Economy in Regional Perspective*, p. 155.

16. R.W. Davies, *The Development of the Soviet Budgetary System* (Cambridge, 1958), pp. 305-306, N.S. Khrushchev, *XX s"ezd KPSS, Stenograficheskii otchet* (Moscow, 1956), p. 89.

17. Advocates of equal industrial development include A.M. Bagdasarian, *Sovetskii opyt ekonomicheskogo uyravnivaniia natsional'nykh respublik* (Groznyi, 1971), p. 13 and A.K. Zakumbaev, *Metody otsenki urovnia ekonomicheskogo razvitiia soiuznykh respublik i raionov* (Alma-Ata, 1975), p. 14.

18. V.A. Lychagin, *Ekonomicheskie problemy razvitiia natsii i natsional'nykh otnoshenii v SSSR na stadu razvitogo sotsializma* (Saransk, 1975), pp. 119-20 and V. Zlatin and V. Rutgaizer, "Comparison of the Levels of Economic Development of Union Republics and Large Regions," *Problems of Economics*, 12 (June 1969): 6-7.

19. K. Subbotina, *Narodnoe obrazovanie i biudzhet* (Moscow, 1967), pp. 105-106.

20. This point has been emphasized repeatedly in debates on American public policy. See, for example, Ira Sharkansky, *The Politics of Taxing and Spending* (Indianapolis, 1969), pp. 190-98; Robert L. Lineberry and Robert E. Welch, Jr., "Who Gets What: Measuring the Distribution of Urban Public Services," *Social Science Quarterly*, 54, no. 4 (March 1974):700-12; and James S. Coleman, "Problems of Conceptualization and Measurement in Studying Policy Impacts," in Kenneth M. Dolbeare, ed., *Public Policy Evaluation* (Beverly Hills, 1975), pp. 19-40.

21. For a more comprehensive discussion, see Michael Rywkin, "Central Asia and Soviet Manpower," *Problems of Communism*, 28, no. 1 (January-February 1979): 1-13 and Murray Feshbach, "Prospects for Outmigration from Central Asia and Kazakhstan in the Next Decade," in *Soviet Economy in a Time of Change*, pp. 656-709.

22. On the question of differences in regional efficiency, see Spechler, "Regional Developments in the USSR," p. 149 and Whitehouse, "Demographic Aspects," p. 156.

23. Elizabeth Clayton writes, for example, that cultural and biological differences modify the impact of health care policy in different regions (see Clayton, "Regional Distribution of Medical Services in the Soviet Union," paper presented at the annual meeting of the American Association for the Advancement of Slavic Studies, October 1975, pp. 3-4).

24. See, for example, Zwick, "Ethnoregional Socio-Economic Fragmentation," pp. 392-95.

25. This is the strategy used by Echols, "Politics, Budgets, and Regional Equality," p. 261 and by Bielasiak, "Policy Choices and Regional Equality," pp. 396-400.

26. Gillula, "Economic Interdependence," pp. 619-36; Spechler, "Regional Development in the USSR," p. 145; and Nove and Newth, *Soviet Middle East*, pp. 93-97.

27. Zwick reports CVs for the following variables in 1940 and 1970:

	1940	1970
Doctors per capita	0.40	0.22
Hospital beds per capita	0.28	0.09
Kindergarten enrollment per population aged 10 and under	0.56	0.42
Higher education enrollment per capita	0.65	0.17

Zwick also reports that the number of primary-secondary schools per population aged 10 and under grew less equal in this period. However, as we note below, it is not clear that the sheer number of institutions is a useful measure of educational opportunity. These data are from Peter Zwick, "Intrasystem Inequality and the Symmetry of Socioeconomic Development," *Comparative Politics*, 8, no. 4 (October 1976): 507. The conclusion that social welfare spending is not compensatory is fom Zwick, "Ethnoregional Socio-Economic Fragmentation," pp. 392-95.

28. Clayton, "Regional Consumption Expenditures," pp. 27-46.

29. See the list of sources in note 10.

30. The rationale is that urbanization is essentially a process of population concentration and therefore can best be measured with a standard numerical criterion. This definition is offered by Leo F. Schnore, "The Statistical Measurement of Urbanization and Economic Development," *Land Economics*, 37, no. 3 (August 1961): 229-45.

31. Zwick, "Intrasystem Inequality," pp. 506-507.

32. Compare the differences between sown area and agricultural land, for example, in *Narodnoe khoziaistvo SSSR v 1972 g.* (Moscow, 1973), pp. 307, 315.

33. Ibid., pp. 23-31.

34. Zwick, "Intrasystem Inequality," pp. 507, 510.

35. This is based on the number of students in school per population aged 5-14: the CV equals 0.04 for 1970 and 0.07 for 1959 (no comparable data were available for earlier years). The source for the number of students is *Narodnoe khoziaistvo SSSR v 1972 g.*, p. 633 and for the number of children, *Itogi vsesoiuzoi perepisi naseleniia v 1970 g.*, 2: 16-75.

36. Problems in interpreting budgetary data are explored in more depth in Donna Bahry, "Measuring Communist Priorities: Budgets, Investments, and the Problem of Equivalence," *Comparative Political Studies*, 13, no. 3 (October 1980): 267-92.

37. Republic budgets, for example, accounted for only 47 percent of expenditures on economic development in 1970 and in 1975 (*Gosudarstvennyi biudzhet SSSR in biudzhety soiuznykh respublik, 1971-1975 gg.* [Moscow, 1976], p. 31).

38. See the list of ministries provided by Jerry F. Hough and Merle Fainsod, *How the Soviet Union is Governed* (Cambridge, Mass., 1979), pp. 412-17.

39. Investment and population data are from *Narodnoe khoziaistvo SSSR v 1972 g.*, pp. 9, 484 and budget data from *Gosudarstvennyi biudzhet SSSR i biudzhety soiuznykh respublik, 1966-1970* (Moscow, 1972), p. 33.

40. This is the basic difference among the works listed in note 6.

41. In 1960, the ratio of the highest ranking republic (Latvia) to the national average was 139, while the ratio of the lowest ranking region (Kirgizia) to the USSR average was 0.84—an absolute difference of 55 points. In 1970, the corresponding republics were Latvia and Uzbekistan, and the corresponding ratios were 126 and 74, respectively. The absolute difference in that year was 52 points, indicating that regional disparities had lessened slightly. That is the conclusion offered by Schroeder, "Regional Differences," p. 183.

42. This method is employed by Morton in "What Have Soviet Leaders Done," p. 170. For 1960, average housing space in developed regions (including the RSFSR, Ukraine, Belorussia, Latvia, Estonia, Lithuania, Moldavia, and Georgia) equaled 9.83, while the average for the remaining seven republics equaled 7.81. For 1970, the averages were 11.84 and 9.16, respectively.

43. The CV, however, can assume two forms, and there are differing opinions about their relative advantages. One form is weighted by the size of each republic's population, which is appropriate if we want to emphasize the equality of people rather than regions. If people in the Baltic region, say, far surpass the rest of the Soviet population in health care or housing, a weighted CV would attach little importance to the differential, because the Baltic republics represent so small a share of the total Soviet population. By the same token, a smaller gap between Russia or the Ukraine and the other republics would have a far greater impact, making the coefficient larger simply because of their respective population sizes. An unweighted CV is appropriate if our real interest is in *republics* as units of analysis. In this case, if the Baltic republics surpass the others, an unweighted CV attaches just as much importance to the gap as it would to a difference between any other regions. Since both Soviet and Western authors focus on republics as units of analysis, we chose here to use unweighted coefficients (except in our example on industrial production, where the only data available were weighted CVs).

44. Education expenditures are from *Gosudarstvennyi biudzhet SSSR, 1966-1970*, p. 38.

45. Spechler, "Regional Developments in the USSR," p. 146.

46. Holubnychy, "Some Economic Aspects of Relations," p. 65.

47. Koropeckyj, "Equalization of Regional Development," p. 79.

48. Silver, "Levels of Sociocultural Development," pp. 1618, 1637.

49. Ann Sheehy, "Some Aspects of Regional Development in Soviet Central Asia," *Slavic Review*, 31, no. 3 (September 1972): 555.

50. For an excellent analysis of Baltic nationalism, see V. Stanley Vardys, "The Baltic Peoples," *Problems of Communism*, 16, no. 5 (September-October 1967): 55-64 and Tönu Parming, "Population Processes and the Nationality Issue in the Soviet Baltic," *Soviet Studies*, 32, no. 3 (July 1980): 398-414.

51. Iu. V. Arutiunian, "Konkretno-sotsiologicheskoe issledovanie natsional'nykh otnoshenii," *Voprosy filosofii*, 1969, no. 12, pp. 135-36; Juris Dreifelds, "Latvian National Demands and Group Consciousness Since 1959," in George W. Simmonds, ed.,

Nationalism in the USSR and Eastern Europe in the Era of Brezhnev and Khrushchev (Detroit, 1977), p. 142; Parming, "Population Processes and the Nationality Issue," pp. 407-10.

52. Karl Deutsch, *Nationalism and Social Communications* (Cambridge, Mass, 1953). Although Deutsch modified his views in later writings, the basic thrust of his work does involve a predictive model linking modernization to social and political integration. Two important studies of Soviet regional development that test hypotheses drawn from Deutsch's theoretical constructs are: Brian Silver, "Social Mobilization and the Russification of Soviet Nationalities," *American Political Science Review*, 68, no. 1 (March 1974): 45-66 and J. Dellenbrandt, "Regional Differences in the Soviet Union," Research Center for Soviet and East European Studies, Uppsala University, 1977.

53. See, for example, Walker Connor, "Nation Building or Nation Destroying?" *World Politics*, 24 (April 1972): 319-55 and Anthony H. Birch, "Minority Nationalist Movements and Theories of Political Integration," *World Politics*, 30 (April 1978): 325-44.

54. Iu. V. Arutiunian, "Ethnosocial Aspects of the Internationalization of Way of Life," *Soviet Sociology*, 18, no. 2 (Fall 1979): 7.

55. Ibid.

56. Ibid., pp. 7-8.

57. Silver, "Social Mobilization," pp. 59-64 and Brian Silver, "Language Policy and Linguistic Russification of Soviet Nationalities," in Jeremy R. Azrael, ed., *Soviet Nationality Policies and Practices* (New York, 1978), pp. 250-306.

12

The Evolution of Soviet
Fiscal Federalism

Donna Bahry

Center-local relations are rarely static in any modern state. The real distribution of money and programs among levels of government is constantly in flux as new problems arise and political conditions and leaders change. According to Soviet theorists, that is precisely the way it should be: in their view, there is no single right way to divide tasks and budgets among central, republic, and local government agencies. Instead, the Soviet system ought to be reorganized often as society develops and circumstances dictate (Piskotin 1981; Shirkevich 1972). Western scholars have taken a similar if less positive view of Soviet needs. Grossman (1963:107) has argued, for example, that determining the optimal degree of centralization is the "chief persistent systemic problem" in a Soviet-type or command system.

Soviet history certainly bears out the difficulty of finding a single long-term solution. Nearly every decade since 1917 has witnessed attempts to redivide programs and funds between center and periphery. Leaders from Stalin to Gorbachev all presided over reforms, though the magnitude of change and the room for maneuver both seem to have grown narrower over time.

This chapter examines the changes in the federal system and their impact on the economic role of republic governments. The changes are tracked by measuring the republics' share of budget funds (which, in Soviet practice, also includes local budgets) since 1924.[1] I will be looking at expenditures, revenues, and transfer payments from Moscow to assess the evolution of "fiscal federalism" and the rise of the republics in the Soviet system. The distribution

Published in Bahry, Donna, *Outside Moscow: Power, Politics and Budgetary Policy in the Soviet Republics* (New York, NY: Columbia University Press, 1987), ch. 2. Reprinted with permission from the publisher.

of expenditures can reveal how much of the business of government has come under republic jurisdiction through the years, and can therefore offer insight into the changing degree of centralization in the Soviet system. The size and sources of republic budget revenue over time also say a good deal about the constraints under which republic officials operate and the revenue needs that bring them to Moscow seeking additional funding.

Budget data do, however, need to be interpreted with caution. . . . [T]he budget does not include all the funds that Soviet planners actually spend. And what is included is not always clear: defense expenditures are the most notable example, but there are also others, such as agricultural subsidies, that are hidden in budgetary residuals.

Budget figures prove to be much clearer on the vertical allocation of funds, by revealing how much of direct budget outlays are left in republic and local hands. The division of funds between central and lower governments should not, of course, be equated with the real division of power. The fact that republic governments account for nearly half of all budget expenditures hardly makes them coequal partners with Moscow. Central controls are greater than any simple tally of budget funds would indicate. Yet the data can tell us when and how the controls have changed—whether the responsibilities entrusted to regional politicians have expanded or contracted. Budget funds can be of substantial value in mapping the repeated attempts to alter center-regional economic relations.

CENTRALIZATION IN SOVIET BUDGET EXPENDITURES

The most striking feature of budget allocations between Moscow and the republics is the uneven pattern over time—the dramatic peaks and valleys in the republic share. Budget revenues have followed a similar path, with the same peaks and valleys in the degree of centralization. Reforms in the federal system have had a profound impact on the way funds are distributed between center and periphery.

Soviet fiscal federalism has gone through several stages, with an emphasis on increased central control during the First Five-Year Plan (1928-32), the war, and during the last years of Stalin's rule. There have also been several eras when central controls became less restrictive. Moscow's share of the budget dropped during the Sovnarkhoz reform, of course, but also during the mid-1930's, when a brief campaign was mounted to counteract the hypercentralization that the First Plan had produced. In contrast to these rather dramatic changes, the period since the Sovnarkhoz reform has been one of relative stability.

The history of these various stages offers a revealing look into the transformations of center-regional relations since the NEP. During the 1920s, after the formal creation of the federal system, Moscow and the republics accounted for roughly equal shares of the state budget. Moscow's share included exclusive jurisdiction over defense, foreign affairs, and foreign trade. Other functions, such as industry, agriculture, transport, communications, labor, finance, and Rabkrin (Workers' and Peasants' Inspection) were officially under joint central and republic ("union-republic") jurisdiction. Still others, such as public education, health care, social security, housing, and municipal services were left to republic and local administration (Okrostvardidze 1973; Kochumov 1982). However, what was clearly divided on paper was ambiguous in practice. The joint union-republic programs were a gray area with the rights and duties of each level never very clearly specified, and with leaders in the periphery complaining about frequent central encroachment on the functions formally assigned to lower levels (Bescherevnykh 1976). The confusion was aggravated by continual reorganizations. Individual enterprises and other institutions were shifted from one level of government's jurisdiction to the other, creating havoc in the still underdeveloped budgetary system (Davies 1958a).

The ratification of the First Five-Year Plan (FYP), with its headlong rush to industrialize and collectivize, quickly put an end to the ambiguities. Stalin's rapid development strategy led to a massive increase in the state budget, most of it concentrated at the national level (Tulebaev 1973). Total expenditures quadrupled just between 1928 and 1932 (from .878 to 3.800 billion rubles), while central government expenditures increased by almost six times (from .533 to 3.005 billion rubles). During the same period, republic expenditures barely doubled.

In the stampede toward industrialization, Moscow shifted major republic-level programs to direct central jurisdiction. The bulk of the republics' responsibilities in agriculture, light industry, transport, communications, and professional-technical education were taken over by the central government. Agriculture was transferred from republic to union-republic control in 1929, and light industry and higher and technical education were reorganized along the same lines in 1931 (Aspaturian 1950; Sullivant 1962). And of course the bulk of industrial production came under national jurisdiction. Thus, for example, by 1932 over 90 percent of the government's expenditures on industry came from the all-union budget (D'iachenko 1978:296).

All told, sweeping centralization cut the republic share of the budget from 44 to just 26 percent between 1926-27 and 1932 (D'iachenko 1957:577). The republic share of spending for industrial development dropped from 19.6 to 7.2 percent; in agriculture, republic expenditures declined from 64.6 to 29.1 percent of the total; and in transport and communications, the regional share went from 11.6 to 7.0 percent (D'iachenko 1957:577). At the end of the First FYP, republic and local governments retained a major role only in health care, primary and secondary education, welfare, housing, and municipal services.

Thus the contours of the centralized administrative machine had already been established by 1932. Moscow was to absorb even more functions during the war: conversion to a wartime economy, temporary losses of territory, and the squeeze on civilian services all cut republic expenditures to less than 15 percent of the total in 1942. And when military expenditures declined and the system had reconverted to a civilian economy, Moscow's share of the budget remained higher than it had been before the war. It was even on the increase at the time of Stalin's death, while both the republics' share of the budget and the absolute level of republic expenditures dropped in 1951 and 1952.

Yet the Stalin era was not one of unremitting increases in centralization. The early 1930s did witness a brief retreat, when the Central Executive Committee (TsIK) moved to counteract excessive central controls by restricting further transfers of republic programs to the central government's jurisdiction and reassigning some health and education expenditures from central to republic and local administration (Davies 1958a). Together, these measures gave a modest boost to the republic share of the Soviet budget during the mid-1930s, but the effect was soon reversed with the onset of the war.

By the early 1950s, the war and postwar reconstruction had left the republics with only a fifth of the total budget. Republic leaders had major responsibility only for health, education, welfare, housing, and municipal services. Even in these areas, Moscow exercised stringent control over budget funds, down to the number of pupils enrolled in school and the amount to be spent on them (Davies 1958a).

. . . [T]he combined succession struggle and economic crisis in 1953 unleashed a number of proposals to reduce the administrative burdens on Moscow. The first of them to be implemented was a plan for consolidating the many overlapping ministries that had multiplied under Stalin: those responsible for domestic and for foreign trade were merged, as were ministries in machine-building, electrical equipment, and other fields of production. All told, over 50 ministries were amalgamated into 25 (Vvedensky 1958).

However, the consolidation failed to produce any measurable economic improvement, and as the initiative shifted to Khrushchev, the result was a more sweeping attempt to cut back the central bureaucracy and enhance the role of regional and local officialdom. The new tack was explained in an article in the December 1953 issue of *Kommunist* (Shitarev 1953): while stoutly defending the need for centralization the author emphasized that the center could only be as strong as the subnational officials who carried out party policy. Strengthening the role of leaders in the periphery would in theory enhance Moscow's power as well.

By 1954, the new line brought the transformation of all-union ministries into union-republic or republic ones, and the devolution of programs and funds in everything from ferrous metallurgy, coal, and oil to machine-building from central to republic administration (Sabirov 1966). Within two years, republic governments were responsible for enterprises producing 55 percent of Soviet industrial output (*Narkhoz* 1960:214).

The new leadership also reduced some of the stringent central controls over republic expenditures. As of May 1955, Moscow was to approve only the totals for major spending categories in republic budgets, leaving the republic governments themselves to decide how funds were to be distributed within categories and within the republics (Sabirov 1966; Khimicheva 1966). The republics were also granted the right to retain any above-plan revenues they could generate, to determine how revenues and expenditures would be divided among localities, and to set administrative boundaries for local governments under their jurisdiction (Okrostvaridze 1973; *Spravochnik partiiinogo rabotnika* 1957:458-59). By 1957, the Sovnarkhoz reform turned economic administration over to 105 regional councils, 94 representing oblasti in the largest republics—the RSFSR, Ukraine, Uzbekistan, and Kazakhstan—and one each in the other eleven republics.

In addition, the reforms under Khrushchev included several other major changes in planning and budgeting. The regime cut back on the number of indicators to be included in national economic plans, and simplified procedures for planning both costs and labor. Moscow also raised the cutoff point for "above-limit" investment projects. Before 1953, any new project of 1.5-10 million rubles or more (the exact limit depended on the sector involved) required specific approval from the center; under the new regime, the limits were raised to 5-25 million rubles (Davies 1958a).

The post-Stalin leadership also upgraded social welfare programs in the mid-1950s, and this too added to the programs and funds under regional administration. The pension system was revamped in 1956 and education was reorganized in 1958, with both measures pumping up regional expenditures. Agricultural investment climbed, and the increasing emphasis on consumer policies pushed republic expenditures even higher.

Altogether, these changes in federal organization and in priorities gave the Soviet republics a vastly increased share of the budget. Republic governments had accounted for only 6 percent of budgetary expenditures on industry in 1950; by 1958, their share had jumped to 76 percent. In agriculture, they had claimed only 26 percent of expenditures in 1950; but by 1958 they accounted for 95 percent. And by 1960, 94 percent of Soviet industrial output came from enterprises under republic or regional administration (*Narkhoz* 1960:214).

This is not to say that Moscow had given up its controls. On the contrary, the planning process was still centralized. Ministries had been dismantled, but many of their tasks had been absorbed by Gosplan and Gosbank, thus keeping control over the allocation of resources in central hands. Yet as the many criticisms of the Sovnarkhozy revealed, the reform did indeed allow regional officials more power—if only the power to evade or alter central priorities. Regional leaders were accused of hoarding resources and neglecting deliveries outside their own territory: since their primary obligation was to meet the local plan, machinery and supplies designated for export to other sovnarkhozy were diverted to local needs instead (Katsuk and Onipko 1961).   Complaints of localism and of investment "fetishism" among regional officials thus began almost immediately after the Sovnarkhoz reform was adopted.

Sovnarkhoz officials were also subtly redefining national economic choices, diverting investment and budget funds from central priorities to local needs. Some were reprimanded for shifting resources into consumer goods and services, thereby taking funds and materials away from the more traditional priorities of heavy industry.   The reprogramming of funds took on major proportions: in Karaganda, Sovnarkhoz officials siphoned 25 million rubles from heavy industry to build a vocational school, swimming pools, and a host of other public facilities.[2]   Some local leaders, given the means, upgraded social benefits—a visible and surely popular means of responding to local needs.

Complaints arose too over the sheer administrative confusion that accompanied the Sovnarkhoz experiment.   Top officials in the old ministries had been reassigned to Sovnarkhozy throughout the country, but many did not show up for their new assignments (Swearer 1959).   Counting the ones who did, there were still too few people with the requisite expertise to fill all the key posts in 100-plus economic regions (Kosygin 1965).

The distortions introduced by the Sovnarkhoz system quickly prompted the consolidation of individual economic regions and the strengthening of controls at the top.   By 1962, the original 105 sovnarkhozy had been amalgamated into 47; centralized state committees had assumed the responsibility for coordinating various branches of the economy from Moscow; and corresponding Gosplan departments had been expanded to provide more central control (Bergson 1964). The ultimate consolidation, of course, came in 1965 with the repeal of the Sovnarkhoz system and the return to branch administration.

Since then, territorial reorganizations have been less pronounced, and attention has focused more on restructuring the ministerial system. The two major efforts of the Brezhnev era—the Liberman and the ob"edinenie reform—both cut into the role previously accorded to regional leaders. The Liberman reforms, by emphasizing internal rather than budgetary financing in state enterprises, cut the total share of Soviet public expenditures passing through the state budget—thereby shifting some fiscal responsibilities from regional to enterprise or ministry control (Tulebaev 1973).   The association reforms of the 1970s followed a different strategy but had similar effects on republic finances: given their emphasis on consolidation within and across different economic sectors, they resulted in the elimination of several republic branches from union-republic ministries.   The reforms also complicated the process of integrating plans and solving problems between local factory management and local officials: with decision-making authority (and khozraschet status) pushed up the hierarchy to the level of an association, local officials now found themselves having to deal with a higher and more distant bureaucracy to resolve the same questions (Todorskii 1979).   In addition, limits for new investment projects were lowered to give Moscow more direct control over funding, and the number of products to be planned directly by Moscow increased (Dyker 1983). The net result was an upward trend in the degree of centralization, as the division of budget funds between the center and republics suggests. Nevertheless, the republics' share of the budget—and their share of responsibilities—is still larger than it was at any point in the Stalin era.

SECTORAL DIFFERENCES IN BUDGETARY CENTRALIZATION

Judging from the evidence of the budget, Soviet leaders have indeed lived up to the dictum that the federal system ought to be reorganized frequently. While the effect on the republics' share of total expenditures has been dramatic, it has also been far from uniform from one sector of the economy to another. . . .

In the economic realm, the peaks and valleys follow much the same path as total expenditures: extreme centralization during the First FYP, the war, and the late Stalin period, coupled with a marked shift toward the republics during the 1950s and especially the Sovnarkhoz period. Yet the patterns vary across individual sectors: the republic share of industrial expenditures peaked during the Sovnarkhoz reform and then dropped radically, while republic involvement in agriculture continued at a much higher level even after the Sovnarkhoz experiment ended. The republic share of transport, communications, and trade expenditures also continued to increase well after 1965.[3]

Republic responsibility for social welfare programs has been more stable. Basic social services have consistently been provided by regional and local governments. The chief exception is in social security, where the central government's provision of veterans' and survivors' benefits after the war temporarily gave it the lion's share of expenditures. As war-related benefits diminished in importance and new social welfare programs came onto the agenda, the republics once again assumed the primary role in the social welfare budget.

DIFFERENCES IN BUDGETARY CENTRALIZATION AMONG REPUBLICS

The budgetary turbulence has also had varying effects on different republics (Tulebaev 1973). Because of the dramatic changes in the allocation of industrial expenditures to different levels of government, predominantly industrial regions have experienced more fluctuations in their budgets than predominantly agricultural ones. The more the industry in the republic—especially major industry—the more the size of the republic budget has been influenced by the reorganizations described above.

In every republic, the devolution from 1953 onward inflated republic-level economic expenditures. Funds that each region had previously received through the central budget were now counted in republic budgets instead, and official statistics for republics' economic expenditures tripled overnight.[4]

However, when the Sovnarkhoz reform was revoked the impact varied from one republic to another, depending on the sectors dominating each region's economy. Since industry experienced the most dramatic recentralization, the most industrialized regions—such as Russia and the Ukraine—saw an absolute drop in republic economic expenditures (especially because heavy industry was now to be administered almost wholly by the central government).[5] These republics still received industrial funds from Moscow—in fact, their total investment allocations increased—but now the amount would be counted in the center's rather than the republic's budget. Other regions experienced far less of a change in their finances, since their economies concentrated more on sectors (such as light industry and agriculture) that continued to be relatively less centralized even after the return to ministerial administration.

The history of Soviet fiscal federalism is thus one of continual reorganizations, all in an effort to retain and yet modify Moscow's controls over the periphery. Recasting the administrative apparatus proved to be a substitute for more fundamental changes in economic priorities and planning.

This is not to say that the reorganizations have had no impact; certainly reforms in the economic structure of Soviet center-regional relations have had substantial effects on the role of governments outside Moscow. Indeed, the experience with the sovnarkhozy suggests that devolution may have worked only too well: given even a very limited increase in operational authority, regional leaders showed an inclination to siphon resources away from centrally defined priorities to local uses, some of them in the consumer sector. These local "deviations" suggest that, from Moscow's vantage point, the risks of decentralization may go beyond the simple loss of direct political control over the periphery. Decentralization also threatens to undermine the Kremlin's fundamental economic priorities.

REVENUES

Just as the republic share of Soviet expenditures has fluctuated over time, so too has the allocation of revenues between Moscow and the republics. Each transfer of programs between central and regional jurisdiction raises the question of funding sources for republics and localities, which have traditionally relied on less income-elastic taxes and fees. Moscow has claimed the more lucrative sources of budget revenue. Thus governments below the national level share the same predicament as their counterparts in the West: an imbalance between basic sources of revenue and demand for public services and programs.

The regional and local "revenue problem" has dogged Soviet leaders since the beginnings of the Bolshevik regime, prompting a good deal of experimentation with the tax system. The timing of these experiments corresponds closely to what was happening to central and regional expenditures.

During the 1920s, each level of government relied on different sources of revenue. For the center, the main sources of income were excises on consumer goods and taxes on industry, which grew apace as the economy recovered from the devastation of the Civil War and the NEP moved into full swing. In contrast, republic and local governments were allocated direct taxes on personal incomes and agriculture, and nontax revenues such as stump and license fees (Plotnikov 1954). These sources proved to be far more limited in raising budgetary income. Direct taxes on individuals appeared to be a political liability to the new regime, and at first were employed less as a means of raising income than as a device for regulating private economic activity (Millar and Bahry 1979). The literature on taxation was filled with references to tax policies as weapons in the struggle against the bourgeois class. And political imperatives aside, direct taxes were simply difficult to collect for a financial system lacking the organization and personnel needed to keep track of what people were earning and what they owed (D'iachenko 1978). Thus central revenues grew more rapidly than did republic and local ones during the 1920s, creating a budgetary shortfall at the republic and local level.

Moscow's initial solution was to provide central subsidies to the republics (and republic subsidies to the localities.) But subsidies drew increasing fire for undermining fiscal responsibility: regional and local officials seemed to be more concerned with getting a larger subsidy than with exploiting their own sources of revenue (Okrostvaridze 1973). Consequently, Moscow turned to the principle of tax-sharing, giving both republic and local governments a fraction of national tax revenues collected in their territory. Regional and local officials now were to have a stake in seeing that national revenues were collected promptly and efficiently.

Yet in spite of the concern with fiscal responsibility in the periphery, promptness and efficiency were nearly impossible. There were simply too many taxes to monitor, and the organization of the financial system was still precarious at best in outlying regions. In the course of the NEP, Moscow adopted a profusion of new taxes on agriculture, industry, trade, incomes, and local property, with over 60 different taxes imposed on industry alone (D'iachenko 1978; Sabirov 1966). And these were to be collected by a Commissariat of Finance that was still barely organized in the periphery. The further one traveled from Moscow, the more difficult it was to find effective fiscal administration. Officials in Turkestan could not find enough qualified people to staff local finance departments, and Soviet accounts complain of disorganization and corruption. (Sabirov 1966). In the Caucasus, regional officials rarely were able to prepare a realistic budget until the fiscal year was over (Okrostvaridze 1973).

The disarray increased rapidly when the new five-year plan in 1928 multiplied revenue needs. Budget projections called for a dramatic increase in expenditures; but the revenue system, with its confused array of taxes, was slow and cumbersome in responding. The very process of tax collection proved costly: enterprises often needed special staffs on hand to decipher the welter of tax regulations and rates, and to keep accounts for each tax separately (D'iachenko 1978). The pressures led to a major reform of the tax system in 1930, with 61 taxes on industry and trade merged into 2—a turnover or excise tax chiefly on agricultural and consumer goods and extractive industries, and a profit tax on the proceeds of socialized industry (Plotnikov 1948).[6] Enterprises were to pay taxes to the level of government holding jurisdiction over them, and since Moscow now had direct jurisdiction over most of industry, agriculture, trade, transport, and communications, revenue collection became a highly centralized affair. It was now up to the national Commissariat of Finance to make sure that taxes were paid. Regional and local governments would no longer be responsible for the major work of the revenue system, and would instead receive subsidies to balance out the limited expenditures they were to make.

The reform unquestionably streamlined the revenue system, and thereby overcentralized it as well. The Finance Commissariat simply could not keep adequate and timely account of the tax obligations of all the enterprises and ministries now under central jurisdiction. Payments were frequently delayed and sometimes evaded altogether (Plotnikov 1948). Moreover, the Finance Commissariat's attempt to enlist republic and local assistance in checking on tax compliance at the local level met with little success, since—as financial authorities complained—regional and local officials had little incentive to help collect revenues that would flow to the central budget (Bescherevnykh 1960).

Together these difficulties prompted further reforms in 1931. Revenue collection was decentralized, with the republics now assigned to collect the turnover tax and allotted a percentage of the receipts collected within their borders, to give them an incentive for tracking down every ruble owed. In this connection, the tax offered central planners a key advantage over other revenue sources: it was essentially a fixed payment based on production or sale of goods and could be planned with relative ease (Millar and Bahry 1979).[7] That made it a useful source for shoring up republic revenues, and it became the main means of balancing republic budgets; the percentage retained in each region was recalculated each year to cover the gap between the expenditures planned for the republic and the available locally generated revenue sources. The percentage of the tax retained in each republic thus varied across regions and from year to year. The higher deductions went to the least developed republics, where other taxes such as agricultural and personal income taxes yielded too little to cover spending needs (Kudriashov 1962). The same principle has continued to operate over time: the Central Asian republics keep almost 100 percent of the turnover tax revenues they collect, while more industrialized regions—such as the RSFSR, the Ukraine, Latvia—hand over roughly half of their turnover tax receipts to the all-union budget. In effect, the tax serves as a major device for redistributing revenues and financing economic development in less advanced regions.

The tax reforms of the 1930s thus affirmed several basic principles that would subsequently guide revenue allocations among different levels of government (Bescherevnykh 1976). Most direct taxes on the population and "local" revenues such as license and stump fees were to be left wholly to republic and local governments, where they could be spent visibly on local needs (Davies 1958a). In addition, profits from enterprises under republic subordination were to go to republic budgets. Other taxes, especially the more lucrative ones such as turnover taxes, were to be shared by Moscow as it saw fit each year in order to balance republic budgets. Soviet budgetary law thus came to distinguish between "assigned" (*zakreplennye*) revenue sources—those that were collected by and left at a single level in the budget hierarchy—and "shared" (*reguliriuiushchie*) sources—those divided up among different levels. This system was supposed to minimize the need for subsidies to the republics and to ensure their fiscal responsibility (Kudriashov 1962). They now kept a percentage of the revenues generated within their borders, and had a stake in seeing that every ruble was collected on time (Shirkevich 1972).

Since revenue sources were now to be divided according to the need to cover expenditures, republic shares of both revenues and expenditures came to be virtually identical. When central government spending climbed during the war, so too did the national share of tax revenues. Agricultural taxes were raised, and personal income taxes increased and shifted from a local source to one shared by the center and the localities. Poll or head taxes were also imposed on able-bodied adults, as was an additional tax on bachelors and childless families, and these too were shared, though the bulk of the revenues went to the center (Allakhverdian et al. 1966).

The Sovnarkhoz experiment had the opposite effect. When economic administration was turned over to regional councils, agricultural taxes and income taxes on cooperatives were transferred from the all-union to the republic budget, and republic deductions from bond revenues and from turnover and personal income taxes were raised to give the republics additional revenue (Bescherevnykh 1960). Through all the changes, however, one thing has remained constant—Moscow's penchant for keeping the most lucrative revenue sources and assigning regional governments the bulk of taxes collected directly from the population. Soviet leaders can therefore exploit the fact that most of the taxes paid by individuals are plowed back into the social welfare and cultural programs that republic and local governments provide. The "tax bite" gets softened by linking it directly to visible local benefits.

By relying on the turnover tax to balance republic budgets, Moscow has also left regional leaders highly dependent on a few key economic sectors for the bulk of their revenue (Dosymbekov 1971). The tax, which alone accounts for 40 percent of republic budget revenues, is collected primarily from the extraction of natural resources and from agricultural and consumer products (Vasilik 1982; Miroshchenko 1974). Other taxes on these same sectors provide an additional 20 percent of republic revenues: the bulk of the profit payments collected by republic budgets are derived from agricultural and consumer products, since these are the sectors predominantly under republic jurisdiction.[8]

A bad year on the farms or in the extraction of natural resources therefore cuts significantly into the short-term funds available to republic budgets—and thus into the means for financing social welfare, consumer services, and other social cultural programs funded by republic governments. Consequently, Soviet fiscal federalism links republic programs closely with the success of the primary sectors in Soviet economy (Pavlenko 1983).

INTERGOVERNMENTAL TRANSFERS

Given all the changes in the republic share of expenditures and in the revenue system, Soviet planners have had to rely on subsidies and transfers to the republics as something of an unfortunate necessity. For the most part, however, Moscow's revenue-sharing scheme has tended to keep the total amounts doled out to republic governments rather low.

Over the years, Moscow has used three types of transfers to help meet regional expenditure needs: "subventions" or grants-in-aid to cover operating expenditures; categorical grants (*dotatsii*) to finance specific projects such as public buildings, highways, etc.; and "means" (*sredstva*) to cover programs jointly financed by Moscow and the republics (such as elections) and to cover funding needs unforeseen at the start of the fiscal year. (Avetisian 1979; Kudriashov 1962).[9]

Each of these has played a somewhat different role at different times. Subventions were chiefly used during the 1920s and 1930s, to cover expenditures in less developed regions, where local revenue bases were so limited that even 100 percent deductions from all-union revenues were inadequate to balance the budget (Kudriashov 1962). In the mid-1920s, for example, republic budgets in Turkmenia, Uzbekistan, and the Transcaucasus were all covered by subsidies from Moscow (Bescherevnykh 1976). These grants-in-aid to the republics were phased out as rapid development pushed economic tasks out of republic budgets and as tax bases expanded in outlying areas, bringing more revenues into republic coffers.

Additional grants (*dotatsii*) were also used in the 1920s and 1930s to help supplement regional budgets, providing capital for duly planned investment projects in outlying regions (Sabirov 1966).[10] These too have become less important with time, although they are still used on occasion to provide central assistance to republic governments on a project-by-project basis (Avetisian 1979; Tulebaev 1973).

In contrast, "means" have varied in importance, especially since the Stalin era. The reasons are not totally clear, because Soviet accounts do not provide any exhaustive breakdown of what this category represents. We do know, however, that it differs from subventions and subsidies, since it represents adjustments made after the plan and budget have already been adopted (Avetisian 1979). It includes some ad-hoc subsidies to cover emergencies, such as a revenue shortfall caused by a bad harvest, not anticipated in the annual plan or budget. It also covers finances for some joint union and republic government activities. In addition, "means" also represent a budget escrow account, including revenues from any enterprise that is transferred between central and republic jurisdiction after the fiscal year has started. Since revenue from the enterprise has already been built into the corresponding expenditure plan at the "old" level of government, it is kept there temporarily, but under the label of "means" rather than under regular budget accounts until a new plan and budget are drawn up the following year.

This use of "means" as an escrow account helps to explain the erratic pattern; transfers peaked as a share of republic revenues in 1957—the year that the Sovnarkhoz reform transferred economic programs and funds to the republics. And they dropped radically when the Sovnarkhoz reform was revoked. In fact, the net flow of "means" for several regions during 1966 and 1967 was negative: payments to the central budget exceeded transfers received—as we would expect at a time when economic responsibilities were being recentralized.[11] Thus to the extent that "means" simply count functions transferred between Moscow and republic governments, true subsidies from Moscow are used sparingly.[12]

Wherever possible, then, Soviet leaders have tried to avoid subsidies to the republics, in favor of tax-sharing schemes to give regional leaders the proper incentives to be fiscally responsible. In view of the fact that most planned transfer payments to the republics have been eliminated, the strategy has worked. Yet this very incentive to fiscal responsibility is also a powerful inducement to lobby—not for a larger subsidy but for a strong tax base. The greater the local industry, the more turnover taxes and profits potentially available for republic budgets (Piskotin 1971; Voluiskii 1970). Central Asia offers a case in point, with some economists arguing that their republics have been deprived of needed turnover tax revenue because local products are shipped to other (mostly European) republics for processing; turnover taxes on such products flow into the other republics' coffers, rather than the local republic budget (Tulebaev 1973; Iskanderov 1969; Ketebaev 1986). They have suggested that the processing ought to be done locally, thereby giving the local economy the revenue benefits and, not so incidentally, providing jobs for local workers.

The structure of the federal system also gives regional leaders reason for concern over the revenue potential of the primary sectors of the economy. Since so much republic budget revenue derives from agriculture and natural resources, republic leaders find themselves heavily dependent on these branches to keep funds flowing for other republic programs. And . . . they figure prominently on regional agendas.

References

Allakhverdian, D.A. et al. 1966. *Soviet Financial System*. Moscow: Progress.

Asputarian, Vernon. 1950. "Theory and Practice of Soviet Federalism." *Journal of Poitics* 12(1):20-51.

Avetisian, I.A. 1979. *Voprosy territorial,nogo finansovnogo planirovaniia*. Erevan: Izd-vo Erevanskogo Universiteta.

Bergson, Abram. 1964. *The Economcis of Soviet Planning*. New Haven: Yale.

Bescherevnykh, V.V. 1960. Razvitie sovetskogo biudzhetnogo prava. Moscow: Izd:vo Moskovskogo Universiteta.

___. 1976. *Kompetentsiia Soiuza SSR v oblasti biudzheta*. Moscow: Iuridicheskaia literatura.

Davies, R.W. 1958. *The Development of the Soviet Budgetary System*. Cambridge: Cambridge University Press.

D'iachenko, V.P. 1957. "Sovetskai sistema finansov i kredita v bor'be za sotsialisticheskoe pereustroistvo ekonomiki i postroenie kommunizma v SSSR." In L.M. Gatovskii, ed., *Sovetskaia sotsialisticheskaia ekonomika, 1917-1957*. Moscow: Politicheskaia literatura.

Dosymbekov, S.N. 1971. "Uchastie soiuznykh respublikh v upravlenii promyshlennost'iu soiuznogo podchineniia." *Sovetskoe gosudarstvo i pravo* no. 2, pp. 62-69.

Dyker. 1983. *The Process of Investment in the Soviet Union*. Cambridge: Cambridge University Press.

Grossman, Gregory. 1963. "Notes for a Theory of the Command Economy." *Soviet Studies* 15:101-15.

Iskanderov, I. 1969. *Problemy razvitiia tekstil'noi promyshlennosti v Uzbekistane*. Tashkent:Fan.

Katsuk, M. and N. Onipko. 1961. "Struggle Against Localism." *Current Digest of the Soviet Press* 13(2):30-31. Translated form *Sotsialisticheskaia zakonnost'* (1960) no. 11, pp. 47-50.

Ketebaev, K.K. 1986. "Nekotoie voprosy sostavleniia finansovnogo balansa respubliki." *Finansy SSSR*, no 1, pp. 46-50.

Khimicheva, N.I. 1966. *Pravovye osnovy biudzhetnogo protsessa v SSSR*. Saratovosk: Izd-vo Saratovskogo Universiteta.

Kochumov, Ia. Kh. 1982. *Konstitutsiia SSSR i problemy upravleniis ekonomisheskim i sotsial'nim razvitiem soiuznoi respubliki*. Ashkhabad: Ylim.

Kosygin, A.N. 1965. *Pravda*, September 28, 1965, p. 1.

Kudriashov, R.A. 1962. *Raspredelenie dokhodov mezhdu biudzhetami*.

Millar, James R. and Donna Bahry. 1979. "Financing Development and Tax Structure Change in the USSR." *Canadian Slavonic Papers* 21(2):166-74.

Miroshchenko, S.M. 1974. "O nekotorykh voprosakh naloga s oborota." *Financy SSSR*, no. 10, pp. 23-31.

Okrostvaridze, I.E. 1973. *Biudzhetnaia sistema i biudzhetnye prava Gruzinskoi SR*. Tbilisi: Metsniereba.

Piskotin, M.I. 1971. *Sovetskoe biudzhetnoe pravo*. Moscow: Iuridicheskaia literatura.

___. 1981. Demokraticheskii tsentraizm i problemy sochetaniia tsentralizatsii i detsentralizatsii." *Sovetskoe gosudarstvo i pravo* no. 5, pp. 39-49.

Plotnikov, K.N. 1948. *Biudzhet sotsialisticheskogo gosudarstvo*. Moscow: Gosfinizdat.

Sabirov, Kh. 1966. *Iz istorii* gosudarstvennykh finansov Uzbekistana. Tashkent.

Shirkevich, N.A. 1972. *Rol'biudzheta v razvitii ekonomiki i kul'tury soiuznykh respublik*. Moscow: Financy

Shitarev, G. 1953. "Demokraticheskii tsentralizm i rukovodiashchia deiatel'nost' partiinykh organov." *Kommunist* no. 18, pp. 51-66.

Sullivant, Robert. 1962. *Soviet Politics and the Ukraine, 1917-1957*. New York: Columbia University Press.

Swearer, Howard R. 1959. "Khrushchev's Revolution in Industrial Management." *World Politics* 12:45-59.

Todorovskii, Iu. V. 1979. "Relations of Territorial and Regional Soviets with Associations Not Subordinate to Them." *Soviet Geography: Review and Translation* 18:61-78. Translated form "Vzaimootnosheniia kraevykh, oblastnykh sovetov s nepodvedstvennymi ob"edineniiami." *Sovetskoe gosudarstvo i pravo* (1978), no. 9.

Tulebaev, T.T. 1973. *Problemy territorial'nogokompleksnogofinansirovaniia*. Alma-Ata: Kazakhstan.

Vasilik, O.D. 1982. *Gosudarstvennyi biudzhet SSSR*. Kiev: Vishcha shkola.

Voluiski, N.M. 1970. *Svodnyi finansovyi plan*. Moscow: Financy.

Vvdensky, G.A. 1958. "The New Economic Setup: The Organization of Soviet Industry, 1917-1958." *Caucasian Review*, no. 6, pp. 37-53.

Notes

1. Technically, local budgets were considered separate from the "state budget" of the union and the republics until 1938, although in practice local finances were regulated from above. In 1938, the de jure situation was brought into line with actual practice, and all levels were consolidated into a system of unified budgetary accounts. Since then data on the state budget of each union republic have included all subordinate local finances. All the references and data here on "republic budgets" thus include all subordinate local finances. Transfers are treated as revenues of the donor, and as expenditures of the recipient level of government.

2. An account is provided in a Central resolution, "O grubykh narusheniiakh gosudarstvennoi distaipliny v ispol'zovanii kapital'nykh vlozhenii i faktakh proiavleniiamestnichestva so storony otdel'nykh rukovoditelei sovnarkhozov" reprinted in *Spravochnik sekretatia PPO* (1960:199-203).

3. Note that the housing and municipal expenditures represent the republic and local share of the state budget for these items; they do not include resources allocated by ministries to house their own employees.

4. Sabirov (1966:207) demonstrates the effect in Uzbekistan with rare data comparing total budget expenditures in the republic versus expenditures only through the republic budget. Total expenditures on Uzbekindustrila development were 83.5 million rubles in 1951-55, but only 21.8 percent of the total (18.2 million rubles) was channeled through the republic's own budget. In 1956-58, total budget spending on Uzbek industrial development reached 163.2 million rubles, but now 135.3 million rubles (82.9 percent of the total) were channeled through the republic's budget. Had we looked only at the

increase in the amount of the republic budget, we would conclude—erroneously—that industrial expenditures had grown sevenfold in just a few years.   In reality, total expenditures only doubled, but with more of the total counted in the republic's own budget.

5. In the RSFSR, the republic's budget expenditures on industry dropped from 7.6 to 2.1 billion rubles just between 1965 and 1966; and in the Ukraine, the republic budget for industry dropped from 2.7 to 2.3 billion rubles (*Gosbiudzhet* 1972:110, 118).   But total investment in industry (by central as well as republic agencies) increased in both regions (see *Narkhoz* 1967:625).

6. Ironically, tax rates and payment schedules grew very quickly.   By 1938, Soviet officials were complaining that the turnover tax had 2,500 assessment rates, and that individual producers often found themselves paying varying amounts even for similar items.   The Commissariat of the Food Industry, e.g., had to contend with 1,387 rates for its different products (*Second Session* 1938:20).

7. In contrast, the other major revenue source, profit payments, created something of a problem for financial officials, since profitability varied not only with plan fulfillment but with cost of production, and these were more difficult to anticipate in drawing up plan and budget for the following year.

8. This includes profit payments from republic-subordinate enterprises, farms, and trade establishments; income taxes on cooperatives and collectives; and agricultural taxes (*Gosbiudzhet* 1982:46-48).

9. Some accounts of budgetary policies during the prewar years also include shared taxes under the label "transfers," making the total appear to be much higher.

10. D'iachenko (1978) shows that the bulk of such grants, at least for the 1920s, went to Central Asia, and that they amounted to as much as half of some republic budgets.

11. In 1967, for examplke, Ukrainian budget figures indicate receipt of 577.8 million rubles in "means" from the central budget, but in the same year the Ukraine also transferred 1,045.3 million rubles *to* the central budget in connection with the recentralization of industry (*Gosbiudzhet* 1972:117-118).   See also the accounts of other republic budgets in *Gosbiudzhet* (1972).

12. This is not true for local budgets, however.   Despite continual warnings in the budgetary literature that subsidies undermine fiscal responsibility, revenue bases for many local governments continue to be too low to support expenditure needs, and subsidies are common below the republic level.   For a discussion of the problems, see Khesin (1976) and Rusin (1974).

PART V

LANGUAGE

Academic debates about Soviet language policy center on what motivates the policy of Russification (understood here as the spread among nonRussians of the use of the Russian language in public life), whether it is deliberate and coherent, policy, and whether it is successful. Leninist ideology, Soviet imperial aspirations, and practical concerns have all been identified as elements motivating language policy. In Leninist ideology, the withering away of national differences jeopardizes national languages; all nationalities of the USSR would therefore be able at least to communicate in Russian, and at most, they would choose Russian as their first language. One could argue that ever since Stalin recognized the importance of linguistic unity for preserving empires, Soviet regimes have attempted (but failed) to force linguistic assimilation upon the non-Russians.[1] There is a consensus that this attempt was successful during Stalin's time, when, for example, the Cyrillic alphabet was imposed on non-Russian languages. Some scholars, however, emphasize the egalitarian component of past Soviet language policy (i.e., developing non-Russian languages and literature) and also recognize the more practical goal of Soviet language policy: to try to establish a lingua franca in a country in which more than a hundred languages are spoken.

Another important question addressed in scholarly debates is how non-Russians respond to Soviet language policy when its goal is to increase the use of Russian. Russification has proved a highly sensitive issue among non-Russians because at stake is the language of public life and professional communication and—in the Estonian case, for example—the survival of their nation. The high priority national front movements accorded native language use attests to the volatility of this issue.

The brief passage by John Dunlop sketches the trends he sees in the pursuit of linguistic Russification and the forces that favor it. Contrary to the popular view, Russian nationalists discourage Russification in order to preserve the sanctity of the language. Committed ideologies are more likely to push for linguistic Russification.

Two chapters in Part V assess the success of Soviet language policy in teaching Russian to non-Russians. Jonathan Pool's chapter outlines the general issues involved in language planning and points out that two main goals of Soviet language policy—establishing Russian as an efficient means of communication and preserving the distinctiveness of non-Russian languages—work at cross-purposes. The Soviet Union is to be credited for making minority languages, many of which were not written languages before the Revolution, into truly modern languages, but Pool tells us how Stalin's reversal of this policy robbed non-Russian languages of their distinctiveness. Soviet regimes have fared less well in their efforts to accomplish the first goal, especially in the union republics. Indeed, Pool foresees the era of "quindecalinguism," when there will cease to be a language of universal communication in the USSR. Fighting this tendency too forcefully, however, risks arousing nationalist sentiment. The language policy that can best guarantee stability among nationalities is a steady "asymmetric bi-lingualism," with non-Russians increasingly learning Russian without abandoning their native languages.

Barbara Anderson and Brian Silver present a slightly different argument. Like Pool, they characterize Soviet language policy as bi-lingual rather than aimed at Russification, but—unlike Dunlop—they believe it is wrong to say that the Soviet Union applied a single policy of either multilingualism or Russification uniformly across the country in any given period since 1934. Their study of trends in the use of native languages in education shows that the key factor determining whether or not native languages are taught in schools is the political status of the relevant nationality. One that has its national homeland in a union republic is more likely to have the option of studying in its native language at higher levels in the educational system than a nationality that has only an autonomous republic or oblast. A nationality's population size and density is another, but weaker, predictor of native language education: The larger or more concentrated the group, the more likely the opportunity of receiving a native language education. Anderson and Silver stress the subtlety of Soviet language policy and insist that the Soviet regime is not pursuing a policy to eliminate the use of non-Russian languages. What is also important, though, is how non-Russians themselves view the government's efforts. The political demonstrations on language issues that Dunlop discusses, as well as the intense revival of native language as a political issue after 1988, testify to the sensitivity of this issue.

Notes

1. Ivan Dziuba makes the most forceful arguement in either Soviet or Western literature that the Soviet Union consistently sought to Russify non-Russians and to impoverish and expunge non-Russian languages (see Ivan Dziuvba *Internationalism or Russification* [New York: Monad Press, 1974]. See also Roman Szporluk, "Nationalities and the Russian Problem in the USSR: An Historical Outline," *Journal of International Affairs* 27:1 (1973), pp. 22-40).

13

Language, Culture, Religion, and Cultural Awareness

John Dunlop

On April 14, 1978, the main streets of Tbilisi witnessed an unusual and stormy demonstration.   A crowd of some five thousand strong—mostly student youth—massed and then marched noisily from the university to the building of the Georgian Council of Ministers.   Their purpose: to contest a new draft constitution for the republic of Georgia that omitted reference to Georgian as the state language.   The mood among the young people was so volatile that, according to an account published in the *New York Times*, the potential for bloodshed was "averted by a Russian general in charge of security who . . . reported that the situation was ugly, and suggested that it would be wise to yield on the language issue."[1] The next day the offensive clause was reformulated, and similar changes were hastily made in the draft constitutions for the republics of Armenia and Azerbaijan.

Three years later, on April 14, 1981, a date that by this time had come to symbolize Russification, several months of student unrest in Georgia reached their peak. Large numbers of young people attempted to assemble in Mtskheta, the ancient capital of Georgia, to engage in common prayer for their nation. Apprised of these plans, the KGB and militia sealed off the roads to the city, denying access even to pedestrians, and forbade trains to stop at Mtskheta station. Due to an oversight, however, some three hundred demonstrators nevertheless succeeded in reaching the ancient church of Svetitskhovlei in Mtskheta, where, after listening to taped recordings of ancient Georgian hymns they knelt down, joined in the recitation of Our Father, and prayed for Georgia.

Reprinted from *The Last Empire: Nationality and the Soviet Future* edited by Robert Conquest, with permission of Hoover Institution Press. © 1986 by the Board of Trustees of the Leland Stanford Jr. University.

At the same time, in Tbilisi, a chain of militia and KGB men cordoned off the city's main cathedral, letting no one in. Over a hundred students subsequently signed a letter to First Secretary Shevardnadze of the Georgian Communist Party, deploring the actions of the authorities.[2]

The tumult in Georgia has involved more than merely students. In 1976, for example, at the Eighth Congress of Georgian Writers, Revaz Djaparidze excoriated Georgia's minister of education for suggesting that such subjects as history and geography be taught henceforth in Russian, that all textbooks be published in that language, and that dissertations and their defenses be translated into Russian. Djaparidze's speech was greeted by a quarter-hour of applause, and the audience refused to permit the minister to answer him. When First Secretary Shevardnadze spoke, he was interrupted by angry shouts as he sought to allay fears of Russification.[3]

As such incidents attest, language, culture, religion, and national identity are clearly and inextricably connected in the mind of contemporary Georgians. But recent evidence suggests that this also holds true for a number of other minority nationalities of the Soviet Union and, increasingly, for an important segment of ethnic Russians as well.

THE ISSUE OF LANGUAGE

Why, one might ask, is the Soviet government so obviously courting trouble by seeking to russify such an ancient and nationally self-conscious people as the Georgians? To a large degree, the rationale can be traced to Marxist-Leninist ideology as it has been applied in the Soviet Union since 1917. From the very beginning, the Soviet state has been viewed by its leaders as a unitary body whose underlying principle, proletarian internationalism, allowed no room for national differences and aspirations. Despite numerous tactical zigzags, beginning with the NEP, this concept of nations as ultimately ephemeral has never been abandoned by the Soviet leadership. The twenty-second party congress under Khrushchev even advanced the radical term *sliianie* (fusion), implying a biological homogenization of the Soviet nationalities. Khrushchev's successors have been more cautious, preferring blander phrases such as *polnoe edinstvo* (full unity [of Soviet nationalities]), but, despite tactical fluctuations, the Brezhnev regime evidenced little real concern for the survival of nations. Hélène Carrère d'Encausse has pointed out that the Soviet leader most aware of the enduring and refractory quality of the Soviet nationalities was Stalin, who made "Great Russian chauvinism" one of his tools.[4] Coercion—including—if necessary, the uprooting of whole peoples was Stalin's equivalent of Khrushchev's naive belief in a future "fusion" of nationalities.

If one accepts the premise that nations are transitory entities, it follows that their means of communication, languages, are no less ephemeral. A unitary state grounded in an ideology containing the whole truth about man and society needs a single lingua franca to ensure mind control and internal security and for

administrative efficiency in general. Through this common language of the one
state, citizens are molded and transformed by a single ideology,
Marxism-Leninism. Commentators have noted that the utilization of Russian for
such a purpose comes at a considerable price to the language itself.
"Associatively," Jonathan Pool observes, "Russian belongs to the Russian
people, but it is also the 'language of Lenin.'"[5]   Lithuanian poet Tomas
Venclova has formulated the problem well: "Russian to a growing degree is seen
not as Russian, but as 'Soviet' and large groups of Russians themselves perceive
it in just this way. The fact is that Russian is more connected with the official
ideology, than non-Russian languages of the Soviet Union." Serving as the
language of politics and ideology, Russian "has experienced the retroactive and
destructive influence of that secondary semiotic system."[6]

Ideology is thus a factor pushing the Soviet leadership to Russify the minority
nationalities of the USSR. But economic and demographic considerations are
perhaps even more important today. As is well known, the fertility rate of
ethnic Russians and Eastern Slavs is not keeping pace with that of Central
Asians and other non-Slavs. Serious manpower shortages are already being felt
in Soviet industry and agriculture. Manpower-surplus areas, such as Central
Asia, must thus become donors to manpower-deficit areas, such as Western
Siberia, if Soviet military-industrial expansion is to continue. But if
non-Russians are to be integrated successfully into the Soviet economy, they
must be taught Russian and, optimally, be Russified. Yet the 1970 census
offered disturbing evidence that certain Soviet nationalities, particularly Islamic
peoples of Central Asia, were being recalcitrant even about learning Russian as
a second language. This was almost a kind of sabotage and too
dangerous—because of its possible links with "bourgeois nationalist" aspirations
and even separatist inclinations—to be permitted to continue. As a result, the
Soviet leadership decided in the 1970s to press ahead with, and speed up, the
process of Russification.

The Soviet regime, of course, has long been encroaching upon the language
rights of its minority peoples. In 1958, for example, Khrushchev's notorious
Thesis 19 suggested that the study of local languages by aliens, that is, Russian
living in the non-Russian republics should be made optional. Thus asymmetric
bilingualism was recommended as the desired norm. As Michael Rywkin has
noted, this reform was one that even Stalin never attempted, since in his period
Russians living outside the RSFSR were required to learn local languages.[7] In
Latvia, Thesis 19 caused a tremendous stir and was heatedly debated in the
republic's press. The Latvian Supreme Soviet, in a rebellious move, actually
increased the number of compulsory hours for the study of Latvian in the
republic's schools (May 1959).[8]   After a purge of Latvian "national
communists," however, Khrushchev's recommendation became policy in Latvia,
as elsewhere in the USSR. The results of this asymmetry were demonstrated

by the 1979 census: only 3.5 percent of ethnic Russians claimed to have fluency in the language of any other Soviet people.

By the late 1970's, the Brezhnev regime had apparently decided upon an even more intense policy of Russification. The removal of Podgorny, who may have been a Ukrainian Nationalist sympathizer, from the Politburo in 1977 perhaps removed the last obstacle to such initiatives. By a decree of the Council of Ministers of the USSR issued in October 1978, Russian was introduced into the lower grades of all elementary schools in the USSR. It is a measure of the perceived political sensitivity of this decree that it was promulgated in secret. (There was nothing novel in this procedure, of course: major new legislation on religion, introduced in 1962, was not published in the Soviet Union until 1975.)[9] According to one account, the October 1978 decree was delivered to educational officials by special courier, with instructions that it be read and memorized on the spot and then returned to the courier; party Central Committee bureaus in the republics were, in turn, to issue detailed confidential decrees embodying the new policy.[10] The decree of the Estonian Bureau was eventually leaked and published by Estonian emigrés in Sweden.

In May 1979, the regime went a step further, organizing a major theoretical conference in Tashkent on the topic "The Russian Language—The Language of Friendship and Cooperation of Peoples in the USSR." In this case, too, elaborate attempts were made to keep the agenda secret—it was mandated, for example, that the conference's draft documents be kept in safes. The recommendations (which, this time, were leaked by the Lithuanians) included the proposal that ministries of education introduce the teaching of Russian to five-year olds in non-Russian kindergartens. The recommendations went beyond mere language instruction: Russian was to be used in play and various extracurricular activities at school, and parents were to be encouraged to make consistent use of Russian at home. School newspapers, excursions, and discussions of television programs and films were to be conducted in Russian.[11]

These extraordinary measures show that the regime was not as concerned as many Western analysts had thought it would be over the reaction to such bullying tactics by the republican elites. The Brezhnev leadership was clearly willing to take a calculated risk: to Russify aggressively in the hope of rejuvenating a stagnant economy and thwarting "bourgeois nationalism" and separatism in the future. Understandably, the Tashkent recommendations created a stir in the minority republics. Five thousand Lithuanians protested the recommendations in a petition to the Central Committee, and an open letter by Estonian intellectuals scored, among other manifestations of Russification, "the hyperbolic and inept propaganda campaign pushing the teaching of Russian in schools and kindergartens."[12]

In the midst of this heavy-handed campaign of Russification, a minor tactical retreat on the language front was sounded by Brezhnev at the twenty-sixth party congress in 1981. On that occasion, he urged that the linguistic and cultural needs of migrant workers in the Soviet Union be cared for. From other statements in his address, it was clear that Brezhnev was seeking to encourage the migration of Central Asians and peoples of the Transcaucasus to Siberia and the Far East.[13] This unexpected solicitude for the linguistic and cultural needs of migrants should not be seen as blunting the thrust of Russification. Brezhnev was surely aware that migrants are more apt eventually to assimilate, linguistically and culturally, than "stay-at-homes," even though Islamic peoples have historically been less likely to assimilate than others.

During his brief tenure as general secretary, Andropov showed himself to be a believer in a Soviet melting pot in which the national distinctions of the peoples of the USSR would be submerged. In December 1982, he made his first major speech since becoming party leader. This statement was devoted to the sixtieth anniversary of the formation of the USSR, and in it Andropov advanced the highly controversial merger theory *(sliianie)*, according to which the peoples of the Soviet Union will merge into one entity, *sovetskii chelovek* (Soviet man).[14] Brezhnev, it should be noted, had carefully avoided this term, no doubt because it had earlier caused trouble for Khrushchev.

How successful has the Russification process been from the regime's point of view? Fragmentary data available from the 1979 census suggest mixed results. Actual linguistic assimilation of non-Russians has been proceeding very slowly. (Furthermore, as the case of the Jews demonstrates, linguistic assimilation does not necessarily betoken ethnic reidentification.) In 1959, 59.3 percent of Soviet citizens—54.5 percent of the population was ethnically Russian—gave Russian as their native tongue, hence 4.8 percent of the population had been linguistically assimilated; in 1970, this figure rose to 5.3 percent and in 1979 to 6.2 percent.[15] Due to fertility trends, however, the actual percentage of native speakers of Russian vis-à-vis the populace as a whole has declined slightly, from 59.3 percent in 1959 to 58.6 percent in 1979.

In a few important cases, linguistic assimilation seems to be proceeding quite rapidly. More than a quarter of Belorussians (25.8 percent in 1979) now do not speak Belorussian as their native language; in 1970, this figure was 19.4 percent. As for Ukrainians, 82.8 percent were native speakers of Ukrainian in 1979, as opposed to 85.7 percent in 1970—a decline of 2.9 percent. For obvious reasons, the Russification of Eastern Slavs enjoys a high priority with the regime. In the case of the Ukraine, where, as the Shelest incident showed, nationalist tendencies can manifest themselves among the top party elite—Russification is undoubtedly viewed as being engaged in a particularly important race with centrifugal forces.

Other Soviet peoples appear to be resisting linguistic assimilation with considerable success. In the 1979 census, Lithuanians showed no change from the 1970 census in the linguistic assimilation of their populace (97.9 percent were native speakers of Lithuanian). The number of native speakers of Estonian and Latvian dropped only 0.2 percent each (to 95.3 and 95 percent, respectively). In view of the regime's desire to Russify the Baltic—especially Latvia and Estonia, with their large numbers of migrants—these census figures seem to show determined resistance on the part of the Balts.

The adoption of Russian as a second language cannot in itself be construed either as assimilation or ethnic reidentification. Nevertheless, from the regime's point of view, it is obviously a necessary first step in a desirable process, a step the leadership has been anxious to promote. One striking instance of growth in the knowledge of Russian as a second language is that of Uzbekistan. In 1970, a mere 14.9 percent of Uzbek respondents claimed fluency in Russian—in 1979, the figure stood at 49.3 percent, a jump of 34.4 percent. Michael Rywkin is correct in drawing our attention to the fact that the assessment of fluency in Russian depends on the respondent and that, as a result, "It is quite possible that demographically vigorous Uzbeks, feeling ethnically secure, tend to exaggerate their own knowledge of Russian."[16] It is nevertheless clear that a major effort must have been made over the period 1970-1979 in Uzbekistan to increase fluency in Russian. Uzbeks are the most populous Central Asian people, and Tashkent is the showplace capital of the Soviet Islamic world. It is symbolically important that, of all Soviet peoples, Uzbeks should learn Russian, and quickly.

Contrary to what is often believed, even by specialists, Russian nationalists were not happy with the campaign of Russification that was pursued by the Brezhnev and Andropov regimes. Indeed, even such an ardent foe of Russification as Ivan Dziuba, author of the seminal study, *Russification or Internationalism? (1965),* singled out Russian nationalist writers Vladimir Soloukhin and Leonid Leonov for strong praise as principled opponents of Russification.[17]

Virtually all present-day Russian nationalist spokesmen are "polycentric" nationalists, that is, they regard all peoples and their cultures as of intrinsic worth. As official nationalist Ilya Glazunov puts it: "I believe that world culture has nothing to do with Esperanto but is a bouquet of different national cultures."[18] A contributor to *Veche,* the important samizdat journal that served as a forum for Russian nationalism in the early 1970s, assails the thoughtless policy of seeking to create a "Soviet nation" and attacks the "elemental Russification" taking place in the borderlands.[19] Such spokesmen insist that undue significance should not be ascribed to the fact that Russian is the language of state, that the Russian language represents no more than a kind of emasculated and cliché-ridden Esperanto. Alexander Solzhenitsyn, among others, has frequently scored the decline and degeneration of the Russian language during the Soviet period.

Which are the elements in the party leadership who are seeking to Russify the minority nationalities? Marxist-Leninist ideologues of the Ponomarev orientation would seem to have few scruples about the process, and neither would devotees of the defense-heavy industrial complex. "The speedy urbanization of Central Russia," Mikhail Agursky notes perceptively, "is a question of life or death for the military industrial complex . . . They are not afraid of the Soviet melting pot for, even without traditional Russian culture, this melting pot is essentially Russian for them."[20]   Groping for a term, Agursky calls this group "progressive" or "radical" Russian nationalists, but I would disagree. A *Russian* nationalist, I would contend, cannot be indifferent to the demographic, social, and spiritual well-being of ethnic Russians, to their language and culture. Let us rather call these elements "Soviet patriots," since their essential concern is expansion of the USSR's military and industrial might.[21]

One other ramification of the language issue deserves mention. Western broadcasts to the Soviet Union—by the Voice of America, Radio Liberty, the BBC, Deutsche Welle, and so on—serve as the Soviet populace's only reliable source of information concerning both domestic and foreign events, and they could serve, potentially, as a means for the West to help bring about desirable changes in Soviet politics. Russian language broadcasts, however, present a particular problem. Since Russian is both the lingua franca of the Soviet federation and the native language of 137 million ethnic Russians, the directors of such broadcasts have been unable to decide whether they should design their programs for an ethnic Russian audience or for the Soviet populace as a whole. The temptation has been to opt for ethnically "neutral" programming, a tactic that ignores or downplays the cultural and religious needs of the dominant nationality of the Soviet Union. (A number of Russian nationalist dissenters, including Solzhenitsyn and Father Gleb Iakunin, the imprisoned cofounder of the Christian Committee for the Defense of Believers' Rights in the USSR, have commented on this paradox.)[22] It has been argued persuasively that the present practice runs counter to the real needs of the contemporary West. . . .

Notes

1. *The New York Times*, December 21, 1979, p. 2.

2. *Russkaia mysl'*, September 3, 1981.

3. Ronald Grigor Suny, "Georgia and Soviet Nationality Policy," in Stephen F. Cohen, Alexander Rabinowitch, and Robert Sharlet, eds., *The Soviet Union Since Stalin*, (Bloomington: Indiana University Press, 1980), p. 219.

4. On the Soviet concept of nations, see Hélène Carrère d'Encausse, "Determinants and Parameters of Soviet Nationality Policy," in Jeremy Azrael, ed., *Soviet Nationality Policies and Practices* (New York: Praeger, 1978), pp. 39-59.

5. Jonathan Pool," Whose Russian Language?" in Edward Allworth, ed., *Ethnic Russian in the USSR* (New York: Pergamon, 1980), p. 239.

6. Tomas Venclova, "Two Russian Sub-Languages and Russian Ethnic Identity," in Allworth, ed., *Ethnic Russia*, pp. 250-251.

7. Michael Rywkin, *Moscow's Muslim Challenge* (Armonk: M.E. Sharpe, 1982), pp. 95-96.

8. Juris Dreifelds, "Latvian National Demands and Group Consciousness Since 1959," in George W. Simmonds, ed., *Nationalism in the USSR and Eastern Europe* (Detroit: University of Detroit Press, 1977), p. 138.

9. Walter Sawatsky, "Secret Soviet Lawbook on Religion," *Religion in Communist Lands*, (Winter 1976): 26.

10. Yaroslav Bilinsky, "Russian Nationalism and the Soviet Empire" (Paper prepared for the thirteenth national convention of the American Association for the Advancement of Slavic Studies, Asilomar, Calif., September 20-23, 1981), p. 20.

11. Kestutis Girnius, "The Draft Recommendations to the Tashkent conference," Radio Liberty Research Paper (hereinafter RLRP) 189/79, June 19, 1979, pp. 3-5.

12. Bilinsky, "Russian Nationalism and the Soviet Empire," p. 40.

13. Roman Solanchyk, "New Turn in Soviet Nationalities Policy, *Soviet Analyst*, April 15, 1981, pp. 4-5. See also the discussion of this speech in Boris Meissner, "The 26th Party Congress and Soviet Domestic Politics," *Problems of Communism*, May-June 1981): 19-22.

14. Iu. V. Andropov, "Shest'desiat let SSSR," *Pravda*, December 22, 1982, pp. 1-2. Andropov's speech also appeared in a booklet edition of 3 million copies, published by Izdatel'stvo Politicheskoi Literaury in December 1982. For a discussion of the relationship of his speech to the nationalities issue, see Ann Sheehy, "Andropov Speaks on Nationalities Policy," RLRP 510/82, December 21, 1982, and "Andropov and the Merging of Nations," RLRP 516/82, December 22, 1982; and Roman Solanchyk, "Merger of Nations: Back in Style?" RLRP 84/83, February 18, 1983.

15. Bilinsky, "Russian Nationalism and the Soviet Empire," p. 9. For the results of the 1979 census, see *Naselenie SSSR po dannym vsesoiuznoi perepisi naseleniia 1979 goda* (Moscow: Politizdat, 1980).

16. Rywkin, *Moscow's Muslim Challenge*, p. 97.

17. Ivan Dziuba, *Internationalizm ili Rusifikatsiia?* (Amsterdam: Suchasnist', 1973), p. 234. This edition is a Russian translation of the Ukrainian original. For an English translation, see *Internationalism or Russification?* (London: Weidenfeld and Nicolson, 1968).

18. Interview with followers of Father Dimitrii Dudko, published in *Vol'noe slovo* 33 (1979).

19. Russkoe reshenie natsional'nogo voprosa," *Veche*, no. 6, Arkhiv samizdata (AS) 1559, pp. 9-10.

20. Mikhail Agursky, "The New Russian Literature," Soviet and East European Research Center, Hebrew University of Jerusalem, Research Paper no. 40 (July 1980), p. 15.

21. Their relative lack of concern for the demographic, social and moral plight of ethnic Russians would distinguish adherents of this tendency from present-day National Bolsheviks, whereas their lack of emphasis on ideology would set them apart form neo-Stalinists.

22. See Aleksandr Solzhenitsyn, "O rabote russkoi sektsii Bi-Bi-Si," *Kontinent* 9 (1976): 210-23; Viktor Sokolov," Zapiski radioslushatelia," *Kontitnent* 12 (1977): 268-86; "Open Letter to the Directors of Radio Stations 'Voice of America,' BBC and 'Deutcshe Welle,'" *Documents of the Christian Committee of the Defense of Believers' Rights in the USSR* (1979), 3:342-43.

14

Soviet Language Planning: Goals, Results, Options

Jonathan Pool

Whenever governments have tried to intervene in the everyday linguistic behavior of their peoples, the tendency of language to resist deliberate planning has been manifest. The Soviet Union is a superb case for the study of language policy, because the government has been extraordinarily ambitious in its attempts to reshape an extremely complex linguistic situation. In this study we shall see what makes the Soviet language situation a challenge to policy makers; how the Soviet leadership has tried to change mass linguistic behavior; where its principal language policies have succeeded and failed; and what policy options exist for the future.

THE SOVIET LANGUAGE SITUATION

The language situation of the Soviet Union is one of the most complex in the world. The 1970 census enumerated 104 nationalities, ranging in size from the 441 Aleuts to the 129 million Russians. It took 20 nationalities to account for 95 percent of the Soviet population. With a few exceptions, each listed nationality has a different characteristic language. Some of the members of each of these nationalities spoke its language as their mother tongue, according to the census, although the figure varied from a low of 13 percent among the Karaites (a Jewish minority of 4,571 persons originating in Persia, having a Turkic language, and inhabiting mainly Crimean and Lithuanian cities) to a high of 99.8 percent among the Russians. On the average, however, 94 percent of the Soviet population had a correspondence between declared nationality and mother tongue, thus making the languages of the USSR relatively "communalistic."[1]

Not only are there many mother tongues, each spoken by a substantial portion of the Soviet population, but they belong to a wide spectrum of language families. Besides Slavic and other Indoeuropean languages, the Soviet Union has at least a million people natively speaking languages in each of four unrelated families: Altaic (including the Turkic group), Uralic (including Estonian), South Caucasian (including Georgian), and North Caucasian (including Chechen).

The people of the Soviet Union have not learned each other's languages in large enough numbers to overcome this diversity of mother tongues. In the 1970 census 22 percent of the population claimed fluency in at least one Soviet language besides the native one.[2] Russian is by far the most widely known second language, but knowledge of it is far from universal. In 1970 it was called their mother tongue by 59 percent of the people, and those claiming second language fluency in it brought the total to 76 percent. Thus there is still a major language barrier to overcome, particularly for a regime wanting to communicate intensively with every citizen.

The resolution of language problems in the USSR is made more difficult by the legacy of gross inequality among languages. During its last 45 years, both before and after the beginning of constitutional government in 1905, the Russian Empire pursued almost without interruption a policy of Russian colonization and land acquisition in non-Russian regions, cultural russianization of non-Russians, and government with even less representation of non-Russians than of Russians.[3] One result was the supremacy of the Russian language and its association with Russian domination. In this situation, while unity and efficiency both seem to demand the spread of Russian, any policy that gives supreme status to the traditionally dominant tongue and its already privileged speakers transgresses the norm of national equality.

The features of this situation can be found, individually, in other countries as well. The Indian census, for example, lists more than 1,000 "languages," about 18 of which are required to take in 95 percent of the population; and there are large numbers of speakers of languages in four unrelated families.[4] In Belgium, as in many other linguistically plural countries, two citizens with different mother tongues do not have a very great likelihood of possessing a *means* of communication. French-speaking people in Quebec want to learn English largely for economic gain, but with the language come memories of conquest and exploitation. The Soviet situation is composed of elements found elsewhere, but in a combination that would challenge even modest efforts at language planning.

THE POSSIBILITIES OF LANGUAGE PLANNING

"Language planning" refers to systematic policies designed to maintain or change existing language situations. Languages have been created, revived, destroyed, reformed, and manipulated as far back as the fifth century B.C.,[5] so the Soviet Union is certainly not the first country in which this kind of planning has been practiced. Language planners have attempted to control the statuses, roles, and functions of languages in society (such as which language is made official, which languages are taught in schools, or how the speakers of minority languages are treated); they also have made plans for preserving or reforming the vocabularies, sound systems, word structures, sentence structures, writing system, and stylistic repertoires of languages.

Language planning has various goals. Some of the most common are to bring about linguistic unity, to preserve or create linguistic distinctiveness or uniqueness, to make certain languages or their speakers equal, to make one language or its speakers superior, to develop a language so it can be used for new purposes, and to make a language more efficient as a tool of communication or more beautiful as a medium of expression. These goals have such consequences as national unity, educational progress, or a wider gap between elites and masses.

Even in fairly simple situations, language planning has its limits. Perhaps the chief one is the reluctance to engage in language planning, partly a product of the traditional belief that language is an organic entity with which people should not or cannot tamper. Where an authoritative agency is intent on changing the language situation, limits are still imposed by the rate at which people can learn new language habits, the systematic and interrelated nature of each language, and the costs, as well as undesired by-products, of successfully implementing a policy whose outcome depends on changes in mass, everyday, partly automatic behavior. Language planners usually strive for several goals at once, but these often prove to be incompatible. Because of these contradictions and the strong emotions that language as a political issue generally arouses, and because the opposing sides in language controversies tend to be cut off from each other by language differences, language planning is often accompanied by fierce conflict and efforts at obstruction.

THE SOVIET EFFORT AT LANGUAGE DEVELOPMENT

In spite of the obstacles to comprehensive language policy making that history has revealed, the leaders of the Soviet Union have attempted to do more than ignore or merely cope with their intricate language situation. They have pursued a series of very ambitious programs, making the USSR probably the best available case in which to study the limits, other than lack of ambition, that language planners face.

Selecting from a multitude of possible goals, the Soviet leadership has made two major and overlapping thrusts.[6] The first began in the 1920's and was aimed at the development of languages other than Russian for mass use in education, the communications media, and public and professional life. The second thrust began in earnest about 1938, with the aim of universalizing the knowledge of Russian among the Soviet population. These two efforts have conflicted with each other and have often varied in intensity, but both continue today.

The first effort, which we might call the multilingual development effort, began while the Bolsheviks were still trying to put the pieces of the Russian Empire back together. The initial impetus was Lenin's struggle to stamp out the oppressive behavior of Russian settlers, soldiers, and administrators in the periphery and to bring the eastern peoples of Russia, as a model for eastern peoples everywhere, into full participation while reasserting firm central control. In this respect Lenin was opposed to most of the rest of the Bolshevik movement, which regarded Russian dominance as a natural and desirable concomitant of centralization.[7] Of the other two principal leaders, Leon Trotsky showed little concern for the importance of national rights, and Iosif Stalin believed that they had to be sacrificed to the inevitably incompatible aim of unitary government. Lenin almost singlehandedly insisted that both aims could, and must, be achieved.[8]

Besides intense political opposition, Lenin faced situational obstacles in most of the country that became clearer as the first, simplistic policies for implementing national equality began to fail. To accomplish the end result of full participation in public life by hitherto suppressed peoples, substantial numbers of those peoples had to be trained for administrative and technical roles, and their languages had to be used in the running of institutions where they lived. These goals in turn required that non-Russians learn to read and write, while Russian administrators, if Moscow were to maintain its governance over the outlying territories, had to learn the languages that were being made official. Thus each language had to be given a writing system or, if it had one that made mass literacy very difficult (such as the Arabic writing systems of the Turkic languages), a new writing system had to be devised. Hence, even when Lenin persuaded the Party and administration to undertake serious efforts at derussianizing the peripheral institutions, these efforts achieved little when there were broken links in the chain of preconditions.

In addition, the push from the center was not consistently strong. During the New Economic Policy the desire to avoid offending non-Russian nationalities implied that they should continue to be brought into the Party and government; but central funding and guidance for the educational and language-development prerequisites mostly disappeared, leaving much of the initiative in local hands. There was enough central coordination of experts in language planning, however, to produce a general pattern for the whole country.[9]

Within the resulting effort at multilingual development, we can distinguish four main components. First, about 40 speech varieties with no writing systems (except, in some cases, systems known only to missionaries or scholars) have been standardized and graphized.[10] This means that in each case the rules of the linguistic code of some group have been party written down, a writing system has been devised for that code, and the code has been adopted as the language of formal speech and writing for those in the group and, often, those speaking a number of neighboring or related dialects as well. Most of these graphizations took place in the 1920s and early 1930s, and used the Roman alphabet, with modifications. It should be noted that this requires more than the mindless extension of some other language's writing system to the unwritten language. It requires investigating the latter's meaningful sound distinctions and its rules for combining meaningful elements into words, and then devising a set of symbols suitable for representing these. The complexity of the task undertaken by Soviet language planners becomes clearer when we consider that the Cyrillic alphabet, which is currently used for writing 60 of the 66 written Soviet languages, and which needs only 33 symbols for Russian, contains a total of 201 distinct symbols when the modified letters used to represent the non-Russian sounds in the other 59 languages are taken into account.[11]

Second, about 45 languages have had their writing systems thoroughly transformed. For about half of these, the authorities have carried out two such transformations, most commonly a change from an Arabic or Cyrillic alphabet to a Roman one, followed in 1938–40 by a change to (or back to) a Cyrillic writing system. "Transformation" here means a transition from one genetic type of alphabet to another, such as from Arabic to Roman or Roman to Cyrillic. In 1929 and 1930 there was serious discussion of converting Russian itself to a Roman alphabet, but this idea was abandoned.[12] A third component of the multilingual development effort has been the eradication of illiteracy, pursued in the only practical manner: teaching people how to read and write in their native languages, once these have been furnished with writing systems. At the time of the October Revolution, only about half the population aged 9-49 was literate; and among some large categories, such as Central Asian rural Muslim females, literacy in this age group was between 0 and 5 percent. By 1959 the rate was no lower than 93 percent in any republic for any sex/urban-rural combination.[13] Literacy among rural females aged 9-49 in Uzbekistan and Azerbaidzhan, for example, has risen as shown below.[14]

Year	Uzbekistan	Azerbaidzhan
1897	0.2%	1.5%
1926	1.2	5.8
1939	70.2	70.6
1959	97.5	96.1
1970	99.6	99.3

The fourth major element in this effort has been to develop the terminologies of 14 Soviet languages other than Russian, to publish teaching materials in them, to employ them as media of instruction at all educational levels, and to use them for advanced professional communication and public affairs. In particular, these are the languages whose namesake territories have the status of union republics, and the primary locus for use of any such language is intended to be the corresponding republic.

This is the component most actively pursued at present and whose outcome is most in doubt. It appears that no one is planning to graphize any additional Soviet languages; only reforms, rather than basic transformations, of the writing systems of currently written languages are being discussed.[15] Literacy cannot rise appreciably, since it already stands at nearly 100 percent. The major question for multilingual development, then, boils down to this: In schools, workplaces, government, and media outside the RSFSR, how far and when will the use of the 14 major non-Russian languages expand and/or contract?

The two areas for which the most data on language selection are available are publishing and education. Rosemarie Rogers has analyzed the former and found that the quantity of publications in the 14 major languages, relative to the number of their native speakers, is substantial, but also substantially lower than it is in Russian.[16] Her statistical analysis shows that 18.0 percent of all copies of non-periodical publications in Soviet languages were in non-Russian languages in 1970 (up from 16.1 percent in 1959) and that, theoretically, this gave a native Russian speaker about 3.2 times as many copies in his language as a non-Russian native speaker (down from 3.6 in 1959). The ratio of non-Russian to Russian publications varies considerably according to whether one measures it in copies or in titles, and with the category of publication. In general, however, the Russian preponderance is greater at higher levels of specialization. For example, while the Russian advantage is 1.8 to 1 in primary and secondary school textbooks, it is 10.3 to 1 in higher education texts. Even more striking are the differences among the non-Russian languages. The Baltic languages have the highest publication rates, followed by the Transcaucasian languages. The advantages in access to copies in the native language, calculated from Rogers' figures, and using the rate for Russian as the unit value, were as follows in 1970:

Estonian	1.37
Latvian	1.21
Russian	1.00
Lithuanian	0.66
Georgian	0.55
Armenian	0.44
Kazakh	0.42
Uzbek	0.41

Ukrainian	0.39
Turkmen	0.37
Moldavian	0.36
Tadzhik	0.34
Kirghiz	0.34
Azerbaidzhani	0.32
Belorussian	0.19

In education, as suggested by the textbook publication figures above, the 14 major non-Russian languages have attained more use at lower than at higher levels. Over-time statistics permitting an accurate assessment of the language situation at all educational levels are not available, but there is enough evidence to conclude that a large majority of pupils outside the RSFSR who are native speakers of the nominal languages of the republics in which they live receive their primary and secondary instruction in those languages. Two published figures are that 68 percent of all Kazakh and 94.5 percent of all Azerbaidzhani pupils in their respective republics were taught in their national languages in the late 1960s (1966-67 and 1968-69, respectively).[17] These figures can be indirectly checked by comparing the number of pupils being taught in the republic language with the number of eligible children in the republic. In Table 1, a rough estimate of this comparison appears for each republic, except for Latvia and Armenia, for which data were not found.

The table shows that the number studying in the language of each republic is close to what we would expect if all eligible young people were in school and being taught in that language, except in Kazakhstan and Belorussia. Even in those two republics, at least two-thirds of the number of eligible children in the population were in native-language classes. In light of the table, the two figures for Kazakhstan and Azerbaidzhan cited above do not appear to be exaggerations. From the evidence available, we must conclude that the retreat of the major non-Russian languages as vehicles of instruction in the face of the relentless penetration of Russian, which seemed only a few years ago to be the dominant trend, did not last; instead, these languages have been largely consolidated as the teaching media for those who speak them as native tongues, and even, in some republics (or so it seems), for substantial numbers of others.[18]

There is evidently far more to be done before the republic languages penetrate higher education to the same degree. Probably for this reason, comparative statistics are not available, other than those on textbook publishing mentioned above. Iu. D. Desheriev states that since 1940, all higher educational institutions in the Ukraine have conducted instruction in both Ukrainian and Russian, but says nothing about the number of enrollees in each language. He also claims that certain figures on the rising educational level of the Ukraine population "bear witness to the fact that higher education in the Ukrainian language has become the property of all sections of the Ukrainian population"

—unfortunately a non sequitur doing nothing to refute the dissident claims of systematic official bias against the Ukrainian language.[19] Desheriev does, however, present a list of 27 specialized fields in the basic and applied natural and social sciences, as well as humanities, in which instruction in Ukrainian has been given.

More helpful are Desheriev's data on the situation in Uzbekistan. In 1968-69 about 70 percent of the 68,820 students there were studying in Uzbek. In 1969-70 about 9,000 out of the 15,000 students at Tashkent State University were doing the same, including unspecified numbers of Russian as well as Kazakh, Karakalpak, Tadzhik, and other students. Uzbek has been more widely used in the social than in the natural sciences, and in the latter more in the first years than the last years of study.[20]

Still more detailed data are available about the language situation at Azerbaidzhan State University, in Baku, the major institution of higher education in that republic.[21] A.N. Baskakov's figures imply the following distribution of students between the two sections of that university:

Nationality of Student

	Azeri	Non-Azeri	Total
Azeri	N = 7,260	N = 1,140	
	Row% = 86.4		
Section	Col.% = 75.6		
of University			

It is impressive that three-fourths of the Azerbaidzhani students at the university are receiving their training in Azerbaidzhani; but it is astonishing that almost half of the non-Azerbaidzhani students are doing the same, since Russians are almost never taught in any language but their own. To understand this figure we would need to know the distribution across sections of each major non-Azerbaidzhani group, including the students from 16 foreign countries reported to be studying there.[22] Since 95 percent of the teaching faculty are Azerbaidzhanis,[23] one can imagine the possibility that they attract non-Azerbaidzhanis into the Azerbaidzhani section by teaching better in their native language, or by providing a more complete program of courses in that section. If the non-Azerbaidzhanis studying in Azerbaidzhani include some native speakers of Slavic languages, perhaps they elect to study in a second language for predominantly "integrative" motives, such as those that typify English-speaking Canadians wanting to learn French.[24] If they plan or expect to remain in Azerbaidzhan, their enrollment may also reflect a belief in their future need for competence in the republic language. Information about the attitudes of students in the different language sections of a university such as Azerbaidzhan State would help to interpret the enrollment data and also would contribute to the comparative study of language choice.

It remains to be seen how far the Soviet government will go in giving a complete repertoire of modern roles to each of the 15 republic languages. According to Desheriev, those languages are already the "main" media of higher education in Uzbekistan, Georgia, Azerbaidzhan, Lithuania, and Armenia.[25] In these and most of the other republics, he says, work is being done or a trend is observable toward the increased use of the republic language, at the expense of Russian, as the medium of instruction in higher education. Since several capitals are becoming proportionally more populated with members of the republic nationality,[26] the national compositions of the student bodies in those republics presumably are changing in the same direction. If so, the educational efficiency of using the republic language as the medium of higher instruction is increasing rather than decreasing.

The amount that has already been accomplished is enormous, compared with similar efforts elsewhere. New states attempting to officialize even one language generally have stumbled for years around a vicious circle: inadequate manpower to develop the language to train the manpower to . . . . [sic][27] Languages must be reduced to writing if literacy is to be achieved. Textbooks must be published and native teachers trained if a language is to be the medium of instruction in schools and universities. Before textbooks can be published, thousands of concepts must be incorporated into the terminology of the language, a laborious process that, in the Soviet Union as elsewhere, has required innumerable hours of consensus building among linguists and subject specialists, while also leading to deep conflicts. The Soviet Union claims to be pushing this process ahead for 15 of its languages, and there is evidence to support this claim.

THE CAMPAIGN FOR MASS KNOWLEDGE OF RUSSIAN

The second thrust of language planning in the USSR has been an effort to make Russian a universally usable medium of domestic communication. (Parallel to this has been an effort to promote Russian abroad as well, but we need not consider this aspect here.) Essentially all Soviet leaders, including Lenin, have considered a knowledge of Russian by members of other nationalities to be a desideratum, either because they favored Russian hegemony or because they recognized that the spread of Russian would facilitate communication, control, and the dissemination of knowledge and cultural creations. Initially, however, Lenin apparently succeeded in persuading the rest of the leadership, in debates that had begun years before the October Revolution, that the voluntariness of the spread of Russian was much more important to the fate of the regime than the fact of the spread.[28] His sensitivity to the feelings of the non-Russians began to lose its impact on policy as soon as he became incapacitated by illness in 1922.[29]

By the late 1930s militant opposition to the regime had been disarmed; native-language literacy had reached a high level; and the Stalin administration's policy of cultural proletarianization had assumed the form of russianization, partly for the purpose of winning more support from the largest nationality. Linguistic manifestations of this policy included the cyrillicization of the writing systems of most Soviet languages, the promotion of direct borrowing from Russian as the way to develop the terminologies of other languages, and (as of 1938) the compulsory study of Russian in non-Russian schools.[30] As many Soviet commentators have pointed out, learning Russian is of course easier if one's first language is written with the same alphabet and if it has many Russian-derived words in its vocabulary.

The policy of cyrillicization was carried out fairly rapidly: it began in 1936 and was largely completed by 1941. It omitted those languages that had substantial literatures in, and popular loyalties to, other scripts (Latvian, Lithuanian, Estonian, Armenian, Georgian, and Yiddish). The resulting alphabets have caused considerable discontent. In their haste to complete the job, linguists made many decisions later viewed as obviously mistaken. Further, whether by design or because of uncoordinated work, they often created an unnecessary multitude of symbols for basically identical phonemes. Given their desire to make alphabets correspond with the Russian one, in some cases they omitted symbols for making distinctions fundamental to speakers of the language in question—for instance, long versus short vowels in Turkmen. On the other hand, the desire to make alphabets correspond to the sound systems of the target languages led to the omission of some unneeded Russian letters, which distressed those who favored the preservation of Russian spellings in words borrowed from Russian. Disputation about these problems continues today among Soviet linguists, and occasionally the alphabet of a language is reformed.[31]

The effort to achieve terminological uniformity through use of Russian as the universal source of borrowed words has aroused considerable anxiety. One index of this is the tendency for Soviet linguists both to advocate and to oppose this policy whenever they discuss the problem.[32] In general there are three widely practiced policies: (1) borrowing without alteration, (2) borrowing with phonological modification to fit the patterns of the borrowing language, and (3) translation of the concept with morphemes already present in the language.

Alphabets seem easy to impose on users of a language, but imposed vocabularies can be evaded more easily. Soviet writers on language policy never complain that someone is reverting to the Roman, Arabic, or Mongolian alphabet. There are many complaints, however, that "artificial" native words are being substituted for Russian borrowings, not only in private speech but even in published and broadcast material. If the rates of publication in non-Russian languages continue to expand, vocabulary control will become more difficult, especially if the proportion of Russians knowing other Soviet languages remains minute.

In the extreme case of Moldavian, it appears that vocabulary policy is not working at all. Authoritative Soviet language planners have strenuously emphasized the intimate historical contacts between Moldavian and the Slavic languages, as part of the effort to deny that Moldavian and Romanian are competing standards of the same language, thus deflating Romania's territorial and emotional claims on the Moldavian SSR.[33] In spite of a clear policy of linguistic differentiation, Nicholas Dima has found a dramatic exodus of Slavic - origin words from Moldavian publications since the late 1940s. At present, there are hardly any more Russian borrowings in literary Moldavian than in literary Romanian, and new terms being coined in Moldavia are Romance-based.[34] Developments like this may well make the cognitive task of learning Russian more difficult. On the other hand, language learning may depend more on attitudes than on cognitions; and a perception of Russians as benevolent supporters of authentic, independent, flourishing national languages might more than compensate, in positive attitudes, for the barriers raised by differences in vocabulary.

This brings us to the question of how well non-Russians learn Russian in the USSR. In 1956 an experienced observer of Soviet life wrote: "On the basis of available data it seems safe to predict that within a relatively short time, perhaps ten years, almost all Soviet citizens will have a good speaking and writing command of Russian."[35] Today more data are available, and there is less basis for such confidence. The mammoth Soviet literature on this subject seems to add up to the claim that everyone is learning Russian, combined with the lament that few people are learning it well. Baskakov summarizes the customarily cited reasons: "the limited amount of instructional literature, the shortage of instructional and scientific manpower, the unavailability of modern technology for language teaching, and the inadequate development of the methodology of teaching Russian." Sometimes, for example, a certain grammatical concept is taught in the Russian courses before the pupils have reached the same concept in their native-language curriculum.[36]

A four-year comparative study of Azerbaidzhan, Lithuania, Estonia, and the Buriat ASSR has attempted to quantify the knowledge of Russian in selected places in those republics and to describe in detail the results of linguistic interference, that is, distortions in second-language competence attributable to the first language.[37] This study used ethnographic methods, questionnaire surveying, written testing, and tape-recorded interrogation to supplement the usual aggregate statistics. It paid some attention to the use of Azerbaidzhani and other languages as second languages, as well as Russian.

In Azerbaidzhan the study examined Zakatala *raion* (district), where Azerbaidzhanis far outnumber all other nationalities and the population is 83 percent rural. Of about 20,000 pupils in the *raion*, 5 percent are Russians and

0.6 percent are Armenians; they are taught in Russian. The others (Azerbaidzhanis, Avars, Tsakhurs, Georgians) study in Azerbaidzhani. The investigators intensively surveyed two village schools and found that 16 of the 30 teachers in one, and 23 of the 44 teachers in the other knew only Azerbaidzhani. No students were found in these schools who could speak errorless Russian.[38] Rural pupils in the second, third, and fourth grades were found to know only half the vocabulary required by the curriculum. Among fourth through eighth graders, it was found that only 14 percent of the rural pupils claimed to read books or listen to radio programs in Russian.[39] When asked how well they knew Russian, pupils in the ninth and tenth grades of Azerbaidzhani schools in the city all claimed to be fluent, but only a small minority made this claim in the rural remainder of the *raion*.[40] Azerbaidzhanis' knowledge of Russian is considerably better by the time they begin their higher education, although the disadvantage among those whose schooling was in Azerbaidzhani and among those coming from rural homes remains considerable. In the survey of university and pedagogical institute students, half of those from rural areas claimed to have trouble speaking Russian. The study found many mistakes in the Russian even of upperclassmen.[41]

Students following the regular program of instruction in Russian, which begins halfway through the first grade in Azerbaidzhani schools, were found to have major deficiencies in the language. Tests of Russian competence in several schools revealed, however, that errors in Russian were reduced to insignificant numbers among pupils who had attended preschools conducted in Russian.[42] On the basis of these findings, Baskakov recommends Russian preschools, especially in rural areas without Russian-speaking populations.[43]

The Lithuanian part of the study concentrated on language knowledge and language choice among both Lithuanians and Russians. Each group tends to have a proportion knowing the other group's language that is positively associated with the proportion of the population in the area belonging to the other group.[44] The *raion* chosen for fieldwork has a Lithuanian preponderance (68 percent), with the only other large groups being Russians (20.3 percent) and Poles (10.2 percent); but the minorities are spread very unevenly across the *raion*. In one bilingual collective farm, when meetings are held each person speaks in Lithuanian or Russian, whichever he prefers. Another observed regularity was that the language of a ceremony or festive occasion is whichever language any monolinguals in the group speak.[45] But the language of interaction can also be determined by anticipated reactions, by following the lead of the person who speaks first, or by deferring to someone with "high social status."[46]

In the settlement of Deguchiai, with 62 percent Lithuanians, 250 residents were surveyed; all of them except 6 women over age 60 were orally bilingual. Competence in written Russian was widespread only among those Lithuanians aged 50 and younger. Almost all Lithuanians watched movies in Russian, fewer listened to Russian radio programs, and fewer still (22 percent) read Russian books—the same percentage as that of Russians who read books in Lithuanian.[47]

The investigation of achievement in Russian showed substantial discrepancies between curriculum demands and pupil performance in Lithuania, but they were not as serious as in Azerbaidzhan. By the end of the third grade, most pupils knew 80 to 90 percent of the required vocabulary, but only 2 percent were able to pronounce Russian without a strong Lithuanian accent. Curriculum goals were met by about 50 percent of the pupils in oral Russian, by about 33 percent in reading, and by about 25 percent in writing.[48] Satisfaction of curriculum demands in vocabulary fell to about 75 percent of the required words by the eighth grade. In one translation test given to 50 pupils, 8 of the 12 worst scorers came from rural homes, while 80 percent of the perfect scorers came from urban homes.[49] As Lithuanians progress through the educational system their competence in, and use of, Russian grows. But the discrepancies between curriculum demands and achievement, between urban and rural achievement, and between the fluency derived from contact learning and the deficient knowledge derived from school learning remain. One-quarter of a tested group of students in higher education institutions could not say *anything* in Russian. Students from areas with small Russian populations made many mistakes in Russian and did not satisfy even secondary school requirements. Reading skills were superior to speaking skills, but still 16 percent of the students were not acquainted with even the most basic Russian terms in their own areas of study.[50]

The Estonian section of the comparative study furnished a wealth of ethnographic detail about language behavior in the Ryuge village soviet in Vyru *raion*, located in the southeastern corner of the republic. The national composition of the population is almost entirely Estonian, and the Estonian language prevails throughout. "In the store, the restaurant, and other establishments, strangers are usually addressed in Estonian (even if the speaker knows excellent Russian), on the assumption that everyone surely knows Estonian.[51]

In the *raion* capital of Vyru, the investigators studied the Russian school and industrial plant. Few Estonians attended the former, but most of the pupils knew Estonian as a second language. In the plant, the work force was 70 percent Estonian, with Russians making up most of the remainder; but knowledge of Russian among the Estonians was considerably more frequent than vice versa. It appears from the figures given in the analysis that non-Estonian workers in the plant who had lived in Estonia for 15 years or more were more likely to know the language than not; those who had lived there ten years or less were more likely not to know it than to know it. Russians ignorant of Estonian and Estonians ignorant of Russian both explained their monolingualism by the fact that they never needed the other tongue, since those with whom they dealt in service establishments were bilingual.[52]

The result of such bilateral linguistic self-sufficiency is the atrophy of the second language. This was vividly revealed by the study when higher education students were tested in Tartu and Talinn in 1968. Of the 1,065 students tested, faculty members in Russian language, who did the initial grading, gave marks of "excellent" to 1.5 percent, "good" to 22.3 percent, "satisfactory" to 31.4 percent, and "unsatisfactory" to 44.9 percent. The investigators reanalyzed the graded test papers and found grammatical errors, however, in 5 of the 16 "excellent" papers. In 99.0 percent of the 1,065 cases, therefore, "these students had not yet reached the first level of full bilingualism, even though the Russian curriculum in Estonian schools (2nd to 11th grades, exceeding 1300 hours of instruction) unconditionally anticipates the complete mastery of the Russian grammatical system and active control over a vocabulary of several thousand lexemes."

The students who were tested were also given questionnaires about their knowledge and use of Russian. Of the 709 who returned questionnaires, 53 (7.5 percent) claimed that they "freely command the Russian language" (the same wording that appears in the USSR census); but the investigators' analysis of their test papers allowed them to grant this level of competence to only 10 of these 53 (18.9 percent).[53] Calculated the other way, only 20.1 percent as many rated themselves fluent were so rated by their professors. If this same ratio applies to the whole Estonian population's ability to assess its competence in Russian, then the percentage of Estonians in Estonia who were fluent in Russian as a second language in 1970 was not 27.8 percent, as reported in the census, but about 5.5 percent. Others, too, have argued that the census overstates the number of bilinguals.[54]

Contrasting with the situations in Azerbaidzhan, Lithuania, and Estonia, the Buriat ASSR emerges from the four-republic study as a case of officially encouraged assimilation. Most education takes place in Russian. A minority of rural elementary schools, and one urban school, use Buriat as the medium of instruction; but "taking into account multitudinous requests from parents," the Buriat ASSR Supreme Soviet passed a resolution in 1973 urging that Buriat as a language of instruction be limited to the first four grades rather than five. In schools that teach in Buriat, pupils are expected to know more than 2,000 Russian words by the end of the third grade, while in schools with Azerbaidzhani (also an Altaic language) as a medium of instruction, the envisioned vocabulary is only 925 words.[55] Party and other organizations support the "initiative" of Buriat parents who choose to send their children to Russian schools from the first grade on, and Russian is taught to Buriats in a "zeroth grade" to prepare them for the Russian medium. The investigators studied a state farm that ran its formal meetings in Russian even though only 2 percent of the members were Russians. Buriats on the farm, talking among themselves, used Buriat until they came to a technical or sociopolitical subject, whereupon they would switch to Russian.[56]

Thus, there is a clear contrast between the limited spread of Russian where the alternative is one of the 15 republic languages, and the rampant penetration of Russian elsewhere. Both policies and results appear to make a sharp distinction between these two kinds of non-Russian languages.

PROSPECTS AND PROBLEMS

At the present time the two major thrusts of Soviet language policy appear to be moving toward success and failure in different arenas. The first effort—for multilingual development—has made remarkable strides toward completion or self-sustaining "takeoff" for 14 major languages in their respective union republics. It has faded, however, for other languages and in other territories. The second effort—to universalize competence in Russian—is moving quickly toward success among citizens who do not speak one of the 15 favored languages, and also among those whose native languages are closely related to Russian, or who are displaced from the home republic of their mother tongue. But gross gaps exist in the remaining republics between plans and performance—gaps that will not necessarily become easier to close as the republic languages expand their utility at the expense of Russian. If the observed trends and policies continue, the USSR will move in the direction of being a quindecanational and quindecalingual state. Russian will be the Russian national language and—for those who need it—the Soviet link language, but not the universal, unique language of the union. Fourteen other national languages will thrive under conscientious cultivation; but a hundred minor tongues will slowly shrivel, officially unlamented, into extinction.

No one can be sure, however, that the existing policies will stay in place. Language policy is a controversial issue with high stakes, possibly including the very survival of the USSR. Let us look, therefore, at three new policies that could possibly become predominant, and see whether they could change the current linguistic trends.

First, Soviet leaders may decide that they want to prevent the entrenchment of quindecanationalism and quindecalingualism, whether because of the victory of a russophilic faction, concern about the costs of linguistic multiplicity, or fear that secessionist movements would inevitably arise. They might thereupon decide to make an all-out effort to russianize the Soviet people completely. If the withering away of all languages but Russian became the official policy, would it succeed? One answer is that this will happen even if, or even because, no such policy is announced. If all non-Russians were to succeed in learning Russian as a second language, the instrumental utility, or at least the essentiality, of their native languages would decline. They might then, if instrumentally motivated, cultivate their Russian at the expense of their other languages. This change would be assisted by the electronic and print media, which would respond to the fact that everybody can be reached in Russian by offering more and better material in Russian. This would further increase the utility of Russian, inducing more parents to send their children to Russian-medium schools, after which they would be likely to raise their children with Russian as the home language, especially if they married across native-language lines.

Two main forces, however, would act to retard the switch to Russian. One is the existence of fairly homogeneous and expanding non-Russian communities. Until the rural population is reduced to a small fraction of its present size, this residential segregation can be expected to persist, preserving enclaves of minority languages that will not be changeable without coercion. Birth-rate projections indicate that the non-Russian nationalities will increase their share of the Soviet population for several more decades.[57] The second force against russianization is the attitudes of the non-Russian elites. This force is likely to grow, rather than shrink, as industrial development and urbanization proceed. The perceived importance of its language among the elite of a subordinate group tends to be low when initial contact with a more advantaged language group is made. Once those who wish to learn the latter group's language have done so and some permanent assimilation to that language has begun, it begins to be perceived as a threat to the survival of the native language. It is difficult to predict how far a movement of native language consciousness would go in a particular Soviet nationality, but the movement probably would become strong as soon as virtually all of the group's population had a moderate command of Russian and a substantial trend toward the selection of Russian-medium education by parents had set in. Thus, when attitudes are taken into account, assimilation may be a self-regulating mechanism.

We must also consider another scenario. The unique role of Russian as the language of intergroup contact and individual mobility may some day be seen as an unfair and un-Leninist privilege granted to one nationality. The "voluntary" acceptance of assigning that role to Russian may deteriorate. Soviet publications already recognize that monolingualism among Russians obstructs the development of favorable attitudes and relations between Russians and others.[58] On the basis of these beliefs, a new policy might emerge: either (1) bilingualism for all except RSFSR Russians or (2) universal bilingualism among the Soviet population (with RSFSR Russians learning the other Soviet language of their choice).

Could such a widespread bilingualism develop, even with complete government support? One can safely assume that the utility of a knowledge of Russian under all foreseeable conditions within a continued Soviet political order will remain much higher than the utility of a knowledge of any other Soviet language. Thus the serious question is whether any policy could succeed in making all Russians, or even all Russians outside their own republic, bilingual. There are hardly any cases of widespread reciprocal bilingualism in the world. Spanish-Guarani bilingualism in Paraguay and English-Afrikaans bilingualism among the white population of South Africa are both high, but neither is the result of a deliberate government policy imposed in a situation where such bilingualism was previously absent.

A recent attempt to turn asymmetrical bilingualism into reciprocal bilingualism has been made in Canada, preceded by millions of dollars worth of feasibility studies. There, although the main effort has been confined to federal civil servants, who have been given encouragement, help, and incentives to learn the other official language, and although this other language (French) has international prestige, recent studies indicate that the program of bilingualization has been a massive failure and that almost the only really bilingual officials remain those whose native language is French.[59] A comparison of the Soviet and Canadian censuses shows that Russians claim to know non-Russian languages considerably less than English Canadians claim to know French, if we control for the ethnic composition of the districts they live in. For example, a Russian surrounded by 98 percent non-Russians has a 5-10 percent likelihood of knowing their language, while an English Canadian living in an area that is 98 percent French-Canadian has a 70-80 percent likelihood of knowing French.[60]

On this basis it would seem less likely that a policy of reciprocal bilingualism could work in the USSR than in Canada. The facts that no major language in the USSR besides Russian has international status, and that many are linguistically very distant from Russian, add to the expected difference. The main force operating in the other direction is the greater capacity for rewarding, sanctioning, and controlling possessed by the Soviet authorities; but the policy in question would surely test this capacity. To the extent that the policy (or the prevailing patterns of natality, migration, and manpower demands[61]) drove Russians from other republics back to the RSFSR, this migration would endanger the plan by depriving both Russians and non-Russians of the most crucial precondition for effective language learning: an environment in which the other language is common and useful.

Finally, there is yet a more extreme policy that has roots in Soviet tradition, and whose roots are not yet dead: a policy of letting—and helping—a hundred languages bloom. The mainstream of Soviet writings on the minor languages asserts that their preservation as living tongues is not per se a good thing. On the contrary, the most common view welcomes the tendency for speakers of these languages to become bilingual and then raise their children with Russian (or one of the other 14 union republic languages) as the native language. The belief in substantive cultural uniformity, expressed through different languages as mere alternative codes, negates the basis for valuing, as thinkers like J. G. von Herder, Benjamin Lee Whorf, and George Steiner have done, the multiplicity of languages major and minor. But the strenuous admonitions of Lenin against any kind of coercion and any degree of privilege among nations and languages provide a legitimate basis for criticism of the mainstream viewpoint.

V.A. Avrorin best exemplifies this criticism with his harsh attack on the works of F.P. Filin, Iu.D. Desheriev, and O.P. Sunik, who, he says, in both describing and praising the extermination of minor languages, have on the one hand falsified the facts and on the other hand advocated a policy of ethnic and linguistic inequality that is Kautskyite rather than Leninist. Avrorin argues that the state should help all speech communities make real use of their constitutional equal rights and should stop falsely assuming that their languages are in the process of dying out.[62] Even those in the mainstream who promote assimilation assert that it is voluntary, and that it actually strengthens rather than weakens the smaller languages, both internally and in terms of the roles they play. Although it may be hard to understand how "The observed transitions from monolingualism to bilingualism, and from there to monolingualism based on communication among nationalities, in no way imply the dying out of nationality languages,"[63] the fact that authorized publications on nationality policy say such things shows that the relevant public still attaches value to languages as entities. Avrorin implies such an evaluation when he says:

> Then Iu. D. Desheriev includes in this same group of hopeless, dying languages Andi and Didoi in Dagestan; Iazguliam and Ishkashim in the Pamirs; Udegei, Orok, Karaite, Chulym, Dolgan, etc., in other words, it seems, all the non-written languages of Soviet ethnic groups. Yet these are a little *more* numerous than the written ones—not in people, of course, but precisely in peoples.[64]

There is not enough experience anywhere to let us foresee the fate of a panlinguistic promotion movement in the Soviet Union if it were to obtain party and government support. As V. N. Durdenevskii remarked in 1927, Karl Kautsky's prediction that the Ossetians, the Kalmyks, and others were destined to go the way of the Bretons and the Basques was wrong on both counts: neither Soviet nor Western minorities disappeared.[65] Soviet writers on both sides of this fence agree that conscious intervention is assuming an increasing share of the ability to determine what happens to languages. There is some evidence that concern about the preservation of languages and cultures grows stronger again with the advent of the postindustrial syndrome, even in the Soviet Union.[66] If both these relationships hold, then the cultivation of minor languages could be both a popular and a successful policy.

In the meantime, under current conditions the politically most acceptable compromise seems to be slow progress toward stable, asymmetric bilingualism, with non-Russians increasingly learning Russian but not abandoning their original languages. This guarantees to each group what it cares most about: to the Russians a widespread and increasing ability to communicate with non-Russians without having to learn another Soviet language; to the non-Russians the continued and even growing vitality of their national languages; and to the political leadership the ability to avoid announcing alarming plans for the long-run linguistic future. As long as this progress is slow, the direction of movement can be a source of comfort to all; and the expectation that this movement will continue for many years can gratify the leaders. As soon as the movement stops or changes directions, new fears are likely. If the learning of Russian by each new generation of non-Russians retrogresses, there will be fears of separatism. If the intergenerational loss of the other 14 republic languages in favor of Russian begins to become substantial in comparison with the expansion caused by population increases, the fear will be one of absorption. But if the Soviet Union, by making good on its claim that Russian and the other republic languages are symbiotic rather than antithetical, can show that neither fear is warranted, it may provide a unique model for reconciling complete linguistic unity with a high degree of linguistic diversity.

Notes

1. Ali A. Mazrui, *The Political Sociology of the English Language: An African Perspective* (The Hague: Mouton,1975), p. 70.

2. *Itogi vsesoiuznoi perepisi naseleniia 1970 goda* (Moscow: Statistika, 1973), 4: 20-22.

3. Richard Pipes, *The Formation of the Soviet Union* (rev. ed.; Cambridge, Mass.: Harvard University Press, 1964), chs. 1-2; Jaan Pennar, Ivan I. Bakalo, and George Z. F. Bereday, *Modernization and Diversity in Soviet Education, with Special Reference to Nationality Groups* (New York: Praeger, 1971), pp. 23-35.

4. For a comparison of these two situations, see Ram Gopal, *Linguistic Affairs of India* (Bombay: Asia Publishing House, 1966), pp. 233-39.

5. Alfred Cooper Woolner, *Language in History and Politics* (London: Oxford University Press, 1938), pp. 78-79; Winfred P. Lehmann, ed., *Language and Linguistics in the People's Republic of China* (Austin: University of Texas Press, 1975), p. 42.

6. Jacob Ornstein, "Soviet Language Policy: Continuity and Change," ch. 3 in *Ethnic Minorities in the Soviet Union*, ed. Erich Goldhagen (New York: Praeger, 1968), also divides Soviet language policy into two stages but sees them as sequential periods. For a four-stage periodization, see E. Glyn Lewis, *Multilingualism in the Soviet Union* (The Hague: Mouton, 1972), pp. 66-80; for a five-stage one, see M.I. Isaev, "Iazykovaia politika i iazykovoe stroitel'stvo v kul'turnoi revoliutsii," in *Razvitie iazykoy i kul'tur narodov SSSR v ikh vzaimosviazi i vzaimodeistvii*, ed. N. A. Baskakov and R. G. Kuzeev (Ufa: Bashkirskii Filial, Institut Iazykoznaniia, Akademiia nauk SSSR, 1976), pp. 57-66, see 65-66.

7. Pipes, op. cit., p. 277.

8. Ibid., pp. 280-81.

9. Alexander G. Park, *Bolshevism in Turkestan 1917-1927* (New York: Columbia University Press, 1957), pp. 178-89, 363-64.

10. K. M. Musaev, *Alfavity iazykov narodov SSSR* (Moscow:Nauka, 1965); N. A. Baskakov, ed., *Voprosy sovershenstvovaniia alfavitov tiurkskikh iazykov SSSR* (Moscow: Nauka, 1972); V. I. Lytkin, "Osnovnye protsessy v formirovanii i razvitii finnougorskikh

i samodiiskikh iazykov v sovetskuiu epokhu," in *Zakonomernosti razvitiia literaturnykh iazykov narodov SSSR v sovetskaiu epokhu: osnovnye protsessy vnutristrukturnogo razvitiia tiurkskikh, finnoyugorskikh i mongol'skikh iazykov*, ed. N. A. Baskakov (Moscow: Nauka, 1969), pp. 239-67; K. M. Musaev, "Izopyta sozdaniia pis'mennostei dlia iazykov narodov Sovetskogo Soiuza," in *Sotsiolinvisticheskie Problemy razvivaiushchikhsia stran*, ed. Iu.D. Desheriev et al. (Moscow: Nauka, 1975), pp. 243-59; A. Kalimov, Neskol'ko zamechanii o putiakh razvitiia dunganskogo iazyka," in ibid., pp. 328-32.

11. Musaev, *Alfavity*, pp. 80-82 and passim. As Soviet scholars themselves have since noted, not all these symbols were necessary. But while they attribute the excess diversity of alphabets to poor organization, some others see it as a deliberate plot to split the speakers of related dialects into relatively impotent groups: Paul B. Henze, "Politics and Alphabets in Inner Asia," in *Advances in the Creation and Revision of Writing Systems*, ed. Joshua A. Fishman (The Hague: Mouton, 1977), pp. 371-420.

12. V. I. Lytkin, "Komi-Zyrianskii iazyk," in Baskakov, *Zakonomernosti*, pp. 302-51, see 328.

13. Jonathan Pool and Jeremy Azrael, "Education" (part A), in *Handbook of Soviet Social Science Data*, ed. Ellen Mickewicz (New York: Free Press, 1973), ch. 6, pp. 137-58, see p. 139.

14. Iu. D. Desheriev, *Zakonomernosti razvitiia literaturnykh iazykov narodov SSSR v sovetskuiu epokhu: Razvitie obshchestvennykh funktsii literaturnykh iazykov* (Moscow: Nauka, 1976), p. 116; A. N. Baskakov, "Usloviia razvitiia azerbaidzhansko-rusisskogo dvuiazychiia," in *Razvitie natsional'no-russkogo dvuiazychiia*, ed. Iu. D. Desheriev (Moscow: Nauka, 1976), pp. 35-54, see p. 38; Pool and Azrael, loc. cit.

15. See Baskakov, *Voprosy*.

16. Rosemarie Rogers, "The Soviet Audience of Book and Other Publishing," paper presented at the Fifth National Convention of the American Association for the Advancement of Slavic Studies, Dallas, Texas, March 1972, pt. II. Cited with permission. Revised figures kindly furnished by Professor Rogers have been used here.

17. Desheriev, *Zakonomernosti*, p. 143; Baskakov, "Usloviia," p. 39. See also Brian Silver, "Bilingualism and Maintenance of the Mother Tongue in Soviet Central Asia," *Slavic Review* 35 (1976): 406-24, see 408.

18. See Pennar et al., op. cit., pp. 263, 293, 315, for evidence of the previous trend. I am indebted to Brian Silver for calling this contrast to my attention. Table 7. 1 probably overestimates the ratios in general by assuming that the only eligible children are native speakers of the republic language who also belong to the republic nationality.

19. Desheriev, *Zakonomernosti*, p. 73; Ivan Dzyuba, *Internationalism or Russification?* (2nd ed.; London: Weidenfeld and Nicolson, 1970).

20. Deshirev, *Zakonomernosti*, pp. 121-22.

21. A.N. Baskakov, "Chetvertaia stupen' azerbaidzhansko-russkogo dvuiazychiia," in Desheriev, *Razvitie*, pp. 315-35, see 316. I have used the total figure of 12,000 students, although the author says "more than 12,000"; the ratios are not affected.

22. Faig Bagyrov, rector, Azerbaidzhan State University, personal communication, April 1975. Professor Bagyrov also stated that the university had 14,000 students, of whom 70 percent were in the Azerbaidzhani Section—both reasonably consistent with Baskakov's figures.

23. Baskakov, "Chetvertaia stupen'," loc. cit.

24. John C. Johnstone, *Young People's Images of Canadian Society*, Studies of the Royal Commission on Bilingualism and Biculturalism, 2 (Ottawa: Queen's Printer, 1969), pp. 86-87.

25. Desheriev, *Zakonomernosti*, pp. 121, 176, 198, 218, 340.

26. S. Bruk, "Natsional'nost' i iazyk v perepisi naseleniia 1970 g.," *Vestnik statistiki* 5 (1972): 42-53, see 47.

27. See, for instance, Richard Noss, *Higher Education and Development in South-East Asia: Language Policy* (Paris: UNESCO and International Association of Universities, 1967).

28. Park, op. cit., p. 178; Pipes, op. cit., pp. 45-46.

29. Pipes, op. cit., p. 282.

30. Robert Conquest, *The Nation Killers* (London: Sphere Books, 1972), pp. 133-34; Lewis, op. cit., p. 198.

31. Baskakov, *Voprosy*; Musaev, *Alfavity*; Henze, op. cit.

32. Jonathan Pool, "Developing the Soviet Turkic Tongues: The Language of the Politics of Language," *Slavic Review* 35 (1976): 425-42, see 435-39, 441-42.

33. N.G. Korletianu, "Moldavskii literaturnii iazyk dosovestskogo perioda," in *Zakonomernosti razvitiia literaturnykh iazykov narodov SSSR v sovetskuiu epokhu: Vnutistrukturnoe razvitie staropis'mennykh iazykov*, ed. Iu. D. Desheriev (Moscow: Nauka 1973), pp. 163-69, see 167-69.

34. Nicholas Dima, "Moldavians or Romanians?" ch. 3 in *The Soviet West: Interplay between Nationality and Social Organization*, ed. Ralph S. Clem (New York: Praeger, 1975), pp. 38-39, 42-43. See also Henze, op. cit., p. 405, on Uzbek.

35. Frederick C. Barghoorn, *Soviet Russian Nationalism* (New York: Oxford University Press, 1956), p. 92.

36. Baskakov, "Chetvertaia stupen'," pp. 316, 334. See also Lewis, op. cit., pp. 202-03; and M. Mobin Shorish, "The Pedagogical, Linguistic, and Logistical Problems of Teaching Russian to the Local Soviet Central Asians," *Slavic Review* 35 (1976): 443-62.

37. Desheriev, *Razvitie*.

38. Baskakov, "Usloviia," pp. 43-45.

39. A.N. Baskakov, "Vtoraia stupen' azerbaidzhansko-russkogo dvuiazychiia," in Desheriev, *Razvitie*, pp. 235-47, see 236.

40. A.N. Baskakov, "Tret'ia stupen' azerbaidzhansko-russkogo dvuiazychiia," in Desheriev, *Razvitie*, pp. 279-85, see 279.

41. Baskakov, "Chetvertaia stupen'," pp. 317-18.

42. A.N. Baskakov, "Pervaia stupen' azeraidzhansko-russkogo dvuiazychiia," in Desheriev, *Razvitie*, pp. 184-201, see 185-87, 198.

43. Baskakov, "Chetvertaia stupen'," p. 335.

44. V. Iu. Mikhal'chenko, "Usloviia razvitiia litovskorusskogo dvuiazychiia," in Desheriev, *Razvitie*, pp. 54-71, see 58.

45. Ibid., pp. 67-68.

46. Ibid., pp. 70-71.

47. Ibid., pp. 68-69.

48. V. Iu. Mikhal'chenko, "Pervaia stupen'litovsko-russkogo dvuiazychiia," in Desheriev, *Razvitie*, pp. 201-13, see 211-13.

49. V. iu. Mikhal'chenko, *Razvitie*, pp. 248-57, see 250.

50. V. Iu. Mikhal'chenko, "Chetvertaia stupen'litovsko-russkogo dvuiazychiia," in Desheriev, *Razvitie*, pp. 335-51, see 337-39.

51. I.A. Selitskaia, "Usloviia razvitiia estonsko-russkogo dvuiazychiia," in Desheriev, *Razvitie*, pp. 72-85, see 80.

52. Ibid., pp. 82-85.

53. A.K. Reitsak, "Chertvaia stupen' estonsko-russkogo dvuiazychiia," in Desheriev, *Razvitie*, p. 351-65, see 351-53.

54. Murray Feshbach and Stephen Rapawy, "Soviet Population and Manpower Trends and Policies," in *Soviet Economy in a New Perspective*, ed. John P. Hardt (Washington, D.C.: U.S. Government Printing Office, 1976), pp. 113-61, see 48. But see also M.N. Gubogio, "Etnolingvisticheskie protsessy," in *Sovremennye etnicheskie protsessy v SSSR*, ed. Iu. V. Bromlei et al. (Moscow: Nauka, 1975), ch. 8, p. 306. Brian Silver has argued (personal communication) that the census question presumably refers to oral, not written, fluency, and that grammatical writing ability is an unfair criterion, since even many native speakers would fail to meet it.

55. A.A. Darbeeva, "Pervaia stupen' buriatsko-russkogodvuiazychiia," in Desheriev, *Razvitie*, pp. 222-33, see 222; Baskakov, "Pervaia stupen'," p. 185.

56. A.A. Darbeeva, "Usloviia razvitiia buriatsko-russkogo dvuiazychie," in Desheriev, *Razvitie*, pp. 85-102.

57. Feshbach and Rapawy, op. cit., pp. 122-23.

58. M.N. Gubogio, "Etnolingvisticheskie kontakty i dvuiazychie," in *Sotsial'noe i natsional'noe*, ed. Iu. V. Arutiunian (Moscow: Nauka, 1973), ch. 4, p. 268.

59. Paul Lamy, "Language Conflict and Language Planning in Canada," paper presented at the annual meeting of the Canadian Sociology and Anthropology Association, Quebec, May, 1976.

60. *Itogi vsesoiuznoi perepisi naseleniia 1970*, IV; Stanley Lieberson, *Language and Ethnic Relations in Canada* (New York: Wiley, 1970), p. 135.

61. Feshbach and Rapawy, op. cit.

62. V.A. Avrorin, *Problemy izucheniia funktsional'noi storony iazychia* (Leningrad: Elm, 1975), p. 210-41.

63. F.K. Kocharli and A.F. Dashdamirov, eds., *Sovetskii narod i dialektika natsional'nogo razvitie* (Baku: Elm, 1972), p. 329.

64. Avrorin, op. cit., p. 211.

65. V.N. Durdenevskii, *Ravnopravie iazykov v sovetskom stroe* (Moscow: Institut Sovetskogo Prava, 1927), p. 19.

66. Jeffrey A. Ross, "An Analysis of the Emergence of Ethnicity in the Politics of Post-Industrial Society," paper presented at the Seventeenth Annual Convention of the International Studies Association, Toronto, February 1976.

15

Equality, Efficiency, and Politics in Soviet Bilingual Education Policy, 1934-1980

Barbara A. Anderson and Brian D. Silver

As both a means of communication and a symbol of identity with the past and future of a nation or an ethnic group, language can evoke strong popular feelings.   For governments of multi-ethnic countries, language policy is potentially one of the most divisive issues. The adoption of one or more state or official languages and the suppression or neglect of other languages can have a variety of purposes, such as promotion of national unity, dominance by particular ethnic or cultural groups, or development of an efficient common medium of mass communications (Fishman, 1968).   Whatever the goals or the probability of their attainment, granting or denying official status to a particular language is commonly regarded as a measure of the government's commitment to the survival of that language's bearers as a distinct ethnic group.

Perhaps more than any other aspect of language policy, provision of formal education in a child's native language reflects a government's commitment to the maintenance of distinct ethnic identities. As Knappert (1968, p.63) has written, "The language of the school is the language of the future." Although the Soviet Union has had longer and more extensive experience with bilingual education than any other country in the world, this experience has been little studied in the West. Even the large English-language literature devoted to Soviet education, including the special literature that appeared in the immediate post-Sputnik period, has given scant attention to education in other languages than Russian. One reason Western scholars have paid so little attention to education in the non-

Published in *American Political Science Review*, 78: 4 (December 1984), pp. 1019-1039. Reprinted with permission from the publisher.

Russian languages is the lack of systematic and comprehensive data on such education.

We have developed a new set of data on the trends in schooling in the non-Russian languages from 1934-1980. These data indicate whether or not non-Russian languages were used at various levels in Soviet primary and secondary schools. The data also allows us to examine factors that can account for differences in the treatment of the non-Russian languages.

Most Western scholars have viewed Soviet education policy as supporting a single minded course toward russification of non-Russian children. Our data suggests that this view does not accurately portray Soviet school-language policy. At the same time, Soviet official doctrine as embodied in such documents as the USSR Constitutions and the Party programs has consistently maintained that all languages are accorded equal rights. Our data suggests that this view, too, does not accurately describe actual school-language policy.

Although the Soviet authorities have not described the actual decision rules that have guided central policy regarding native-language schooling, we have adduced from the Soviet literature three principles that might have guided the provision of native-language schooling: equality, efficiency, and political status. We test hypotheses implied by each of the principles in order to determine how well each decision rule can account empirically for the treatment of the non-Russian languages over time.

BACKGROUND

Ethnic Diversity of the USSR

In 1979, the Soviet population numbered 262 million, only 52% of whom are ethnic Russians. Twenty-two ethnic groups had a population of at least one million (USSR, Ts.S.U., 1980). Approximately 90 ethnic groups, which, following Soviet practice, we refer to as nationalities, are officially recognized as indigenous to the USSR.[1]

The Soviet state is federal in form, with the primary territorial divisions representing the official territories of particular nationalities, as is reflected in the territorial names. More than 50 ethnic groups are recognized as the titular nationalities of administrative-territorial units in the federal state-structure. There are 15 soviet socialist republics(SSRs), also called union republics, that are the official homelands of nationalities such as the Russians, Ukrainians, Uzbeks, Armenians, and Latvians. Below the level of union republic there are 20 autonomous soviet socialist republics (ASSRs), also called autonomous republics. Autonomous republics are located within and are administratively subordinate to the union republics. Sixteen are located within the Russian Republic (RSFSR). At the next lower level there are eight provinces (*avtonomnye oblasti*) or AOs, six of which are in the RSFSR. There are ten autonomous districts (*avtonomnye okrugi*) or ADs, all of which are located in the RSFSR.

Almost every one of the 90 indigenous ethnic groups has its own traditional language. The languages of the Soviet nationalities are extremely diverse, coming from five main genetic language families (Indo-European, Uralic, Altaic, Caucasian, and Paleoasiatic) and numerous subgroups within those families (Comrie, 1981).

Development of Soviet Language Policy

Official Soviet policy has long balanced a concern for extending the role of the Russian language with a reluctance to stir up nationalistic resentments. In addition, language is usually cited by Soviet theorists on nationality relations as the best example of what is meant by national form in the slogan describing non-Russian cultures in the USSR as "socialist in essence and nationalist in form." Both for these reasons and as a mechanism for mobilizing support by non-Russians for the new regime, from the early 1920s to the mid 1930s the Party pursued a policy of indigenization (*korenizatsiia*) that included recruitment of local government leaders and of Party members from the non-Russian (local) populations and promotion of the local languages in schools and in government administration (Fainsod, 1963, pp. 362-363).

After the revolution of 1917, the Soviet government embarked on a massive program to provide secular schools to the non-Russian nationalities, with their languages serving as the languages of instruction. A special section of the Commissariat of Enlightenment responsible for developing schools using the non-Russian languages was established by decree of the Council of People's Commissars on October 31, 1918 (USSR, Sovnarkom, 1973, p.145).

In the 1920s and the 1930s, non-Russian (national) schools flourished in the larger- and medium-sized republics and provinces. By the middle of the 1930s, native language schools were operating in all regions of the country, and in 1934 textbooks were printed in 104 languages (Sovetkin, 1958, p.11).

During the 1920s, the Soviet government Latinized the existing scripts of all indigenous languages with the exception of the three major Slavic languages (Russian, Ukrainian, and Belorussian), which continued to use Cyrillic scripts, and of Armenian and Georgian, which used their distinctive long-established non-Latin-based scripts.[2] In the mid-1920s, the government also adopted a policy of creating Latin-based scripts for the previously scriptless (*bespis'mennye*) languages of almost 30 small ethnic groups. (Iakovlev, 1931)

Promoting the Latin script rather than the Cyrillic script as the "new alphabet" in the 1920s was one way in which the communist regime sought to distinguish its nationality policy from the russificationist policy of the Tsars. Until 1936, when the Communist Party Central Committee criticized those responsible for the Latinization of the alphabets for making this policy an absolute, proposals to create or preserve Russian-based alphabets could be resisted and effectively criticized as reflecting "great-Russian chauvinism" or an "old russificationist policy" (Kreindler, 1982, p.8; Zak & Isaev, 1966, pp. 11-12).

By the late 1930s a campaign was begun to teach Russian language in schools, and the alphabets of most languages were shifted from a Latin to a Cyrillic script to facilitate this process. The Cyrillization of the scripts was justified as facilitating the learning of Russian as a second language by people whose native language was not Russian. This new emphasis on the learning of Russian was strengthened by a decree of the Council of People's Commissars on March 13, 1938, "On the Obligatory Study of Russian Language in Schools in the National Republics and Provinces," which made the study of Russian mandatory in all non-Russian schools.

The next significant legislative change in the role of different languages in the Soviet schools was the Education Law of 1959, which introduced the idea of "voluntary choice in both the language of instruction (the primary medium of instruction) and the study of other languages as subjects (Bilinsky, 1962, 1968). Although the 1959 law may appear to have eliminated the obligatory study of the Russian language, in practice it apparently provided a form of democratic legitimation for reductions in the provisions of native-language schooling through the exercise of free-choice by the parents of non-Russian children. After the 1959 legislation, there were apparently widespread and substantial reductions in the use of non-Russian languages as media of instruction in schools (Silver, 1974).

Since the late 1970s, there has been a special campaign, supported by new legislation, to increase the quantity and to improve the quality of Russian language instruction among non-Russians (Feshbach, 1981; Kreindler, 1982; Solchanyk, 1982). Some Western scholars maintain that this recent effort, along with the major legislative steps taken in 1938 and 1959, demonstrates that the long-term goal of Soviet language and nationalities policy has been the elimination of the use of the non-Russian languages (e.g., Carrere d'Encausse, 1980; Conquest, 1967; Kreindler, 1962; Solchanyk, 1982).

A key problem with this line of reasoning is that it ignores the fact that Soviet nationalities policy, as expressed both in formal doctrine and in actual administrative practice, has always displayed significant tendencies that run counter to a policy of russification. For example, even the Third Party Program of 1961, which is often cited as providing doctrinal legitimation for an accelerated effort to bring about the *sliianie* (blending) of nationalities, did not use the term *sliianie* at all. Although the Program stated that ethnic distinctions will eventually disappear and a single *lingua franca* will be adopted by all the nationalities, it also stated that "the obliteration of national distinctions, and especially of language distinctions, is a considerably more drawn-out process than the obliteration of class distinctions" (USSR, CPSU, 1962).

Many scholars assume, or at least give the impression, that whenever there has been an increase in the study of Russian in the non-Russian schools, there has been a commensurate decrease in the study of the group's non-Russian language. A policy of bilingualism may thereby be misinterpreted to be a policy of eliminating the non-Russian languages. Although making Russian a mandatory subject of study may have promoted not only bilingualism but also loss of the mother tongue, the actual impact of this policy cannot be understood without an understanding of the roles of both Russian and the traditional (non-Russian) languages in the school curriculum of non-Russian children.

Unfortunately, the published evidence on the status of particular non-Russian languages in the schools over time is scattered and incomplete. We have systematic, although incomplete, evidence only for 1940, 1958, and 1972. In the late 1950s, Sovetkin (1958, p. 23) provided clearcut evidence that there was a hierarchy of educational opportunities in the native language for members of different nationalities in the RSFSR. Some non-Russian nationalities had native-language schools available through complete secondary school (ten years). Others had such schools available only through a maximum of 7, 4, 2, or fewer years. According to Sovetkin, the number of years of native-language schooling available to the different nationalities was essentially established by the 1931-1932 school year. In addition, a monograph published in 1948 by the Ministry of Education of the RSFSR reported that in 1940, except for some small ethnic groups in Siberia, all non-Russian nationalities in the RSFSR had primary schools (classes 1-4) in the native language. But the "incomplete secondary school" classes (5-7) and "complete secondary school" classes (5-10) "for the most part . . . were still not indigenized" (Konstantinov & Medynskii, 1948, pp. 301, 310). In 1940, the incomplete secondary schools were nativized in only eleven languages. The "complete secondary schools" (10-year schools) were nativized in only two languages. Finally, the Minister of Education of the RSFSR published an article concerning non-Russian schooling in 1972 which presented figures that, when contrasted with those reported for 1940 and 1958, showed that the status of the languages of nationalities indigenous to the RSFSR was deteriorating (Danilov, 1972; Silver, 1974).

Although these three sources provide helpful information, published sources can provide the basis of a comprehensive account of the languages used in the RSFSR only for 1940, 1958, and 1972, and not for other years or for schools outside the RSFSR; nor do the sources provide information on the rationale for a differentiated treatment of the non-Russian languages. Nonetheless, this evidence is helpful in indicating that a very large number of non-Russian languages have been used as languages of instruction in Soviet schools and also that Soviet school-language policy has long been a highly differentiated one.

DECISION RULES IN THE ALLOCATION OF NATIVE-LANGUAGE SCHOOLS

The actual administrative rules guiding whether or not native-language schools were to be set up and at what grade levels (and in which subjects) in the curriculum a given language might be used have seldom been discussed publicly by Soviet officials.

In 1918 a rule was introduced by the Council of People's Commissars that called for the establishment of native-language schools for national minorities whenever there were at least 25 pupils at a given grade level who spoke that language (USSR, Sovnarkom, 1973). Although this rule may explain the liberal development of the national schools in the 1920s, the administrative rules operative in more recent years are less clear. In fact, a rarely cited portion of the March 13, 1938, decree making study of the Russian language mandatory in schools, states that:

> The native language is the basis of instruction in schools of the national republics and provinces, that exceptions from this rule occurring in some autonomous republics of the RSFSR can have only a temporary character, that the tendency to convert the Russian language from a subject of study of a language of instruction while at the same time infringing on the native language, is harmful and incorrect (cited in Sovetkin, 1958, p. 15).

Occasionally, Soviet writers on language planning use verbal formulas that have the tone of administrative decision-making rules. For example, after explaining how parents in a multinational setting might exercise their freedom of choice concerning the language of schooling for their children, Khanazarov (1963, p. 173) states:

> Here we speak not of regions of compact settlement of a single nationality in other republics. In such regions the question of language of instruction is resolved simply. Here national schools operate in which instruction is conducted in the language of a compactly settled monolingual population (*kompaktno zhivushchego odnoiazychnogo naseleniia*) or in some other languages according to the parents' wishes.

Based on writings by Soviet scholars, we propose three decision rules or principles that might describe the actual policy on native-language schooling at various dates.

The Equality Principle

The dominant theme in official Soviet doctrine concerning the non-Russian languages has been that each nationality is free to use its traditional language. Article 121 of the 1936 Constitution of the USSR guaranteed citizens the right to instruction in schools in their native language. Article 36 of the 1977 Constitution assures citizens "the opportunity to use the mother tongue and languages of other peoples of the USSR." Article 45 assures citizens "the opportunity for school instruction in their native language." We call this basic official doctrine the equality principle.

Strictly speaking, the equality principle has not been followed, since in official practice Russian is clearly preeminent among the languages of the USSR. Russian has been described in numerous official speeches, documents, and scholarly writings as unique among Soviet languages. Since the adoption of the Third Party Program in 1961, Russian often has been referred to as the "internationality language of discourse" (*mezhnatsional'nyi iazyk obshcheniia*) of the peoples of the USSR.

In view of the special role of Russian, instead of applying an absolute equality standard to Soviet school-language policy, we define a modified egalitarian standard along two dimensions: the greater the number of nationalities that are provided with some form of native-language instruction, the more egalitarian is school-language policy, and the greater the number of school years (the higher the class level) in which the non-Russian languages are used either as the primary medium of instruction or as a separate subject of instruction, the more egalitarian the policy.

The Efficiency Principle

A second principle that might explain use of non-Russian languages in schools is the principle of economic efficiency. The efficiency argument has two aspects. From the perspective of the child or the child's parents, it is an inefficient investment of personal resources to study in a language that has limited utility in the job market or that cannot offer a full range of cultural opportunities. From the perspective of the state, it is inefficient to expend substantial resources to develop the capacity to teach in languages that are used by only a small number of persons and thus can play only a limited role in the modern economy, in science and technology, and in disseminating the cultural achievements of the society as a whole.

Soviet scholars frequently offer arguments consistent with the efficiency principle to explain why the Russian language is the preferred *lingua franca* of Soviet nationalities and why the smaller nationalities often have limited opportunities for native-language schooling. For example, after explaining that in the early 1930s instruction was organized in the languages of many small ethnic groups, Khanazarov (1977, p. 133) writes:

> Further development of school affairs made plain to the smaller people, nationalities, and ethnic groups the inexpediency (*netselesoobraznost'*) and practical unwarrantedness (*neopravdannost'*) of the splintering of schools and instructional classes by language of instruction. Parents became convinced in practice of the unprofitability (*nevygodnost'*) of instructing their children in languages that are not widely used. In those languages there is an extremely small number of speakers, which greatly lowers the pay-off of the education received.

Others state that there is no contradiction between the principles of equality and efficiency. For example, Tsamerian (1973, pp. 241-242) writes:

In our country all languages are equal under the law and develop freely. This is well known to everyone. But on the basis of this could one assert that all languages of the peoples of the USSR (including even language-dialects, which are spoken by only a few thousand or hundred people) have identical possibilities, fulfill identical functions in the development of cultures in general, and of art and literature in particular?

Speaking of the equal rights of languages, it is impossible also to forget about the objective functional possibilities of each language.

On the basis of Soviet literature, we propose two efficiency hypotheses. First, the larger the population size of a group, the greater the likelihood that its traditional language will be used either as the medium of instruction or as a separate subject of study in schools or both, and the higher the class level in which the language will be used. Second, native-language schooling will be more likely to be provided if a large number of group members are compactly settled than if they are not.

The Political Principle

In its broadest application, the political principle would determine opportunities for native-language schooling according to the roles assigned to the nationalities by the country's top political leaders. For example, Armstrong (1968) has constructed a model of Soviet nationalities policy that assigns specific roles to ethnic groups based on the groups' potential utility in realizing the goals of the top Communist Party leaders.

The establishment of the USSR as a federal system may be viewed as a pragmatic concession by the Bolshevik Party to the non-Russian nationalities as part of an effort to consolidate control of the non-Russian regions. The initial reasons for the organization of the USSR into a federal system were the subject of an extended scholarly debate in the USSR during the 1960s (Hodnett, 1967). However, formal recognition of a nationality's territoriality probably reflected some willingness to make concessions in the cultural sphere, especially the possibility of using the group's traditional language in schools, mass media, and governmental affairs.

We use the status of a nationality in the territorial-administrative hierarchy of the Soviet Union as an indicator of its political status. Thus, nationalities with titular areas that are union republics are assumed to have a higher political status than those whose titular areas are autonomous republics. Autonomous republic nationalities are assumed to have higher status than autonomous province nationalities which in turn rank higher than autonomous district nationalities. All nationalities with formal status rank higher than those without any formal territorial status in the federal system.

Official recognition of nationalities is shown in other ways besides formal territorial status. For example, official disfavor was shown for those nationalities that were forcibly moved from their official homelands during

World War II because of their alleged collaboration with the Nazi invaders (Conquest, 1970; Nekrich, 1978; Wimbush & Wixman, 1975). All the so-called deported nationalities lost native-language schooling from the date of their deportation in 1943-1944. After their political rehabilitation in the late 1950s, native-language schooling was restored for most of these groups. But formal territorial status does not mirror perfectly the current attitude of the Party leaders toward a particular nationality; for example, although Jews are an AO-level group, and although there were native-language schools in Yiddish, Tat, and Bukharan Jewish until the late 1930s, Soviet Jewish groups have not been provided with native-language schools since World War II.

The formal administrative-territorial status of a group is an unambiguous, official, centrally determined, and highly stable characteristic of a nationality. If formal status in the federal system can be shown to be systematically and strongly related to school-language policy, then this policy can be said, on the whole, not to be idiosyncratic or geared to the peculiarities of each separate nationality.

We therefore hypothesize that the higher the formal political status accorded a nationality in the federal structure, the more likely the nationality is to receive some native-language schooling and the higher the grade level in which that group's traditional language can be used either as the primary medium of instruction in the schools or as a separate subject of study.

DETERMINING THE STATUS OF NON-RUSSIAN SCHOOLS

In addition to the three sources mentioned earlier, we have two other sources of systematic information about native-language schooling: curricula and bibliographies of school textbook publication.

School Curriculum Plans

For some years and regions, we have curriculum plans that list the number of hours in the school program mandated for particular subjects of study (e.g., USSR, Minpros, 1976, 1979, 1980). These reports describe the different curriculum plans for the non-Russian (national) and Russian schools, and they demonstrate the recent increase in the number of hours mandated for Russian-language study in the non-Russian schools.

In addition, these published reports show that, at least in recent years, in the non-Russian republics and provinces there have been three main types of primary and secondary educational schools:

1) Russian schools where Russian is the primary medium of instruction and where the local languages are not studied. We call these *Russian schools Type 1*.

2) Russian schools where Russian is the primary medium of instruction, but where the language of a non-Russian nationality is studied as a separate subject. These are officially called "Russian schools where the language of a republic,

autonomous province or autonomous region nationality is studied as a separate subject according to parents' wishes." (Sometimes they are also referred to as "national schools with Russian as the language of instruction.") We call these *Russian schools Type 2.*

3) Non-Russian (national) schools where one or more non-Russian language serves as the principle medium of instruction for almost all subjects (except Russian and foreign languages), and where Russian language and literature are studied as separate subjects. We call these *Type 3 schools.*

Western scholars often assume that there is only one kind of Russian school in the Soviet Union, in which the entire curriculum is taught in Russian and members of non-Russian nationalities study alongside Russian children. These model curricula show that there is more than one kind of "Russian school" and that some native-language schooling is available in the Type 2 Russian schools.

Kashin and Chekharin (1970, p. 108) attribute the appearance of "national schools with Russian language of instruction from the first class" in the RSFSR to the 1959 Soviet education law. We think this form of school is a consequence of the provision of the 1959 law that gave parents the formal right to choose the language of instruction for their children, as well as to decide whether children in Russian-language schools would study their native language as a subject (Bilinsky, 1962).

Textbook Publication

Although the model school curricula are useful, we do not have them for all years or for all groups, and we know that the plans described in the model curricula have not been followed for some groups to whom they ostensibly apply. Therefore, we also use data on textbook publication by language to construct a consistent, systematic set of data reflecting school-language policy toward a large number of nationalities over a long period of time. The data and the methods of developing them have not been described before.

The All-Union Book Chamber (*Vsesoiuznaia knizhnaia* palata) publishes *Knizhnaia letopis' (Chronicle of Books)* weekly and *Ezhegodnik knigi SSSR (Book Annual of the USSR),* annually which report data on virtually all books, including school textbooks, published in the Soviet Union. The All-Union Book Chamber only began to report information on books published outside the Russian republic in 1934; before that, even for the RSFSR, the Central Book Chamber of the RSFSR did not identify books by language. Thus we depict the status of native-language schooling from 1934 through 1980; we used both *Knizhnaia letopis'* and *Ezhegodnik knigi* for information about the languages in which school textbooks were published for mathematics, natural science, language, and literature.

We assume that the use of a given non-Russian language in math or science textbooks is a good indicator that the language is the primary medium of instruction for at least some schools, because if these subjects are taught in a given non-Russian language it is reasonable to infer that most other subjects are also taught in that language. Accordingly, for each year between 1934 and 1980 we code the highest class level for which any math or natural science textbook was published in a given language.

If only one or two subjects are taught in a group's traditional language, they are likely to include a course on the group's language or literature. We assume that publication of such textbooks indicates that at least the language was studied in some schools; therefore, we also coded the highest class level for which any language or literature textbook was published in each non-Russian language. Since the language may well have been used in other subjects as well as in language or literature, this measure indicated the minimum use of the language in schools.

In a few cases, we found that math or science textbooks in a given language were available for a higher class level than language or literature textbooks. To take this apparent anomaly into account, we used the higher of the figures for math-science or language-literature textbooks published in that language as our operational measure of the highest class level in which the language was employed in at least one subject.

We coded this information for 101 ethnic groups, 81 of which are considered officially to be indigenous to the Soviet Union (see Table 15.A1). The technical appendix presents details concerning the coding procedures and case selection.

THE LOCUS OF DECISION MAKING

Because our data do not reflect the proportion of children from each nationality who actually obtained schooling in their group's traditional language, we do not address the question of the distribution of children among Type 1 and Type 2 Russian schools or Type 3 national schools. Such information would be useful, and in the absence of systematic official data, this distribution might be estimated from information in *Knizhnaia letopis'* on the size of the press run, the *tirazh*, of school textbooks by subject in different languages. Although use of the *tirazh* information for this purpose is neither simple nor straight-forward, we hope to use it in future research.

Data on the highest level in which different languages are used are important in their own right. Children who find that they cannot complete secondary or even primary school without studying most, and perhaps all, subjects in a language other than their own nationality's traditional language, are likely to view their language, and perhaps their nationality, as lacking a future. The use or lack of use of the native language in school convey a powerful message.

The class levels and subjects for which particular languages are to be used are likely to be determined by the central authorities rather than by local school officials. USSR and republic ministries of education are responsible for the preparation and allocation of educational resources, including teachers and textbooks. This is a probable legacy of the centralization of control over curricula, textbook publication, and overall educational administration during the early 1930s (Fitzpatrick, 1979).

Translating, printing, and distributing school textbooks in each subject and training individuals to teach these subjects in various languages involved major long-term financial commitments that are likely to be determined centrally. In any given year and for any given subject, class level, and language, there is usually only a single title printed. Therefore, the highest class levels for which textbooks have been published in each language probably reflect a commitment by central political authorities concerning the amount of official support to provide for each language.

At the same time, since the 1959 Soviet education law was enacted, many references have appeared in the Soviet educational literature to the importance of taking local conditions, such as parental wishes and the extent of bilingualism among the children, into account when determining the language of instruction. In many cases, however, the real choice offered to parents may not be "In what language should your child study?" but rather "What type of school should your child attend?" A leading Soviet critic of some of the policies and practices used in Soviet languages planning has noted that education workers often present the choice to parents incorrectly (Avrorin, 1972, pp. 56-57):

> Instead of asking about the desired language of instruction [education workers] usually ask: "Do you want your children to know Russian?" Having received a positive response, and in the overwhelming majority of cases it naturally would be a positive one, the questioner concludes the conversation: "This means that you want your children to attend a Russian school." But in fact this conclusion, from the standpoint of elementary logic, cannot withstand any kind of criticism. It would be correct only in the situation when it was known in advance that the children already had a satisfactory command of Russian before entering school.

References to mistakes by local school administrators who pushed non-Russian children who were inadequately prepared into either Type 1 or Type 2 Russian schools are quite common (e.g., Avrorin, 1972, p. 56; Desheriev, 1968, pp. 60-61; Kirdiashkin, 1973, pp. 77-79; Tsydypov, 1965, p. 170). For example, after describing in detail the procedures for choosing the correct language of instruction in a district, Kirdiashkin (1973, pp. 77-79) explains what happened in the Mordvinian ASSR in 1969-1971:

> The process of transition of Mordvinian primary schools to Russian language of instruction began in 1959.
> The Minister of Enlightenment of the RSFSR developed and distributed to the locales three curricula: the curriculum of the Russian school, the (unified) curriculum plan of the national school, and the curriculum of the 1-8th classes of Russian schools where pupils according to the parents' wishes study the language of the basic nationality.

Rybkinskaia secondary school of Kobylkinskii district is Mordvinian. In the 1969-1970 school year it worked according to the curriculum of the Russian school, with children not studying the native language. Upon checking, it became apparent that the children had low achievement (*uspevaemost'*) in the Russian language. The director of the school [in explaining] the unsatisfactory knowledge of Russian among the pupils, stated: "Our school is national, children have weak command of Russian speech. We work according to the curriculum of the Russian school, but this is difficult for the children." In the 1970-1971 school year, the Rybkinskaia secondary school went over to the curriculum of the national school, but the earlier error in choice of curricula is reflected to this day in the quality of knowledge of the children.

This example illustrates the tension created by the 1959 education law between the long-term commitment to central planning of education and the simultaneous commitment to local decision making that is supposed to take local conditions into account. These tensions and problems in policy implementation are likely to occur when a centralized effort is made to shift the medium of instruction from a non-Russian language to Russian, especially when the necessary conditions for an effective shift are missing.

TRENDS IN NATIVE-LANGUAGE SCHOOLING
Egalitarian Hypothesis

There has been a strong egalitarian element in Soviet school-language policy; 83 of the 101 nationalities included in the data set had schooling where the group's own language was used at least as a subject of study at the level of class 1 or beyond during at least one year between 1934 and 1980.

Thirteen of the 18 nationalities that did not have any native-language schooling during this period were classified in the 1926 Soviet census as not having a literary language. All of them have small populations and reside in either the Soviet Far North or the Caucasus. Twenty-one nationalities that officially lacked a literary language in 1926 received some native-language schooling between 1934 and 1980.

The presence of non-indigenous (foreign) nationalities in the data set presents an analytic problem because, in light of practice in most countries, it is not reasonable to expect the Soviet government to provide native-language schooling for many different foreign groups. Even so, native-language schooling has been provided during some years to members of such foreign nationalities as the Poles, Uighurs, Hungarians, Czechs, Kurds, Assyrians, Chinese, and Koreans.

We concentrate in the remainder of the analysis on the nationalities that are indigenous to the USSR, because it is for these groups, more than for foreign groups, that the logic of Soviet language policy should be examined. We use the official Soviet definition of indigenous groups as used in recent census reports. (See Table 15.A1.)

If we exclude the 20 foreign nationalities, 81 indigenous groups remain, 67 of which (83%) had schooling in which their group's traditional language was used at least as a subject through at least the first class for at least one year between 1934 and 1980. Judging by our data on publication of math or science textbooks, the same 67 nationalities also had schooling at some time in which their group's traditional language was the primary medium of instruction.

Although impressive, these figures give only a superficial picture because they answer only a simple question: Between 1934 and 1980, how many nationalities ever had schooling in which their group's traditional language was used as the medium of instruction or as a subject of study at any class level? It is also important to know how the availability of native-language schooling has changed over time, and whether, on average, the class levels for which native-language schooling has been provided have followed any trend.

To answer these additional questions, we broke the 47-year time series into nine periods, for each of which (and also for the entire 1934-1980 time span) we calculated the number of indigenous nationalities that had schools in which math or science textbooks (abbreviated as M) used the group's traditional language, an indication that the group's language was the primary medium of instruction. We also calculated the number of nationalities that had schools where language or literature textbooks (abbreviated as L) used the traditional language, and those where the group's traditional language was used in either math-science or language-literature (abbreviated as H—higher of M or L).

The results of these calculations, given in Table 15.1, show that the heyday of non-Russian schools was before World War II. During the 1934-1940 period, 64 nationalities had schools in which math-science was taught in their traditional language, and 65 had schools where instruction in language-literature was given in that language. The number of nationalities with schools where math-science (M) was taught in their traditional language has declined substantially since 1934-1940. There were approximately 50 such languages between 1946 and 1965; after that, the number dropped in each succeeding period and reached a low of 35 in the 1976-1980 period, just over half the prewar number.

The pattern of use of the non-Russian languages as subjects of study is very different. In every period since 1945, about 53 nationalities have had schools where their group's language was at least a subject of study (H), about 82% of the prewar number. However, the disappearance of schools in which the non-Russian language is the primary medium of instruction indicates that increasingly over time the Type 3 (national) schools have been replaced by Type 2 schools.

We also want to know the highest class level for which native-language schooling was available. In Table 15.2, we examine the class levels for all groups that had native-language schooling at some time, i.e., the 67 groups from the last row of Table 15.1. For each period, for the 67 indigenous groups that ever had some native-language schooling, we computed the average of the highest grade in which math or science textbooks were published (M). We also computed the average of the highest grade in which either math-science or language-literature textbooks were published (H). In Tables 15.2-5, preschool texts are coded as .5 years to take some account of the difference between preschool native-language schooling and no native-language schooling.

Table 15.2 shows that of those indigenous nationalities that ever had traditional-language schooling, the average maximum class level in which the group's language was available as the primary medium of instruction (M) declined from 5.48 years in the 1934-1940 period to 3.21 in 1976-1980. A substantial drop in the average occurred during World War II, probably as a result of disruptions in the production of textbooks and in the operation of Soviet schools during those years. After World War II, the level rebounded, although it never regained the prewar level. The average has declined steadily in each period since 1951-1955.

In contrast, non-Russian languages have been increasingly available at least as a subject of study (H). The average maximum class level in which the group's language was available at least as a subject of study has risen since World War II; by 1956-1960, the level exceeded that achieved in 1934-1940 (6.21 vs. 5.94), and by 1976-1980, it reached 6.93 years.

To summarize, at the same time that availability of some instruction in the non-Russian languages has increased, there has also been substantial erosion in the use of the non-Russian languages as the primary medium of instruction in the schools. It would appear that the non-Russian languages are increasingly being reduced to use as a subject of study in Russian-language schools—the Type 2 Russian schools. But there is substantial intergroup variation in the extent to which this is taking place, and obviously, an equality principle cannot explain this differential treatment. We therefore turn to the evidence for the operation of the efficiency principle and the political principle.

The Efficiency Hypothesis

One indicator of the efficiency of providing native-language schooling to a given nationality is the size of the population. In addition, the more members of a nationality who live close to each other, the more efficient it is to provide schools in that group's traditional language. Although our current data do not allow us to test the effects of residential concentration in cities and rural districts, where central policies are implemented in native-language schooling, we attempt to measure the effects of geographic concentration on the availability of native-language schooling. Geographic concentration is expressed here as the number of members of each nationality who resided in that nationality's titular area (republic, province, or district) in 1959.

If the efficiency principle is the basis for deciding which nationalities were provided with native-language schooling, the larger the group's population, and the more members of the given nationality who reside in the group's titular area, the higher the class level for which traditional-language schooling in that group's traditional language will be available. Accordingly, we calculated Pearson correlation coefficients in turn between a) the natural log of the group's 1926 population size, the natural log of the group's 1959 population size, and the natural log of the number of group members in 1959 living in the group's titular area, and b) the two basic native-language school policy measures at various dates for the indigenous nationalities. We use the natural logarithm of population because the distributions of the population size variables are highly skewed.

Panel A of Table 15.3 shows the coefficient of determination (r^2) between the measures of 1926 and 1959 population size and the highest school class in which the group's traditional language was used to teach math-science (M). Panel B presents the analogous coefficients between population size and the extent to which the group's traditional language was used at least as a subject of study (H). In each panel, the first two rows of figures use the entire population of the nationality in the USSR in 1926 and 1959, while the third row uses the population of the nationality in 1959 living in its own titular republic, province, or district, if it had one. We show the coefficient of determination rather than the Pearson correlation coefficient in order to make Table 15.3 more comparable with the proportion of variance explained (R^2) in Tables 15.4 and 15.5. All of the correlation coefficients were positive, as expected.

Using either the 1926 or the 1959 population of the nationality, more than 80% of the 1934-1940 variance in each measure of native-language schooling can be accounted for by population size. The explanatory power of population size is nearly as great for the 1941-1945 period. These large proportions of explained variance indicate that during the heyday of the national schools, the provision of native-language schooling was highly consistent with an efficiency principle.

Over time, the correlation between the 1926 population variable and both native-language schooling variables remains fairly strong but gradually weakens. For the math-science schooling variable (M), the r^2 with the 1926 population measure drops from .841 in 1934-1940 to .503 in 1976-1980. For the language-literature or math-science schooling variable (H), the proportion of variance explained drops from .830 to .557.

Such an attenuation of correlation is to be expected, since the time periods for which the language policy is measured become increasingly distant from 1926. But the declining correlation does not result solely from the time lag between the population and language-policy measures, because the relation between policy and the 1959 population measure follows a similar pattern. Whether population is measured in 1926 or 1959, its correlation with school-language policy decreases in magnitude over time.

Table 15.3 also shows that geographic concentration is an important factor for native-language schooling; as measured by the size of the population that lived in its own titular area, geographic concentration maintained a consistently strong relation over time with the math-science measure (M), but generally weakened in its relation with the math-science or language-literature measure (H). Thus, whether or not a group is compactly settled affects differentially whether a nationality's traditional language was used as the primary medium of instruction or only as a subject of study. The statistical results are consistent with the interpretation that providing instruction in a given non-Russian language in one subject (i.e., language-literature) is relatively inexpensive, but maintaining an entire curriculum in a given non-Russian language is only reasonable when a large number of pupils from the same non-Russian nationality live close to each other.

The Political Hypothesis

To examine the extent to which the provision of native-language schooling has varied with the territorial status of the nationality, we classify all of the indigenous nationalities according to their current status: union republic (SSR), autonomous republic (ASSR), autonomous oblast' (AO), autonomous district (*avtonomnyi okrug*—here abbreviated AD), and other indigenous nationalities (here abbreviated as IND).

Figures 1 and 2 show for each period the average highest school year in which textbooks in the nationality's traditional language were published either in math-science or language-literature (H) or in math-science (M), for nationalities grouped by their formal political status. The extent to which schooling has been available follows distinctive paths related to the group's formal political status, and the status groupings always remain in the expected rank order. The highest school year is always lower on average for the ASSR nationalities than for the SSR nationalities, the corresponding figures for the AO nationalities are lower on average than those of the ASSR's during each period, and the figures for AD nationalities are lower on average than those for the AO groups, but higher than those for the IND nationalities.

Figure 1 depicts the average highest class levels in which the non-Russian languages were used in school at least as a separate subject (H). It demonstrates the steady increase since World War II in the class levels in which the languages of all groupings of AO status and higher were used in schools. After lagging behind the SSR nationalities by over three class levels in the 1934-1940 period, the ASSR nationalities improved their position to such an extent that in the 1976-1980 period it nearly matched that of the SSR nationalities. The AO nationalities followed a similar upward trajectory over time, but lagged behind the ASSR nationalities. In contrast, after a decline in the status of their languages between 1934-1940 and 1941-1945, both the AD and IND groups have experienced little change.

The trends in the use of the non-Russian languages as the medium of instruction are very different from the trends in use as a separate subject. Figure 2 shows that all groupings except the SSR nationalities have experienced steady reductions over time in the highest school year in which the groups' traditional languages were used as the primary medium of instruction. This generalization is only slightly modified by observation of the brief recovery after World War II for the non-SSR groupings.

We infer that native-language education for the ASSR- and AO-level nationalities is increasingly taking place not in the national schools but instead in the Russian schools with the (non-Russian) native language as a separate subject. In contrast, for the AD- and IND-level nationalities, traditional-language schooling is disappearing completely; children in these nationalities are increasingly attending only Type 1 Russian schools.

The upward trends in Figure 1 run counter to the common supposition in the West that the non-Russian languages are disappearing from use in the educational system. The downward trends in Figure 2, however, are consistent with the Western supposition of increasing russianization of the bulk of the school curriculum for members of non-SSR nationalities. Thus, it is inappropriate to suppose that any single pattern of change applies to all Soviet ethnic groups.

THE RELATIVE IMPORTANCE OF
EFFICIENCY AND POLITICAL STATUS

We now test more rigorously to what extent the formal political status of the nationalities accounts for the extent of native-language schooling over time; i.e. are the differences among political status groupings more important than the differences within political status groupings? Once this theory is determined, the combined and the relative effects of the efficiency and the political status factors on traditional-language schooling can be assessed.

To conduct these tests, we first calculated the multiple correlation between the measure of formal political status and the measures of school-language policy. We estimated regression equations using as the dependent variables alternately the average for each period of the highest class levels in which textbooks were published in math-science (M), and the average for each period of the highest of language-literature or math-science (H). For independent variables, we created dichotomous variables representing the different levels of territorial status of the indigenous nationalities: SSR, ASSR, AO, and AD. The results of these calculations are presented in Table 15.4.

As expected, Table 15.4 shows that the formal political status of the nationalities is strongly related to the availability of native-language schooling. For simplicity, we do not show the coefficients for the individual independent variables, all of which are positive or not statistically significant. Also, in every case the effects of the set of dichotomous variables as a whole are statistically significant.

Political status accounts for between 67 and 85% of the variance in school-language policy. During most periods, political status is more highly related to the use of the group's traditional language as a subject of study than as the primary medium of instruction. More important for our analysis, the relation between formal political status and the provision of native-language schooling has maintained its strength over time.

Thus the variation among political status groupings is far more important than the variation within political status groupings in accounting for the differential provision of native-language schooling, and the trends depicted in Figures 1 and 2 capture the vast majority of the experience of the particular nationalities within each political status grouping.

Comparing the figures in Table 15.4 with those in Table 15.3 shows that for both aspects of school-language policy, population size has become a weaker predictor of the provision of native-language schooling over time, whereas formal political status has become a slightly stronger predictor. The relative strength of the two predictors can be compared more directly by estimating a series of multiple regression equations that include indicators of both kinds of factors simultaneously.

For each period we estimated multiple regression equations using alternately each of the school-language policy measures as dependent variables and using as independent variable both the natural log of the 1959 population and the set of dichotomous variables representing the formal political status of the groups. (Table 15.5).

Table 15.5 is organized in the following manner. Panels A and B are analogous to Table 15.4. They show the proportion of the variance in school-language policy explained (R^2) by 1959 population alone, by the set of political status variables alone, and then by the population variable and the political status variables together. For example, in 1951-1955, for M, the population variable alone can explain 62.3% of the variance, the set of political status variables alone can explain 70.9% of the variance, and the two kinds of variables together explain 71.8% of the variance. Panels C and D in Table 15.5 present the probabilities that the additional variance explained by each of the factors (after the other has already been taken into account) is owing to chance alone. We adopt the conventional criterion for determining whether a variable has a non-random effect, which is a significance level of .05 or less.

Table 15.5 shows for the 1934-1940 period not only that population size by itself accounts for a greater proportion of the variance in each measure of school-language policy than does political status by itself, but also that the two factors together explain only a slightly greater proportion of the variance than does population alone. Population size is also a more powerful predictor of school-language policy than is formal political status for the 1941-1945 period. Just the opposite is true for every period after World War II. In the postwar years, not only does the formal political status of the nationality by itself explain a large proportion of the variance in the provision of schooling in the non-Russian languages than can group population size, but once political status is taken into account, population size explains only a negligible (and statistically non-significant) additional proportion of the variance.

This change in the relative importance of the efficiency and political factors is shown by the p values in Panels C and D of Table 15.5. For both H and M, the p values for population size before 1946 are statistically significant—they are less than .05 and in fact are .000, that is, less than .0005. from 1946 through 1980, the p values for population size are always larger than .05, and the p values for the political status variables as a group are always smaller than .05.

Thus, Table 15.5 suggests that between 1934 and 1945, the operative decision rules for the provision of native-language schooling hinged less on the formal territorial status accorded the nationalities in the 1936 Constitution than on the practical efficiency of organizing such schooling. Additional support for this interpretation is that the extent to which a nationality had schooling in its traditional language in the 1934-1940 period is strongly related to whether the group already had a written language in 1926 ($r = .714$).

Over time, however, the policy of providing schooling in the non-Russian languages was related less to consideration of economic efficiency and more to the hierarchical organization of the Soviet federal state. Thus, differences in formal administrative-territorial status appear to be associated with real policy differences, independent of the population size of the nationalities.

This does not mean that population size had only a temporary effect on the availability of schooling in the non-Russian languages. On the contrary, in results not shown here, we found that population size is related to school-language policy in the postwar era in three ways. First, 1926 population size is positively related to the political status of nationalities, which in turn affects the availability of native-language schooling. Second, there was substantial inertia in provision of native-language schooling. To the extent that school-language policy during 1934-1940 was determined more by group population size than by group political status, population has a persistent indirect effect on later native-language schooling opportunities. Third, a nationality's population affects school-language policy even in the postwar years through the number of group members residing in the nationality's titular area.

IMPLICATIONS FOR UNDERSTANDING
SOVIET NATIONALITIES POLICY

The best way to characterize the Soviet Union's policy toward the use of the non-Russian and Russian languages in education with a simple phrase is that it is a "bilingual education policy." Since World War II, the number of languages used as the primary medium of instruction in schools has decreased, and also there has been a substantial reduction in the highest class levels in which the non-Russian languages have been used in this capacity. But the non-Russian languages still have an important place in the curriculum.

The number of nationalities able to study their traditional language as a separate subject in at least some schools was not much smaller in 1976-1980 than in 1934-1940 and has not changed since 1941-1945. More important, the average highest class level in which the non-Russian languages are taught as subjects of study has increased since 1934-1940. If the only intention had been to eliminate the use of the non-Russian languages, there would have been no reason to increase the highest grade level at which non-Russian languages could be studied as a subject.

We describe Soviet school-language policy as one of bilingual education rather than of linguistic russification because we regard use of language in the curriculum even as a subject of study as an important source of support for that language. In this respect we take issue with the implicit argument of many other Western scholars, who seem to regard the use of languages as the primary medium of instruction as the only meaningful support for the non-Russian languages and their use as subjects of study as inconsequential.

Our attention to use of the languages as subjects of study is grounded in part on empirical analyses that indicate that availability of the languages as subjects of study is often sufficient to retard the shift to Russian as native language. If the medium of instruction was Russian but the group's traditional language was available as a separate subject, group members tended to acquire Russian as a second language but to retain the group's traditional language as native language (Anderson & Silver, 1982).

The data on use of the non-Russian languages in schools are not consistent with the patterns of policy shift suggested by others. Whatever changes may have occurred in the official theoretical formulas on Soviet nationalities policy, our evidence on school language policy supports neither the depiction of official policy as shifting back and forth between a centralist (pro-Russian) and a peripheralist (pro-non-Russian) emphasis (Lewis, 1972), nor the depiction of official policy as moving inexorably in a russificationist direction (Kreindler, 1982), nor the description of the policy as absolutely egalitarian (Isaev, 1970).

If the policy had shifted between a centralist and peripheralist emphasis, we would not have found a monotonic decrease over time in the number of nationalities whose traditional languages were used as the medium of instruction. Nor would we have found a monotonic increase in the average class levels in which the non-Russian languages served as subjects of study.

If the policy had moved inexorably toward greater russification, we would not have found nearly complete stability over time in the number of languages taught as subjects of study, and we would not have found that these languages are used at increasingly higher levels of the school curriculum. Nor would one find that in many of the union republics, such as Uzbekistan, the roles of the local languages have substantially increased over time (Fierman, 1982).

If the policy were completely egalitarian, Soviet authorities would not have extolled the virtues of the Russian language to such an extent, and there would not be the high degree of asymmetry in the emphasis given to the non-Russian and the Russian languages in the school curricula in recent years (Kreindler, 1982; Solchanyk, 1982). Although a great many non-Russian nationalities have been provided with instruction in their traditional languages, these nationalities have not been treated identically. In all periods since at least 1934, school-language policy has differentiated among the non-Russian nationalities either on the basis of their population size, their geographic concentration, or their political status.

Based on our data analyses, we identify three main periods in the evolution of Soviet policy concerning the non-Russian languages in the schools: 1917-1938, 1938-1959, and 1959-1980. The first period begins with the October Revolution and ends roughly with the 1938 decree that made Russian a mandatory subject of study in school, the second begins with the decree on Russian-language instruction and ends with the adoption of the 1959 education law, and the third period runs from the 1959 education law to the present.

Consistent with the interpretation of several Western scholars, we characterize the first period as an egalitarian period, during which an enormous effort was made to construct new alphabets, open non-Russian schools, and limit the role of the Russian language in the non-Russian areas. The model national school was one in which all subjects were taught in the native language of the non-Russian pupils.

The second period was one of differentiated bilingual education. During this period Russian became a mandatory subject of study in the non-Russian schools, but the model non-Russian school remained one in which the non-Russian language was the primary medium of instruction. It became more acceptable for non-Russians to attend Russian-language schools. As educational attainment increased and as greater numbers of non-Russians started to attend secondary schools, the earlier differentiation of native-language schooling opportunities was more or less frozen into established policy. About 50 languages of indigenous non-Russian nationalities were used as the medium of instruction.

The third period, one of highly differentiated bilingual education, dates from the 1959 education law, which nominally changed the study of the Russian language by non-Russians from an obligatory to a voluntary act and gave parents the right to choose the language of instruction for their children. In this period, the model non-Russian schools divided into two main types: the traditional national schools, where the non-Russian groups' languages served as the primary medium of instruction and where Russian was studied as a separate subject, and the national schools with Russian as the main language of instruction, but where the non-Russian groups' languages might be studied as separate subjects.

There was a sharp decline in the 1960s and 1970s in the number of languages that served as the primary medium of instruction as well as in the highest class level in which the non-Russian languages might serve in that capacity. To preserve their groups' traditional languages as the primary medium of instruction, groups had to have a large population and to be concentrated geographically. Formal status in the federal system became more closely linked to the use of the non-Russian languages as the medium of instruction.

Not only does Soviet school-language policy between 1934 and 1980 not fit the patterns described by other scholars, it does not fit any simple pattern. The differentiation in the treatment of the non-Russian nationalities and the partially countervailing trends in different aspects of school-language policy show the policy to be far more subtle than is conventionally understood. One should therefore expect any impact of this policy on language use and language loyalties also to be differentiated, both across nationalities and across generations. Moreover, the impact of Soviet school-language policy cannot easily be separated from the effects of other aspects of Soviet nationalities policy or from the effects of the enormous social and demographic changes since 1917. The effects of these other factors on the linguistic behavior are also likely to be differentiated and complex.

TECHNICAL APPENDIX

Choice of Nationalities for Analysis

To be included in the analysis, ethnic groups had to be listed both among the approximately 190 *narodnosti* (peoples) identified in the 1926 Soviet census and among the approximately 125 *natsional'nosti* (nationalities) in the 1959, 1970, or 1979 Soviet censuses, or be the titular nationality of a territorial unit during the period 1934 to 1980. The first criterion was adopted because we wanted to learn how many of the 1926 *narodnosti* that are still considered to be distinctive nationalities ever had native-language schooling. Using these criteria, 101 nationalities qualify. The qualifying nationalities are given in Table 15.A1.

To increase the comparability of population data on the nationalities over time, in cases where 1926 census *narodnosti* (peoples) were classified in later census reports as subgroups of a larger *natsional'nost'* (nationality), we combined the reported 1926 populations of the relevant *narodnosti*.

Special Coding Procedures

For some years and for some nationalities (principally the Baltic nationalities), complete secondary schooling requires 11 years rather than the USSR norm of 10 years. Also, for many ethnic groups, especially in recent years, the only textbooks available have been designated for preschool. We have recoded 11 years as 10 years so that a score of 10 indicated complete secondary education. We also assign preschool a value of 0.5, to take some account of the difference between no native-language schooling and preschool classes in the language.

For the Mari, Mordvinians, and Ossetians, books have been reported published in more than one dialect (or language). In each case, textbooks published in either dialect (language) are combined in the coding.

In official Soviet practice, the Kabardians and Cherkess are regarded as different nationalities, but they have the same traditional language. We have assigned identical scores to the Kabard and Cherkess languages in each year, based on the highest class level in which texts were reported published in Kabard, Cherkess, or Kabard-Cherkess. Furthermore, in the 1926 census report, no Cherkess are listed; instead, the ethnonym *Adygei* was used to refer to all who were later officially designated as Adygei or Cherkess, and books were officially listed as published in Cherkess or in Kabard-Cherkess during most years since 1934. We attribute 1926 census characteristics of the Adygei (such as population size) also to the Cherkess.

The Karachai and Balkars have the same traditional language. We assign the highest class level attributed to Karachai, Balkar, or Karachai-Balkar identically to both the Karachai and the Balkars.

Although there are strong differences among dialects of Finnish, Finnish has been used as the literary language of the Karelians (Comrie, 1981, pp. 97-98), and in some years the entries in *K.L.* have been given as "Finnish (Karelian)." For the years before World War II (i.e., preceding the creation of the Karelo-Finnish Soviet Socialist Republic), we assigned to both Karelians and Finns the higher of the class levels reported for either Karelian or Finnish.

For the prewar years, some textbooks were listed as published in Latgal, which is a dialect of Latvian (Comrie, 1981, p. 147). We have coded all references to Latgal or Latvian as Latvian.

When books are listed as published in the Tat language, the entry in *K.L.* is given as "Tat (Mountain Jewish)." Hence, we attribute these books to the Jewish Tats rather than to the Moslem Tats.

Smoothing of Data

We use a smoothed data series rather than the raw data. The scores that we assign to a given language in a particular year represent the highest reported figure for that language among that year and the two contiguous years. This procedure is used for the entire time series, except for 1934 and 1980, when data are only available for one contiguous year.

References

Anderson, B. A., & Silver, B. D. Changes in linguistic identification in the U.S.S.R., 1959-1979. Presented at the Annual Meeting of the Population Association of America, San Diego, April, 1982.

Armstrong, J. A. The ethnic scene in the Soviet Union. In E. Goldhagen (Ed.), *Ethnic minorities in the Soviet Union*. New York: Praeger, 1968, pp. 3-49.

Avrorin, P. A. Dvuiazychie i shkola. In P. A. Azimov, Iu. D. Desheriev & F. P. Filin (Eds.), *Problemy dvuiazychiia i mnogoiazychiia*. Moscow: Nauka, 1972, pp. 49-62.

Bilinsky, Y. Education of the non-Russian peoples in the USSR, 1917-1967: An essay. *Slavic Review,* 1968, *27,* 411-437.

Bilinsky, Y. The Soviet education laws of 1958-1959 and Soviet nationality policy. *Soviet Studies,* 1962, *14,* 138-157.

Carrere d'Encausse, H. *Decline of an empire: The Soviet socialist republics in revolt.* New York: Newsweek Books, 1980.

Comrie, B. *The languages of the Soviet Union.* Cambridge: Cambridge University Press, 1981.

Conquest, R. *The nation killers.* London: Macmillan, 1970.

Danilov, A. Mnogonatsional'naia shkola RSFSR—prakticheskve voploshchenie leninskoi natsional'noi politiki. *Narodnoe obrazovanie,* 1972, *12,* 21-25.

Desheriev, Iu. D. Problema funktsional'nogo razvitiia iazykov i zadachi sotsiolingvistiki. In F. P. Filin (Ed.), *Iazyk i obshchestvo.* Moscow: Nauka, 1968, pp. 55-81.

Desheriev, Iu. D, & Protchenko, I. F. *Razvitie iazykov narodov SSSR v sovetskuiu epokhu.* Moscow: Prosveshchenie, 1968.

Fainsod, M. *How Russia is ruled* (Rev. ed.). Cambridge, Mass: Harvard University Press, 1963.

Feshbach, M. Demography and Soviet society: social and cultural aspects. Unpublished, 1981.

Fierman, W. The view from Uzbekistan. *International Journal of the Sociology of Language,* 1982, *33,* 70-78.

Fishman, J. A. Sociolinguistics and the language problems of the developing countries. In J. A. Fishman, C.A. Ferguson & J. Das Gupta (Eds.), *Language problems of developing nations.* New York: Wiley, 1968, pp. 3-16.

Fitzpatrick, S. *Education and social mobility in the Soviet Union, 1921-1934.* Cambridge: Cambridge University Press, 1979.

Hodnett, G. The debate over Soviet federalism. *Soviet Studies,* 1967, *18,* 458-481.

Iakovlev, N. Itogi unifikatsii alfavitov v SSSR. *Sovetskoe stroitel'stvo,* 1931, *8,* 105-117.

Isaev, M. I. *Sto tridtsat' ravnopravnykh (o iazykakh narodov SSSR).* Moscow: Nauka, 1970.

Kashin, M. P., & Chekharin, Ie. M. (Eds.). *Narodnoe obrazovanie v RSFSR.* Moscow: Prosveshchenie, 1970.

Khanazarov, K. Kh. *Sblizhenie natsii i natsional'nye iazyki v SSSR.* Tashkent: Izdatel'stvo Akademii nauk Uzbekskoi SSR, 1963.

Khanazarov, K. Kh. *Reshenie natsional'no-iazykovoi problemy SSSR.* Moscow: Nauka, 1977.

Kirdiashkin, V. V. *Mordoviia na puti vseobshchemu srednemu obrazovaniiu.* Saransk: Mordovskoe knizhnoe izdatel'stvo, 1973.

Knappert, J. The function of language in a political situation. *Linguistics,* 1968, *39,* 59-67.

Konstantinov, N. A., & Medynskii, Ie. N. *Ocherki po istorii Sovetskoi shkoly za 30 let.* Moscow: Izdatel'stvo Ministerstva prosveshcheniia RSFSR, 1948.

Kreindler, I. The changing status of Russian in the Soviet Union. *International Journal of the Sociology of Language,* 1982, *33,* 7-40.

Lewis, E. G. *Multilingualism in the Soviet Union.* The Hague: Mouton, 1972.

Nekrich, A. *The punished peoples*. New York: Norton, 1978.

Silver, B. D. The status of national minority languages in Soviet education: an assessment of recent changes. *Soviet Studies*, 1974, *26*, 28-40.

Solchanyk, R. Russian language and Soviet politics. *Soviet Studies*, 1982, *34*, 23-42.

Sovetkin, F. F. *Natsional'nye shkoly RSFSR za 40 let*. Moscow: Izdatel'stvo Akademii pedagogicheskikh nauk, 1958.

Tsamerian, I. P. *Teoreticheskie problemy obrazovaniia i razvitiia sovetskogo mnogonatsional'nogo gosudarstva*. Moscow: Nauka, 1973.

Tsydypov, Ts. Ts. Buriatskii iazyk v shkole. In G. D. Sanzheev, et al. (Eds.), *Razvitie literaturnykh iazykov narodov sibiri v sovetskuiu epokhu*. Ulan Ude: Buriatskoe knizhnoe izdatel'stvo, 1965, pp. 167-172.

USSR, Communist Party (CPSU). *XXII S'ezd Kommunistiheskoi partii sovetskogo soiuza: stenograficheskii otchet*. Moscow: Politizdat, 1962.

USSR, Ministerstvo prosveshcheniia RSFSR (Minpros RSFSR). *Sbornik instrukstii Ministerstva prosveshcheniia RSFSR*. Moscow: Prosveshchenie, 1976-1980.

USSR, Sovet narodnykh kommissarv (Sovnarkom). O shkolakh natsional'nykh menshinstv," Decree of 31 October 1918. In *Narodnoe obrazovanie v SSSR (obshcheobrazovatel'naia shkola): sbornik dokumentov, 1917-1973 gg*. Moscow: Pedagogika, 1973, p. 145.

USSR, Tsentral'noe statisticheskoe upravlenie (Ts.S.U.). *Vsesoiuznaia perepis' naseleniia 1926 goda*. Moscow: Gosplan, 1928-1931.

USSR, Ts.S.U. *Itogi vsesoiuznoi perepisi naseleniia 1959 goda*. Moscow: Gosstatizdat, 1962-1963.

USSR, Ts.S.U. *Naselenie SSSR (po dannym vsesoiuz noi perepisi naseleniia 1979 goda)*. Moscow: Politizdat, 1980.

Wimbush, S. E., & Wixman, R. The Meskhetian Turks: a new voice in Soviet Central Asia. *Canadian Slavonic Papers*, 1975, *17*, 320-340.

Zak, L. M., & Isaev, M. I. Problemy pis'mennosti narodov SSSR v kul'turnoi revoliutsii. *Voprosy istorii*, 1966, *2*, 3-20.

Notes

    1. We adopt the classification of nationalities as foreign or indigenous used in recent Soviet censuses.

    2. For a description of the development of Soviet language policy, see Comrie (1981) and Conquest (1967).

Table 15.1 Number of Indigenous Non-Russian Nationalities that Had
Native-Language Schooling (N=81).

Type of Schooling	Number with Group's Language Used to Teach Math-Science (M)	Number with Group's Language Used to Teach Lang.-Literature (L)	Number with Group's Language Used for EITHER Math-Science or Lang.-Literature (H)
Period			
1934-1940	64	65	65
1941-1945	49	44	51
1946-1950	50	51	52
1951-1955	50	49	51
1956-1960	52	55	55
1961-1965	47	52	52
1966-1970	39	49	49
1971-1975	36	53	53
1976-1980	35	53	53
Ever 1934-1980	67	67	67

Note: In this table, a nationality is considered to have native-language schooling only if there was a textbook in the groups' traditional language for the first class or higher; preschool texts do not qualify a group for inclusion.

Table 15.2 Mean Highest Grade of Native-Language Schooling among Indigenous Nationalities that Ever Had Such Schooling ($N=67$)[a]

Type of Schooling	(M) Group's Language Used in Math-Sci. (Mean)	(L) Groups's Language Used in Lang.-Lit. (Mean)	(H) Group's Language Used in EITHER Math-Sci. or Lang.Lit
Period			
1934-1940	5.48	5.38	5.94
1941-1945	4.10	4.10	4.66
1946-1950	4.74	5.14	5.50
1951-1955	4.92	5.29	5.48
1956-1960	4.57	6.18	6.21
1961-1965	4.26	6.35	6.36
1966-1970	3.63	6.22	6.23
1971-1975	3.43	6.85	6.85
1976-1980	3.21	6.93	6.93

[a]Estonians, Latvians, Lithuanians, and Tuvinians are excluded from calculations for 1934-1940 but included for other periods.

Table 15.3 Proportion of Variance in School-Language Policy Explained by Population, for Indigenous Nationalities by Period

	1934-1940	1941-1945	1946-1950	1951-1955	1956-1960	1961-1965	1966-1970	1971-1975	1976-1980
A. Math-Science Schooling (M)(r^2)									
1926	.841	.760	.618	.615	.642	.612	.557	.530	.503
(N)	(77)	(77)	(77)	(77)	(77)	(77)	(77)	(77)	(77)
1959	.808	.766	.634	.623	.676	.843	.582	.560	.540
(N)	(77)	(77)	(81)	(81)	(81)	(81)	(81)	(81)	(81)
TR59	.692	.757	.654	.629	.762	.740	.702	.687	.666
(N)	(43)	(43)	(47)	(47)	(47)	(47)	(47)	(47)	(47)
B. Higher of Math-Science or Language-Literature Schooling (H)(r^2)									
1926	.830	.778	.602	.593	.626	.578	.613	.582	.557
1959	.801	.785	.626	.605	.677	.664	.646	.608	.607
TR59	.650	.785	.588	.548	.634	.618	.599	.508	.486

The table cells are coefficients of determination (r^2) between the population measure in either 1926 or 1958 and the given type of native-language schooling in each period: Math-or-Science and Higher Math-Science and Language-Literature.

TR59 is the natural logarithm of the number of people living in their titular area in 1959, for those groups having titular areas in 1959. Where nationalities were titular or co-titular for more than one territory (Buriats, Ossetians, and Nenets), the figures represent the total population of that nationality living in all titular areas of that group.

Table 15.4 Proportion of Variance in School-Language Policy Explained by Social Status, for Indigenous Nationalities ($N=77$)

	1934-1940	1941-1945	1946-1950	1951-1955	1956-1960	1961-1965	1966-1970	1971-1975	1976-1980
A. Math-Science Schooling (M)(R^2)									
	.711	.752	.702	.709	.792	.816	.777	.772	.796
B. Higher of Math-Science or Language-Literature Schooling (H)(R^2)									
	.741	.770	.686	.671	.850	.799	.822	.831	.818

The coefficients are R^2 values between the formal territorial-political status of the nationality and the highest class level in which math-science or language-literature textbooks were published in each period. Political status is measured by dummy-variable terms expressing the four different levels of territorial status.

Table 15.5 Proportion of Variance in School-Language Policy Explained by 1959 Population and Political Status

	1934-1940	1941-1945	1946-1950	1951-1955	1956-1960	1961-1965	1966-1970	1971-1975	1976-1980
A. Math-Science Schooling (M)(R^2)									
1959 Population	.808	.766	.634	.623	.676	.643	.582	.560	.540
Political Status	.711	.752	.702	.709	.792	.816	.777	.772	.796
Population & Status	.823	.813	.717	.718	.801	.819	.784	.778	.801
(N)	(77)	(77)	(81)	(81)	(81)	(81)	(81)	(81)	(81)

B. Var. Expl. in Highest of Math-Sci. or Lang.-Lit. Schooling (H) (R^2)

	1934-1940	1941-1945	1946-1950	1951-1955	1956-1960	1961-1965	1966-1970	1971-1975	1976-1980
1959 Population	.801	.785	.626	.605	.677	.664	.646	.608	.607
Political Status	.741	.770	.686	.671	.850	.799	.822	.831	.818
Population & Status	.831	.833	.699	.682	.853	.808	.825	.832	.821

C. Sig. of Additional Var. Expl. in (M) by Separate Factors (*p* value)

	1934-1940	1941-1945	1946-1950	1951-1955	1956-1960	1961-1965	1966-1970	1971-1975	1976-1980
1959 Population	.000	.000	.061	.129	.076	.255	.151	.162	.171
Political Status	.199	.003	.000	.000	.000	.000	.000	.000	.000

D. Sig. of Additional Var. Expl. in (H) by Separate Factors

	1934-1940	1941-1945	1946-1950	1951-1955	1956-1960	1961-1965	1966-1970	1971-1975	1976-1980
1959 Population	.000	.000	.086	.124	.242	.080	.231	.408	.271
Political Status	.020	.001	.001	.001	.000	.000	.000	.000	.000

Table 15.A1 Nationalities Included in Data on Native-Language Schooling by Official Territorial Status in 1980 and by Population Size, 1926 and 1959

Level of Official Territory	Nationality	Population 1926	Population 1959	Native Schools 1934-1980
Union Republic	Ukrainians	31,194,976	37,353,930	Yes
	Belorussian	4,738,923	7,923,488	Yes
	Uzbeks	3,988,740	6,015,416	Yes
	Kazakhs	3,969,007	3,621,610	Yes
	Azeris	1,712,921	2,939,728	Yes
	Armenians	1,568,197	2,786,912	Yes
	Georgians	1,812,191	2,691,950	Yes
	Lithuanians	41,463	2,326,094	Yes
	Moldavians	278,905	2,214,139	Yes
	Lativans	151,410	1,399,539	Yes
	Tadzhiks	981,441	1,396,939	Yes
	Turkmenians	763,940	1,001,585	Yes
	Estonians	154,666	988,616	Yes
	Kirghiz	762,736	968,659	Yes
Autonomous Republic	Tatars	3,311,241	4,764,504	Yes
	Chuvash	1,117,419	1,469,766	Yes
	Avars	197,392	270,394	Yes
	Lezgians	134,529	223,129	Yes
	Darghins	125,764	158,149	Yes
	Kumyks	94,549	134,967	Yes
	Laks	40,380	63,529	Yes
	Tabasarans	31,983	34,700	Yes
	Nogais	36,274	38,583	Yes
	Rutuls	10,495	6,732	No
	Tsakhurs	19,085	7,321	Yes
	Aguls	7,653	6,709	No
	Mordvinians	1,340,415	1,285,116	Yes
	Bashkirs	713,693	989,040	Yes
	Udmurts	514,222	624,794	Yes
	Mari	428,192	504,205	Yes
	Chechens	318,522	418,756	Yes
	Ossetians	272,272	412,756	Yes
	Komi	226,383	287,027	Yes

Level of Official Territory	Nationality	Population 1926	Population 1959	Native Schools 1934-1980
Automous Republic	Buriats	237,501	252,959	Yes
	Yakuts	240,709	233,344	Yes
	Karakalpaks	146,317	172,556	Yes
	Karleians	248,120	167,278	Yes
	Ingush	74,097	105,980	Yes
	Tuvinians	-	100,145	Yes
	Kalmyks	133,652	106,066	Yes
	Abkhazians	56,957	65,430	Yes
Autonomous Province	Jews	2,672,499	2,267,814	Yes
	Kabardinians	139,925	203,620	Yes
	Karachi	55,123	81,403	Yes
	Adyegei	65,270	79,631	Yes
	Khakasy	45,608	56,584	Yes
	Altais	50,951	45,260	Yes
	Balkars	33,307	42,408	Yes
	Cherkess	65,270	30,453	Yes
Autonomous District	K o m i - Permiaks	149,488	143,901	Yes
	Evenks	39,488	24,151	Yes
	Nenets	17,566	23,007	Yes
	Khanty	22,306	19,410	Yes
	Chukchi	13,037	11,727	Yes
	Mansi	5,754	6,449	Yes
	Koriaks	7,439	6,287	Yes
	Dolgans	656	3,931	No

Figure 1

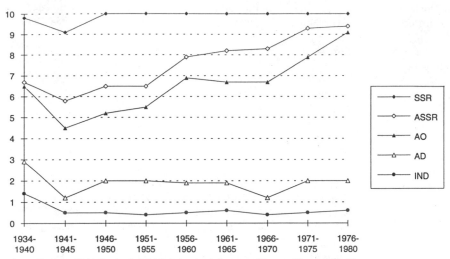

Highest Grade for Which Textbooks in Math-Science or in Language-Literature Were Published in the non-Russian Group's, for Indigenous Groups by Level of Political Designation, 1934-1980 (H)

Figure 2

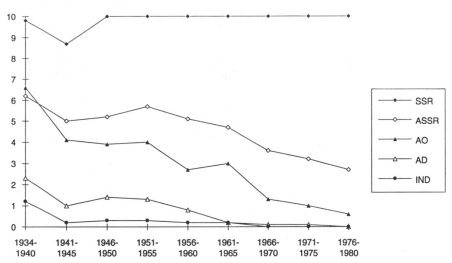

Highest Grade for Which Textbooks in Math-Science Were Published in the non-Russian Group's Language, for Indigenous Groups and by Level of Political Designation, 1934-1980 (M)

PART VI

NATIONALISM

AND NATIONALIST MOVEMENTS

Throughout this volume, scholars posit that the Soviet government used a variety of policies to prevent economic grievances, language, republic elites, and other factors from contributing to nationalism. Indeed, for decades no nationalist movement challenged Moscow's rule. In assessing the political costs of nationalism, Mary McAuley suggested in 1984 that nationalism was a threat only when channeled into nationalist movements confronting Moscow with "a range of demands for autonomy."[1] This situation was unlikely under a stable Soviet regime that could prevent nationalist intelligentsias from reaching out to broader communities. As long as nationalist expression was forced underground and confined to small circles of dissidents, they could not mobilize nationalist movements. Quite unexpectedly, however, in 1988-1991 such movements began to present an immediate danger to Soviet stability. The chapters in Part VI explain the sudden emergence of nationalist movements and suggest the factors that previously held them check.

Most scholars agree that coercion was crucial in preventing the formation of nationalist movements. In his 1987 book, *Will the Non-Russians Rebel?* Alexander Motyl concluded that "[b]ecause they *cannot* rebel, non-Russians *will not* rebel."[2] The retraction of the security forces from public life and the sanctioning of independent political groups that accompanied *perestroika*, however, created the "political space" necessary for opposition forces to organize. Nationalist movements mobilized (first in the Baltic republics and in Armenia), and they now govern many of the post-Soviet republics.

Teresa Rakowska-Harmstone's chapter (which first appeared in 1974) uses modernization theory to explain the rise of a "new type of nationalism" in the USSR. In this new nationalism, clashes between Moscow and the republics exacerbate "old ethnic antagonisms," which Soviet policy failed to expunge. Indeed, Soviet economic, language, and elite policies aimed at integrating Soviet nationalities and building a modern socialist economy, she argues, exposed inequalities among Soviet nationalities, made non-Russians want to fight assimilation, and unwittingly spawned nationalism. National territorial units (mainly the union republics) helped preserve national distinctiveness and gave national elites—the linchpin of her argument—something to fight for. Created by Soviet regimes to facilitate modernization, national elites increasingly turned to their national heritage in order to gain legitimacy among their national constituents and "thus form a power base vis-à-vis Moscow." The drive for economic efficiency ended the policy of economic equalization, and persisting regional inequalities bred frustration among minorities. The process of linguistic Russification only reinforced a sense of ethnic identity and nationalist sentiment, (especially among republic elites), for which the new media provided a forum for expression.

Rakowska-Harmstone distinguishes two types of this new nationalism: Orthodox nationalism seeks wider autonomy within the political system; unorthodox nationalism rejects the Soviet system and champions secession. She finds orthodox nationalism pervasive in the Soviet Union but contends that it poses no threat to stability. The danger is that, given the right conditions, orthodox could be transformed into unorthodox nationalism and could tear apart the USSR. This danger exists, she contends, because the Soviet regimes failed to build a consensus among nationalities on the legitimacy of Soviet rule.

In contrast, Gail Lapidus's 1984 article assumes that the Soviet political system enjoyed legitimacy, and argues that destabilizing nationalist movements were unlikely to form for four reasons. First, ethnicity was not the sole, or even the most important, identity that motivated political behavior. Soviet citizens have overlapping identities based on education, gender, and other social categories, and could therefore be loyal to their ethnonational group and still be patriotic to the Soviet state. Lapidus's understanding of nationalism resembles Rakowska-Harmstone's concept of orthodox nationalism: Most nationalist strategies were devoted to working within the political system. Second, unlike Rakowska-Harmstone, Lapidus's discussion of the political issues that spark nationalist hostilities against Moscow—economic equality, elites policy, language—points not to cumulative problems that galvanize nationalist moments, but to conflicts that "create diverse and cross-cutting cleavages"; these conflicts are not the same in every republic. Third, Lapidus (like McAuley) believes that elites and the masses have diverse interests that do not necessarily coincide, and fourth, she sees no overriding issue that could spur non-Russians to unite in a single struggle against Moscow.

Lapidus's argument does not neglect the constraints the earlier Soviet political system imposed on the mobilization of nationalist moments. Organization, Lapidus recognizes, is the sine qua non of any movement, and the Soviet regime's coercive apparatus and its monopoly over all forms of organization and public communication dim the prospects for organizing a nationalist movement.

As noted earlier, Gorbachev's reforms removed the impediments to organizing nationalist movements that the Soviet political system had imposed. Indeed, Stanley Vardys begins Chapter 18 by noting that glasnost made possible the rise of Sajudis, the Lithuanian popular front movement that now governs Lithuania. The movement began as a campaign to support Gorbachev's reforms, and intended mainly to make the Party and government more accountable to the public. The Lithuanian Communist Party's conservatism and ineptitude in managing republic politics, however, resulted in the radicalization of the movement's demands.

Intellectuals at the Lithuanian Academy of Sciences, angered at the Party's business-as-usual fashion of electing delegates to the 1988 Nineteenth CPSU Conference and deeply concerned over environmental problems, created Sajudis. Its program originally consisted of orthodox nationalist demands: control over republic resources, instituting the Lithuanian language as the national language of the republic, and the like. As the movement gained enthusiastic, widespread public support, the Party remained paralyzed, refusing to acknowledge and come to terms with the strong nationalist sentiment that drew the public to Sajudis. More generally, Vardys points out, the Party did not know how to react to this new public pressure, and by the time it was willing to make concessions to nationalism, it was too late.

August 1988 marked a turning point in the radicalization of the movements. Sajudis led a public meeting denouncing the Molotov-Rippentrop Pact and demanding the publication of the secret protocols that provided for Soviet annexation of the Baltic republics. The movement allied itself with dissidents, declared Lithuania an occupied state instead of a member of the Leninist federation, and began to make demands for the primacy of Lithuanian laws over USSR laws. Sajudis thus became an unorthodox nationalist movement. Its adherents continued to dominate politics, dealing the Party an embarrassing defeat in the March 1989 elections to the USSR Congress of Peoples' Deputies. The movement made demands directly to Moscow for wider republic autonomy, but Moscow, like the Lithuanian Communist Party, reacted too slowly and lost control of events. By July 1989, Sajudis's program was calling for complete independence from the USSR.

Moscow faced a very different situation in Nagorno-Karabakh, but there too, the Party, as in Lithuania, was ill-equipped to deal with the demands of the nationalist movement and consequently lost control over events. The target in this case was not Moscow, at least not at first. Ronald Suny points out that the movement for independence in Nagorno-Karabakh (like Sajudis) saw itself as "acting in the spirit of *glasnost* and in support of *perestroika.*" *Glasnost*, Suny notes, "allowed pent-up political frustrations" to be vented, and key among them was the ancient inter-ethnic rivalry between Armenians and Azerbaijanis over Nagorno-Karabakh. Suny outlines three phases of the crisis, during which the Party lost control over events and, as a result, lost Armenia, one of its most faithful allies in the Soviet federation. After the first phase, which culminated in the Sumgait riots in February 1988, the Karabakh Committee called not only for control of Karabakh to be transferred to Armenia but also for an end to corruption in the Party, democratization, social justice, and economic reform. The Party responded ineptly to these demands, and in June 1988 the Karabakh Committee—transformed into the Popular Armenian Movement, which currently governs Armenia—lodged demands for Armenian sovereignty. At the end of the constitutional phase, the USSR Supreme Soviet refused to grant Armenian control of Karabakh, and the movement focused its anger on Moscow. The anti-Armenian pogroms in Azerbaijan in November and the earthquake in December 1988 marked the third phase, during which the movement broadened its goals and became an anti-Party organization.

Roman Szporluk's chapter asserts that the most important ethnic issue in the USSR is the relationship between Russians and the Soviet state, because "non-Russians formulate their nationalist agendas on what they perceive as the role of the Russians in the Soviet state." The Russians are not necessarily the enemy in the struggle for autonomy and freedom from bureaucratic centralism, but their identity had unfortunately merged with the identity of the USSR.

Szporluk identifies two main groups of Russian nationalists. First, empire-savers identify Russia with the Soviet Union and wish to preserve the empire at all costs. Amid the demise of Marxism-Leninism, this group could turn to other ideologies to justify its rule, for it subordinates ideology to geographical imperatives. Second, nation-builders reject Soviet socialism, but are a more heterogeneous group. Some advocate models of Russia based on culture and tradition; others envision Russia as a democratic nation-state.

Szporluk believes that, in order for nationalist tensions to subside, Russians themselves have to realize that their enemy is the empire, against which non-Russians are also struggling. He advocates the institutional separation of the RSFSR from the USSR and believes that a democratic, progressive model for Russia could form the basis of a new Russian identity. The RSFSR indeed followed this path in 1990-1991 when it confronted Moscow with a slew of legislation that contradicted USSR laws, refused to contribute funds from the USSR budget, and declared its economic and political sovereignty.

Notes

1. See Mary McAuley, "Nationalism and the Soviet Multi-Ethnic State" in Neil Harding, ed., *The State in Socialist Society,* (Albany: State University of New York Press, 1984), pp. 179-210.

2. Alexander J. Motyl, *Will the Non-Russians Rebel? State, Ethnicity, and Stability in the USSR* (Ithaca: Cornell University Press, 1987), p. 170.

16

The Dialectics of Nationalism in the USSR

Teresa Rakowska-Harmstone

Addressing the 24th Congress of the Communist Party of the Soviet Union (CPSU) in the spring of 1971, General Secretary Leonid Brezhnev proudly affirmed the emergence of a new Soviet socialist nation forged from among the ethnic mosaic of the old Russian Empire. "In the years of socialist construction," he declared, "*a new historical community of people*—the Soviet people—arose in our country."[1]

Close examination of Soviet society reveals, however, that this statement reflects more official *desiderata* than reality, for it can be argued that an increasingly assertive ethnic nationalism among the non-Russian minorities of the USSR has emerged as a major conflict area in Soviet domestic politics. Not only has the traditional sense of separate identity on the part of major ethnic groups failed to disappear, but it has begun to transform itself into modern nationalism.[2] This development—unanticipated and contrary to the basic assumptions of Marxism-Leninism—appears to constitute a challenge to the party leadership. Furthermore, in responding to this challenge, the CPSU leaders have yet to formulate policies capable of effectively reversing the trend whereby national polarization of the various Soviet peoples has advanced faster than their common consciousness of a new Soviet nationhood.

The forces of minority nationalism in Russia were recognized by Lenin and other leaders of the 1917 Bolshevik Revolution, who believed that nationalism was a part of the social superstructure at the capitalist stage of historical development but were confident that it would be replaced by a new "internationalist proletarian consciousness" free of nationalist elements once

Published in *Problems of Communism*, 23: 3 (May-June 1974), pp. 1-22. Reprinted with permission from the publisher.

socialism was achieved. When nations on the periphery of the former Tsarist empire attempted to break away, the Bolsheviks decided to reincorporate them by force rather than allow dissolution of the new Soviet state. The USSR Constitution of 1924, adopted after heated debate between "assimilationists" and "autonomists,"[3] continued to recognize the separate identity of the minorities under a federal formula which represented a pragmatic compromise for the period of transition pending implementation of reforms necessary to establish the new socialist society. This formula called for a political system "national in form and socialist in content." In practical terms, this meant the establishment of a federal institutional structure in which the more important national groups would be accorded the forms of statehood,[4] but their exercise of real autonomy would be severely circumscribed by the monopoly of power exercised by the sole, unitary CPSU.[5] In the existing historical context, moreover, Great Russian political, social and cultural elements dominated the "socialist" part of the formula from the outset. Ethnic Russians not only constituted a majority of the Soviet population but also enjoyed a clear predominance within the CPSU and in the leading social strata.[6] This left little room for and input from the smaller and, in most cases, relatively less developed national groups.

In the years since the establishment of the Soviet state, party policies have indeed wrought major transformations in the economic and social fabric of the country. Powerful integrative forces were released through the process of industrialization and the accompanying expansion of mass education and intensive political socialization. At the same time, however, the retention of a federal administrative framework safeguarded the territorial loci and formal ethnocultural institutions of most minorities, thereby preserving the bases for potential manifestations of national attitudes.

It is this question of attitudes which is crucial today both for the leaders of the CPSU and for students of the national problem in the USSR. Has the construction of a new socialist material base resulted in the predicted growth of "proletarian internationalism" and a corresponding decline in the sense of separate national identity, or has the crystallization of nationalist attitudes among Soviet-reared generation of minority peoples eclipsed nascent "Soviet patriotism?" Is ethnic nationalism only a vestigial attitude among old historic nations such as the Ukrainians, Georgians, and Armenians, one that will wither away and present no threat to the future unity of the Soviet Union, or is it a new phenomenon which is present even among people who, at the time of the Revolution, had only an inchoate sense of a common culture? If, as will be argued, the latter is the case, then nationalism is on the increase and cannot strictly be classified as a survival of the past (even if it is nurtured by the traditional soil); rather it must be considered an integral feature of the new society and, improbable as it may seem, an outgrowth of the very policies of social mobilization that were designed to eliminate nationalism. If this is the case, what sorts of policies are likely to further or, conversely, to reverse this trend? In attempting to address these complex questions, the following analysis will first examine recent data bearing on the progress of Soviet society towards the goals of equalization and integration, then look at the evidences of contemporary nationalist attitudes and at the "pressure points" where these sentiments manifest themselves in conflict with authorities and policies at the center, and finally assess the responses of the ruling party in the post-Stalin period.

Before proceeding, however, it is important to establish a working definition of nationalism and to indicate the major forms that it has taken in the Soviet context. Without repeating the complex debate over the proper definition of this phenomenon, the author prefers to use the one formulated by Rupert Emerson:

> The simplest statement that can be made about a nation is that it is a body of people who feel that they are a nation. . . . To advance beyond it, it is necessary to attempt to take the nation apart and to isolate for separate examination the forces and elements which appear to have been the most influential in bringing about the sense of common identity which lies at its roots, the sense of the existence of a singularly important "we" which is distinguished from all others who make up an alien "they." This is necessarily an overly mechanical process, for nationalism, like other profound emotions such as love and hate, is more than the sum of the parts which are susceptible of cold and rational analysis.[7]

This broad definition highlights the crucial attitudinal dimension, the "we-they" dichotomy. In the Soviet context, further definitional refinement is required if one is to gauge whether or not minority self-assertion has reached the stage of separatism. For this purpose a distinction will be made between "orthodox" and "unorthodox" nationalism, the first involving the pursuit of political, economic and cultural autonomy *within* the system, the second characterized by advocacy of secession and independence and/or rejection of the system's ideological mold.

THE RESULTS OF PROGRESS

Let us turn, then, to a brief survey of recent data bearing on the success or failure of Soviet policies on economic and social mobilization as they relate to the solution of the nationality problem. Has the party been able to equalize the economic and social status of the diverse national groups in the USSR? Have successes in this area been sufficient to shift the focus of the aspirations of members of minority nationalities from the achievement of particularist goals to the pursuit of a broader common good? Have the social and economic changes introduced since 1917 proven functional or dysfunctional as regards national integration?

When one examines the results of five decades of centrally-determined economic policies aimed at all-Union integration and internationalization, one discovers that national disparities are still significant.[8] The growth pattern of each national area was largely predetermined by its level of development at the outset of the Soviet experiment. European Russia (including the Ukraine), which was the most advanced area and provided the lead-off base for development, remains the "effective national territory" (to use the geographers' term). . . .

Efforts to combine the conflicting goals of rapid economic growth predicated on efficient investment and proportional development on the one hand, and of equalization of the other, have generally worked out in favor of the former. Considerations of strategic and foreign policy, too, have inclined economic policymaking in the same direction. Thus, although official policies have resulted in disproportionately high growth indexes for those republics initially most backward, these areas continue to lag significantly behind the economic core regions in the overall level of development. Measured in terms of income, savings, and trade turnover per capita, the relative level of economic development tends to slope downward, geographically, from northwest to southeast, with the Baltic republics ranked first, the Central Asian regions last, and the Slav and Caucasian republics in the middle[9]—a pattern which reflects little change in the relative standings of the various national groups since 1917.

Of even greater significance is the finding that the tendency toward equalization of regional levels of development observable before World War II and on through the mid-1950's appears to have reversed since 1958.[10] In part this shift in priorities reflects strategic considerations—i.e., the need to develop Eastern Siberia and the Far East in view of the threat from China. In addition, economic priorities have been increasingly determined by the leadership's preoccupation with economic efficiency and integrated growth of an "intensive" nature.[11] Although marginal areas such as the Caucasus and Central Asia have become more important economically in the last half-century and boast growing labor surpluses, it is the European core area which remains the optimal area for further economic development. Current priorities, then, would seem to weigh against a resumption of the policies of equalization which worked to close the gap in earlier periods.

A review of some aspects of social development reveals a similar pattern of overall progress but little real change in the relative standing of national groups in terms of such indicators as urbanization or the proportion of population with secondary or higher education. Even though the 1970 census revealed that the USSR had finally reached a point where a majority (56 percent) of the population was urban, there was a substantial variation in the degree of urbanization among the different nationalities. Only four republics (the Russian Federation, Armenia, Latvia, and Estonia) and only three ethnic groups (Russian, Armenians, and Jews) exceeded the USSR average. With the exception of the Russian Federation and Armenia, the proportion of urbanization for all inhabitants of each republic was higher than the proportion for the titular national group (see the accompanying figure).

Although one should qualify the observation by noting that portions of each national group live elsewhere than in their titular republic, such differentials as compared to that of the whole population of their own republics emphasize the fact that urban areas tend to be dominated by nonindigenous national groups, mostly Russians. This fact imparts ethnic overtones to the antagonism over disparities in the quality of urban *vs.* rural life, disparities which seem to grow faster than the rate of rural-urban migration.[12]

This problem has been particularly acute in the southeastern potions of the USSR where a combination of high fertility rates and low skill-levels has created large rural labor surpluses even while there have been shortages of skilled manpower in urban-industrial centers. The rate of migration from the countryside to the cities in Central Asia was only 5 per 1,000 population in 1970, the lowest for any region of the Soviet Union.[13] The deficiency in urban skilled labor has been filled by immigration from other parts of the country, a phenomenon which not only contributes to urban-rural ethnic conflicts, but also diverts migration from northeastern regions where central planners have tried to direct it.

Turning to mass education, one discovers an enormous expansion of opportunities since the Revolution, student/population ratios now being comparable or higher than those in the developed Western countries. This development has resulted in a rapid growth of educated indigenous elites; yet, here too, the broad achievements registered have not changed relative cultural rankings. The Georgian, Latvian, Armenian, Estonian and Ukrainian republics continued to lead in student/population rankings as of the 1970-1971 academic year. Only five national groups (the Jews, Georgians, Armenians, Russians, and Azerbaidzhani) exceeded the nationwide average of 18.95 post-secondary-school students per 1,000 people in that year. The first four of these, plus the Latvians and Estonians, led in the proportion of members belonging to the scientific elite. As a rule, the Central Asians and Moldavians have ranked at the bottom in such statistical comparisons.[14]

As a recent study of sociocultural development among Soviet minorities concluded, progress towards equalization has been

> ... strongest for the least demanding indicator (incomplete secondary eduction) and especially for the younger age cohorts. Once one compares the equalization of higher educational attainment and skilled manpower, whether for entire nationalities or for their urban and rural population separately, one observes significant remaining dispersion among nationalities.[15]

Another study aptly summed up the implications of this blend of considerable progress and continued inequality:

Any plan for long range equality would have to institute radically dissimilar treatment which would involve favoring of the less advanced at the expense of the more advanced. What is crucial to the future is whether the relatively equal treatment over time, a factor promoting integration, is a more powerful determinant of psychological perceptions than the unchanging position in the rank-ordering of republics, a factor which might well breed perceptions of frustration and apathy.[16]

DEMOGRAPHIC ISSUES

Recent demographic trends are likely to intensify rather than alleviate problems and perceptions of inequality. The 1970 census revealed that recently population growth has been most dramatic in the less advanced republics. According to one analyst, the coefficient of reproduction (or net reproduction rate) in Central Asia and Azerbaidzhan is 2.0, the highest in the USSR, indicating doubling of population in these regions in the next 30 years.[17] This has important implications for manpower (as noted above), for the age composition of the population in the given republics, and for the future of official policies of "internationalization," *i.e.,* efforts to dilute ethnic separateness and increase the sense of a common identity among the diverse peoples of the USSR.

With regard to age composition, the 1970 census indicated that persons under 20 years of age constituted between 52 and 56 percent of the population of the four Central Asian republics and Azerbaidzhan, compared to only 29 to 38 percent of the population in the RSFSR, the Ukraine, Belorussia, and the three Baltic republics.[18] The census also revealed that the natural increase of local population has come to replace migration as the major source of population growth east and south of the Urals in the last decade,[19] thus dimming the prospects for "internationalizing" the population of the national republics by the migration of other nationality groups, predominantly Russians or other Slavs, into these republics—a policy long pursued by Moscow. Still further, the census showed both a decline in the Great Russian majority's share in the total USSR population (from 54 percent in 1959 to 53 percent) and an upsurge in the share accounted for by the peoples of Central Asia and the Caucasus (from 10 to 13 percent). Moreover, in all the Central Asian and Caucasus republics—including the highly "internationalized" (*i.e.,* Russified) Kirgizia and Kazakhstan—the titular nationality group increased its share of the republic's population at the expense of the Russians in the period between 1959 and 1970.

In the area of intermarriage, "internationalization" has also proceeded slowly, except in the cases of intermarriage between members of different Slavic groups and between Russians and Jews. According to a Soviet ethnographic report in the early 1960's, in the case of marriages between Russians and members of other groups it has been less uncommon for Russian women to marry men of other nationalities than for Russian men to marry women of the local nationality, especially in Central Asia where marriages of the latter type have been almost unknown.[20] (Recently Soviet sources have published information indicating a higher proportion of national intermarriage in the cities and among educated individuals,[21] perhaps with the hope of encouraging this trend.)

It is also apparent that the consistent party policy of promoting Russian as the *lingua franca* of the USSR and of the new Soviet culture, while successful in superficial terms, has generally not resulted in the anticipated degree of cultural and ethnic assimilation. The 1970 census revealed that some 128.8 million Russians and 13 million non-Russians speak the Russian language as their native tongue, and another 41.9 million non-Russians declare Russian to be their second language. Thus, 76 percent of the total population is now able to communicate in Russian. Nevertheless, 93.9 percent of Soviet citizens continue to regard their respective national languages as their native tongue. In 13 of the union republics, more than 90 percent of the titular national group speak the local language as their native tongue (only in the Ukraine and Belorussian are the figures lower: 86 and 80 percent, respectively). The figures range from 60 to 90 percent for the large non-Russian minorities within the Russian Federation; however, only 32.5 percent of the Poles and 17.7 percent of the Jews listed their national language as their primary tongue.[22] Commenting on these phenomena, Rein Taagepera has observed:

> . . . the 1970 census results suggest that the Soviet leaders have been quite successful in establishing Russian as *lingua franca*, except in Central Asia. But a clear-cut retreat of national languages on the local and private-life level has taken place only in the European republics and in the case of the diaspora nations. In all other regions, the fusion process has been slow at best, and a quiet crystallization of national languages is a definite possibility.[23]

A recent study by Brian Silver noted a number of factors that seem to contribute to the retention of linguistic homogeneity, even where bilingualism (*i.e.*, knowledge of Russian as well as of the native language) is high. The existence of a national-administrative apparatus, local language schools, and local cultural facilities in the union republics has been important. Religion has also been a factor inhibiting linguistic assimilation, primarily in Moslem areas, but also to some extent in Catholic and Protestant areas in western regions (Orthodox groups have assimilated linguistically much more readily). Urban residents appear more amenable to linguistic assimilation into Russian, but Silver cautions against the assumption that urbanization and social mobilization necessarily lead on from linguistic assimilation to a loss of ethnic identity. He suggests that mobilization may also enhance the awareness of separate identity on the part of the new national elites.[24]

THE NEW NATIONALISM

What one finds, then, is a modernizing Soviet society in which the party has engaged in extensive mobilization of the population with the stated purpose of equalizing the lot of the diverse nationalities and effecting their ultimate internationalization. However, resistance to linguistic and cultural assimilation has remained strong, with a marked tendency toward the continuation, or even a strengthening, of traditional ethnic allegiance, in the face of assimilatory pressures from Moscow. The failure of government policies to achieve the goal of equality may well have contributed to a resurgence and intensification of national feelings based on perceptions of real or imagined discrimination in development policies and in the urge to press particular demands on the central authorities. The merging of such attitudes with traditional ethnic antagonisms and the desire to preserve distinct cultural heritages seems to be providing the basis for the growth of a qualitatively new form of nationalism.

That nationalism exists in the Soviet Union and that it is taking on new forms has been tacitly admitted by no less an authority than General Secretary Brezhnev. In a December 1972 speech commemorating the 50th anniversary of the formation of the USSR, the party leader admitted that "nationality relations even in a society of mature socialism are a reality that is constantly developing and putting forth new problems and tasks." His concluding remarks on nationality issues were particularly revealing:

> Finally, comrades, there are also objective problems in our federal state—such as finding the best paths for the development of individual nations and nationalities and the most correct combination of the interests of each of them with the common interests of the Soviet people as a whole.[25]

We have seen above that the objective problems of equalizing the levels of development of the individual national minorities remain unresolved. And judging from the intense attention paid to nationalist manifestations in a series of top-level republic party ideological conferences held in the six months following Brezhnev's anniversary address, there is a growing national assertiveness among the country's ethnic minorities which must owe a considerable portion of its impetus to these very unresolved issues. In Soviet press accounts of these meetings, one reads official critiques of a wide range of activities either explicitly or implicitly branded as nationalist—from "survivals" of traditional cultural patterns, economic "localism" and "parochialism akin to nationalism" to "chauvinism," "national narrow-mindedness" and outright "nationalism."[26]

On the basis of such evidence, it is clear that strong tensions exist within Soviet society and that they have a tendency to express themselves in nationalist terms. Moreover, as pointed out above, there are indications that this nationalism is of a new variety. Thus, although Soviet sociological surveys conducted in the early 1960's indicated that urban dwellers were generally less inclined to display "nationalist prejudices" than rural dwellers, nationalist feelings in the cities were more prevalent among professional people and intellectuals, some of them young and highly educated—perhaps a reflection of job competition among elites of various nationalities.[27] Here, one is dealing with a new type of nationalism which—while drawing on attitudes from the past—has been generated by conditions arising in the context of modernization and mobilization of Soviet society.

There are three crucial factors underlying the emergence of this new form of nationalism in the Soviet state: (1) the formation of indigenous modern elites who seek sources of legitimacy in their own unique national heritage and in establishing ties with people of their national group; (2) the existence of the federal system, which affords a political-administrative apparatus through which these minority elites can pursue their national-group interests and objectives; and (3) the continued political, economic and cultural hegemony enjoyed by the Great Russian majority and the national chauvinism manifested by this group vis-a-vis the minority nationalities. Let us address each of the factors briefly.

The principal focus of the new nationalism lies in the new indigenous elites composed of articulate citizens with modern skills, the very product of official policies of mobilization and social transformation. These elites, whose ranks are growing rapidly even among the least developed national minorities owing to the broad educational opportunities made available are now beginning to find themselves frustrated politically and economically. Within their own national areas, they are in competition with the Russians and other outsiders for control of jobs and local decision-making, and their relative input into decision-making at the all-Union level is even lower. In addition to these economic and political pressures, the native elites also sense a constant effort to impose Russian cultural models on them under the guise of spreading Marxism-Leninism. They react by turning to the surviving "old heritage," not only in order to preserve it against Russian inroads but also in order to forge a link with other members of their national group and thus form a power base vis-a-vis Moscow.

This process has been facilitated by the continued existence of the federal structure of the USSR—a system devised, ironically, as only a temporary measure pending the creation of a socialist and internationalist society. The nationality-based units of the federal political-administrative system have provided the minority elites with both the bases and the means for pursuing national-group interests.

As noted above, a strong administrative-territorial base has proved important in the ability of major nationalities (in the union republics and also in Tataria) to withstand powerful pressures toward assimilation. Groups without such strong autonomous geographical and political units have tended to be more susceptible to assimilation, as evidenced particularly by the experience of internal diaspora of groups such as the Jews and the Poles. (It should be noted that assimilation does not necessarily entail loss of ethnic identity, a fact demonstrated in the case of the Jews, to be discussed later.)

Moreover, the very complexity of the federal administrative structure affords numerous opportunities for evading central directives and promoting local interests. It is not surprising that party leaders tend to equate efforts of minorities in the republics to pursue their own national interests with manifestations of localism, for, in the dynamics of Soviet nationality relations, the strains of conscious political nationalism unquestionably intermingle with the complex jockeying for administrative, economic and regional advantage typical of many modern societies. This may explain why there has been such complicity in manifestations of republic self-interest by republic party and government leaders whether they are members of the indigenous nationality or outsiders (mostly Great Russians.) As long as the federal system remains intact, the strands of localism and nationalism will remain inextricably interwoven.

The final critical factor in the growth of nationalist attitudes in contemporary Soviet society is the predominance of the Great Russian majority. Its very weight and omnipresence in the political, economic and cultural realms contribute to the growth of the minorities' sense of ethnic separateness, and—what is perhaps more important—these objective factors are reinforced by the persistence of Great Russian nationalism itself. The latter, deeply rooted in historical Russian attitudes toward non-Russian peoples, involves a paternalistic posture colored by the sense of a Russian *mission civilisatrice* and of the special and superior worth of the Russian heritage and culture. For all the efforts at internationalization and assimilation, the Soviet (Russian) authorities still require that every citizen's passport contain an identification of his ethnic background—a category which is filled in at birth and is extremely difficult to change thereafter. An ethnic bias is also implicit in official exploration of means to limit the explosive growth of population in Moslem Central Asia and to revitalize birth rates in European Russia, in order, one suspects, to preserve the Great Russians' majority status in the total population.[28]

THE NATIONALIST CHALLENGE

To summarize, the new nationalism results from a dual process involving (1) a change in content as a result of superimposition of new conflicts on top of old ethnic differences, and (2) a shift in the main locus of nationalistic impulses to the new national elites. Old ethnic antagonisms have been reinforced by powerful new conflicts between the demands of the center and the aspirations of the various national groups. And the force of nationalism seems to be on the rise in a dialectical process of challenge and response—with integrationist and assimilationist pressures resulting in nationalistic challenges to the central leadership, which responds with policies that unwittingly engender greater nationalism.

The nationalist challenge to the center is manifested in three broad areas: (1) pressure for broader political autonomy; (2) pressure for greater allocation of investment resources to local projects and for more authority to plan and manage republic economic activity; and (3) pressure for greater freedom to promote local national cultures.

Pressures for broader political autonomy are seen in the effort of local elites to obtain control of the power structure and decision-making in their republics and to achieve fair representation for themselves and their local needs at the all-Union level. Since at least the 1930's, national groups have sought to influence the appointment and promotion of personnel under the so-called *nomenklatura* (key jobs filled by specific party decisions) in order to "pack" local decision-making organizations with local people. Perhaps the most explicit admission of such practices surfaced in the 1973 meeting of the Georgian republic's party activists, where it was reported:

> In Abkhazia [the Abkhazskaya ASSR] a half-baked "theory" according to which responsible posts should be filled only by representatives of the indigenous nationality has gained a certain currency. . . .[29]

Problems of personnel promotion and distribution involve not only political *nomenklatura* but increasingly affect a whole range of positions in the economy. This is particularly true where the native population is growing but its skill-levels are low and specialist positions are filled by skilled labor from other parts of the Soviet Union. Such in-migration not only causes local job displacement but also retards the training of local specialists, both resulting in intensified ethnic antagonisms. Such feelings apparently motivated some leaders of the Adzharskaya Autonomous Republic of Georgia to contemplate forgoing economic development rather than risk an influx of alien persons. As reported in the press,

> . . . there were executives who urged the Adzhar Party organization to reject proposals . . . to build new factories and plants and to develop resorts and tourism, basing their advice on the premise that this would lead to migration of people from other republics. . . .[30]

Local autonomy is also promoted by sabotaging or simply failing to comply with all-Union policies considered undesirable. Practices of this kind—particularly in the economic realm—are apparently so common that they are regarded, except in the most flagrant cases, as no more than venial sins. The local elites also contrive to bypass lines of central control by forming local "backscratching" groups and "family circles" and by cultivating factional "pull" in Moscow.[31] There exists, in fact, considerable room for maneuver by skillful republic-level leaders in the massive tangle of conflicting laws, regulations and jurisdictions of the Soviet administrative system.[32]

The drive to maximize local autonomy is observable in all republics, whether or not the level of indigenous participation in the power structure is high (as in

Georgia and the Ukraine) or the leadership is highly "internationalized" (as in Kazakhstan and Kirgizia). Nationalism, nepotism and corruption figured among the charges leveled against republic leaders purged in Azerbaidzhan, Kazakhstan and Latvia in the early 1960's; in the Ukraine, Kazakhstan and Georgia in 1965 (in conjunction with a post-Khrushchev realignment of the leadership); in Azerbaidzhan in 1969; and in Latvia, the Ukraine and Georgia in 1972 and 1973.

Nationalist deviations also appear to have figured in the April 1972 removal of Piotr Shelest from the CPSU Politburo and from the post of First Secretary of the Communist Party of the Ukraine (although the formal complaint was his hard-line opposition to the policy of detente with the West). Shelest evidently displeased the central party leadership by taking a relatively indulgent line toward Ukrainization in the cultural realm and by promoting the Ukraine's regional economic interest.[33] A scathing critique of a Shelest book *(Our Soviet Ukraine)* appeared in *Kommunist Ukrainy* (Kiev) in April 1973, accusing Shelest of failing to show "the favorable influence exerted by Russian culture on the development of Ukrainian literature, art and music . . ." and of treating a number of Ukrainian developments in isolation from the country's overall development both before and after the October Revolution. The article asserted:

> There are obvious elements of economic autarkism in the book. They are harmful because they may stimulate nationalist illusions and prejudices. In general, the book places inordinate emphasis on the special features of Ukrainian history and culture.[34]

Similarly, although economic mismanagement, corruption, and permitting free enterprise to flourish were given as the principal reasons for the removal of V.P. Mzhavanadze as an alternate member of the CPSU Politburo and First Secretary of the Georgian CP in December 1972, subsequent criticisms of developments in the Georgian republic strongly suggest that alleged nationalist "deviations" of a political nature—such as attempting to run the republic as if it were an independent fief—also figured in the case against him.[35]

In the realm of economics, there is evidence that republic leaderships have become increasingly aggressive in pressing the central planning authorities to approve prestigious local projects and to grant their republics larger shares of centrally-allocated resources, while at the same time they have sought to minimize the extent of their republics' respective contributions to the all-Union kitty.[36] Belorussian First Secretary P. Masherov confirmed such phenomena in an authoritative discussion of nationality relations published in October 1972. He wrote, in part:

> In economic relations, this type of anomaly [*i.e.*, nationalistic and parochial tendencies] may be expressed, on the one hand, in a special kind of parasitism, in the desire to receive as many assets and capital investments from the all-Union funds as

possible, and, on the other hand, in the belated and incomplete fulfillment of obligations to the country as a whole, in the absence of proper concern for ensuring on-time inter-republic cooperative deliveries and the best and most efficient utilization of allocations from all-Union funds, as well as of local resources and assets.[37]

The type of haggling that this causes is suggested by an item from Ukrainian *samizdat* (unofficially distributed) materials. According to one account, USSR State Planning Committee officials encounter great difficulties in finalizing plans for capital investment with the Ukrainian Council of Ministers because these republic organs "always stubbornly try to increase capital investment funds, basing their demands on production quotas which the Ukraine contributes to the all-Union fund. They openly speak of being robbed."[38] The demands of the individual republics, however, vary according to their particular situations. The Central Asian republics, for example, appear to press for greater allocations of capital investment funds in order to diversify their economies and become something more than producers of raw cotton.[39] By contrast Latvians and Estonians frown on greater investment allocations because they fear that these will inevitably bring in more Russians. It appears, moreover, that a higher level of republic economic development relative to other regions of the USSR does not necessarily mean a decline in economic nationalism. For one thing, the Baltic republics and the Ukraine—the most developed areas of the country—tend rather to compare their economic levels with those of their neighbors to the west, in Scandinavia and Eastern Europe, where standards are still higher. On the other hand, the republics of Central Asia may find less cause for dissatisfaction in making comparisons with their Asian neighbors. Moreover, regardless of relative levels of development, each republic wants to have a say in the process of planning and resource allocation, and beyond this it is not uncommon for republic officials to try to promote local economic interests by resorting to such practices as nonfulfillment of plans and quotas, unauthorized diversion of resources, falsification of reports, and illegal deals.

ASSERTING NATIONAL CULTURES

While the political and economic manifestations of nationalism described above are of serious concern to the Soviet central leadership, perhaps the most abrasive and explosive area of national relations in the USSR is that which encompasses nationalistic pressures in the cultural realm. What is involved here is the assertion of cultural autonomy in such areas as the writing of national histories and in artistic and literary expression. While all of these tendencies existed in fact or *in potentia* prior to the advent of the Soviet system, the processes of modernization and mobilization may, paradoxically, have both intensified and facilitated their expression by making clearer the inequalities between different national groups, by providing modern techniques of communication, and by creating or revitalizing some of the very forms (*e.g.*, language, national historiography, literary movements, etc.) through which nationalist sentiments have become increasingly expressed. The renascent national cultures have gained further strength through resisting the simultaneous and insistent propagation of official "Marxist" (or Russian) cultural models from Moscow.

The dynamics of this process may be traced through the development of national historiographies. Research and writing on the national history of the diverse minority groups has unquestionably been fostered by the Soviet system's stress on education and publishing. Even while encouraging the writing of national histories (in a genuine observance of the policy of permitting the national cultures to "flourish"), the central leadership has always insisted that such works be written through the prism of class criteria with the clear injunction that the national heritage be interpreted from the perspective of two distinct historical "streams"—one "progressive" and the other "reactionary." In practice, this meant historical distortion by interpreting any self-assertion of a minority vis-à-vis Russian encroachment as "reactionary." The battle for more objective historiography has been fought since the 1930's, but particularly after 1956 (when greater freedom of interpretation was granted) there surfaced "incorrect" (i.e., unapproved) interpretations of history in a number of republics. "Nationalist deviations" in the recent works of Georgian, Ukrainian, Kirgiz, and Armenian historians came under particular fire in late 1972.[40] A. Yakovlev, in a particularly strong diatribe, blasted "attempts to prettify and whitewash certain representations of bourgeois nationalism, attempts found in a number of publications dealing with Ukrainian bourgeois nationalists, the Georgian Mensheviks, the Social Federalists, and the Armenian Dashnaks."[41]
. . .

The profusion of such works of nationalist historiography, as well as of a wide range of literary and artistic works with "incorrect" or "nationalist" orientation, involved not only a large number of members of the creative and academic intelligentsia, but also of media and publishing houses. One can only assume that republican party hierarchies either found no great fault with these developments or even actively sponsored them, as in the Shelest case.

Closely related to the development of cultural-ethnic differentiation has been the continued or increased adherence of minorities to traditional religions. Religious faith and observances have formed an integral part of the growing national identity of most of the ethnic minorities of the USSR, a linkage which is recognized by the Soviet leadership.[42] Thus, the Roman Catholic religion has been an integral part of Lithuanian nationalism, and similar roles have been played by the Uniate Church in the western Ukraine, to a somewhat lesser extent by the ancient Orthodoxy of Georgia and Armenia, and by Lutheranism in Estonia and Latvia. For the peoples of Central Asia, as well as the Tatar, Azeri Turks, and others, Islam has provided a unifying bond and a mark of distinctiveness which has helped to insulate them against the most integrative impact of social change. Moreover, the pressure of official atheism to eradicate such "vestiges of the past" has unquestionably tended to generate a reactive adherence to these very cultural forms and to spur demands for the freedoms of religious worship and education guaranteed under the Soviet constitution.

DIFFERENCES OF DEGREE

Surveying the overall picture of nationalist pressures, one observes a striking growth in the visibility of these pressures in the last decade. Latent but suppressed earlier, ethnic nationalism appears to have come into its own in recent years, perhaps under the catalytic effect of the succession struggle following Stalin's death in 1953 and the Khrushchev "Thaw" of 1956-57. It appears that there is hardly a union republic which has not manifested "orthodox" nationalism, *i.e.*, the conscious pursuit of greater political, economic and cultural autonomy within the framework of the existing system. In each case, a new national elite of intellectuals, including members of the local power apparatus, has acted as the standard-bearer of the new sense of national identity. The degree to which the broad masses identify with this new nationalism remains an open question, although there is evidence that in even the most backward republics the rural masses do identify consciously with national traditions.[43]

The intensity of "orthodox" nationalism varies. Among the historic nationalities, such as those of the Baltic states (incorporated into the USSR in the 1940's) or the Georgians or Armenians, the sense of national identity has not only been preserved but has strengthened. The Ukraine, with its more than 40 million nationals and its economic base, is a special case. Also a historic nationality, the Ukrainians experienced some loss of national self-awareness in the 1930's, but a vigorous revival has taken place in the last two decades, perhaps under the stimulus of the incorporation of the western Ukraine as a result of World War II. Whatever the reasons, the Ukrainians seem at the forefront of the national reawakening, and solution of the national problem in the Ukraine is crucial for the Soviet leadership, because, if the Ukrainians were successfully assimilated, pressures from other minorities would be of only marginal importance.

In Central Asia and also to a degree in Azerbaidzhan, development of a sense of separate ethnic identity was long circumscribed by the cultural unity of Islam within the Turkestan territorial base. However, all Moslem nations have experienced a rapid growth of modern nationalism in the Soviet period. National consciousness there is most clearly visible in the cultural sphere, but it is beginning to exert pressure in the political and economic spheres as well. The Kirgiz and Kazakhs, more modernized perhaps than the others and a minority in their republics, and the Uzbeks (the largest Moslem nationality) boast the most articulate native elites. . . .[44]

[A]s the case of the Soviet Jews illustrates, it is one thing to become highly assimilated and another to renounce one's ethnic identity. The Soviet Jews are dispersed throughout the Soviet Union without any significant administrative-economic base, almost totally urbanized, highly mobilized, widely habituated to using the Russian language, and accustomed to expressing themselves in Soviet cultural modes (in part as a result of restrictions on cultural autonomy not experienced by most minorities). Nevertheless, in recent years growing numbers of Jews have reasserted their ethnic identity, and many have even signaled their rejection of the Soviet system by choosing to emigrate to Israel.[45] It should be emphasized, however, that the situation of the Jews in the Soviet context is unique, both because of the existence of a powerful external force of ethnic identity—Israel—and because of the failure of the Russians and other national groups in the Soviet Union to afford the Jews genuine social acceptance.

Of course, the Jews are not the only national group in the Soviet Union to exhibit "unorthodox" nationalism. Such examples of separatism and rejection of the system, however, appear to have surfaced only in isolated pockets. Ruthlessly suppressed, unorthodox nationalism is known to observers in the West mainly through *samizdat*. Such forms of nationalism apparently emerge where a historical sense of national identity coincides with a strong cultural stimulus, such as religion. It has been observed in the Ukraine, in Lithuania, and among the Crimean Tatars, and also to a lesser extent in Latvia and Estonia.

For example, there were waves of nationalist unrest and consequent arrests in the Ukraine in 1966-67 and again in 1972. In March 1972, some 17,000 Lithuanian Catholics sent a memorandum to the United Nations Secretary General protesting persecution, and two months later troops were required to suppress rioting in Kaunas following the self-immolation of two other Lithuanian youths.[46]

The formation of underground groups or even the circulation of nationalist or religious *samizdat* also constitutes clear evidence of unorthodox political dissent. A number of such underground groups existed in the Ukraine in the 1960's, some as a continuation of wartime independence-seeking groups, as exemplified by the Ukrainian National Liberation Front.[47] In the summer of 1973, copies of *Lietuvos Kataliko Baznycios kronika* (A Chronicle of the Lithuanian Catholic Church) and an appeal to world Communist parties from the Crimean Tatars (with 105 pages of handwritten signatures) were disseminated in the West. Smaller-scale attempts at establishing underground organizations and at distributing *samizdat* in the republics of Latvia and Estonia were also reported.[48]

THE OFFICIAL RESPONSE

That the Soviet leadership is aware of and concerned about nationality relations in the USSR is beyond dispute. Politburo ideological specialist Mikhail Suslov has singled out ethnic antagonism as one of the three major conflicts standing in the way of the building of communism in the Soviet Union,[49] and a 1972

CPSU Central Committee resolution recognized the national problem as "one of the critical sectors in the struggle between socialism and capitalism."[50]

In examining the official nationality policy of the Soviet leadership, there is little need to review the various phases of that policy prior to 1953. . . .

[C]ontinued ethnic pressures did gain some recognition at the 20th CPSU Congress in 1956. First Secretary Khrushchev at that time transferred some federal powers to the republics and also permitted the rehabilitation of some purged national leaders and certain minorities removed from their ancestral homelands during World War II. However, the intensification of ethnic pressures that ensued soon brought a reaction which was heralded by the removal of various republic leaders in 1959 for "localism" and "nationalistic tendencies." Even the 1957 reform in economic management, instead of benefiting the local interests of the republics, proved to be a measure that made them more and more a superfluous link in the management chain.[51]

Khrushchev reacted to the challenge of growing ethnicity by amending the official theory of national relations. In the new Party Program, adopted in 1961 at the 22nd CPSU Congress, it was stated that in the new period on Communist construction,

. . . the nations will draw still closer together, and their complete unity will be achieved.[52]

The new formula was cast in dialectical terms, affirming that separate national cultures were to flourish by a "drawing together" (*sblizhenia*), stressing cultural phenomena common to all Soviet groups until the final dialectical leap to "merger" or "achievement of complete unity" (*sliianie*). Presentation of the new formula was accompanied by pointed remarks on the "obsolete character" of federal state forms.[53]

Ethnic elites were far from happy with the new formula, and there is reason to suspect that counterpressures from this sector were a factor in Khrushchev's fall in October 1964. Certainly his successor made some prompt tactical concessions to the republics, including restoration of traditional lines of administrative jurisdiction in economic management and paying lip service to the need for all republics to develop their national fronts and cultures. References to a "merger" of nationalities were dropped, although official statements continued to evoke the concept of "drawing together." In addition, during the late 1960's the chairmen of republic supreme soviets were made *ex-officio* members of the USSR Council of Ministers. The same principle was applied to presidents of republic supreme courts and planning committees.

Nevertheless, the "drawing together" formula continued to be in vogue and emerged as a leading theme in the deliberations of the 24th CPSU Congress, held in the spring of 1971, where Brezhnev called for an intensive ideological and educational campaign to foster popular understanding of the concept. He also condemned "nationalism and chauvinism, national narrow-mindedness and conceit in any form whatsoever," and made references to the pivotal role of the Russians in Soviet society.[54]

The uncertainty among the Soviet leadership concerning how to deal with this major domestic issue is evident in Brezhnev's 50th anniversary speech. In it, he stated bluntly:

> . . . the party regards as impermissible any attempt whatsoever to hold back the process of the drawing together of nations, to obstruct it on any pretext or artificially to reinforce national isolation. . . .[55]

Yet the whole tenor of the General Secretary's address reflected the strength of nationalist pressures as he took obvious pains to justify the "special historical role" of the Russian Federation within the USSR and to remind people in republics such as the Ukraine, the Baltic states, and Kazakhstan that their progress and development has been possible only because of membership in the multinational socialist state. At the same time, Soviet publications carry critiques of the revival Slavophile (extreme Great Russian nationalist) conceptions and caution that the process of "drawing together" is a long-term matter, in which "tactful and attentive consideration" should be paid to the interests of each nation and nationality."[56]

Amidst this climate of official ambivalence, the national problem has continued to grow in magnitude. This fact has come sharply into focus since the 50th anniversary of the Soviet Federation in December 1972, as a proliferation of authoritative statements in political and professional journals has attested to the leadership's recognition of the dimensions of the problem and to its determination to prevent a further growth of ethnic nationalism.[57] Yet there seems to be no agreement on what major new policies will be needed to turn the tide. . . .

THE FUTURE OF THE REPUBLICS

Revival of active discussion of the need to revise the Soviet Constitution to reflect new circumstances may be an indirect response by the party leadership to the persistent national problem. Constitutional revision became quite topical in 1961 and was mentioned again at the time of the 23rd CPSU Congress in 1966, but has been on the back burner of political priorities. In his 50th anniversary speech, however, General Secretary Brezhnev brought the matter back to the forefront, promising that a draft of the new Constitution would be made public for discussion prior to the next party congress (presumably to be held sometime in 1975 or shortly thereafter).[58] While no portions of the new document have been published, the discussion of possible provisions has afforded certain scholars a forum for suggesting that the ethnically-based territorial units are becoming obsolete and that in the field of economic administration increased centralization is a necessity.[59] Other commentary suggests that while the union republic units will be retained, their laws will be brought into even stricter conformity to all-Union legislative norms.[60] While such proposals are not necessarily definitive, their publication can be construed as a veiled threat to the position of the republics and their native elites.

According to one Western observer, the most threatening—and hence most controversial—aspect of the discussion lies in calls for more centralization of the economy. These have evoked counterappeals for "safeguarding of the republics' rights in this field. . . ."[61] Of course, this issue emerges in more concrete forms than mere discussion of possible constitutional verbiage. There is a strong policy commitment by central leaders, including Brezhnev, to increased centralization of economic management. . . .

This orientation has colored discussions and implementation of various recent reforms in industrial management in the USSR, once again revealing conflicts at the all-Union and at the union-republic levels. A new law on industrial associations (*obedineniia*), published April 3, 1973, in *Pravda*, raised anew the specter of industrial management organs whose competence extends over plants in more than one republic (the *sovnarkhozy* established by Khrushchev in 1957 were an earlier attempt at creating efficient horizontal coordination of industrial management regardless of existing administrative-territorial divisions). In discussing the reordering of industrial management, a *Pravda* editorial of May 13, 1973, spoke of a 3- or at most 4-link system of economic management. While this account specifically mentioned a union-republic link, it stressed the point that

> . . . the administrative boundaries and departmental subordination of enterprises and organizations must not serve as obstacles to the introduction of more effective methods of management. . . .

Other commentary has been even more explicit in suggesting that the republic-level organs of industrial management (ministries) be eliminated where expedient.[62] Compromise proposals have suggested that republic links be eliminated in the chain of management in heavy industry and retained in areas such as production of consumer goods, where local needs should be more directly represented.[63] Regardless of the final outcome of this heated debate, it is clear that republic prerogatives in the realms of economic planning and management face diminution.

What one finds, then in surveying the state of national relations in the Soviet Union today is unquestionable evidence of growing modern nationalism among the major minority peoples. This nationalism is most often expressed by native elites in the context of the nationally-based union republics and is directed against the dominant force of the Great Russian majority, which continues to exercise it historical hegemony in the land.

It has long been the hope of the CPSU leadership that the edge of minority nationalism will become blunted under the impact of policies of social mobilization and economic growth.   Yet, although social mobilization may encourage integration and certain types of assimilation to the Soviet (Russian) model, it also seems to have the contrary effect of promoting awareness of national identity on the part of major Soviet minority groups. As for efforts to consolidate and streamline all-Union planning, administration and management, these have encountered strong resistance on the part of republic elites who recognize the threat posed by such measures to their own prerogatives. Moreover, the chances for success of yet another attempt at streamlining the economy are very slim in view of the very vastness of the Soviet Union and the complexity of its administrative apparatus.   Thus, it is unlikely that there will be a dramatic economic advance capable of erasing remaining inequities.

OPTIONS AND OUTLOOK

Therefore, the swelling tides of nationalism seem to be on a collision course with party policies. The leadership seems to lack a clear consensus on how to proceed on this thorny issue.   Indeed, the available options are far from attractive.

Theoretically, the Soviet leadership might choose to eliminate the federal structure, which provides much of the focus for modern nationalism, disperse members of the new national elites, and engage in mass resettlement of populations in order to physically achieve "internationalization" of the populace. Such a policy, though fully legitimate in ideological terms and perhaps having some few adherents at the highest levels, would require a vast terror apparatus of the Stalinist variety and would almost inevitably cause an upheaval which the system could not sustain. It seems extremely unlikely that the more rational and cautions members of the CPSU leadership, let alone those members of the Politburo and Central Committee whose power base is in the union republics, would even seriously consider such a course of action. . . .

[I]t would seem unlikely that the Soviet leadership would alter the federal structure of the Soviet Union, at least as it appears on paper. . . .

Short of abolishing the republics, the central authorities can, however, move to further concentrate administrative authority in Moscow. Amid the discussions of constitutional revision and of reform in the chain of economic management there are numerous indications that the overlapping jurisdiction of all-Union and union-republic administrative organs is viewed as inefficient. This duplication of administrative competence is quite likely to be eliminated in at least some instances by the abolition of republic-level organs, a move which will further reduce the room for maneuver of the various republic elites.

The Soviet leadership has so far been spared the burden of dealing with simultaneous and concerted pressure from all major nationality groups. There is little evidence of coordination among nationalities, partly because the rate of growth of national consciousness varies from group to group, and also because of interminority antagonisms which are on the upswing. Moreover, as long as there exists a measure of "collective leadership" in the central party leadership, there would seem to be some mechanism for adjustment of republic pressures through factional groupings in that leadership. In this environment, we have seen the growth of influence of at least some republics, most importantly the Ukraine. Even with the setback administered to the Ukrainians in the Shelest affair, one can envisage the possibility of further increases in the influence wielded by major republics—or even groupings of smaller republics—in Moscow's corridors of power. . . .

In sum, given current conditions, one can anticipate a continued growth of national awareness among the Soviet minorities -- despite or even because of the policies of the ruling elite in Moscow. Such attitudes will prove increasingly disruptive, but not necessarily destructive of the existing political system. Although from time to time, perhaps with growing frequency, nationalist aspirations will be expressed in "unorthodox," separatist ways, the leadership should have little difficulty quashing such extreme manifestations under normal conditions. However, in the case of a major upheaval or external stimulus such as an international conflict, these isolated cases of separatist nationalism may come to displace more orthodox nationalist attitudes. The lessons of the Great Fatherland War (World War II) are perhaps instructive. That conflict revealed the absence of a broad consensus among the minorities regarding the legitimacy of the Soviet system and its fundamental principles, and diverse national groups opted for separation when the opportunity seemed to arise. Whether or not a suitable consensus has been built in the subsequent thirty years is doubtless a troublesome question for the Soviet regime. It cannot be answered here with any certainty, but the portent appears negative.

Notes

1. See *The Current Digest of the Soviet Press* (Columbus, Ohio—hereafter, *CDSP*), Vol. 23, No. 14, p. 3. Original emphasis.

2. "Modern nationalism" refers to nationalism manifested by Soviet-educated national elites, in contrast to attitudes of traditional elites, now largely extinct.

3. See Richard Pipes, *The Formation of the Soviet Union: Communism and Nationalism, 1917-1923*, rev. ed., Cambridge, Mass., Harvard University Press, 1964.

4. The USSR currently contains 15 union republics, 20 autonomous republics, 8 autonomous provinces (*oblasti*), and 10 national regions (*okrugi*) as territorial units for major national groups. For a listing, see *Narodnoe Khoziaistvo SSSR v 1970 g.* (The USSR National Economy in 1970), Moscow, Statistika, 1971, pp. 27-32. Size alone does not guarantee a major ethnic group its own union or autonomous republic: of the 22 national groups numbering a million or more in the 1970 census, three—Germans, Jews and Poles—do not have their own union or autonomous republic, whereas small

groups such as the Yakuts or Udmurts do. Other factors, such as compactness of settlement, geographic location (a unit must be located on the USSR international border to be a union republic), economic unity, and "a common psychological make-up" are the official conditions for autonomous status. Unlisted, but also important, are political considerations. Geographic dispersion is an important reason for the absence of a Jewish republic. Although a minor administrative unit—the Jewish Autonomous Province, or Yevreyskaya Autonomous Oblast—was established in the far eastern reaches of the USSR (along the Amur River in Khabarovskiy Kray), the Jews have not been drawn to that locale and have remained dispersed throughout the USSR. The political factor is evident in the case of the Germans and the Crimean Tatars, who had republics prior to World War II, when they were deported *en masse*. Despite their official rehabilitation in the 1960's their autonomous status was not restored, nor were they allowed to return to their original areas of settlement.

5. Despite the national forms of its organization, the CPSU has never operated on federal principles. As Frol Kozlov told the 22nd Congress in 1961, "It must . . . be made clear that the CPSU is not a federation of parties or party committees. It is a centralized organization." Charlotte Saikowski and Leo Gruliow, Eds., *Current Soviet Policies IV: The Documentary Record of the 22nd Congress of the Communist Party of the Soviet Union*, New York and London, Columbia University Press, 1962, p. 205. This unitary principle was declared as early as 1919 when the party program demanded strict compliance with central decisions by "all sections of the party, irrespective of their national composition." See TsK RKP (b), *Rossiiskaia Kommunisticheskaia Partiia (bolshevikov) v resolutsiiakh ee sezdov i konferentsii, 1898-1922gg.* (The Russian Communist Party [Bolshevik] in Resolutions of its Congresses and Conferences, 1898-1922), Moscow, 1923, p. 253.

6. See Pipes, *op.cit.*, pp. 277-78. Despite the influx of non-Russians into the membership of the CPSU, the weight of Great Russians in the leading bodies of the party and government administration remained disproportionately large. See, for example, Adburakhman Avtorkhanov, "Denationalization of the Soviet Ethnic Minorities," *Studies on the Soviet Union* (Munich), new ser., Vol. 4, No. 1, 1964, pp. 74-99; Seweryn Bialer, "How Russians Rule Russia," *Problems of Communism* (Washington, DC), September-October 1964, pp. 45-52; and Yaroslav Bilinsky, "The Rulers and the Ruled," *ibid.*, September-October 1967, pp. 16-26.

7. *From Empire to Nation: The Rise to Self-Assertion of Asian and African Peoples*, Cambridge, Mass., Harvard University Press, 1960, p. 102.

8. See David Hoonson, "The Outlook for Regional Development in he Soviet Union," *Slavic Review* (Seattle), No. 3, September 1972, pp. 535-54.

9. *Attitudes of Major Soviet Nationalities*, Cambridge, Mass., Center for International Studies, Massachusetts Institute of Technology, Vol. 5, Tables 15-17, pp. CT-24 to CT-26, and Ellen Mickiewicz, Ed., *Handbook of Soviet Social Science Data*, New York, Free Press, 1973, Introduction, pp. 1-47. Moldavia constitutes a low-ranking exception on the European end; Kazakhstan, a high-ranking exception on the Asian end.

10. See V. Holubnychy, "Some Economic Aspects of Relations Among the Soviet Republics," in Eric Goldhagen, Ed., *Ethnic Minorities in the Soviet Union*, New York, Praeger, 1968, pp. 50-120; I.S. Koropeckyj, "Equalization of Regional Development in Socialist Countries: An Empirical Analysis," *Economic Development and Cultural*

Change (Chicago), No. 21, October 1972, pp. 68-86; and Anne Sheehy, "Some Aspects of Regional Development in Soviet Central Asia," *Slavic Review*, No. 3, September 1972, pp. 557-58.

11. Discussing the 9th Five-Year Plan, Premier A.N. Kosygin stated: "The plan must be based on a single integrated conception of the country's development over the long range future, including the determination of the most important social and political goals." See *CDSP*, Vol. 25, No. 3, p. 7.

12. See for example, Mickiewicz, *op. cit.*, p. 5.

13. See an interview with the well-known Soviet demographer V. Perevedentsev in *Zhurnalist* (Moscow), January 1973, pp. 34-37, tr. in *CDSP*, Vol. 25, No. 19, pp. 18-19.

14. See Tables 18-21 in *Attitudes of Major Soviet Nationalities*, Vol. 5, pp. CT 27-30.

15. Brian Silver, "Level of Sociocultural Development Among Soviet Nationalities: A Partial Test of the Equalization Hypothesis," a paper delivered at the 1973 Annual Meeting of the America Political Science Association, New Orleans, Sept. 4-8, 1973, p. 24.

16. Mickiewicz, *op. cit.*, p. 60.

17. See Roman Szporluk, "The Nations of the USSR in 1970," *Survey* (London), Vol. 17, No. 4, 1971, p. 68.

18. *Attitudes of Major Soviet Nationalities*, Vol. 5, Table 5, p. CT 14. See also Rein Taagepera, "National Differences within Soviet Demographic Trends," *Soviet Studies* (Glasgow), April 1969, pp. 478-83 and 489.

19. J.A. Newth, "The 1970 Soviet Census," *Soviet Studies*, October 1972, pp. 200-22. (According to Newth, the share of total population living east of the Urals rose form 27.8 percent in 1897 to 43 percent in 1970.)

20. *Ibid.*, p. 219, and the unsigned article, "Mixed Marriages in Central Asia and Kazakhstan," *Central Asian Review* (London), No. 1, 1963, pp. 5-12.

21. See *Literaturnaia gazeta* (Moscow), Jan. 24, 1973, tr. in *CDSP* Vol. 25, No. 22, p. 13, and William Mandel's paper at the 1972 AAASS Conference in Dallas, which was reported in *New World Review* (New York), January-February 1974, pp. 23-25. According to *Literaturnaia gazeta*, 102 of every 1,000 marriages in the USSR were of mixed nationality as of 1959, while the figure was 144 in Kazakhstan. Mandel reports that the figure was roughly 200 in Tashkent in the same year and that one-third of the mixed marriages involved local women.

22. For details see *Narodnoe Khoziastvo SSSR v 1972 g.* (The USSR National Economy in 1972), Moscow, Statistika, 1973, p. 15. Moscow has continued to promote Russian-language schools and instruction in Russian in local-language schools wherever feasible in the national republics. This policy has been hampered not only by shortages of Russian-language teachers and textbooks in many national areas, particularly in the southeastern regions, but also by resistance on the part of parents and local administrators charged with implementation of all-Union legislation. See, for example, V. Asputarian, "The Non-Russian Nationalities," in Allen Kassof, Ed., *Prospects for Soviet Society*, New York, Praeger, 1968.

23. "The 1970 Census: Fusion or Crystallization of Nationalities?" *Soviet Studies*, October 1971, pp. 220-21.

24. "Ethnic Identity Change Among Soviet Nationalities," an unpublished Ph.D. thesis (Political Science), University of Wisconsin, Madison, 1972, pp. 8-9.

25. *Pravda* (Moscow), Dec. 22, 1972, tr. in *CDSP*, Vol. 24, No. 51, pp. 6, 9.

26. Accounts from these meetings were translated in *CDSP*, Vol. 24, No. 38, pp. 27-28, and Vol. 25, No. 11, pp. 13-16, No. 13, pp. 5-6, No. 16, pp. 4-10, and No. 22, pp. 11-12.

27. As reported in the *New World Review*, January-February 1974.

28. See, for example, Szporluk, *loc. cit.*, p. 69, and Helen Desfosses Cohn, "Soviet Population Policy," *Problems of Communism*, (Washington, D.C.), July-August 1973, p. 43.

29. Report from a meeting of the Georgian republic party *aktiv, Zarai vostoka,* (Tbilisi), April 27, 1973, tr. in *CDSP*, Vol. 25, No. 16, p. 5.

30. *Ibid.*

31. For a discussion of local cliques, see the report of the Georgia party meeting, *ibid.*
. . .

32. For some idea of the imprecise division of authority among ministries of republic and of all-Union competence, see M.I. Piskotin, "Functions of a Socialist State and the Administrative Apparatus," *Sovetskoe gosudarstvo i pravo* (Moscow), October 1973, pp. 3-11; V.F. Kotok and N.P. Farberov, "The USSR Constitution—the Evolving Basic Law of Society and of the State," *ibid.*, June 1973, pp. 3-12; I.O. Bisher, "Ministries of the Union Republics: Pressing Problems," *ibid.*, May 1973, pp. 28-35; M.G. Kirichenko, "The Juridical Nature of the Principles of Legislation of the USSR and of the Union Republics," *ibid.*, April 1974, pp. 18-26; and M. Solomentsev, "Under the Leninist Banner of the Friendship of Nations," *Kommunist* (Moscow), January 1973, pp. 21-38.

33. Shelest is reported to have circulated Ivan Dzyuba's *Internationalism or Russification*—a scathing condemnation of nationality policy, cast in Leninist terms—among secretaries of oblast party committees in the Ukraine; to have protected for a time the known dissenter Vyacheslav Chornovil; and to have favored Ukrainization of the educational system and easing of restraints on Ukrainian historiography and literature. See, for example, *Soviet Analyst*, June 8, 1972 and *Ukrainsko Slovo* (Paris), Sept. 24, 1972.

34. Tr. in *CDSP*, Vol. 25, No. 25 p. 22.

35. See the report from the meeting of the Georgian party *aktiv, loc. cit.* A report from a Georgian CP Central Committee meeting noted that "certain executives have divided the republic into spheres of influence, assume patronage over certain districts, cities, and party organizations, and have their so-called "pets" and privileged individuals . . ." (*Zaria vostoka*, Feb. 28, 1973, tr. in *CDSP*, Vol. 25, No. 13, p. 5.).

36. See, for example, Violet Connolly, *Beyond the Urals*, London, New York and Toronto, Oxford University Press, 1967, and Leslie Dienes, "Issues in Soviet Energy Policy and Conflicts over Fuel Costs in Regional Development," *Soviet Studies*, July 1971, pp. 26-58.

37. "Several Traits and Features of National Relations in Conditions of Mature Socialism," *Kommunist*, No. 15, October 1972, tr. in *CDSP*, Vol. 24, No. 46, pp. 1-5

38. Politicheskii dvenik" (Political Diary), *Sobranie Dokumentov Samizdata* (Collection of Samizdat Documents), New York, Vol. 20, AS 1002, p. 33.

39. Christian Duevel notes some hints of resistance by Central Asian leaders to increases in cotton-production quotas for their republics; see "Some Cryptic Remarks by Brezhnev in Tashkent," *Radio Liberty Dispatch* (New York), Sept. 28, 1973.

40. For example, U. I. Sidamonidze was criticized for a book on the role of Georgian Mensheviks in the period of revolutionary consolidation, and A. I. Menabde, for attempting to rehabilitate "nationalist deviationists by condoning their struggle against the Transcaucasian Federation" (see *CDSP*, Vol. 24, No. 44, p. 5). Kirgiz historians K. Nurbekov and R. Turgunbekov drew criticism for various works including their joint 1969 monograph, The Formation and Development of the Sovereign State of the Kirgiz People (ibid., Vol. 25, No. 12, p. 17). In the Ukraine, R. P. Ivanova's monograph on 19th century Ukrainian national liberation leader M. P. Dragomanov and N.P. Kisyenko's book on the Zaporozhe Cossacks were accused of nationalist deviations (*ibid.*).

41. "Against Antihistoricism." *Literaturnaia gazeta*, Nov. 15, 1972, tr. in *CDSP*, Vol. 24, No. 47, pp. 6-7. In this article Yakovlev also attacks Great Russian chauvinism.

42. See complaints of republic party leaders above; also the comment in a *Pravda* editorial of Sept. 15, 1972: "We still encounter attempts to present religious practices as a feature of national distinctiveness and to depict the nonobservance of religious holidays as all but apostasy from the 'behest of one's fathers," (Tr. in *CDSP*, Vol. 24, No. 27, p. 8).

43. See Barry Rosen, "An Awareness of Traditional Tadzhik Identity in Central Asia," in Edward Allworth, Ed., *The Nationality Question in Central Asia*, New York, Praeger, 1973.

44. See James Critchlow, "Signs of Emerging Nationalism in the Moslem Soviet Republics," in Norton T. Dodge, Ed., *The Soviets in Asia*, Proceedings of the May 19-20, 1972, symposium of the Washington Chapter of the American Association for the Advancement of Slavic Studies and the Institute for Sino-Soviet Studies, George Washington University, Mechanicsville, Md., The Cremona Foundation, 1972.

45. It is difficult, of course, to draw sweeping generalizations about the relationship between assimilation and nationalism even in the case of the Soviet Jews. Zvi Gitelman, a leading authority on Soviet Jewry, notes that the emigration has come both from among urban Jews in the Soviet heartland who are linked with other dissident groups and from such little-assimilated groups as the Georgian Jews (the latter comprise only 3 percent of all Soviet Jews but 30 percent of the emigrants!). These observations were made in an oral presentation at Carleton University on April 3, 1974.

46. For information on nationalist resistance in these and other Soviet republics, see *The Chronicle of Current Events*, published in translation by Amnesty International, London. See also, Vyacheslav Chornovil, *The Chornovil Papers*, New York, McGraw Hill, 1968; Ivan Dzyuba, *Internationalism or Russification?* London, Weidenfeld and Nicolson, 1968; John Kolasky, *Two Years in Soviet Ukraine*, Toronto, Peter Martin Associates, Ltd., 1970; and Michael Browne, Ed., *Ferment in the Ukraine*, London, Macmillan, 1971.

47. See Victor Swoboda, "The Western Republics," in the collection "Ethnic Pressures in the Soviet Union," *Conflict Studies* (London), No. 30, December 1972. The front reportedly attempted to enlist Chinese aid to appeal to Western journalists to protest political arrests in the Ukraine in the summer of 1973.

48. See Albert Boiter, "Soviet Dissent and *Samizdat:* Summer 1973," *Radio Liberty Dispatch*, Oct. 17, 1973.

49. "The Social Sciences—a Combat Arm of the Party in the Building of Communism," *Kommunist*, January 1972, pp. 18-30.

50. "Preparations for the 50th Anniversary of the Formation of the Union of Soviet Socialist Republics," *Partiinaia zhizn* (Moscow), No. 5, March 1972, p. 12.

51. See the author's "The Dilemma of Nationalism in the Soviet Union," in John W. Strong, Ed., *The Soviet Union under Brezhnev and Kosygin*, New York, Van Nostrand Reinhold Co., 1971, pp. 115-34.

52. *Current Soviet Policies IV*, p. 26.

53. *Ibid*. The impermanent, tactical nature of federal forms was commented on by P.G. Semenov in "The CPSU Program for the Development of Soviet National-State Relations," *Sovetskoe gosudarstvo i pravo*, December 1961, and B. L. Manelis, "V.I. Lenin's Development of the View of Marxism on Federation," *ibid.*, No. 4, 1962

54. See General Secretary Brezhnev's report at the 24th CPSU Congress, *loc. cit.*

55. *Loc. cit.*

56. On the first point, see A. Dymshits, "Against Yielding in the Ideological and Esthetic Struggle," *Kommunist*, No. 11, July 1972; and A. Yakovlev, "Against Antihistoricism," *loc.cit.* On the latter point, see P. Fedoseev in *Pravda*, Oct. 20, 1972, tr. in *CDSP*, Vol. 24, No. 42, p. 19. and V. P. Sherstobitov in *Isoriia SSSR* (Moscow), No. 3, May-June 1972, tr. in *CDSP*, Vol. 24, No. 44, p. 15.

57. See the author's article, "Recent Trends in Soviet Nationality Policy," in *The Soviets in Asia, op. cit.*

58. *Loc. cit.*

59. See, for example, Kotok and Farberov, *loc. cit.* and A. Kositsyn, "The Government of a Mature Socialist Society," *Kommunist*, No. 6, April 1973, pp. 59-70. The latter article makes no mention whatsoever of federalism.

60. Kirichenko, *loc. cit.*

61. Paul Wohl in *The Christian Scientist Monitor* (Boston), Dec. 14, 1973, p. 17.

62. Thus V. Kistanov states: "In a number of instances, the union-republic boundaries and the territorial economic complexes that objectively exist or are in the process of formation do not coincide. . . . It would appear that some forms of associations including several nationalities would be economically expedient in certain cases." (*Voprosi ekonomiki*—Moscow—December 1973).

63. Bisher, *loc. cit.*

17

Ethnonationalism and Political Stability: The Soviet Case

Gail Warshofsky Lapidus[1]

ETHNONATIONALISM AND POLITICAL STABILITY: CHANGING SOVIET PERSPECTIVES

The long-term stability of the Soviet system is critically dependent on how successfully the Soviet leadership deals with its "nationality problem." The USSR is not only the largest multinational state in the world today, but also one of the most complex—comprising over 100 distinct nationalities, 22 of which consist of over one million each. It is thus exceedingly vulnerable to the possible effects of rising ethnonationalism, one of the most potent forces of political instability in developing and industrial societies alike.

Until quite recently, the Soviet system appeared comparatively immune to the impact of ethnic self-assertion. Soviet writings continued to maintain that the Soviet system had finally solved one of the most difficult of all political problems and that, in contrast to its tsarist predecessor, the imperial Russian "prison of nations," Soviet socialism had brought equality, prosperity, and harmony to the ethnically diverse population of the USSR.[2] This optimistic assessment is no longer tenable. It has been replaced, in recent years, by the more somber recognition that, from the Baltic to Central Asia, rising ethnic self-assertion constitutes a growing political challenge. The sociocultural transformation and rapprochement of Soviet nationalities is increasingly recognized to be a far more problematic and lengthy process than was earlier anticipated, and national identity a more enduring and less malleable social phenomenon than was initially assumed. The optimism of Khrushchev's

Published in *World Politics*, 36: 4 (July 1984), pp. 355-80. Reprinted with permission from Johns Hopkins University Press.

assertion, at the 22nd Party Congress in 1961, that "the Party has solved one of the most complex of problems, which has plagued mankind for ages and remains acute in the world of capitalism to this day—the problem of relations between nations,"[3] has been superseded by Brezhnev's more somber recognition at the 26th Congress in 1981 that, although

> the Soviet nations are now united more than ever. . . . this does not imply that all the problems of the relations between nationalities have been resolved. The dynamics of the development of a large multinational state like ours gives rise to many problems requiring the Party's tactful attention.[4]

This sober reassessment was reaffirmed in even stronger terms by Yuri Andropov in December 1982, on the occasion of the anniversary of the creation of the USSR. In a major address on national relations Andropov reminded his audience:

> [Soviet] successes in solving the nationalities question certainly do not mean that all the problems engendered by the very fact of the life and work of numerous nations and nationalities in the framework of a single state have disappeared. This is hardly possible as long as nations exist, as long as there are national distinctions. And they will exist for a long time, much longer than class distinctions.[5]

Growing recognition by the Soviet leadership that sociocultural change and long-term rapprochement among Soviet nationalities demand patient and delicate social engineering, and that "the successful construction of communism will depend to a significant degree on a correct policy in the realm of national relations,"[6] has been responsible for greater encouragement and support of empirical social research on ethnic processes. This concern was already evident during the Brezhnev years, which saw a marked expansion of the range of activities of the Institute of Ethnography in Moscow and its republic-level counterparts. The establishment, in 1969, of an All-Union Council for the Study of Nationality Problems (headed by the Institute's distinguished director, Yulian Bromlei) not only gave high-level visibility to these efforts, but provided an institutional framework for joining scholarship to policy formation.[7] Andropov took the final step in explicitly linking social research to current political concerns in his December 1982 speech when he called, for the first time, for the formulation of a "well-thought-out, scientifically substantiated nationalities policy."[8] Up to then, Soviet "nationality policy" had been the by-product of other functional concerns—one dimension of policies primarily focused on education, or resource allocation, or political recruitment, or demographic behavior. Now, Andropov appeared to be calling for the formulation of an explicit, coherent, and comprehensive strategy in which the "nationality question" stood at the very center.

ETHNONATIONALISM AND POLITICAL STABILITY:
CHANGING WESTERN VIEWS

While the nationality problem has come to occupy an increasingly important place on the Soviet policy agenda in the 1980s, it has become a central preoccupation, if not a virtual obsession, in Western analyses of the Soviet system. The potential impact of politicized ethnicity went largely unrecognized in the scholarship of the 1950s and 1960s, partly for reasons common to the broader social science literature on nation building, and partly resulting from specific features of the development of Soviet studies. The totalitarian model, with its focus on the capacity of a monolithic state to bring about a well-nigh atomization of society, left little room for explorations of the potential bases of social solidarity, including ethnicity. To be sure, the nationality problem was not completely neglected, but its absence from the classic textbooks of the period is striking.[9] Even in specialized studies, the predominant emphasis on Soviet domination and exploitation tended to reinforce rather than challenge the reigning paradigm.

The shift in Western approaches to the Soviet nationality problem was the result partly of internal changes in the Soviet system precipitated by de-Stalinization, and partly of shifts in the focus of Soviet studies that these changes invited. As the emphasis on "revolution from above" was modified by rediscovery of society, and as the image of a monolithic regime gave way to a concern with interest groups and the policy process, the attention of specialists was directed to the potential bases of solidarity and cleavage and their implications for Soviet politics.[10] Investigation of the extent to which affiliation might itself constitute an independent basis—however limited—of collective action thus represented a logical evolution of new lines of inquiry.

At the same time, internal developments within the USSR—beginning with the ethnic self-assertion facilitated by Khrushchev's "thaw"—offered ample evidence that the quest for collective identity had been temporarily silenced, but hardly obliterated, by the repressive policies of the Stalin era. The development of the dissident movement, which included an important national component, focuses new attention on the sources of alienation in the Soviet system; at the same time, the rising tide of protests in the Baltic republics, the Ukraine, among the Crimean Tatars, and in Georgia, in addition to the emigration of some 400,000 Soviet citizens (mainly Germans, Armenians, and Jews) gave further impetus to a reassessment of the position of minorities in the Soviet multinational system. Most recently, the rise of Islamic fundamentalism in the Middle East, with its heightened salience for Soviet domestic and foreign policy in the wake of events in Iran and Afghanistan, together with the astonishing demographic vitality of Soviet Central Asia revealed in the 1959 and 1970 censuses, has brought these regions to the forefront of scholarly as well as policy concern.

As a consequence of these developments, Western scholarship on the USSR has taken on two new features in recent years. The first is a preoccupation with the destabilizing potential of politicized ethnicity, epitomized in the titles of two recent best-selling books: *L'Empire Eclaté* by Hélène Carrère d'Encausse and *The Islamic Threat to the Soviet State*, by Alexandre Bennigsen and Marie Broxup.[11] The second feature is a shift in the focus of interest and the perception of Soviet vulnerability, from the more developed and Westernized regions of the USSR—the Baltic and the Ukraine—to Soviet Central Asia.

In the view of these and other observers of the Soviet scene, a resurgence of nationalism among both the non-Russian and Russian nationalities of the USSR poses a growing threat to the long-term stability of the Soviet system. These scholars argue that a convergence of exogenous and internal developments, though differing in their configuration from one republic to another, is contributing to the growing confidence and self-assertion on the part of local elites in the non-Russian republics, particularly those of Central Asia, and to a growing resentment over the lack of political autonomy and other attributes of nationhood. Pressures for Russification also generate increased resentment and in some cases, anxiety, about its threat to national identities. The growth of centrifugal tendencies, whether or not they are likely to culminate over the long run in ethnonational movements or demands for secession, poses increasingly serious problems of management for the Soviet state.

The increasing self-assertion of the non-Russian nationalities has, in turn, contributed to the growth of a Russian nationalism that views the Russian people as the victims of rather than the beneficiaries of the Soviet multinational empire. The rise of Russian nationalism poses a strategic problem rather than one of management: its impact could be decisive for the system as a whole. Ethnic Russians possess a strong and cohesive sense of nationhood, and combine domination of the central organs of power with the dispersion of settler communities throughout the entire territory of the USSR (concentrating in the major cities of the non-Russian republics). Their growing impatience and resentment, therefore, if successfully translated into pressures on the Soviet leadership to promote integrationist policies and to resist further concessions to the non-Russian nationalities, could galvanize still-dormant forces and upset the precarious balance that has characterized Soviet nationality policy in recent years.

The dangers that a rise in ethnonationalism would pose for the Soviet system are substantial. Such a rise would threaten the unifying force of Soviet patriotism, provide a social base for the organization of activities directed against official values and policies, rule out reforms that entail a significant degree of decentralization, challenge the unitary structure of the Party and military, and strengthen ties of affinity and loyalty with regions and peoples outside the Soviet borders, from Poland to the Muslim East. The ultimate danger, of course, is that of political fragmentation: it is to this prospect that much of the recent Western discussion has been devoted. Indeed, in the view of a considerable number of Western scholars and policy makers, the scope and intensity of rising ethnonationalism is likely to become unmanageable: Richard Pipes, among others, has explicitly predicted that "sooner or later the Soviet empire, the last multinational empire, will fall apart roughly along the lines of today's republics," and Alexandre Bennigsen has given it only 10 to 20 more years.[12]

This burgeoning Western literature on the implications of politicized ethnicity for the future stability of the Soviet system, however, contains a number of implicit and unexamined assumptions about national consciousness and about the character of Soviet nationality policy that deserve to be held up to critical scrutiny. The first is the tendency to treat national identity as a primordial, objective fact rather than as a subjective condition. Although many features of Soviet policy—such as the passport system—treat nationality as if it were a rigid ascriptive category, Soviet reality is far more complex. In many instances, particularly although not exclusively involving the smaller nationalities, national identity has a more dynamic and fluid quality.[13] Migration, intermarriage, and changes in group boundaries alter older definitions of identity. For a growing number of Soviet citizens, the question of which of several possible identities, or levels of identity, is perceived as a core identity, and in what contexts, is a problematic issue. Moreover, to assume that national affiliation is the single most salient identity of the Soviet citizen is to ignore the degree to which national identities overlap with other social identities and the degree to which their salience varies not only among individuals but with specific situations. One of the major tasks of further research is to identify the conditions under which national identity assumes high salience, and to assess the features of Soviet policy that either contribute to or minimize such developments.

A second shortcoming of much of the current literature is the tendency to treat the preservation of distinct national identities as fundamentally incompatible with Soviet goals. As John Dunlop has expressed it: "From the very beginning, the Soviet state has been viewed by its leaders as a unitary body whose underlying principle, proletarian internationalism, allowed *no room for national differences and aspirations.*"[14] In a similar vein, Alexandre Bennigsen asks whether, by the year 2000, "The children of today's Muslims will still belong to the world of Islam or will have been transformed into Soviets—*totally liberated from the perezhitki [vestiges] of the past and indistinguishable from their Russian comrades.*"[15] Such formulations posit simplistic and exaggerated dichotomies that are totally at variance with historical experience as well as with Soviet reality—both of which demonstrate the resilience of traditional cultures and values and illustrate the importance of distinguishing acculturation from assimilation. Moreover, those who assume ethnic homogeneity to be the operative objective of a monolithic Soviet approach, and the preservation of any elements of national distinctiveness to be a defeat for the Kremlin's goals, ignore shifts in Soviet policy over time, internal differences within the Soviet elite, and even the gap between aspirations and real possibilities. They also ignore the way in which the Soviet regime exploits ethnic cleavages to reinforce central power and does not merely deplore them.[16]

Because the perpetuation of national consciousness is viewed as incompatible with the effort to forge a new Soviet identity, a number of observers have concluded, as Seweryn Bialer puts it, that "the polarization of the Soviet peoples along ethnic lines is increasing faster than their identification with, and consciousness of, a new Soviet nationhood."[17] This assertion, quite apart from the question of whether there is an empirical basis for either supporting or challenging it, assumes an inherent conflict between ethnic consciousness and Soviet citizenship, and treats the relationship between them as a zero-sum game.

Finally, a number of observers fail to distinguish between national sentiment, a strong attachment to or exaltation of a national group, and nationalism, a political doctrine or movement—a distinction that sophisticated Soviet analysts seek to maintain.[18] Assuming the political salience of ethnicity to be self-evident rather than problematic, and treating politics as a dependent variable, such writers anticipate a virtually automatic unfolding of ethnic self-assertion and project it forward to political destabilization. They fail to explain variations in the apparent intensity of national feelings among different groups over time, and from one situation to another. They ignore or minimize the social and political forces—repression excepted—that may either propel or limit the politicization of ethnicity, or may indeed result in demobilization. They fail to consider the entire range of possible outcomes short of the disintegration of the Soviet empire along the lines of its constituent national republics. And they neglect the capacity of the Soviet system to satisfy, channel, or manage ethnonationalism in ways that reduce its potential for instability.

In this paper, I will propose a somewhat different framework for assessing the implications that rising ethnonationalism has for Soviet political stability. I will argue that the preservation of important features of national identity is not of itself incompatible with Soviet goals; that the political salience of ethnicity in the USSR is not self-evident and automatic, but varies over time and among contexts, and is constrained and shaped by complex factors; that the capacity of the Soviet system to manage ethnonational assertion in ways that reduce or eliminate its potential for instability is a critical variable in any assessment of Soviet prospects in the years ahead.

NATIONAL IDENTITY AND SOVIET PATRIOTISM

The widespread tendency to assume that Soviet policy is devoted to the total eradication of national distinctiveness ignores what is perhaps the most striking development in the evolution of Soviet views about the relationship of nationalism and socialism: the growing recognition of the ubiquitousness and durability of national identity. From the initial opposition of socialism to nationalism in the 19th century writings of Marx and Engels, to the "Austro-Marxism" of Renner and Bauer, to the Leninist "federal compromise" which granted political-administrative recognition and limited cultural autonomy to a variety of national groups, to the ambiguous Stalinist formulation of the dialectical relationship of the "flowering" (*raztsvet*) and "rapprochement" (*sblizhenie*) of nations, to the current reformulations of the very definition of a "nation," the fundamental trend of Soviet theory and practice has been its accommodation to the reality of national attachments. National identity is increasingly recognized to be a far more stable and less malleable social phenomenon than was initially assumed in socialist theory, and national differences are treated in recent Soviet writings as enduring, if not actually indestructible characteristics.[19]

The precise balance to be struck between integrationist and pluralist approaches to Soviet nationality policy remains the subject of continuing ideological and political controversy. Two opposing "tendencies," with conflicting diagnoses, goals, and policy recommendations echoing the early debates between Rosa Luxemburg and the Austro-Marxists, still contend for influence over doctrine and policy; the first advocates more rapid integration and assimilation of the non-Russian nationalities, and the second the more flexible adaptation of the Soviet system to the social and cultural characteristics and needs of its varied groups. But the expectation of complete merging (*sliianie*) of national groups into a single Soviet entity—as distinct from the increasing economic, political, and ideological integration of separate national entities—has been postponed to a very distant future, and in some cases explicitly repudiated, in authoritative Soviet pronouncements. A leading Soviet specialist on national relations recently commented:

> It is no secret that in the early 1960s there was an exaggeration in the literature about the results achieved in the rapprochement of nations; certain scholars manifested nihilism in interpreting the national factor in the life of peoples and even began to search for the road to merger in the "visible " future.[20]

A 1969 editorial in the Party's theoretical journal, *Kommunist*, clearly distinguished between the concepts of rapprochement (*sblizhenie*) and merger (*sliianie*):

> Each Soviet nation and nationality brings its own weighty contribution to the successful construction of the new community. In the process of creating communism they attain an all-round flourishing and ever closer rapprochement with one another. For all nations the common characteristics increase in all spheres of the material and spiritual life of the Soviet people. *However, the rapprochement of nations and their international unity should not be viewed as merger. The elimination of all national differences is a long process, and it is possible only after the complete victory and consolidation of communism in the entire world.*[21]

The renewed and explicit use of the term *sliianie* in December 1982 by Andropov, in a passage quoting directly from Lenin, was linked to the assertion that these changes will occur only in the very distant future, if at all. In a series of writings on national relations which preceded Andropov's speech, R.I. Kosolapov, a leading Party theoretician and editor-in-chief of *Kommunist*, noted pointedly:

> It seems to me that the idea of the merger of nations has suffered in large part from a vulgar-utopian interpretation which assumed that merger meant the total eradication of all linguistic and ethnic differences among national groups. . . . *But why impute a meaning to Lenin's concept that it doesn't have?*[22]

In a striking passage, Kosolapov argued:

> As the 26th CPSU Congress pointed out, social classes will largely disappear while we are still in the historical period of developed socialism. The same cannot be said of socialist nations, which are more stable social and ethnic entities. As for the racial, national, and ethnic differences among major population groups and individuals, these will undergo substantial changes, of course, as a result of migration and the constant intermixing of the population, but in principle they are indestructible. Only given this condition can we realistically conceive of the future merger of nations.[23]

As a corollary of this view, and in contrast to the oft-repeated assertion that Soviet policy seeks to make "state" and "nation" coterminous, Soviet writings insist on the *distinction* between existing nations and the supranational Soviet community. The term *sovetskii narod*, widely used in official writings in recent years to describe a new form of community, is properly translated as "the Soviet people" rather than "the Soviet nation"; in the Soviet conception, it "does not abolish or supplant socialist nations and national distinctions."[24] The Soviet multinational system thus might more properly be viewed as one which recognizes the simultaneous existence of two cultures, corresponding to two different levels of identification: an inclusive "civic culture" based on universal membership in the Soviet political community and emphasizing a unified economic system, political integration, and a shared ideological orientation, and a variety of "group cultures," based on distinct national identities and drawing sustenance from the political recognition and limited cultural autonomy granted to them. National sentiment, or loyalty to an ethnonational group, is clearly distinguished from patriotism, or loyalty to the Soviet state. Although there may well be particular circumstances in which the two come into conflict, there is no reason why they should be incompatible in principle.

Indeed, far from being treated as a necessarily threatening or destabilizing trend, the growth of national consciousness in the Soviet Union in recent years has been endowed with historical legitimacy in authoritative writings. An article in a recent issue of *Istoriia SSSR* insisted, "the growth of national self-consciousness and national feelings is a lawful regularity [*zakonomeren*] under socialism and cannot be considered as a form of nationalism."[25] This position was reaffirmed by Andropov when he stated, in his December 1982 speech, "Life shows that the economic and cultural progress of all nations and nationalities is accompanied by an inevitable growth in their national self-awareness.[26]

THE POLITICAL SALIENCE OF NATIONAL IDENTITY

The historical experience of a wide range of multinational societies suggests that the politicization of ethnicity is not a unilinear and automatically unfolding process, but the function of specific catalysts in the sociopolitical environment without which ethnonationalism would remain a latent or relatively marginal force. Moreover, the politicization of ethnicity is a two-way process: the relevant actors include not only ethnic groups or elites but also central political elites, and the forms, scope, and intensity of ethnonationalism vary with specific institutions, policies, and socioeconomic conditions. An assessment of the potential scope and limits of ethnonationalism in the USSR therefore requires a close examination of the issues that have served as catalysts of national tensions in the Soviet context and the nature of the cleavages they have crystallized. To the extent that those cleavages are cumulative and mutually reinforcing, their potential for political instability is commensurately enhanced.

A series of issues bearing directly on the resources, power, and status of different nationalities lies at the heart of current tensions and debates; we can touch on each only briefly here. The first is the nature and future of the federal system itself, and the balance to be struck between a unitary and centralized as opposed to a federal or pluralist conception of the Union. This classic center-periphery conflict, which pits the interests of republic elites against those of the center, has its origins in the fundamental tension built into Soviet nationality policy from the earliest days of the Soviet state. Forced to grapple with the tsarist legacy and to combine political centralization with some form of administrative and cultural autonomy, Lenin opted for a federal system that granted limited political-administrative recognition to major existing national groups, fostered the creation of new nationalities, and committed the Soviet leadership to their economic and cultural development. This arrangement provided an organizational context, a political legitimacy, and a cultural impetus for the assertion of group interests, values, and demands and even served to shape group identities. At the same time, the centralization of economic power and political control in a unitary Party organization dominated by a largely Slavic elite, and pursuing a cultural policy that contained a strong component of Russification, undercut the commitment to diversity and provoked intensified national consciousness and self-assertion on the part of the non-Russian nationalities.

Despite the fact that the republics are formally endowed with many attributes of sovereignty, it is ultimately the center that defines the scope and limits of their jurisdiction; large areas of economic life are excluded from their direct control.   Nonetheless, both the nature of the functions performed by the republics and, indeed, the very sanctity of the original federal arrangement have been the subject of continuing controversy.   Under Stalin, several republics and autonomous areas were arbitrarily abolished; in some cases—as in the Crimean Tatar, Kalmyk, and Chechen-Ingush republics—their populations were forcibly removed.[27]   Although theses abuses were exposed and denounced by Khrushchev, they were not fully rectified; and it was during Khrushchev's rule that the Karelo-Finnish Republic lost its status as a union republic.   During the Brezhnev era a prolonged controversy over the status and powers of the union republics again erupted; it delayed the adoption of the 1977 Constitution. Although the debate appeared to revolve around the question whether Lenin viewed the creation of the federal structure as a temporary and tactical expedient or an expression of a durable political principle, more sensitive policy problems lurked beneath the surface.

Advocates of reducing the role of the republics further, or of eliminating the federal principle altogether, urged their case on grounds of economic rationality (holding that existing boundaries were an obstacle to optimal economic planning); as a matter of political control (arguing that retention of the federal structure impeded political integration); and as a response to demographic trends (which had reduced the titular nationality to a minority in several union and autonomous republics).   Defenders of existing federal arrangements cited Lenin on their behalf and asserted that the federal system had by no means exhausted its utility and that its retention was a precondition for further rapprochement among nationalities.   Their insistence on the need for an exceptionally careful and sensitive approach was coupled with the scarcely veiled warning that ill-considered measures would inflame national prejudices.   While the new Constitution preserved the existing structure—although with some diminution of the republics' autonomy—Brezhnev's report about the discussions did not challenge the principle of a unitary system but indicated only that major changes were inexpedient at the time.[28]   Behind the scenes the debate continues, however, with discussions of the durability of the republics and the conditions under which they might become superfluous in the future forming a crypto-dialogue with considerable economic and political stakes.

The pace and pattern of economic development have constituted a second subject of real controversy, pitting the interest of different regions of the USSR against each other.   Within the framework of a unified national economy based on regional specialization and a "fraternal division of labor," local elites have called for a more diversified and balanced pattern of economic growth within their republics, greater authority over economic and social development within their boundaries, and greater reliance on indigenous labor rather than on Slavic immigrants. Moreover, declining rates of economic growth are exacerbating competition for investment among different regions. The emphasis on Siberian development is challenged by advocates of a "European strategy" who call for increased investments in the Western regions of the country because their skilled labor forces, excellent transportation networks, and nearby markets generate higher productivity. Siberian development is also challenged by those who seek increased investment in Central Asia, both to utilize a growing labor surplus and to promote greater equalization of the level of development among republics. But even this competition over resource allocation does not directly threaten the cohesion and stability of the system; it may indeed enhance it by setting the interests of republics and regions against each other in ways that prevent unified resistance to the center.[29]

Cadres policy is a third subject of controversy, involving the sensitive issue of access to positions of political power. The nomenklatura has preserved the dominance of Slavic elites in the key positions of the political, military, and security apparatus not only in the central organs, but in the non-Russian republics as well. For example, while the first secretary of a republic's Communist Party is now customarily a member of the titular nationality, the second secretary, who controls cadre assignments, is usually a Russian or other Slav. Although resentment generated by this situation seldom reaches public expression, there is abundant evidence that local elites are quietly promoting increased representation of local cadres in the political apparatus—and are reaping frequent criticism for substituting "local origins" for merit in appointments and promotions. As Politburo Candidate Boris Ponomarev pointedly remarked at the Riga Conference in June 1982, the authorities in every republic "serve the interests of all its laboring peoples regardless of whether they belong to the titular nationality."[30]

This issue is all the more delicate because of earlier Soviet encouragement of "affirmative" action in access to higher education and desirable jobs outside the political apparatus. Throughout the history of Soviet rule, considerable efforts have been made to foster the emergence of indigenous elites in the non-Russian republics whose loyalty and cooperation would add legitimacy to Soviet rule. Preferential access to higher education and professional positions, particularly in the cultural arena, have helped to create a new native intelligentsia that has a stake in the achievements of Soviet power. At the same time, the process of modernization brought with it a major influx of Russian and other Slavic settlers into urban centers in the non-Russian republics. They provided needed technical and administrative skills and, in return, enjoyed career opportunities and living conditions far above those they might have attained in the provincial capitals of the Russian republic.

During the long period of economic and educational expansion, when opportunities for rapid upward mobility were widespread, these trends generated little friction between the local populations and the Slavic settler communities which led relatively separate lives.   In recent years, however, shrinking opportunities have intensified the competition for scarce positions and have provoked controversy over whether the preferential treatment of local nationalities is justifiable under present conditions.   In a veiled protest against the squeezing out of Russians from republic-level organs, one of several recent articles in *Nauchnyi kommunizm* (in good Leninist form, using members of national minorities to attack local chauvinism) declared:

> Under conditions of mature socialism, when actual equality of nations and nationalities has been achieved in all spheres of life, when the population of the republics has become multinational, and the Russian language as a medium of international intercourse has become widespread, there is no longer any need in the selection of cadres to give preference to representatives of the indigenous nation to the detriment of the nationalities living in a given republic. Today an unconditional carrying out of the policy of "indigenization" of the party apparatus would mean a limitation of the interests of the non-indigenous nationalities, the forgetting of the fact that all inhabitants of this or that republic, regardless of nationality, are the bearers of the statehood of a given national republic and make a contribution to the development of its economy, science, and culture. . . . Consequently, neither absolutization or exaggeration of national identification, nor ignoring it or national nihilism is permissible in cadre policy.[31]

The central leadership has sought to steer a delicate balance between these two positions.   Brezhnev was clearly alluding to the problem in his speech to the 26th Party Congress when he tactfully stated, "The population of the Soviet republics is multinational.   All nations, of course, have the right to be adequately represented in their Party and state organs.   Needless to say, the competence and moral and ideological makeup of every candidate must be carefully scrutinized."[32]   Andropov expressed a similar concern in his 60th anniversary speech:

> We are not talking about any formal norms of representation, of course. An arithmetic approach to the solution of such problems is inappropriate. But we must consistently seek to ensure that all nationalities present in a given republic be properly represented at various levels of Party and soviet agencies. Consideration of business, moral and political qualities, courtesy, thoughtfulness, and great tact in selecting and placing cadres are especially necessary in conditions of the multinational composition of the union and autonomous republics.[33]

This set of issues creates a complex mosaic from republic to republic, pitting the demands of the titular nationality of a given republic against the interests not only of the Russian settler communities but often of other minority nationalities as well. It is therefore no accident that criticisms of the preferential treatment of local elites link the interests of local Russians and non-Russian minorities together as victims of these exclusionary practices.

If excessive "nativization" is a source of concern in the political apparatus, the opposite problem prevails within the Soviet military, where the need to recruit more non-Russian (and especially Central Asian) officers conflicts with the need for Russian-fluent and technically skilled cadres. Recognizing that the prevalence of units in which non-Slavic troops are commanded by Slavic officers is a built-in source of tension, military leaders have called for increased efforts to recruit and train non-Russian officers in greater numbers. As a recent article in a Soviet military journal put it, "the party constantly points to the necessity to be concerned that all nationalities of the country are adequately represented in military training institutions and in the Soviet officer corps."[34] The differing requirements of different institutions and republics thus precludes the formulation of a uniform cadres policy and makes it likely that the issue will be a continuing subject of controversy in the years ahead.

Demographic policy has become yet another catalyst of interethnic tension in recent years. With demographic trends no longer being treated as a natural process and increasingly as a subject of attempted official regulation in the USSR, the direction of state policy has become the object of intense public interest and controversy. The vitality and potential political "weight" of different national groups are deeply engaged by this issue. Nationalities experiencing declining birth rates—the Russians, the Balts, and the Ukrainians—express growing fear and anxiety over the perceived threat to their national identity and focus their criticism on central policies that have constituted, in their view, a contributing element in this decline. On the other hand, those nationalities with high birthrates—particularly those of Central Asia—find in this demographic vitality a source of pride and self-confident assertiveness, as well as a rationale for the allocation of increased resources and greater political representation to their region.

Moreover, in a situation where sharply contrasting regional demographic trends are linked to differences in the cultures, values, and socioeconomic opportunities of distinct national groups, and where the policies involve not only the allocation of material resources but also intervention, however indirect, in the most sensitive domains of group and personal behavior, the effort to develop a nationwide population policy is an inherently delicate undertaking. Unavoidably, the discussions focus on the most sensitive and potentially divisive issue of all: the question of whether this policy should be regionally—and, by implication—ethnically differentiated. In the past few years, a number of leading economists and demographers largely centered in Moscow have advocated the pursuit of a differentiated policy which would seek to increase birthrates in regions suffering from decline while attempting to control and limit them in regions of high population growth.[35] Opponents of such a policy have argued, in the words of a distinguished Kazakh demographer, that a "differentiated population policy is by its nature and intent a discriminatory policy,"[36] which runs counter to key features of Soviet nationality policy and constitutes a direct violation of Leninist norms.

The decisions taken at the 26th Congress of the CPSU in 1981 represented a compromise between the two positions. The inherent sensitivity of this issue, however, as well as the tendency to structure interests and issues along dichotomous lines that correspond to fundamental ethnic cleavages, make it highly likely that demographic policy will continue to serve as a precipitant of ethnic tensions in the years ahead.

The status and recognition accorded various nationalities—whether in the treatment of their languages, history, cultural monuments, or customs and traditions—has been a fifth source of tension and conflict. Language policy has become especially sensitive in recent years as demographic trends combine with military requirements to make the expansion of Russian language training an increasingly urgent central priority. While basic instruction in the local languages is guaranteed in the non-Russian republics, Russian remains the official language and its study as a second language is compulsory in non-Russian schools. Moreover, upward mobility—especially in the scientific, political, and military arena—requires that local elites master the Russian language and cultural norms; Russians, on the other hand, are not required to learn the languages of the republics in which they live and work—a source of widespread local resentment. Under these conditions, recent shifts in language policy that are intended to give further impetus to the study of Russian, but which threaten the status of the local language, have generated not only widespread resistance but even mass demonstrations in several instances, and have prompted the leadership to shroud new initiatives in utmost secrecy.[37]

While the language issue has proven to be the single most sensitive catalyst of national protest, cultural assertion takes far broader forms. Russian and non-Russian elites alike are engaged in exploration as well as in glorification of their "roots." The resurrection of folk heros, both ancient and modern, including those previously under opprobrium; the purification of national languages and exclusion of foreign borrowings; the evocation of group achievements; the concern with preserving the group's environment, both cultural and natural; and the defense of local traditions, from religious practices to family behavior—all involve an assertion of developing cultural identities and an effort to convert cultural traditions into a political resource.

Although many aspects of this development have a conflictual aspect, it would be a mistake to exaggerate the degree of polarization involved or to assume a uniform situation from republic to republic. Georgia, the Baltic republics, and the Ukraine have offered more open resistance to measures that threaten national languages; in Central Asia, where the cultural divide between the indigenous and

Russian communities is especially great and the prospects for large-scale assimilation are minimal, such measures do not represent the same threat, nor do they evoke as strong or visible a reaction. Moreover, although local cultural elites—particularly from intellectual, professional, and student milieus—have been in the forefront of efforts at national self-assertion in the USSR as elsewhere, there are many for whom career interests are bound less to the fate of national languages and cultures than to upward mobility in a largely Russian scientific, technical, and administrative environment. Finally, it should be borne in mind that cultural self-assertion by national elites is part of a process of political bargaining as well as of conflict: cultural traditions are converted into a political resource in a within-system competition over power, wealth, and status.

All these problems could well be exacerbated by several emerging trends and issues in Soviet political life. The succession process, which promises heightened competition and instability at the apex of the political system, could increase the temptation of rival claimants to exploit nationality policy in order to build political support. Declining rates of economic growth are also likely to make the management of ethnic relations more difficult; competition over the allocation of limited resources among various republics as well as within them is likely to grow. In the past, an expanding economic pie mitigated both the costs of empire, on the one hand, and the resentment of exploitation, on the other. When economic circumstances are strained, rival groups will confront each other's claims more directly. This trend is highlighted in a striking article in the prominent journal *Soviet State and Law*. The essay conveys the widespread sense of grievance among Russians by cataloguing a whole succession of central policies—from family allowances to agricultural procurement prices—which transfer resources from the Russian heartland to unspecified "outlying regions." "As for budget policy," the authors complain, "not once in the entire existence of the Soviet state has the Russian republic benefited by a subsidy from the all-Union budget, as several other republics have."[38]

Major shifts in the relative "weight" of different regions, resulting from demographic trends or new technologies, compound the problems of low growth. A more flexible deployment of resources between the older industrial regions and the emerging "sun belt" is vitally needed, but as American experience suggests, such shifts are politically difficult to achieve. Moreover, the prospect of reduced social mobility in the decades ahead is especially conducive to increased ethnic tensions as the competition for educational and professional advancement sharpens. Differential birthrates are producing a rapidly growing cohort of young people in the Muslim regions of the USSR who will confront a stable but well-entrenched cohort of their Slavic counterparts. Short of massive investments in industrialization and social infrastructure to generate new job opportunities and forestall a deterioration of living standards, increased competition is likely to intensify ethnic prejudice.[39]

The increasing salience of foreign policy in Soviet domestic affairs may also interact with ethnic assertiveness. The greater involvement of the Soviet Union in the outside world during the past two decades has exposed the Soviet population to a wider variety of influences, values, and experiences than was the case when official media held an unchallenged monopoly. The Baltic population could follow events in Poland on Scandinavian television transmission; in the case of Central Asia the orientation of Soviet policy toward the Middle East has been accompanied by the emergence of Tashkent as a showcase of Soviet achievement. The proliferation of officially sponsored technical, cultural, and even religious delegations, the increasing reliance on Central Asian cadres in technical and diplomatic roles, and, most recently, the dispatch of Soviet armed forces and administrative personnel into Afghanistan, have created both opportunities and problems for Soviet policy. The gains derived from using members of minorities to expand Soviet influence abroad are undeniable, but recent developments have also rekindled traditional anxieties about divided loyalties. . . .

This brief discussion of some of the major issues around which ethnonational grievances have centered demonstrates the considerable difficulties that stand in the way of forming ethnonational movements able to bridge the diverse backgrounds, interests, and objectives of their constituencies. The conflicts outlined here create diverse and cross-cutting cleavages rather than cumulative and mutually reinforcing ones. They span a broad spectrum, including the competing claims and interests of center and periphery, of different regions against each other, of local elites of the titular nationality against those of the Russian settler community (often itself allied with other minority nationalities), as well as of conflicting views within local as well as national elites. With the possible exception of the Baltic republics and the Ukraine, where in deteriorating economic conditions it is at least conceivable that protest movements could join working-class unrest to national grievances, considerable difficulties clearly stand in the way of defining issues "which strike responsive chords simultaneously among elites and masses and serve to link the concerns of different strata in a coherent ethnic movement."[40]

STRATEGIES AND GOALS OF NATIONAL SELF-ASSERTION

The widespread tendency of Western observers to assume that political instability, if not outright secession, is the natural and logical outcome of rising national consciousness neglects the broad repertoire of potential strategies and goals available to ethnonational elites. Especially in light of the severe constraints on the political mobilization of ethnicity imposed by the Soviet system, it is important to be mindful of the full gamut of possibilities available to those who wish to identify themselves with some form of national self-assertion in the USSR.

At the individual level, national elites are presented with a variety of options. They include assimilation, whether in the form of identifying with the dominant group and its culture, or by actually altering one's ethnic identity; maximizing individual power through political mobility or by acting as a broker between the two cultures; or linking one's personal fate to that of one's nation and defending or asserting its distinctive traits. The ethnonational groups face a parallel range of possibilities, such as the promotion of cultural or political nationalism in its various manifestations; mobilization for increased autonomy, communalism, or resources; or outright secession at the far end of the political spectrum.

Of this entire gamut of possible strategies, by far the most widespread in the Soviet context are those devoted to working within the system. They encompass center-periphery bargaining designed, on the part of the participant group, to enhance its resources, power, and status as well as the reliance on bureaucratic politics and clientele relationships to modify centrally imposed policies in the course of implementation. The degree of direct pressure that any group can exert on the center is, in turn, the product of several factors. The most important have been the responsiveness of a given leadership as well as of the central elite to group pressures; the overall "weight" of the particular group in the system as a whole; its role in key positions of economic, political, and military power; its control over strategic resources; and the availability of exogenous political forces willing and able to offer effective support to its goals or to provide leverage on its behalf. In short, the scope, the strategies, and the outcomes of national self-assertion are highly diverse, variable, and problematic. They will, moreover, be shaped in important ways by the particular constraints imposed on its expression by Soviet institutions and practices.

THE POLITICAL MOBILIZATION OF ETHNICITY IN THE USSR: CONSTRAINTS AND PROSPECTS

The long-term prospects for ethnonational resurgence in the USSR are constrained by both intrinsic and systemic factors. First, as I have already noted, there are significant intrinsic constraints on the political mobilization of ethnicity in the Soviet Union as elsewhere; the repertoire of potential ethnic identities and their salience varies among individuals and in different situations. Furthermore, individuals have multiple and overlapping identities and roles based on gender, socioeconomic status, age, and institutional affiliation of which ethnicity is only one, and not necessarily the most important. Under normal conditions, education and profession are likely to be more significant determinants of attitudes and behavior than ethnicity *per se*. Moreover, neither national elites nor masses share homogeneous and unified attitudes or aspirations; these divisions complicate still further the task of mobilizing large populations around a single issue.

An additional constraint on the political mobilization of ethnicity in the USSR is the absence of a single overriding cleavage on which such mobilization might center.   The issues that pit the interest of Russians against those of the non-Russian nationalities form only a small part of a much larger spectrum. Divergent historical and political experiences have shaped the attitudes of different non-Russian nationalities toward the Russians; for some, the Russians represent allies or protectors against traditional enemies. In other cases, regions and republics compete over the allocation of resources.   And even within the same national republic, ethnic communities may be divided over key issues, such as the importance and value of religious traditions or the desirability of further modernization, with its attendant Russification, for example.   The dissident groups themselves are internally divided; Jewish and Ukrainian activists have more than once accused the civil rights movement of being insufficiently concerned with the national question, while Russian nationalists hold widely divergent views about the costs and benefits of empire.   Thus, the existence of multiple cross-cutting cleavages that are not cumulatively and mutually reinforcing constitutes a major asset for the regime in the management of ethnic relations.

Another Soviet asset turns on matters of comparative size, consciousness, integration, and demands on the system among national groups.   The most "advanced" Soviet nationalities—the Baltic states of Lithuania, Latvia and Estonia, absorbed into the Soviet Union during World War II—which are likely to make the greatest demands and are potentially the least "digestible," are numerically the smallest.   The potential demographic weight of the Central Asian republics, on the other hand, is offset in the short run by their more parochial, underdeveloped, and self-sufficient way of life that makes comparatively fewer demands on the system.

Furthermore, the very nature of the Soviet regime imposes severe constraints on the political mobilization of ethnicity (as, indeed, on the mobilization of any other subculture or group identity), through a combination of coercion, repression, control, co-optation, competition, and concessions.   Any potential national movement faces a political regime with an exceptionally highly developed mechanism of control. Repression and the threat of repression have remained central components of Soviet nationality policy.   They are used to prevent the organization of dissident movements, outlaw their activities, ban their publications, and to arrest and try participants.   In addition, the management of dissidence includes efforts to ridicule and discredit potential participants in such movements by defining their concerns as non-issues, by labeling their spokesmen as fanatics or anti-Soviet accomplices of Western imperialism, or by warning of the disastrous political and economic consequences that might follow from any effort to disengage a constituent unit from the federal Union.   Official statements are not above depicting many national languages and cultures as relatively primitive and limited, unlikely to receive full international recognition on their own; they may even imply that nationalist movements would deprive these groups of the cultural status and economic benefits that derive from their association with the larger Union. An official monopoly over all forms of organization and association as well as the overall means of public communications is a further impediment to the expression of demands outside official channels; the effort to assign military conscripts outside their regions ensures the loyalty of the armed forces and makes possible their use in local disturbances. To the extent that a solid organization is a *sine qua non* of any potential ethnonational movement, prospects for such an organization inside the USSR are exceedingly slim.

Quite apart from the coercive restraints on the politicization of ethnicity, the Soviet regime also appeals to normative and material interests. The leadership goes to considerable lengths to emphasize the way in which members of non-Russian nationalities derive substantial benefits from working within the system. Unlike classic colonial systems, the Soviet Union proffers full and equal citizenship, providing symbolic recognition and genuine opportunities for participation and advancement of the non-Russian nationalities in exchange for loyalty and partial assimilation. Having initially destroyed traditional local elites and eliminated the economic and political bases of alternative centers of power, the Soviet system proceeded to train, promote, and co-opt new indigenous sub-elites and to reward them for their collaboration and loyalty. In the absence of any major threats to the viability of the Soviet system, these new elites are more likely to direct their energies toward within-system demands than toward secession.

Displacement and depoliticization are especially useful instruments for the management of ethnic tensions. The enormous expansion of cultural and scientific elites in Central Asia is not only a way of rewarding and co-opting local elites, but of channeling ethnic aspirations away from more sensitive political and administrative domains. Similarly, the toleration of societies for the preservation of historical and cultural monuments reflects a recognition that they constitute a comparatively harmless alternative to other forms of ethnic self-assertion. . . .

The regime has also employed a strategy of avoidance in a number of areas. By concentrating its efforts at control of the "commanding heights," and avoiding direct assaults on local customs and norms when they are marginal to central priorities, it has reduced the potential for counterproductive confrontations. The treatment of Islam within the USSR is a telling illustration: thanks to its control of the recruitment, training, and activities of official religious elites, and to an active campaign of antireligious propaganda, the Soviet leadership can afford to tolerate a considerable degree of private religious observance.

Another major device in the management of national relations is the exploitation of alternative lines of cleavage and solidarity. By emphasizing class rather than ethnicity as a fundamental social division, by promoting contacts across ethnic boundaries among different professional groups—from writers and artists to natural and social scientists—and by exploiting conflict among ethnic groups as well as divisions within them, the Soviet leadership has sought to create solidarities that transcend ethnic boundaries and to exploit cleavages that cut across them. It has also largely avoided creating situations which activate ethnic identities in politically destabilizing ways.

Finally, the Soviet leadership has motivated ethnic elites to participate in and benefit from the system, rather than to exacerbate ethnic conflict. By exploiting external threats (particularly from China directed at Soviet Central Asia), by pressing the view that any conflict would detract from the economic well-being of the whole, and by making clear that the acquisition or retention of political power depends upon collaboration with central elites, the Soviets have emphasized the benefits of the present system as well as the dangers of fragmentation. For all these reasons, although the political salience of national self-assertion is likely to increase significantly over the next decade, and to pose increasingly difficult problems of management for the Soviet elite, rising nationalism, in the absence of a major military conflict on Soviet territory, is unlikely to pose a serious threat to the stability of the Soviet system.

Notes

1. I should like to thank the Lehrman Institute, the National Council for Soviet and East European Research, and the Kennan Institute of the Woodrow Wilson International Center for Scholars for supporting the larger project of which this article forms a part, and Amy Saldinger and Denis McCauley for their research assistance. This article has also benefited greatly from the insights and suggestions of participants in the Lehrman Institute seminars, and from the helpful comments of Jeremy Azrael, Seweryn Bialer, Alexander Dallin, Paul Goble, Don Horowitz, and Ellen Jones.

2. Typical of a voluminous body of such writings is the assertion that the USSR has created a "fundamentally new social and international community . . . a single and friendly family of over 100 nationalities jointly building communism," based on "friendship, equality, multi-faceted fraternal cooperation and mutual assistance." P.N. Fedoseev, *Leninizm i natsional'nyi vopros v sovremennykh usloviiakh* [Leninism and the National Question in Contemporary Conditions] (Moscow: Polizdat, 1974), 357-58. All translations are by the author unless otherwise noted.

3. *Pravda*, October 18, 1961, p. 1.

4. *Pravda*, February 24, 1981, p. 3.

5. *Pravda*, December 22, 1982, pp. 1-2.

6. P. Paskar', "Sovetskii narod—novaia sotsial'naia i internatsional'naia obshchnost' liudei" [The Soviet People—a new social and international community of people], *Kommunist Moldavii*, No. 12 (December 1982), p. 82.

7. For a useful discussion of the creation and activities of the Council, see Paul Goble, "Ideology, Methodology, and Nationality: The USSR Academy of Sciences Council on Nationality Problems," paper delivered at the National Convention of the APSA, Washington, D.C., August 1980. In recent years, Party organizations in a number of republics have created additional bodies to coordinate research and policy on nationality problems.

8. *Pravda*, December 22, 1982, p. 2.

9. See, for instance, the work of Merle Fainsod, Alex Inkeles, and Raymond Bauer, John N. Hazard, Leonard Schapiro and Adam Ulam, and among recent writings, Jerry F. Hough. Inkeles and Bauer's *The Soviet Citizen* (Cambridge: Harvard University Press, 1961) is particularly instructive as a case in point. Although their study demonstrated extraordinary prescience in anticipating many of the key developments of the Khrushchev period on the basis of refugee interviews, it failed to anticipate the emergence of a significant dissident movement in general and of national protest in particular.

10. Cleavages based on functional specialization, for example, are explored by Milton Lodge, *Soviet Elite Attitudes Since Stalin* (Columbus, Ohio: C.E. Merrill, 1969) and in H. Gordon Skilling and Franklyn Griffiths, eds., *Interest Groups in Soviet Politics* (Princeton: Princeton University Press, 1971); on policy orientation, by Franklyn Griffiths, *ibid.*, and by Donald Kelley, "Environmental Policy-Making in the USSR: The Role of Industrial and Environmental Interest Groups," *Soviet Studies*, 28 (October 1976). For a review of these approaches, see Gail W. Lapidus, "The Study of Contemporary Soviet Policy-Making: A Review and Research Agenda" (Workshop on Contemporary Soviet Policy-Making, Berkeley, Calif., 1980).

11. Carrère d'Encausse, *L'Empire Eclaté* (Paris: Flammarion & Cie, 1978), trans. by Martin Sokolinsky and Henry LaFarge as *Decline of an Empire: The Soviet Socialist Republics in Revolt* (New York: Newsweek Books, 1979); Bennigsen and Broxup, *The Islamic Threat to the Soviet State* (London: Croom Helm, 1983).

12. Pipes, in Carl Linden and Dimitri K. Simes, eds., *Nationalities and Nationalism in the USSR: A Soviet Dilemma* (Washington, D.C.: Georgetown Center for Strategic and International Studies, 1977), 10; interview with Bennigsen in *Ruskaia mysl'*, June 23, 1983, p. 5.

13. See, in particular, Frederik Barth, ed., *Ethnic Groups and Boundaries* (Boston: Little, Brown, 1969).

14. Dunlop, "Language, Culture, Religion, and National Awareness," paper delivered at Hoover Institution Conference on Soviet Nationality Problems, Stanford, Calif., April 1983 (emphasis added).

15. Bennigsen and Broxup (fn. 10), 140 (emphasis added).

16. For a perceptive treatment of this theme, see Cynthia Enloe, *Ethnic Soldiers: State Security in Divided Societies* (Athens: University of Georgia Press, 1980).

17. Bialer, *Stalin's Successors* (New York: Cambridge University Press, 1980), 208.

18. Anthony Smith, *Theories of Nationalism* (New York: Harper & Row, 1971), 168. A similar Soviet view is found in E. Bagramov, *Natsional'nyi vopros v bor'be idei* [The National Question in the Struggle of Ideas] (Moscow: Politizdat, 1982), 6-7: "Socialism draws a solid line between the concepts of 'national' and 'nationalistic.' The former is preserved and developed under socialism."

19. For a more comprehensive treatment of this thesis, see Gail W. Lapidus, "The 'National Question' in Soviet Doctrine: From Lenin to Andropov," paper presented at the Lehrman Institute, New York, March 16, 1983. See also Walker Connor, *The National Question in Marxist-Leninist Theory and Strategy* (Princeton: Princeton University Press, 1984).

20. M.I. Kulichenko, *Raztsvet i Sblizhenie natsii v SSSR* [The Flowering and Rapprochement of Nations in the U.S.S.R.] (Moscow: Mysl', 1981). Similar critiques of authors who oversimplify the process of *sliianie* are found in I.P. Tsamerian, *Natsii i natsional'nye otnosheniia v razvitom sotsialisticheskom obshchestve* [Nations and National Relations in Developed Socialist Society] (Moscow: Nauka, 1979), 178-82, and K.K. Karakeev, I. Ia. Kopylov, and R. A. Salikov, *Problemy upravleniia stroitel'stvom sovetskogo mnogonatsional'nogo gosudarstva* [Problems of Administration in the Construction of the Soviet Multinational State] (Moscow: Nauka, 1982), 250.

21. "Torzhestvo leninskoi natsional'noi politiki," [The triumph of Leninist nationality policy], *Kommunist* (No. 13, 1969), 10 (emphasis added).

22. Kosolapov, "Klassovye i natsional'nye otnosheniia na etape razvitogo sotsializma" [Class and national relations in the stage of developed socialism], *Sotsiologicheskie issledovaniia* (No. 4, 1982), 10 (emphasis added). These views were also presented at a major conference in Riga on "The Development of National Relations in the Conditions of Developed Socialism" in June 1982.

23. *Ibid.*, 15 (emphasis added).

24. M.A. Morozov, *Natsiia v sotsialisticheskom obshchestve* [The Nation in Socialist Society] (Moscow: Politizdat, 1979), 41. In a similar vein, a recent article in *Kommunist Moldavii* argues that,

contrary to the false claims of bourgeois ideologists, the Soviet people do not consider themselves as some sort of "Russian-Soviet nation" in which the ethnic features of the non-Russian peoples are said to have dissolved and disappeared. In reality the international community does not replace the national one, but encompasses it. . . . The development of the USSR proves that the nation is now the definitive form of social development. Even under socialism, it is within the framework of the nation that production and all other social relations . . . exist.

D. Ursul, "Raztsvet i sblizhenie sovetskikh natsii—torzhestvo leninskoi natsional'noi politiki [The flowering and rapprochement of Soviet nations—the triumph of Leninist nationality policy], *Kommunist Moldavii* 11 (November 1982), 88.

25. Z.S. Chertina, "Burzhuaznye istoriki o novoi istoricheskoi obshchnosti—sovetskii narod" [Bourgeois historians on the new historic community—the Soviet people] *Istoriia SSSR* 6 (November-December 1982), 195.

26. *Pravda*, December 22, 1982, p. 2.

27. See, e.g., Alexander Nekrich, *The Punished Peoples* (New York: Norton 1977).

28. For a discussion of the earlier controversies, see Grey Hodnett, "The Debate over Soviet Federalism," *Soviet Studies* 18 (April 1967), 458-81. Brezhnev's report of October 4, 1977 to the Supreme Soviet on the discussions of the draft constitution states that a number of proposals were advanced to introduce a reference to the existence of a single Soviet nation, to liquidate or sharply curtail the sovereignty of union and autonomous republics, and to establish a unicameral Supreme Soviet by abolishing the Soviet of Nationalities, but that such proposals were resisted as premature (*Izvestiia*,

October 5, 1977). See also A. Shtromas, "The Legal Position of Soviet Nationalities and Their Territorial Units According to the 1977 Constitution of the USSR," *Russian Review*, No. 3 (July 1980), 265-72. For an informative Soviet treatment of current debates over the nature and future of the federal arrangement, see Karakeev and others (fn. 19), 260-98. For an example of advocacy of expanding the powers of the republics, see A. Agzamkhodzhaev, "Demokraticheskii tsentralizm i sovetskaia federatsiia," [Democratic centralism and the Soviet federation], *Sovetskoe gosudarstvo i pravo*, No. 7 (July 1983), 24-31. Agzamkhodzhaev is Dean of the Law Faculty of Tashkent State University and a corresponding member of the Uzbek Academy of Sciences. Virtually no published advocacy of altering the federal system has appeared since the late 1960s either in official or *samizdat* writers.

29. Local elites are not themselves united on these issues, and policy differences cut across both indigenous and Russian elites. See, for example, the study by Teresa Zimmer, "Ethnic Identity and Policy-Making in Soviet Uzbekistan," paper presented at AAASS meeting, September 1981, Asilomar, Calif.

30. B.N. Ponomarev, "Leninskaia natsional'naia politika KPSS na etape razvitogo sotsializma i ee mezhdunarodnoe znachenie" [The Leninist nationality policy of the CPSU at the stage of developed socialism and its international significance], in *Vospityvat' ubezhdennykh patriotov-internatsionalistov: Po materialam Vsesoiuznoi nauchno-prakticheskoi konferentsii "Razvitie natsional'nykh otnoshenii v usloviiakh zrelogo sotsializma."* *Opyt i problemy patrioticheskogo i internatsional'nogo vospitaniia* [Rearing Convinced Patriot-Internationalists] (Moscow: Politicheskaia literatura, 1982), 20.

31. G.T. Tavadov, "O razvitii natsional'nykh otnoshenii v SSSR" [On the development of national relations in the USSR], *Nauchnyi kommunizm* 5 (September-October 1981), 11-21. . . .

32. *Pravda*, February 24, 1981, p. 7.

33. *Pravda*, December 22, 1982, p. 2.

34. Lt. Gen. Ye. Nikitin, *Agitator armii i flota*, No. 23, 1982, 10-14.

35. For a fuller account of these discussions, see Gail Warshofsky Lapidus, *Women in Soviet Society* (Berkeley: University of California Press, 1979), chap. 8, and Cynthia Weber and Ann Goodman, "The Demographic Policy Debate in the USSR," *Population Development Review* 7, (June 1981), 279-95.

36. M.V. Tatimov, *Razvitie narodonaseleniia i demograficheskaia politika* [Population Development and Demographic Policy] (Alma-Ata: Nauka, 1978), 4.

37. For a discussion of the controversy provoked by Khrushchev's initiatives in 1958-1959, see Yaroslav Bilinsky, "The Soviet Education Laws of 1958-59 and Soviet Nationality Policy," *Soviet Studies* 14 (October 1962), 138-57. More recent conflicts are reviewed in Roman Solchanyk, "Russian Language and Soviet Politics," *Soviet Studies* 34 (January 1982), 23-42.

38. G.I. Litvinova and B. Ts. Urlanis, "Demograficheskaia politika Sovetskogo Soiuza" [The demographic policy of the Soviet Union], *Sovetskoe gosudarstvo i pravo* 3 (March 1982), 38-46.

39. The inverse relationship between upward mobility and ethnic prejudice, and its special salience in the more educated, intelligentsia strata, is clearly demonstrated in the research of Iu. V. Arutiunian, "Konkretno-sotsiologicheskoe issledovanie natsional'nykh otnoshenii" [Concrete sociological research on national relations], *Voprosy filosofii* 12

(December 1969), 129-39. The potentially divisive impact of economic issues on nationality relations can be seen with greater clarity in studies conducted in Yugoslavia; see Steven L. Burg, *Conflict and Cohesion in Socialist Yugoslavia* (Princeton: Princeton University Press, 1983) chap. 2.

40. Donald L. Horowitz, "Multiracial Politics in the New States: Toward a Theory of Conflict," in Robert J. Jackson and Michael B. Stein, eds., *Issues in Comparative Politics* (New York: St. Martin's Press, 1971), 172.

18

Lithuanian National Politics

V. Stanley Vardys

The process of social, economic, and political change in Lithuania defies simplistic characterizations frequently found in Western media. If pressed for labels, one can best identify it as an articulate movement toward national independence and democracy. What began in large measure as an initiative for democratization to support the renewal of socialism has become a movement for national liberation, for seeking emancipation both from the Soviet empire and Soviet socialism. Independent groups seek to dismantle the Communist Party's monopoly of power in favor of a pluralistic social and political order. These goals have quickly won grass-roots support among almost all segments of Lithuanian society.

The purpose of this article is to examine the origins and scope of this unprecedented development and to highlight the interplay between the main actors of the drama, namely the Lithuanian Reconstruction Movement (*Lietuvos Persitvarkymo Sąjūdis*), the Communist Party of Lithuania (CPL), and the leadership of the Communist Party of the Soviet Union (CPSU). Because the play is not over and because the actors are still changing their scripts, observations and especially conclusions on the outcome can be only tentative. However, enough material exists to allow discussion of the meaning of this process of change for Lithuania and for the Soviet Union as a whole.

POPULAR DEMANDS FOR CHANGE

The rise of Sąjūdis and of other social groups that drive the current process of change in the republic was made possible by the policy of *glasnost'* enunciated by Soviet leader Mikhail Gorbachev. Pushing for badly needed economic reform, Gorbachev chose democratization and glasnost' as tools to subject

Published in *Problems of Communism*, 38: 4 (July-August 1989), pp. 53-77. Reprinted with permission from the publisher.

regime bureaucrats to some measure of popular control and to promote social initiative and creativity. The three Baltic popular fronts use this rationale for legitimizing their programs, which have gone far beyond *perestroyka* (restructuring) as defined by Moscow. "We are convinced," the three movements stated in a joint declaration of May 14, 1989, "that alongside the process of broadening openness, mass democratic movements are the only guarantee for the continuation and irreversibility of the radical restructuring of society."[1] The use of the word "radical" shows that the Lithuanians and the other Balts seek to interpret *perestroyka* in the spirit of their own political cultures. The Lithuanians seek a pluralistic society, not merely the "pluralistic socialism" Gorbachev intends. In the economic realm, Moscow has confronted "radical" demands concerning private ownership and management. Finally, the quest for political and economic change takes place in an atmosphere of revived Lithuanian national consciousness. Georgijus Efremovas, a leading member of *Sąjūdis*, has remarked that "democratic liberation movements usually are closely connected to the national idea that will likely be institutionalized in the Baltic region. To battle against the victory of this idea is immoral, imprudent, and hopeless."[2]

Western observers may be correct in arguing that in Lithuania and in the other Baltic countries, Gorbachev sought to mobilize energies generated by popular movements of national liberation for "constructive purposes,"[3] that these popular revolutions can be "co-opted," or that for the tolerance thus far shown by Moscow, the Baltic nations, including Lithuania, "will reward him by leading the country in economic restructuring."[4] Gorbachev was probably also convinced that the CPL and the other Baltic parties would be able to ride the tiger of resurgent nationalism instead of being devoured by it.

Although *glasnost'* led to a resurgence of nationalist sentiments and the emergence of reform groups in Lithuania, these have been conditioned by two elements of Lithuanian political culture: first, a deep commitment to historic national values and the tradition of national resistance to occupying powers and, second, the brief experience of democracy in the interwar period.

These elements of Lithuania's political culture require further comment. Lithuanian opposition to the first Soviet occupation in 1940-41 culminated in a successful revolt against Stalin's regime a day after the Germans attacked the Soviet Union. A provisional government emerged, which declared independence. The Nazi invaders snuffed out the independent regime, pushing the rebels and their supporters into the underground.[5] Yet, Lithuanian anti-Nazi resistance, with the exception of the Communists, was non-violent. Passive resistance groups, however, sabotaged or frustrated more than one German war policy. Then, after the return of the Red Army, anti-Soviet partisans took up arms against the Communists.[6] Guerrilla war, little noticed in the West, lasted from 1944 to 1952 and cost tens of thousands of casualties. Mass deportations and inhuman persecution by Soviet authorities accompanied this warfare.

Lithuania's short-lived experience with democracy colored popular understanding of reform. People are still alive who remember genuine elections and political competition. Historical memories of free elections do not necessarily serve the interests of the reformers in Moscow.

The dissidents and their decades-long struggle cannot be forgotten either. In the 1970's and 1980's, Lithuania produced more dissident publications per capita than any other Soviet republic. The Helsinki Group, the Catholic Committee for the Defense of Believers' Rights,[7] and other groups showered the government with petitions and complaints of human rights violations. Politically, the most memorable was the appeal of 1979 condemning the Molotov-Ribbentrop Pact of 1939 and demanding that the Soviet and German governments denounce the treaty and its political consequences and restore independence to the Baltic states. The Catholic rights movement also was especially strong and articulate.[8]

Taken together, Lithuanian nationalism, democratic traditions, and dissent provided the basis for a program much different from and more far-reaching than the CPL's and the CPSU's efforts at *perestroyka* and democratization. It was inevitable that popular demands for change would quickly outstrip the limited efforts of the regime to engineer directed change from above.

THE CPL

At first, neither party leaders nor, surprisingly, many party intellectuals and mangers wanted to commit themselves to a reform process that was likely to involve considerable political risk. Several factors explain this attitude. First, Soviet rule has been less threatening to the survival of the Lithuanian nation in Lithuania than it has been for the Estonians and the Latvians in their titular republics. The proportion of Lithuanians among the population of the Lithuanian SSR has remained a steady 80 percent, even after the 1989 census. The percentage of Russian immigrants remained under 10 percent, as in the 1960's and 1970's. Second, Lithuanians are generally cautious and not usually aggressive. Doubting the permanence of Gorbachev's rule and cynical as a result of previous experiences with Moscow's "reform" efforts, most Lithuanians were slow to take the newly developing situation earnestly enough to risk taking initiatives. Moreover, some degree of fear, apathy and alienation had come to characterize almost all members of the population. Finally, the CPL leadership, especially after the death of First Secretary Antanas Sniečkus in 1976, fell into the hands of mediocre *apparatchiks*. Petras Griškevičius, who took over as first secretary after Sniečkus's death, conceded that *perestroyka* was a "revolutionary process" but had a very conservative understanding of *glasnost'*. Certain public criticisms, according to Griškevičius, "obstructed harmonious common efforts." It was permissible to reexamine the past, but historical events had to be judged from "class positions." Griškevičius frowned upon historians who sought to fill in historical "blanks spots."[9]

Griškevičius died on November 14, 1987. On December 1, a new first party secretary, Ringaudas Songaila was promoted to this position from the chairmanship of the Presidium of the Lithuanian Supreme Soviet. The new first secretary, whose tenure proved to be short-lived, followed in his predecessor's footsteps and predictably kept the brakes on *glasnost'*. Thus, on January 26, 1988, a report of the CPL's Central Committee plenum intoned old tunes: the party had demonstrated weakness combatting "alien" philosophies, it did not stress "international" and "class-conscious" education; "atheistic education" was unsatisfactory; "nationalist and clerical extremists" were not receiving sufficient rebuff. The plenum avowed that it was necessary to "unmask demagogues and opportunists who seek to speculate with democracy and public opinion for their selfish interests and for the purpose of discrediting reconstruction."[10]

Attacks on the dissidents and the nationally conscious intelligentsia followed. Thus, the CPL daily, *Tiesa*, intensified its propaganda against *The Chronicle of the Catholic Church of Lithuania*, a *samizdat* publication that had been periodically appearing for 16 years and had attracted world-wide attention to the persecution of the Catholic Church and its believers.

Songaila's regime then took various police measures, some of them violent, to prevent the Lithuanians from observing the 70th anniversary of Lithuanian independence on February 16, 1988.[11] Concentrations of military and police personnel, especially in the capital city, made public meetings and demonstrations impossible. The regime apparently considered the occasion a crucial challenge not only because the authorities knew of local plans for the celebration but also because President Ronald Reagan had issued a proclamation supporting Lithuanian independence and inviting a commemoration of the anniversary.[12] A large group of United States senators also had written to Gorbachev asking that Soviet authorities not interfere with the festivities.[13] At the same time, Soviet President Andrey Gromyko had come to Vilnius in early February to denounce "the lunatics abroad" who did not understand how "mighty" Soviet power in Lithuania was.[14] However, none of these activities stopped the independence commemoration by the people. Banished from the streets and meeting halls, demonstrators flooded churches, where special masses were said and sermons preached. Songaila's regime then went after the pastors who had allowed such "anti-Soviet" acts.

NATIONALLY CONSCIOUS INTELLIGENTSIA

Groups of Lithuanian intellectuals and writers had become restless prior to Griškevičius's death. As if to test the new leadership that succeeded Griškevičius, on December 1, 1987, at a meeting of the Writers' Union, a group of leading critics and poets took to task the editor of their professional weekly *Literatūra ir Menas* (Literature and the Arts), which is published by the Ministry of Culture and the Writers' Union. One writer protested the editor's fear of publishing a collective letter that took issue with some ideas expressed in an article written by one of the republic's leaders.   A poet, Sigitas Geda, complained about censorship and demands that he change his poetry before publication; and Vytautus Kubilius, a highly respected but ideologically deviant literary critic, told the gathering that "society is indignant about [*Literatūra ir Menas*'s] facelessness, writers are ashamed to contribute, members of the editorial board are resigning one after another, while the leadership of the Writers' Union keeps the 'best relations' with the editors.   This decaying newspaper can be revived only by contributors who think originally and courageously.   Are the reserves of Lithuanian intellectual talent so poor that we can not find our own V. Korotich or M. Chaklays?"[15]   Antanas Drillinga, the editor of *Literatūra ir Menas*, survived for another year, but the newspaper soon became one of the flagships of *glasnost'* and *perestroyka* in Lithuania.   Another writer, the irascible and aggressive Communist Vytautas Petkevičius, who demonstrated his loyalty to Moscow by fighting against the partisans for the establishment of Soviet rule, loudly insisted that despite the breezes of reform the atmosphere for creative activity in the republic was "still unfavorable." He bluntly put the responsibility for the situation on the CPL "activists, men of little talent who parrot some memorized slogans." He advised the party "to put them in their place" and never again "to allow them to drown out the creative and sane mind of our nation."[16]

Soon, however, Lithuanian "Korotiches" and "Chaklays's" began to make their appearance in the weekly *Gimtasis Kraštas* (Native Country) and the daily *Komjaunimo Tiesa* (Truth of the Komsomol).   The first was originally published for the consumption of Lithuanians abroad, but it was distributed at home as well.   The editor, Algimantas Čekuolis, made the weekly extremely popular by publishing unflinching exposés of the system's sins.   Čekuolis's political connections indicated that some elements of the republic's leadership had decided that the time had come for Lithuania to implement *glasnost'* even though it involved political risks.

In late 1988 and early 1989, the intellectuals were busily meeting among themselves to discuss possible courses of action.   At an Artists' Union meeting, for example, Arvydas Juozaitis, a philosopher at Vilnius University, read a remarkable lecture on national sovereignty, which became widely known and admired.   At its plenary meeting of April 4, 1988, the Writers' Union proposed that the Lithuanian language be declared the official language of the republic and that every year a day of remembrance be held for Stalin's victims.   In the literary journal *Pergalė*, Romualdas Granuskas published a short story showing that collective farms were organized by force and that the life of collective farm workers from generation to generation was drenched in alcohol and death.   The tragic state of Lithuania's environment received much more attention, although it reflected negatively on bureaucrats in both the republic and in Moscow.   Also in April, new questions were raised about Lithuanian history during the crucial period from the late 1930s to the early 1950's.   For example, Stalinist cruelty was held responsible for the 1944-52 partisan war. This finding exonerated the partisans from the charge of "banditry" and elevated their struggle to a legitimate, albeit mistaken, defensive action.[17]

PRINCIPAL PLAYERS

Before highlighting the dramatic political interplay that on May 18, 1989, culminated in a formal declaration of sovereignty and proclamation of the ultimate goal of complete independence by the Lithuanian Supreme Soviet, it is necessary to identify and characterize the main actors in the Lithuanian political drama: the CPL, the leaders of the CPSU, and especially the new "informal" groups. The first two are known entities. Unknown are the grass-roots organizations that have mushroomed since mid-1988. Foremost among the independent organizations is *Sajŭdis*. Others were either spawned by *Sajŭdis* or organized to oppose some or all of *Sajŭdis*'s goals. Still others organized themselves independently. The list of such organizations is long, but most important are the Lithuanian Freedom League and *Vienbé-Yedinstvo-Jednośĉ*, which is made up largely of Russians and Poles. Finally, it is also necessary to include the Catholic Church, an institution that has long represented and defended aspirations of the Lithuanian people.

Sajŭdis

As noted above, *Sajŭdis* is the main engine that drives social and political change in Lithuania. The organization was established by party and non-party intellectuals to consolidate all segments of society for implementing *perestroyka* in Lithuania.[18] *Sajŭdis* was born in the Lithuanian Academy of Sciences, which on May 23, 1988, established a commission to propose changes in the Lithuanian SSR constitution needed to accommodate *perestroyka*, democratization, and *glasnost'*.[19] Three days later, the Academy hosted two distinguished Estonian economists from the Estonian Academy of Sciences, who discussed the newly organized Estonian People's Front and the Estonian model for economic self-government. Other meetings followed that considered the establishment of a reform group similar to the Estonian People's Front.

Determination to form a popular front was solidified by two events, namely the election of CPL delegates to the 19th Conference of the CPSU and decisions taken by Moscow on the expansion of the Lithuanian chemical industry.[20] The delegates to the party conference were elected "the old way," that is, they were appointed by the CPL leadership—contrary, party progressives claimed, to the CPSU Central Committee's instructions. The Lithuanian party thus showed itself unaffected by the new spirit of *glasnost'* and democratization. Moscow's economic managers betrayed a similar spirit. On June 2, the Lithuanian government announced that central ministry authorities had unilaterally decided to speed up the expansion of giant chemical industries in Jonava Kėdainiai and

Mažeikiai—cities that already were choking from pollution and where further enterprise expansion had been forbidden by the Lithuanian government. By riding roughshod over Lithuania's leadership, Moscow's ministries provoked many elements inside and outside the Lithuanian power structure to action.

On June 3, scientists, writers, artists, and professionals of various specialties flooded the Academy of Science's auditorium to vent accumulated grievances and to discuss a course of action. The meeting elected an "initiative group" consisting of 36 prominent scholars and intellectuals to organize a movement for the support of *perestroyka*.[21] *Sajūdis* was born. Half the membership of the "initiative group" consisted of party members. This fact signaled, of course, a split in the ruling party and also may have indicated a certain restlessness among segments of the Lithuanian *nomenklatura* itself.

It is clear that *Sajūdis* was born not in cooperation with the party leadership but against its wishes. The CPL distrusted the new organization because it deprived the party of its "leading role" in Lithuanian society. The "initiative group" was even rumored to be hostile to party leaders because it refused to welcome a section chief of the CPL Central Committee at a meeting to which the *apparatchik* came uninvited.[22] However, the new group merely sought independence from the party; it was not inimical to the party. In fact, *Sajūdis* attempted to certify its loyalty by deciding that it would not accept "people who had attempted to propagate extremist ideas."[23] These "extremists," of course were dissidents, many of whom had spent years in prisons or concentration camps. Eventually, however, *Sajūdis* became a mass organization; participation (it had no formal membership) was opened to all, including dissidents and former political prisoners.

The new organization used the summer for a feverish and skillful mobilization of public support and on October 22-23, 1988, held its founding congress in Vilnius. Its 1,121 delegates were chosen by professional organizations of the republic, and from political, cultural and social groups.[24] For example, the Lithuanian Freedom League was allocated seven seats in the Congress; the Catholic clergy also received a quota of delegates.

The congress was a middle-class gathering, dominated by intellectuals. Occupationally, the largest group of delegates consisted of scientists, artists, writers, and other professionals. Educationally, more than 77 percent of the delegates were university graduates.

The meeting was also very much a Lithuanian gathering. According to nationality, the delegates were 96 percent Lithuanian, .08 percent Russian, 0.6 percent Jewish, and 0.9 percent Polish, with 11 percent from other ethnic minority backgrounds. If compared to minority percentages in the population, the Russians and Poles were much underrepresented, because the delegates were elected from groups supporting *Sajūdis* and such groups enjoyed little support among the Russian and Polish minorities.

The congress elected a Diet (*Seimas*) of 220 members, which in turn chose *Sąjūdis*'s governing council, consisting of 35 people. Initially, *Sąjūdis* refused to choose a president; however, political developments soon made such a choice necessary.

The congress decided against a formal organization because it would involve the creation of a "bureaucracy," which no one wanted. Thus, in contrast to the Latvian Popular Front, *Sąjūdis* does not have dues-paying membership, only participants and activists, the latter running its local organizations. Only lists of activists are kept. As a result, the Movement's leadership can only estimate the group's size. In March 1989, *Sąjūdis*'s president, Professor Vytautas Lansbergis, who was chosen for that position in November 1988, put the organization's membership at 100,000 to 500,000.[25]

Programmatically, *Sąjūdis* has undergone changes from the time of its inception on June 3, 1988. It was radicalized as a result of its fierce and competitive interplay with the CPL. In October 1988, at the time of its founding Congress, the Movement professed as its goal the "support and deepening of *perestroyka* initiated by the CPSU;[26] achievement of "sovereignty" in all areas of Lithuanian life within a "Leninist" Soviet federation; and the goal of "pluralist society" with no organization "usurping" political power. Other programmatic goals included Western-style guarantee of civil rights, eradication of Stalinism, research and reporting on the crimes of the Stalin period, and punishment of those responsible. Finally, although *Sąjūdis* avoided the topics of foreign relations and military affairs, it nevertheless postulated that "Lithuania has to become part of the nuclear-free zone of Europe and its territory must be demilitarized."[27] Were this goal attained, Lithuania would no longer belong to the Warsaw Pact; neither would Soviet troops be stationed on its territory.

Sąjūdis went on record as a group that "considers national consciousness and expression as independent values and as important factors of social renewal."[28] In concrete policy terms, *Sąjūdis* supported controls on immigration into the republic and the declaration of Lithuanian as the republic's official language. (The organization also sought to guarantee minorities the right to use and develop their languages and cultures.) The program further opposed "state monopoly" over culture, and demanded the establishment of a "national" school system and broad cultural contacts with foreign countries. Normalization of relations with the Catholic Church and other religious denominations, and the abolition of state-sponsored atheist indoctrination were other important parts of the political program.

In the all-important economic field, *Sąjūdis* advocated an equally comprehensive program. It sought complete self-management for the republic and demanded that Lithuania participate in the all-Union economic system as a distinct economic unit. It advocated Lithuania's control over its economic resources, finances, and currency. *Sąjūdis* also promoted "pluralistic" ownership, which meant that it sought legalization of private ownership. *Sąjūdis* also advocated the idea of direct relations with foreign enterprises and economic institutions. Finally, *Sąjūdis* exhibited acute concern for the state of the Lithuanian environment. *Sąjūdis* contended that the central government in Moscow ought to help clean up Lithuania's environment by compensating the republic for ecological damage previously inflicted by its policies.

Sąjūdis was formally legalized on March 16, 1989.

The Lithuanian Freedom League

The other organization that has moved the process of change, although its influence has been of a less direct nature, is the Lithuanian Freedom League (*Lietuvos Laisvės Lyga*). It has visibly affected the interplay between *Sąjūdis* and the CPL. The League (LFL for short) was born in the underground. First mentioned in 1978, for a decade the League was not heard of. Even its existence was questioned. Its members reemerged in 1987, the first among civic groups to test the credibility of *glasnost'* and democratization. On August 23, 1987, the League's members sponsored the commemoration of the anniversary of the signing of the Molotov-Ribbentrop Pact, a public demonstration that shocked Griškevičius's conservative leadership. The League also provoked Songaila's regime into giving official approval for public discussion of Stalin's purges, deportations and crimes by staging—without a permit—a demonstration in remembrance of the May 1948 deportations from Lithuania. This gathering—although drowned out by the loudspeakers playing music and dispersed by police—nevertheless took place on May 22, 1988.

The League's goals have not changed since the days of its underground activities. As its information bulletin states, these goals are, first, to raise Lithuanian national consciousness and, second, to promote uncompromisingly the idea of independence.[29] In the underground, the League published *samizdat*, registered violations of human rights, and organized protests against Soviet policies. Above ground, it united with six other groups into the Association for Lithuania's Independence (*Lietuvos Mepriklausomybės Sąjunga*) and, as indicated, has been rather conspicuous in the public eye. The other members of the Association are the following small groups: The Movement for Lithuania's Independence, the Lithuanian Democratic Party, the Christian Democratic Party, the Lithuanian Helsinki Group, the Lithuanian National Youth Association, and the Committee for the Rescue of Political Prisoners. The League subscribes to the principles of *glasnost'* and democratization, and it supports most of the program of *Sąjūdis*. However, the League has differed with *Sąjūdis*'s early interpretation of "sovereignty." The League has consistently advocated full independence, by which it means Lithuanian control not only of domestic but also of foreign and defense policies.

In contrast to *Sąjūdis*, whose supporters are distinguished party and non-party intellectuals, the League is led by former political prisoners and former partisans of the 1944-52 period. Some Catholic clergymen are also active in its leadership. Its core support comes from former dissidents, political prisoners, partisans, and deportees.

The League's main achievement has been to radicalize *Sąjūdis* and even certain elements in the CPL. The League's goal of complete independence has been virtually embraced by *Sąjūdis* and finds support among some party leaders. However, *Sąjūdis* has disapproved of the League's confrontational tactics, which the League's dissident leaders have favored as a result of their decades-long struggles with Communist authorities. Nevertheless, 38 percent of *Sąjūdis* Diet favored close cooperation with the League, while 49 percent supported cooperation only if the League changed its tactics.[30]

Vienybė-Yedinstvo-Jedność

Although smaller minorities—the Jews, Belorussians, Tartars, Karaims, and other—generally supported reforms as advocated by *Sąjūdis*, the Russians and the Poles—with exceptions, of course—made alternative policy proposals on some burning issues, such as having Lithuanian be the official language of the republic.

The massive and emotional currents of national rebirth intimidated these minorities and led, after the founding congress of *Sąjūdis*, to the establishment of *Vienybė-Yedinstvo-Jedność* (Unity), an "informal" organization supposedly open to all nationalities but actually composed mostly of Russians and Poles. The avowed purpose of *Yedinstvo* was to articulate and defend the interests of the Russian and Polish minorities. At first, *Sovetskaya Litva* and *Czerwony Sztandar*—the Russian and Polish dailies published in Vilnius—served as forums for this unlikely Russian-Polish coalition.

On November 11, 1988, the republic's press published a declaration adopted at the new group's founding meeting that explained its objectives.[31] The program of *Yedinstvo* was orthodox in comparison to that advocated by *Sąjūdis*. It came out in clear support of the CPL's leading role, professed loyalty to *perestroyka* as defined by the CPSU leadership, favored the "mutual enrichment" of national cultures, and opposed discrimination on the basis of national background. In its only concrete policy proposal, *Yedinstvo* strongly objected to the adoption of Lithuanian as the official language of the republic.

Yedinstvo representatives attribute the rise of their opposition to *Sąjūdis*'s insensitivity to Russian and Polish needs. In fact, *Sąjūdis* has made mistakes, but its declarations have been liberal in attitude toward minorities. Most of Lithuania's Russians and Poles are working-class people who feel intimidated by the sea of Lithuanian flags and other symbols of national awakening. In addition, the Russians are mainly immigrants and therefore feel insecure.

Russians and Poles must feel threatened by a language decree requiring all state employees to learn Lithuanian in two years. Many Russians have never gained or intended to gain proficiency in Lithuanian, although they intended to live permanently in the republic. Neither group willingly accepts minority status despite the fact that in Lithuania they are indeed minorities.

In a public demonstration on February 12, 1989, which took place in Vilnius and was attended by a crowd estimated at 80,000, *Yedinstvo* threatened workers strikes and refusal to pay CPL membership dues if the decree on Lithuanian language, which was passed on November 19, 1988, was not rescinded in two weeks.[32]   Other demands voiced at various meetings, which attracted thousands, included a proposal that people of all nationalities have a right to use their native language in all government, economic, social, and political establishments, that students in special and higher educational institutions be taught in their native languages, and that autonomous territories be established for each minority nationality.

Associations of smaller nationalities, namely the Lithuanian Jewish Cultural Association, the Jewish Association "Tkuma," Belorussian "Syabryna," Tartar, Latvian, Estonian, Mordvinian, Karaim, and German societies, and the Ukrainian Community of Lithuania denounced the February 12 meeting as the embodiment of "Great Russian chauvinism" and *Yedinstvo* itself as a negative organization that opposed efforts by all of Lithuania's nationalities to restrain "the pretentious monopolistic claims" of the center (Moscow). The statement of these national groups supported the implementation of the decree making Lithuanian the official language.[33]

In its founding conference of May 13-14, 1989, extremists from the city of Vilnius led by Valeriy Ivanov, an official of the *Znaniye* society, captured *Yedinstvo*. As a result, the organization split, many delegates walked out, and two dozen leading figures, including some founding members, withdrew from the organization altogether, denouncing the conference as an "example of how extremism endangers democracy."[34]

In February, impressed by the ability of *Yedinstvo* to stage a demonstration with 80,000 participants, Lithuanian authorities had promised that it would be consulted and given the opportunity to influence the drafting of legislation that was to implement the language law.[35] The group's split in May has, however, considerably reduced its ability to influence political change in Lithuania. Time will tell whether it can recover.

It should be stressed that the case of Lithuania's Polish minority is different from that of its Russian minority. In May, a separate association of Lithuania's Poles was established. A lively dialogue developed between the Polish minority representatives, on the one hand, and republic authorities and *Sąjūdis*, on the other. In Warsaw, on June 26, 1989, Lithuanian party chief Algirdas Brazauskas and Polish party leader Wojciech Jaruzelski signed an agreement committing the Lithuanian and Polish communist parties to extensive cooperation, including numerous exchanges, which will presumably profit Lithuania's Polish minority.[36] On July 10, 1989, Lithuania's Supreme Soviet appealed to the Poles, asking them to withdraw legislation passed in some districts of Vilnius region declaring Polish autonomy.[37] A law on minority rights is in preparation. However, *Yedinstvo* leader Ivanov, who wants Moscow to transfer administration of Vilnius to the Russian Republic, continues to claim that *Yedinstvo* represents the Poles.

The Catholic Church

Among societal institutions that have influenced political change, it is necessary to include the Catholic Church. Under the Soviet regime, the Church—once a powerful institution in Lithuanian society—found itself separated from public life, with its adherents physically persecuted. Some of the bishops were shot; others, together with one-third of the clergy, were deported to labor camps. Preparation of new clergymen was severely limited, and the religious press was banned. State-sponsored atheistic propaganda conveyed through schools, the media, and public institutions further undermined the Church's influence. Practicing believers faced discrimination in public and professional life.[38]

But the Church stayed close to the people, identified itself with the population's spiritual, social and cultural needs, and thereby survived. It also warranted respect as Lithuania's only surviving national institution and has served as a trustee for national traditions. During the Brezhnev era, Catholic churchmen nurtured a civil rights movement, undertook petition drives, and produced *samizdat* publications. According to Jonas Mikelinskas, a distinguished writer, of all Lithuanian institutions, the Catholic church was the "most consistent and persevering laborer for society's democratization, for human dignity and spirituality."[39] In some ways, indeed, it prepared the ground for the current social, national, and even political renewal. The Church came out of the ordeal of almost half a century of suppression strong enough to command attention. Both *Sąjūdis* and the CPL have vied for its support.

The Church's attitude toward *Sąjūdis* and the process of national renewal and political change was unclear; in the early summer of 1988 it was not participating in the reform movement. But its absence did not last long. *Sąjūdis* reserved a number of seats for clergymen at its founding meeting on October 22-23, 1988. Festive occasions sponsored by the reform movement do not occur without a Mass or a benediction.

The CPL leadership itself began periodic meetings with church hierarchy representatives in late 1987. Since that time the regime has made several concessions to the Church, thereby hoping to win Church support for its own program of *perestroyka*.

The Church's general attitude toward social and political change in Lithuania was outlined by Reverend Vaclovas Aliulis, chairman of the Church's Liturgical Commission, at the founding congress of *Sąjūdis*.[40] He said that the Catholic bishops supported the main objectives of *Sajūdis* on questions of human and civil rights, social justice, education for national awareness, culture, ecology, and economic development. The bishops believed that the nation itself, without outside interference, should choose its political system. They sought regime recognition of ecclesiastical self-government according to canon law. The bishops further suggested the abolition of the Council on Religious Affairs—an instrument used to control the churches—whose functions, in their view, violated the principle of separation of church and state.

The Church insists on the same right to propagate its beliefs that the atheist government has in propagating its world view. The bishops also support children's access to religious instruction and education. Finally, they advocate the creation of private schools and suggest that the principle of separation of church from school, now embedded in constitutional law, ought not to apply to private educational institutions.

Reformers both outside and inside the CPL have received the Church's support. However, the Church does not directly participate in politics. *Sajūdis* generally supports the rights of the Church and its appropriate place in society, but President Landsbergis stressed that in contrast to Poland, the Lithuanian reform movement did not develop around the Church; instead, he argues, the Church came to the movement.[41]

THE DRAMA

Following the establishment of the initiative group of *Sajūdis* on June 3, 1988, Lithuania's social and political life became extremely active and intense.[42] Intellectuals and professionals had broken the ice for a wide range of discussions, meetings, demonstrations, ecological marches, Lithuanian language festivals, and planned and unplanned rock music festivals. New associations and publications appeared with a vengeance. But the political stage was dominated by the struggle for influence over policymaking between *Sajūdis* and the CPL.

Sajūdis did not have a formal role in the system. It functioned as an "informal" organization, but quickly was accorded legitimacy by the Lithuanian people. The movement became powerful by virtue of the public support it could mobilize for its purposes. In the age of *glasnost'* and reform, the CPL could not disregard such power.

The struggle for influence, however, differed from competition for power in Western systems. Two factors account for the differences. First, although *Sajūdis* had the allegiance of the people and relied on private donations for support, the CPL had control over the media, law enforcement agencies, and significant financial resources. Second, both *Sajūdis* and especially the CPL had to take an outside player into account, namely the CPSU leadership—Moscow's approval was needed for whatever policies were hammered out in the competition between the two groups. The CPSU leadership had its own ways of participating in the process, and ultimately it alone could ratify the results of the competition. In other words, *Sąjūdis* and the CPL could not themselves decide the final outcome of their contest. The CPL's position was further complicated and weakened by the fact that many of its own most distinguished intellectuals, artists, writers, and other professionals had actively joined the "other" side. On the one hand, the circumstance indicated a party split and weakened the ruling group. On the other hand, it also facilitated control and influence of *Sąjūdis* and the building of a consensus without an apparent loss of face. Indeed relations between the Movement and the CPL reflected both a struggle for power and a process of consensus-building.

One can distinguish between several periods in this relationship. Once *Sąjūdis* was founded, it attempted to marshal its forces. In turn, the CPL attempted to contain *Sąjūdis*'s influence, if not win control over it. Thereafter, both forces moved toward accepting for Lithuania the federalist model developed in Estonia. After the CPL, under pressure from the CPSU, derailed that effort, bitterness, disappointment, and conflict followed, which radicalized *Sąjūdis* and spelled defeat for the CPL. After elections to the Congress of People's Deputies in March 1989, cooperation reemerged as reflected in a mutual desire to embrace the Estonian model and then proceed toward independence.

SĄJŪDIS GATHERS STRENGTH

Sąjūdis used the summer of 1988 to establish a strong base of popular support, reaching out to the masses and providing an umbrella for diverse points of view. It relied on mass meetings, demonstrations, and public events—all announced by word of mouth—to spread the message. Meetings were held to discuss such burning issues of the day as justice for those who had been deported and maltreated by the authorities, elimination of pollution and ecological dangers to health and safety, the question of "sovereignty," the Molotov-Ribbentrop Pact of 1939, the status of the Lithuanian language, economic independence, the restoration of normal relations with the Catholic Church, the correction of abuses and mistreatment of Lithuanian recruits in the armed forces, and the release of political prisoners. Equally important was the search for the historical truth about deportations, the partisan war, collectivization, and Lithuania's occupation and annexation in 1940. These public meetings became occasions for venting anger, and expressing the pent-up emotions accumulated through five decades of oppressive Soviet rule.

On June 24, *Sąjūdis* called an open "send-off" meeting—attended by 50,000 people—with Lithuanian party delegates elected to the 19th CPSU Conference. At the demonstration, the speakers voiced dissatisfaction with the secret elections of the delegates by a plenum of the CPL's Central Committee. *Sąjūdis* also released a statement that resembled the CPSU's understanding of *perestroyka* and demonstrated early programmatic restraint. The group endorsed the ideas of the 27th Congress of the CPSU and suggested that the 19th Party Conference decide how to ensure actual rule by the soviets (the government), as distinguished from the party, and how to restore republic sovereignty in accordance with the Leninist "concept of the nature of the Soviet Union." *Sajūdis* also called upon the conference to "secure guarantees" for the democratization of the party and the government, approve policies for the protection of the environment, establish republic citizenship, regulate immigration into the republic, declare Lithuanian the official language of the republic, guarantee autonomous development of republic education and culture, reestablish constitutional courts at the all-Union and republic levels, and ensure opportunities for "direct" republic relations with foreign countries.[43] When calling for reforms, *Sajūdis* formulated its suggestions with reference to party policies and used a generally accepted phraseology for that purpose.

Encouraged by the success of the June 24 meeting, *Sajūdis* organized a "reception" for the delegates returning from the party conference in Moscow. This meeting—on July 9—attracted 100,000 people. More flags and patriotic speeches were made.

The apex of mass demonstrations was reached on August 23 at the Vingis Park in Vilnius, where an estimated 250,000 people attended a public meeting to commemorate and discuss the signing of the Molotov-Ribbentrop Pact. These numbers exceeded all expectations. The meeting featured a taped speech by independent Lithuania's last foreign minister, Juozas Urbšys, who was still alive in Kaunas but too frail to attend. He negotiated with Stalin and Molotov in 1939 and told the story of the imposition of Soviet rule on Lithuania. The gathering soundly denounced Stalinism. One speaker said that "a religion has not yet been invented that could forgive all the crimes of Stalinism."[44] Another suggested that "if tsarism created a prison of nations, Stalinism established a 'slaughterhouse of nations'."[45]

The meeting demanded publication of the text of the Molotov-Ribbentrop Pact with its secret protocols, the opening of archives, the rewriting of history texts for schools, and the restoration of republic sovereignty. The last demand would ensure that Soviet laws would not be valid in Lithuania unless they were approved by the republic's Supreme Soviet or a popular referendum. The meeting also demanded rehabilitation of deportees, payment of compensation to the deportees by the republic and the all-Union government, and a release of political prisoners. The emotional occasion was significant in still another way. By organizing it, *Sajūdis* aligned itself squarely with the dissidents who in 1979 had demanded denunciation of this pact by both the Soviet Union and Germany.

Thus, the meeting demonstrated a shift from the rather modestly stated requests of autonomy of June 24 to discussions of national self-determination implied in the exposure of the Molotov-Ribbentrop Pact. *Sajūdis* had shifted its priorities from the needs of *perestroyka* as defined by Moscow to the requirements for reform as defined by the Lithuanians.

In the summer of 1988, the CPL was disoriented and seemed unable to understand the needs of Lithuanian society. The CPL leadership also was leery of *Sajŭdis* and watched its spreading influence with great apprehension.[46] Only occasional voices, such as that of Brazauskas, then a Party Secretary, at the meetings on June 24 and July 9, favored concessions to patriotic sentiments, but even Brazauskas confessed to confusion when he first saw national flags flying. The party seems to have been hoping, as secretary of the Vilnius University party organization Professor Bronius Genzelis suggested, that somehow everything would pass and that it would not be necessary to resolve the emerging dilemmas.[47]

Songaila and Nikolay Mitkin, the Lithuanian first and the Russian second secretaries, apparently decided to contain and slow down *Sajŭdis* and to combat "nationalist" forces within the movement and outside of it. On June 17, *Sajŭdis*'s leaders met with Party Secretary Lionginas Šepetys, the one-time Lithuanian cultural tsar, and on June 23, they met with First Secretary Songaila. Neither meeting led to mutual understanding. The regime denied *Sajŭdis* access to all state media and failed to give its activities fair and unbiased coverage. Party and government authorities in Vilnius, Kaunas, and many provincial localities hindered *Sajŭdis*'s activities. Local party officials frequently demanded that party members who joined *Sajŭdis* resign from the CPL; in some cases, their party membership was simply terminated.

Despite the CPL's hard line, Songaila had begun to march to the beat of Gorbachev's drums: the government began a study of models for future economic self-management by the republic; plans to revise the republic's constitution to reflect this change began in May. Moreover, the program of the CPL delegates to the 19th Party Conference did not much differ from *Sajŭdis*'s program at that time. At the conference, Songaila even dared to suggest making Lithuanian the official language of the republic.

Yet, at the 19th Party Conference, although he made some concessions to the opposition in the cultural sphere, Songaila condemned informal groups that, in his words, wanted to move "outside of our political system" or to "dictate their will to party organizations." He also demanded greater party influence over their activities.[48] At the party meeting with returning conference delegates, Songaila stressed that only those contributions that really strengthen and rejuvenate socialism were acceptable. He condemned the activities of informal groups that "undermined" socialist foundations, "incited" people, "encouraged national hostilities," and thus, distracted people from the "burning issues of the day." Songaila complained of too much *glasnost'* in some official publications, which printed "unfounded assertions of doubtful ideological value."[49] A week later, party bureaucrats explicitly criticized *Sajŭdis* for not "rebuffing" nationalists who wanted to join *Sajŭdis* activities and denounced the movement's cooperation with the Lithuanian Freedom League.

Thus, the CPL failed to understand or to accept the fact that reform and autonomy promoted from below would be undergirded by Lithuanian nationalism. After all, for 50 years the CPL had combatted Lithuanian nationalism. Furthermore, *Sajūdis* challenged the party's vanguard role. The regime bureaucrats knew reform was inevitable, but they alone wanted to decide its pace. Unused to public pressures, they did not know how to react to *Sajūdis's* initiatives and to the emergence of large public manifestations of Lithuanian nationalism. Revelations engendered by *glasnost'* had cost the CPL credibility, prestige, and deference.

Moscow soon became concerned with the developments in the republic. On August 11-13, Aleksandr Yakovlev, Gorbachev's closest ally in the Politburo, visited Vilnius to sort out the situation. He arrived from Riga where he had conducted talks with Latvian leaders. However, Yakovlev did not give comfort to the Lithuanian party leadership. He strongly supported *glasnost'*, insisting that eventually everything would have to be revealed one way or another. He also prodded the CPL leadership to become more active in directing change, to avoid confrontation, and to harness the "national factor" as a force for reform.[50] This last admonition required the CPL's co-optation of national traditions.

Yakovlev's visit led Lithuanian party leaders to satisfy several national demands. On August 18, the old national flag and anthem gained co-equal status with state (communist) symbols.[51] On August 20, the government published a decree that established Lithuanian geography and history as separate instructional subjects in schools, stipulated that pre-school children would be taught in their native language, that teaching of Russian would not begin until the third grade, and that teachers of Lithuanian in Russian schools would receive the same 15 percent salary bonus that teachers of Russian in Lithuanian schools have been receiving for years.[52] These moves reversed the Russification of education begun after the Communist takeover. Chairman of the Council of Minister Vytautas Sakalauskas also announced that the Lithuanian government had ended financial support for the installation of the third nuclear reactor at the Ignalina nuclear plant and stopped further construction until questions of safety would be satisfactorily answered. This act in defiance of the central ministries was unprecedented. Furthermore, Second Secretary Nikolay Mitkin publicly stated that CPL members could remain in *Sajūdis*, inasmuch as the latter was not an opposition party. He also permitted non-party members to participate in party meetings.[53] It also seems that Yakovlev's visit, as well as a public boycott of the newspaper, spelled the dismissal of Albertas Laurinčiukas (a former TASS correspondent and author of an anti-American play) as editor-in-chief of *Tiesa*. *Sajūdis* had targeted him and his staff for his newspaper's biased reporting of *Sajūdis* activities. Finally, after Yakovlev's visit, the CPL allowed television coverage of some of *Sajūdis's* activities. Thus, Lithuanian television broadcast a program summarizing the demonstration of August 23, which commemorated the signing of the Molotov-Ribbentrop Pact of 1939. Although the program was considered biased and distorted by many, at least the television silence regarding Sąjūdis was broken.

To clear the air and discuss such issues as political prisoners, glasnost', and the activities of the KGB, the leaders of Sąjūdis met with the chairman of the Lithuanian KGB, Eduardas Eismuntas, on August 30. According to Eismuntas, the three-hour meeting helped to produce "more mutual confidence" but, he said, "in many circles the Movement is [still] viewed with suspicion." He expected Sąjūdis to "mature," but advised it to acknowledge publicly the party's primacy and its own merely auxiliary role. Eismuntas emphasized that Sąjūdis should stress cooperation by using not only "national" (Lithuanian) but also "state" flags and symbols. It should also reject "carriers of infection." Eismuntas could not understand why Sąjūdis "closely collaborated" with the Lithuanian Freedom League and other organizations of "anti-Soviet disposition." Eismuntas also thought that Sąjūdis should recruit more non-Lithuanians into its ranks and leadership.[54]

The meeting with Eismuntas indicated that the CPL had not withdrawn its objections to the "national" aspects of the movement's activity. Indeed, the armistice between Sąjūdis and the party leadership did not continue for long. On September 14, the CPL Bureau delivered a blistering attack on the organization, arguing, among other things, that Sąjūdis did not represent the entire population of Lithuania, was "mono-national," cooperated with "extremists who openly propagate separatist sentiments," and that some of its adherents maintained contact with "Western radio 'voices' and with the reactionary part of Lithuanian emigration."[55]

Sąjūdis had no equivalent forum for response, but in its bulletin, the prominent lawyer and Sąjūdis leader Kazimieras Motieka, who had resigned from the party, dryly noted that the "republic's party leadership is upset that the Movement fights for perestroyka much more actively and decently" than did the CPL.[56]

Songaila's and Mitkin's preoccupation with the defense of the prerogatives of the party apparatus and with the hunt for "nationalists" in Sąjūdis and society very shortly backfired on the party and even derailed their own personal careers.

On September 28, the irrepressible Lithuanian Freedom League organized a meeting in Vilnius to mark the anniversary of the day on which Hitler "traded" Lithuania to the Soviet sphere of influence in 1939. The League had asked the administration of the city of Vilnius for a permit to hold the meeting, but the permit was refused on the grounds that the League was an "anti-Soviet" organization. Despite the prohibition, 10,000 people gathered in Gediminas Square, but as soon as Antanas Terleckas, one of the leaders of the LFL began to speak, about 500 riot police and troops from the Ministry of the Interior, wearing helmets and plexiglass shields, charged the crowd and began forcibly to disperse it. The police attacked the crowd four times in 20 minutes. The crowd formed a column and marched to the shrine of Our Lady of the Dawn; then most of the column returned to the square, where another violent confrontation broke out between police and demonstrators. The police struck with rubber truncheons; the demonstrators replied with stones and bricks. A number of demonstrators were beaten up; some policemen also were hurt. Ten demonstrators were injured and 25 were arrested.[57]

The violent police action greatly angered the public. The incident, after a summer of very peaceful gatherings, became a scandal. Songaila received blame because the police could not have been used against the demonstrators without his approval. *Sajūdis* demanded an investigation, and on September 29, demonstrated in front of the Central Committee building. At the 13th plenum of the Central Committee convened on October 4, Professor Bronius Genzelis, secretary of the Vilnius University party organization, declared that responsibility for the incident lay not only with LFL leader Terleckas, but "most of all [with] our Central Committee. It is slowly losing the people's confidence; it is responsible because it does not attempt to understand the process of development in our country." Genzelis ended his speech by suggesting that First Secretary Songaila "think over whether he is capable of leading the republic's party organization."[58]

The CPL daily *Tiesa* did not report Genzelis's implied suggestion that Songaila resign, but by October 20, Lithuania had a new first secretary. Algirdas Brazauskas, a long-time secretary for industrial affairs, was chosen to lead the party at the Central Committee plenum on October 20. Secretary Nikolay Mitkin was apparently eased out somewhat later, to be succeeded by Vladimir Berezov, a Russian with Lithuanian roots, whose father had served as director of a Lithuanian vocational school in the interwar period. At the massive farewell meeting of May 20, 1989, for the departure of Lithuania's deputies to the Congress of People's Deputies, Berezov said that he would not be "Moscow's *Gauleiter*" (regional governor in Nazi Germany, meaning henchman) in Lithuania.

THE HONEYMOON PERIOD

The founding Congress of *Sajūdis* on October 22-23, 1988, was held under the sign of peace with the CPL. The gathering was a massive festive occasion telecast live on the Lithuanian television network. Radio provided a simultaneous translation for the non-Lithuanian speaking population.[59] The emotionalism of the congress itself was heightened by a torch parade held at night, and by a Catholic Mass, celebrated in front of the cathedral at Gediminas Square, and attended by thousands of non-delegates. Never before under Soviet rule had such a religious event been allowed in public; neither had such an event ever been televised.

The congress adopted over two dozen resolutions that addressed a wide range of issues, from demands for the republic's sovereignty, to a request for help for Arturas Sakalauskas, a Lithuanian soldier whose maltreatment by the Soviet Army had become a national cause célèbre and a subject of a documentary produced by a Leningrad film studio.

The CPL was prepared for this gathering. In Algirdas Brazauskas, it had a party leader committed to *perestroyka*. A respected man and political moderate, Brazauskas was known as a defender of the republic's interests and was received enthusiastically by the congress. In his speech to the Congress, Brazauskas revealed that three days previously, that is, before his appointment as first secretary was announced, he had seen Gorbachev. Brazauskas reported that the General Secretary sent greetings to the Lithuanian people and that he considered *Sąjūdis* a "positive" force for *perestroyka*. The party leader opined that a single party system has room for societal associations. He admitted that the CPL had made mistakes concerning the *Sąjūdis*, but that a "more objective" evaluation had emerged in the last two Central Committee plenums. In appealing to the congress, he asserted that "on matters of principle we think alike."[60] Therefore, the CPL and *Sąjūdis* should be able to cooperate. Brazauskas urged discussions.

Brazauskas reminded his audience how far the CPL already had gone to meet the public's demands as expressed by *Sąjūdis*. The use of traditional national symbols had already been authorized, but in a more substantive move, on October 21—a day before the congress convened—the Presidium of the republic's Supreme Soviet passed a decree that rehabilitated all, not just some, deportees from 1941-52 and ordered compensation for "economic damages" inflicted upon them at the time.[61] Moreover, in a press conference with foreign and Soviet journalists held on the eve of the congress, Brazauskas praised the Church's contribution to *perestroyka*, and Lionginas Šepetys announced that St. Casimir church in Vilnius, which had been converted into a museum of atheism, was to be returned to religious use and proposed that the Vilnius cathedral—which had been transformed into an art museum—be shared by the government and the Church.[62] (During the congress, however, because Cardinal Sladkevičius did not like that idea, an announcement was made that the cathedral would be returned to the Church.) Brazauskas also promised reconstruction of the monument of three crosses that towered over Vilnius until 1951, when it was dynamited. The monument was erected in 1916 to commemorate the early Christian martyrs in Lithuania. The promise pleased the Lithuanian as well as Polish population. It was fulfilled in June, 1989.

The party's moves were well-received, although, because they came late, the CPL did not get much credit for this welcome shift in policy. The credit, by and large, went to *Sąjūdis*, which had requested such changes. Yet, *Sąjūdis* and the party seemed to share similar political views on a number of important issues, namely, the desirability of economic autonomy, revision of the republic's constitution, and some aspects of the new national electoral law.

However, the euphoria and the era of good feeling the congress had generated lasted no longer than six weeks. Disagreement emerged over the concept of sovereignty and, more specifically, over the tactics to achieve it. Ultimately, the rupture was caused by the Kremlin. A brief review of the proposals for economic autonomy and the proposals for changes in the constitution will help elucidate the new conflict.

On October 5, *Tiesa* published the "principles" for the organization of the republic's economic self-government. These principles had been agreed on September 21-23 at a meeting in Riga of the chiefs of state planning agencies and the economists of the academies of sciences of all three Baltic republics.[63] The document was a result of inputs by economists close to all the Baltic popular fronts as well as by official government agencies. The Baltic statement also addressed the issues of sovereignty and federalism, thus affecting the newly drafted revision of the Lithuanian constitution (on this last point, see below).

The Baltic model radically differed from Moscow's basic requirements for revised economic management in the republics. The Balts proposed—contrary to all-Union provisions—that the title to all land, mineral resources, outer shelf, forests, and space in their territory belong to the republics. Management, regulation, and use of these resources were to be decided by republic supreme soviets, not by Moscow.[64] Banks, enterprises, transportation, energy industries, and communications networks were no longer to be subordinated to central management. The government in Moscow, according to this model, would manage only defense industries, which would be run on the basis of long-term contracts between the republic governments and the all-Union government.

The central government in Moscow was to have only delegated powers, which would cover defense and foreign relations. Certain deductions would be made from republic budgets to finance their operation. The republics would also share in the financing of other programs common to the entire country or to several republics.

Republic jurisdiction would extend to all local government and to questions of economic management. Such jurisdiction would cover economic policies; republic and local budgeting; social, economic and demographic development; taxation; prices; wages; and incentives. Republics further would have the power to control banks and circulation of money, to establish currency, and to set rates of exchange. The ruble would still be acceptable as common currency in the all-Union market. Republics would independently decide all questions of international economic activity.

These "principles' were endorsed by the *Sąjūdis* congress. They also enjoyed the party's support because the chairman of the state planning committee obviously could not have signed the Riga agreement without the CPL's sanction.

In addition to the document outlining the principles of desired economic organization, *Sajŭdis* and the party also had to consider a draft of a new Lithuanian constitution. This draft was prepared by a group of scholars under the sponsorship of the Lithuanian Academy of Sciences for the purpose of establishing a legal framework for the new economic model and to reflect changes necessitated by *perestroyka* in the political, social and cultural spheres. The first draft was completed on September 21; a second, amended draft was approved by the Diet of *Sajŭdis* on November 13.[65]   These two drafts contained some interesting differences; for example, only the second draft mentioned the party at all, although not in a "vanguard" role. The second draft also assumed the existence of private schools that would not be bound by the legal separation of church and school.

On the question of sovereignty, the second draft was more precise and direct. The legal basis of relations with Moscow's central government and with republics would be contractual. Defense, foreign affairs, and all-Union budgets would belong to a "mixed" jurisdiction; delegation of these functions could be withdrawn from the center "if the activities of the USSR organs contradicted the interests of the Lithuanian SSR." Lithuania would have the right to secede. Article 70 provided that Soviet laws would be valid only if they did not "contradict the constitution of the Lithuanian SSR." This draft was submitted to the Supreme Soviet of the republic with an expectation that it would be considered at its November 17 meeting.

Finally, yet another item of immediate importance was Gorbachev's proposed amendments to the USSR constitution and the draft of the new electoral law. The *Sajŭdis* Diet resolved, on November 13, that these amendments were "undemocratic and contrary to the spirit of the 19th Party Conference" and therefore ought to be rejected. Similarly, *Sajŭdis* argued that the electoral law was an "undemocratic" document, because it did not "guarantee equal voting rights to people nor equal representation of republics but instead strengthens the bureaucratic system of governance."[66]   *Sajŭdis* held that the highest representative institution in the USSR ought to be composed of an equal number of deputies from each union republic, elected by universal and direct suffrage.

The strong criticism represented the culmination of furious efforts by *Sajŭdis* to persuade Gorbachev that it was imperative to postpone consideration of his proposals.   On November 2, *Sajŭdis* sent Gorbachev a telegram asking postponement.   On November 8, representatives of all three Baltic popular fronts met in Riga where they articulated opposition to the constitutional amendments, defined the legal guarantees needed for economic autonomy, and decided to appeal to the people to sign a massive petition to the Kremlin. On this occasion, the three movements restated their support for the Soviet Union as a whole.[67]

On November 9, *Sąjūdis* leaders met with First Secretary Brazauskas and other top republican officials. It seems that these officials did not advocate an outright rejection of the amendments but rather a postponement of their consideration. That evening on television, *Sąjūdis* speakers appealed for signatures to a petition demanding that the consideration of the proposed amendments be postponed. The appeal was made after reading and discussing the declaration agreed in Riga. Within a week, *Sąjūdis* collected 1.8 million signatures. As Jonas Mikelinskas later said, this petition was really a popular referendum on the question of independence from Moscow.[68] Some 75 percent of the republic's adult population supported postponement.

Party leader Brazauskas and most of his colleagues supported economic autonomy and shared many of *Sąjūdis*'s criticisms of Moscow's constitutional amendments and the proposed electoral law. In the presence of CPSU Politburo member Nikolay Slyun'kov, Brazauskas blamed the republic's increasing economic difficulties on the central ministries and insisted that only the economic independence of the republic could facilitate economic recovery.[69] Brazauskas also agreed with *Sąjūdis* that Gorbachev's proposed amendments betrayed "a tendency to seek further centralization of government and economic management" and suggested that their adoption would create additional difficulties for the promised expansion of union-republic rights. He called the new centralism "impermissible."

Brazauskas also criticized the electoral system.[70] Like the *Sąjūdis* leaders, he suggested that the announced procedures and rules would "practically" eliminate direct and secret elections. He thought it regrettable and unfair that the republic's representation in the Council of Nationalities of the USSR Supreme Soviet would be reduced to seven. Brazauskas criticized as well the rules governing election of delegates to the Congress of People's Deputies from social organizations of all-Union status were allowed to elect delegates from the republics (via their branches in the republics), and not those headquartered in the republics.

RUPTURE OF CONSENSUS

The CPL's support for the revision of Lithuania's constitution must have been very fragile because it quickly crumbled under pressure from Moscow. As noted earlier, the Kremlin had become concerned with Baltic developments in the summer of 1988. Moscow's anxieties sharply increased after the Riga agreement of September 21-22 on the principles of Baltic economic autonomy. Although Gorbachev averred that the Lithuanian developments were a "normal" part of the *perestroyka* process,[71] organized opposition to Gorbachev's constitutional amendments, it seems, alarmed the Kremlin.

Two days after the beginning of the campaign for the petition to postpone consideration of changes in the USSR constitution, three Politburo members arrived in Tallinn, Riga, and Vilnius, respectively, to restrain Baltic opposition.

Victor Chebrikov visited Estonia, Vladimir Medvedev went to Latvia, and Nikolay Slyun'kov visited Lithuania. Slyun'kov was not as direct as Chebrikov was in Estonia—most likely because he found more cautious attitudes among Lithuanian party leaders—but he publicly warned against "overemphasizing" national concerns. Socialist pluralism could tolerate diversity of views only if it strengthened "socialism instead of ruining it." Renewal was possible only if reform did not weaken "the unity of republics," but reinforced it.[72]

On November 17, the Estonian Supreme Soviet adopted amendments to the republic's constitution according to which all-Union legislation would come into force in Estonia only after it had been ratified by the Estonian Supreme Soviet. Brazauskas was immediately called to Moscow to be warned against following Estonia's example. Brazauskas very likely met with the Politburo "experts" on the Baltics, namely Slyun'kov, Chebrikov, and Medvedev. Gorbachev was on a state visit to India at the time.

The Lithuanian party acceded to Moscow's demands. To be sure, at its November 18 session, Lithuania's Supreme Soviet changed Articles 77, 168, and 169 of the constitution to make Lithuanian the official language and to legalize the old flag and anthem. The legislature also counseled the USSR Supreme Soviet to postpone consideration of amendments to the all-Union constitution until republics had rewritten their own constitutions, and it criticized Gorbachev's electoral law. However, the Lithuanian Supreme Soviet refused to declare Lithuanian law sovereign.[73] The republic's Supreme Soviet did not reject outright the needed revision of the Lithuanian constitution but skirted the issue. Chairman of the Supreme Soviet Lionginas Šepetys simply refused to accept motions to revise Articles 11, 37, and 70 of the current constitution.[74]

Representatives of *Sajŭdis* who attended the session were incensed and angry. The crowd outside the Supreme Soviet building, which was waiting in a festive mood for the anticipated declaration of sovereignty, became furious after learning of the decision. Deputies emerging from the building were treated with hostility. TASS poured salt into the Lithuanian wound by reporting that the Lithuanians "rejected" the Estonian proposal. Denials by *Sajŭdis* and by the republic's leaders, including Brazauskas, could not correct the distortion spread in the all-Union media. For the supporters of reforms, the Supreme Soviet's decision meant "betrayal of Estonia," a "stab in the back to Estonia," and even "treason." The decisions on the Lithuanian language, flag, and anthem were no consolation.

Brazauskas tried to repair the damage. On November 19, in a dramatic television speech that he reportedly had great difficulty in preparing, the First Secretary tried to explain that the adoption of provisions on legal sovereignty and precedence of Lithuanian laws would have been "confrontational," and that in actuality they would "legalize secession" and indicate a "refusal to obey USSR laws." "The road to sovereignty," he said, "is extremely complicated, enormously long, and all our actions must come from a deeply felt sense of responsibility. Quick, thoughtless decisions would only hurt us in pursuing the main goal."[75] Brazauskas suggested that ratification of sovereignty would bring an adverse turn in "cadres policy," meaning that Moscow would send outsiders to manage Lithuanian affairs.

Brazauskas also evidently appealed to Cardinal Sladkevičius for help. The Cardinal obliged by writing a statement "to the believers" in which he expressed support for an "unstoppable" process of change. But Cardinal Sladkevičius stressed that on the road of change, "of great importance will be our own determination, resolution, tenacity, and unhurried, wise steps toward ever new achievements." This statement, published on the front page of *Tiesa* on November 21 seemed to endorse Brazauskas's plea for patience.

The decision by the Supreme Soviet shattered the newly established cooperation between the CPL and *Sajūdis*. The Party acknowledged that *Sajūdis* was not merely an auxiliary helper to the party or a lobbyist but a political competitor. "There is a contest going on," confirmed Brazauskas. "Sometimes [*Sajūdis*] must learn to lose. We [the party], too, sometimes lose."[76]

But *Sajūdis* did not want to lose. It reacted to defeat swiftly, loudly, and decisively. *Sajūdis* leaders quickly turned to lobbying Supreme Soviet deputies for a special session of the legislature on November 25, before the meeting of the USSR Supreme Soviet. *Sajūdis* gained the support of 57 deputies, but because the number was far lower than the required 117, ultimately the CPL leadership prevailed. *Sajūdis* then blasted the leadership of the legislature for "procedural violations" that frustrated the original vote, and censured three leaders of the Supreme Soviet responsible, in its view, for manipulating these procedures: Chairman Vytautus Astrauskas, Secretary Jonas Gureckas, and Chairman of the Supreme Soviet Lionginas Šepetys. Eventually, all three paid the price for their timidity. *Sajūdis*'s Council now vowed to use its political power in various forms of "moral" protest. On November 20, in a declaration of its "moral independence," the group stated that

> no political requirements of the situation can restrain the free will of Lithuania. Its will is its highest law. Only Lithuania can decide and execute its laws. Until this principle becomes a legal norm, only those laws will be respected in Lithuania that do not restrain Lithuanian independence. Disobedience to laws that violate our independence may incur juridical responsibility but they do not transgress morality.[77]

This strong reaction caused dissension within the ranks of *Sajūdis* despite the fact that the statement of "moral independence" was adopted nearly unanimously by an expanded meeting of the governing Council. Long discussions evinced unanimity on the goal of sovereignty for Lithuania, but they also revealed disagreements over its meaning and over the tactics by which sovereignty was to be achieved. To breach the emerging schism, which was immediately exploited in the official press, the Council adopted a declaration of unity, clarified the nature of membership in *Sąjūdis*, and elected Landsbergis president.

The Council agreed that its decisions were to be unconditionally binding on its membership. This action meant that obligations emanating from membership in the party or from any other institution would not override the decisions of *Sąjūdis*.[78] Thus, from its first real political crisis, *Sąjūdis* emerged as a stronger, more united organization, ready to do battle with the party using all legal means, and persuaded that political power lies in moral strength.

On November 18, the CPL won a pyrrhic victory. Actually, while winning in the Lithuanian Supreme Soviet, it lost in the country. It proved impossible to please both Moscow and the Lithuanian people. The CPL could no longer command support from all its members. It could expect support only from veterans, other orthodox Soviet groups, and from *Yedinstvo*. But the Russo-Polish group, too, was upset because of the CPL's support for the establishment of Lithuanian as the official language of the republic.

The party, however, needed help. In November, the Supreme Soviet in Moscow approved the proposed constitutional changes and the regulations for the elections to the Congress of People's Deputies. The CPL would have to win these elections. With *Sąjūdis* now in clear opposition, winning seats in the new Congress of People's Deputies would be an extremely difficult task for the Communist party of Lithuania.

To strengthen the party's starting position in the forthcoming electoral competition, First Secretary Brazauskas chose to continue the party's reconciliation with religious and nationalist forces. By then, virtually all political prisoners had been released. Christmas became a legal holiday. At the end of December, Commissioner for Religious Affairs Petras Anilionis informed Bishop Julijonas Stepanavičius that he would be allowed to return to Vilnius to resume his duties as administrator of the diocese from which he was banished in 1961. Soon to be elevated to Archbishop by Pope John Paul, Stepanavičius solemnly returned to his cathedral on February 5, 1989.[79] On the same day, the first issue of an independent Catholic magazine was allowed to appear with a print-run of 100,000 copies.

Restoration of patriotic Lithuanian traditions also continued. The Ministry of Education endorsed a project for reorganizing education into a "national school" system, philosophically different from the old ideologically oriented communist institution, i.e., one that would place greater emphasis on Lithuanian history and geography and not require instruction in Marxism-Leninism or atheism. This project, courageously explained at a Moscow conference on education, won supporters among educators from other national republics but incurred the wrath of central ministry officials in Moscow. Then, while celebrating the 70th anniversary of the establishment of the short-lived Soviet power on December 16, 1918, Brazauskas rehabilitated the "bourgeois" declaration of Lithuanian independence, which occurred on February 16, 1918, declaring—contrary to 50 years of propaganda—that it was a progressive event because it signified restoration of the tradition of Lithuanian statehood.[80] He also painted a rather favorable picture of independent Lithuania's development, emphasizing the progress achieved in education, culture, and the economy. This speech was a prelude to the declaration of February 16 as a legal holiday, which came on January 25.[81] Thus, this anniversary, whose commemoration was brutally suppressed by police in 1988, would henceforth be officially celebrated in Lithuania.[82] Ironically, the party again did not receive much credit, if any at all, for these concessions. The public suspected the CPL of seeking to co-opt religious and national traditions for its own purposes.

At the same time, the CPL also tried to limit *Sajūdis*'s emerging power and influence. This effort also failed. Speakers at a conference of the Vilnius party organization noted a worsening in relations between the party and *Sajūdis*.[83] Brazauskas admitted "disharmony" after the Supreme Soviet session of November 18 but urged "consolidation" of forces with *Sajūdis* to advance republic autonomy, for which Brazauskas judged the situation in the Soviet Union to be rather "favorable."

However, although Brazauskas spoke of peace, his colleagues in the party and government followed a different course. The *Sajūdis* bulletin *Atgimimas* announced that it was being subjected to censorship as of mid-December.[84] The state television network curtailed its cooperation with the reform movement. The government temporarily froze *Sajūdis*'s deposits held in a bank account on grounds that not all formalities had been met. Signs also appeared that the party might decide to screen nominations at the regional level for the Congress of People's Deputies, as provided by law. Fearing that the party might use this means to eliminate opposition candidates, *Sajūdis* warned the authorities to disregard the option Moscow had allowed. Newly appointed party Second Secretary Vladimir Berezov publicly labelled *Sajūdis* an "opponent" and a "critic," although he considered it a "positive" factor that prodded the party and government to make better decisions. Berezov thought, however, that *Sajūdis* lacked such qualities as *glasnost'*, democracy and tolerance of the opinions of others.[85]

THE ELECTION CAMPAIGN

In this climate of mistrust, *Sajūdis* and the CPL prepared for the scheduled electoral campaign. Lithuania was to elect 10 deputies from territorial-population districts, 32 from national-territorial districts and 16 from organizations. Popular electoral competition would decide the fate of 42 deputies.

Few doubted that the party's candidates would be contested by *Sajūdis* nominees. The non-party forces, however, were not united on the question of participation in elections. The Lithuanian Freedom League, the Christian

Democratic Party, and the Helsinki Group attempted to persuade *Sajŭdis* to stay out of the electoral process. The League considered the elections illegal because it held that Lithuania was an occupied country and, furthermore, the League doubted the honesty of the process. In the view of the LFL leaders, the party would not allow candidates other than its own to win. *Sajŭdis* rightly considered this view mistaken.

In the electoral campaign, *Sajŭdis* candidates were at a disadvantage. For the most part, the official media either did not cover their activities or did so in a most perfunctory manner. However, *Sajŭdis* candidates managed to compensate for these obstacles with hard work—meetings of voters in every town or hamlet, getting acquainted with the people, and listening to their concerns.

At first, *Sajŭdis* nominated candidates in all electoral districts against all party candidates, including against Brazauskas and Berezov. However, after the campaign heated up and it became likely that these two leaders would be defeated, *Sajŭdis* withdrew its candidates against the two party leaders. *Sajŭdis* positively evaluated both men for their views, as well as for their personal and leadership qualities. Moreover, *Sajŭdis* apparently did not want to embarrass them, lose the leading official spokesmen for the republic at the Moscow parliament, and weaken their power to negotiate with the CPSU leadership.

The party published its electoral platform in *Tiesa* on January 26. It expressed support for *perestroyka*, and opposed "anti-socialist" programs and "conservative forces." The platform promoted the plan for economic self-government starting in 1990, called for respect and mutual understanding in church-state relations, and advocated "pluralism" of opinions, democracy, and *glasnost'* founded on the "common values of mankind."

Sajŭdis could and did accept much of what the CPL sought. But *Sajŭdis* advocated private farming, regarding which the CPL hedged, and military service in national units stationed on republic territory.

The two platforms differed on the meaning of sovereignty. Interestingly, the antagonists shared the slogan "Lithuania without sovereignty is Lithuania without a future." Each side, however, understood the slogan differently. According to the party, sovereignty meant the

> opportunity of independently deciding all questions of political, economic, social and cultural life; realization of the right of self-determination by the Lithuanian people; preservation of national identity. Sovereignty means an exclusive right to our land, natural and cultural resources and treasures; our own constitution and the laws; citizenship, state language and freedom to maintain relations with the other Soviet republics and with foreign countries.

In its electoral platform, the party related the concept of sovereignty to the "concept of a Leninist Soviet federation." *Sajŭdis*'s views on republic sovereignty more directly espoused the idea of an independent state. "The

Lithuanian nation," *Sajŭdis* said, "has an old and strong tradition of statehood that it never renounced of its own free will; it therefore has the natural and inalienable right to reestablish independent Lithuania." *Sajŭdis* contends that the Russian republic and the other Soviet republics must respect the peace treaty that Lenin signed with Lithuania on July 12, 1920, recognizing Lithuania as an independent state. *Sajŭdis* called upon the Soviet government to publish and declare null and void the Nazi-Soviet agreements of 1939 and 1940, which opened the way "for the occupation and annexation of the Lithuanian Republic." With the establishment of a sovereign Lithuania, relations with the USSR were to be regulated by treaties and Lithuanian laws were to override all-Union laws on republic territory.

This statement was further augmented by a declaration of "spiritual independence" by *Sajŭdis*'s Diet on February 16, 1989.[86] In a brief statement, the movement's leaders said that although Germany and the USSR annexed Lithuania by force and conspiracy in 1939-40, "international recognition of Lithuanian independence is still valid." *Sajŭdis* stated that its goal was "to reestablish state sovereignty, not limiting progress toward it by partial achievements." The organization based its claims on Gorbachev's speech at the United Nations on December 7, 1988, in which he was perceived to have stressed the right of national self-determination. *Sajŭdis* further advocated social justice, humanism, democracy, and cultural autonomy for Lithuania's ethnic minorities. It favored "traditional neutrality in a demilitarized zone of Europe." It also supported universally recognized human and citizenship rights that give Lithuania's citizens the right independently to choose their own form of government. Thus, *Sajŭdis*'s platform made clear that the movement strove for complete independence from the Soviet Union, although it was prepared to accept some ties to Moscow regulated by treaties.

Concerned with the fortunes of his party in the election campaign,[87] at the next CPL Central Committee plenum on February 21, Brazauskas raised the question of how far *Sajŭdis* should be allowed to go. Brazauskas accused *Sajŭdis* of tiptoeing toward the policy line advocated by the Lithuanian Freedom League. He said that *Sajŭdis* had changed since June 1988. The Movement, the First Secretary charged, wants Lithuania to be involved not only in *perestroyka*, but also in "national liberation." This program raises questions, he warned, about "the prospects for further cooperation." Brazauskas cautioned that only common goals could assure cooperation and only unity could help Lithuania. Currently, "*Sajŭdis* is pushing Lithuania into ruin."[88]

The First Secretary then revealed the degree to which the party had lost control over the media, the youth, higher education, the Academy of Sciences, and even its own membership. Printing houses and the media behave as is they were not owned by the state or the party, he complained. We should stop, Brazauskas said, blackening and defaming the reputations of party leaders and the party itself, which now goes on in all the media. It is also time, Brazauskas continued, to stop excessive criticisms of the past. Laws should be passed punishing those who violate rules on meetings and demonstrations. He blamed *Sąjūdis* for ethnic polarization because it supposedly did not welcome non-Lithuanians and seemed to be incapable of dissociating itself from extremism. Brazauskas' speech was followed by others demanding a similar or stronger measures to reestablish control."[89]

The plenum reflected the bitter electoral struggle between the party and *Sąjūdis*. The party's words simply did not inspire confidence. It was also burdened by responsibility for past repressive policies when it acted as both the puppet and as the hatchet man for the rulers in the Kremlin. Revelations of opposition to *Sąjūdis*, to independence, and to *glasnost'* in the Central Committee plenum further impaired the party's credibility.

Why did the party threaten to muzzle *Sąjūdis*? Juozas Kuolelis, an old *apparatchik* dismissed from his position as chairman of the Lithuanian State Television and Radio Committee, put his finger on the main reason for the party's behavior. He suggested that the electoral campaign did not favor the CPL's candidates, and therefore it was not very optimistic about its chances for electoral success.[90]

The elections took place on Easter Sunday, March 26, an unfavorable election day for non-Communist forces in a Catholic country. However, despite the holy day and the boycott by the Helsinki Group, the Lithuanian Freedom League, and the Lithuanian Democratic Party,[91] 82.5 percent of the voting population cast their ballots. The level of participation in Lithuania was a little lower than in Latvia and Estonia, but very impressive under the circumstances.

For the CPL, the election results proved disastrous. Election casualties included two Central Committee secretaries, the chairman of the republic's Council of Ministers, the chairman of the Presidium of the Supreme Soviet, some ministers, district party secretaries, and the mayors of the cities of Kaunas and Vilnius.

Sąjūdis's candidates won in 36 of 42 electoral districts.[92] Because *Sąjūdis* did not contest the candidacies of Brazauskas and Berezov, the party could claim to have won only four contested electoral seats. If one adds those of its supporters who were elected by "societal" organizations, *Sąjūdis*'s total was even higher.

Sąjūdis winners included eight writers, several economists, scientists, lawyers, and professionals, and one worker. One of the movement's deputies was a Russian professional (Nikolay Medvedev), elected in a heavily Lithuanian district in Kaunas by a comfortable margin, and a Jewish writer (Yakov Kanovichus), elected in a run-off in Vilnius. The ethnic factor apparently worked for a Russian nominee of the CPL (Gennadiy Konoplev) in Vilnius and a Polish professor (Ivan Tikhonovich) of the Vilnius Pedagogical Institute, who was supported by *Yedinstvo*.

Surprisingly, the CPL took its defeat in stride. Immediately after the election, party Second Secretary Berezov explained that the party lost simply because the voters "categorically voted against the old times and the old order."[93]   In discussing specifics, Berezov said that the party lost votes because it could not shake off the responsibility for "old mistakes."   The CPL's last Central Committee plenum also scared some voters who concluded that the old times were returning.   Berezov further blamed the party's failure on its local organizations, which proved unaccustomed to seizing the initiative. Crediting the fervent commitment of *Sąjūdis* followers, the Secretary concluded that the elections were won by "those who went to the people."

Berezov was not pessimistic about the future prospects of the party.   The electoral campaign, he said, drew the party's and *Sąjūdis*'s positions closer to one another. *Sąjūdis* candidates, he noted, did not propagandize "maximalist" demands.   Moreover, in his view, *Sąjūdis* candidates became more realistic about the actual possibilities for implementing their election platform in Lithuania.

REEMERGENCE OF CONSENSUS

After appraising the new situation, *Sąjūdis* and the CPL quickly began to search for a new understanding.   Some newly elected deputies from *Sąjūdis* immediately asked for an appointment with Gorbachev, but settled for a session with Anatoliy Lukyanov, Gorbachev's deputy, who ostentatiously sought to impress the Lithuanians with his knowledge of Lithuanian culture and circumstances in the republic.[94]   They discussed problems of misinformation about Lithuanian events in the central press, the slow action on reform in Moscow, the Molotov-Ribbentrop Pact, and the Soviet socialist model. Lukyanov was anxious to know whether *Sąjūdis* recognized the party's leading role and advised the Lithuanians to concentrate on economic problems. He suggested Moscow's principles for economic self-management as a guide for action, although *Sąjūdis* economists tried to persuade him that the application of those principles would not stimulate the economy. The Baltic model was more radical than Lukyanov was apparently willing to accept.

Probably the first public indication that a new wind had begun to blow was an announcement by the CPL's historical commission that Moscow had come to acknowledge the existence of secret protocols to the Molotov-Ribbentrop Pact of 1939 and that the time was approaching when those protocols were going to be "denounced."[95]   Shortly thereafter, the public's curiosity was aroused by an article published by Lionginas Šepetys, the chairman of the Supreme Soviet and former party secretary for propaganda, in which he asserted that if the November 18, 1988, Supreme Soviet session were held in 1989, the results would be different.   He also spoke of a new status for the CPL and even of "party pluralism."[96]   A week later, on May 11, First Secretary Brazauskas, together with his colleagues from Estonia and Latvia, took part in a Politburo meeting in Moscow. Brazauskas revealed that the Politburo discussed the question of economic self-management and made an evaluation of the "events of 1939-40." According to Brazauskas, Gorbachev "understood" the importance of economic autonomy. Brazauskas was certain that the Politburo would soon do more on this question.[97] The next day the Presidium of the Supreme Soviet of the Lithuanian SSR decided to convene the 11th session of the legislature on May 18 to consider amendments to Articles 11, 31, 37, and 70 of the Lithuanian constitution. Ratification of these amendments would represent a declaration of republican sovereignty. Representatives of *Sajūdis* actively participated in preparations for this session.[98] It seems reasonable to assume that Brazauskas discussed this matter when meeting with the CPSU Politburo in Moscow.

Thus, the party and *Sajūdis* finally reached consensus to do what could have been accomplished on November 18. Indeed, when the Supreme Soviet met on May 18, exactly six months after rejecting the concept of sovereignty, the mood was at once solemn, happy, and expectant. The legislature easily approved the revisions of the constitutional articles, declaring that all land and resources in the republic's territory shall belong to the republic, not to the USSR; that Lithuania shall have its own form of citizenship and shall control immigration; that all citizens of the Lithuanian SSR shall possess all the rights and freedoms guaranteed by the constitution, laws, and international "legal acts"; and finally and most important, that only laws adopted by the Supreme Soviet of the Lithuanian SSR or by a referendum shall be valid in Lithuania.[99] Laws and "legal acts" adopted by the USSR would be valid only if confirmed and duly registered by the Lithuanian Supreme Soviet. The Soviet could also limit or reject such legislation. In fact, during the same session, the legislature declared invalid a decree passed on March 21, 1989, by the USSR Supreme Soviet that increased taxes on private automobiles.[100]

The Supreme Soviet adopted several other documents, the most important of which was the "declaration of Lithuanian state sovereignty." This document is a virtual proclamation of independence, and is one more indication that the CPL made further concessions to *Sajūdis*. The declaration averred that Lithuania first arose as a state in the 13th century and reestablished itself in 1918. "The restored statehood was recognized by many nations in the world," the declaration stated, "and also by Soviet Russia, which renounced all claims to the Lithuanian state and territory by a treaty signed with Lithuania in 1920."[101] However, on the basis of the Molotov-Ribbentrop Pact of 1939 and the additional secret protocols,

> the sovereign Lithuanian state in 1940 was illegally annexed by force to the Soviet Union and lost political, economic and cultural independence. The government of the USSR currently ignores even the goal of economic independence of the republic.

Thus, the only way out of this situation, the declaration continued

is by regaining state sovereignty, which today is a clearly manifested goal of the Lithuanian nation and an inalienable right of nations that can materialize only under conditions of free national self-determination. The Supreme Soviet of the Lithuanian SSR declares that from today, after amending Article 70 of the constitution of the Lithuanian SSR, the only valid laws in Lithuania are those adopted or confirmed by its Supreme Soviet. Future relations with the USSR and other states shall be established only by international agreements. These aims of the Lithuanian people are directed neither against the rights of nations nor against their legitimate interests.

Finally, the Supreme Soviet approved a law on economic self-management to which the party and *Sajūdis* essentially had agreed in the fall of 1988. Thus, as of January 1, 1990, a new model for economic independence was to be implemented in the republic.

According to published reports, all these measures were adopted by a vast majority of delegates. Constitutional revisions apparently won unanimous agreement. Two deputies—the chief of the Lithuanian KGB and the editor of party journal *Komunistas*—voted against the Supreme Soviet's declaration of sovereignty. Three deputies abstained.[102]

The crowd outside the Supreme Soviet building waited for 14 hours for the deputies to appear. This time the deputies received greetings and flowers. A new wave of euphoria swept over the city.

Why did the Lithuanian authorities change their minds? Why did the Supreme Soviet adopt not only the constitutional amendments, but also a declaration of sovereignty that was every bit as radical as the "spiritual" declaration of independence by *Sajūdis* on February 16? What transpired between February 16 and May 18 to change the views of Brazauskas and the rest of the republic's leadership?

Some answers can be extrapolated from contextual comments made by party or *Sajūdis* leaders. According to Supreme Soviet Deputy Romualdas Ozolas, the authorities "had no other choice but to do what was needed by all."[103] In other words, they had to accede to the demands of the majority, which expressed its will in the March elections.

Other, more specific factors may explain the evolution in the CPL's thinking from November to May. First, the party finally faced the fact that the movement for *perestroyka* had changed into a movement for "national rebirth," whose goal was sovereignty.[104]

Second, the votes were a reaction to Moscow's indifference to Lithuania's quest for economic independence. Neither the central authorities nor most Soviet economists wanted to hear about the Lithuanian plan; neither did the central press open its pages for explanations of the plan by Lithuanian specialists.[105] The Lithuanian government addressed Moscow four times in the previous six months on this question, and it was rebuffed each time. Thus, "Lithuania was forced to take the steering wheel in its own hands."[106] Central authorities apparently felt threatened by the proposed changes, so they disputed the expected effectiveness of such reforms.

Third, some leaders foresaw a possible reemergence of "dogmatism" and assimilationist nationality policies that would again stifle the development of native culture.[107] *Perestroyka*, as pursued by Moscow, was believed to be moving too slowly to avoid setbacks. Thus, Moscow needed to be pushed, and the CPL leaders believed that they had better push for independence while circumstances in Moscow favored its success. It also was noted that Estonia's declaration of independence in November did not have the repercussions threatened by Politburo member Viktor Chebrikov, nor did it endanger the Estonian party leadership. On the contrary, the Estonian cause became better known and respected throughout the world.

Fourth, the CPL leadership came to understand that only active and strong party support for the republican independence could ultimately restore the party's credibility.[108] Thus, the CPL sough to identify itself with the political will of the Lithuanian people.

MOVEMENT TOWARD INDEPENDENCE

Following the declaration of sovereignty, the people and the party made further concrete moves toward independence and toward greater political and social pluralism. Lithuanian branches of the writers', artists', and other unions quickly broke ties with the center and legally registered themselves as independent Lithuanian organizations. An Olympic Committee was established even before the declaration of sovereignty was adopted, with the hope that it would be accepted as an independent national organization by the International Olympics Committee. In June 1989, the Lithuanian Komsomol became "Lithuania's Communist Youth Organization," instead of being a branch of the "all-Union Leninist Communist Youth League." New associations and newspapers, which competed with those sponsored by the authorities, mushroomed. Ties were resumed with the emigration, especially in the United States and Canada.

The CPL could not remain unaffected by its low standing with society. Its current condition is abysmal. According to a poll conducted in May 1989 by the Center of Public Opinion Research of the Lithuanian Academy of Sciences, the CPL received a positive rating of only 22 points (out of 100), while *Sajŭdis* received 68 points, and the Lithuanian Freedom League received 15. Brazauskas, however, fared better (84) than *Sajŭdis* President Landsbergis (70) or Gorbachev (63).[109] The status and the role of the party became a subject of ever-increasing discussion in the press. Moreover, the party's primacy in the political system was rejected in the draft of the republic's new constitution originally prepared by the Academy of Sciences and then revised by *Sajŭdis*. The Vilnius University party organization proposed that the party itself renounce its leading role, accept the existence of other political parties, and seek to reorganize the all-Union party into an association of communist parties of the Soviet republics.[110] A secretary of a Kaunas party organization has come out strongly for political pluralism. "A multiparty system," he wrote, "would much better allow the expression of political interests of diverse social groups and more adequately would reflect the expectations and hopes of diverse nationalities."[111] He considers that "currently Lithuania is going through a transitional period characterized by political differentiation, which eventually will crystallize into political movements. . . . It is time . . . we prepare formulas for cooperation with other political forces in parliamentary conditions."

In the fall of 1988, Brazauskas condemned demands that the CPL seek broad autonomy from the CPSU or even become an independent party. However, he now has accepted the necessity for discussion of this issue and of the idea of calling a special conference to resolve questions about the party's status and role in society and to formulate a new relationship with the CPSU. At the request of many party organizations, Brazauskas wants the conference to discuss such issues as the party's internal reorganization, democratic centralism, and minority rights, and to develop a policy on such questions as a multi-party system and the role of private property. The party already moved toward acceptance of private property by approving an economic self-management plan with provision for private property and by sponsoring, in June 1989, the adoption of new farm legislation that allows private cultivation of farms of 10 to 50 hectares (22 to 110 acres). Hired labor will be allowed, inheritance rights will be guaranteed, and questions of farm sales will be discussed and resolved later.[112]

A party conference to resolve these problems is scheduled to meet in the fall of 1989. The Central Committee plenum on June 24, however, cautiously indicated that the party would remain loyal to Leninist-type socialism and would seek more autonomy, rather than secession from the CPSU.[113] Yet the forces demanding the CPL's complete independence are very strong and the outcome is, therefore, uncertain.

PROSPECTS

The Lithuanian developments of 1988-89 bear strong resemblance to Czechoslovakia's "Prague Spring" of 1968 and put the Kremlin in a similar quandary: should it use all available means to compel Lithuania (as well as Latvia and Estonia) to remain in the empire, or should it satisfy itself with less than imperial influence over the Baltic republics?

The lines in Lithuania have been clearly drawn. *Sąjūdis* reconfirmed its commitment to independence both at the historical meeting of Baltic popular fronts in Tallinn on May 13-14 [114] and after the return of Lithuania's deputies from the convocation of the Congress of People's Deputies in June. On June 12, *Sąjūdis* and its allies began a signature drive for a petition to the government of the USSR, the Federal Republic of Germany, the German Democratic

Republic, and the Secretary General of the United Nations demanding that "the USSR abolish the consequences of the Molotov-Ribbentrop Pact, withdraw its occupation forces from the Baltic states, and allow the peoples of those states to determine for themselves what political and social system Lithuania, Latvia and Estonia shall have."[115] Three days later, the republic officials appealed to the population not to sign the petition, because the international situation makes the demand for withdrawal of Soviet military forces "illusory."[116] Party leader Brazauskas expressed concern and "sadness," suggesting that such an ultimatum cannot be taken "seriously."[117] Nevertheless, on June 17 and 18, *Sajŭdis* spokesman Romualdas Ozolas went on television, without the CPL's permission, to appeal for signatures. Thus, the challenge to Soviet centralism has turned into a challenge to Soviet imperialism.

As was discussed above, when the question of independence first arose in the summer of 1988, Aleksandr Yakovlev derided the notion, claiming that the Baltic republics were not economically viable.[118] Gorbachev favorably greeted the *Sajŭdis* congress of October 22-23, but his response to the challenge of independence first came on February 14, 1989, when he said that "those who demand Lithuania's secession from the Soviet Union are either people consumed by personal and career ambition or they are simply extremists. They generally do not support socialism."[119] More recently, Moscow's attitude was indicated in the May 22, 1989, issue of *Pravda*, which contained an article by Reyn Myullerson of the Institute for Law and Government at the Tallinn conference declaration on the right to independence and its appeal to the United Nations as a "march forward into the past." In Myullerson's view, demand for sovereignty was an "anachronism," and confederation, moreover, was an obsolete form of government organization.

Moscow's negative attitude toward independence derives from ideological, political, and economic concerns. Separation of the Baltic states would further expose the failure of Marxist-Leninist socialism, a political system that the peoples of these republics seek to dismantle. Secession of the republics would also badly reflect on the Soviet Union's foreign image. Finally, although it publicly pays homage to economic decentralization, Moscow does not desire the devolution of actual control over the economy. Thus, the Lithuanians have been extremely frustrated by Moscow's attempts to thwart the Baltic economic proposals. "We constantly feel resistance from the central management institutions. Neither the Council of Ministers nor the State Planning Committee wants to understand the economic and political importance of these questions," Brazauskas said on June 24. Moscow itself has no constructive proposals. In the meantime, the "standard of living is sinking. Stores are getting more and more empty."[120]

General Secretary Gorbachev has recently hardened his position. Using the violent ethnic clashes in the Caucasus and Central Asia as an excuse, in a specially taped television speech on July 1, he raised the specter of the dissolution of the Soviet state. He clearly opposed Baltic independence, although he did not mention the Balts by name. In Gorbachev's view, "there exists now in the Soviet Union an integrated complex of people's economy based on division of labor and cooperation on a national, all-Union scale. All regions of the country are very closely interconnected." To cut these ties would mean "cutting up a living body."[121] He charged that demands for separation are demands for "economic autarchy" and "spiritual isolation." Gorbachev, in other words, believes that the needs of the empire take precedence over economic acceleration and modernization as the Balts understand it.

The peaceful revolution in the Baltic nevertheless has provoked the CPSU leadership to try to address the Baltic concerns. Gorbachev now stresses that a reorganization of the Soviet federation is necessary and that the implementation "of the principles used by Lenin as a foundation for the union of republics" is required to resolve most of the country's nationality problems.

Recently, two important concessions were made to Baltic republics. First, in June, the Congress of People's Deputies created a commission for the study and appraisal of all Stalin-Hitler agreements of 1939-40 concerning the Baltic states. Gorbachev chose Aleksandr Yakovlev to chair this commission.[122] The commission was supposed to report before August 23, 1989, the 50th anniversary of the signing of the Molotov-Ribbentrop Pact.

Second, on July 27 (one is tempted to think it happened in response to the new Baltic petition drive), the USSR Supreme Soviet endorsed the Baltic plan for economic self-management as proposed by Lithuania and Estonia.[123] The approval did not come without a floor fight, during which some deputies and government officials expressed fears that economic independence of the Baltic republics would be merely the first step toward political independence from the Soviet Union. The law authorizing self-management, however, will come up for passage by the USSR Supreme Soviet only in October.

The latter action justifies Brazauskas's optimism and uplifts the CPL's standing in Lithuania. It remains to be seen whether the recommendations of the Yakovlev commission will dovetail with the Supreme Soviet's approval of economic independence and will be used by Gorbachev to define a "special" place for the Baltic republics in the Soviet Union.

Internally, all of these developments are bound to affect the legitimacy and fortunes of the Lithuanian Communist Party and also to test the unity of *Sąjūdis* as a political force. The future remains uncertain, but *Sąjūdis*, Baltic deputies to the Congress of People's Deputies, and Gorbachev have all demonstrated the ability to compromise. Pressured by economic difficulties and the need for Baltic economic cooperation, Moscow may accept a status for the Baltic countries similar to the autonomous status that the Duchy of Finland had in Imperial Russia from 1809 until the reign of Nicholas II. However, the Balts would see such a status as only the first step toward full emancipation.

Notes

1. "Appeal to the Democratic Movements of the Soviet Union," a telefaxed statement secured by Lithuanian Information Center, Brooklyn, New York (hereafter—LIC).

2. *Komjaunimo Tiesa* (Vilnius), May 1, 1989.

3. *The Observer* (London), Oct. 23, 1988.

4. *The New York Times*, Sept. 2, 1988.

5. The best account of the rebellion in English has been written by Zenonas Ivinskis, in V. Stanley Vardys, Ed., *Lithuania Under the Soviets*, New York, F.A. Praeger, 1965, pp. 61-84; see also Seppo Myllyniemi, *Die Neuordnung der baltischen Länder 1941-1944* (The New Order in the Baltic Countries 1941-1944), Helsinki Societas Historical Finlandiae, 1973, pp. 72 ff.

6. See V. Stanley Vardys, "The Partisan Movement in Postwar Lithuania," *Slavic Review* (New York), September 1963, pp. 499-522; Kęstutis Girnius, *Partizanų kovos Lietuvoje* (Partisan Battles in Lithuania), Chicago, I Laisvę Fondas, 1987.

7. The Helsinki Group was established in 1976 to monitor Soviet violations of civil rights guaranteed by the Conference on Security and Cooperation in Europe in 1975. It had ultimately lost effectiveness because of the arrest and emigration of its members. The Helsinki Group was revived in 1988. The Catholic Committee for the Defense of Believers' Rights was created in the underground shortly after the election of Pope John Paul II as head of the Roman Catholic Church. It monitored and wrote petitions in cases involving freedom of religion. Its leaders were arrested. The members of the Committee were Catholic clergymen for the most part, but the scope of its work went beyond the Catholic Church.

8. See V. Stanley Vardys, *The Catholic Church, Dissent and Nationality in Soviet Lithuania*, Boulder, CO, and New York, East European Quarterly/Columbia University Press, 1978.

9. See his article, "The Focus of *Perestroyka* Is Man," *Pergalé* (Vilnius), February 1987, pp. 3-11 passim.

10. *Tiesa* (Vilnius), Jan. 29, 1988.

11. See the interview with General Stasy Lisauskas, the Minister of the Interior, in *Gimtasis Kraštas* (Vilnius), Apr. 7-13, 1988, pp. 1-2.

12. See Saulius Girnius, "Commemorations of Independence Day," in Radio Free Europe-Radio Liberty (hereafter—RFE-RL), *Radio Free Europe Research* (Munich), Baltic Area Situation Report No. 3, Mar. 24, 1989.

13. Ibid.

14. See *Tiesa*, Feb. 3-6, 1988.

15. *Literatūra ir Menas* (Vilnius), Dec. 1, 1987, pp. 2-5. Vitaliy Korotich is the editor of the liberal magazine *Ogonek*, and Riga poet Maris Chaklays is editor of the Latvian literary publication *Literatūra un Māksla*.

16. *Švyturys* (Vilnius), No. 24, December 1987, p. 8.

17. See Saulius Girnius, "Debate on Lithuanian History Continues," RFE-RL, *Radio Free Europe Research*, Baltic Area Situation, Report No. 2, Feb. 16, 1988; and "A Reevaluation of the Partisan War," ibid., Baltic Area Situation Report No. 5, May 20, 1988.

18. Ibid., p. 2.

19. *Sajūdžio Žinios* (Vilnius), No. 2, 1988, p. 1.
20. Ibid.
21. Ibid.
22. Ibid., p. 4.
23. *Gimtasis Kraštas*, June 9-15, 1988, p. 3.
24. *Atgimimas* (Vilnius), No. 7, Nov. 15, 1988, p. 7.
25. Interview in *Tygodnik Powszechny* (Kraków), Feb. 5, 1989, p. 5.
26. *Atgimimas*, No. 3, Oct. 15, 1988, pp. 6-7 passim.
27. Ibid.
28. Ibid.
29. *Lietuvos Laisvés Lyga* (Vilnius), No. 1, Nov. 10, 1988, pp. 1 ff.
30. Press release of April 7, 1989, by Lithuanian Information Center, New York.
31. *Tiesa*, Nov. 11, 1988.
32. Ibid., Feb. 14, 1989.
33. See *Gimtasis Kraštas*, Mar. 30 - Apr. 5, 1989, p. 7.
34. *Tiesa*, May 18, 1989; see also *Sovietskaya Litva* (Vilnius), May 16, 1989.
35. *Tiesa*, Feb. 14, 1989.
36. Ibid., July 2, 1989.
37. Ibid., July 11, 1989.
38. See Vardys, *The Catholic Church. . .* , pp. 89-127.
39. *Gimtasis Kraštas*, May 11-17, 1989, p. 4.
40. *Atgimimas*, No. 8, Nov. 22, 1988, p. 8, and No. 9, Nov. 29, 1988, p. 4.
41. *Tygodnik Powszechny*, Feb. 5, 1989, p. 5.
42. Justas Paleckis, former Soviet diplomat and current CPL Central Committee division chief for ideology, in *Kamjuanimo Tiesa*, May 19, 1989, p. 4.
43. Text in *Gimtasis Kraštas*, June 16-22, 1988, p. 3.
44. *Atgimimas*, No. 1, Sept. 16, 1988, p. 15.
45. Ibid., p. 14.
46. In addition to those already mentioned, a number of other mass meetings were held in the summer and early fall. A series of rock music festivals sponsored by *Sajūdis* took place in July. An ecological rally on August 2 in Kaunas that was attended by 500,000 people requested a halt to the installation of a third Chernobyl-type nuclear reactor at the Ignalina power plant. It also demanded the expenditure of 100 million rubles on construction of a water purification plant in Kaunas. *Sajūdis* also sponsored a new ecological group, *Žalieji* (the Greens). On September 16-17, 10,000 activists formed a human chain around Ignalina. Finally, *Sajūdis* sponsored a boycott of dairy products to force better quality control. On these matters, see *Radio Free Europe Research*, Baltic Area Situation Report No. 10, Sept. 9, 1988, pp. 21-22, and No. 11, Oct. 5, 1988, pp. 19-21; and press release of the LIC, Sept. 19, 1988.
47. *Tiesa*, Oct. 11, 1988.
48. Ibid., July 2, 1988.
49. Ibid., July 9, 1988.
50. Secretary Nikolay Mitkin, ibid., Aug. 23, 1988.
51. Ibid, Aug. 18, 1988.
52. Ibid., Aug. 20, 1988.
53. Ibid., Aug. 23, 1988.

480 V. Stanley Vardys

54. *Sąjūdžo Žinios*, No. 33, Sept. 5, 1988, Sept. 16, 1988.

55. *Tiesa*, Sept. 14, 1988.

56. *Sąjūdžo Žinios*, No. 39, Sept. 20, 1988, p. 2.

57. Saulius Girnius, "Police Disperse Demonstration," RFE-RL, *Radio Free Europe Research*, Baltic Area Situation Report, No. 11, Oct. 5, 1988, p. 23-25; *The Chicago Tribune*, Sept. 29, 1988, *Tiesa*, Oct. 1, 1988.

58. *Tiesa*, Oct. 11, 1988; *Atgimimas*, No. 3, Oct. 15, 1988, p. 3.

59. *Tiesa*, Oct. 21, 1988.

60. Ibid., Oct. 23, 1988.

61. Ibid., Oct. 22, 1988.

62. Ibid.

63. *Atgimimas*, No. 2, Oct. 10, 1988, p. 13.

64. *Tiesa*, Oct. 5, 1988.

65. Text of the first draft in *Atgimimas*, No. 2, Oct. 10, 1988, pp. 7-12; second draft in ibid., Nov. 15, 1988, pp. 2-6.

66. See *Atgimimas*, No. 7, Nov. 15, 1988, p. 6.

67. Ibid., No. 6, Nov. 11, 1988, p. 5.

68. *Literatūra ir Menas*, June 17, 1989, p. 2.

69. *Tiesa*, Nov. 16, 1988.

70. Ibid.

71. Ibid.

72. Ibid., Oct. 22, 1988.

73. Ibid., Nov. 16, 1988.

74. See *Atgimimas*, No. 8, Nov. 22, 1988, p. 3.

75. *Tiesa*, Nov. 20, 1988.

76. Ibid.

77. *Atgimimas*, No. 8, Nov. 22, 1989, p. 5.

78. Ibid., No. 9, Nov. 29, 1988, pp. 2-3.

79. *Tiesa*, Feb. 7, 1989. Anilionis was replaced in early January as Commissioner for Religious Affairs by Kazimieras Valančius, who promised to correct mistakes made in church-state relations. Valančius said that henceforth these relations would be characterized by "constructive dialogue rather than confrontation, as in the past." See ibid., Jan. 13, 1989.

80. Ibid., Dec. 17, 1988.

81. Ibid., Jan. 26, 1989.

82. Ibid., Feb. 17, 1989. The festivities took place in Kaunas and were sponsored by *Sąjūdis*. Events included a solemn Mass, rededication of the renovated Freedom Monument, and a meeting of *Sąjūdis*'s Diet. Guests from the other Baltic republics and Lithuanian diasporas abroad attended. Except for Brazauskas, regime officials were not invited.

83. Ibid., Dec. 6, 1988.

84. *Atgimimas*, No. 11, Dec. 16, 1988, p. 1.

85. Ibid., No. 13, Dec. 30, 1988, p. 3.

86. Ibid., No. 7, Feb. 17, 1989, p. 1.

87. In a special election held in January to fill vacant seats in the republic's Supreme Soviet, *Sajŭdis* candidates won in all four districts. This election gave the CPL a bitter taste of things to come.

88. *Tiesa*, Feb. 23, 1989.

89. Ibid. For example, Kęstutis Zaleskas, first secretary of the Vilnius city party organization, denounced *Sajŭdis*'s February 16 declaration as "adventurist" and "extremist." Secretary of the Presidium of the Supreme Soviet Jonas Gurieckas argued that all city and local publications produced by *Sajŭdis* should be closed down, that *Atgimimas* be allowed to remain open but be subject to censorship, that enterprises and organizations should not be allowed to make financial contributions to *Sajŭdis*, that the law governing demonstrations should finally be confirmed, and that *Sajŭdis* should be allowed to telecast only taped programs.

90. Ibid.

91. The last group advocating left-of-center and nationalist policies.

92. See the election results in *Tiesa*, Mar. 29 and April 11, 1989.

93. *Komjaunimo Tiesa*, Mar. 30, 1989.

94. *Tiesa*, Apr. 11, 1989.

95. Ibid., Apr. 21, 1989.

96. Ibid., May 3, 1989.

97. Ibid., May 13, 1989.

98. Ibid.

99. Ibid., May 19, 1989.

100. Ibid., May 24, 1989. At its May 18 session, the Lithuanian Supreme Soviet also snubbed Moscow by electing Jonas Sabutis, a former high official in the republic's Procuracy, to the position of secretary of the Presidium of the Supreme Soviet. Sabutis had been fired from the Procuracy three months earlier for his refusal to become the "Lithuanian Vyshinskiy." (Andrey Vyshinskiy was Stalin's prosecutor in the notorious show trials of the 1930's.)

101. Ibid., May 19, 1989.

102. Ibid., May 24, 1989.

103. Ibid., May 21, 1989.

104. Ibid., May 3, 1989.

105. Ibid.

106. *Gimtasis Kraštas*, May 25-31, 1989, p. 2.

107. *Tiesa*, May 3, 1989.

108. Interview with Justas Paleckis, the new chief of the Central Committee's ideological Department, *Konjaunimo Tiesa*, May 19, 1989.

109. Ibid., June 16, 1989.

110. *Universitas Vilnensis* (Vilnius), No. 12, 1989, cited in *Gimtasis Kraštas*, May 25-31, 1989, p. 3.

111. *Kauno Tiesa* (Kaunas), No. 98, cited in *Gimtasis Kraštas*, May 25-31, 1989, p. 3.

112. On these measures, see *Tiesa*, May 19 and July 5, 1989.

113. Ibid., June 28, 1989.

114. The three popular fronts sponsored a Baltic Assembly in Tallinn on May 13-14, 1989. Party leaders stayed away from this meeting but did not deny it media coverage. Many guests and journalists from Eastern Europe and the West attended the meeting as well.

It proved to be a very important gathering, as the Baltic popular fronts moved toward greater unity. They fully agreed on their national political purposes, urged economic integration of their economies and pledged mutual help for resolution of problems and difficulties.

The Assembly adopted a number of crucially important documents. The first, a declaration of the rights of the Baltic states, demanded political independence in "a neutral, demilitarized Balto-Scandia." The second, a declaration of economic independence, criticized the failure of *perestroyka* to curb economic decline, control inflation, and maintain the standard of living. It also rejected Moscow's proposed general principles for reforming economic management as "incapable of taking the economy out of the crisis." This document again suggested approval of the Baltic economic model adopted in Riga on September 23, 1988, with economic self-management to begin in 1990.

In the appeal to heads of state of members of the Conference on Security and Cooperation in Europe, to the Secretary General of the United Nations, and to the Chairman of the Presidium of the Supreme Soviet of the USSR, the Assembly requested that the USSR "renounce and declare null and void" the Molotov-Ribbentrop Pact of 1939, and that everyone "heed the aspirations of our nations to self-determination and independence."

A statement on Stalin's crimes demanded that the Soviet government pay compensation to the victims of repression and that organizations that participated in the genocide—the statement listed the OGPU, GPU, NKVD and "others"—be declared criminal and that the perpetrators of crimes be made public and tried like the Nazi criminals at Nuremburg.

Furthermore, the Assembly demanded that Moscow disband the troops under the Ministry of the Interior and limit the use of the armed forces strictly to defense against external enemies. Finally, the Assembly sent a telegram to the Supreme Soviet and the Politburo supporting *perestroyka*.

The documents were released by the LIC.

115. For a text, see the press releases of the *Sajŭdis* Information Agency, *Draugas* (Chicago), July 18 and July 26, 1989. *Sajŭdis*'s allies in this undertaking are the Lithuanian Freedom League, the Christian Democratic, Democratic, Social Democratic, Nationalist, and "Greens" political parties; the newly established Lithuanian Workers' Association; the Helsinki Group; the Political Prisoners Defense Committee; and the Lithuanian branch of the International Association for the Defense of Human Rights.

116. *Tiesa*, July 15, 1989.

117. Ibid.

118. *The New York Times*, Oct. 28, 1988.

119. *Tiesa*, Feb. 17, 1989.

120. Ibid., June 25, 1989.

121. Ibid., July 2, 1989; *The New York Times*, July 2, 1989.

122. Commission membership is listed in *Tiesa*, June 4, 1989. The group included four Lithuanian deputies.

123. See *The New York Times*, July 27 and 28, 1989.

19

Nationalism and Democracy in Gorbachev's Soviet Union: The Case of Karabagh

Ronald Grigor Suny

On a clear night in the spring of 1988 twenty thousand people quietly marched through the streets of Erevan, capital of Soviet Armenia. For six hours they made their way reverently through the dark town, in disciplined columns, quietly chanting "Karabagh, Karabagh." United by an intense feeling of national purpose and encouraged by the new atmosphere of *glasnost'*, the Armenian demonstrators calculated that peaceful protests in support of *perestroika* might reunite with its homeland a small piece of Armenian territory separated from their republic. All hopes were placed on Gorbachev and the new reformist leadership in Moscow, which had repeatedly called for redress of the crimes of the Stalin era and greater sensitivity to the problem of nationalities. In the beginning the demonstrators in Erevan flew, not the provocative tricolor of the shortlived independent republic (1918-1920), but the red flag with blue stripe of Soviet Armenia. They carried portraits of Gorbachev, and their defiant yet loyalist placards warned the Moscow leadership that "Karabagh is a test of *perestroika*." Their mood was buoyant and optimistic, at least for the first weeks of the movement. Only with repeated disappointments at the decisions taken in Moscow and Baku (the capital of Azerbaijan), the distorted reporting of the events in the central media, and the consistent refusal to grant the basic demand of the Armenians did the mood in Stepanakert (the capital of Karabagh) and Erevan turn bitter. The enthusiasm for *perestroika* evaporated and was replaced by cynicism and depression. Within months of the first

---

Published in *Michigan Quarterly Review*, 28: 3 (Fall 1989), pp. 15-36. Reprinted with permission from the publisher.

demonstrations, hopes had been dashed, and the Armenian loyalists turned bitterly against Gorbachev. By year's end when the Soviet leader flew to Armenia to comfort the victims of the devastating earthquake of December 7, the hostility directed at him personally completed the estrangement between one of the most consistently pro-Russian peoples of the USSR and the leaders in the Kremlin. In a year marked by stunning international triumphs, his skillful direction of the Nineteenth Party Conference, and the isolation of his principal foe within the Politburo, the crisis over Karabagh—and the subsequent nationalist stirrings in other parts of the USSR—represented the most frustrating political failure for Gorbachev.

Unlike the national struggles in the Soviet Baltic, which have been largely constitutional and free from popular violence, the Armenian-Azerbaijani conflict over the autonomous region of Nagorno-Karabagh (Mountainous Karabagh) has been far more volatile, less manipulable by political authorities, and more subject to rapid and unpredictable escalation. At first seen in the Western press as one more example of nationalist protest against the policies of the Soviet government, and then as the latest expression of an "ancient enmity" between neighboring Muslims and Christians, the Karabagh conflict was in fact from the beginning a layered problem—in part structured by quite separate religious and cultural allegiances, in part based on the uneven social and political development of Armenians and Azerbaijanis. Rather rapidly the more perceptive reporters noted that the demonstrators in Erevan and Stepanakert were not particularly hostile to the central Soviet authorities or anti-Russian in their expression but were acting in the spirit of *glasnost'*, in support of Gorbachev's policies of *perestroika* and *demokratizatsiia*, and directing their particular grievance against the neighboring republic of Azerbaijan. A nationalist struggle for recovery of ethnic irredenta was combined with a broader movement for political reform and ecological survival.

Like most conflicts in the Caucasus, the Karabagh problem has a long historical pedigree. A mountainous region at the easternmost edge of the great Armenian mountain-plateau stretching through eastern Anatolia, Karabagh had been in ancient and medieval times part of the kingdom of the Caucasian Albanians. This distinct ethno-religious group, now long extinct, had converted to Christianity in the fourth century and drew close to the Armenian Church. Over time its upper classes were effectively Armenized. When the Seljuks invaded Transcaucasia in the eleventh century, a process of Islamization began that resulted in the conversion of the peoples of the plain to the east of Karabagh to Islam. These people, the direct ancestors of present-day Azerbaijanis, spoke a Turkic language and adopted the Shi'i brand of Islam dominant in neighboring Iran. The mountains remained largely Christian, and in time the Karabagh Albanians merged with the Armenians. The central seat of the Albanian church at Gandzasar became one of the bishoprics of the Armenian church, and the memory of the once-independent national religion was preserved in the stature of the local primate, who was called Catholicos.

Semi-independent Armenian princes governed Karabagh, called Artsakh by the Armenians, until the early nineteenth century when the Russian empire annexed the region from Iran. Through the century of tsarist rule Karabagh was linked administratively to the richer areas to the east, to the agricultural plains and to Baku with its oil fields. With the revolution, the Karabagh Armenians expressed their interest in joining independent Armenia, but the Azerbaijanis, supported by the Turks, forced the Karabaghtsis to remain in the new state of Azerbaijan. With the defeat of the Ottoman Empire in late 1918 and the establishment of British hegemony over eastern Transcaucasia, the solution to the Karabagh question was again delayed when the British prevented an Armenian annexation of the region.

When the Communists took over Baku and established the Soviet republic of Azerbaijan in 1920, the new government promised that Karabagh would be ceded to Soviet Armenia. Once again, however, expediency overruled ethnic self-determination when the key decisions were taken by the Caucasian Bureau of the Russian Communist Party (Kavbiuro) in July 1921. On the third of July the Kavbiuro resolved to attach Mountainous Karabagh to Soviet Armenia. Mysteriously, two days later, the Bureau reversed itself "considering the necessity of national harmony between Muslims and Armenians, the economic linkage between upper and lower Karabagh, and its permanent ties to Azerbaijan."[1] The region was to be given broad autonomy with its administrative capital at Shusha. Recently Soviet Armenian historians have insisted that Stalin and the Azerbaijani party leader Nariman Narimanov pressured the Kavbiuro to pass the new resolution. Narimanov, a contemporary Armenian version claims, threatened that if Karabagh did not remain in Azerbaijan, the Azerbaijani Council of Ministers would resign. The Armenian Central Committee protested (July 16, 1921) against the decision, but to no avail. Armenian party leader, Aleksandr Miasnikov, told the First Congress of the Armenian Communist Party six months later that "the last session of the Kavbiuro can be characterized as if Aharonian [an Armenian nationalist leader], Topchibashev [a Muslim nationalist], and Chkhenkeli [a nationalist Georgian Social Democrat] were sitting there. Azerbaijan declared that if Armenia demanded Karabagh, then we will not give them kerosene."[2]

For sixty years Karabagh remained an enclave within Azerbaijan, an anomaly in the Soviet system—the only autonomous national region with a majority that was of the same ethnicity as a neighboring Soviet republic yet was not permitted to join that republic. Discontent with Azerbaijani rule grew, as discrimination against Armenian language, culture, and contacts with Soviet Armenia became a persistent practice. Armenians believed that Azerbaijan preferred to invest economically in regions where its own nationality were a majority rather than in Karabagh where 75-80% of the population was Armenian. Confident that they were culturally superior to the Muslims, the Armenians generally kept themselves separate from Azerbaijani society. Intermarriage between the two peoples was extremely rare. Yet the repressive and dictatorial state during the Stalinist years precluded growing resentments and tension from leading to open protests. Armenians moved out of Karabagh over the years or migrated to the new capital of the region, Stepanakert. The city of Shusha, once an Armenian cultural center, became almost entirely Azerbaijani. In 1959 Armenians made up 84.4% of Karabagh's population. Twenty years later they were only 76%. Azerbaijanis were almost a quarter of the region's population, yet relations between the two communities were hostile. Karabagh Armenians indicated to the census takers that they overwhelmingly preferred Russian as their second language to Azeri.

With the end of the worst excesses of Stalinism and the establishment of a more tolerant regime under Khrushchev, political expression often took the form of ethnic nationalism. Through the 1960s Armenian discontent coalesced around key ethnopolitical issues: the genocide of 1915 at the hands of the Ottoman Turks, the recovery of national cultural themes in literature and art, and the question of Karabagh. The limits of permissible expression were continuously tested through the 1960s and 1970s. In Karabagh itself intellectuals, even prominent members of the Communist party, and ordinary citizens began to petition and write letters to officials. In 1960 rumors spread that Karabagh would be ceded to Armenia, but the Soviet government responded by stating that only Azerbaijan could make such a concession. In 1963, 2500 representatives of Karabagh signed a petition to party secretary Nikita Khrushchev complaining of cultural oppression and economic discrimination. Khrushchev refused to deal with the issue. Violence broke out in Karabagh, and it was reported that eighteen Armenians were killed and protesters at Erevan State University arrested.

With the fall of Khrushchev in October 1964 and the coming to power of the more conservative Leonid Brezhnev, dissent from orthodox political views crossed more frequently into semi-legal and illegal activities. In April 1965 the first massive demonstrations took place in Erevan to mark the 1915 genocide. The crowds called for "our lands," in Azerbaijan as well as Turkey, to be returned. The following year a small underground dissident group, the National Unity Party, called for the unification of Karabagh and Nakhichevan, another historically Armenian region now in Azerbaijan, with Armenia. Unlike Karabagh, Nakhichevan was very largely Azerbaijani in population, and while claims were raised on historic and cultural grounds, the demographic argument could not be made as it could for Karabagh. In 1977 Sero Khanzatian, a leading novelist and a prominent member of the Armenian Communist Party, wrote a strong letter of protest to Brezhnev calling for the incorporation of Karabagh into Armenia. There was no reply. In December of that year demonstrations once again took place in Karabagh.

When Mikhail Gorbachev came to power in March 1985, the gradual expansion of political expression provided an opening for the pent-up political frustrations of Armenians. Three major issues overlapped in a series of rapidly-developing events:

1. the growing concern over the environmental pollution of the Armenian republic and the danger facing Armenians from the nuclear plant at Metsamor, near Erevan;

2. the perennial issue of Karabagh;

3. the pervasive corruption and stagnation in the republic connected with the long reign of the party chief Karen Demirchian.

Throughout the Soviet Union concern over the environment has been tied to the growing ethno-nationalist anxiety over the developmental policies of the Soviet government. Since Stalin's First Five-Year Plan the central planners in Moscow have been able to override regional and republic concerns about the cultural or environmental impact of large-scale, rapid industrialization. In some republics, such as Latvia and Estonia, demographic imbalances have resulted from the in-migration of Russian workers to man the new plants located in their republics. In Armenia the threat of another Chernobyl was matched by the poisoning of the air by a mammoth chemical industry located in the Erevan bowl and the damage done to Lake Sevan by ill-considered engineering projects. In March 1986, 350 Armenian intellectuals urged Gorbachev to close the nuclear plant in Armenia. Those demands were raised again in two demonstrations held in Erevan in October 1987. This time environmental issues were closely connected, as in the Russian and other republics, with patriotic sentiments about the homelands and the defense of Armenian national rights. The environmental movement gave the Armenians a popular, broad-based issue that mobilized significant numbers of people but which did not yet appear to threaten political authority.[3]

At the same time the political leadership in Armenia was being undermined both from within and from above. From the time that Gorbachev came to power—with his campaigns against corruption and stagnation—the days of the Armenian Communist Party leadership, unchanged at the highest level since 1974, seemed to be numbered. Central party press reports were highly critical of Armenia, and at the July 1987 plenum of the Central Committee of the Armenian party the party organization was criticized for corruption and favoritism. The first secretary of the Hrazdan district committee, Haik Kotanjian, spoke of the growth of a "shadow economy," of falsification of reports, of bribery, and called for the resignation of First Secretary Karen Demirchian.

Inexplicably Demirchian clung to power, and the Moscow leaders did not decisively intervene. In December 1987 Demirchian gave a perfunctory report to the Central Committee that *Pravda* reported as "somewhat critical, mostly placid; in any event the speaker constantly radiated confidence that everything is going as it should."[4] Just as the meeting was ending, with the party elite rallying around Demirchian, a high party official, S. M. Khachatrian (chairman of the Party Control Commission), insisted on being allowed to speak. Through shouts from the floor and cries of slander, Khachatrian told of bribetaking in the police apparatus, the punishment of lower-level cadres while high party bosses went unscathed. The police and the courts were working with illegal, underground businesses, and all of this was overlooked by the party. Khachatrian argued that "a tightly knit group of people who owe their posts to the Party" were "opponents of restructuring" and were responsible for these problems. He was followed by Kotanjian, who repeated his charges of July and claimed that the situation had gotten worse in the meantime. *Glasnost'* and *perestroika* were making little headway in Armenia. "Just try to figure out from the local newspapers what is going on in Armenia," Kotanjian challenged. "You can't do it. The most urgent, acute problems are hushed up. People are forced to content themselves with rumors. In Erevan, for example, spontaneous demonstrations were held in defense of the environment. There was not a word about them in the press. Irreconcilable disputes flared up at a plenary session of the republic Writers' Union, but the official report distributed to the newspapers was laconically worded."[5] When he requested that Moscow look into the situation, Kotanjian was denounced by the meeting—accused of careerism, pseudopatriotism, political adventurism, and schizophrenia. Twenty-four speakers attacked him, and only the representative from Moscow tried to turn the discussion away from Kotanjian.[6]

Unified around Demirchian the Armenian Communist elite managed for another five months to thwart the exponents of *perestroika* who wanted to reform the party and replace Demirchian with a leader more in the Gorbachev mold. At this moment, with Moscow alienated from the local Communist leaders and a growing discontent with "business as usual" within Armenia, the Armenians of Karabagh took their fate into their own hands. A year earlier, in October 1987, there had been reports of violence against Armenians in Karabagh. Armenians and Muslim villagers in Chardaklu had clashed at about the same time that Heidar Aliev, the highest ranking Muslim in the USSR and a former party chief of Azerbaijan, was removed from his seat on the Politburo in Moscow. About 1000 Armenians had responded in Erevan with a public demonstration, just a day after 2000-4000 had marched to protest pollution. The situation seemed more fluid, the potential for change more palpable.

In January 1988 a petition with tens of thousands of names was sent by the Karabagh Armenians to Moscow, asking for a referendum to be held in Karabagh on the future of the region. Rumors began to spread that Karabagh's status would be changed. While traveling in the United States, several prominent Soviet visitors—Sergo Mikoyan, son of the late president of the USSR Anastas Mikoyan, and Zori Balayan, correspondent for the prestigious *Literaturnaia gazeta*—indicated that conditions were favorable for a solution to the Karabagh question. It was reported that Gorbachev had appointed a special commission, with thirteen delegates from Karabagh and four from Moscow, to look into the question. On February 13, 1988, the Karabagh Armenians began demonstrations in Stepanakert. Six days later they were joined by mass marches in Erevan. On February 20, the Soviet of People's Deputies in Karabagh voted 110-17 to request the transfer of Karabagh to Armenia. This unprecedented action by a regional soviet (usually nothing more than a rubber stamp "parliament") directly contradicted official party policy.

Through the following week tens of thousands of demonstrators marched in Erevan, bringing the city to a halt. Estimates of the crowds went as high as 1,000,000. Along with portraits of Gorbachev and Soviet Armenian flags, banners included appeals to Moscow for justice, calls for Armenian unity, and votes of no confidence in the Armenian government. The demonstrations were orderly and well-organized, but tensions escalated rapidly in Karabagh. Rumors spread that thousands of Azerbaijanis were marching toward Stepanakert, burning buildings on their way.

The central Soviet government was slow to react and seemed always to be two steps behind the accelerating events. On February 18 Gorbachev offered to hold a special Central Committee meeting to discuss Soviet policy toward the nationalities in general. The Politburo decided against allowing Karabagh to join Armenia, and representatives of the Central Committee, Georgii Razumovskii and Petr Demichev, were sent to Stepanakert to state the official opposition to any attempt to remove Karabagh from Azerbaijan. On February 25 Soviet army troops arrived in Erevan, and that same day four Armenian deaths were reported in Karabagh. The only concession made to the Karabaghtsis was the replacement of longtime party boss Boris Kevorkov, who had been compromised by his subordination to the Azerbaijanis, by Henrik Poghosian, a man who would soon prove to be a popular spokesman for the aspirations of Karabagh Armenians.

As the crisis escalated, Gorbachev intervened personally, calling for calm and reaffirming the proverbial "friendship between the peoples." He met with Zori Balayan and Silva Kaputikian, a well-known poet, and requested that they carry his message to Armenia that a moratorium on demonstrations be declared for one month while the party considered the issue. Balayan later reported that "Gorbachev did not suggest any repressions or the use of force." "He told us to return to Erevan and that he will do everything to put out the fire." Leaving with the impression that "we had reached our goals," Balayan spoke to the crowds in Erevan, the next day, February 27, and the protesters agreed to suspend the demonstrations for one month.[7] Demonstrations, however, continued in Stepanakert.

Obliquely Gorbachev had remarked to Balayan and Kaputikian that they should consider the tens of thousands of Armenians living in Baku. Oblivious to any apparent danger to his countrymen, Balayan had answered "So what?" Suddenly and ferociously, on February 28, riots broke out in Sumgait, an Azerbaijani industrial town of 220,000 on the Caspian. For two days mobs roamed the streets attacking, beating, and killing Armenians. By the time military forces were called in to quell the riots, at least thirty-one people, most of them Armenians, had been killed.

The reasons for the Sumgait riots remain unclear. They appear to have been triggered by a radio report from Baku in which a Moscow prosecutor had stated that two Azerbaijanis, one 16, the other 23, had been killed and others wounded in clashes with Armenians in Agdam earlier in the month. Armenians strongly suspect that local officials allowed the killings to go on for several days with little real effort to stop them. There are even suspicions of premeditation and prior organization. Whatever the reality behind the rumors, the dimensions of the hatred had only been vaguely sensed before Sumgait.

Though the hostilities between the two peoples are colored by their religious differences, they have deeper cultural and social origins. Muslims ruled in eastern Transcaucasia since the Middle Ages, and Christians lived as subject peoples until the coming of the Russians in the early nineteenth century. The great majority of the Azerbaijanis, however, lived in villages, poor, ruled by their khans and beks, subject to the religious instruction of their mullahs. The Armenians of eastern Transcaucasia, on the other hand, living in town, making up what little working class and middle class existed, benefited disproportionately from the economic advances during the century of tsarist rule. The former social dominance of the Muslims ended, and by 1900 Armenians held the key economic and political positions in Baku, Tiflis, and other cities.

Among the Muslims a sense of social inferiority in the changing environment of autocratic capitalism coalesced into anti-Armenian feelings. The Azerbaijanis remember the clashes in 1905 and the "March Days" in Baku, 1918, when Bolsheviks allied with Armenian nationalists brutally put down a Muslim revolt. They fear Armenian claims to what they hold to be Azerbaijani territory (Karabagh and Nakhichevan) and harbor deep-seated resentments toward Armenians whom they consider to have had unfair advantages over Azerbaijanis. The Azerbaijanis' perception that Armenians are a powerful, influential people close to the centers of Soviet power who have imperial designs on Azerbaijani territory were reinforced by the open demands for Karabagh. Velayat M. Kuiev, Azerbaijani writer and deputy director of the Azerbaijan Literary Institute in Baku, told a Western journalist that the Armenians "have better connections," citing Zori Balayan and Abel Aganbegyan, the economist-advisor to Gorbachev. "Lately the Armenian nationalists, including some quite influential people, have started talking again about 'Greater Armenia'." "It's not just Azerbaijan," he went on. "They want to annex parts of Georgia, Iran, and Turkey." Azerbaijanis have their own claims to Karabagh, said Kuiev: "There is a town there called Shusha which is the native land of many Azerbaijani writers and composers. Practically all of the Baku intelligentsia come from Karabagh."

The violence, he concluded, should be blamed on "inflammatory statements" by Armenians. "The Armenians have always been the first to start conflicts."[8]

Armenians had a different historical and social experience. Displaced from their former positions of dominance in Baku during the years of Soviet rule, Armenians either migrated to their own Soviet republic or contented themselves with a subordinate role in the economic and political life of the Azerbaijani republic. Yet they maintained positions of influence based on their skills and education and developed attitudes of superiority to the Muslims. Many Armenians hold that Azerbaijanis are a primitive and savage people, barely civilized by the Soviet experience, and the bloody days in Sumgait only confirmed these views. As a people that suffered genocide at the hands of the Ottoman Turks and the loss of three-quarters of historic Armenia to the Turkish republic, the Armenians were desperate to prevent the loss of "orphaned" Karabagh. Besides the memory of genocide, they remember the clashes with Azerbaijanis in 1905, the massacre of 20,000 Baku Armenians in September 1918 by Azerbaijanis, and the perennial grievances over Karabagh.

With Sumgait the first phase of the Karabagh crisis came to an end. The situation in Transcaucasia had been radically altered. The possibility of a peaceful transfer of Karabagh to Armenia now became remote, and attitudes on both sides hardened. The idea that a mediated settlement satisfactory to both parties might be reached was now utopian. Yet for the next few months the Soviet government, as well as the Armenians, sought some kind of "constitutional" solution. With the palpable danger of further violence, many in Erevan urged caution. But the crude attacks in the press on the Armenian demonstrators as "anti-socialist" and the failure to condemn strongly the Sumgait pogrom fueled emotions in Karabagh and Armenia.[9] The party leader and mayor of Sumgait were dismissed, and trials of the leading participants began, but Armenians were angered by official efforts to picture the Armenian and Azerbaijani actions as equivalent. The movement in Erevan split between those who wished to continue the demonstrations and those, like the writers Balayan and Kaputikian, who spoke out against continuation. To many, continuing the protests appeared to challenge Gorbachev and to endanger his policies of reform. The protest leaders decided to cancel a planned demonstration for Saturday, March 26. A peaceful general strike was called instead, but there was little response to it. When Soviet authorities arrested Paruir Hairikian, a long-time dissident who headed the Union for National Self-Determination and advocated an independent Armenia, several demonstrations were held to protest his arrest.

Tensions rose in May when news of the trials of those who had participated in the Sumgait riots reached Armenia. Talekh Izmailov, an Azerbaijani, was sentenced to fifteen years for beating Shahen Sarkisian, an Armenian, to death. Armenians and Azerbaijanis fought one another in the Armenian town of Ararat. Crowds gathered in Baku and Erevan. This time Moscow reacted immediately, sending troops and dismissing the first secretaries of Armenia and Azerbaijan.

Demirchian was replaced by Suren Harutiunian, a party functionary who had worked for six years in Moscow and could distance himself from the political "mafia" that ran Armenia. Kiamran Bagirov was succeeded by Abdul-Rahman Vezirov, a diplomat who had been out of the country for over a decade and therefore was untainted by the corruption in Azerbaijan.

The crisis simmered through the spring while Gorbachev consolidated his personal position within the Kremlin leadership. In March and April he fended off a challenge from more conservative forces who had instigated a letter from a Leningrad woman criticizing the anti-Stalinist campaign. In June he chaired the Nineteenth Party Conference, which endorsed much of his reform program but made little headway on the question of nationalities. On June 15, the Supreme Soviet of Armenia consented to the entry of Karabagh into the Armenian republic, but two days later the Supreme Soviet of Azerbaijan rejected the transfer of Karabagh. Since the Soviet constitution requires the approval of both republics' parliaments in order to change the boundaries of republics, the constitutional solution had reached an impasse.

Demonstrations and a general strike continued in Stepanakert, even after Soviet troops were brought into the city in June, and the local leadership of the movement, the *Krunk* (Crane) Committee, continued to operate. The Karabagh Communist organization voted to raise the issue of Karabagh's transfer to Armenia. The provincial soviet of Karabagh decided to secede from Azerbaijan and noted that the most acceptable action would be to implement the June 15, 1988 decision of the Armenian Supreme Soviet that consented to the entry of Karabagh into the Armenian republic. The Soviet Executive Committee was instructed to take up the question of renaming the region the Artsakh Autonomous Province. That same evening the Azerbaijan Supreme Soviet called this decision unconstitutional and declared that resolution of Karabagh's status was the prerogative of the Azerbaijani republic.[10]

In Erevan as well hunger strikes and round-the-clock demonstrations kept the pressure on the Armenian Supreme Soviet to declare its support for Karabagh's entry into the republic. The Armenian Communist Party, largely discredited in the eyes of much of the population, was losing authority to the growing movement in the streets, which while focusing on Karabagh also raised the issue of greater democracy in Armenia. Harutiunian's time was limited, and the difficulty of reforming the corrupt party apparatus seemed insurmountable. When Armenian delegates returned to Erevan from the Nineteenth Party Conference, they first appeared on Erevan TV and then went directly to a rally on the square in front of the opera. Thousands were present, and a stormy debate ensued. The crowd was dissatisfied with Harutiunian and other delegates for not raising the Karabagh issue in Moscow. The "Strike Committee" called for a general strike and demanded the immediate resolution of the Karabagh question, transfer of the trials in Sumgait to the USSR Supreme Court, and full information about the reported poisoning of female workers in a garment factory in Masis.[11] The crowd discussed closing down the railroad station and the Zvartnots airport. Demonstrators marched to the airport and occupied the buildings. Airplanes landed but could not take off. With the airport effectively in the hands of the demonstrators, soldiers and police moved into the airport (July 5) and began beating people until the airport was cleared. The marchers moved back toward Erevan and were caught between the airport and another column of soldiers. More beatings ensued, and one young man was shot when he tried to take a picture. Troops closed off the opera square. Thirty-six people were hospitalized.

The break between the crowds and the officials was complete. Rallies were held wherever possible. On July 9 troops again closed off the opera square, and the police suggested that the square near the Hrazdan Stadium be used for rallies. The organizers refused, and two days later a massive rally was held before the Matendaran, the manuscript library at the foot of Lenin Street. Speakers urged the people not to go back to work, at least not until after July 18, the date set for the session of the USSR Supreme Soviet on the Karabagh question. The Armenian delegation to the Nineteenth Party Conference was sharply attacked for not standing up for national interests.[12]

The Armenian Communist Party faced the most serious challenge to its authority since 1921, a challenge from its own mobilized people and their chosen leadership, the Karabagh Committee. Made up of nationalist intellectuals, many of them members of the Communist Party, the Karabagh Committee tried to guide the mass movement in peaceful and disciplined actions. Ashot Manucharian, an assistant principal of a secondary school, soon emerged as a leading figure.[13] He and his colleagues were deeply critical of the existing state/party regime in Armenia. At a rally in mid-July, Committee member Vano Siradegian asked the crowd rhetorically, "To what state can the top-official gangsterism that has been ruling this country for 70 years now, and Great Russian stupidity, bring us? This is not just a tragedy for our country, it's a tragedy for the whole world."[14]

The Karabagh Committee called for democratization, social justice, economic reform, and national sovereignty. Referring to itself as the "Popular Armenian Movement," the Committee announced its objective as "a sovereign Armenian republic, in the framework of a Soviet confederation, and based on de facto autonomy and respect for equality between the republics." On the eve of the Supreme Soviet meeting the Committee called for the re-election of party and trade union committees.[15]

With no solution possible on the Caucasian level, all attention focused on the meeting of the presidium of the USSR Supreme Soviet on July 18. Much of the session was broadcast on television, and the whole country had the opportunity to watch the first open discussion of the nationality question. G. M. Voskanian, vice-chairman of the Presidium of the USSR Supreme Soviet and chairman of the presidium of the Armenian Supreme Soviet, spoke on the history of

Karabagh, mentioning that it was Stalin who changed the original intent of the
Kavbiuro to have Karabagh and and Nakhichevan in Armenia. He noted that
if the resolution to prevent Karabagh's entry into Armenia is adopted, "it will
cause both pain and disappointment among the Armenian people, since the entire
Armenian people had expected that, in examining this question, we would be
guided by the directives in the Party conferences' resolutions." He called for
a compromise.

Gorbachev, who was presiding, challenged Voskanian. "What do you see as
a compromise? I think we must find a decision that does not infringe on either
the Armenian or the Azerbaijani people and does not put them in a situation in
which it can be said that one side won while the other side was defeated."

The chairman of the Azerbaijani presidium, S. B. Tatliev, noted that 200,000
Armenians in Baku had signed a petition expressing alarm over recent events.
"The idea of detaching the Nagorno-Karabagh Province from the Azerbaijani
republic is not justified politically, economically or juridically," he went on.
"The separation of Nagorno-Karabagh from the remaining part of the entire
Karabagh zone and from our entire republic would mean the deliberate
destruction of a historically evolved single complex." He requested that "all
necessary measures be taken to put an end to the disturbances and other
unlawful actions in the Nagorno-Karabagh Autonomous Province and the full
range of powers be used to introduce order there."

The new party chief in Karabagh, Poghosian, dissented from the views of his
party superiors: "The past 65 years have been years of oppression of the
province's Armenian population." Karabagh is seven times closer to the
Armenian border than Nakhichevan is to the Azerbaijani border. There are no
close economic ties between mountainous and lowland Karabagh, though
Karabagh is in general dependent on Azerbaijan. Poghosian's appeal was
echoed by Academician Viktor Hambartsumian, who attacked the leadership of
Azerbaijan for not taking any serious steps toward improvement.

For the Armenians the hero of the day was Sergei Hambartsumian, the rector
of Erevan State University, who boldly stated that an historical injustice had
been committed, and that part of the Armenian people, against their will, found
themselves in an autonomous formation that was created outside Soviet Armenia.
He praised the mass movement of the Armenians and their faith in the victory
of reason and justice, though he condemned the events at Zvartnots airport,
work stoppages, and hunger strikes. Gorbachev attacked Hambartsumian for not
having "a hint of compromise" in his speech. Hambartsumian replied: "We fear
another Zvartnots airport incident. We fear exploding bombs, weapons and the
like. We have to fear all this." Gorbachev warned against escalation: "There
are just as many Azerbaijanis living in Armenia as there are Armenians living
in Nagorno-Karabagh. Well, are we going to create an autonomous province
there too?" When V. A. Petrosian, head of the Armenian Writers' Union,
called Sumgait an attempt at genocide, Gorbachev bristled: "You know what that

word implies, the weight it carries. You are making accusations that you will regret for the rest of your life. "

More moderate was the position of Harutiunian, the First Secretary of Armenia, who called for compromise solutions: "Such options might take the form of placing Nagorno-Karabagh under the temporary jurisdiction of central Union agencies or the Russian republic, transforming the province into an autonomous republic, or sending to Nagorno-Karabagh special authorized representatives of the Central Committee of the Communist Party of the USSR, the USSR Council of Ministers and the Presidium of the USSR Supreme Soviet."

Gorbachev sided with the hardliners, like Politburo veteran Shcherbitskii, who declared that the situation was becoming "anti-Soviet" and giving comfort to foreigners. Coming down hard on the Armenians, Gorbachev said that the events around Karabagh are "a cunning maneuver on the part of those who want to impede restructuring, a maneuver designed to distract people from the problems that in fact must be solved in these republics: personnel questions and the struggle against negative phenomena, the shadow economy and favoritism." He opposed territorial changes, though he acknowledged that mistakes had been made sixty-five years ago when the state was formed. He praised Vezirov and said "we are hearing more self-criticism from the representatives of Azerbaijan and less from the representatives of Armenia." But his constant theme was the danger presented by nationalist conflicts to *perestroika* and democratization:

> In general, to put it bluntly, we are going through a time of trials. Will restructuring hold up in this situation? Restructuring demands the utmost solidarity of people, but we are being offered discord and national distrust. Restructuring demands democratization and openness, but here we see, under the banner of democratization, shameless pressure on labor collectives and on the population of the republics by irresponsible individuals, and even pressure on bodies of power, including the Presidium of the USSR Supreme Soviet. . . . Victory in this question can only be a common victory. . . . We regard any isolation of the Armenian population of Azerbaijan from Armenia in the sphere of culture, education, science, information and spiritual life as a whole to be inconceivable. Azerbaijanis living in Armenia should be surrounded with the same kind of attention, in exactly the same way and in equal measure.

The resolution of the Presidium passed: Armenia's request that Karabagh be joined to Armenia was rejected on constitutional grounds. It was acknowledged that the rights of the Karabagh people had been violated, and the Supreme Soviet was to send representatives to Karabagh to work with the representatives of Azerbaijan and Armenia.[16]

The "constitutionalist phase" of the struggle was over. The party's position was cool and pragmatic, intended at calming the situation in the short run more than arriving at a permanent or a "just" solution. The first imperative was to prevent a repetition of Sumgait, and certainly the effect of any resolution on Soviet Muslims was considered. But for Armenians such "even-handed" treatment was grossly insensitive to the injustices they had suffered from the Azerbaijanis. Both in Stepanakert and Erevan Armenians greeted the Moscow resolutions with hostility and depression. Much of their anger was focused at Gorbachev and his failure to assess the Sumgait events morally and politically. Rallies were held around the clock, and the Karabagh Committee declared the Moscow resolution to be unacceptable.

Many Soviet intellectuals sympathized with the Armenian position, and though they so stated in public addresses (e.g., Iurii Afanas'ev on his visit to Ann Arbor in October 1988) they were unable to express their support in print. When asked why he had not reported on the Karabagh events, the activist editor of the popular Moscow magazine *Ogonek*, Vitalii Korotich, told a Spanish interviewer:

> In my twin capacity as an honest journalist and a responsible politician, I find myself in a professional quandary. . . . On three occasions I sent correspondents there and they all brought me material that made it obvious that one side was right and the other was not. . . . Whatever I do, I prompt a reaction by the Armenians against the Azerbaijanis, or vice versa. . . . You see, I could repeat what other newspapers write in articles calling for internationalist friendship, but such calls will not be heeded.

Later in the interview he made it clear that he had been appalled by the events in Sumgait and said that "the struggle for democracy is a struggle against Sumgait."[17]

After the July session of the Supreme Soviet Moscow began to implement its solution to the Karabagh crisis along two lines: the "restructuring" of Karabagh itself and the containment of the growing nationalist opposition in Armenia. On July 20, the outspoken dissident, Paruir Hairikian was stripped of his citizenship and expelled from the Soviet Union. The most fervent advocate of Armenian separatism, Hairikian had, in fact, not been a primary force in the Karabagh movement, but had been marginalized by the leaders who rejected his call for independence. Two days later a long article in *Izvestiia* attacked the Karabagh Committee as a subversive organization:

> Their primary aim was to seize power through destabilizing the economy and public life of Armenia. Taking advantage of the fact that the previous leadership of the Armenian Communist Party Central Committee had let the initiative slip from its hands and had yielded its position step by step, the members of the "committee" created ramified organizational and political structures. "Karabagh sections" are operating at virtually every enterprise, institution and educational establishment, and

in a number of cases they have crushed Party organizations, councils of labor collectives, and management. Local police are collaborating with the Committee.[18]

The Bureau of the Armenian party noted that the danger of the Karabagh Committee to primary party committees had not been perceived and ordered the activity of the Committee to be investigated, especially the behavior of Communists who were drawn into it.[19]

While the Armenians had not achieved all of their goals in Karabagh, the actual policy of the Soviet state benefited them far more than the Azerbaijanis. It was widely conceded that Azerbaijan had discriminated culturally and economically against the Armenians in the region. Following the July decision, the central government sent Arkadii Volskii to Karabagh as its representative with extraordinary powers. Azerbaijani officials lost their authority in the region, and from July until a more radical decision was taken in January 1989 a gradual but steady separation of the region from Azerbaijani control was implemented. De facto Azerbaijani sovereignty over Karabagh ended, even as the enclave remained within the Republic of Azerbaijan. Both Volskii and First Secretary Harutiunian met with members of the Karabagh Committee to appeal for calm and time to find a more permanent solution to the Karabagh conflict.

Yet, with the most fundamental decisions about the eventual disposition of Karabagh postponed, the hostilities between Armenians and Azerbaijanis intensified. Azerbaijani refugees from Armenia drifted into Karabagh, and local Armenians feared that an attempt was being made to increase the Muslim population in the area.[20] In mid-September, a busload of Armenian students taking food supplies to Stepanakert was surrounded in the village of Khodzhaly by Azerbaijanis who attacked them with rocks and gunfire. Armed Armenians from Stepanakert went to Khodzhaly, and the ensuing battle could only be halted by the intervention of police and internal security (MVD) troops. Demonstrations started up again, and a state of emergency (*osoboe polozhenie*) was declared in Karabagh. Curfews were imposed, and all public gatherings banned. MVD troops cleared the streets.

In Erevan sympathy strikes were organized, and one million people gathered to hear Hrant Voskanian, the president of the Armenian republic, promise that officials would consider calling another meeting of the Armenian Supreme Soviet to discuss annexation of Karabagh.[21] The crowd decided to hold a general strike until the meeting was held. On September 22, troops and armed vehicles were deployed in the center of the city, even as the demonstrations continued. In an extraordinarily frank broadcast, a television correspondent reported that the local Communist authorities had lost control in Armenia and that the initiative was with the Karabagh Committee.[22]

Soviet news reports, usually hostile to the Karabagh movement, revealed a growing militance among its leaders. Siradegian told the crowds: "The chief mistake made on February 26 was to end the strike from a position of strength.

. . . We are not a whining nation but a fighting, belligerent one. . . . We must stop holding explanatory talks and speak only from a position of strength given us by our unity." Another Committee member, Levon Ter-Petrosian, called for Armenian military units in the republic. And Samvel Georgisian dramatically announced that Armenia stands "on the brink of destiny, and from now on let us not hear the word 'comrade'. . . . Moscow's stooges cannot rule Armenia, they are the enemy's local staff. . . . It has long been known that Moscow's interests are at variance with our interests. This means that we must openly declare war. . . ." Manucharian condemned the deployment of troops in Erevan: "Those who are sending the Army here again should know that the Armenian people regard that army as a colonial force."[23]

For another two months the Karabagh movement and the Soviet authorities coexisted uneasily. Demonstrations and strikes occurred under the eyes of the troops. At the same time soldiers were called upon to protect refugees and to supply food to isolated villages.[24] Agdam, an Azerbaijani provincial center near Karabagh, received 177 Azerbaijani refugee families, about 1000 people, from Stepanakert. It was reported that Azerbaijani villages in Karabagh were not being supplied with food, and food convoys under military guard had to be organized from Azerbaijan proper. At the same time Armenian refugees from Shusha fled to Stepanakert.[25]

In late November the situation began to deteriorate rapidly. Rallies were held in Baku when it was reported that a cooperative formed at the Kanaker Aluminum Plant in Armenia had begun the construction of a workshop in the health resort of Topkhana in Karabagh without the knowledge of the Azerbaijani republic agencies. On November 22, at about 5 p.m., crowds in the large Azerbaijani city of Kirovabad surrounded the city's party committee (Gorkom) building. The Gorkom called for help, and soldiers arrived. They cordoned off the building, but were insulted and threatened. Stones were thrown. A grenade exploded, and three soldiers were killed, others wounded. That evening more than 70 attempts were made to set houses and cars on fire or to "stage pogroms" in Armenian houses or apartments. The local police did nothing; the local party had lost control; and the army was forced to intervene, confiscating firearms and arresting 150 people.[26] A state of emergency was declared in Baku, Kirovabad, and Nakhichevan.

Nearly a year of Armenian protests and demands for Karabagh had, by the fall of 1988, mobilized Azerbaijanis to defend what they considered the territorial integrity of their republic. Protests were sporadic and violent until late November when they took on a more organized, mass form in Baku. Resentment about the silence of the central newspapers in reporting Azerbaijani viewpoints led the Baku printers on November 25 to refuse to print that day's *Izvestiia* and other Soviet papers.[27] Crowds gathered outside Government House, 20,000 during the night, 500,000 during the day. Suddenly, as if on cue, the crowd would chant "Karabagh." In Lenin Square bonfires burned.

Though the square was completely surrounded by soldiers carrying submachine guns, the rally organizers and hunger strikers maintained a vigil through the night. The hunger strikers demanded: transfer of the Sumgait case to Sumgait, arrest of the nationalist committee in Karabagh (Krunk), and the end of the construction in Topkhana.[28] The demonstrators called for the implementation of the decision of July 18, 1988—retention of Karabagh within Azerbaijan (but not in the *pro forma* way it has been retained) and protection for Azerbaijanis in Armenia. In the square people wore red headbands with "Karabagh" cigarette packs on their lapels. Green banners of Islam and even portraits of Ayatollah Khomeini were occasionally raised.[29] An unofficial organization, Varlyg, raised issues of ecology and the inattention to questions of the native language and history. Another organization called Ana (Mother) was formed by women to support the demands of the Azerbaijani young people, but to counsel patience and return to work.[30]

In general the Azerbaijani movement was led by workers, rather than intellectuals, and expressions of hostility toward the privileged could be heard. One of the most influential leaders was the lathe operator Neimat Panakhov, a principal spokesman on Lenin Square. In Azerbaijan as in Armenia, Karabagh was the initial point around which other social and cultural issues swirled. Among the complaints in Baku were claims that Azerbaijani workers, even those with families, were not given apartments when they came into towns from the countryside and were forced to live in dormitories. The targets of these resentments were the relatively privileged Armenians. As one newspaper reported, "It used to be that men coming from outlying areas to work at the plant would live in dormitories and their wives and children couldn't even get residence permits to join them. . . . Gradually, other problems snowballed as well. There was a demand that those responsible for this situation be found. And found they were—in the person of representatives of the Armenian nationality, who were said to be undeservedly using things that there weren't enough of for the Azerbaijanis themselves. . . . In that situation, a spark was enough to set off an explosion." Panakhov managed to have an audience with the new party chief Vezirov and to convince him to release more than eighty apartments to workers.[31]

An article in *Pioner Azerbaidzhana* applauded the school children who left school to join the rallies: "Classes have been canceled in most Baku schools. Groups of youngsters run to the square, not wanting to fall behind their parents or their older brothers and sisters. These wonderful children-patriots' anger, anxiety and resolve and the innocent and serene looks on their faces—all of which seem not in keeping with their ages—touch the heart, and we say with pride: 'Well done!'. . . . When the homeland is in trouble, when encroachments are made on its land, the descendants of Babek, Kyor-ogly, Dzhevanshir, Nabi and Khadzhar are prepared for struggle and exploits in the name of the people."[32]

With news of disturbances in Azerbaijan, the Armenian Supreme Soviet broke off its session. A round-the-clock rally was taking place in the opera square. People demanded that the deputies resume their session. On November 24, some deputies of the Armenian Supreme Soviet gathered at the opera and took up matters that remained on the abrogated session's agenda, including amendments to the USSR Constitution. The Presidium of the Supreme Soviet called the opera meeting unlawful and announced that the session would be resumed after the situation was normalized. The new violence in the countryside and the militance of nationalist leaders on both sides stimulated a new flood of refugees at the end of November and the beginning of December.[33] Armenians began to move from Azerbaijan to Armenia, many of them settling in Leninakan, Kirovakan, and other towns of northern Armenia.

On the eve of his leaving for his first visit to the United States, Gorbachev warned publicly that nationalist conflicts threaten *perestroika.* "We are one family, we have a common home," he said, "and we have accomplished much thanks to concerted effort."[34] He appealed for an end to confrontation: "The principle of a solution is: There should be neither 'victors' nor 'vanquished,' and neither side should bear a grudge . . . [Redrawing the boundaries] is impermissible in current conditions. . . . At the same time, one cannot justify the position of Azerbaijan's former leadership, which committed numerous deviations from the Leninist principles of nationalities policy with respect to the Nagorno-Karabagh Autonomous Region."[35] At the same gathering in Moscow Volskii, the representative of the Central Committee and the Presidium in Karabagh, reported to the deputies that the economy of the region was in

> an extremely neglected state, especially in the social area, with respect to the satisfaction of people's priority needs for housing, water and power supply, medicine and food. There is no excuse for the individuals who brought this mountainous area, where good, hard-working people live, to such a state. . . . A start has been made on overcoming the estrangement and artificial alienation of the Armenian part of the population from Armenia in the sphere of language, culture and education. . . .

Volskii was disturbed that the economic and social improvements had not lessened ethnic tensions:

> Before leaving for this session, we watched a television broadcast of an essentially anti-Armenian rally that has been going on in Baku in recent days. To say that it made a painful impression tells less than half the truth! It is a horrible spectacle that insults our world view. . . . I cannot fail to mention the openly irresponsible behavior of the mass news media—in both Azerbaijan and Armenia. For example, Armenian television offered the following assessment of events in Baku. I quote: 'These rallies show the whole gist, the whole psychology of the Azerbaijanis. There is nothing in their hearts but atrocities and killing.' Is it really possible to speak of an entire people in this way? The activity of Baku television also cannot be called anything but

political blindness, if not worse. In recent days, it has taken the same path. A steady stream of threats and insults addressed to the Armenians pours from the screen. They balk at nothing.[36]

Neither appeals to reason nor piecemeal reforms were adequate to stop the escalating violence in Transcaucasia. Incidents broke out daily. Near the railroad station in Baku, a crowd of 1500 people tried to beat up an Armenian. Troops intervened in incidents in various parts of the city; 417 people and 63 vehicles were detained.[37] The army was used to remove Azerbaijanis from Armenia for their safety. Some had fled into the mountains. A government commission for the refugees in the Caucasus, to be headed by V. E. Shcherbin, began operation in early December. And then nature intervened.

On December 7, at 11:41 a.m., an earthquake of the magnitude of 6.9 on the Richter scale hit northwestern Armenia, destroying large parts of Leninakan, Kirovakan, and almost the entire towns of Spitak and Stepanakert. A shallow earthquake with several heavy aftershocks of 5.8 and 5.2, it was particularly devastating to newly-built, prefab, and concrete slab buildings. At first it was thought that 50,000 had perished, then the toll estimate rose to 100,000, until it settled at about 25,000. Hundreds of thousands were homeless. With Gorbachev in New York and the international press spotlight on him, his decision to return home immediately carried the world's attention toward Armenia. Offers for aid poured in. A commission of the Politburo in Moscow, headed by Prime Minister Nikolai Ryzhkov, traveled to Armenia to coordinate rescue operations. The Karabagh Committee organized its own efforts at aid from headquarters in the Writers' Union in Erevan. A fierce competition between the official and unofficial rescue efforts began, and in the chaos of the first days the Karabagh Committee made its own appeals to prominent Armenians, like Charles Aznavour and Governor George Deukmejian of California, to organize relief efforts in Europe and America. In reality the Karabagh Committee had become a second government in Armenia, one with more popular support and credibility than the Communist Party and the Soviet government. If one accepts Lenin's definition, a revolutionary situation existed in Armenia: the old rulers could no longer rule in the old way, and the ruled were no longer willing to be ruled in the old way.

On December 10, the official day of mourning for the victims of the Armenian earthquake, Gorbachev arrived in Erevan. That same day hundreds of women, reacting to broadcasts calling for adoption of Armenian orphans by people in other parts of the Soviet Union, gathered before the Writers' Union. However well-meaning the appeals, they had failed to take into account a deep-seated fear among Armenians about the loss of their orphans, a fear located in memories of the loss of children to Turks, Kurds, and Arabs during the genocidal marches of 1915. With the agreement of the military commandant of Erevan, Manucharian spoke to the women and announced an agreement with the Soviet authorities not to remove any orphans from the republic. That evening a new military commander was appointed in Erevan, and the leading members of the Karabagh Committee were arrested.[38] The government had evidently decided to use the crisis as an opportunity to end the operations of the Karabagh movement and to restore authority to the ruling party.

While still in Erevan Gorbachev gave an interview, castigating the Karabagh movement:

> Residents of Armenia were standing on the street. I stopped, and we had a good conversation. The people were all worried, very worried. They were taking it hard. I shared with them the fact that I had been simply astounded by what I had seen, by the magnitude of the disaster that had befallen people. And suddenly, right here in Erevan. I was asked: What kind of relations are we going to have, what kind of dialogue are we going to establish with the unofficial organizations? Again, the subject was Karabagh. You know, I told them just what I thought, in rather sharp language, perhaps. First of all, I said to them: Stop. Look at the calamity that has befallen both the Azerbaijanis and the Armenians, look where they are being pushed and at the point they have already reached—blood is being spilled. Now so great a disaster has struck that the whole country, the whole world, is stunned by what happened in Armenia, by what has befallen the Armenian people. And here is a person in the capital of Armenia asking me what kind of dialogue we are going to set up with unofficial organizations. Only a person devoid of all morality could do such a thing. . . .
>
> I think that there is such a thing as a Karabagh problem. The problem has roots, and it has become exacerbated because at a certain stage the former Azerbaijani leadership took an incorrect attitude toward the Karabagh population, an attitude that was not in the spirit of Leninist traditions and sometimes was simply inhuman. This offended people. We condemn this.[39]

A new stage had been reached in the Karabagh crisis. The leadership in Moscow had decided that repression was necessary, ironically, to preserve the movement toward democratic reforms. As Gorbachev told a group in Erevan, "We are at the brink of a precipice. Any further, one more step, and we plunge into the abyss. . . . We agreed to let both sides think about how to calm Nagorno-Karabagh for a while." The use of martial law ended the worst outbreak of violence temporarily and gave the regime time to rebuild its support. Prominent leaders, like the head of the Armenian Church, Vazgen I, were recruited as spokesmen supporting the government. When Ryzhkov met with Vazgen I, the Catholicos reported that "everywhere in Armenia people are expressing feelings of great respect for M. S. Gorbachev, who, putting off all other matters, came to Armenia, visited the disaster areas and gave moral support to all the people. It is impossible to forget this."[40]

By January 1989 the Karabagh movement had come to a temporary halt, with the positions of the government and the committee completely opposed.

Gorbachev was firm in his refusal to change republic borders but equally committed to reform for Karabagh. Nineteen eighty-eight was the year he had been forced to recognize the nationality issue as one of the most serious on the Soviet agenda. In January 1989 he told a meeting of intellectuals that "at some stage we began to rest on our laurels, believing that all questions had been resolved. There was even a proposal to begin the virtual fusion of nations. At one time I managed only with great difficulty to withstand pressure from certain men of science who were trying to force this dangerous directive into the Party Program now in effect. . . ." He indicated that various solutions were possible, but nothing that leads to "the kindling of nationalistic passions" or "national isolation and exclusiveness." He favored the "national" but not the "nationalistic."[41] Most importantly, he would use whatever means at his disposal to preserve and enhance the prestige and power of the Communist Party.

Before his arrest in early January, Ashot Manucharian gave an interview from hiding to *L'Express* and wrote up his own account of what had happened since the earthquake. He noted his surprise that foreign news reports referred to the Karabagh movement as "narrowly nationalistic." "In reality," he explained, "starting from the question of Karabagh, the thrust of the movement quickly broadened into a democratic, anti-mafia campaign. And that is the reason for the fierce attacks on our Committee. The point is that the Soviet mafia is found within the political power structure." The mafia survives because of the principle of appointing officials from above and would be eliminated by real democratic choice.[42] For the Karabagh Committee nothing short of full democratization would be acceptable.

In mid-January 1989 Karabagh was placed under a special administration. A committee, chaired by Volskii and directly responsible to the central Soviet government, replaced the local soviet. This interim solution to the Karabagh issue dealt with one of the demands of the Armenians—the end of the 65-year-long Azerbaijani domination of Karabagh. The issues of full democratization remained. While the coming months may witness an improvement in the lives of the Karabagh Armenians and give the state more time to consider a more permanent solution, this temporary resolution of the Karabagh question places the broader issues of democratic reform and cultural development in Armenia more squarely on the table. At the moment it is still too early to predict whether the current policy of repression of the democratic movement will succeed in Armenia or whether, as in Poland, the government will eventually be compelled to open a dialogue with the popular forces for reform.

Notes

1. *Nagornyi Karabakh, Istoricheskii spravka* (Erevan: Izdatel'stvo Akademii nauk Armianskoi SSR, 1988). pp. 32-33.

2. Ibid., p. 33.

3. Elizabeth Fuller, "Is Armenia on the Brink of an Ecological Disaster?" *Radio Liberty Research*, RL 307/86, August 5, 1986; "Armenian Authorities Appear to Yield to 'Ecological Lobby'," ibid., RL 130/87, March 30, 1987; "Armenian Journalist Links Air Pollution and Infant Mortality," ibid., RL 275/87, July 14, 1987 [on Zori Balayan's article in *Literaturnaia gazeta*, no. 26, June 24, 1987]; and "Mass Demonstrations in Armenia Against Environmental Pollution," ibid., RL 421/87, October 18, 1987.

4. *Izvestiia*, January 6, 1987; *Current Digest of the Soviet Press* [henceforth CDSP], XL, 1, February 3, 1988, p. 17.

5. *Pravda*, January 18, 1988; CDSP, XL, 3, February 17, 1988, p. 5.

6. *Izvestiia*, January 6, 1987; CDSP, XL, February 3, 1988, p. 17.

7. Jackie Abramian, "An Interview with Zori Balayan," *The Armenian Weekly*, July 16, 1988, p. 7.

8. *New York Times*, March 11, 1988. p. 4.

9. *Pravda*, March 21, 1988.

10. *Izvestiia*, July 14, 1988, p. 3; CDSP, XL, 28, August 10, 1988, pp. 18-19.

11. *Izvestiia*, July 5, 1988; CDSP, XL, 28, August 10, 1988, p. 16.

12. *Izvestiia*, July 12, p. 3; CDSP, XL, 28, August 10, 1988, p. 18.

13. Other members of the Committee included his colleague, Samson Kazarian, a teacher in the same school; Hambartsum Galstian, a researcher in Erevan City Soviet's sociological research laboratory; Rafael Kazarian, a corresponding member of Armenian Academy of Sciences; Vano Siradegian, a member of Armenian Writers' Union; Levon Ter-Petrosian, a doctor of philosophy; Samvel Gevorkian, television commentator; Aleksan Hakopian, a researcher in the Institute of Oriental Studies of the Academy of Sciences; Vazgen Manukian, an instructor at Erevan State University; Babken Araktsian, department head at the university; David Vardanian, a senior researcher at the solid-state branch laboratory; and Igor Muradian, a senior researcher at the Armenian Gosplan Economic Planning Research Institute.

14. *Izvestiia*, July 22, 1988, p. 6; CDSP, XL, 30, August 24, 1988, p. 17.

15. *Pravda*, July 21, 1988, p. 6; CDSP, XL, 30, August 24, 1988, p. 16.

16. *Pravda* and *Izvestiia*, July 20, 1988; CDSP, XL, 29, August 17, 1988, pp. 1-11, 31-32.

17. *La Vanguardia*, discussed in Bodhan Nahaylo, "Vitalii Korotych on 'Undemocratic' Conditions in Ukraine, on Sumgait, and on 'Pamyat'," *Radio Liberty Research*, RL 400/88, September 5, 1988.

18. *Izvestiia*, July 22, 1988, p. 6; excerpts in CDSP, XL, 30, August 14, 1988, pp. 16-17.

19. *Pravda*, July 25, 1988, p. 8; CDSP, XL, 30, August 24, 1988, pp. 18-19.

20. Bill Keller, "Soviet Region Hit by New Ethnic Unrest and Strike," *New York Times*, September 16, 1988.

21. "Armenian Strikers Hold Rally," *New York Times*, September 21, 1988.

22. Bill Keller, "Parts of Armenia are Blocked off by Soviet Troops," *New York Times*, September 23, 1988.

23. *Pravda* September 28, 1988, p. 6; CDSP, XL, 39, October 26, 1988, p. 10.

24. *Pravda*, October 4, 1988, p. 6; CDSP, XL, 39, October 26, 1988, p. 11.

25. *Pravda*, October 2, 1988, p. 6; CDSP, XL, 39, October 26, 1988, p. 11.

26. *Krasnaia zvezda*, November 26, 1988, p. 6; CDSP, XL, 48, December 28, 1988, p. 11.

27. *Izvestiia*, November 25, 1988, p. 3; CDSP, XL, 48, December 28, 1988, p. 9.

28. *Komsomol'skaia pravda*, November 27, 1988, p. 2; CDSP, XL, 48, December 28, 1988, p. 11.

29. Felicity Barringer, "1,400 Arrests Reported in Tense Armenian Capital," *New York Times*, November 29, 1988.

30. *Bakinskii rabochii*, November 27, 1988, p. 3; CDSP, XL, 48, December 28, 1988, p. 14.

31. *Krasnaia zvezda*, December 24, 1989; CDSP, XL, 52, January 25, 1989, pp. 9-10. Panakhov was arrested in late December 1988.

32. *Pioner Azerbaidzhana*, November 25, 1988; *Komsomol'skaia pravda*, December 1, 1988, p. 4; CDSP, XL, 48, December 28, 1988, p. 12.

33. *Bakinskii rabochii*, December 3, 1988, p. 4; CDSP, XL, 48, December 28, 1988, p. 15.

34. "Address of Soviet Leader: 'We Are One Family'," *New York Times*, November 28, 1988.

35. *Pravda* and *Izvestiia*, December 4, 1988, pp. 1,3; CDSP, XL, 49, January 4, 1989, pp. 13-14.

36. *Pravda* and *Izvestiia*, December 2, 1988, pp. 1-3; CDSP, XL, 51, January 18, 1989, pp. 16, 27.

37. *Bakinskii rabochii*, December 3, 1988, p. 4; CDSP, XL, 48, December 28, 1988, p. 15.

38. Manucharian was released when he said that as an elected member of the Armenian Supreme Soviet he had immunity, and he immediately went into hiding.

39. *Pravda*, December 12, 1988, pp. 1-2; CDSP, XL, 50, January 11, 1989, p. 4.

40. *Pravda*, December 16, 1988, p. 8, carried the complete text of a 1000-word address by Vazgen to Armenian believers.

41. *Pravda*, January 8, 1989; CDSP, XLI, 1, February 1, 1989, pp. 7-8.

42. Ashot Manucharian, "How it Happened," *The Armenian Mirror-Spectator*, April 8, 1988, pp. 8, 10. This report was originally written on December 18, 1988. Manucharian himself had defeated a member of the mafia in the parliamentary elections. He was then offered 100,000 rubles if he would give up the campaign. Later he received death threats.

20

Dilemmas of Russian Nationalism

Roman Szporluk

The present state of ethnic relations in the Soviet Union, writes Aleksandr Zharnikov in the June 1989 issue of *Kommunist*, results from the literal collapse of the "command-administrative system." This system had consistently undermined the principle of self-determination of nations, replacing it with the concept of the Russians as "elder brother" of the other Soviet peoples. This substitution lies at the root of recent expressions of anti-Russian sentiments. It is not surprising, argues Zharnikov, that the sins of the compromised command-administrative system tend to be attributed in some degree to the "elder brother," i.e., to the Russian people. Unfortunately, there are also people who deliberately "speculate" on the problems of their nations—and which nation has no problems?"—and try to make the "elder brother" responsible for all their troubles.[1]

Zharnikov's is only one of many voices that have explicitly or implicitly argued recently that the relationship between the Russian nation and the Soviet state—let us call it the Russian national problem—is *the* central ethnic problem in the Soviet Union today, not least because it also defines the nature of the other nationality problems in the USSR. For the non-Russians tend to formulate their own agendas in light of their perception of the status and role of the Russian nation in the Soviet state.

If this is the case, then the roots of the Russian problem go deeper than the bankrupt command-administrative system or Stalinism. After all, it is commonplace to view Stalin, and by extension the present Soviet system, as a continuation of the tsarist, imperial pattern of inter-nationality relations. Thus, the search for solutions to current nationality problems must go back to the relationship established in tsarist times between the state and the Russian nation.

Published in *Problems of Communism*, 38: 4 (July-August 1989), pp. 15-35. Reprinted with permission from the publisher.

Moreover, a genuine normalization or "regularization" of the Soviet nationality situation requires above all that the Russian national problem be properly defined—and resolved.

There is a large and growing body of writings on Russian nationalism in particular, and on Russian political thought in general. The most recent addition to it is a collection of insightful essays by John Dunlop, Darrell Hammer, Ronald Suny, Andrei Sinyavsky, and Alexander Yanov in a special edition of the *Radio Liberty Research Bulletin* entitled "Russian Nationalism Today."[2] These and other scholars have also produced studies of diverse currents in the broad phenomenon of past and present Russian nationalism. Under the Romanov empire, there were Slavophiles, Westernizers, and adherents of "Official Nationality," as well as *pochvenniki* Pan-Slavs, liberal nationalists, and integral nationalists. In the contemporary Soviet Union, Dunlop discerns liberal nationalists, centrists, a nationalist Right, including the National Bolsheviks, and so forth. For his part, Yanov carefully distinguishes between nationalism, chauvinism, and patriotism:

> Patriotism, chauvinism, and nationalism have one thing in common: they are all manifestations of love of one's country. Yet, distinctions are evident—at least in the Russian context. A patriot loves his country, but this does not prevent him from loving humanity. A chauvinist loves his country but dislikes humanity, especially if it is of Jewish origin. A nationalist loves his country but sees humanity as an invading force ready to conquer it—with the Jews in the vanguard.[3]

While the conceptual distinctions of Yanov, Dunlop, and other scholars help to clarify intellectual currents in contemporary Russian nationalism, the present essay proposes to focus on a question they do not consider—namely, what do Russian nationalists, patriots, or chauvinists mean by the country they claim to love? Is one Russian patriot's "Russia" the same as the "Russia" of another patriot (chauvinist, nationalist)? Moreover, this "geographic" question will be linked to a political theme developed by Sinyavsky in his discussion of the acuteness of the nationality problems facing the Soviet government. Sinyavsky writes:

> The main reason for this can be summed up in a single word—"empire": first, the Russian empire, shaped in the course of centuries and inherited by the new order; then, the Soviet empire, built on the ruins of the old order, consolidated and extended as a world power. Today, it is the only empire in the world and unique as a country in terms of the sheer extent of its territory and number of its constituent peoples. Of necessity, being an empire complicates the nationality problem to an unusual degree.[4]

Sinyavsky also notes that "Soviet ideology has collapsed in ruins, and whatever attempts are made to revivify it, it will never imbue life with higher meaning. Soviet society today . . . is without ideals."[5]

It is worth noting that in his speech before the Congress of People's Deputies in Moscow on June 5, 1989, Andrey Sakharov characterized the Soviet situation in exactly the same way. Even as the country finds itself "in the throes of spreading economic catastrophe and a tragic worsening of interethnic relations," Sakharov said, "one aspect of the powerful and dangerous processes at work has been a general crisis of confidence in the country's leadership . . . accumulating tensions could explode, with dire consequences for our society." With regard to nationality problems, Sakharov said: "We have inherited from Stalinism a constitutional structure that bears the stamp of imperial thinking and the imperial policy of 'divide and rule'." Among the victims of the imperial system Sakharov counts not only the non-Russian nations but also the Russian nation, which "had to bear the main burden of imperial ambitions and the consequences of adventurism and dogmatism in foreign and domestic policy."[6]

Such opinions on the present condition of the USSR are heard with increasing frequency and intensity both inside and outside the USSR. In a much discussed article in *Literaturnaya Rossiya* published in 1988, Yuriy Afanas'yev claimed to see an "ideological vacuum" in the Soviet Union resulting in what he called an "identity crisis" of society. He attributed the crisis and the "vacuum" to the "systematic destruction of collective memory" perpetrated under Stalin and Brezhnev. Yet, historical memory is the pivotal formative component of social and group identity. Afanas'yev directly attributed the rise of what he called "chauvinist, anti-Semitic groups, like the extremists from Pamyat'," to that destruction of historical memory.[7]

Alain Besançon has concluded that, with the bankruptcy of Marxism-Leninism, the only alternative source of legitimacy is the empire, regardless of how anachronistic it may be:

> Once the ideological magic has been destroyed, there would only be one source of magic left—the imperial or colonial legitimacy of the Russian people in a world that today is entirely decolonized.[8]

Is Besançon necessarily right? Are the Russians incapable of defining themselves as other than an imperial nation?

EMPIRE OR NATION-STATE

The Bolshevik victory in the Civil War stopped what in 1917-1919 looked like the natural process of disintegration of the Russian empire into a number of independent nation-states that had started following the February (March) Revolution of 1917. As we see now, this victory also prevented Russia's evolution into a "normal" nation and state.[9] The subsequent Bolshevik attempt to transcend altogether the dialectic of nation and nationalism by establishing class as the basic referent, and class solidarity as the principle of new legitimacy and identity, failed. Instead, the imperial model was restored in a communist guise, with the Russian nation being elevated to the rank of "elder brother," but itself becoming an object of manipulation by Stalin and the system he created. The establishment of communist regimes in Asia and Eastern Europe after World War II extended the power and influence of the Soviet state beyond anything the tsars had ever achieved. But the establishment of the "socialist bloc" did not end the Soviet Union's reliance on the promotion of Russia. It was not until after 1945 that the "Russia First" slogan became paramount in philosophy, culture, science, and so on, first in the Soviet Union and then in Eastern and Central Europe. Domestically, the annexation of the Baltic states, Western Belorussia, and Western Ukraine further complicated the already existing nationality problem—as has become especially evident under glasnost'. The extension of communism beyond the borders of the USSR, and the territorial expansion of the Soviet state in turn tied the Russians more closely to the problems of both the "inner" and the "outer" empires, thereby inhibiting even more their search for national self-definition.

This legacy makes the question "What is Russia?" even more complex. But the present map of Soviet and Russian politics will become much clearer if one distinguishes between two basic responses from the Russian people to the question—that of "empire-savers" and that of "nation builders."

"Empire-savers" regard the present Soviet Union in its current boundaries as the proper and legitimate national "space" of the Russian nation. Indeed, some of them may extend it to the Soviet bloc. They may and indeed do differ profoundly about how they would like to see that country governed, how non-Russians should be treated in it, and so forth. But they all share the conviction that the USSR is in essence a synonym for Russia and consider the preservation of its political unity as a Russian (or Russian-dominated) state to be their primary political goal. That they may include extreme right-wingers and no less extreme left-wingers is not as important as the fact that they all agree on this fundamental point.

On the other side are those Russians who think of Russia as something very different from the USSR—as a geographical, historical, and cultural entity that does not encompass what they themselves recognize to be non-Russian lands and nations, even if these are part of the USSR. The geographical extent of Russia is not identical for all "nation-builders." Unlike the empire-savers, some nation-builders exclude the Baltic states from Russia but include the Caucasus; others exclude both of these but include Ukraine and Belorussia, and so on. What unifies them is a basically national position and the political goal of establishing a Russia that is a nation-state. Their goal is not to save, reform, transform, or modernize the empire but to establish in its place a Russian and a number of non-Russian nation-states. Insofar as nation-builders envisage close ties between Russia and some or all of the other "successors"—and some Russian nation-builders are in favor of such ties—they want *Russia*, and not the imperial center, to be a party to such arrangements.

It is impossible to determine how many Russians prefer empire-saving to nation-building or vice versa. But it is remarkable that in a recent article called "Preservation of the Empire or Self-Preservation by Way of National Sovereignty—The Main Problem of the Russian People," Vladimir Balakhonov formulates the Russian national dilemma in these same terms,[10] which suggests that the issue is entering the political agenda.

"EMPIRE-SAVERS"

It is essential to keep in mind that this broad designation encompasses ideas and programs, individuals and organizations, which in most other respects have little in common, and may disagree and oppose one another on some fundamental matters. But this fact does not make "empire-saving" a meaningless concept. When the chips are down, all empire-savers (it would be much simpler to call them "imperialists," but this term has now become one of abuse) agree that the preservation of the territorial integrity of the state is more important than anything else.

The classical expression of this approach is to be seen in the post-1917 phenomenon of "National Bolshevism," a designation describing those Russian anti-communists in the Civil War who opted for the Bolsheviks because they saw the latter as the only force capable of saving the empire. Private property, independent courts, freedom of religion, representative government—all these could be given up in exchange for "Russia's" retention of Ukraine, the Caucasus, or Central Asia. For the National Bolsheviks, a smaller but democratic Russia was no consolation for the loss of the empire.

Among today's most obvious empire-savers are the military and the police, the state and party bureaucracies, members of other "all-Union" structures and apparatuses, such as foreign ministry or cultural officials engaged in foreign relations. Imperial nationalism offers an ideological justification for the dominant position of the central bureaucracy (and its departmental and territorial subdivisions). For the Moscow bureaucracy, the whole of the USSR, be it Estonia or Armenia, Russia "proper" or Moldavia, Ukraine or Uzbekistan, represents the canvas for its "creative" undertakings. The ministries of nuclear power stations and of water irrigation, not to mention the State Planning Committee, embody this imperial perspective and vision. A song that was popularized by the official media during the era of "stagnation" (and now is criticized for its wrong attitude) reflects "artistically" the same imperial outlook, especially in this much-quoted refrain: "Not some house, not some street—my address is the Soviet Union."

Some of today's empire-savers may continue to believe that the political system established by Lenin and Stalin is the best for the Soviet Union. As a matter of principle, they may question whether political freedom is a desirable goal in any circumstances, and they are certain to oppose political freedoms when these threaten the unity, and thus indirectly the territorial integrity, of the Soviet state. Indeed, some may go even further and favor some kind of military or fascist-style dictatorship that would abandon Marxist-Leninist ideology openly and completely. For our purposes, they are empire-savers, because they consider the USSR to be a Russian state. But right-wing extremism is not the only "empire-saving" outlook today. It may even be the least important, although it is very vocal.

Other empire-savers seem to favor Western, liberal-democratic, and constitutional institutions for the Soviet Union. Indeed, when some of those "liberals" think of their ideal Russia, they envisage a polity closely resembling what they imagine the United States to be. That their empire would be a liberal one, would have independent courts, would accept equality of all citizens before the law (without regard to ethnic origins, national background, religion, and so forth), is of course praise worthy. But what is decisive in this outlook is that it treats the non-Russian peoples—and the Russians too—as subject to decisions made in Moscow—and not by those peoples themselves. Some of these "imperial" admirers of America are prepared to allow local and regional autonomy in their state, and they even discuss the possibility of basing such autonomy on what they see as the most significant aspect of the American model: dissociation of ethnicity *from territory.*

Some of the "Westernizers" go even farther. They openly proclaim their own desire for a total separation of ethnicity from politics and the state, for making nationality, as it were, a private matter of concern only to individuals, rather than having it be a factor affecting the state structure. Again, some Soviet scholars seem to think that this ideal is realized in the United States.[11]

There are grounds to surmise that the current line of the center in the face of rising ethnic nationalisms is to defuse the threat coming from the larger nations by having Moscow assume the role of defender of smaller nations, and especially of scattered national and religious groups living among the non-Russian peoples. This policy would serve two purposes. It would weaken union republics by granting their citizens the right to go to Moscow for justice, and it would create a new mission for the old apparat—which would become the protector of ethnic and human rights all over the USSR, in the same old centralized way to which it became accustomed while admittedly doing other things. The newly appointed head of the Ethnography Institute of the USSR Academy of Sciences, Valeriy Tishkov, for one, is against "absolutizing" the rights of the union republics over the rights of other entities such as autonomous republics or national districts.[12] Indeed, the center seems, in self-defense, to be advocating the granting of broader rights to the subdivisions of the union republics, presumably in order to give Moscow more things to do, and not because the Moscow bureaucracy now consists of converts to libertarianism and individualism.

Whether empire-savers are fascist or liberal, extremist or moderate, atheist or Orthodox, their "geography" is the same—it is an imperial geography, and their Russia is co-extensive with the empire. But why should the hoped-for liberal empire be called Russian? Why should it not have the "Soviet" or some other non-ethnic designation? Recent Soviet discussions help answer this question.

The historical failure of the Soviet system is openly conceded today. The declaration of the Congress of People's Deputies issued in June 1989 speaks about the present "crisis" of the Soviet Union. It is admitted that the Soviet system has failed to defeat capitalism in their historic "great contest." This failure has called into question the concept of the "Soviet people." If a new Soviet civilization has not been created, as is also being admitted, then in what sense are the peoples living in the USSR a *Soviet people*?[13]

The empire-savers are noticeably concerned to preserve the concept of a "Soviet people." But when one examines their arguments closely, one discovers that the "Soviet people" they defend is a form of the Russian nation. Academician Yulian Bromley (until 1989 director of the Ethnography Institute) defined the "Soviet people" as a real community that is held together by common socialist features. He called it a "meta-ethnic community."[14] In a January 1989 article, Bromley recognized that demands for greater use of "national"—which in the Soviet usage means subnational or local or regional—languages in the non-Russian republics of the Soviet Union are legitimate. But he stressed the necessity of continuing and expanding the use of Russian throughout the USSR. Revealingly, Bromley referred to the publication of fiction and poetry in non-Russian languages as indicating the growth of the "nationally specific" as opposed to the "general," which means that he considers the publication of fiction and poetry in Russian to represent the "general," that is, the integrating or internationalizing tendency.[15]

Bromley attributes "international" qualities to the Russian language, and by extension to the Russian ethnos, even though to an outsider there would appear to be no more internationalism in the Russian language than there is in Georgian or Abkhazian. One may well ask whether a poem praising Lenin in Armenian would be "nationally specific," while one written in Russian, praising Nicholas II, would be "general and integrating" just because it was written in Russian. Absurd as this may be, such categorizations lay at the root of imperial thinking in Stalin's time—and seem to be alive today. The Estonian scholar Jaan K. Rebane has recently made the point that in this view, the "internationalist" (i.e., Soviet) or "general" means one ethnically specific aspect—the Russian.[16]

Bromley's reference to the non-Russian languages as expressing the "specific" and his assumption that Russian stands for "the general" shows quintessential Russian imperial thinking, and makes it clear why it is a Russian, and not a Soviet, imperial thinking. It is based on the assumption that Russian ethnicity is not in the same category as all the other ethnicities in the USSR: it is above them, it is a distinguishing feature of the "universality" of Sovietism. This approach holds that the unity of the USSR is based on the non-Russians' submergence in—not their integration as equals with—Russia.

What some other prominent figures understood by "internationalization" became clear from a speech by Yevgeniy M. Primakov given at the 19th Party Conference in June 1988. Primakov proposed the establishment of "international structures" by means of a "rotation of cadres along horizontal lines in the whole country," a move made imperative by the "lessons from recent events in Azerbaijan and Armenia." Primakov argued:

> Only through such a horizontal transfer of party and economic personnel will it be possible to create a single international fusion in the Soviet Union, one that will be more monolithic than the sum of national [i.e., ethnic] formations that gravitate toward seclusion.[17]

Academician Primakov did not explain who would implement such a transfer of cadres. The new political reforms in the USSR seem to make the decision as to who shall head a given party or economic organization subject to elections. This would mean that Moscow could no longer appoint or transfer leading cadres from one republic or region to another. It is obvious that Primakov's plan would require retention of the power of appointment by the center.

Exchange of cadres between republics was a standard theme in the Brezhnev and Andropov times, and Mikhail Gorbachev himself also used to endorse it, at least until the January 1987 plenum of the Central Committee, after which this topic seems to have disappeared from his public pronouncements. But in April 1989, Adbul-Rakhman Bezirov, first secretary of the Azerbaijan Central Committee, spoke strongly in favor of an exchange of party officials between republics and the center, although from a different perspective than Primakov's. His complaint was that for years no party officials from his republic had been called to serve in Moscow.[18]

Academician S. L. Tikhvinskiy, an influential historian, insisted at an academic conference in 1987 that it was necessary to develop new forms of inter-republic cooperation in the scholarly sphere. Tikhvinskiy stressed the need to "resolutely overcome the harmful tendency to divide science (*nauka*) into Ukrainian or Azerbaijani, central or peripheral." According to him, only one, Soviet, historical science existed, and it was "firmly grounded" in Marxism-Leninism and socialist internationalism.[19] It is worth noting that Tikhvinskiy spoke about Soviet scholarship and about internationalism, but did not deny the existence of a Russian historical science. One suspects that he identified Russian with Soviet or "internationalist" scholarship, even though it was hard in 1987, and impossible in 1989, to ignore the fact that Russian historical writing is not firmly grounded in either Marxism-Leninism or in socialist internationalism.

Some scholars do not have Tikhvinskiy's or Primakov's inhibitions about explicitly identifying "Soviet" with "Russian." Examples of uninhibited Russian imperial thinking may be found in the symposium "Democracy is Conflict," published in the monthly magazine *Vek XX i Mir*. Doctor of Philosophical Sciences A. Prigozhin was refreshingly open in characterizing the Russian nation as the "patron-nation" (*narod-patron*) of all the Soviet peoples. Prigozhin thought it quite self-evident and normal that the Russians should form the highest leadership of the country (i.e., of the USSR), and should predominate among the heads of the state's central agencies, in the USSR Academy of Sciences, the Central Committee of the CPSU, and so forth. He even thought that in the non-Russian national republics, Russian leaders should "also occupy a special position."[20] Clearly, for Prigozhin, being "Russian" means embodying and personifying the general or universal, the "Soviet," in the Soviet Union. By the same token, the other ethnic elements in Prigozhin's scheme of things represented the "specific," or particular, in other words, something local, subordinate, and inessential.

"NATION-BUILDERS"

One of the consequences of the Soviet Union's identity crisis is the current rise of ethnic assertiveness in many regions of the country. Dissatisfaction with the Soviet system, general disillusionment with the empty promises of a better "Soviet way of life," and the search for alternative explanations of the current problems and ways of solving them lie behind the present processes in which ethnic communities "construct" and "reconstruct" themselves.

Among the nations in search of an identity and purpose are the Russians. They are increasingly asserting themselves—and defining themselves—as a Russian nation and, especially important, as a nation that exists independently of the state, which in this case means the empire. Some of the emerging Russian nationalists take pains to diss ociate the Russian nation from the Soviet state's record not only in the 1930s, but also in the 1920s. Indeed, some are repudiating even the immediate post-revolutionary years. The process of reevaluation of history has assumed sufficiently large proportions to raise the possibility of a "divorce" or secession of Russian nationalism from the Soviet state and Marxist-Leninist ideology. If the trend continues and gains in scope, it may lead to the dissolution, "ungluing," or coming apart of what has been called by some Russia's "national communism."

More than 20 years ago, Mark G. Field defined national communism as "the search, on the part of a nation that has recently emerged as a major world power on the world scene, for a national and cultural identity." National communism, he wrote, rested on "the fusion of the doctrinal bases of the communist movement and identification of the interests of that movement (which is, in essence, supra-national) with the interests of the Russian nation." Field saw the sources of that "fusion" in the recognition by the Soviet leaders that "no proletarian revolution was in sight and the resulting decision (primarily Stalin's) to build 'socialism in one country'." Stalin considered Russia the bastion of the communist movement and held that "anything that added to the strength of Russia as a nation (industrialization, for example) was good for the movement."[21]

It is a separate question whether Stalin ultimately proved to be "good" for the world communist movement; what is relevant here is that more and more people openly say now that Stalin's regime was very bad for Russia. Bad not just for the Russian "landlords and bourgeoisie," for kulaks or even peasants in general, but also bad for Russia in the sense of the entire people and country. This theme has long been heard from declared anti-communists, for example, Aleksandr Solzhenitsyn, who in the early 1970s, when he was still in the USSR, used to be the most prominent spokesman for this assessment of communism's relationship to Russia. While Solzhenitsyn criticized communism on behalf of the old, Orthodox Russia, certain extremist chauvinist elements among the dissidents criticized the Soviet past and present from another vantage point. They blamed the Soviet state's negative aspects on the Jews, Zionists, Freemasons, and so on, but professed their profound loyalty to "genuine" Soviet socialism (under which term they also understood Stalinism).[22]

Today, many people are convinced that Russia is hopelessly behind when compared with other Soviet republics (not to mention foreign countries), and it is frequently said or implied that the ruling party, the state, and the ideology are to blame. Many examples can be cited to illustrate this pervasive mood, but a few will have to suffice. The well-known "village" writer Vasiliy Belov, speaking as a candidate for the USSR Congress of People's Deputies, said: "The ill-considered collectivization of the '30's inflicted great losses not only on the peasantry but also on the whole Russian people [*narod*]. According to my information, the Russians now constitute less than one half of the country's [population]." Belov complained that despite this fact, some scholars claimed that the Russians were characterized "by some special kind of aggressiveness." Those unnamed scholars even "dare to say that there exist special medical means to treat this aggressiveness. I was deeply angered to hear such statements at one very representative conference."

Belov was no less critical of the government's conduct of foreign trade under the terms of which, he said, the Soviet Union exports its best goods, which are not accessible to the Soviet population, and buys industrial machinery from abroad, thus perpetuating the country's traditional role as a backward nation dependent on the foreigners' "technology of yesterday." (Belov assumed that foreigners do not sell their most up-to-date products). If such practices continue, the country risks becoming a "colony."[23]

In an article in a series remarkably called "Who Is to Blame or What Is to be Done?" Yuriy Chernichenko referred to Russia (meaning the RSFSR, not the USSR as a whole) as a country that was the dirtiest in all of the USSR and in all of Europe, being dirtier in the Soviet era than in the early 19th century when the poet Mikhail Lermontov had called Russia "*nemytaya Rossiya*" (unwashed

Russia). Chernichenko said it was time to "wash up" Russia (*otmyt' Rossiyu*), and he drew a direct connection between the sorry state of Russia and the rule by party bureaucrats who headed a "purely totalitarian regime, an administrative regime."[24]

It is not unusual to identify Russian nationalism with the most extreme, fascist, or racist ideas and groups. This point of view is erroneous. Fascism, racism, and extremism are not the only Russian-proposed alternatives to the ideology of communism and the present Soviet political system. There are many diverse currents in Russia, and it would be an impossible task to classify them without crude oversimplification. For the purposes of this discussion, however, let us rather consider several different models envisaged for Russia, each of which has at its source its proponents' sense of alienation from the present system.

First, there are those Russians who reject communism and Sovietism and who look for an alternative in a nationalism rooted in culture, especially in religion. The second model of Russia proposes a democratic, liberal, Western-style modern nation-state. A third model is advanced by those who are critical of the imperial structure of the Soviet Union and expect a change for the better if the RSFSR were to become a full-fledged republic. Their opposition to "Moscow"—read the Stalinist bureaucratic and centralized machine—lead these Russians to call for a basic change in the status of the Russian Soviet Federated Socialist Republic within the Soviet Union. They seem to believe that the national needs of the Russians might be addressed and met if the RSFSR acquired an identity that was separate from the USSR and its governmental, party, and other organizations.

RSFSR-Nationalism

Let us begin with the third model, which is anti-empire but is not anti-socialist or anti-Soviet in principle. It calls for an institutional rearrangement for the RSFSR that would amount to the removal of the Russian nation from the position of imperial nation in the USSR. An interview given recently by the secretary of the Moscow Writers' Union, Anatoliy Zhukov, to *Literaturnaya Rossiya* conveys well the mood of those "RSFSR Russians." Zhukov cited some of the ethnic problems arising in Central Asia, the Baltic states, Armenia and Azerbaijan, as well as the rise of "Russophobia" in Kazakhstan and elsewhere, and attributed them to neglect of the specific conditions in those particular regions. These republics could not deal with their problems adequately because they lacked the freedom to run their own affairs. When asked if this was also true of the Russian Federation, Zhukov responded:

Of course. Why should we be an exception? But we are an exception. In Russian schools, for example, Russian history is not being taught, there is only the history of the USSR. We do not have our own republic academy of sciences, we do not have our own republic party or Komsomol central committee, there are no [republic–rank] trade union organs, and no congresses are held. The Russians are last in the number of specialists with college education and in the number of scientists per 1,000 of population, our countryside has been ruined, our birth rates have fallen, our national culture has been almost destroyed. What is this if not an exception? We do not even have a capital of our own—we "share" one with the whole of the country.[25]

It goes without saying that Zhukov's statements are not always accurate. For example, he seems not to know that Ukrainian schools do not teach a subject called "Ukrainian history." What is more interesting is that Zhukov—and other Russian critics who complain that Russian history is not taught in Russian schools—do not think that what is being presented as the "history of the USSR" is a history of Russia. What is called "history of the USSR" in Soviet textbooks is principally the history of the tsarist state. When critics of this kind of history say they want a history of the Russian people, the Russian nation, they are revealing a belief that the story of the grand princes and tsars is not real Russian history. Indeed, some dispute the propriety of calling the pre-1917 history a history of the "USSR" (which is what Soviet historians do, and not only in textbooks but also in scholarly works). Thus, in a letter to the journal *Nash Sovremennik*, Colonel (Ret.) I. A. Zaichkin and Major-General of the Air Force I. N. Pochkayev, called it absurd to have book titles like, "History of the USSR: Feudal Epoch." On the pre-1917 era, they said, there should be histories of *Russia* and of other nations.[26]

Admittedly, there is nothing politically subversive in such proposals. However, Russian demands of this kind are frequently presented by individuals who combine them with chauvinistic, including anti-Semitic, views. Thus, a letter to the 19th Party Conference signed by a group of Russian cultural figures contained a demand for ethnic quotas in those RSFSR institutions that the letter-signers wanted to have established.[27] (Incidentally, like Zhukov, the authors of this letter seem convinced that in the non-Russian republics, the histories of the respective nations are taught. This, as mentioned above, is certainly not the case now in Ukraine, and it seems most unlikely to be the case in Belorussia and a number of the other republics.) The Russian "cultural figures" charged that the absence of RSFSR structures (they also included in their list the KGB and academies of the sciences and arts) perpetuates a "Zionist-Trotskyist program," which they describe as follows: "A federation for the 'nationalities' with separate centers for them, but without one for the Russians." They said that Lenin had protested this program—evidently without success. "And so the Russians have now proved to be without rights in their own country!"[28]

The support for some of the Russian national desiderata by professed anti-Semites and reactionaries should not obscure the fact that not all of these desiderata are objectionable. While it would obviously be wrong to restrict employment in a Russian academy of sciences by ethnic quotas, the idea of establishing such a new academy is not discriminatory per se. Indeed, if realized, it might help to develop Russia and at the same time help to dissociate "Sovietism" from the Russian people as the Soviet Union's allegedly dominant master nation, or "patron-nation" in Prigozhin's phrase. Indeed, some years ago similar Russian demands circulated in *samizdat* and were then supported by leftists.[29]

One such idea that constantly reappears and seems to bother Russians of all political persuasions is the dual role of Moscow as capital of the USSR and the RSFSR. Many Russians complain that Leningrad has fallen from the rank of an imperial capital to that of a regional center. The question of the status of Leningrad was again raised quite recently in *Literaturnaya Gazeta* and *Literaturnaya Rossiya*. Writing in the latter, the Leningrad writer Feliks Dymov recalled that one of Stalin's charges against the Leningrad party leaders in 1949-50 was their proposal to move the capital of the RSFSR to that city. (Stalin regarded this as separatism.) Although Dymov did not take a definite stand in favor of such a move, he deplored the low ranking of the former capital, which, he said, in population, scientific potential, and industrial output, was far ahead of the 14 union republic capitals.[30]

Nation as Culture

No current of contemporary Russian opinion whether unofficial or "legal," has attracted Western scholars more than the complexities of Russian national-religious and "culturalist" thought. Indeed, there are Russian thinkers who want to explore and affirm the importance of the Orthodox religion and the Orthodox Church in the history of Russia, and who consider this spiritual aspect a formative influence on modern Russian identity. These thinkers disagree profoundly among themselves in their specific assessments of individuals and events in Russia's spiritual history, and even more profoundly on the implications of Russia's past for its present spiritual and political problems. Their ideas deserve attention.

Until very recently, most of those cultural and national debates were conducted among the intelligentsia on the pages of "thick" journals. In the past year or two, however, formal organizations have emerged seeking to promote their respective visions of a culturally-defined Russia among the general public. One might see in these emerging structures initial attempts to give an institutional shape to the different ideas of Russia. It is evident that these organizations are characterized by diverse approaches to the questions of Russian national identity, the territorial shape of "Russia," and the empire.

Remembering that such distinctions lack precision, especially because a certain overlap is evident in the positions of the groups in question, let us first mention those that concentrate their attention on Russian culture broadly defined but make it clear that they do not claim for Russia any special position in relation to the other nationalities in the Soviet Union.

One such organization was founded in June 1989 under the name of "National [or People's] Home of Russia" (*Narodnyy dom Rossii*). The "National Home" expressly limits its sphere of operation to the RSFSR, and its programs aim at "the revival of the spiritual, social, cultural, and socio-economic life of the Russian Federation." It wants to achieve this goal by freeing the energies of a society that had for long lived under "the oppression of a totally prohibitive system."[31]

Another Russian national initiative that emphasizes its autonomy from the state is the "Russian Encyclopedia Cultural Center." The projected Russian encyclopedia is to be devoted to all aspects of Russian history, culture, and civilization, and will not attempt to be a universal encyclopedia of the kind represented by the *Great Soviet Encyclopedia* or the comprehensive encyclopedias published in the union republics. The Russian encyclopedia planners insist on their independence from the state.[32]

John Dunlop draws attention to two other recent nationalist initiatives in the cultural area. Both are remarkably political—not to say "imperial"—in their "cultural" concerns. One of these is called "Foundation for Slavic Writing and Slavic Cultures" (*Fond slavyanskoy pis'mennosti i slavyanskikh kul'tur*) and includes among its founders individuals whom Dunlop calls "conservative Russian nationalists." As he puts it, the Foundation is "pan-Slavic in orientation."[33] Dunlop notes that the Foundation, launched in March 1989, has among its more than 80 sponsoring organizations the Writers' Union of the RSFSR as well as those of Ukraine and Belorussia, the academies of sciences of Ukraine and Belorussia, as well as numerous Russian and general Soviet organizations. He thinks that the "de facto goal of the new organization appears to be to cement relations among Russians, Ukrainians, and Belorussians." Only secondarily, according to Dunlop, is the Foundation concerned with Slavic and/or Orthodox nations abroad.

Dunlop quotes from a statement by Dmitriy Balashov, "the well-known Russian nationalist historical writer," who expressed this view: "The question of the day...is whether the 'supra-ethnic' state created by ethnic Russians can be preserved." It would be lamentable, Balashov said, "if the miracle of Russian statehood should be consumed by 'chaos'." This and similar statements led Dunlop to the following general observation: "Conservative Russian nationalists are concerned about the future political fragmentation of the Soviet empire. They are attempting to shore up the Eastern Slav nucleus of the USSR."[34]

The other organization discussed by Dunlop is the "Association of Russian Artists," also organized in early 1989. Dunlop notes that the Association's primary aim is to "combat separatist minority nationalist tendencies threatening the unity of the Soviet Union," and he quotes from a declaration of the Association to support his assessment:

The once-powerful union of the peoples of Russia, joined together by the idea of steadfast unity, is experiencing a difficult period, during which, under the guise of demagogic slogans, nationalist groups are seeking to break up and destroy the unity of peoples.[35]

Recently, Boris Tsarev, the Association's business manager, declared that the organization supported the free development of all nationalities even though its own focus was on Russian culture. The Association firmly defends the unity of the USSR, which it views as a product of historical development that has produced a "brotherhood" of all peoples living in a common state. Tsarev warned the non-Russian nationalities against (unnamed) elements who work for the destruction of the USSR and aspire to establish their domination "over all nations."[36]

At least two other Russian nationalist organizations began their existence in the spring of 1989. The Union for Spiritual Rebirth of the Fatherland (*Soyuz dukhovnogo vozrozhdeniya Otechestva*) was officially organized in Moscow on March 16-17, 1989. According to *Moskovskiy Literator*, the organizing session was attended by some 200 delegates from "patriotic associations and organizations" of Moscow, Leningrad, the Volga region, the Urals, Siberia, Belorussia, Ukraine, and Kazakhstan, as well as by representatives of the Russian Orthodox Church. The organization's listed "founders" include the *Sovetskaya Rossiya* Publishing House, the Lenin Library, the Scientific Council for Problems of Russian Literature in the USSR Academy of Sciences, a kolkhoz in Chuvashia, and "eighty patriotic associations from regions of the Urals and Siberia."[37]

One week after the initial announcement, M. Antonov, president of the Union for Spiritual Rebirth, publicly explained the Union's goals. The Union expects resolution of the country's crisis "only on the condition that there is a moral rebirth of every nation of our great Fatherland." Only those patriotic organizations that have actually shown by deeds that they support socialism and the preservation of the independence of the country, and that support the party in its *perestroyka* policies, may join the Union. The manifesto of the Union, which was published next to Antonov's article, was directed to "Our compatriots, fellow Russian (*rossiyane*) brothers and sisters, all nations which have flourished in our Fatherland."[38]

Judging by the text of the Manifesto and Antonov's article, the Union is a strongly nationalistic, anti-Western, and anti-liberal body that appeals simultaneously to communist and Russian nationalist slogans. It would not be unfair to call the Union a nationalist-socialist organization, envisioning the "Fatherland" as a multinational country led by Russians. As if one such Union were not enough, many of the same organizations that sponsored the Union for Spiritual Rebirth were behind the establishment, also in March 1989and also in Moscow, of yet another body, namely, the "Moscow Russian Patriotic Society

'Fatherland'"   (*Moskovskoye   russkoye   patrioticheskoye   obshchestvo
"Otechestvo"*).   The Moscow Society clearly sees itself as an ethnic
organization, as shown by its use of the adjective *russkoye*, not *rossiyskoye*, the
former being an ethnic or personal designation, the latter a territorial one in
which non-Russian citizens of the Russian Republic can also be included. Its
program advocates the establishment of a Russian (meaning RSFSR) television
network and a Russian academy of sciences, and several other causes.   It
stresses "military-patriotic education" and includes on its board at least one
military officer.[39]   In its stronger emphasis on Russian ethnicity, the
Association differs from the Union for Spiritual Rebirth, which is clearly
interested in extending its activities throughout the entire Soviet Union.

   This brief and of necessity superficial review of recent Russian initiatives
nevertheless reveals a rise in nationalist sentiment and concerns and testifies at
the same time to the confusion about what kind of country it is that the Russians
are envisaging. Some of the positions mentioned here closely parallel those of
the empire-savers, although the empire-savers prefer to call themselves Soviet
rather than Russian, even when they really mean Russian. Other positions are
more clearly concerned with Russia proper, the RSFSR. But those "culturalist"
nationalists who stress Orthodox religious factors and who emphasize the
Russians' ties to their fellow Slavs appear to be rather oblivious to the fact that
the Russian Republic is the homeland of several Muslim nations, including the
Volga Tatars, who form a large nation not only by RSFSR but also by all-Union
standards. The culturalists' neglect of the non-Slavs within Russia, and their
accenting of Ukrainian and Belorussian affinity with the Russians—some of them
imply that the three nations are really one—seem to betray an "empire-saving"
rather than a "nation-building" orientation.

Russia as a Democratic Nation-State

   The third model of Russia is that which is beginning to take shape in the
thinking of the activists and theorists of the national democratic movement of
Russia. As of the summer of 1989, the Russian democratic movement has not
created all-Russia structures comparable to those already existing in the Baltic
states or even those emerging in Ukraine and Belorussia. But "popular" or
"national" fronts have already been created in the Urals, in Yaroslavl',
Leningrad, and most recently, in Moscow. It is only a matter of time, one
imagines, before they coalesce into a Russian popular front.

   It is also conceivable that these fronts will unite to proclaim the establishment
of an "all-Union"—rather than a Russian—popular front, thus setting up the
Russians in a position of leadership once again. If this happens, Russian
democrats will be following in the footsteps of the Bolsheviks as well as of their
democratic predecessors in pre-1917 Russia, who until the very last declined to
identify themselves simply as "Great Russians."   On this subject, the
recollections of Paul Milyukov, written in the 1920s, are very revealing. He

recalled how before the 1917 revolution, non-Russian nationalists asked the Russian democratic intelligentsia to redefine its national identity as a precondition for cooperation. In asking the Russians to become "Great Russians," i.e., to define themselves in ethnic terms rather than as a group representing the whole empire, the non-Russians argued that this redefinition would make it possible for all parties to act as equals. But by defining themselves as "Russian" in an imperial rather than a national sense, in the view of the non-Russians, Russian democrats were making a claim to superiority and leadership (*pervenstvo*) over the other nationalities. In Milyukov's retrospective view, the Russian intelligentsia could not have acted other than it did, since yielding to those demands required "undoing" Russian history.[40] In other words, it required denying legitimacy to that product of Russian history that Milyukov and his fellow intellectuals really valued—the empire.

Will the Russian intelligentsia in the 1990s agree to do what its predecessors refused to do in the 1900s? The article by Balakhonov mentioned earlier is remarkable for addressing, in the most explicit manner possible, the necessity to dissociate the Russian nation from imperial ambitions, thereby possibly giving the answer that Milyukov was unable to give.[41] If Balakhonov's proposal for the solution of the "Russian question" were implemented, it would not only allow the non-Russian peoples of the USSR to become free but, in the words of Milovan Djilas, would also mean "the emancipation of the Russian nation from the present (and often unwillingly borne) burdens of empire." In a conversation with George Urban, Djilas put his view of the Soviet-imperial versus Russian-national problem in the following way:

> We are talking about the natural expiry of an unnatural tyrannical regime which is bound to come, as surely as the British and French empires had to face their demise when the time was ripe. The Russian people would benefit the most. They would gain a free and more prosperous life and yet remain, undoubtedly, a great nation. You see, the Communist system has forced the Russian people into a state of sulking introspection which seeks outlets in xenophobia, petulant demonstrations of national superiority—or, at the opposite end, maudlin admissions of national inferiority. I firmly believe that a reduced but self-confident, opened-up democratic Russian state would induce much less brooding in the Russian people and make them a happier race, to the extent that Russians can be happy. Imagine what it would mean for free men and women everywhere to see this last bastion of universal unfreedom go the way of all tyrannies.[42]

Let me summarize the most important points of the Balakhonov proposal—bearing in mind that at least some of his ideas are also being debated and presumably shared by the Democratic Union, which may well be the first major Russian political force that is both national (or "nationalist") and liberal, pro-Western, and democratic. For complex and deep historical reasons, Balakhonov argues, Russian national consciousness has become tied to the idea of empire (which also happens to be an autocratic, centralized state). In these deep historical recesses he sees the source of most recent expressions of "imperial ideology." Balakhonov also thinks that the extremist positions of Pamyat' are rooted in an imperial-statist outlook.

The primary task of the Russian nation, Balakhonov writes, should be to reshape its national consciousness. The Russians need to fathom the value of democracy and to see that Russia's "voluntary withdrawal from the 'large empire' of the USSR" will be beneficial to the Russian people. The Russians ought to understand, too, that the "small empire—the RSFSR," which he says forms the core of the "large empire," should also be dismantled.

Specifically, Balakhonov proposes the formation of three or four Russian-speaking states out of those parts of the RSFSR where the Russians predominate. Those democratic and sovereign states would include: (1) Russia proper, embracing Moscow and historic Russian lands to the west of the Urals, where the Great Russians and the Russian state originally were formed; (2) West Siberia; (3) East Siberia (although he takes into account the possibility that there would be a single Siberian state); (4) the Russian Far East. Balakhonov thinks that the creation of independent states in Siberia and the Far East would enable the Russian nation to participate in, and benefit from, the development of the "Pacific Community" in the 21st century. In any case, he is sure that the dismantling of the empire would benefit both the non-Russians and the Russians themselves. Indeed, he thinks that some Russians already acknowledge this possibility: "Both in Russian Siberia and in the Far East, voices are already heard in favor of their economic, state-political, and cultural autonomy, in favor of reducing their dependence on the supercentralized administration."[43]

But Balakhonov recognizes that his plans are not likely to win mass support in the foreseeable future. He therefore thinks that the most urgent task is to advance a restructuring of the Russian people's consciousness, because most Russians still remain under the influence of an imperial mentality. "The imperial instinct of the Russians is exceptionally strong, and as yet, we simply do not imagine a form of existence other than the framework of the present empire from Brest to Vladivostok." Because the Russians themselves have not been under foreign rule for many centuries, they do not understand what national oppression means and accordingly do not sympathize with the national-liberation movements of dependent nations. Nevertheless, the Russians will have to accept the fall of the empire as a result of which they will become free themselves—or they can try to preserve the empire but in doing so they will deprive themselves of freedom. The latter course might ultimately lead to the rise of a "great-power Russian Nazism."[44]

Balakhonov is not a lone voice. *Atmoda*, the newspaper of the National Front of Latvia, recently published a speech before the Baltic Assembly by Boris Rakitskiy, vice-president of the Soviet Sociological Association. As quoted in *Literaturnaya Rossiya*, Rakitskiy said:

The Russian democratic movement, I assure you, is concerned now precisely with its inability to penetrate into the thicket of popular consciousness in order to try to root out its imperial component. This consciousness is great-power consciousness in form, but slavish in content. But we are working, we are trying on our part to support your efforts.[45]

In his article "To Russian Society on Russian Problems," Aleksandr Kazakov called upon his compatriots to stop identifying their fatherland with the state and "the authority." The Russian people have to learn, Kazakov said, not to mistake their love for their native land with love of the state and its political, military, and economic might. The Russians should work above all for "the revival of a national Russia" (*natsional'naya Rossiya*).[46]

It is impossible to determine at this stage how widely ideas like Balakhonov's, Rakitskiy's, or Kazakov's are supported. Balakhonov himself began to speak out in the 1970s in favor of dismantling the Soviet empire and replacing it by a Russian democratic nation-state as one of the empire's successors—and was punished for it at the time. Irrespective of how widely his ideas are shared, he is certainly right in paying attention to the political prospects of regional movements within the Russian republic, including those in the ethnically-Russian core of the RSFSR.

If the Russian nation ever frees itself of its "imperial mentality," by which Balakhonov and his fellow-thinkers claim it is dominated, this will not happen as a consequence of some kind of massive intellectual revolution originating in Moscow or Leningrad. It is more realistic to suppose that the change will begin along the path that many are apparently already taking in "the provinces," where regional "popular fronts," like those already formed in the Urals, various Siberian centers, and in European Russian provincial capitals, are being established.

Some signs point to a democratic Russian nationalism—a democratic Russian national consciousness—taking shape in organized form. The Democratic Union appears to be a Russian, not an "all-Union," organization. On March 12, 1989, it held a demonstration in honor of the first revolution of 1917, and the participants, according to *The New York Times*, carried Russian flags of a pre-Soviet vintage. Just as the Balts and the Ukrainians celebrate various dates in 1918 as their national independence day, so democratic Russians seem to have adopted the March 1917 anniversary as a Russian national holiday to mark their nation's emancipation from tsarism.[47]

March 1917 is not a date Russian nationalists in the RSFSR Writers' Union (not to mention the Pamyat' Society or its fellow travelers) would choose for a Russian national holiday. Some of them are more critical of those who overthrew the tsar in March 1917 than they are of those who seized power in November 1917.[48] It is easy to understand why this should be so: the liberals, radicals, and democrats inaugurated the disintegration of the empire; the Bolsheviks restored it.

NON-RUSSIAN RESPONSES

The debate about Russian identity is not an internal Russian national affair. The questions that the Russians ask themselves evoke reactions from their fellow citizens of other nationalities. One type of response relates to the status of the RSFSR. Another deals with the Russian ideas about relations between the Russian nation and the two other East Slavic nations. Most important of all is the question of Russian versus Soviet identity. It is under this last rubric that Russian-Jewish relations are being debated.

Those Russian nation-builders who think of the Russian republic solely as the national homeland of the Russians seem to pay scant attention to the fact that the RSFSR includes about 20 autonomous republics, including the Tatar, Bashkir, Daghestan, and Yakut ASSR's. Those Russian culturalists who are preoccupied with the question of Slavic unity, especially East Slavic unity, and stress the religious, Orthodox contribution to Russian identity, also seem oblivious to the fact that even if the Russian nation as they define it is Slavic and Orthodox-Christian (the latter at least in tradition), many millions of citizens of Russia (the RSFSR) are neither Slavic nor Orthodox.

It is commonly known that the coterie of ethnic Russian nationalists grouped around *Nash Sovremennik* is anti-Semitic. *Nash Sovremennik* had also been involved in conflicts with Georgian writers. But, as Julia Wishnevsky has noted, the non-Russian members of the RSFSR Writers' Union, especially Tatars and members of the nationalities of the Soviet North, also have made it clear that they have "no time for Russian nationalism." At the 1988 RSFSR Writers' Union plenum, they protested about discrimination against their nations in favor of Russians in their ethnic homelands, in wages, occupations, and cultural matters. They also objected to discrimination within the RSFSR Writers' Union itself, pointing out that *Nash Sovremennik*, the journal of the Union, did not have a single non-Russian on its editorial board.[49]

Some non-Russians propose that the RSFSR should become a real federation, which it is in name but not even in its formal constitutional structure. The so-called autonomous republics do not enjoy any autonomy, and most of the Republic, considered as ethnic Russian territory, does not have any even formally autonomous organs. To correct this problem, a deputy from the Evenki autonomous district to the Congress of People's Deputies proposed the establishment in the Russian Republic parliament of two chambers: a chamber of the Republic and a chamber of nationalities.[50]

The Tatars, Russia's largest non-Russian nation, wish to go farther in trying to improve their position. In late 1988, the journal of the Tatar party committee, *Slovo Agitatora*, published a draft of the program of the "Tatar Civic Center," which is the Tatar counterpart to the national fronts familiar from the

Baltic republics. The draft demanded that the sovereign rights "of the people of the Tatar ASSR" be realized, that the people of the "Tatarstan" be equitably represented in the government of the USSR and RSFSR, and that the rights of the Tatar ASSR be gradually widened, eventually making Tatarstan a union republic.[51] In May 1989, the congress of the Tatar ASSR Writers' Union unanimously voted to ask an upcoming plenum of the CPSU Central Committee to grant the Tatar ASS the status of union republic. It was noted at the congress that only 12 percent of Tatar children in Tataria study Tatar in school, and only 7 percent of Tatar children in the entire RSFSR do so. The Tatars clearly hope that this situation will change for the better if their republic is raised in status. Among other issues discussed were matters of history: speakers called for a reassessment of an official condemnation of the "Sultan-Galievist" national deviation and for the repudiation of the 1944 CPSU resolution that branded Tatar history of the medieval period (the period of the "Mongol Yoke" in Russia) as "reactionary."[52]

Acknowledging the validity of many complaints of the non-Russian nationalities (of which those cited above are only examples), a group of Russian writers, including M. Alekseyev, V. Belov, Yu. Bondarev, and V. Rasputin, published an appeal entitled, "We have a Common Fate." These writers thanked various Bashkir, Tatar, Chuvash, and Mari writers by name for not blaming the Russian nation for their own nations' plight. The Russian authors also issued a call for the restoration of national and cultural rights, including language rights, to all nations living in Russia. They specifically endorsed a prompt establishment of a Tatar newspaper in Moscow, "where hundreds of thousands of Tatars live." They called on regional Russian-language literary journals as well as local radio and television to cover the life of "fraternal nations."[53]

However welcome these declarations may be to the non-Russians of the RSFSR, it is doubtful that they address their most important concerns. And, in any case, statements in defense of the Tatars or the Peoples of the North need to be weighed against those which emphasize the Slavic and Orthodox character of "Russia." This in itself would tend to promote a sense of second-class citizenship among the non-Russians. There is no evidence suggesting that many influential Russians are prepared to accept today the ideas of Eurasianism, a current in Russian cultural and political thought in the 1920s-1930s that proposed to redefine Russian identity in a fundamental manner by establishing a new entity of "Eurasia." In it, the Russians were to be fully equal with the peoples of the former empire's Asian possessions, such as the Volga Tatars. The only well-known figure who speaks in favor of Eurasian ideas today, but without calling himself a Eurasian, is Lev Gumilev.[54]

As might be expected, the resurgence of Russian nationalism, which expressed itself in the publication on a mass scale of such Russian 19th-century historians as Nikolay Karamzin (1766-1826), Sergev Solov'yev (1820-79), and Vasiliy Klyuchevskiy (1841-1911), was watched with great attention by the Ukrainian intelligentsia. However gratifying the works of these and other historians might be to Russian national feeling, they are bound to displease the Ukrainians, who think of themselves as a separate nation from the Russians. The Russian history presented by these pre-1917 scholars is one that assumes that all Eastern Slavs are, and have been throughout their history, one Russian nation—albeit with regional differences and characteristics—which found its authentic expression in the tsarist state. In other words, these Russian histories of the pre-1917 period, which are now becoming accessible to the general public, are helping those who favor an imperial model of Russia. Karamzin believed that the tsarist state was the most perfect expression of the national character of Russia, and even the title of his magnum opus, *History of the Russian State*, conveys this idea. In the words of Anatole G. Mazour, Karamzin's work "is not even a history of the state—it is a rhetorical, panegyrical narrative that endeavors to prove the autocracy alone has bestowed all the blessings that the Russian empire ever enjoyed." Mazour quotes the famous Pushkin epigram on Karamzin to illustrate how the contemporaries of the historian understood the political message of his work:

In his "History," beauty and simplicity
Prove without bias
The necessity of Autocracy
And the charm of the whip.[55] . . .

Mykhaylo Hrushevsky (1866-1934), unlike Karamzin and the latter's Russian successors, Solov'yev and Klyuchevskiy, was not a "statist" but a "populist" and a "federalist." While working as professor of Ukrainian history at the University of L'viv (then in Austria's province of Galicia), where he was appointed in 1894, Hrushevsky became active in many scholarly projects, the most important of which was a multi-volume history of Ukraine. Hrushevsky's life was dedicated to demonstrating that the Ukrainian people, who, he thought, constituted a society distinct from the state, have had a history of their own, even when they lacked a state. That history should not be subsumed under some artificial formula of a broader "all-Russian" or imperial history. (Hrushevsky thought that the history of the Russian people also should not be reduced to the history of the Muscovite and imperial state, and his position on this subject had sympathizers among Russian historians.)

Hrushevsky was also a political activist. In March 1917, he became the head of the Ukrainian Central Rada and held that post until the overthrow of the Rada in the Skoropadsky coup of May 1918. During Hrushevsky's tenure, Ukraine proclaimed its independence from Russia in January 1918 and then signed a peace treaty with Germany and Austria-Hungary at Brest-Litovsk in February 1918. (The Soviets signed "their" Brest treaty in March.) In 1924, with Moscow's consent, Hrushevsky returned to Kiev from his Vienna exile. As was to be expected, he again played a highly visible public role. But as Stalin launched his attack on Ukraine, Hrushevsky was exiled in 1931 to Moscow. He died under somewhat mysterious circumstances in 1934.

Hrushevsky had been attacked even in his lifetime, but after his death he became a symbol of Ukrainian "bourgeois nationalism" and "fascism." After 1937, no work by Hrushevsky was published in the USSR and the historian's name gradually disappeared from books and journals. A modest attempt to bring Hrushevsky into the realm of scholarly and public discourse was made in the 1960s, but it ended soon and in any case never resulted in the re-publication of his writings. In the 1970s, Ukrainian scholars were simply forbidden even to mention his name.[56] This background information allows one to appreciate the significance of Zahrebel'nyi's "raising the matter" of Hrushevsky in 1988. Zahrebel'nyi's question has since been answered in the affirmative in his homeland. The most important work of Hrushevsky, his 10-volume history of "Ukraine-Rus'," has not been republished, but some of his other writings have been serialized in literary journals.[57]

Literary journals have become the forum for what amounts to a Ukrainian-Russian debate on a number of questions, including the legacy of Kievan Rus'. The debate on Kievan Rus' began when a corresponding member of the USSR Academy of Sciences, O. Trubachev, declared that it should be called a Russian, and not an "East Slavic" state, and that its culture, including its language, should be called Russian.[58]

One might add that the Russian-Ukrainian dispute about Kiev is not limited to the question of its identity in the Middle Ages. A leading Moscow journal, *Novyy Mir*, in its April 1989 issue published a selection of essays by the prominent Russian historian and philosopher G. P. Fedotov (1866-1951), including the previously unpublished "Three Capitals." That essay contains the following passage about the third of the three capitals in question, which touches on the very essence of the Ukrainian-Russian relationship:

> It seems strange to speak about Kiev in our times. Until very recently, we ourselves used to renounce Kiev's glory and infamy, tracing our descent from [the banks of] the Oka and the Volga [rivers]. We ourselves gave Ukraine away to Hrushevsk'kyi and paved the way for Ukrainian separatists. Did Kiev ever occupy the center of our thought, of our love? A striking fact: modern Russian literature has completely left Kiev out.[59]

As for the debate inaugurated by Trubachev, it has since moved to a literary journal published in Moscow, *Druzhba Narodov*.[60] The debate has expanded in scope to examine traditional Russian attitudes toward the Ukrainian language, culture, and history. . . .

The view that Stalinism, Khrushchevism, and Brezhnevism-Suslovism (these designations are used in the Ukrainian press) continued tsarist policies toward

Ukraine is expressed with increasing openness. Borys Kharchuk, for example, claimed to see a direct and uninterrupted line from Peter the Great's ban on Ukrainian printing in 1920, to Alexander II's decrees of 1863 and 1876 (which respectively restricted and banned the use of Ukrainian in publishing), to Stalinist and Brezhnevian anti-Ukrainian measures.[61] . . .

It is quite clear that these "historical" controversies and celebrations are really about the present status of Ukraine in the Soviet Union. Some commentators do not even pretend otherwise. Thus a Kharkiv writer, Radiy Polons'kyi, in an article written in late 1988, quotes from notes he made in 1974-77, which, he said, contained the following passage: "What used to be considered chauvinism and Ukrainophobia now is called internationalism. People whom Lenin used to call great-power bullies now call themselves Leninist-internationalists."[62] Such people, Polons'kyi went on, continue to be active in the period of glasnost' and *perestroyka*. Polons'kyi described Yevgeniy Primakov's project to develop "international structures" via a "rotation of cadres along horizontal lines" as a plan "to artificially mix nations." It is clear to Polons'kyi that "national nihilism" has supporters in high places.

In Polons'kyi's opinion, such a position derives from two different sources. One is the tsarist idea of "one and indivisible Russia" and comes from the past. The other source of inspiration to the "Brezhnevite-Suslovist" policy comes "from outside": the United States of America. The Brezhnevites were impressed by the American model because the American nation is based on a non-national—"extra-national"—principle, and because the American nation represents a conglomerate of people who are united by a common, English language. But "our pseudo-ideologists" have forgotten, says Polons'kyi, that "the great American nation" has behind it "powerful historico-geographic and socio-economic factors of long duration, and not armchair fantasies of power-hungry individuals." Second, and more important, the Brezhnevites "have ignored" the will of the Soviet peoples, including the unflinching will of Russia itself to remain Russia, and not to dissolve itself in a conglomerate. "As we now see," Polons'kyi observed, "they have not succeeded."[63]

Precisely because they fear for their own survival as a nation, Ukrainians are among the most vocal supporters of the restoration of Russia as a full-fledged republic in the form of the RSFSR. The . . . poet-politician Oliynyk, for example, went so far in defending Russia's rights as to complain that Russia did not have a separate seat in the United Nations, which it obviously much deserved. He also said that Russia needs its own Central Committee, its own academy, and all the rest.[64]

The theme of Russia as a republic like the others emerged especially strongly in the speeches of some Baltic deputies to the USSR Congress of People's Deputies. Janis Peters from Latvia, for example, pointed out that the central agencies such as Gosplan also "violate the sovereignty" of Russia, and he wondered why the Russians themselves were not speaking up more in behalf of their republic. "Why is Russia afraid to become independent of the all-Union *diktat*?" Peters asked.[65]

In what was unquestionably the most remarkable analysis of the entire complex issue of the nationalities under the Soviet system presented at the Congress, the Estonian Deputy Klara Hallik argued that the interests of RussiaWhat do "ordinary, the Russian nation, also suffer under the "unnatural" and "antidemocratic" socialism that preserves "habits of imperial thinking."[66] Russian national consciousness suffers because of its "truncated" state structure, whose powers have been taken over by the organs of the USSR. Moscow rules Russia not as a country but as a conglomerate of regions, and Russian identity becomes diluted in an all-Union identity. This impedes Russia's national revival. The struggle against bureaucratic centralism that other republics are waging is, in consequence, mistaken for a struggle against Russia. If a full-fledged institutional structure were created in Russia, the majority of existing all-Union agencies and organization will no longer be necessary.

Hallik also warned against the tendency to confuse integration with centralization and subordination. Only free nations can join the process of integration—and so the centralization being practiced in the USSR runs counter to natural tendencies toward integration. "Russia, let alone Moscow, cannot be considered a center even for Slavic languages, let alone Turkic, Baltic, or Finno-Ugric ones." Similarly, religion and the church are gaining in importance in the contemporary world, but Moscow, the state's capital, is the center for the Russian Orthodox Church alone. For the adherents of Islam, their centers are outside the borders of the state, as they are for Catholics and some other Christians. For Latvians and Estonians, the cultural attraction is to the Scandinavian countries in the Baltic. All Soviet nations should be free to contribute in their unique ways to world culture. Hallik questioned the meaning of various slogans applied to inter-nationality relations in the USSR, including "a strong center and strong republics." What is that "strong center of ours?" Hallik asked. Has some previously unknown "sixteenth republic" been formed in the USSR?[67]

CONCLUSIONS

There is no question that the Russian intelligentsia is giving much thought to the problems of Russian national identity, including the political issues involved in those problems. It is also clear that the non-Russians are pressing for a solution of the Russian problem by means of an institutional separation of Russia from the USSR as a prerequisite for overcoming "imperial thinking" and imperial practices in the Soviet Union.

What do "ordinary" Russians—the *russkiy narod*—think about the matter? Sergey Grigoryants started his recent article on "The Russian National Movement" in the following way: "As yet, a Russian national movement that could become the support of a future democratic state, does not exist in our country."[68]   Although democratic organizations do exist among the Russians, they are relatively weak and often lack a clearly defined national outlook. Grigoryants, who thinks that Pamyat' represents the statist or imperial version of Russian national consciousness taken from the tsarist past, concedes that no counterweight to it has yet emerged that would be both democratic and national. In his view, the political spectrum lacks a force that would promote the cause of a democratic Russia, and focus on the fact that the Russians too are one of the nationalities of the Soviet Union and their national needs should be met as well.   Grigoryants's analysis cannot help but make a historian wonder if those democrats of his acquaintance are not behaving in the same way as did the pre-revolutionary Russian democrats in Milyukov's recollections.[69]

But other historical analogies come to mind as well.   Especially suggestive are the parallels between the problem of "Russia" versus the Soviet state and the problem of German nationalism in the 19th-century Habsburg monarchy up to its fall in 1918.   Allan Janik and Stephen Toulmin drew such parallels in their book, *Wittgenstein's Vienna*, which was published in 1973.   As in the present-day Soviet Union, in the Habsburg monarchy of the late 19th and early 20th centuries, all problems were conceptualized as "national" problems.   Moreover, the Germans in the Habsburg monarchy—just as the Russians today—did not have certain political options available to other nations precisely because of their identification with the ruling center.[70]

A somewhat different parallel suggests itself from the experience of the Ottoman Empire, whose fall did result in the rise of a Turkish nation-state in the old territorial and political core of the empire.   Moreover, much of its periphery had gradually "peeled away" even before the Ottoman Empire disintegrated. Whether "Ottomanization" is in fact a prospect for the Soviet Union in its "inner" empire is another matter, but Timothy Garton Ash believes it is already under way in the East European "outer" empire.[71]

The Soviet Union and Yugoslavia are heirs of the old Habsburg, Ottoman, and tsarist Russian monarchies in that both are facing a fundamental problem of reconciling within their borders nations with Christian and Islamic traditions and their profoundly contrasting ways of life and value systems, according to John A. Armstrong.   Armstrong expects the Christian-Muslim conflict to become a major issue in the coming years not only in Yugoslavia, where it has already been visible for some time, but also in the USSR.[72]

The above may be suggestive and potentially fruitful leads for studying the Soviet nationality problem, but they do not offer any direct help in discerning trends among the population of Russian nationality.   It may be useful, though, to keep in mind the Germans in Bohemia, Slovenia, and other regions of the Habsburg empire before 1918, where indigenous national movements were a threat to the Germans not simply as Germans, i.e., as one of many ethnic groups, but also as representatives of imperial authority.   If this analogy is followed up, then Grigoryants's comments on the Russian reactions in the Baltic area are worth noting. The rise of the "interfronts," or "international fronts," consisting mainly of Russians and other Russian-speaking immigrants, says Grigoryants, should be seen as an expression not of Russian national sentiment but of an "unquestionably Soviet sentiment."[73] In other words, most Russians in Latvia or Estonia view themselves as representatives of the state, of the Soviet-imperial principle, and feel they are living in a potentially rebellious province. They do not view themselves as a (Russian) national minority living in a country that is different from Russia.

It would seem, therefore, that a democratic, "normal" Russian national consciousness has a better chance of emerging in Russia proper, perhaps by developing from some regional autonomist grass roots. There may be reasons to see the workers movement in Siberia in the summer of 1989 in this light. It is evident that the striking miners objected not only to intolerable material conditions but equally strongly to the entire way of life to which they are condemned. They spoke up against bureaucracy, "colonialism," "domination by Moscow," and similar enemies. This would suggest that at stake there are relations between an imperial center and its dependent province.

What role did the intelligentsia have in this conflict? It so happens that in April 1989, there appeared an announcement of the establishment in Novosibirsk of a "Siberian Independent Information Agency." (That announcement was not printed in the official Soviet media.) The inaugural meeting of that "Agency" was attended by representatives of independent journals from Novosibirsk (three publications) and Omsk, as well as by "independent journalists" from Irkutsk, Krasnoyarsk, Novokuznetsk, Kemerovo, and Yakutsk. The declaration adopted at the meeting contains phrases that reveal a sense of a distinct Siberian identity and suggest that it may be assuming a political form. Thus, the declaration protests that Siberia, "which finds itself in a colonial dependence on Moscow authorities," has no mass media of its own and is subject to an "information *diktat*" by all-Union publications. Siberia has to make do with regional media, but lacks media covering Siberia as a whole. It was in order to correct this lack of a specifically Siberian media that the Siberian information agency was founded. The agency's organizers said they would be willing to cooperate professionally with international and national news services interested in covering Siberian affairs. They also hoped that the new agency would be supported by the "Siberian people" (*Sibirskiy narod*) as well as the authorities.[74]

Speeches at the April 1989 plenum of the CPSU Central Committee supplied another kind of evidence that social and economic problems are being perceived in Siberia as in essence problems of regional dependence on the center, which is viewed as the embodiment of the bureaucratic, command-administrative system. The plenum agenda was devoted to assessing the results of the March elections of the Congress of People's Deputies. The elections resulted in defeats of numerous party officials and regional bosses, notably in Leningrad, Moscow, and Kiev, the three largest cities of the Soviet Union. But as one of the losers, the Kemerovo oblast first secretary, noted, the biggest defeats of party officials happened in Siberia and the Far East, "from the Urals to the ocean." The secretary, A. G. Mel'nikov noted that the whole area—30 million inhabitants—suffered from profound social tensions, that "people have come to live much worse," and that the problems were "critical." Mel'nikov cited coal and oil output figures on Siberia's contribution to the economy and complained that despite its importance, Siberia was not treated as a single unit but that its regions were separately managed by central agencies from Moscow, employing administrative-command methods "because we still do not know of any other way" to manage. The only way out of the critical situation was to give Siberia its own rights, its economic and administrative autonomy, and to treat it as an economic partner—and so assure its contribution to the national economy.[75] The appropriateness of these warnings was confirmed by the Siberian strikes.

The key issues for Russian democratic nationalism are also key for all currents of Russian national consciousness. The one to which most attention has been devoted in this article is the attitude toward the state. The second issue, whose urgency and potential destructiveness is daily becoming more apparent, is the social and economic question broadly defined. This somewhat general and academic term covers the most serious and pressing matters of daily life for millions of people: health, ecology, food supplies or rather food shortages, education, wages, housing, work safety—the list goes on. The realization that in all these respects, the Soviet Union lags behind most of the developed world, even certain parts of the Third World, is universal in the Soviet Union. Among the Russians, this awareness is increasingly assuming the form of injured national feelings: "We, the Russians, who have suffered most, we who helped the others in the USSR, in Eastern Europe, Asia, Cuba, Africa, we are now poor and backward."

The resulting anger is directed against many targets. One obvious target is the state and party bureaucracy—"Moscow." Another—the nationalities, such as the Balts and the peoples of the Caucasus. Some elements are explaining the plight of Russia by accusing the "Jews, the international Zionist conspiracy," or "the Masons." These extremists do not blame the state for the present crisis—and for the most part also not the communist ideology per se. Rather, they attribute the sins of the Soviet regime to the Jews who at one time or another occupied important posts in it, and by extension—to Jews as a people.

In such a situation it would seem imperative for the liberal and democratic Russian intelligentsia to make sure that the specifically national or nationalist Russian concerns and issues are not left to the extremists of the Pamyat' kind. Against the right-wing models of Russia, which so prominently feature anti-Semitism and other forms of prejudice, the democrats and liberals need to propose their own democratic, tolerant, and progressive model of *Russia*. They cannot afford to ignore the specific Russian problem as they concern themselves

with general social, economic, or political issues in somewhat abstract terms.
In this regard, the Russian intelligentsia would do well to ponder the
circumstances that in the 1920s had allowed the Fascists in Italy and the Nazis
in Germany to capture considerable popular support by appealing to national
sentiments and traditions.[76]

Clearly, the situation is very critical; and the intellectual and political
confusion, overwhelming. The second question, therefore, that Russian
nationalists, and everybody else in the Soviet Union, have to ask, is: which
ideology and program currently on "the market" will the masses accept as their
own? Like so many thinking Russians are doing these days, Balakhonov quotes
in his article the famous Pushkin lines expressing the poet's dread of "Russian
mutiny, senseless and merciless." To prevent such a "mutiny," the intelligentsia
will have to find a common language with the workers, the likes of whom struck
the mines in Siberia. Will the Russian intelligentsia prove capable of
accomplishing what Polish intellectuals accomplished in the 1970s? As the
world knows, the Polish strikes of 1980 produced Solidarity, not a "senseless
and merciless mutiny."[77]

One of the most insightful analyses of the Solidarity phenomenon was provided
by Alain Touraine, the French sociologist. Touraine sees the historical meaning
of Solidarity, whose rise he believes signals "the end of communist society," in
"setting an alternative agenda of historical action," thereby challenging a major
prerogative that the communist regime had reserved for itself.[78] To follow
Solidarity in this respect will require that the Russian national intelligentsia put
aside its more abstract debates about Orthodox tradition and forget about Zionist
plotters. Instead, the intellectuals in Russia (and in other republics) will have
to think of new ways in which they can help construct a new agenda, an
alternative vision of the future. How they perform this task will help determine
the shape of any new national identity or identities that are likely to emerge in
the USSR. Touraine also offers some instructive thought on identity:

> To the sociologist, identity is . . . no longer an appeal to a mode of being but the
> claim to a capacity for action and for change. It is defined in terms of choice and not
> in terms of substance, essence, or tradition . . . if identity is opposed to the
> organization of social life, it will be marginalized or manipulated by those who direct
> it. On the other hand, the appeal to identity can be considered a labor of democracy,
> an awareness of the effort by which the actors of a social system, that exerts a great
> deal of power upon itself and that is engaged in ceaseless change, attempt to
> determine for themselves the conditions within which their collective and personal life
> is produced.[79]

As this article has tried to show, any effort in this area requires the Russians
to understand that the political entity that many of them now accept as an empire
is the same state that they reject as an oppressive bureaucratic machine.

Notes

1. Aleksandr Zharnikov, "National Self-Determination in Theory and Practice," *Kommunist* (Moscow), No. 9, June 1989, p. 62. Zharnikov is the scientific secretary of the scientific communism section in the Institute of Marxism-Leninism in Moscow.

2. Radio Free Europe-Radio Liberty (hereafter—RFE-RL), "Russian Nationalism Today," *Radio Liberty Research Bulletin* (Munich), Special Edition, Dec. 19, 1988.

3. Ibid., p. 49.

4. Ibid., p. 25.

5. Ibid., p. 33.

6. *Izvestiya* (Moscow), June 11, 1989. Sakharov's address has been translated by Edward Kline; see *The New York Review of Books*, Aug. 17, 1989, pp. 25-26.

7. Yuriy Afanas'yev, "Restructuring and Historical Knowledge," *Literaturnaya Rossiya*, (Moscow), June 17, 1988, pp. 2-3 and 8-9.

8. Alain Besançon, "Nationalism and Bolshevism in the USSR," in Robert Conquest, Ed., *The Last Empire: Nationality and the Soviet Future* (Stanford, CA: Hoover Institution Press, 1986), p. 11.

9. Ibid., pp. 12-13.

10. See *Russkaya Mysl'* (Paris), June 23, 1989, pp. 6-7. Balakhonov's article was originally published in issue No. 13 of *Svobodnoye Slovo*, the independent publication of the Democratic Union.

11. See the various "liberal" views expressed in the round-table discussions entitled, "Democracy Is Conflict: A Search for a Correct Resolution of National Problems in the USSR," *Vek XX i Mir* (Moscow), No. 12, 1988, pp. 8-17.

12. Valeriy Tishkov, "Nations and the State," *Kommunist*, No. 1, January 1989, pp. 49-59.

13. For a fuller discussion of this problem, see Roman Szporluk, "The Imperial Legacy and the Soviet Nationalities Problem," in Lubomyr Hajda and Mark Beissinger, Eds., *The Nationalities Factor in Soviet Politics and Society* (Boulder, Colo.: Westview, 1990).

14. Yu. V. Bromley, "Being a Cohesive Force," *Sovetskaya Kul'tura* (Moscow), June 25, 1988, p. 8.

15. Yu. V. Bromley, "National Problems under Restructuring," *Voprosy Istorii* (Moscow), No. 1, 1989, p. 40.

16. J. K. Rebane, "Let Us Build Together Reasonable Relations," *Kommunist*, No. 4, March 1989, p. 85. This argument is not new, of course, as the title of Ivan Dzyuba's book written a quarter of a century ago—*Internationalism or Russification?*—reminds us.

17. *Pravda* (Moscow), July 2, 1988.

18. Ibid., Apr. 27, 1989.

19. S. L. Tikhvinskiy, "Tasks of Coordination in the Area of Historical Science," *Istoriya SSSR* (Moscow), No. 1, 1988, p. 119.

20. "Democracy is Conflict...," loc. cit., p. 10.

21. Mark G. Field, "Soviet Society and Communist Party Controls: A Case of Constricted Development," in Donald W. Treadgold, Ed., *Soviet and Chinese Communism: Similarities and Differences* (Seattle, WA: University of Washington Press, 1967), p. 196.

22. Alksander Yanov's and John B. Dunlop's many publications provide full documentation and analysis of those currents.

23. G. Sazonov, "Vasiliy Belov: Do Not Be Afraid of Glasnost'," *Pravda*, Mar. 5, 1989.

24. *Znamya* (Moscow), No. 2, 1989, pp. 168-169.

25. Interview in *Literaturnaya Rossiya*, June 2, 1989.

26. "For Objectivity in the History of the Fatherland," *Nash Sovremennik* (Moscow), No. 5, 1988, pp. 186-188.

27. "Letter to the Soviet Government," *Literaturnyy Irkutsk*, December 1988, pp. 4 and 7.

28. Ibid. The authors refer to Lenin's *Polnoye sobraniye sochineniy* (*Complete Collected Works*), Vol. 22, pp. 229-230, to support their assertion. The Soviet scholar, G. I. Kunitsyn, in "Self-Determination of Nations: The History of the Problem and Our Times," *Voprosy Filosofii* (Moscow), No. 5, 1989, pp. 66-86, argues that the Stalinist conception of the role of the Russian nation as the ruling nation of the Soviet state was put into practice after 1917, and that this was done in direct violation of Lenin's view. By depriving the RSFSR of the normal state structure of Soviet republics, and by placing Russia directly under central authorities, Stalin restored the pre-revolutionary great-power, imperialist concept, but he disguised it under revolutionary terminology. (See especially pp. 76-78). There is not a word about "Zionists" or "Trotskyists" in Kunitsyn's balanced and well-documented account.

29. Roy Medvedev wrote more than 10 years ago: "It is a fact that the national life of Russians is hampered to a far greater degree than that of, say, Armenians, Georgians, and the Uzbek peoples."

"Thus, for example, the villages and hamlets of basically Russian districts are in an immeasurably more neglected condition than the villages of Ukraine, Moldavia, the Transcaucasus, and the Baltic. Furthermore, Russians are basically deprived of their capital. As the capital of a multi-national Union, Moscow has almost lost its traits of a national Russian city, a capital of Russian lands such as it was prior to the Revolution. The more European, industrial, and bureaucratic Petersburg was the capital of the Empire. This transformation of Moscow into an international center devoid of clear national lines is by no means a positive consequence for the whole Russian nation."

"At present, the weakening of the national foundations of Russian life is neither legal [*zakonomernyy*—meaning, a natural process], nor progressive."

"How could not only the preservation but also the development of the distinctive originality of the Russian people be furthered? This is a question that demands social analysis. Let us note, first of all, that the old proposal of separating the capitals of the USSR and the RSFSR, for which many people were condemned under Stalin, is not so fruitless. Similarly, it is necessary to undertake wide-ranging and urgent measures for upgrading agriculture and culture in basically Russian districts, especially in the center and the north of the European areas of the RSFSR." See "What Awaits Us in the Future? (Regarding A. I. Solzhenitsyn's Letter)," in Michael Meerson-Aksenov and Boris Shragin, Eds., *The Political, Social, and Religious Thought of Russian "Samizdat"—An Anthology* (Belmont, MA: Nordland, 1977), pp. 77-78.

30. Feliks Dymov, "Permit Whatever Is Not Forbidden!" *Literaturnaya Rossiya*, No. 24, June 17, 1988, p. 3. See also a report on the symposium, (whose participants included D. S. Likhachev and N. A. Tolstoy), "A Great City with a Provincial Fate?" *Literaturnaya Gazeta* (Moscow), Mar. 2, 1988, p. 10.

31. S. Galayeva, "National Home of Russia," *Literaturnaya Rossiya*, No. 25, June 23, 1989, p. 18.

32. See the interview with the chairman of the board, corresponding member of the USSR Academy of Sciences Oleg Trubachev, in *Literaturnaya Gazeta*, Mar. 22, 1989, p. 5; and a report entitled "Plans for a Russian Encyclopedia," in *Literaturnaya Rossiya*, Apr. 14, 1989. p. 3.

33. John B. Dunlop, "Two Noteworthy Russian Nationalist Initiatives," RFE-RL, *Report on the USSR* (Munich), No. 21, May 26, 1989, p. 3.

34. Ibid., pp. 3-4.

35. *Moskovskiy Literator*, Dec. 16, 1988, p. 3, as quoted by John B. Dunlop.

36. Boris Ivanovich Tsarev, "By the Force of Russian Brotherhood," *Literaturnaya Rossiya*, June 16, 1989, p. 11.

37. *Moskovskiy Literator*, Mar. 24, 1989, p. 1; and *Literaturnaya Rossiya*, Mar. 31, 1989, p. 10.

38. M. Antonov, "From the Standpoint of Socialism," *Moskovskiy Literator*, Mar. 31, 1989; and "Appeal of the Union of Spiritual Rebirth of the Fatherland," ibid.

39. "Thinking of the Homeland, of Russia," *Literaturnaya Rossiya*, Mar. 31, 1989, p. 10; and "Fatherland—the Highest Good," ibid., June 23, 1989, p. 14. The former source calls the organization a "movement" (*dvizheniye*); the latter, a "society" (*obshchestvo*).

40. P. N. Milyukov, *Natsional'nyy vopros—Proiskhozhdeniye natsional'nosti i natsional'nyye voprosy v Rossii* (The National Problem—The Origins of Nationality and National Problems in Russia), no place of publication, Biblioteka izdatel'stva "Svobodnaya Rossiya," 1925, pp. 116-117.

41. Vladimir Balakhonov, "Preservation of the Empire or Self-Preservation by Way of National Sovereignty—the Main National Problem of the Russian People, *Russkaya Mysl'*, June 23, 1989, pp. 6-7.

42. "Djilas on Gorbachev (II): Milovan Djilas and George Urban in Conversation," *Encounter* (London), November 1988, p. 30.

43. Balakhonov, loc. cit., p. 6. Suggestions about subdividing the RSFSR have appeared in an official Moscow weekly, *Literaturnaya Gazeta*. See Vladimir Sokolov, "Democracy and Borders: Concepts," August 2, 1989.

44. Ibid., p. 7.

45. *Literaturnaya Rossiya*, June 30, 1989, p. 14.

46. Ibid.

47. *The New York Times*, Mar. 13, 1989.

48. Julia Wishnevsky, "*Nash Sovremennik* Provides Focus for 'Opposition Party'," *Report on the USSR*, Jan. 20, 1989, p. 30.

49. Ibid., pp. 5-6.

50. M. I. Mongo, *Pravda*, June 7, 1989.

51. "Theses for the Preparation of a Platform of the Tatar Civic Center," *Slovo Agitatora* (Kazan') Nos. 23-24, December 1988, pp. 34-35.

52. Kamilla Yunusova, "Responsibility, As Never Before," *Literaturnaya Rossiya*, June 2, 1989, p. 10.

53. Ibid., May 26, 1989, p. 5.

54. For a discussion of Eurasianism see my "The Search for Identity in Russia and Eastern Europe," *Cross-Currents: A Yearbook of Central European Culture* (Ann Arbor, MI), No. 9, forthcoming in 1990.

55. Anatole G. Mazour, *Modern Russian Historiography* (Westport, CT: Greenwood Press, 1975), pp. 81 and 85.

56. For Hrushevsky's life, times, and writings, see Thomas M. Prymak, *Mykhailo Hrushevsky: The Politics of National Culture* (Toronto, Buffalo, and London: University of Toronto Press, 1987), and his "Hrushevsky and the Ukraine's 'Lost' History," *History Today* (London), January 1989, pp. 42-46. On the prohibition to mention Hrushevsky's name in Ukraine (but not in Russia, where scholars had been free to cite his writings), see Vasyl' Skurativs'kyi, "Protective Immunity—Ethnography," *Literaturna Ukraina*, July 21, 1988, pp. 3 and 5. Without saying so directly, Skurativs'kyi implies that the ban on Hrushevsky's name went into effect when Petro Shelest was replaced by V. V. Shcherbyts'kyi as Ukrainian Communist Party first secretary. Two contrasting stands on the Ukrainian historian and politician are revealed in Serhiy Bilokin', "Hrushevs'kyi," ibid.; and V. Sarbey, "How Are We to Treat M. Hrushevs'kiy," *Radyans'ka Ukraina* (Kiev), Aug. 27, 1988. Bilokin' treats Hrushevsky in the same way as the non-Marxist historians of Russian are treated in Russia. Sarbey views the historian primarily as a dangerous enemy of the Soviet state, although he, too, recognizes the scholarly value of Hrushevsky's work.

57. See Mykhailo Hrushevs'kyi, "Memoirs," *Kyiv* (Kiev), No. 9, 1988, pp. 115-49, and subsequent issues; and idem, "The Cultural-National Movement in Ukraine in the 16th-17th Centuries," *Zhotven'* (L'viv), No. 1, 1989 (and subsequent issues). *Vitchyzna* (Kiev) began the publication of Hrushevsky's work dealing with the Cossack period in its January 1989 issue.

58. O. Trubachev, "The Slavs: Their Language and History," *Pravda*, Mar. 27, 1987.

59. G. P. Fedotov, "Three Capitals," *Novyy Mir*, No. 4, 1989, p. 215.

60. Trubachev in *Druzhba Narodov* (Moscow), No. 5, 1988, and his response in "On the Union of Language and other Matters," ibid., No. 9, 1988, pp. 261-64. The same issue contained several critical letters from readers, including one by Bohdan Sen'kiv, who argued that Trubachev's stand implies the subordinate position of the Ukrainian and Belorussian languages vis-à-vis the Russian language in the Ukrainian and Belorussian republics.

Druzhba Narodov's opening of its pages to Ukrainian contributions is important because Ukrainian journals are printed in incomparably fewer copies and, in any case, are not read by the Russian public.

61. Borys Kharchuk, "The World and the Nation," *Prapor* (Kharkiv), No. 10, 1988, reprinted in *Suchasnist'* (Munich), no. 3, 1989, pp. 113-26.

62. Radiy Polons'kyi, "If the Revolution Lives in the Heart," *Prapor*, no. 1, 1989, p. 146.

63. Ibid., p. 152.

64. Quoted in Pavel Emelin, "The Energy of the Word: People's Deputies of the USSR Speak Out," *Literaturnaya Rossiya*, June 16, 1989.

65. *Izvestiya*, June 4, 1989.

66. *Pravda*, June 7, 1989.

67. Ibid. Hallik did not say so, but the slogan "a strong center and strong republics" was coined by Gorbachev.

68. Sergey Grigoryants, "The Russian National Movement," *Russkaya Mysl'*, No. 3775, May 12, 1989, p. 6.

69. But this assessment may be too pessimistic. At least one contemporary critic, and moreover one who is not a friend of the democratic option, speaks of public opinion becoming split into two extremes, one being Pamyat', the other—the Democratic Union. See Sergey Kurginyan, "On the Mechanics of Gliding Down," *Literaturnaya Rossiya*, July 7, 1989, p. 9 and July 14, 1989, p. 2.

70. See Allan Janik and Stephen Toulmin, *Wittgenstein's Vienna* (New York: Simon and Schuster, 1973), pp. 271-72. I discuss their thesis in my article, "Defining 'Central Europe': Power, Politics, and Culture," *Cross Currents: A Yearbook of Central European Culture*, No. 1 (1982), pp. 30-38. For reflections on the German problem under the Habsburgs, see Benedict Anderson, *Imagined Communities: Refections on the Origin and Spread of Nationalism* (London: Verso and NLB, 1983), p. 81.

71. Timothy Garton Ash, "The Empire in Decay," *The New York Review of Books*, Sept. 29, 1988, p. 56.

72. John A. Armstrong, "Toward a Framework for Considering Nationalism in East Europe," *Eastern European Politics and Societies* (Berkeley, CA), Spring 1988, pp. 301-02.

73. Grigoryants, loc. cit., p. 6.

74. "Creation of a Siberian Independent Information Agency," *Russkaya Mysl'*, Apr. 14, 1989, p. 2.

75. *Pravda*, Apr. 27, 1989.

76. See Geoff Eley's chapter, "What Produces Fascism: Preindustrial Traditions or a Crisis of the Capitalist State?" in *From Unification to Nazism: Reinterpreting the German Past*, (Boston, London, and Sydney: Allen and Unwin, 1986), pp. 254-82; see also Roman Szporluk, *Communism and Nationalism: Karl Marx versus Friedrich List* (New York and Oxford: Oxford University Press, 1988), pp. 189-90.

77. According to Bill Keller, writing from Moscow on the strikes in the Ukrainian SSR, "miners who walked out today in the Western Ukrainian city of Chervonograd included in their demands the creation of an independent national coal-miners' union explicitly modeled on the Polish union Solidarity." ("Soviet Strikers Hint at Forming a Free Union Like Solidarity," *The New York Times*, July 21, 1989.) Future events will show whether these demands will acquire substance and whether the workers of Siberia and Donbas will organize unions modeled on Solidarity.

The original Solidarity in Poland had may dimensions—religious and national as well as social and economic. Just as it is too early to tell whether the workers of Siberia feel any definite regional Siberian or national Russian identity, so it is impossible to detect any specific regional or national Ukrainian identity in the workers' consciousness in the Donbas or Western Ukraine. This brings to mind Ukrainian writer Yuriy Shcherbak's recent remark that unlike elsewhere in the USSR, in Ukraine there have emerged not interethnic conflicts but rather a conflict between Ukrainians and those whom Shcherbak calls "Little Russians." (Interview with Yuriy Shcherbak in *Literaturnaya Gazeta*, Jan.

18, 1989, p. 3.) The latter term would describe those ethnic Ukrainians who prefer to consider themselves members of a larger Russian nation while preserving some specific regional Ukrainian features. Thus, the "Little Russians" represent Ukrainian supporters of an "all-Russia" national identity discussed earlier. It would seem, therefore, that in contemporary Ukraine, especially in such heavily Russified areas as Donbas, at least three identities are competing for popular support: Russian, Ukrainian, and "Little Russian." Conceivably, there is a fourth one too—some form of Soviet identity. The possibility of such an identity actually taking shape should not be dismissed a priori, even though the concept itself was originally "manufactured upstairs." For ample evidence on how national traditions and national identities were being "invented," that is, consciously produced (not to say manufactured) in 19th-century Europe and elsewhere, see Eric Hobsbawm and Terence Ranger, Eds., *The Invention of Tradition* (Cambridge: Cambridge University Press, 1988).

78. Alain Touraine, *Return of the Actor: Social Theory in Postindustrial Society*, tr. by Myrna Godzich (Minneapolis, MN: University of Minnesota Press, 1988), p. xix.

79. Ibid., pp. 81-82.

PART VII

COPING WITH THE NATIONALITIES CRISIS

Much of the Western literature on the Soviet nationality question assesses the threat that the multinational structure and national diversity pose to the stability of the Soviet state and hazards predictions on whether, and under what conditions, the nationalities question will push the Soviet state toward disintegration. This issue was the focus of debates as much in the 1970s (and even before) as it is in the 1990s. A key assumption among Western authors who predicted the break-up of the Soviet Union even before the rise of Gorbachev was that the problems that would lead to the disintegration of the USSR were insurmountable and inherent in the Soviet system.[1] Those authors might understand the current crisis as the inevitable crowning of insoluble problems that have plagued the country since its inception. Another view, however, characterizes the nationalities crisis as more directly the result of Gorbachev's reforms, initiated in 1985.[2] The chapters in Part VII describe the crisis and Gorbachev's attempts to cope with it. Their accounts raise the difficult question of whether a reformed federation is compatible with the Soviet political system.

Paul Goble's chapter discusses the dynamic relationship between republic elites, who took advantage of a more relaxed political environment to engage more actively in ethnopolitics and make bold demands, and Moscow elites, who tried to cope with the new political environment. He suggests that the parameters of nationality-related demands are wider in the new, less coercive environment in the Soviet Union, and that not all demands are about independence. As long as the USSR remains a multinational state and relatively free of any widespread use of coercion, some national elites will use certain political resources to advance their interests within the system. Remaining within the system, however, does not mean that they wholly submit to being "Sovietized." Those national elites who seek independence, however, will also engage in ethnopolitics to reach their ends.

Goble recognizes the strength of ethnonational identity and the "relative weakness of other collective identities" but argues that Moscow could, in the absence of the old methods of coercion, work out a new ethnic politics with some nationalists. As a part of this ethnic politics, Moscow would have to set limits on how much the national republics could claim; events have demonstrated, however, that Moscow consistently lagged behind developments in republic politics. Both Goble and Alexander Motyl point out how democratization and *glasnost'* limited Gorbachev's room to maneuver in dealing with nationalist activities. He allowed the Balts and the Armenians to go too far too fast, a policy that preempted the leadership's capacity to set limits on republic activity—especially after the coming to power of counter elites. The subsequent crackdown on nationalist dissent undermined the two programs that framed economic restructuring.

Goble's hope that a new ethnic politics could be established is based in part on new ideas about the role of federal institutions in resolving ethnic conflict. Gorbachev lobbied hard to convince the USSR Supreme Soviet to adopt the draft Union treaty, and the Council of the Federation was to fulfill the role Goble sketches out at the end of his essay. These institutions might have gone some distance in keeping ethnic politics contained, but by the time they took their final legal form, counterelites and political institutions in many republics (supreme soviets and political party leaders) had developed far more radical agendas, such as secession, on which they were unwilling to compromise.

Motyl recasts the problem in more dire terms. There is no space for ethnic politics, he says, for in the absence of a coercive apparatus, nationalist elites will take advantage of decentralization to "pursue increasingly . . . nationalist behavior." The USSR is stable so long as it is not democratic. Motyl argues that the Soviet Union can cohere only with recentralization and a renewed use of coercion, or with a new federation altogether, and that Gorbachev's political and economic reform project set off the nationalist crises that threaten this coherence. Stephan Kux describes Gorbachev's first steps toward renewing the federation in an attempt to contain the crises and preserve the Union. According to Kux, however, the Soviet federation lacks legitimacy and the institutions for conflict resolution required for a federation to work. Drawing on the theoretical literature on federalism, he argues that addressing the threat of disintegration by reconstructing federalism runs against the tradition of using federation building as a way of *building*—as opposed to salvaging—a nation or empire. This view complements Motyl's vision, which suggests that the Soviet Union can endure *only* as an empire.

The search for a new political structure to make the USSR viable leads one to wonder whether the authors addressing the issue of collapse have the same object in mind. Disintegrationists doubted the survivability of a quasi-totalitarian political system in which the Communist Party exercised arbitrary rule and the police wielded unchallenged power. Gorbachev's policies shook loose these two linchpins, and thus undermined the totalitarian system that many people thought characterized the Soviet political system. The kinds of reforms that Kux examines probably would never have been attempted under the regime that the disintegrationists scrutinized. However, that the Soviet Union collapsed as a result (in part, at least) of the failure of democratic reform should lead one to ask whether the disintegrationists were right for the right reasons.

Notes

1. See especially Hélène Carrère d'Encausse, *Decline of an Empire*, Conclusion, pp. 266-275, and Richard Pipes in Carl Linden and Dimitri Simes, eds., *Nationalities and Nationalism in the USSR: A Soviet Dilemma* (Washington, D.C.: Georgetown University Center for Strategic and International Studies, 1977). The disintegrationist versus nondisintegrationist debate is treated by Roeder and Lapidus, in Chapters 7 and 18 respectively. It is worth reiterating here that the nondisintegrationists did not entirely deny the relevance of the variables in the disintegrationists' equation for collapse; rather, they argued that the equation did not "add up," and that other factors accounted for the system's endurance. Alexander J. Motyl wrote in *Will the Non-Russians Rebel: State, Ethnicity, and Stability in the USSR* (Ithaca: Cornell University Press, 1987) that effective coercion would provide the necessary means for the system to continue. Since this means evaporated, the argument for collapse is reasonable, but we should still examine how helpful and accurate the first group is in predicting this particular crisis of the Soviet federation, and how helpful the second group has been in explaining it.

Long before Gorbachev's rise to power, the disintegrationist argument held that the Soviet federation was inherently unstable and that rising ethnic nationalism would make it untenable. In his conclusion to *The Formation of the Soviet Union* (New York: Atheneum, 1974), Pipes (see Chapter 2) set out the framework in which the disintegrationist argument could be placed by identifying the USSR's multiethnic, federal structure as the country's most historically significant feature. The more recent literature (especially that of Roeder and Motyl) bears out this prescient claim, as it identifies the republics' political institutions as springboards for mobilization and collective action by nationalists.

D'Encausse later advanced the argument that the long-standing Soviet policy that aimed at instilling a sense of Soviet identity (*sovetskii narod*) and developing a supranational culture based on loyalty to the Soviet Union failed. The tactical nation-states that the Bolsheviks made of the union republics, autonomous republics, and autonomous regions sponsored ethnocultural development and fostered among national minorities a strong sense of national identity. D'Encausse concludes that, instead of "drawing together," the peoples of the republics, keenly aware of their national heritages, were splitting apart. However, d'Encausse places less emphasis on anti-Soviet or anti-Russian sentiment and finds rather that non-Russian nations desire real autonomy and a strict application of federalism. Moreover, she holds that the concept of "the Soviet People" was doomed because some minority groups were totally incapable of being assimilated, especially the Central Asians. National minorities were not seeking to destroy the Soviet system, but all of the above problems combined to create an impasse from which "the Soviet state seem[ed] incapable of extricating itself" (Hélène Carrere d'Encausse, Decline of an Empire [New York: Harper Colophon Books, 1981], p. 275).

Both d'Encausse (1978) and Gail Lapidus (Chapter 18) focus on national consciousness and national identity, but each has a different assumption about the primacy of national identity and each draws a different conclusion about its impact on the future of the Soviet state.   In 1984, Lapidus emphasized bases of identity other than ethnicity that would motivate individuals' political participation. Motyl bridged the two, accepting some of the premises of the disintegrationists about the inevitability of conflict in the Soviet multiethnic structure and about the desire among non-Russians to rebel.   State coercion, however, denied dissatisfied minority groups the opportunity to garner the political resources necessary for collective action.

2. This is one of the broadest questions in Soviet nationalities studies, and authors on both sides of the debates changed or refined their views over the years.   The chapters in this volume represent views at particular points in the debate, but they cannot represent all the views that have been expressed throughout the past twenty years.

21

Ethnic Politics in the USSR

Paul Goble

The rising tide of national activism in the Soviet Union has led many in Moscow and in the West to draw apocalyptic conclusions. Some have seen the upsurge of unrest as heralding the end of the Soviet empire; others view it as pointing to the end of *perestroika* and the eventual ouster of its author. Although these judgements may ultimately prove prophetic, the current preoccupation with them has detracted attention from a more immediate and interesting development—the demise of the "national question" as traditionally understood in the USSR and the emergence of a distinctly Soviet brand of ethnic politics.

Even now, the use of the term "ethnic politics" in speaking of the Soviet system has a strange ring to it. Until very recently, ethnic issues in the USSR were discussed in terms of the "national question," an ideologically charged concept that set strict limits on what could be discussed and usually precluded the open acknowledgment of real problems. Combined with Moscow's virtual monopoly on political resources, this meant that the various national entities of the Soviet Union had neither the sanction nor the resources to engage in ethnic politics in any meaningful way.[1] Moscow made decisions "behind closed doors" on the basis of its own calculations, carefully concealed any controversy, and used its overwhelming political, economic, and coercive clout to impose its will on the periphery.[2] Under Mikhail Gorbachev, this has begun to change. . . . Moscow . . . no longer observes many of the taboos that [the national question] had imposed. Soviet leaders from Gorbachev on down now routinely acknowledge the existence of serious ethnic problems and, particularly important here, that the groups directly involved should participate in the resolution of these problems. And as the intended or unintended consequence of his policies, Gorbachev has overseen the devolution of certain kinds of political resources

Published in *Problems of Communism*, 38: 4 (July-August 1989), pp. 1-15. Reprinted with permission of the publisher.

from Moscow to the periphery. As a result, at least some national groups now have both the sanction and the resources to engage in political activity, even though Moscow continues to have the upper hand.

In this essay, I wish to explore the outlines of this new phenomenon in the Soviet Union. To do so, I would like to suggest some preliminary answers to three major questions:

• How have Gorbachev's policies transformed the situation, allowing what had been unthinkable just a few years ago to take place on a regular basis?

• What are the resources of and constraints on the major participants, and what strategies has each of them employed to advance its interests in the new environment?

• What forces in the Soviet system tend to buttress the emerging system of ethnic politics, what forces work against it, and how are these likely to play out over the next year?

By doing so, I hope to show that the changes in the Soviet system that have made the new ethnic activism possible may provide the basis for an evolution of the Soviet system in a direction that avoids the two apocalypses mentioned above.

CHANGING THE RULES OF THE GAME

As one Soviet specialist on ethnic relations has observed, Gorbachev could have begun *perestroika* in the area of nationality relations but chose instead to launch it in the economic and political spheres.[3] This is hardly surprising: Gorbachev had little experience or expertise on nationality questions before coming to power, and many of those who currently surround him in the Soviet leadership also lack a background in this area. Had Gorbachev and others in the leadership been more aware of the implications of the country's ethnic mosaic for reform and vice versa, they might not have been willing to take the policy risks needed to shake the system. But precisely because Gorbachev did not focus on nationality issues and did not articulate a specific nationality policy as his predecessors had invariably done, the impact of his other policies on the country's various ethnic communities has been all the greater.[4]

Gorbachev's three man domestic policy thrusts—the reduction of coercion and promotion of *glasnost'*, his presidential and participatory style of leadership, and his overriding concern with efficiency and generally anti-ideological stance—all have had significant implications for ethnic politics.

Gorbachev's reduction of the level of coercion in Soviet society and his "new thinking" in foreign policy, which removes much of the justification for coercion, has contributed to an explosion in public activism throughout the Soviet Union and to a dramatic change in the relationship of republic elites to Moscow and to their respective populations. The frequency with which demonstrations are staged provides a good example. Prior to Gorbachev, few people were willing to engage in public protests, because the risks were high and certain and the chances of reward were virtually nil. Between 1956 and 1985, there was on average one demonstration in the USSR every 18 days; most had fewer than a dozen participants, and focused on elite concerns such as human rights issues. Since Gorbachev came to power, much has changed; the risks of participating in demonstrations have declined and the chances of achieving one's demands have gone up dramatically as Moscow and republic leaderships have proved willing to negotiate with demonstrators. Now, there is approximately one demonstration every three days in the USSR, and its average size is in the thousands.[5] More important, however, is the fact that an ever-increasing share of these demonstrations are nationality-related—reflecting the nationality basis of the system, the strength of ethnic identities, and the relative weakness of other collective identities and ties because of past Soviet policies.

Even more significant is the change in the relationship of republic leaders to Moscow and to their own populations. In the environment of high coercion before Gorbachev, republic leaders were more dependent on and responsive to those above them than to those below them. Moscow could remove republic leaders with impunity, and those below them could be coerced into obedience. This meant that Moscow could rely on republic elites to act as its proconsuls, imposing its policies and deflecting popular anger away from the center. That has changed. In the words of one writer, "The apparatus that was able to command must now learn how to convince."[6] To be effective, republic leaders must now increasingly heed the view of those below them and hence may be ever less responsive to those above. One example is Gennadiy Kolbin, the ethnic Russian whose appointment as Kazakhstan's party chief in December 1986 sparked a major Kazakh protest. While holding this post, he became more Kazakh than his Kazakh predecessor, advancing republic interests far more forcefully that Dinmukhammad Kunayev ever did. He defended his republic against criticisms from the center and presented himself as an expert on ethnic problems of the Kazakhs and the large German minority in Kazakhstan.[7] Or take the case of Moscow trying to impose order in Armenia and Azerbaijan by a change in republic leadership. In each republic, Moscow's new man soon began to articulate many of the same themes for which his predecessor had been let go. Had either failed to do so, he would have been rendered ineffective. This change in the relationship between republic leaders and Moscow has affected even conservative Brezhnev-era holdovers like Ukraine's Volodymyr Shcherbytskyi and Moldavia's Semen Grossu, both of whom have had to go along with at least some national aspirations in order to exercise effective rule.

This development was apparently unforeseen by Gorbachev. Yet, it carries major ramifications. In addition to signifying that the republic leaderships will increasingly line up with their respective populations, it has the potential to heighten ethnic tensions through the lack of a native executor of Moscow's will.

It also reduces Moscow's options for coping with a situation that threatens to get out of control. Indeed, Moscow's decision to impose martial law on much of Armenia and Azerbaijan in 1988 reflected this change as much as it represented a response to the demonstrations, strikes, and communal violence that preceded the decision.

At the same time as coercion has been reduced, Gorbachev has sponsored *glasnost'*—the more open discussion of virtually all issues. By calling attention to past and present problems, this policy has both angered the population and accentuated national differences and conflicts. It is simply not true that Soviet citizens knew about all the things that have been brought out by *glasnost'* but simply could not voice their knowledge; most of them probably had no idea of the scale or even the existence of certain events and developments. Moreover, there is virtually no event in Soviet history whose discussion does not increase national divisions. Collectivization, for example, looks very different in [the] Ukraine and Kazakhstan—where millions died as a direct result of it—than in Moscow, where Russian workers were guaranteed some food through rations. Even the Great Patriotic War, which Moscow views as the best proof of the Soviet Union's unity, divides the people of the Baltic republics—who lost their independence as the result of the Hitler-Stalin Pact—from those who remember the war as a singular achievement.

An organizational feature of the Soviet press is relevant here. To a large extent, it is structured along ethno-linguistic and ethno-territorial lines rather than functional ones. As a result, the press tends to provide each national group with what can only be described as a national perspective on events. And in this way, the press often becomes a stimulus of national activism by providing details on demonstrations and their often successful consequences. The Kazakh press, for example, noted that fewer dismissals of Kazakh officials took place in Alma-Ata following the December 1986 demonstrations than of officials in neighboring republics, where there had been no demonstrations.[8]

Gorbachev's second main decision—to adopt a presidential style and support mass participation—reflects both his weakness in many of the party and state bureaucracies and his own sense of himself as a Soviet man who can make successful appeals to the population as Soviet citizens above all else. His frequent public expressions of impatience with manifestations of non-Russian ethnicity reflect that attitude. His anti-bureaucratic approach has two major consequences. First, it has weakened some central ministries and their party committee branch departments, thus allowing greater scope for independent action by republic leaderships. For example, the republics quickly moved into the foreign trade arena following the dismemberment of the old Ministry of Foreign Trade in Moscow. And second, his attack on republic bureaucracies and the resultant cuts of up to 50 percent in some republic ministry and party organizational personnel have angered many.[9] Some of those dismissed have not been able to make an easy transition, and it is not unlikely that at least a few are now applying their political and bureaucratic skills to help ethnic activists work against the system.

Gorbachev's desire to avoid anything that might call his democratization program into question or offend key constituencies in Moscow and abroad, plus his desire to mobilize the population against bureaucratic constraints, has also had significant consequences for ethnic groups. First, it has led him to support virtually all forms of popular activism at least initially, even when a more sober assessment might have suggested another course of action. This has encouraged ever more groups to take up various causes. Second, because various national groups—such as the Armenians and the Baltic nationalities—have been able to count on some restraint on the part of the center, they have often gone further than Moscow could ultimately tolerate and have had to be reined in sharply later. This has led to a situation in the republics where everyone is uncertain about just what will happen next.

While Gorbachev has not been very effective at setting limits, he has had the good fortune to have some colleagues who are. And as will be seen below, this fact may help to constrain the centrifugal forces that he appears to have set loose. At the same time, some of his political reforms may have the effect of isolating extremists. In Leningrad, for example, a Russian nationalist candidate of *Pamyat'* suffered a serious defeat in a working-class Russian constituency that might have been expected to support him, precisely because he was not equipped to make the pledges of constituency service that the winners did.[10] And in the Baltic republics, the people's fronts' candidates are generally more moderate and even cautious than their supporters.

The third major thrust of Gorbachev's policy package is his promotion of efficiency and an essentially anti-ideological stance. Gorbachev's approach necessarily works against some, if not all, demands of non-Russians. For example, he has undercut the affirmative-action programs in the republics, on the grounds that they are inefficient and a form of "reverse discrimination."[11] He has attacked, even killed, major "gigantist" projects like the Siberian river diversion. While these projects were opposed by Russians and would have been extremely expensive, they would have constituted major interregional, and hence interethnic, transfers of resources. And his support for some sort of republic *khozrashchet* (self-financing) is at least partially intended to make every republic pay its own way. If this policy were ever to be implemented, it would create a vast new number of winners and losers, and this would, in turn, result in protests of various kinds.

While Gorbachev is clearly a committed Marxist-Leninist, his attacks on Marxist-Leninist theory and on much of Soviet history as well as his generally technocratic approach have called into question the legitimating principle of the multinational Soviet state and opened the door to various choices and activism that ideology heretofore had proscribed.[12] Besides legitimating the USSR, Marxism-Leninism served to curb non-Russian nationalism and many forms of

Russian assertiveness. To the extent that the constraints inherent in Marxism-Leninism are lowered or removed, both Russians and non-Russians are likely to become more active, to explore their unique pasts, and to engage in activities that will exacerbate interethnic tension. In the absence of institutional protections, the smaller ethnic groups will tend to suffer disproportionately more at the hands of the more numerous and now less constrained Russians. Such a development could additionally delegitimate the regime for the non-Russians and might force a return to a more repressive and Russian-nationalist rule.

At the same time, the reduction of the importance of Marxist-Leninist ideology has had several positive consequences in both official and unofficial realms. Officially, it has allowed the regime to explore a far broader range of options to cope with its problems.[13] Thus, for example, Moscow copied India's practice of seizing direct control of ethnically troubled regions when it imposed direct rule from Moscow on Nagorno-Karabakh in January 1989. And it has encouraged officials to risk experimenting with various kinds of ethnic organization that they otherwise might have rejected, such as allowing the hitherto ideologically suspect application of extraterritorial cultural autonomy, a policy that could give groups living outside their home area some native-language institutions. Outside the official realm, the benefits have been far greater. All ethnic groups have been able to explore aspects of their history and identity that had formerly been completely out of bounds—such as religion—and to articulate new ideas on the basis of sources that Marxism-Leninism would have declared beyond the pale.

Taken together, these three thrusts have launched but not yet institutionalized a new system, one that can be described as a form of ethnic politics. Gorbachev's general approach has provided various non-Russian groups with important political resources of a distinctive but important kind—primarily in the information area—and the sanction to engage in political negotiations on a variety of levels. Moreover, his tolerance for the expression of divergent views has meant that many old issues have been allowed to surface and to mobilize larger portions of the population. And his policies themselves have created new winners and losers, many of whom clearly believe that they must act quickly before it is too late to defend or oppose the new situation.

PLAYING THE GAME

The variety of ethnic communities that have responded to these changes is exceeded by the diversity of their responses. Virtually all of the USSR's more than 100 nationalities have become political actors who resort to various tactics ranging from strikes and demonstrations, to constitutional argument and elections, to behind-the-scenes maneuvering. Any simple enumeration of all these actions would almost certainly hide the forest in the trees, and any imposition of a single analytical framework would necessarily oversimplify a complex and fluid situation.[14] In order to avoid these particular problems, I have adopted a structural-functionalist approach, one that seeks to identify the major underlying patterns without making any claim to absolute comprehensiveness. As a first step, I want to examine the ways in which Gorbachev's reforms have transformed the specific characteristics of the three major players—non-Russians, Russians, and Moscow—into political resources and constraints and then to consider the special strategies each has adopted to pursue its goals.

Before doing that, however, I want to make three general observations about this approach lest I be misunderstood. First, while each of these three players occupies a distinct functional position in the system, none is internally homogencous. Each has opponents within its own group and allies in the other two, and the resultant cross-cutting allegiances have allowed the current system to emerge. For example, many non-Russian literary elites line up with Gorbachev even as conservative republic party leaders ally themselves with Moscow conservatives,[15] and reformers in non-Russian areas may look to Russian reformers even to the point of being willing to accept the imposition of an Estonian "Kolbin."[16] Nonetheless, considering each group separately in functional terms remains a useful approach because it helps us to understand the current pattern of ethnic politics in the USSR and to predict its future course of development.

Second, ethnic politics, as I have said, requires some distribution of political resources, but this distribution need not be fixed or equal. In the Soviet Union, it is neither. Moscow's position remains supreme, and its leaders could end the current game of ethnic politics at any time. This indisputable fact clearly limits Soviet ethnic politics. However, Moscow's reluctance to end the game because of the enormous political costs at home and abroad provides a basis—albeit still a fragile one—for participation by the other groups. And just as this ethnic politics has emerged over the last several years, so too can it be expected to evolve, expanding or contracting in turns, in the future. In such a situation, all participants will regularly test the limits of the permissible, mistakes will occur, and explosions that could break the system remain possible.

Third, ethnic politics takes many forms, with any given player often practicing several forms at once. Prior to Gorbachev, ethnic elites did press for change, but because they generally had to act behind the scenes and had few resources beyond personal ties, their efforts were seldom effective. Now that they can "go public," mobilizing support in the streets as it were, there is a risk that only their public face will be noticed and that their other forms of political activity will be ignored or downplayed. This had already led to some serious misunderstandings by both participants and observers. A recent case in point: in February 1989, the Lithuanian Restructuring Movement, *Sajŭdis*, issued a dramatic call for independence and then shortly thereafter withdrew its candidates from races against the republic's top leaders, virtually guaranteeing the election of the latter. One way to read these events is to see the call as genuine and the subsequent withdrawal simply as the result of pressure from Moscow. However, a more fruitful and accurate way to view them is as a part of a complex negotiating situation in which the *Sajūdis* elite first moved to hold its political base and then made a concession in the interest of both its future influence on republic leaders and its desire to reduce further the role of Moscow in this situation. Keeping track of several balls in the air at the same time is not an easy task for either players or observers, but that is precisely what makes the new ethnic politics in the USSR so intriguing.

THE NON-RUSSIANS

The most fragmented of the three major players is the non-Russian half of the Soviet population which embraces more than 100 nationalities, each with its own internal subdivisions, characteristics, and goals. Despite this, all share certain fundamental functional statuses and thus can be usefully considered as an entity.

The extent of political activism by particular nationalities is often explained by the specific characteristics of the group involved. Thus, the Estonians are active because their small numbers pose fewer problems for Moscow, their political culture inclines them to public participation especially now that coercion has declined, and their local elites have been less tightly supervised than some others and hence are more ready to articulate national demands and mobilize the population. Ukrainians, on the other hand, are seen as less active. Their relative quiescence so far is explained by Moscow's insistence on a tighter grip on this largest non-Russian group, the absence of a strong participatory streak in Ukrainian political culture, greater restrictions on alternative elites as well as the greater organizational difficulties in reaching out to a much larger republic.[17] Such explanations are useful, but even more important, they point to a more general approach, one that considers these basic factors across the entire spectrum of non-Russian groups.[18] Such an approach has greater explanatory and predictive power and will be used here. Specifically, I will examine five characteristics of non-Russian ethnic communities in the USSR—size, (both absolute and relative), institutional completeness, political culture, distinctive problems and goals, and the ability to form alliances via the media and in other ways—showing in each case how the characteristic functioned as a resource and constraint before Gorbachev and how it works now.

Size

The non-Russian nationalities range widely in size, and this factor alone has profound political consequences. A dozen peoples claim fewer than 2,000 members, while the Ukrainians number nearly 50 million. Both before Gorbachev and now, the larger nationalities tended to do better in closed politics, where their official elites can bargain from a position of strength without appearing to threaten the system. These elites are less well-equipped to participate in more open politics both because Moscow keeps a close watch on them and because they need to maintain tight control over alternative elites lest the latter frighten the center. Conversely, smaller nationalities have done less well in closed politics but have been more successful in open activism. Behind closed doors, their official elites have had little to bargain with, but because both Moscow and the Russians are less fearful of their activism, both official and unofficial elites have the opportunity and incentive to employ newly available forms of protest.

Relative size is important in three other respects. First, most ethnic politics in the USSR takes place not between one national group and Moscow but among the various non-Russian groups. While size does not determine who will win, it often helps to find allies or to simply overwhelm their opponents. Second, within a given area, a nationality small on the all-Union scale may be dominant and within limits behave more like a majority than a minority group. An example of the former is the on-going clash between Uzbeks and Tajiks in Central Asia; of the latter, the behavior of titular nationalities in the Baltic states. As will be seen below, a corollary of this is that from a functional perspective, Russian minorities in non-Russian areas can be expected to take on the characteristics of a minority both ideologically and institutionally. Thus, Russians in Estonia make their claims as a threatened minority and have organized for political action just like non-Russians in other republics. And third, the larger the nationality involved, the more credible—and more threatening to Moscow—are demands for national autonomy or secession.

Institutional Completeness

This factor has both an official and unofficial aspect, each of which can function as a resource or constraint depending on specific conditions. Prior to Gorbachev, official recognition in the form of an ethnic territory meant that the nationality involved would at least nominally have officials who could push its interests behind the scenes. In practice, however, it also meant that these officials blocked direct participation by nationalities and could be counted on to try to keep any counter-elites in their place. As a result, in the past, some groups without their own republics, such as the Jews and the Crimean Tatars, were in a better position to advance distinctly national demands than groups that had republics.

Now this has changed.[19] Republic elites have had to seek a rapprochement with the dominant nationality in their charge and to represent its concerns precisely because in most cases they cannot apply the kind of coercion they regularly had applied in the past. Moreover, these elites may even see popular activism as a useful adjunct to their own efforts to survive in office, as was the case with the official organization of the Alma-Ata demonstrations in December 1986, or to advance a specific program with which they agree, such as appears to be the case now in Estonia. Consequently, republic status has become a much more valuable political resource, and it is no surprise that some nationalities lacking this status now want it, while others want their existing low-level status upgraded.

Equally important in evaluating how a group will approach ethnic politics is the unofficial aspect of institutional completeness—whether or not cultural, economic, and other elites exist within a particular national community who can articulate its interests, provide credible alternatives, and mobilize the population. Most large republic nationalities have such elites, but many smaller ones do not. Under conditions of heavy coercion, this factor was relatively unimportant because the political role of such groups was extremely restricted; but now, many small groups have entered the political arena precisely to achieve that kind of institutional completeness. They see it as necessary for their continued national existence and for protection against Gorbachev's efficiency drive.

Political Culture

Prior to Gorbachev, the authoritarianism of the state was supported by the often authoritarian political cultures of the most numerous national groups, both Russian and non-Russian; where this was absent, coercion made up the difference. Now, perhaps the greatest resource any ethnic group could have for playing ethnic politics, and the one that Gorbachev seeks to promote to achieve his broader aims, is a participatory political culture, one that approves activism, tolerates diversity, and is willing to live with complexity and uncertainty. However, virtually none of the nationalities except perhaps the three small Baltic nations appears to have a fully participatory political culture at the mass level. Therefore, few will find it easy to mobilize the masses in the absence of the former level of coercion that provided the sticks, and in view of the poor performance of the economy, which might have provided the carrots. All this will change—and, recent developments suggest, it will take place more quickly than many had expected.

Problems and Goals

Prior to Gorbachev, non-Russian groups were severely limited in their ability to engage in public discussion of their particular problems and were virtually precluded from setting forth goals different from the center's. This is not now the case, as the result of the decline in coercion, the loosening of ideological strictures, and the rise of a freer republic press under *glasnost'*. The range of problems and programs discussed is enormous, from the radical to the trivial, from Moscow-threatening to Moscow-supportive, from the vague to the extremely specific. While some republics share the same concerns and goals, the overlap is far from total, limiting the ability of these groups to form alliances and Moscow's ability to respond to them in a generalized and undifferentiated way.

The nature of individual national problems and goals has a profound impact on the ability of a group to participate in public political activism. Where, as in the Baltic states, the programs are generally simple and clear, mobilization is relatively easy despite the disapproval of many in Moscow. But in Central Asia, where the programs are complicated and seemingly counterintuitive (Central Asians need a stronger center not a weaker one to be able to achieve their aims), rallying the population is difficult, and the central authorities can use this situation to their advantage against the groups involved. No simple matrix is possible, and an open recognition of this very complexity provides a useful and necessary correction to the often-heard assumption that all non-Russian groups have the same ultimate objectives, that they are travelling along a single continuum to them, and that extrapolation from the most extreme groups today provides a reliable prediction of the behavior of others in the future.

Alliance Formation and Media Access

These two closely-related factors have always been important; that is why Moscow has traditionally worked so hard to limit them. Even before Gorbachev, those groups that could easily form broader alliances—such as the Central Asia-Moscow construction industry tie to push Siberian river diversion—have generally been more successful than those non-Russian groups that could not make such alliances; and those with attentive and important sympathizers abroad and/or regular access to the foreign media—such as the Jews, Germans, and Armenians—have enjoyed a protection and resource that others did not have. Under Gorbachev, a far larger number of groups have used the more open Soviet media to assist their efforts.

This last point is especially important. The press in the non-Russian republics has changed dramatically over the last decade. Ten years ago, an Estonian typically learned about Ukrainian developments only very occasionally and only via channels in Moscow; now, his newspapers, like those in all other union and autonomous republics in the USSR, are likely to feature a daily column on developments in other republics and most of the news items are written by Estonian or Ukrainian journalists. As a result, each nationality knows far more about the others and can more easily find the bases for cooperation. Moreover, because any new policy or practice can be seen as a precedent and any differential treatment of republics seen as discrimination, this development also affects Moscow's ability to cope with the periphery. It is no accident that in 1987, when the Armenians launched their drive for the transfer of Nagorno-Karabakh to the jurisdiction of the Armenian republic, only about two dozen other nationalities thought of making similar territorial demands; now, that number is over 50 and likely to grow. And as the full extent of the Chernobyl' disaster finally leaked out, it is not surprising that activists in all republics with nuclear power plants stepped up their drives to shut them down.

Singly and in combination, these five factors affect which groups will participate in ethnic politics and how. They suggest that one of the most dramatic kinds of ethnic activism—mass demonstrations and general strikes—is likely to remain confined to the small Baltic republics and Armenia, which have a tradition of participatory political culture, powerful attentive publics at home and abroad, and a major role to play in Gorbachev's campaign to change the Soviet Union and especially its image abroad. These factors also suggest that other groups are more likely to adopt other available strategies in the pursuit of their goals, strategies that better reflect their special conditions and promise greater results, or to decide to remain outside of ethnic politics as described here. Without any pretense at comprehensiveness, I would now like to review the five most interesting non-Russian strategies: demonstrations, organizational innovation, media manipulation, alliance formation, and capitalizing on opportunities available in the system. Finally, I would like to consider another strategy which is not really part of ethnic politics, but which may be an important limiting factor in the elaboration of these politics—namely, communal violence.

Demonstrations

The most visible aspect of this new politics—mass demonstrations—requires the least additional comment. Nevertheless, three observations appear to be in order to correct some misconceptions. First, mass demonstrations are not a particularly good barometer of either ethnic activism or ethnic influence. By themselves, they may even be a sign of a group's weakness, a confession that this is the only way to get attention. Sometimes a demonstration may help—witness the results the Crimean Tatars have achieved—and sometimes not. Moreover, for many groups lacking a participatory tradition, strikes or anomic violence—something Moscow may find far easier to control—may represent a functional equivalent. Consequently, a decline in the number and size of public demonstrations . . . may not reflect a receding of ethnic mobilization or influence but rather its institutionalization. Indeed, if a group can act in other ways, demonstrations may simply be a useful adjunct or threat rather than the best way to proceed.

Second, demonstrations are almost never simply the manifestation of popular attitudes. Very often, an individual demonstration may reflect the efforts of more than one group and be directed to more than one end. The situation in the Caucasus in 1988 is a classic example. Various groups were seeking to use the demonstrations to protect their positions, advance *perestroika*, or make demands for systemic change.[20] An even more obvious example of this competitive situation in organizing demonstrations was provided when Gorbachev visited Ukraine in February 1989.[21] Thus, it is a major mistake to assume that all demonstrations in a particular republic reflect only one point of view. Instead, they reflect mobilization efforts by various elites—Moscow, republic officials, Russians, and non-Russians.

And third, as has been indicated repeatedly above, demonstrations generally have appeared and will continue to appear where they support the policies of Moscow or republic elites—or can be presented as such—and will tend not to take place elsewhere. Because of Gorbachev's interest in Western Europe, the Baltic nationalities have and know they have far more leeway than other groups. This fact underscores an important point: given Gorbachev's program, attention by both Western media and Western governments has already played a key role in the rise of ethnic politics in the USSR and will likely continue to do so in the future.[22]

Media Management

To a remarkable degree, Soviet control of the population before Gorbachev was based on control over information. Attempts by small elites to circumvent this system of control, via *samizdat* or other means, were never very successful because they could not reach large audiences. Now, given Gorbachev's policy of *glasnost'* and the economic incentive the media have to reach and hold an audience, that has begun to change. Widespread competition has emerged among key elites to reach the population, other republics, and Moscow, as well as foreign audiences. Although examples of this competition are numerous, I will discuss only three: The Baltic youth press, the competition between Armenians and Azeris in Moscow, and the use of Western reporters by Uzbeks.

The Baltic republic Russian-language youth newspapers are the most radical papers in the Soviet Union and those most widely subscribed to outside their home areas. More than 100,000 people outside of Latvia now read *Sovetskaya Molodezh'* every day. Why are these newspapers so popular? It is because of their willingness to take risks, such as publishing interviews with Boris Yel'tsin and Andrey Sakharov (or printing soft-core pornography), and their desire to hold an audience in their home republics by publishing a large amount of information on popular activism. Not surprisingly, given that these papers have become virtual mouthpieces for the people's front organizations, Moscow has tried to rein them in. The most dramatic effort came last fall, when the authorities announced that Russian-language papers from Estonia and Latvia would not be available for subscription outside their home republics. This step, taken at the behest both of military officers who were upset at the publication of articles critical of the army and of Siberian party secretaries who confiscated earlier issues containing the Yel'tsin interview, provoked a storm of criticism in the Baltic republics and outside. Significantly, the article about the decision to rescind the order ran under the caption, "They're Reading the Youth Paper in Washington," a reflection of the influence of attentive foreign publics on what happens in the Baltic republics.[23]

A second example, and one that is almost comical, involved the competition between Armenians and Azeris in Moscow trying to reach other republics, Moscow, and the West with their respective cases during the Nagorno-Karabakh crisis. The Armenians started with an enormous advantage: a large Armenian population in Moscow, a sympathetic Russian intelligentsia, and preexisting channels to the West, via both Armenian cultural institutions and the Armenian permanent representation in Moscow. The Azeris had none of these advantages: there are only a few thousand Azeris in Moscow, the Russian intelligentsia is generally hostile, and the Azeris have few contacts with the West, except for Turkey. Soon, however, the Azeris went to work. Initially, they organized a local Moscow library and then created a Moscow Society of Students and Graduate Students from Azerbaijan to reach out to Western journalists. Then, they sought and received support from the Turkish government, which allowed them access to formerly closed military archives in order to support Baku's claim to Nagorno-Karabakh. And finally, they launched a series of foreign tours and visits to other Soviet Muslim republics to shore up support.[24] So far, they have won few converts, but their effort continues and may inspire others.

But perhaps the most interesting example of all is provided by the activities of the Uzbeks. A leader among other nationalities in publishing news about other republics in their local papers, the Uzbeks have recently learned the utility of the foreign press in support of their national demands. Despite being attacked for providing information to *The New York Times*, the Uzbek intellectuals have continued to supply material via this channel, and it is almost certain that the demonstrations in Tashkent that led to the removal of the Mufti Babakhan from leadership of the Religious Directorate for Central Asia and Kazakhstan would not have been possible had the foreign press corps not been informed of the demonstrations in advance. (Moscow may not have been unhappy either, given Babakhan's bad relations with foreign Muslims, but the manner of his removal doubtless troubled even those wanting his ouster.)[25]

Organizational Innovation

The most important strategy over the long term is likely to be the elaboration of new political institutions as channels to mobilize publics and to enhance their ability to influence the regime. Here, I would like to point to two of the most interesting of these institutions, the first very familiar but generally misunderstood, and the second virtually unknown but capable of becoming a model for a variety of other groups.

The people's fronts that began in the Baltic republics but later found resonance in many other republics, at least at the elite level, are the most misunderstood organizations of the Gorbachev era. They were not created to be alternative party groupings, nor are they simple expressions of popular will. Instead, their creation and evolution reflects the conjunction of three interests: Moscow's interest in pressuring recalcitrant republic governments and using the republics as a model of what can be done elsewhere; republic government interest in co-opting the nationalists and preventing a further radicalization of the population; and alternative-elite interest in finding a means to enter into a dialogue with the authorities from some sort of independent base. All the evidence suggests that the creation of people's front organizations was taken reluctantly; one Estonian commented that the Balts began such organizations in order to have some chance of changing the party only after the expulsion of Yel'tsin from the Politburo in 1987.[26] To a certain extent, however, all three interests have been met by these organizations, but because radical nationalists in each republic have penetrated the organizations, the people's fronts in the Baltic republics have gone further than was anticipated. Nevertheless, their leaderships remain far more moderate and responsible—given Baltic conditions—than leaderships of groups not so sponsored and organized might have been. In all three Baltic republics, the people's front leaderships now play a key role in ethnic politics, simultaneously reining in radicals, maintaining their own bases of support and pressuring the authorities on some issues, and making concessions on others lest Moscow intervene. . . .

Alliance Formation

The alliances that have been formed in the Gorbachev era, some of which have already been discussed, are diverse both in composition and in purpose. Some have been formed within a republic between alternative elites and officials, others spread across the USSR, and still others are with foreign groups. Some may be official, others unofficial; some the regime has encouraged, and some it clearly fears. Let me give several examples. First, the Volga Tartars have renewed their effort to build a Tatar-dominated entity in the Middle Volga-Urals region, this time one based on common interests rather than, as with Sultan Galiyev in the 1920's, on any common ideology.[27] Second, some groups have taken the lead in instructing other groups: the Jews are helping the Tajiks in Uzbekistan to organize, and the Balts are providing guidance to all other national elites who see the people's front strategy as useful.[28] Third, drawing on the Armenian model of using the diaspora to support its demands, virtually all non-Russian nationalities have stepped up their interest in and contacts with co-nationalities, with the Azeris playing up the fact that they have 15 million ethnic brothers in Iran, and the Balts highlighting their ties with American Baltic groups. Fourth, regime-sponsored interrepublic economic and academic bodies have taken on a life of their own, serving as an important pipeline of unofficial contact. And fifth, all nationalities are learning to use such contacts in symbolic terms. Not accidentally, Russians in the republics have sought to play on their ties to Russians in Moscow, and every time Moscow has seemed to be on the verge of making a decision on the Caucasus, the Azerbaijani party leadership visited or was visited by Central Asian party leaders, a very unsubtle reminder of ties among Muslims who might be offended if Moscow sided with Armenia.

Using the System

In addition, non-Russians have been remarkably adept at taking advantage of a number of opportunities offered by the system to pursue their goals. Three areas seem especially important. First, they have successfully used the new electoral system and legislative bodies to mobilize public opinion and advance their causes. Intriguingly, they have employed virtually all the tricks known in Western elections—from gerrymandering districts to reduce the representation of other groups, to publishing special campaign literature. Second, republic elites are increasingly exploiting both Soviet law and the constitution to manipulate the system, often against Moscow's interests. . . . And third, they have taken advantage of the decay in certain republic party organizations either to penetrate them or to launch, with little opposition, alternative groups. For many non-Russians, the traditional Soviet question, *"Kto kogo?"* no longer means "Who will defeat whom?" but rather, "Who will be co-opted by whom?"

Communal Violence

Although not a strategy within ethnic politics as understood here, communal violence may perform an important role for some groups as well as be an important element in defining the limits of ethnic politics. Certain groups can conceivably benefit from communal violence—it could invite central intervention and repression from which those groups would benefit—and so might see violence as a strategy. But the more important point here is that many Russians are likely to fail to distinguish clearly between violence and other forms of ethnic activism, and thus become ever more supportive of those who promise to restore law and order.

THE RUSSIANS

The Russians operate under some unique constraints. For most of Soviet history, their dominance could not be acknowledged; even now, it is difficult to speak of it openly. And the lack of a Russian republic party organization has meant that the political goals of the Russian nation were either mediated by officials who necessarily had an all-Union perspective or were taken up by groups outside the political system. As a result, the Russians and their spokesmen were and continue to be misunderstood.[29]

The Russian half of the Soviet population is the overlooked element in Soviet ethnic politics in a double sense. On the one hand, the Russians are an important political resource for systemic stability by virtue of their size and political culture. On the other, the Russians are increasingly an actor in ethnic politics, a role rewarding to them but profoundly threatening to other nationalities.

Like the other two actors in Soviet ethnic politics, the Russians are subdivided in a variety of ways. The most important one for present purposes is between Russians living in the RSFSR and those living in other republics. As mentioned above, Russians living in the Russian Republic suffer from two important constraints. Because they lack many of the political and cultural institutions that nations in other republics have, their behavior is not mediated through such institutions and instead is subject to officials who, even if Russians themselves, must be attentive to broader concerns. Second, because Russians form so large a portion of the population and conceive of the entire USSR as their own country in important respects, many activities that they engage in, which would be described as ethnic activism if they took place in non-Russian areas, are considered only in functional terms by both the Russians themselves and many observers. This has two major consequences. First, it means that much of Russian activism is misclassified as something else and that only certain extreme groups are viewed as expressing the Russian position. Thus, *Pamyat'* is often equated with Russian nationalism, when it is in fact only a minuscule part of a broad spectrum of Russian nationalism and is detested by many Russian nationalists. Second, it means that Russian activism by Russians in the RSFSR is both more frustrated by all-Union calculations and less constrained by republic elites than activism of other groups.

More immediately interesting, because they are more likely to appear as ethnic political actors in the near term, are the nearly 30 million Russians who live in the non-Russian republics. Although they see the republics as part of their homeland and thus provide an important social and political glue to the system, they often tend to behave like non-Russian groups in response to local majority nationalities. Thus, for example, Russians in the Baltic republics have formed a variety of social and political institutions in order to defend and advance their interests, which may serve as an important incubator of ethnic assertiveness for other Russians. From Moscow's point of view, Russians from non-Russian republics may have some important utility in playing ethnic politics, but a too open reliance on them when the ideology that served to cover Russian control is being downplayed and when popular mobilization is going on carries with it enormous risks that the authorities may not be willing to bear. As a result, those Russians in the republics who have always viewed themselves as representatives of the center may be cut loose or, what amounts to the same thing, made to feel that they have been cut loose. If this happens they could become further radicalized and even more difficult to control.

MOSCOW

The third and last of the major participants, Moscow, requires the least comment. The general thrust of Gorbachev's approach and the problems associated with it have already been described, and only three general observations are needed here. First, Moscow is deeply divided; it is split both among a variety of players who seek different alliances depending on interests and, even more important, between those committed to this new ethnic politics and those who either do not understand it or do not see it as desirable. Because of Moscow's position in the game, the attitudes of the latter are not unimportant.

Second, Moscow is the only one of the three players that is currently having to adjust to a somewhat diminished status. As has been observed, this situation derives from policy rather than institutional or cultural change and is less dramatic than it sometimes might appear. The major institutional supports of the system and therefore of Moscow—the party, the army, and the KGB—are still very much in place; the central leadership has at its disposal a variety of levers to effect its will; and finally, Moscow remains the only one of the players with the capacity to unilaterally end the game—which enables it to set important limits on the range and type of ethnic politics that can take place.

Third, Moscow faces major tasks requiring the elaboration of new strategies. From the point of view of its own interests, the central authorities need to recognize that the situation is not as serious as it sometimes appears and that it is not impossible to adopt regionally specific policies. Use of force in one area, such as the Caucasus, need not mean its broader application, and tolerance of Baltic activism need not mean tolerance of analogous developments elsewhere. In short, Moscow must learn to live with diversity and to avoid overreacting to specifics.

The authorities must also set explicit limits as to what is permitted. As was noted above, Gorbachev has been reluctant to do so, but since the 19th CPSU Conference in June 1988 and, more particularly, since the Armenian earthquake and the resultant establishment of the Ryzhkov Commission,[30] Moscow has moved to set such limits. Its failure, however, to distinguish between legitimate forms of political protest that must be protected and illegitimate ones, such as communal violence, that must be suppressed, continues to create problems—as recent violence in Central Asia and the Caucasus shows. And finally, the authorities must start to channel in new ways those forces that have been mobilized—for example, via institutional innovations and by political methods such as agenda-setting, control of communication, and manipulation of economic resources and reform.

AVOIDING AN APOCALYPSE

Can this ethnic politics continue and develop? Or must it end in one of the two apocalypses outlined at the beginning? According to the old rules of the game as understood both in Moscow and in the West, apocalypse would be inevitable. But according to these same rules, many if not all of the developments just described would be impossible by definition. Obviously then, the rules have changed, if not totally, then to a significant degree, and so too must our expectations about the outcome.

The first apocalypse—the disintegration of the USSR—remains just as unlikely now as it was in the past. Despite a willingness to tolerate more diversity in the Soviet republics than ever before, Moscow would clearly sacrifice almost all its other policy goals in order to maintain the integrity of the Soviet Union. And the second apocalypse—a return to significantly greater repression—needs to be rethought. The USSR is not now and is not likely in the future to become a liberal society in Western terms, so discussions about a "return" to repression are misplaced. At the same time, a simple restoration of the past—be it Brezhnevism or Stalinism—probably is impossible, except at costs far beyond the ability of the authorities to pay. As a result, we are likely to be entering a period where there will be a series of ratchet-like adjustments of freedom and repression, as both Moscow and the other actors feel the situation out. No one event is likely to mark a turning point in either direction, and we will have to develop tolerance for a certain amount of messiness if we are to understand the situation.

In this last section, I would like to examine not what would guarantee or institutionalize ethnic politics or what would kill it, but rather focus on those forces, both endogenous and exogenous to ethnic politics itself, that are likely to lead to the contraction of the current ethnic political arena or to its expansion to new areas and players. I wish to conclude by pointing to five areas.

There are three endogenous and three exogenous forces that are working or would work toward the contraction of ethnic politics. The endogenous ones are: the usual objection that Soviet nationalities are not ethnic groups in the Western sense; expanded activism, and especially communal violence directed against Russians by large groups such as the Ukrainians that might appear to threaten Moscow's ability to control the situation; and ethnic unrest within the key agencies supporting the system—the party, the military, and the KGB. While it is true that Soviet nationalities are not equivalent to American ethnic interest groups, it is also true that under certain conditions they will behave like them. The two most obvious of these conditions are an awareness that secession is not a real option and a belief that participation in the system provides real benefits. Except for the three Baltic nationalities, the Western Ukrainians, and still small sections of a few other groups, all Soviet ethnic communities appear to share this understanding; and even the exceptions may participate as ethnic groups in order to advance their interests. However, should Moscow's behavior lead them or the others to have doubts about either condition, the situation could change quickly. At the present time, the other two endogenous factors appear to be under control: Moscow has supported a far more repressive approach in Ukraine that elsewhere, and it does not yet face any serious ethnic divisions within the military and the KGB. The three exogenous factors that limit or might limit ethnic politics are: a political culture that does not tolerate diversity; a collapse of the Soviet economy or serious unrest in Eastern Europe; and the ouster of Gorbachev for reasons other than tolerating ethnic activism. These are more serious, but considered in this way, the countervailing forces can be identified as well.

There are also three endogenous factors and three exogenous ones supporting the maintenance or even expansion of the system of ethnic politics. The endogenous factors include the benefits both Moscow and the various other players have already derived from participation in ethnic politics; the role of the Russians as a ballast to untrammeled activism by others; and changes in the political culture itself. While the last is slow, there is obvious evidence of movement that could help to stabilize the situation. The three exogenous factors include significant expansion of the economy (admittedly not likely in the short run); Gorbachev's own agenda, particularly in foreign policy, that requires domestic change; and significant losses by conservative groups in the leadership for other reasons. Again, by dividing the supportive factors this way, we will be in a better position to assess future change.

How are these diverse forces likely to play out in the near term? The first thing to say is that the much-delayed Central Committee plenum on nationalities is not going to solve anything. Indeed, holding a plenum on nationality issues as such may initially cause more problems than it solves by raising expectations that the regime cannot meet and by creating gridlock as various players advance their demands and seek alliances. A more useful approach might have been that employed by Lenin, who sponsored more limited meetings between the Central Committee and representatives of particular regions in order to thrash out policy. Perhaps the Ryzhkov commission in the Caucasus suggests Moscow is beginning to think in these terms.

Nevertheless, the pre-plenum discussions as reported in *Kommunist* and elsewhere provide useful indications of the directions in which Moscow is likely to move, both at the plenum and beyond. The most obvious of these are:

• *True bilingualism.* Non-Russians will have to learn Russian as before, but Russians living in the non-Russian republics will have to learn the language of the titular nationality. In the short run, this step will be extremely popular in the periphery, but because it may lead many Russians to leave non-Russian areas, it could ultimately weaken Moscow's control and thus is likely to be resisted.

• *Economic reform.* Republics are likely to receive what they say they want: republic *khozrashchet*, but this will not be a transfer of power and will not always work simply for the benefit of the nationalities. Many republics will come out losers because they currently depend on central aid, and many nationalities will discover that if they have to pay their own way, they will not be able to maintain some of the institutions, cultural and otherwise, that they now have.

• *Strengthened federalism.* This is the area of greatest debate. Further devolution of power to the republics is likely, although it may be combined with recentralization in some areas, such as key economic sectors. The existing federal system is likely to be simplified, with some autonomous soviet socialist republics raised to union-republic status, and sub-union-republic groups put in a single category. At the same time, a variety of mechanisms to protect extraterritorial groups—for example, through the creation of regional national soviets or republic supreme soviets of nationalities, or through the expansion of central supervision of ethnic rights for individuals—is likely. And the republics are likely to receive greater official representation in the center via the permanent representations or other devices.

• *A "nationalities" court.* Moscow does not now have a mechanism for resolving interethnic conflicts that is both institutionalized and not directly linked to the highest leadership circles. Such an institution is very much needed, but its exact form is still undecided—precisely because of indecision regarding the powers to be granted it. Some advocate making the Supreme Soviet of Nationalities into such a body; others have called for the reestablishment of some kind of USSR Ministry of Nationalities along the lines of the old People's Commissariat for Nationalities (*Narkomnats*); and still others want a series of commissions to handle this within the party. Some action is likely both because the top leadership wants to deflect this issue onto others, and because the current arrangements regularly break down.

• *Expanded non-Russian participation in the Politburo and USSR Council of Ministers.* Moscow will almost certainly elevate some republic party leaders to the Politburo as candidate members, both to increase the non-Russians' sense of participation and to divide these elites. Gorbachev's earlier moves against non-Russians at the center had the effect of uniting republic elites; now he appears set to reverse course, something at which he has proved remarkably adept.

The result of the plenum will not be some "solution" to the nationality problem. The days when it could be declared "solved" are over. The best Moscow and the two other players can hope for is an institutionalization of the current messiness and a growing acceptance of limits by all three. To the extent that this happens, the rise of ethnic politics in the USSR may point to a more thoroughgoing reconceptualization of Soviet political life, one likely to draw as much on *Plunkitt of Tammany Hall* as on *What is to Be Done?*

Notes

1. Complex ethnic politics were played earlier, but generally this happened behind the scenes and more often at the local than the all-Union level. For a remarkable description of just how rough such politics often were, see M.A. Gasparyan, "Neither a Persian Yoke, nor an Arab Sheikhdom, nor a Turkish Yataghan," *Russkaya Mysl'* (Paris) May 20, 1988, p. 7.

2. The quote and a description of the transformation under Gorbachev is found in Algis Prazauskas, "'Why Nations Rebel? . . .'", *Druzhba Narodov* (Moscow), No. 8, 1988, pp. 207-08.

3. Galina Starovoytova in a roundtable discussion entitled "Democracy is Conflict" in *Vek XX i Mir* (Moscow), No. 12, 1988, p. 8.

4. See Paul Goble, "Gorbachev and the Soviet Nationality Problem," in M. Friedberg and H. Isham, Eds., *Soviet Society Under Gorbachev*, Armonk, NY, M.E. Sharpe, 1987, pp. 76-100. Cf. Ann Sheehy, "Non-Russian Representation in the Politburo and Secretariat," Radio Free Europe-Radio Liberty Research (hereafter—RFE-RL), *Radio Liberty Research* (Munich), RL 439/87, Oct. 20, 1987, and "Upping Russian Representation in Soviet Parliament," ibid., RL 474/88, Oct. 31, 1988.

5. These calculations are based on Ludmilla Alekseyeva, "Mass Unrest in the USSR," unpublished manuscript, 1987; and reports in the *samizdat* journals *Ekspress Khronika* and *Glasnost'* The latter are now conveniently summarized on a weekly basis in the Paris *Russkaya Mysl'*.

6. *Rigas Balss* (Riga), Oct. 4, 1988.

7. See Gennadiy Kolbin's remarks in *Izvestiya* (Moscow), June 24, 1988, and in *Freundschaft* (Tselinograd), July 5, 1988.

8. Kolbin implied this in *Izvestiya*, Aug. 24, 1988. See also *Kazakhstanskaya Pravda* (Alma-Ata), 1978-88, passim.

9. TASS (Moscow), Feb. 21, 1988; and Dzintra Bungs, "Restructuring the Republic Government: The First Phase," RFE-RL, *Radio Free Europe Research* (Munich), Baltic Area Situation Report, SR/5/88, May 20, 1988.

10. *Leningradskaya Pravda* (Leningrad), Feb. 2, 1989. I am indebted to Blair Ruble for calling this article to my attention.

11. Leokadiya Drobizheva used this term to criticize past Soviet practices and to urge a "nationality-blind" approach to hiring and administration. See *Moscow News*, May 31, 1987.

12. See Yuriy Feofanov's assertion that "no one seems to question the precision of the accusation about a 'collapse of ideology'," in ibid., June 18-25, 1989, p. 3; Valentina Khardeva-Alekseyeva, "Toiling Youth in Conditions of Economic Reform," *Obshchestvennyye Nauki* (Moscow), No. 3, 1989, pp. 206-14; and especially Vladimir Shubkin, "A Difficult Farewell," *Novyy Mir* (Moscow), No. 4, 1989, pp. 165-84.

On the import of this change, see Bohdan Nahaylo, "Change in Russian Views on the Nationality Problem?" *Radio Liberty Research*, RL 456/88, Oct. 2, 1988; and Paul Goble, "Can Anyone Solve the Soviet Nationality Problem," talk at the Kennan Institute for Advanced Russian Studies, The Woodrow Wilson Center, Washington, DC, January 23, 1989.

13. See the outline for future Soviet research on domestic and foreign ethnic problems in *Voprosy Istorii* (Moscow), No. 9, 1987, pp. 97-118, and the sources cited therein.

14. Among the best Soviet discussions of this diversity are M. Guboglo, "Internationalist Upbringing: Achievements and Pressing Problems," *Kommunist Moldavii* (Kishinev), No. 11, 1987, pp. 45-53; P.I. Goryayev, "On the Reasons for National Manifestations in Soviet Society," *Nauchnyy Kommunizm* (Moscow), No. 9, 1988, pp. 40-46; G. Pyadukhov, "Inter-National Relations: Toward an Analysis of the Reasons for Individual Negative Phenomena," *Kommunist Kirgizii* (Frunze), No. 12, 1988, pp. 27-32;

and Yu. Bromley, "National Problems under Restructuring," *Voprosy Istorii*, No. 1, 1989, pp. 24-41.

15. The possibility of such a "vendée" was first raised in *Komsomol'skaya Pravda* (Moscow), June 17, 1988. Since then, it has been raised many times.

16. This possibility was raised by Edgar Savisaar, the head of the Estonian People's Front. Writing in the December 1987 issue of *Raduga* (Tallinn), p. 56, he concluded that radical change may require outsiders not locked into the old ways by local ties. In short, even Estonia might need a "Kolbin" (who replaced Kunayev in Kazakhstan in December 1986) to get things moving.

17. For a discussion of the impact of size in determining republic behavior see Goble, "Readers, Writers and Republics: A Structural Approach to Non-Russian Literary Politics," in M. Beissinger and L. Hajda, Eds.,

18. Ukraine represents an exception because of its overriding importance to the system. For useful discussions on this point, see Roman Solchanyk, "Lvov Authorities Begin Criminal Proceedings Against Ukrainian Activiists," *Radio Liberty Research*, RL 327/88, July 26, 1988; Bohdan Nahaylo, "Lvov Authorities Resort to Old Methods in Breaking Up Unauthorized Meetings and Religious Services," ibid., RL 355/88, Aug. 13, 1988; and especially idem, "Vitalii Korotich on 'Undemocratic' Conditions in the Ukraine, on Sumgait and on *Pamyat*'", ibid., RL 400/88, September 5, 1988.

19. See Goble, "Gorbachev and the Soviet Nationality Problem," loc. cit.

20. For more details, see the special reports of the US Department of State, Bureau of Intelligence and Research, "Crisis in the Caucasus," *Soviet Nationalities Survey* (Washington, DC), No. 15 (1988) and No. 16 (1989).

21. The demonstrations by intellectuals in Kiev against Shcherbytskyi clearly enjoyed Moscow's backing; those in L'viv against the General Secretary represented a response by republic officials; and demonstrations in the run-up to the Congress of People's Deputies elections represented a protest against both.

22. See Goble, "Gorbachev and the Challenge of Russian Nationalism," German-American Papers on the Gorbachev Reform Program, Washington, DC, Kennan Institute for Advanced Russian Studies, 1989, pp. 129-33.

23. *Molodezh' Estonii* (Tallinn), Jan. 3, 1989.

24. *Molodezh' Azerbaydzhana* (Baku), July 30 and Dec. 12, 1988.

25. *Pravda Vostoka*, (Tashkent), Dec. 15, 1988.

26. On the role of Yel'tsin's ouster, see *Molodezh' Estonii*, Oct. 18, 1988.

27. B. Zheleznov, "Ways of Perfecting Soviet State Autonomy," *Kommunist Tatarii* (Kazan'), No. 11, 1988, pp. 18-19.

28. On the remarkable collaboration of Jews and Tajiks, see *Komsomol-i Tajikistan* (Dushanbe), Jan. 6, 1988, trans. in British Broadcasting Corporation, *Summary of World Broadcasts* (London), Apr. 6, 1988.

29. For a more thorough discussion, see the source cited in fn. 22.

30. Formation of a special commission of the Politburo headed by Politburo member and Chairman of the USSR Council of Ministers Nikolay Ryzhkov to deal with the Armenian disaster was announced on December 7, 1988. Other Commission members are Politburo member and party secretary Nikolay Slyun'kov, Defense Minister Dmitriy Yazov, and Yuriy Batalin and Lev Voronin, deputy chairmen of the USSR Council of Ministers. See TASS International Service in Russian, Dec. 7, 1988, trans. in Foreign

Broadcast Information Service, *Daily Report: Soviet Union* (Washington, DC), Dec. 8, 1988, pp. 51-52.

22

The Sobering of Gorbachev: Nationality, Restructuring, and the West

Alexander J. Motyl

The massive nationalist demonstrations that erupted in Soviet Armenia in February 1988 surely surprised Mikhail Sergeyevich Gorbachev as much as they perturbed him. For seven decades, the Armenians had all the makings of a model Soviet nationality. Materially satisfied and politically loyal, they had not been a major policy concern since the early 1920s, when they opposed the Red Army's takeover of their independent state. Literally overnight, the demonstrations changed the image the Armenians presented to the rest of the world. A watershed in the development of the republic, the demonstrations transformed Armenia from an exotic backwater into a paragon of popular mobilization.[1]

If as many as 1 million Armenian demonstrators were manifestly infected by nationalism, then it is likely that the virus is much more virulent than Soviet officials have been willing to admit. As disturbing as this fact must be for the Kremlin, it would be a gross error for Western observers to conclude that the Armenian events herald an incipient nationalist rebellion or an impending civil war. Rather, the importance of the demonstrations lies in what they hold for Gorbachev's program of restructuring (*perestroika*) the Soviet system. The demonstrations are a foretaste of the side effects of *perestroika* and suggest that the "national question" of the Soviet Union may prove to be the rock on which Gorbachev's reforms may founder. As Gorbachev has haltingly come to realize, he confronts a dilemma: On the one hand, *perestroika* is necessary to revive the

Published in Seweryn Bialer, ed., *Politics, Society, and Nationality Inside Gorbachev's Russia* (Boulder, CO: Westview, 1989), pp. 149-174. Reprinted with permission from the publisher.

system; on the other, it is likely to aggravate the national problem and, in the long run, to threaten Soviet stability.

THE NON-RUSSIANS AND CENTRAL AUTHORITY

Western policymakers, scholars, and journalists have often treated the Soviet national question as a peripheral concern. Moscow in general, and the Kremlin in particular, are perceived as "where the action is," with the result that non-Russians are reduced to nonissues. This perception is not only erroneous, but also pernicious. By skewing Western understanding of the Soviet Union, it can but negatively affect Western policy towards that country as well.

What does the phrase "the Soviet national question" mean? It refers to the political, socioeconomic, and cultural interplay among the Russian-dominated Party-state, the dominant Russian majority, and the subordinate non-Russians. That interplay consists in a perpetual tug of war between the centralizing and decentralizing tendencies built into the Union of Soviet Socialist Republics at its founding in the early 1920s. The Soviet federal system is the product of the confrontation from 1917 to 1921 between a Russian-led Communist Party based in the largely Russian cities as well as the working class and a variety of non-Russian nationalist forces drawing on the non-Russian countryside for support. The Bolsheviks eventually won, to a large extent because of their ability to win non-Russian allies by promising them the "right to self-determination up to separation." Although separation (or, in U.S. terms, secession from the Union) was declared counterrevolutionary once the "dictatorship of the proletariat" has been established and the bourgeois bases of national enmity putatively abolished, the political and ideological imperative of granting the non-Russians a degree of self-rule and cultural autonomy remained. A system of ethnically designated administrative units and republican branches of the Party was constructed, one that has survived largely unchanged to this day.

Today, approximately one-half of the 275 million inhabitants of the Soviet Union are non-Russians.[2] Like the Russians, fourteen nations inhabit so-called union republics, and more than thirty others live in autonomous republics, provinces, and regions. Each non-Russian republic has its own Party organization, Council of Ministers, Supreme Soviet, constitution, flag, hymn, and capital city. The Ukrainian and Belorussian republics even have seats in the United Nations, the International Labor Organization, UNESCO, and other international organs.[3] Although Soviet propaganda holds that the republics are sovereign entities bound together in a voluntary federation, their sovereignty is largely symbolic while their dependence on Moscow is very real. Although the reins have been loosened since Iosif Stalin's rule, political power is still lodged in the central organs of the Communist Party and government apparatus in Moscow, and Russians continue to dominate the system politically, socially, and culturally.

Appearances to the contrary notwithstanding, the republics and their populations do, in fact, play an important role in the Soviet system in general and the process of formulation of policy in particular. First, republican elites influence central policies by making substantive contributions to the decisionmaking process and by implementing resulting measures according to their own cultural perceptions and local requirements. Second, the very presence of the non-Russian republics demands of Moscow that it adopt ethnic policies that are specifically designed to meet their needs and address their demands. Third, the non-Russians and their sensitivities always figure in Moscow's calculations of popular reactions to its policies because virtually every technically nonethnic issue in the USSR—economic efficiency, labor supply, education, and so on—has an ethnic component that must be considered by Kremlin policymakers.

These three points illustrate the contradictory nature of the relationship between the non-Russians and central authority. On the one hand, the non-Russians willingly participate in the policy process, attempt to utilize it for their own advantage, and thereby legitimize both the status quo and their subordinate status within it. On the other hand, Moscow remains constantly fearful that non-Russian initiative will get out of hand, translate into rejection of Moscow's supervision, and spark bona fide separatist tendencies. Although non-Russian elites generally support the system and consider themselves Soviet, the Kremlin's fears are not groundless. World War I and II testify to the fact that non-Russian loyalty to Moscow is a function of its ability to maintain control over the periphery. By the same token, national communism—or the tendency of local Communists to pursue "national roads" to communism—has flourished when the Party-state has retreated to the "commanding heights" of the polity or economy, as it did in the 1920s and 1960s. To sum up, it is the proclivity of the non-Russians to define their own interests and go their own way whenever Moscow permits them to do so by relinquishing some central control.

It is not an exaggeration to say that preventing and containing non-Russian nationalism—the belief in and pursuit by non-Russians of political independence—is the main purpose of Soviet policy toward the non-Russians. Although both nationalist beliefs and nationalist behavior are anathema to the Soviet authorities, the latter, logically, is deemed to be more unacceptable. Nationalist beliefs are the target of frequent invective, but they cannot alone undermine the state. Nationalist behavior, by contrast, can, and has therefore always been repressed by the Soviet authorities, quickly and usually violently.

As the Soviets realize, however, nationalist behavior can be pursued out of conviction, expedience, or necessity—that is, both by bona fide believers in political independence and by nonbelievers who rationally respond to political and economic incentives and disincentives by acting *as if* independence and sovereignty were their primary goal. Indeed, the history of the international Communist movement suggests that even ostensibly internationalist goals may be best pursued—some would say, can *only* be pursued—within a nationalist framework. Coping with the subjectively nationalist behavior of genuine separatists is relatively easy for a superpower with the apparatus of a formidable secret police.[4] It is far more difficult to manage the objectively nationalist behavior of the seemingly loyal Soviet elites. Here, repression alone is insufficient because the root of the problem—the political-economic conditions that induced these elites to pursue national communism in the first place—must be addressed. But these very conditions are the crux of the Kremlin's dilemma. If, as I shall argue, the circumstances that drive non-Russian elites to place the interests of their own nations above all else are the unintended consequence of central policies, then such policies have built-in limits on their ultimate success. Indeed, to use the language of Marxian dialectics, they may well result in their own negation.

THE NATURE OF PRESENT-DAY
NON-RUSSIAN REPUBLICS

The most striking characteristic of the non-Russian republics today is the enormous progress they have made since the early 1920s. These previously illiterate peasant societies with little industry and tiny intelligentsia all now possess, to varying extents, well-educated populations, large working classes, extensive economic bases, and self-confident and increasingly assertive elites. Soviet propaganda may or may not be correct in attributing this progress to socialism, but one thing is certain: Developed non-Russian republics represent a qualitatively new challenge for the Soviet leadership. The 1986 Party Program implicitly accepted this view by stating that the "nationalities question *inherited from the past* has been successfully solved in the Soviet Union."[5] The political, economic, and cultural resources now possessed by the republics translate into increasing influence and weight in the Soviet system and its policy process. The national question has come into its own, not only as a policy problem but also as a central concern.

Politically, the last two-and-a-half decades have seen the rise of formidable republican Party machines. The dismantling of Stalinism, Nikita Khrushchev's subsequent encouragement of greater non-Russian representation in central and local Party-state organs, and Leonid Brezhnev's policy of "stability of cadres" have combined to create pockets of political autonomy outside Moscow. Non-Russia elites have rushed to fill this vacuum by establishing their own ethnic networks and extending local control over as much of a republic as possible. Uzbekistan's Sharaf Rashidov, Kazakhstan's Dinmukhamed Kunayev, the Ukraine's Vladimir Shcherbitsky and Petr Shelest, Georgia's Vasilii Mzhavanadze, Lithuania's Antanas Snieckus, and Kirgizia's Turdakun Usubaliyev represent the new breed of republican Party boss willing and able to dish out favors, to advance ethnic personnel, and to establish local bailiwicks not unlike old-fashioned U.S. ward politicians. Although their motives are not nationalistic, these non-Russian elites inevitably place local interests above all-Union ones and generally resist efforts to submit to Moscow's direction. For a conservative politician in Brezhnev's mold, such a locally oriented style may have been of little concern; but for a would-be radical reformer like Gorbachev, republican empire building is inevitably a major problem.

Economically, the decades since Stalin have witnessed the emergence of two related trends. First, there has been a tendency toward economic equalization among the republics. Although vast differences still abound, especially between the industrially advanced northwest and the lagging southeast, the fact remains that the underdeveloped regions of the USSR have made enormous strides thanks to purposeful central policy. Second, serious regional imbalances have emerged, partly as a result of the trend toward equalization. Industry and infrastructure are still largely concentrated in the resource- and labor-poor European part of the Soviet Union west of the Urals. Mineral resources are increasingly found in the industrially undeveloped and sparsely populated Siberia. Surplus labor is concentrated in Central Asia, where industry is weak. Bringing industry, resources, and labor together is of great importance to the Soviet Union's continued growth and modernization. Yet, correcting these regional imbalances while maintaining a commitment to republican equalization will be difficult. Building industry in the south or east means diverting resources from the more prosperous west; modernizing the industrial base in the west, however, means investing less in the south and east. Similarly, inducing Central Asians to migrate to the north and west is problematic in light of their cultural preferences and the lack of incentive given that the standards of living have significantly improved in the "sun-belt" of the Soviet Union. Some kind of balance may well be found, but it will require time and political finesse. Even General Secretary Gorbachev may not possess these in sufficient measure.

The economic problem is exacerbated by a demographic one: the enormous growth rates—three times that of the Soviet average in the twenty-year period from 1959 to 1979—of the Soviet Muslim population in Kazakhstan, Central Asia, and Azerbaijan. Even if, as is likely, the rising curve of Muslim population growth flattens out, the Soviet authorities will have to contend with two problems. First, Soviet Muslims have managed to retain a sense of community and separateness from the Russians in the face of frequent persecution and seven decades of antireligious propaganda. Increased numbers may reinforce their sense of identity at a particularly inauspicious time, as Islamic fundamentalism undergoes a resurgence on the southern borders of the Soviet Union. Second, because of their relatively poor knowledge of Russian, the USSR's lingua franca, the ever-growing cohort of young Muslims poses a special problem for Soviet economic and military planners. A modern economy and army require language proficiency, and although there is no reason that the Muslims should not eventually acquire Russian-language skills, the process is likely to be lengthy and disruptive.

Culturally, the decades since World War II have witnessed an unprecedented expansion of national consciousness among all Soviet ethnic groups, including the Russians. It was not supposed to work out this way according to Communist ideology, which had asserted (as it still continues to do) that "friendship of peoples" and "proletarian nationalism" would grow by leaps and bounds and nations would merge to form a single "Soviet people." Indeed, the opposite has taken place. The ethnic groups of the Soviet Union are more vigorous than ever, and their concern for native languages and cultures is unquestionably on the rise. Although national consciousness does not alone pose a threat to Soviet stability, it can contribute to nationalism, which does. More fundamentally, a growing sense of ethnicity greatly complicates Moscow's management of the system. The more Soviet citizens think and view problems in ethnic terms, the more difficult it becomes for policymakers to ignore the ethnic factor in making policy choices. U.S., Canadian, and European politicians understand these constraints, and we can be sure that their Soviet counterparts do as well.

Naturally enough, education and publishing are two of the Soviet policy issues of greatest importance to the non-Russians. The Soviet ideological commitment to cultural development requires that resources be channeled in support of local languages and publications; the necessity of having a Russian lingua franca and of catering to the cultural wishes of the dominant Russian majority, however, means that Russian language, culture, and values are vigorously propagated as well. Finding a balance between the Russian and non-Russian imperatives has proven to be virtually impossible, with the weight historically having been placed on the Russian side of the scales. As a result, where the authorities and the Russians see only the propagation and inculcation of ethnically neutral Soviet values, or Sovietization, non-Russians see a threat to their ethnic identity—they see Russification. To make matters worse, Moscow's occasional stabs at evenhandedness have often produced discontent among the Russians who resent being treated as the cultural and political equals of the non-Russians.

Education is an especially sensitive area because in the Soviet Union, as in North America and Western Europe, it is a prerequisite of social mobility. Since the early 1960s, the Soviet government has assiduously pursued educational and professional affirmative action for the non-Russians. The number of non-Russians receiving secondary and higher education has greatly increased, a non-Russian professional class has emerged, and the republican bureaucracies have become career paths for the natives. Although social mobility has doubtless contributed to stability, such a massive and rapid expansion of educational opportunities has produced negative effects. It has resulted in a surplus of graduates of sometimes dubious ability; it has also skewed popular perception of the status associated with certain jobs and careers. It is difficult to imagine how the recent Soviet school reform, which hopes to bring the Soviet education system more in line with the needs of a modern economy, can successfully address these problems without at least a partial reversal of affirmative action.

The educational dilemma is further complicated by the fact that the expansion of opportunities for most non-Russians has coincided with—indeed, has probably contributed to—the decline in opportunities for Soviet Jews. Traditionally better educated than most Soviet citizens, Jews came to bear the brunt of Soviet attempts to raise the educational levels of other ethnic groups. Such a policy also dovetailed with official hostility towards Israel, Zionism, and Jews. In any case, a policy of equal educational opportunities may not mix well with a policy of equal results. Some ethnic groups inevitably will do better than others.

Are these problems so great that they pose a threat to the stability of the system? No. Moreover, none of them is insoluble. For all their truculence, Sharaf Rashidov, Dinmukhamed Kunayev, and other republican bosses were in fact ousted, and a similar fate probably awaits Vladimir Shcherbitsky. Some combination of modernization and investment, coupled with Russian-language training, may resolve the problem of regional imbalance without alienating the Muslims. In principle, national consciousness can be channeled in support of the system, while genuine nationalists can always be repressed. It is important for Western observers to avoid the oversimplification they would certainly reject if it were applied to their own societies. Nevertheless, as Soviet society grows more complex and as the republican share of that complexity increases, the impact of the national question on both the system and its policy will grow correspondingly. Dealing effectively, wisely, and humanely with the increasing importance of the non-Russians may be the greatest challenge facing Soviet policymakers in the near future.

GORBACHEV'S EDUCATION
IN THE NATIONALITY ISSUE

If any sphere of Soviet politics illustrates both the manner in which Mikhail Gorbachev has learned while in office and the difficulties attendant upon learning about difficult subjects, it is the national question. Gorbachev is no newcomer to this problem area, if only for personal reasons: His wife Raisa is partly Ukrainian, and Mikhail Sergeyevich himself reportedly speaks some Ukrainian.[6] Moreover, by the time he had been appointed General Secretary in March 1985, he had already accumulated a good deal of working experience with the multinational nature of the Soviet Union.

Until 1978, when Gorbachev was promoted to Moscow, his entire Party career had been centered on Stavropol, an ethnically heterogeneous north Caucasus territory that administratively encompasses an autonomous province inhabited by the Karachai and Cherkess, two small nations subjected to severe repressions by Stalin for alleged collaboration with the Germans in World War II.[7] In fact, Gorbachev made two speeches on the "friendship of peoples" as early as 1972, and despite his position as Central Committee Secretary in charge of agriculture, he was considered sufficiently expert on nationality issues to travel to Lithuania in June 1980, where he delivered an ornate oration on the "Friendship of USSR People—an Invaluable Achievement," in celebration of the fortieth anniversary of Lithuania's annexation to the Soviet Union.[8]

What do these speeches tell us about the early Gorbachev? Only that he expressed the official line. His early pronouncements on the national question are notable only for their dullness, cliches, and naive optimism. They seemed to assume there was nothing more to Soviet national relations than harmony, friendship, brotherhood, and boundless love. New ideas may have been germinating on his mind in the 1970s and early 1980s, but there is nothing in these speeches to indicate that they extended to the question of the Soviet nationalities.

The tenor of Gorbachev's comments concerning nationality changed little after his appointment as General Secretary. His March 11th, 1985, acceptance speech made the obligatory reference to the "steadfast strengthening of the friendship of peoples of our great multinational state."[9] His May 8th, 1985, speech on the fortieth anniversary of victory in World War II repeated the same platitudes that Brezhnev never tired of stating: "The blossoming of nations and nationalities is organically connected to their all-round drawing together. Into the consciousness and heart of every person there has deeply entered the feeling of belonging to a single family—the Soviet people, a new and historically unprecedented social and international community."[10] If anything, the speech was regressive in that Gorbachev unnecessarily praised the "great Russian people" and Stalin for their role in the war. Gorbachev's Russocentric inclinations appeared to surface on June 25, 1985, when in an impromptu talk in Kiev he transposed the USSR with Russia.[11] Whatever the psychological importance of this misstatement, it confirmed that Gorbachev's attitude toward the non-Russians was one of complacency at best and lack of interest at worst.

But things were to change, and radically so. On May 9 and 15, 1985, anti-Russian riots erupted in Latvia's capital city, Riga. In November and December 1985 and in January 1986, meanwhile, in addition to the continuing cleanup in Sharaf Rashidov's former fiefdom, Uzbekistan, major personnel changes were implemented in several republics in preparation for the republican Party congresses planned for early 1986. New Party first secretaries were assigned to Kirgizia, Tadzhikistan, and Turkmenistan; Azerbaijan and Moldavia received new chairmen of their local Supreme Soviets. In addition, new KGB chiefs were appointed in Kirgizia and Kazakhstan, while internal affairs ministers were replaced in Uzbekistan, Tadzhikistan, and Georgia.

The changes were obviously preceded by several months' painful examination and deliberation, an experience that appears to have conflicted with Gorbachev's tranquil image of national relations. Not surprisingly, his own speech at the Twenty-seventh Party Congress in February 1986 reflected his growing doubts about the status of the national question. The six paragraphs Gorbachev devoted to the nationalities contained their share of cliches, but for the first time in his career he spoke openly of "contradictions" and other problems that threatened to undermine the "fraternal friendship of peoples." But what was the Party to do about these problems? At this point, Gorbachev recommended more of the same: uncompromising opposition to nationalism and chauvinism; sensitivity; creativity; adaptability; and other practically meaningless measures. Significantly, the most concrete of Gorbachev's suggestions—opposition to nationalism and chauvinism—was negative. His positive recommendations were so vague as to be worthless as guidelines.[12]

In the months that followed the Party Congress, some rumblings were heard among non-Russian intellectuals, but it was not until mid-December 1986 that Gorbachev's idyllic image of nationality relations was finally shattered. To make matters worse, shock after shock would follow throughout 1987. On December 17-18, mass anti-Russian riots erupted in Kazakhstan's capital, Alma-Ata, after Gennadi Kolbin, a Russian, replaced Dinmukhamed Kunayev, a Kazakh, as Party First Secretary. Thousands of students—many of them Komsomol members—participated, some of them carrying banners calling for autonomy and a U.N. seat for Kazakhstan. Store windows were smashed, cars burned, and policemen attacked.[13] Events such as these were said to take place only in colonialist and capitalist countries, not in the Soviet Union, which, as the Party program insisted, had definitively and completely solved the national question.

At the other end of the country, in Riga, anti-Russian demonstrations took place in late December 1986 and early January 1987. Jewish dissidents participated in several days of protest in Moscow on February 10-13, 1987. Nationalist demonstrations again broke out in the Latvian capital on April 19. Several weeks later, in May, a newly formed Russian chauvinist group, Pamyat' (Memory), staged a series of noisy and ominously anti-Semitic public meetings. Much to the consternation of Jews and other non-Russians, the supporters of Pamyat' appeared to be legion and the authorities' handling of the group relatively lenient. Riga was the site of another disturbance on June 14.

Crimean Tatars besieged Moscow for most of July, demanding the right to return to their ancestral homeland in the Crimea. August 23—the day on which the Molotov-Ribbentrop Pact had been signed in 1939—was particularly tense as nationalist demonstrations took place in the Baltic capitals, Riga, Tallinn, and Vilnius. Then, in early October, an unofficial Ukrainian peace group took to the streets of Lvov. Finally, national unrest climaxed in February 1988, when hundreds of thousands of Armenians marched through the streets of Yerevan demanding that Nagorno-Karabakh, an Armenian-populated province in neighboring Azerbaijan, be annexed to Armenia. So many demonstrations in so short a time are unprecedented in Soviet history, and it is difficult to imagine that they failed to bring Gorbachev to his senses.[14]

The sobering of Gorbachev was evident at the January 1987 Central Committee Plenum. The self-laudatory and complacent tone of his earlier pronouncements was gone. Instead, it was clear that Gorbachev now realized that the roots of the Alma-Ata riots were not unique to Kazakhstan and that the Party had actually made "mistakes" in implementing its national policy. Gorbachev also accused Soviet social scientists of having painted an excessively optimistic picture of national relations, and—in what may have been an indirect form of self-criticism—he said that "it was long not accepted to speak" of mistakes. As refreshing as was Gorbachev's growing sophistication, he again had few positive recommendations. He expressed his support for equitable ethnic representation in Party and state organs, for an intensification of "internationalist education," greater candor, and so on, but all of this was familiar ground. On the other hand, Gorbachev's list of measures he opposed had grown to include "all manifestations of national narrow-mindedness and conceit, nationalism and chauvinism, parochialism, Zionism, and anti-Semitism."[15]

Still, Gorbachev was clearly learning, as became painfully clear in February 1987, when he visited Latvia and Estonia. In contrast to his upbeat 1980 speech in Lithuania, Gorbachev now sounded distinctly apologetic and ill at ease. With no trace of irony, he noted that the "Baltic peoples' road to socialism had been thorny and complex" and that there had been "omissions," "miscalculations," and "strain" in the Soviet Baltic experience. He also felt obliged to compare nationality relations in the Soviet Union with those under "imperialism" and to reject émigré "bourgeois nationalist" insinuations regarding Soviet national policy. No less striking, however, was his complete lack of openness about the shameful circumstances of Stalin's annexation of the Baltic states in 1940.[16] Gorbachev took one step forward only to take one step backward.

A similar dialectic was evident at the close of 1987. Just two months after a frank official statement on the national question appeared in the September issue of the theoretical Party journal, *Kommunist*, Gorbachev retreated to Brezhnevian platitudes in his otherwise groundbreaking November 2 speech commemorating the seventieth anniversary of the 1917 Revolution. This relapse notwithstanding, the *Kommunist* editorial, which may be assumed to represent Gorbachev's own views, remains an important milestone in Gorbachev's political growth. First, the document all but acknowledged that nationality relations were in as much difficulty as was the rest of the Soviet system; the friendship of peoples might be an ideal, but it was certainly not a reality. Second, the continued prominence of national tensions was explained in terms of Russia's backwardness at the time of the revolution—a clear-cut admission that contradictions about the national question were inherent in the system and were not merely "survivals of the past." Third, nationalist disturbances were attributed to "extremists" who misused *glasnost'* and democracy, while the "leading Soviet intelligentsia" was enjoined to be "implacable towards any manifestations" of subjectivism, passions, and political frivolity. Finally, the *Kommunist* editorial addressed non-

Russian language concerns and recommended that both Russian and non-Russian languages—and not primarily the former—be cultivated in the republics and that both Russians and non-Russians be bilingual.[17] As the first substantive official statement on the national question since Gorbachev's appointment, the article was remarkable not only for engaging in public self-criticism, but also for making concessions to the linguistic demands of non-Russians as well as for strongly implying that there were clear nationality-related limits to *glasnost'*.

Regardless of whether these verbal assurances ever become policy, their importance lies in the fact that they are concessions. As Gorbachev's belated call in early 1988 for a special Central Committee plenum on nationality relations indicates, the Kremlin is reacting to and not acting upon the national question. Such meek behavior is clearly atypical for Gorbachev, who generally finds himself in the role of the radical innovator surrounded by lethargic bureaucrats and citizens. That the non-Russian elites have taken the lead in arguing for *perestroika* in national relations and have succeeded in imposing some of their preferences on the Kremlin means that it must be particularly reluctant to tinker with existing national arrangements to the point of deeming them outside the entire reform program.

What can account for this reluctance? Although it would be naive to think that Gorbachev believes all he says about the indissoluble friendship of peoples, it is nonetheless possible that the Soviet leadership acquired an idealized view of nationality relations as a result of its lack of contact with the grassroots of Soviet society in the Brezhnev era. A far more plausible explanation, however, is that Gorbachev has purposely been mouthing platitudes in order to avoid dealing with the Pandora's box of ethnicity. This is a classic example of a nondecision. Soviet leaders know of their country's frequent ethnic conflicts, of Soviet federalism's contradictory nature, and of non-Russian resentment of Russian dominance. These leaders surely understand that restructuring nationality relations is both supremely difficult and dangerously complex in that it can lead to questions regarding the Russian-non-Russian relationship that should not be raised and cannot be answered. Gorbachev's lack of interest in and seeming complacency about the nationalities are thus partly genuine and partly false. On the one hand, he is "confusing wishes for reality," as Soviet propaganda calls such self-delusionary behavior; on the other, he is intentionally avoiding an issue that can only seriously complicate the political, economic, and social reforms he wants to effect.

It is precisely for this second reason that Gorbachev continually emphasizes what should be avoided—such as nationalism and chauvinism—and the limits to *glasnost'*.   Gorbachev knows that *perestroika* inevitably has profound implications for the nationality question. If it upsets the delicate imbalance between central and peripheral authority too much in the direction of the periphery, *perestroika* may also elicit nationalist tendencies and thus create an insurmountable barrier to continued reform.   In view of this possibility, restructuring the national question appears to be far less pressing an issue to Gorbachev than containing it—keeping it within manageable limits and preventing it from disrupting the four pillars of *perestroika*'s support: democratization, *glasnost'*, political renewal, and economic modernization.

All four elements logically go together, and without each of them, *perestroika* would be meaningless. Of course, economic modernization is Gorbachev's highest priority. But Gorbachev has come to understand that modernization is contingent on a renewal of the political system. Administrative effectiveness must be enhanced and political opposition must be quelled for the radical economic measures he envisions to take effect and to work. In turn, political restructuring means mobilizing the support of various elite and popular constituencies through greater publicity and *glasnost'* and increased popular initiative and participation (democratization). All of these are laudable goals, but even laudable goals can have unintended consequences. Unfortunately for Gorbachev, measures to cope with these consequences may be fatal to *perestroika*.

GLASNOST' AND PERESTROIKA IN A NON-RUSSIAN CONTEXT

Glasnost' and democratization inevitably go together because a more open expression of opinions is predicated on the ability to do so. The rights of citizens must be expanded and those of the police and courts curbed. This means that the powers of the secret police, the KGB, must be reduced, even if only temporarily. Gorbachev appeared to have moved in this direction when he announced that a law on "USSR state security" is scheduled to appear in 1990 and when he encouraged the public exposure and censure of a KGB operative in the Ukrainian city of Voroshilovgrad.[18]

The dangers of such a policy are readily apparent. Even a weaker KGB would still be a formidable opponent, but it would mean that political adversaries would have an easier time expressing opinions and organizing oppositionist groups. It was in 1986, for example, long after the Helsinki human rights movement had been crushed, that a Latvian group was established to monitor the state's record on national and civil rights in Latvia. There followed in 1987 the *samizdat* (self-published) journals *Glasnost'* (Moscow) and the *Ukrainian Herald*, the Russian chauvinist group Pamyat', the Initiative Group for the Release of Ukrainian Prisoners of Conscience, the Committee for the Release of Political Prisoners in Armenia, the Committee for the Release of Political Prisoners in Georgia, the Ukrainian peace movement, the Armenian National United Party, the Ukrainian Association of Independent Creative Intelligentsia, the Ukrainian Culturalogical Club, a Soviet branch of the International Society for Human Rights, and a revived Ukrainian Helsinki Group.[19] Where, and whether, to draw the line on such unsanctioned activity is a question that is likely to concern Gorbachev for the rest of his tenure. The longer he waits, the more the dissidents can organize. The swifter his crackdown, however, the sooner the KGB will reassert itself and the more hypocritical will Soviet democracy appear.

The dangers of *glasnost'* must be particularly evident to Gorbachev. Given that *glasnost'* represents the removal of taboos; the expansion of the permissible in literature, journalism, and scholarship; the encouragement of criticism; and the expression of real needs, desires, and values, it is inevitable that some non-Russians will use *glasnost'* to pursue their own ends. This would be acceptable if their perception of the utility of *glasnost'* matched that of the Party and if they restricted their criticism to lazy workers; corrupt bureaucrats; such social ills as drug abuse, violence, and black marketeering; and the like. Matters become far more sensitive when *glasnost'* is extended to nationality issues. Since early 1986, for example, non-Russians from republics as different as Estonia, Belorussia, the Ukraine, Turkmenistan, and Kirgizia have been publicly expressing ideas that would have landed them in prison for "bourgeois nationalist agitation and propaganda" only several years ago.

This new fearlessness was most apparent at the republican writers' congresses held in May and June 1986. Some writers openly called for the purification of foreign (that is, Russian) loan words from local languages; others lambasted the educational and publishing systems for neglecting native languages; still others demanded that true internationalism required that Russians learned to speak the language of the republic in which they live and that republican languages be enshrined in republican constitutions.[20] The following statement by Pavlo Zahrebelny, the First Secretary of the Ukrainian Writers Union, was typical of many that were expressed at the gatherings:

In what things does national dignity manifest itself first of all? From the writer's point of view, it manifests itself in the national character depicted by artistic mastery. Therefore we cannot remain indifferent to such things as the language in which business correspondence is conducted, the language in which technical, scientific, and sociopolitical literature is published or what language is used in kindergartens, in schools, in higher educational establishments, in Komsomol and Pioneer organizations, or how many theatres have already become bilingual, because such an approximate language gives rise to approximate thoughts, approximate feelings, approximate work, and, as a consequence, approximate people. Let us be frank: He whose speaking ability is poor also lives and works badly. One is convinced of this by the example of those drones and punks who have ceased to understand us, who instead of living are "sailing high."[21]

Perhaps most remarkable was the fact that twenty-eight prominent Belorussians, representatives of a nation that most Western scholars had long since dismissed as lacking a sense of ethnic identity, wrote a letter to Gorbachev in December 1986 in which they expressed concern for the "fate of the Belorussian language"

and demanded a return to the policy of linguistic and cultural liberalization of
the 1920s:

   a. Belorussian to be introduced as a working language in Party, state, and local
       government in the republic....
   b. a compulsory leaving examination to be introduced in Belorussian language and
       literature (essay) in secondary schools, and in Belorussian language (dictation)
       in eight-year incomplete secondary schools irrespective of the language of
       instruction.
   c. a compulsory examination for all school-leavers (except for those coming from
       outside the BSSR and USSR) in Belorussian language and literature (essay) for
       entry into all institutions of higher education, and in Belorussian language
       (dictation) for entry into the technical colleges of the republic.[22]

Why is the language issue so important to non-Russians? At one level, the
growing use of Russian is perceived as Russification. The defense of non-
Russian languages thus becomes a defense of national traditions, cultures, and
identities. But there is an even more important dimension to the language
debate. In multinational states, such as the Soviet Union, language is inevitably
politicized, which is probably the major reason that many former colonial states
have retained the languages of the former colonial powers as their national
languages. In the Soviet Union, however, what is officially called the "language
of internationality discourse" happens to be the language of the dominant
nationality, the Russians, so that the use of the Russian language often becomes
a virtual political statement. A non-Russian who speaks only Russian is tacitly
supporting the Soviet status quo; one who insists on using his or her own
language is tacitly expressing dissatisfaction with the existing political
arrangement.[23] In demanding a higher status for their languages, therefore,
non-Russian writers are not concerned exclusively with linguistic issues; they are
engaged in an oblique form of politics and are thereby testing the limits of
glasnost' in a manner that may well alarm the critics of *perestroika* and perhaps
even its advocates.

It is thus of little wonder that such radical demands concerning language are
a source of distress for Gorbachev. Not only are they associated with the
nationalism and chauvinism he is determined to oppose, but by implementing
them, he would surely produce substantial resentment, especially among the
large Russian populations living in non-Russian republics who are generally
ignorant of the local languages. But if non-Russian intellectuals are forbidden
to make such demands, *glasnost'* and the Party's ostensible commitment to
ethnic equality will suffer. If these demands are not met, frustration may well
result.

It may be a sign of things to come that the Belorussian Party leader, Efrem
Sokolov, strongly rebuffed the writers of the Belorussian letter and suggested
they needed enlightenment. Indeed, he asserted, "those who would like to

dramatize the situation should be aware that this does not serve the cause of restructuring."[24]   In an action that was no less indicative of the new spirit of the republics, however, 134 Belorussians ignored Sokolov's admonitions and wrote another letter to Gorbachev on June 4, 1987, in which they repeated the demands of the first letter.[25]

A particularly explosive mixture is that of *glasnost'* and non-Russian history. It is one thing to go over familiar ground and criticize Iosif Stalin and his cult of personality or to reevaluate Nikita Khrushchev, Nikolay Bukharin, and perhaps even Leon Trotsky, all of whom were associated with the Soviet Party-state and its development. It is quite another to delve deeply into non-Russian history and ask awkward questions (that reinforce nationalist tendencies) about the manner in which the borderlands were subdued and annexed. (Recent Soviet willingness to examine the Katyn massacre is a positive development, but it is premised on, and can only improve, the abysmal quality of current Soviet-Polish relations.) Are the Balts to study Stalin's absorption of their countries in 1939? Are the Ukrainians to open the archives on the 1933 famine that may have claimed several million lives? Are the Central Asians to evaluate the Basmachi anti-Soviet guerrilla movement of the 1920s and 1930s, especially in the light of its similarities to the Afghan *mujahidin*? *Glasnost'* has not yet gone that far, but one day Gorbachev must confront these issues and decide how much openness he actually desires.

So far, the outlook is mixed. Gorbachev's speeches in Latvia and Estonia suggest that the "blank spots" in non-Russian history will remain far larger than those in Russian history. More ominous was an otherwise openminded and reasonably argued article written by Alexander Yakovlev, a protégé of Gorbachev known for his opposition to Russian chauvinism, which contained the following passage:

> Recently, sometimes quietly, but also openly, criticism of the Revolution and of Soviet power has been voiced for their supposedly destructive policy vis-a-vis national cultures. The subtext of such arguments contains the thought that the class, socialist approach and proletarian internationalism have in practice proven to be the reason for the "impoverishment " of national cultures. This is political speculation on lack of knowledge and ignorance, as well as a prime result of the fact that the demagogy that repeats bourgeois propaganda fables is not getting a well-argued rebuff from scholarly criticism, which is summoned to defend historical truth.[26]

If Yakovlev's opinions reflect those of Gorbachev, non-Russian *glasnost'* may soon be reduced to a pale shadow of its Russian counterpart. If that happens, disillusionment, protests, and perhaps even repression are sure to follow. When they do, *glasnost'* and with it *perestroika* will be seriously harmed.

Even if Gorbachev can produce both *glasnost'* and democratization in the non-Russian context, he is likely to discover that they will not simplify his task of restructuring the political system. Politically, Gorbachev's goals are to streamline the bureaucracy and to mold it into an effective instrument of government. Naturally, all bureaucrats, both Russian and non-Russian, may be expected to resist such a move, but the problem is likely to be more acute in the non-Russian republics, where entrenched elites, ethnic favoritism, and affirmative action represent a formidable obstacle to Gorbachev's plans of renewal.

Whereas recalcitrant locals can always be purged—although not without difficulty—and non-Russian reformers can usually be found, ethnic favoritism and affirmative action are so ingrained in the republics that these have become a part of the non-Russian political expectations. A policy that emphasizes merit and not nationality in the disbursement of jobs in the Party and state bureaucracy goes against what many non-Russians now consider to be their birthright. Renovating the bureaucracy will thus involve sending an unmistakable signal to the non-Russians, one that they are unlikely to receive with equanimity. Gorbachev's appointment of Kolbin, for example, an able Russian apparatchik with a reputation for getting things done, as Kunayev's replacement in Kazakhstan was precisely such a signal. The ethnic violence that followed may have contributed to Gorbachev's far more cautious attitude toward the Ukrainian Shcherbitsky. Nationalist riots in Kiev would not only be an international embarrassment, but they would also represent a major blow to the legitimacy of the leadership. Obviously, such considerations will not keep Gorbachev from pursuing whatever personnel policy he deems necessary. But the ethnic factor will stand in the way of his search for an ideal bureaucracy and, at the same time, will impede *perestroika*.

The results of *glasnost'*, democratization, and the quest for political renewal indirectly affect the primary goal of *perestroika*—economic modernization—by undermining what Gorbachev believes are its bases. Nevertheless, it is conceivable that substantial modernization could be achieved, albeit at a slower pace, even without the benefits of openness, participation, and efficiency. Unfortunately for Gorbachev, the national question directly casts a shadow, the longest yet, even on economic modernization.

THE REPERCUSSIONS OF DECENTRALIZATION
FOR THE REPUBLICS

Regardless of whether the Soviet economy is currently in a state of crisis, there appears to be little doubt, both among Western and Soviet economists, that it is in the doldrums. Soviet leaders appear to think that the Soviet Union is falling behind the West and is progressively becoming a second-rate power. Modernization is the solution: raising productivity and improving the quality of products by means of better technology, improved management techniques, and greater individual initiative. Gorbachev recognizes that such an economic change may be accompanied only by introducing some elements of the market and thereby decentralizing economic decisionmaking authority and devolving it to lower levels of the system. Some steps have already been taken in this direction. More private activity in the service and consumer-goods sectors is now permitted than in the past, and enterprises may now make more decisions concerning how to allocate their resources, what and how much to produce, and to whom to sell it. But if *perestroika* is to succeed, even greater steps toward decentralization are necessary, with one Soviet economist, Nikolai Shmelev, suggesting that a form of market socialism might have to be introduced.[27] How far Gorbachev intends to go is unclear, but he does appear to believe that decentralization is still in its initial stages.

Decentralization may or may not solve the economic problems of the Soviet Union, but it is certain to produce important consequences for republican participants and institutions.[28] Most basically, decentralization represents a devolution to local levels of information and of decisionmaking. Devolution represents a significant expansion of peripheral authority on its own terms, but it is important for three additional reasons as well. First, devolution cannot be confined to the economic sector alone—to the system of ministries and to the factories attached to them. Political and economic are intertwined in socialist systems, and it is inevitable that economic decentralization will be accompanied by the devolution of information and decisionmaking to peripheral political organizations. Second, a genuine devolution to the periphery of information and decisionmaking is necessarily associated with increased popular participation and initiative. If the periphery is now to solve centrally defined problems, then it must involve greater numbers of people in its information-gathering and decisionmaking processes. Just as the center depends on contributions from the periphery to make decisions, so now the periphery depends on its own "periphery" for contributions. Third and perhaps most important, none of these developments is feasible if central or coercive organs (or both) continue to exert particularly close supervision of events on the periphery. Some kind of thaw is required for information processing on the periphery and peripheral decisionmaking and participation to function semieffectively. For decentralization to work, the center must reproduce at the peripheral level the conditions of decisionmaking that it enjoys—that is, the center must expand the autonomy of the periphery.

Economic decentralization, however, does far more than permit republican actors more freely to pursue their interests as they define them. Decentralization forces peripheral elites to pursue *only* their interests. The purpose and logic of decentralization compel peripheral elites to focus their energies on the territorial unit they administer, the republic; otherwise they would be incapable of implementing the original mandate of decentralization—improved efficiency, better decisions, a smoothly functioning system. Decentralization also arms the periphery. It gives local elites the means effectively to pursue their goals. That is, it provides them with resources or with greater control of resources, such as information, finances, organization, language, ideology, jobs, and cadres. Resources, in turn, convert into rewards and sanctions that permit peripheral elites to mobilize republican support for their policies.[29]

Economic decentralization thus turns the tables on the normal structure of incentives. It rewards efficient self-centered behavior and punishes inefficient self-centered behavior, and rational, non-nationalist republican elites respond accordingly. They come to act *as if* they believed that their unit of governance should be sovereign and its interest paramount, and by acting as if they were nationalists, they become nationalists in spite of themselves. Local elites need not be nationalists, nor must they want sovereignty for their republics. Indeed, as members of the Soviet elite, the *nomenklatura*, they will probably devote themselves to the well-being of the Soviet Union as a whole. Under conditions of decentralization, however, all the incentives go in the opposite direction—that of enhancing the prosperity and modernity of one's own republic and, thus, automatically neglecting the all-union context. Economic decentralization within a centrally directed socialist federal system encourages objectively nationalist behavior, even by non-nationalists or antinationalists. Yugoslavia's constantly warring ethnic republics would appear to confirm the validity of this observation.

Objectively nationalist elite behavior affects the Soviet system in the same way as does the subjectively nationalist behavior of bona fide nationalists. Both accelerate centrifugal tendencies and aggravate the systems's fundamental contradiction between Russian hegemony and non-Russian symbolic sovereignty. Economic decentralization thus contains the seeds of its own destruction. Because decentralization logically leads to the breakup of the Soviet system, Moscow cannot permit decentralization to run its course. At some point, when it perceives that centrifugal tendencies have increased more than the system can bear, Moscow must recentralize, revoke peripheral autonomy, and reduce peripheral resources. In sum, it must retrench. The precise timing of retrenchment will depend on many circumstances—international relations, intraelite conflicts, successions, economic trends, and so on—but at some point a retrenchment must occur if the system is to survive.

This logic will hold equal force if economic centralization is held constant and political decentralization is assumed to occur. The diminution of Party control and supervision of local political organs translates directly into increased peripheral prerogatives, political resources, and objectively nationalist behavior for the reasons I have discussed with regard to economic decentralization. Significantly, the political de-Stalinization initiated by Khrushchev and more or less maintained by his successors means that some political decentralization is now built into the Soviet system. Attempts at economic decentralization under condition of some political decentralization are therefore all the more likely to encourage objectively nationalist behavior and produce national communism.

Both of these forms of decentralization coincided in the 1920s, with nativization and the New Economic Policy, and in the 1950s-1960s, with de-Stalinization and the Sovnarkhoz reform—periods that witnessed a flowering of national communism. Since Khrushchev's ouster, political and economic decentralization have not overlapped to as great an extent as was the case earlier. The Kosygin reforms and their progeny, wholly in fact and partly in intention, were tantamount to economic recentralization, whereas Brezhnevism represented a selective reassertion of some central control on recalcitrant republics such as the Ukraine and Georgia, together with the institutionalization of the political prerogatives of peripheral cadres. This fact, together with the political turmoil that accompanied the Brezhnev succession, enabled Rashidov, Kunayev, Usubaliyev, and other Central Asian satraps to engage in a form of national communism and convert Uzbekistan, Kazakhstan, and Kirgizia into modern versions of the ancient khanates of Khiva and Bukhara.

Mikhail Gorbachev is treading on particularly thin ice because his program combines all the necessary ingredients of objectively nationalist behavior. *Glasnost'* and democratization accelerate political decentralization, and economic modernization is equivalent to economic decentralization. The combination is a potent one, and the visible growth of aggressively national sentiments in all the republics is the first sign of the dangers ahead. Despite the fact that Gorbachev is placing his own supporters into key positions in both Moscow and the periphery, the logic of decentralization within a federal context will drive these elites to pursue increasingly objective nationalist behavior. If so, Gorbachev or his successor will come face to face with the contradictory nature of Soviet federalism, and unless he is willing to preside over the system's disintegration, recentralization of some kind will be inevitable.

To the extent that, as most economists argue, centralization inevitably leads to crises demanding economic decentralization as a solution, the Soviet Party-state would appear to be caught in a vicious cycle of its own making. Just as centralization effectively addresses the problems of economic centralization, so, too, decentralization inevitably sets loose forces that threaten the stability of the system. Can the Soviet Union continue indefinitely in such a cycle? The answer, for better or for worse, is "yes." Because systemic survival is not now or in the immediate future an issue, temporary decentralization can alleviate certain problems, and recurrent recentralization is always a possibility. Some states manage to muddle through for centuries, and most do well for decades. In order to answer this question in the negative, we would have to assume that the crisis requiring decentralization is so severe that anything but complete decentralization will lead to collapse.

Can the vicious cycle ever be broken? Only if one of three conditions is met. The uneven federalism of the Soviet Union would have to be replaced with a more unitary state structure that dissociates administrative units from ethnic groups. Or the uneven federalism would have to be transcended, and a more genuine federation, without Russian hegemony, would have to be established. Or, finally, Soviet socialism would have to work sufficiently well—perhaps with some element of low-level marketization—that it would prevent the emergence of overcentralization. On their own, these conditions are not at present likely to emerge. The non-Russians are not prone to tolerate the abrogation of the rights they do possess; the Party and the Russians are unlikely to give up their elite prerogatives (elites, after all, generally do not self-destruct); and socialism's renewal still seems a long way off at best. Recentralization and repression appear to be inevitable, unless, as I will argue in the concluding chapter of this section, an outside force improves the likelihood that the second and third condition will come into existence.

THE NON-RUSSIANS AND THE WEST

While the side effects of *perestroika* represent a political and economic dilemma for the Soviet Union, they confront the West with a moral one. Specifically, the USSR's difficulties will put the West's putative commitment to human rights and democracy to a severe test. At some point, the West may have to choose between tolerating repression of legitimate non-Russian national aspirations and supporting the destabilization of a superpower and risking bloodshed and, perhaps, war.

The best way for the West to resolve this dilemma is to create the conditions that would enable the Soviet system to escape the vicious cycle described in this chapter. Given that the endorsement of extreme political centralization in the Soviet Union would be tantamount to violating non-Russian human and national rights, the West should opt for a combination of genuine federation and economic reform. In a word, the West should encourage *perestroika* in the non-Russian republics. There are ample incentives for all sides to support this course of action. Such a policy would permit the West to remain sincerely committed to human rights and to peace; this policy would enhance the decisionmaking prerogatives of the non-Russian elites within the Soviet context; and this policy would sweeten the pill for supporters of Russian hegemony and Party centralization by improving *perestroika*'s overall chances of success.

Is such a course realistic? Western policy toward Eastern Europe, which is no less a part of the Soviet empire than are the non-Russian republics, suggests that the answer is a qualified "yes." Whereas the post-World War II U.S. aim of rolling back Soviet control back from Eastern Europe proved to be an illusion, and in reality only drove the Eastern Europeans into the arms of the Soviets, the expansion of interstate and intersociety contacts—all of which were based on Western recognition of Soviet hegemony—improved the quality of life and advanced human rights in most Eastern European countries. Eastern Europe benefitted, as did the West, while the USSR was generally satisfied that its imperial interests in the area were not being threatened. Greater contacts with the West were effective because they attempted to institutionalize and thus make permanent the relative autonomy of the Eastern European countries in the context of their subordinate status within the Soviet bloc. Institutionalization proceeded along the lines of permanent political, economic, and cultural contacts between the Eastern Europeans and the West on the understanding that bridges can only exist to link separate spheres of influence.

A Western policy of bridge building toward the non-Russian republics may well be what is required today. Liberation is unrealistic, repression morally repugnant; genuine and institutionalized limited autonomy coupled with Western recognition of continued Soviet hegemony may be the best for which the non-Russians can hope. Notwithstanding the problematic nature of the Baltic states' international status,[30] a basis for expanding diplomatic relations with other republics exists. All have ministries of foreign affairs, and the Ukraine and Belorussia are represented in a variety of international bodies and are hosts to a number of consulates. The United States has agreed to open a consulate in Kiev, and West Germany may do the same. Academic and cultural relations could also be extended. Here, too, precedents exist, such as the recent establishment of direct relations between the American Council of Learned Societies and the Soviet Ukrainian Academy of Sciences. Most important, now that Soviet enterprises may legally engage in some foreign economic relations of their own, the basis for establishing direct economic bridges, investing in and trading with the republics, the West can contribute directly to economic modernization and thus to the success of *perestroika*, which is a prospect of considerable appeal to Soviet reformers and one that may overcome their apprehensions concerning genuine federalism.

The purpose of bridge building would not be to foment nationalism and encourage the dissolution of the Soviet Party-state. Rather, the goal would be the opposite: to expand and to institutionalize the political, cultural, and economic autonomy of the Soviet republics—of their populations in general and of their nationally minded elites in particular—*within* the Soviet context. By helping the republics to acquire a form of limited, but genuinely national, autonomy—one that falls far short of Finlandization, Polonization, or Magyarization and that more closely resembles Bulgarization—while acknowledging continued Soviet rule over these territories and promoting economic reform, Western policymakers may eventually succeed in sparing Mikhail Gorbachev and themselves the unpleasant choice between repression and disintegration. For the non-Russians, of course, Bulgarization, or the possession of limited autonomy and genuine national identity under the rule of an outside hegemony, would represent an enormous step forward in terms of their cultural, linguistic, economic, and political aspirations—a result of no small magnitude.

Notes

1. For an excellent overview of the Armenian demonstrations and of their repercussions in Azerbaijan, see Elizabeth Fuller, "A Preliminary Chronology of Recent Events in Armenia and Azerbaijan," *Radio Liberty Research*, RL 101/88, March 15, 1988.

2. The largest non-Russian groups, according to the 1979 census, include the Ukrainians (42 million), Uzbeks (12.5 million), Belorussians (9.5 million), Kazakhs (6.5 million), Tatars (6.3 million), Azerbaijanis (5.5 million), Armenians (4 million), Georgians (3.5 million), Moldavians (3 million), Tadzhiks (3 million), Lithuanians (3 million), Turkmen (2 million), Kirgiz (2 million), Jews (1.8 million), Latvians (1.4 million), and Estonians (1 million). *Chislennost' i sostav naseleniia SSSR* (Moscow: Finansy i statistika, 1984), p. 71.

3. See Alexander J. Motyl, "The Foreign Relations of the Ukrainian SSR," *Harvard Ukrainian Studies*, no. 1 (March 1982), pp. 62-78.

4. See Alexander J. Motyl, *Will the Non-Russians Rebel? State, Ethnicity, and Stability in the USSR* (Ithaca, N.Y.: Cornell University Press, 1987).

5. *The Programme of the Communist Party of the Soviet Union* (Moscow: Novosti, 1986), p. 47 (emphasis supplied).

6. *Soviet Nationality Survey*, no. 9 (September 1985), p. 5.

7. On the fate of the Karachai, Cherkess, and other deported nationalities, see Aleksandr M. Nekrich, *The Punished Peoples* (New York: Norton, 1978).

8. M.S. Gorbachev, *Izbrannye rechi i stat'i* (Moscow: Izdatel'stvo politicheskoi literatury, 1987), vol. 1, pp. 50-54, 69-78, 225-236.

9. *Kommunist*, no. 5 (March 1985), p. 10.

10. M.S. Gorbachev, *Ibrannye rechi i stat'i* (Moscow: Izdatel'stvo politicheskoi literatury, 1985), p. 52.

11. *Soviet Nationality Survey*, no. 9 (September 1985), p. 5.

12. *Izvestiya*, February 26, 1986, p. 6.

13. T.K., "Nationalist Riots in Kazakhstan," *Soviet Nationality Survey*, no. 1 (January 1987), p. 3. See also Uwe Halbach, "Perestrojka und Nationalitaetenpolitik. Der Schock von Alma-Ata und Moskaus gespanntes Verhaeltnis zu Mittelasien," *Berichte des Bundesinstituts für ostwissenschaftliche und internationale Studien*, no. 38 (1987).

14. "V Ryzi vidbulasia demonstratsiia," *Svoboda*, June 17, 1987, p. 1; "Russian Nationalists Test Gorbachev," *New York Times*, May 24, 1987, p. 10; "Lithuanians Rally for Stalin Victims," *New York Times*, August 24, 1987, p. 1; "Unofficial Peace Demonstration Broken Up in Lviv, Ukraine," *Ukrainian Press Agency*, no. 6 (October 8, 1987); "Wachsende nationale Spannungen in der UdSSR," *Neue Zürcher Zeitung*, March 13-14, 1988, p. 7.

15. *Kommunist*, no. 3 (February 1987), pp. 28-29.

16. *Pravda*, February 20, 1987, pp. 1-2; *Pravda*, February 22, 1987, pp. 1-2.

17. "Internatsionalistskaia sut' sotsializma," *Kommunist*, no. 13 (September 1987), pp. 3-13. Also Mikhail S. Gorbachev, *October and Perestroika: The Revolution Continues* (Moscow: Novosti, 1987).

18. Vedomosti verkhovnogo soveta SSSR, no. 37 (September 10, 1986), pp. 729-736; *Pravda*, January 4, 1987, p. 3.

19. See "Latvian Helsinki Group Documents," *Ukrainian Weekly*, January 25, 1987, pp. 2,4; Roman Solchanyk, "Former Political Prisoners Form New Human Rights Groups in Ukraine," *Ukrainian Weekly*, October 18, 1987, p. 1; Bohdan Nahaylo, "'Informal' Ukrainian Culturological Club Under Attack," *Radio Liberty Research*, RL 477/87, November 23, 1987; *Glasnost'*, nos. 2-4 (July 1987), pp. 4-5; and "Herald Editors Renew Ukrainian Helsinki Group," *Ukrainian Weekly*, January 17, 1988, p. 1.

20. *Soviet Nationality Survey*, no. 9 (September 1986), pp. 1-5.

21. Ibid., pp. 6-7.

22. "A Letter to Gorbachev from 28 Belorussian Cultural Figures," *Soviet Nationality Survey*, no. 5 (May 1987), p. 8.

23. See Motyl, *Will the Non-Russians Rebel?* pp. 88-106.

24. Roman Solchanyk, "Party Leader in Belorussia Rejects Criticism About Status of Belorussian Language," *Radio Liberty Research*, RL 180/87, May 7, 1987, p. 3.

25. Roman Solchanyk, "An Open Letter to Gorbachev Sent by Belorussian Workers, Intellectuals," *Ukrainian Weekly*, August 30, 1987, p. 2.

26. A. Iakovlev, "Dostizhenie kachestvenno novogo sostoianiia sovetskogo obshchestva i obshchestvennye nauki," *Kommunist*, no. 8 (May 1987), p. 20.

27. "Zu lange herrschte statt des Rubels der Befehl," *Der Spiegel*, no. 25, June 15, 1987, pp. 135-137.

28. On the connection between economic decentralization and political liberalization, see Wlodzimierz Brus, *The Economics and Politics of Socialism* (London: Routledge & Kegan Paul, 1973).

29. On the importance of positive and negative sanctions, see Mancur Olson, *The Logic of Collective Action* (Cambridge, Mass.: Harvard University Press, 1971).

30. For the best discussion of the Baltic states' legal status, see William J. H. Hough III, "The Annexation of the Baltic States and Its Effect on the Development of Law Prohibiting Forcible Seizure of Territory," *New York Law School Journal of International and Comparative Law* 6, no. 2 (Winter 1985), pp. 303-533.

23

Soviet Federalism

Stephan Kux

Mikhail Gorbachev sees his program of *perestroyka* as seriously jeopardized by outbreaks of popular unrest, ethnic clashes, and separatist movements that are occurring in every corner of the inner Soviet empire. The Lithuanian question has achieved as much importance on the East-West agenda as have German unification or nuclear disarmament. Yet the so-called nationalities conflicts cannot be limited to particular issues or areas—or viewed as a function of local phenomena or minority problems. Nationalism, particularism, and separatism are manifestations of more complex problems besetting the USSR. Social, economic, environmental, and political issues are "ethnicized" and vice versa. The explosion of ethnic unrest and the escalation of center-periphery conflicts testify to the inadequate performance of the federal institutions, the breakdown of traditional channels of communication, the failure of internal bargaining processes, and the lack of appropriate mechanisms for a peaceful resolution of domestic conflicts. In brief, they are symptoms of a crisis of Soviet federalism.[1]

In theory, the Soviet Union is constituted as a union of sovereign states or republics bound together in a voluntary federation—like Switzerland or the United States.[2] The constitution describes the USSR as an "integral, federal, multinational state formed on the principle of socialist federalism."[3] Soviet legislation sets down rules guiding the political, economic, and cultural interplay between the Russian-dominated central authority and the predominantly non-Russian union republics. Yet de facto any American town has a larger measure of independence and self-government than a Soviet republic.[4] The tradition of a strong center, the built-in tendencies toward centralization, and the lack of constitutional oversight have in practice resulted in the usurpation of jurisdiction

---

Published in *Problems of Communism*, 39: 2 (March-April 1990), pp. 1-20. Reprinted with permission from the publisher.

by the central authorities, so that few inalienable, exclusive powers are left to the republics. While a republic has the theoretical right to leave the Union, it is not allowed to select the textbooks for its schools or to build a new road without asking for permission from Moscow. The extent of the powers of the republics at any time depends not on guaranteed constitutional rights but on the will of the central authorities to delegate responsibilities to lower levels of administration. As even the "CPSU Nationalities Platform" concedes, the republics' sovereignty is "largely formal."[5] Gorbachev has said that "up to now our state existed as a centralized and unitary state and none of us has yet the experience of living in a federation." The political and economic realities in the USSR "violate the constitutional provisions of the Soviet federation both in letter and spirit." As a result, "the very idea of federation has been seriously compromised."[6]

In recent years, the republics were able, thanks to *perestroyka* and *glasnost'*, to strengthen considerably their political, economic, and cultural resources, as well as increase their weight in the Soviet system and thus change the balance in the center-periphery relationship. The existing pseudo-federal arrangement no longer satisfies the growing aspirations and expectations Gorbachev has aroused in the peripheries. The indecisiveness of the center, the slow pace and contradictory nature of political reform, and the deterioration of the economic situation have accelerated the disintegration of this exceptionally heterogeneous, multi-ethnic empire. Soviet republics have begun to follow the example of the Soviet Union's East European satellites and to question the economic and political bonds linking them to the center. What Gennadiy Gerasimov called the Sinatra doctrine, in reference to the external empire, applies now to the internal one. The regions and republics of the USSR start to do it "their way." Whatever its real content has been in the past, the Soviet federation is currently heading towards its most serious crisis of confidence and performance since the creation of the USSR in 1922.

The Soviet federation lacks legitimacy. In the words of historian Yuriy Afanas'yev, "one must admit that Soviet history as a whole is not fit to serve as a legal basis for Soviet power."[7] None of the non-Russian member states believes that it joined the Union on a truly voluntary basis. The Georgian parliament has recently declared the incorporation of 1922 "null and void."[8] The Baltic republics consider the Molotov-Ribbentrop Pact, the Soviet-sponsored elections of 1940, and the decision of the "puppet parliaments" to join the USSR as illegal and invalid acts.[9] In their view, no contractual relationship exists with the Soviet Union, and therefore no legal basis for their membership in the federation. In Armenia, Azerbaijan, and other republics, parliamentary commissions have submitted reports reviewing the circumstances of their incorporation into the USSR.

GORBACHEV'S AGENDA

While the condition of the federation is viewed as one of the problems besetting the Soviet Union, its reform is also seen as part of the solution. The once despised notion of federalism is becoming increasingly popular among Soviet leaders. As the CPSU Nationalities Platform stresses, the task of resolving ethnic and political conflicts within the USSR is inseparable from building a "completely new federation," from constructing a "common home for all Soviet peoples."[10] Political debates, parliamentary hearings, scholarly literature, newspaper articles, and interviews in the mass media exhaustively discuss the Union's shortcomings, the prospects of federalism, and the specific approaches to reviving the Soviet federation and staving off its collapse.[11] The problem thus defined, Gorbachev attempts to design his nationalities policy in the broader context of constitutional reform, democratization, and devolution of political and economic powers to the republic and local level. The very essence of the Soviet state system is under review, as the Soviet leadership constructs various blueprints for the creation of a "completely new federation."[12]

Gorbachev has presented a package of measures specifically designed to consolidate the political and economic independence of the republics and thus to reinforce the federation. In particular, he intends (1) to extend the jurisdiction and autonomous powers of the union republics and to establish their full autonomy and responsibility in economic, social, and cultural spheres; (2) to draw clearer lines between the jurisdictions of the central authorities and those of republics; and (3) to improve the representation and participation of the republics in decision-making at the all-Union level.[13] The Soviet President seems intent on establishing a loose federation that would put the republics on an equal basis and give them more self-determination.[14] Such a transition to a "true federation" would require a radical transformation of the Soviet Union, its ideology, constitution, and institutions. Gorbachev, the lawyer, stresses that this restructuring should be achieved by legal means, within the existing constitutional framework.[15] The agenda of the Congress of People's Deputies envisages three stages of constitutional reform. The first stage, which has been almost completed, addresses the reorganization of the legislative bodies at the all-Union level. In the current, second, stage, the Congress is redefining the relationship between the central authorities and the republics. The third stage will focus on local government. The on-going constitutional reform and the flood of new laws are thus supposed to lay the "legal base under the edifice of the federation."[16]

THE VIEW FROM BELOW

Recent developments in the Baltic republics and in other regions clearly demonstrate, however, that Gorbachev's policy of federalization has run into a dead end. The periphery sets the agenda on this question, to which Moscow is just reacting or not acting at all. Gorbachev's program has constantly been lagging behind the escalating demands of the republics. When Baltic politicians pressed for a renewal of the federation in 1988, he gave vague promises of political decentralization and economic self-management. In fact, the first stage of constitutional reform resulted in a further strengthening of the central authorities, contrary to his original promises. He met the subsequent Baltic quest for a "loose federation" or "confederation" with promises to renew the federation. Yet the CPSU plenum on nationalities questions planned for early 1989 was repeatedly postponed, and the results of the September 1989 meeting were less than impressive. No timetable was set, no mandate given, and few specific steps were taken to implement the plenum's agenda.[17]

The debate on the second stage of constitutional reform—which was to lay the foundation for a new federative state structure—scheduled for the December 1989 session of the Congress of People's Deputies, was postponed. Instead, President Gorbachev, Prime Minister Nikolay Ryzhkov, and others started to contradict or qualify earlier statements on the future shape of the Soviet state, thereby putting into question their commitment to a "true federation." In an appeal to the Soviet people, the CPSU Central Committee warned against "too hasty steps of constitutional reform."[18] Only in early 1990, after the dramatic developments in the Transcaucasus and after the Lithuanian and Estonian parliaments devised plans for achieving full independence, did the Soviet leadership propose specific measures for reforming the national-state structure.

Kazimiera Prunskiene, Prime Minister of Lithuania, told Gorbachev: "imagine how skeptical we are of a new Union whose plan we have never seen."[19] Vaino Väljas, leader of the Communist Party of Estonia, dismissed Gorbachev's federalization program as a set of half-hearted semi-restructuring measures, "too little, too late."[20]

Meanwhile, the pressure for a reform of the center-periphery relationship is mounting in the Soviet republics outside the Baltic area. The boldness of the Baltic avant-garde, the events in Eastern Europe, and Moscow's use of force in Tbilisi and Baku have had a significant spillover effect on the other republics, where myriad grass-roots organizations have emerged. These highly heterogeneous movements incorporate a broad spectrum of political views and convictions. At the moment, they seem to be concentrating on the newly elected local and republic parliaments, in the hope of furthering their cause by gaining control over parts of the republic government and the communist party. In Ukraine, the Democratic Bloc, a broad coalition of forces including the Popular Movement for Restructuring (Rukh), demands "genuine political and economic sovereignty."[21] Some members of the Democratic Bloc—including members of Rukh, the Ukrainian Helsinki Union, the National Party, and the National Democratic League—openly advocate a separatist agenda.[22] In February, a group of USSR people's deputies from Ukraine submitted a memorandum to Gorbachev calling for a renewal of the Union treaty on the basis of confederative ties.[23] And even Ukraine's Party First Secretary Volodymyr

Ivashko has noticeably stepped up his calls for increased Ukrainian sovereignty within a renewed federation.[24]   After the strong showing of the opposition in the republic elections in March, 1990, pressures for economic and political autonomy and a renewal of the federal institutions are likely to increase. The agendas of the Ukrainian party's reform wing and the moderate forces of the Democratic Bloc have much in common and thus provide the possibility for an alliance between the popular front and reformist communists as emerged in the Baltic republics.

In neighboring Belorussia, the Popular Front *Adradzhen'ne* (Renewal) describes the republic as a "semi-colony that supplies the center," calls for the rebirth of the Belorussian nation, and advocates complete independence.[25] The Moldavian Popular Front has so far refrained from calls for a unification with Romania. It does agree, however, with the Communist Party of Moldavia that the sovereignty of the republic has to be restored, and that only limited powers are to be delegated to the Union authorities.[26]

In Georgia, the popular movement is split among a dozen groups, including historical parties originating in the brief period of independence. The republic communist party has elaborated plans for the restructuring of political and economic ties in a loose federation.[27]   On March 9, 1990, the republic's Supreme Soviet condemned Georgia's forcible annexation to the USSR in 1922 and called for talks on the restoration of its sovereignty.[28] In Armenia and Azerbaijan, the moderate wings of the popular movements call for more autonomy and self-determination, while radical groups advocate outright independence from Moscow. The military intervention in Baku in January 1990 seems to have strengthened secessionist and irredentist forces.

In Central Asia, a heterogeneous mixture of national groups and movements has emerged, and some political movements from the pre-Soviet era have revived. Salient issues include economic problems arising from single-crop cultivation, neglect of national languages and cultures, religion, and the environment. The degree of organization and mobilization is much lower than in western and southern republics; the focus of the movements is limited mainly to local and regional levels. Yet the anti-establishment sentiments are strong, and the potential for spontaneous social unrest is high. In Kazakhstan, the nascent opposition group *Adilet* (Justice) calls for more autonomy at the local and regional level. The Kirghiz popular movement *Ashar* also advocates increased economic autonomy. In Uzbekistan, the main nationalist movement, *Birlik* (Unity), propagates national revival and independence. A moderate wing has reportedly split away and formed a new group, *Erk* (Will). Its program calls for greater economic and political autonomy within the framework of a renewed federation.[29] The Tajik movement *Rastakhiz* (Renaissance), which played a prominent role as mediator in the Dushanbe disturbances, advocates more economic autonomy within a federation. In Turkmenistan, the newly formed *Agzybirlik* (Unity) seems to pursue an agenda similar to that of its Uzbek namesake.[30]

While the various regional movements share common characteristics, namely the demand for a multi-party system and increased autonomy, there is little consultation and coordination on the specific demands.[31] So far, local strength has not been translated into organized influence at the all-Union level. The main advocates for a transformation of the USSR into a loose federation of equal, sovereign states are the reformist forces within the republic communist parties, which seem to have gained in strength in the recent parliamentary elections. None of the dominant, grass-roots forces among the major nationalities, including the Ukrainians, are demanding outright secession. Thus, in most regions, Gorbachev still has a chance of winning over the moderate and isolating the radical forces. If he can demonstrate that national dignity, genuine sovereignty, and economic improvement can be achieved within a revised federal structure, the domino effect of Baltic separatism can be contained.

The decisive question is whether the Russian majority will accept a diminution of its role as primus inter pares in a renewed federation. In an obvious attempt not to stir up Russian nationalist feelings in their own ranks, even the Interregional Group of Deputies, Democratic Russia, and other liberal movements take relatively vague, neutral positions on the federation. The Democratic Platform Group within the CPSU, for instance, calls in very general terms for the "transition from the principle of a unitary state toward a voluntary union of peoples."[32] Some Russians are publicly considering the prospects of a rapidly changed structure of the Soviet Union. Economist Vasiliy Selyunin soberly contemplates the dissolution of the USSR in its current composition and the emergence of "a new, much looser confederation" consisting of Russia, Ukraine, Belorussia, Georgia, Armenia, and perhaps Moldavia.[33] Conservative Russians such as Eduard Volodin or Valentin Rasputin call for the secession of the RSFSR from, or the dissolution of, the Union so that Russia can concentrate on putting its own house into order without the ballast of the other republics.[34]

Most Russian nationalists, however, insist on the preservation of the territorial integrity of the USSR. Organizations such as the RSFSR writers' union, the workers' councils, and conservative publications such as *Nash Sovremennik, Molodaya Gvardiya*, or *Moskva* have suddenly turned into supporters of "true federalism." Non-indigenous Russians in the Baltic republics and elsewhere have formed their own organizations to oppose local demands for secession and support a renewal of the federation.[35] The controversial notion of a renewed federation has become the battle line for conservative Russians living inside and outside the RSFSR.

Whether the RSFSR will voluntarily give up its traditional hegemony remains to be seen. The steps toward democratization, decentralization, de-étatization, and federation suggested up to now would undoubtedly result in a comparative decline of the economic and political role of Russia proper and in the strengthening of the non-Russian republics.

RENEWAL OF THE UNION TREATY

Confronted with these escalating demands, Gorbachev has announced that he will use his new office of the presidency to prepare a new treaty of union (*soyuznyy dogovor*).[36] The form of this new federal contract remains unspecified. The CPSU Nationalities Platform has rejected the idea of a formal treaty comparable to the Treaty on the Formation of the USSR signed on December 30, 1922. Instead, the party suggested the elaboration of a "Declaration on the Union," which would form an organic part of the constitution, but would essentially be a political, rather than a legal document. In the eyes of its opponents, such a political declaration would be a cheap alternative to substantive constitutional reform as envisaged in the proposed Law on Federation (see below). Some voices suggest the dissolution of the old USSR and the creation of a new union, under which each republic would have to decide whether and under what conditions it would rejoin the Soviet federation.

The idea that the USSR will have to return to square one of federation-building raises some fundamental questions. Traditional theories treat federalism within the context of nation- or empire-building.[37] Yet the Soviet Union is currently heading in the opposite direction, i.e., toward the disintegration of a multinational state structure, the dissolution of an empire. As Gorbachev concedes:

> What we must do is win over the federation all over again, by restoring mutual trust and a realization of the advantages of integration. Good relations cannot be established by command or force. What lies ahead is lengthy and painstaking work.[38]

While Gorbachev has been highly successful in convincing an international audience of the existence of a global community confronted with common problems and sharing all-human values and interests, domestically, he has been unable to further a sense of commonwealth and of a common future within a Soviet federation. The perception of a common threat is evaporating. The traditional role of the Union as a security alliance is declining. While the rest of Europe is progressing toward integration, the desire for closer political, legal, and economic relations between the center and the periphery seems to be declining in the USSR. In the eyes of many proponents of local self-determination, the ties with Moscow are an obstacle to, rather than a catalyst for, change. Separation rather than integration appears to many as a panacea.

Despite the signs of a gradual disintegration of the internal empire, of a collapse of its socio-economic basis, in short, of a systemic crisis in the USSR, Gorbachev expresses his "unbridled optimism regarding the future of our multi-ethnic federal state . . . the renewal of our federation and its replenishment with new content."[39]   In his view, the nations of the Soviet Union are united by historical ties; share the dogma and the internationalist tradition of a political movement; rely on a division of labor in a highly institutionalized, integrated "national economic complex"; depend on the central authorities for resource allocations, investments, subsidies, and grants-in-aid; and enjoy the diplomatic, economic, and military advantages that accrue to a superpower.   To cut these ties would mean to "dissect a living body."[40]   In Gorbachev's view, secession from the existing institutions would thus involve considerable costs and risks for the republics, as he recently told the Lithuanians:

> Think a thousand times before embarking on an independent drift, without a compass, without a map, reserves of fuel and a competent crew. You cannot drop people on an iceberg and say, "let them swim."[41]

Yet, rational cost-benefit considerations of political and economic independence, risk avoidance, security, and stability have been poor predictors of change, both in the Third World and Eastern Europe. Moreover, given the progressive decline of the Soviet economy and the gradual disintegration of the traditional institutions, the cost-benefit equations are rapidly changing. The benefits of the old system are disappearing, while the advantages of the new system are not yet visible. Caught between the wreckage of a discredited past and the promise of an uncertain future, Gorbachev is thus facing the difficult task of dismantling the old federal system and giving new content to the notion of the Union without sacrificing the stability and territorial integrity of the country.

Secession

Pressed by developments in the Baltic republics, Gorbachev seems to have opened the door for all republics to leave the Union, but in due time and on his own terms. A law on secession, currently under debate in the USSR Supreme Soviet, defines the disengagement procedures, which include a referendum requiring a two-thirds majority of the population in the republic to vote in favor of independence, a five-year waiting period, and potentially daunting conditions such as huge compensatory payments to the Union by the seceding republic. In the case of Lithuania, Gorbachev has spelled out the price tag attached to independence: territorial claims regarding Klaipeda and Druskininkai near the Belorussian border, more than 21 billion rubles' compensation for investments, outstanding taxes and deliveries, and relocation costs for minorities leaving Lithuania.[42] The obvious aim of the exercise is to bargain for time and to try to frighten the republics into ending their drive for independence. Gorbachev continues to emphasize the importance of "territorial integrity" and to warn that "secession today means to blow up the Union, to set the people against each other, and to sow conflict and blood and death."[43]

Federation or Confederation?

Given the heterogeneous nature of the USSR, the centrifugal forces work at different speeds in the various regions. The Soviet leadership thus faces the difficult task of seeking agreement on a status of the Union and its jurisdiction acceptable to all the union republics and best suited to accommodate a variety of interests and expectations. Gorbachev envisages a "differentiation of federal ties."[44] Under common principles, the place of each republic in a renewed federation "will be unique to itself, taking into account the specifics of the region, each people, their culture and traditions." The Soviet President stresses that "it is better for the center to overdo the concessions to national groupings than underdo them."[45]

Federation, "loose federation," and confederation are the models most discussed, the first being mainly proposed by the Soviet leadership, the latter two by popular fronts in the Transcaucasus, Moldavia, and Ukraine. In Soviet discussions, federation and confederation are frequently described as opposites.[46] It should be noted, however, that the line between a federation and a confederation is fluid, the difference a matter of degree rather than of clearly discernible and mutually exclusive characteristics. In a federation, the member-states delegate relatively more powers to the central authorities than in a confederation. A confederation is not necessarily bound by a common constitution, the legislation of the member-states retains supremacy over confederal law, the states retain their treaty-making powers, and they exercise exclusive or joint control over the armed forces.

A flexible framework of federalization could allow Gorbachev to grant extensive autonomy to the independence-minded Baltic republics, say in the form of a confederation or federation, while retaining closer ties with Ukraine, Siberia, and other parts of the Soviet heartland, and maintaining tight control over the restive Central Asian republics.[47]

However, such a selective, ad hoc approach to federalization poses serious problems. First, a mixture of federative structures would have to be unified in a single constitutional framework. Hence, a selective approach to federalization would nevertheless require substantial constitutional reforms and adjustments in the state structure. Second, it would be difficult to grant special status to some republics without sparking demands for similar treatment by other republics or nationalities. Federations are built on the assumption of equal rights and obligations of the constituent states. The Soviet heartland is likely to be quite sensitive about special favors extended to the periphery. And it is the attitude of the Russian majority that will have a decisive influence over the future shape of the federation. The smaller union republics will also face increased political competition from entities with stronger economies and larger populations at the level of the autonomous republic and below.[48] A reform of the federative structure will have to address the question of how to deal with these demographic and economic imbalances and how to accommodate particularities at all levels without weakening the privileged position of the sovereign member states of the USSR.

Some Soviet specialists suggest a refinement of the criteria for defining the basic entities constituting the federation. Yulian Bromley suggested the break-up of the RSFSR into three or four republics.[49] The geographer Vladimir Sokolov proposed the creation of 50 union republics, representing the main economic and demographic centers and most of the ethnic groups and nationalities, by upgrading the status of existing sub-republic units. The giant RSFSR would be split up into European Russia, the Urals, Western Siberia, Eastern Siberia, the Far East, Transbaykal, and an array of ethnic homelands with union-republic status.[50] Another suggestion was to strengthen the status of the *krays* and oblasts, thereby creating a system of politically and economically autonomous "village-states" (*Khutorgosudarstva*), which would form the constituent units of the federation.[51] Every reorganization of the status and borders of the existing political entities would likely open a Pandora's box of ethnic grievances and further complicate an already complex situation.

The dispute between the center and the periphery is in essence a debate over the degree of sovereignty (*polnovlastiye*) and self-determination (*samoopredeleniye*) of the republics. Both in theory and in practice, the idea of sovereign republics conflicts with the notion of a sovereign union. In Soviet discussions, this conflict is often covered up by slogans such as "combining national and international interests," "equality of all people, equality of all peoples," and "strong center-strong republics."[52] This basic difficulty in reconciling traditional notions of sovereignty with federative structures is not unique to the Soviet Union; it also finds expression in competing doctrines of sovereignty in Western literature on federalism.

How to reconcile the conflicting sovereignties and what sovereignty means in operational terms is widely disputed. The CPSU Nationalities Platform refers to the "Leninist principle of national self-determination," defined as "a complex, multi-layered process of the affirmation of national dignity, the strengthening of political and economic autonomy, and the development of language and culture . . . best expressed as self-management."[53] Advocates of greater independence have a much broader conception of sovereignty and self-determination. For some, sovereignty means autonomy or self-rule within the framework of the Soviet Union, i.e., more jurisdiction and self-government for republic and local governments. For others, sovereignty denotes the achievement of independent statehood.

THE REDISTRIBUTION OF POWERS

The redistribution of powers between the center and the republics is therefore the key issue in the periphery's quest for more sovereignty. It also is at the heart of Gorbachev's program for the renewal of the federation. In the words of the Soviet President, the clear delineation of powers of central and republic bodies "will enable the latter to decide all issues of their life on their own, except issues which they will voluntarily delegate to the jurisdiction of the Union and in the resolution of which they will, incidentally, take part as well through respective political mechanisms."[54]

In Western federations, the division of powers rests on three pillars: the explicit, unambiguous enumeration of powers assigned to the federal authorities and the member-states respectively; the regulation of cases of concurrent competencies; and the existence of independent procedures for enforcement and adjudication of these federal agreements. A renewal of the Soviet federation requires substantial adjustments in all three regards. The USSR has already taken major steps toward giving greater responsibility to the republics in economic, fiscal, and social matters. The Law on Land, the Law on Property, and the Law on Socialist Enterprises further extend the room for self-management and entrepreneurial initiative and provide the USSR's regions with opportunities to extend their economic autonomy and viability. A new feature is that recent legislation at the all-Union level defines only the basic framework, the "fundamentals," leaving the republics considerable freedom to shape their own laws according to local conditions and aspirations.[55]

Law on the Federation

The Supreme Soviet is currently debating the Law on the Foundations of Economic Relations in the USSR, the Union Republics, and the Autonomous Republics, which is supposed to create the basis for a "fundamentally new intra-Union relationship" in the economy and social sphere. The law forms the key part of the second stage of constitutional reform, namely, the revision of Section III of the Constitution, which regulates the distribution of powers within the federation and is therefore dubbed the Law on the Federation. It prescribes the transition of all republics to economic independence and cost-accounting (khozraschet) by 1991. The republics are supposed to have jurisdiction over a broad range of economic and social activities, establish their own budgets, levy some taxes, introduce their own banking system, manage industries previously run by Union ministries, participate on a voluntary basis in all-Union programs, and engage independently in international economic relations.[56] Contractual forms of cooperation between the center and the republics and between individual republics are to have a greater role.

Instead of the traditional regulation of the rights of the republics, the draft limits the competence of the Union and establishes exclusive, inalienable rights for the republics. It is thus based on the assumption of non-centralization, and not—as before—on decentralization from the center. This is in accordance with Article 76 of the USSR Constitution, which has always stipulated that the sovereignty of each republic is limited only in the spheres that are explicitly delegated to the Union. At least in theory, the new legislation attempts to rebuild the pyramid of governmental powers from the bottom to the top. Republics will have the right to suspend decisions by the central authorities that run counter to the law. This provides for a limited supremacy of republic legislation in areas where the republics have exclusive jurisdiction.

In practice, however, as the experience of Estonia, Latvia, and Lithuania with regional *khosraschet* demonstrates, the center's continued reliance on central planning and so-called administrative-command methods conflicts in many respects with the notion of greater economic autonomy granted to the republics. The blueprint for the 1991-95 five-year plan presented by Prime Minister Ryzhkov puts the program of economic decentralization into question. Remarkably, regional autonomy receives only passing attention in Deputy Prime Minister Leonid Abalkin's reform program.[57]

The main obstacle to meaningful economic autonomy is thus the chaotic nature and inconsistency of economic reform in the USSR. Without coherent institutional reform, no diffusion of the power of the central apparatus can occur. The central ministries controlling individual sectors of the economy are not yet abolished. In the Baltic republics, the central ministries continue to control a substantial segment of the economy, namely, enterprises and utilities of "all-Union significance," including power plants, pipelines, railways, shipping lines, and other key industries.

Moreover, the demarcation of the responsibilities between the center and the republics remains ambiguous. Disputes over overlapping competencies abound and make the transition more conflictual than it need be. The Presidium of the Supreme Soviet has interfered repeatedly, for example, by instructing the Baltic republics to adjust pricing, budgetary, and social measures to all-Union legislation.[58] Despite provisions allowing the Baltic republics to set up their own banking and credit system, the Central State Bank announced last December that it was taking full control over savings deposits in the Baltic republics to prevent the republics from using this money to introduce their own currency. In March of this year, the central authorities imposed strict controls on banking activities in the Baltic republics by reinstating central supervision over financial transactions of Baltic banks, declaring checks signed in the Baltic republics as invalid, and, in effect, vetoing joint commercial ventures.[59]

The rapid transition to republic *khozraschet* seems to be driven by political, not economic, considerations. It has to be realized in the absence of a functioning market and in conditions of economic stagnation, inflation, and scarce supplies. Current attempts to protect local markets through the prohibition on selling scarce items to "outside buyers," the setting up of local customs checkpoints, or the introduction of local currencies and surrogate money in the form of certificates are signs that the "national economic complex" is disintegrating into quasi-autarkic entities, or what the Estonian economist Mikhail Bronshteyn calls "closed economic systems at the republic level."[60] Volodymyr Ivashko, first secretary of the Communist Party of Ukraine, complains that "contractual discipline has collapsed like a house of cards." The situation in the economy is such, he continues, "that our republic is compelled, already at this stage, to take measures on its own in order to protect economically its own interests both from the arbitrariness of departments and from our unobliging partners in other regions of the country. This is not us shouting: Save yourselves in any way you can—it is, unfortunately, severe reality."[61]

Interregional conflicts, manifestations of localism (*mestnichestvo*), and mutual recriminations over the value of services and deliveries are increasing, as each region strives to protect relative advantages and privileges. At the second meeting of the Congress of People's Deputies, the Russian Vera Matyukha claimed that 40 billion rubles annually are appropriated from the RSFSR's funds in favor of other republics as a result of nonequivalent trade. Deputies from Central Asia riposted by talking about the enormous losses inflicted on their republics due to artificially low cotton prices and the single-crop economy imposed by the center. And there are also "resentful regions" within the RSFSR, such as Chechen-Ingush, the Komi ASSR, or northern Siberia—areas which are the richest in resources—that are facing social, economic, and ecological disaster. In the absence of a real market system, including wholesale trade and pricing mechanisms, this "bill" of intra-Union trade can never be fully settled, yet there will always be forces ready to exploit the tensions over mutual claims and demands. The current debate on "equivalent exchange" is likely to result in further disruptions, inflationary price wars, delivery boycotts, and economic warfare among the various regions.[62] Competition on economic issues, not unity of interests and views, characterizes the individual regions and republics, a fact that can easily be exploited by central bureaucracies.

The mounting centrifugal tendencies are to a considerable degree a direct consequence of the current socio-economic situation. The result is an explosive fusion of political and ethnic demands with economic grievances. The collapse of the national economic complex seems to be preceding the political collapse of the federation. The renewal of the Union, in turn, largely depends on the success of economic reform and the transformation of the system into a market economy.

Economic Community

If properly implemented, economic self-management by the republics and regions could have a profound impact on the structure of the Soviet state. It would change the traditional approach to macro-economic management and give the notion of (economic) sovereignty new content.[63] The decentralization of economic power would also reinforce tendencies toward a horizontal integration of the Soviet republics. The principle of centralized allocation of resources is gradually to be replaced by direct trade relations among individual republics, regions, and enterprises. Decentralized relations include the use of contractual prices, the auctioning of republic commodities, direct industrial cooperation among enterprises, division of labor, and the creation of trading firms, commercial centers, and trading offices in other regions of the country. The economist Bronshteyn suggests the creation of an economic union modeled on the institutions and mechanisms of the European Community.[64] The promotion of such horizontal relations would reinforce the perception of mutual interests and interdependence and strengthen the perception of commonwealth (*sodruzhestvo*). Gorbachev contends that with the introduction of regional *khozraschet*, each republic will start to recalculate the advantages and disadvantages of membership in the USSR. Lithuania's President Vytautas Landsbergis acknowledges that even after separation, Lithuania will be highly dependent on trade with the rest of the USSR and calls for the conclusion of a treaty on cooperation. The transition to regional self-accounting and self-management thus has a greater role than that of a purely economic incentive. It lays the groundwork for economically and politically more viable republics and for a stronger federation.

Budgetary Authority and Ownership

The redistribution of power and the transition to cost-accountability requires a reorganization of the fiscal system and of ownership arrangements between the center and the periphery. The right to levy taxes and freely dispose of revenues is an important attribute of sovereignty. Independent control over some resources is the precondition for a community's freedom to set its own agenda. The Soviet Union's fiscal system has so far denied to its republics the right to tax and to dispose of revenues, except in accordance with the terms established by the central authorities. In the USSR, finance has been centralized and apportioned to the union republics ("to each according to his needs"). The division of fiscal authority forms a major bone of contention in the current reform of tax legislation. It has an important political aspect, for with the dispersion of resources, the center's ability to support a large apparatus and to sustain the myriad functions performed today will be weakened, and its hegemony will decline. At the same time, the Union will find it more difficult to generate budget revenues to fund all-Union investment projects such as the development of energy resources, or improvements in infrastructure and other collective goods.

The controversy over ownership also continues to be a highly sensitive issue in the federalism debate. Will Tyumen', for example, have full control over its oil fields, Yakutya over its coal, timber, and diamonds, and the Baltic republics over their seaports? The Soviet leadership continues to assume that there is common ownership by the entire "Soviet people," with the central authorities having extensive jurisdiction and utilization rights over public property in the republics. Some politicians argue in favor of a three-tiered ownership structure, namely, republic, all-Union, and joint or shared public property.[65] Economists in Armenia, the Baltic republics, Georgia, Moldavia, Ukraine, and other regions and republics also call for exclusive jurisdiction over their own territory.[66] The Supreme Soviet of the Lithuanian SSR, for instance, amended Article 11 of Lithuania's constitution and so proclaimed Lithuania's exclusive property and utilization rights over natural resources, land, air space, internal and territorial waters, continental shelf, and the 200 mile exclusive economic zone in the Baltic Sea.[67] The question of ownership goes beyond the issue of the control of resources; it is considered a major attribute of territorial sovereignty and reflects the emerging sense of homeland and the growing awareness regarding environmental issues in the republics.

Foreign Affairs

In most federations, the conduct of foreign relations is the exclusive responsibility of the central authorities. In theory, a line is drawn between internal and external sovereignty. In this regard, the USSR is a unique case. In 1944, a constitutional amendment gave the republics the power to enter into relations with other states, conclude treaties with them, exchange diplomatic and consular representatives, and take part in the work of international organizations (Article 80). Accordingly, each republic has its own ministry of foreign affairs.[68] The involvement of the republics in Soviet foreign affairs and foreign economic policy has become an issue in the debate over federation and confederation. Foreign Minister Eduard Shevardnadze has announced that representatives of the republics will be actively drawn into official visits to foreign countries and diplomatic talks dealing with cross-border issues such as trade, economic cooperation, environmental protection, or transportation.[69] The new Law on the Foundations of Economic Relations empowers the republics to open trade missions abroad. The resumption of direct economic ties with neighboring countries is a matter of time. The staff of Soviet embassies and consulates in some countries will be increased to better represent republics with direct interests in those states. At the Ministry of Foreign Affairs in Moscow, a newly established Union Republics Department is charged with improving and coordinating the republics' activities in these spheres.[70]

It is thus likely that the republics will become more assertive in claiming their constitutional right to conduct foreign relations. Since January 1990, Moldavia has negotiated political, economic, and cultural relations directly with Romania.[71] Belorussia and Ukraine have both announced that they will increase their activities in the framework of the United Nations and its specialized organizations. Representatives from the Baltic republics have been active in seeking ties with the United Nations, the Nordic Council, and governments and political, social, and economic organizations of neighboring states.[72] Allowing consulates of neighboring states in the capitals of certain republics is also being discussed, for example, a Finnish consulate in Tallinn, a Swedish consulate in Riga, a Polish consulate in Vilnius.[73] With increased national self-awareness and economic autonomy, it is of great importance for the more independent-minded republics to revive traditional ties with their neighbors and to activate contacts with politically and economically influential émigré communities to help their cause.[74]

This prospect raises interesting questions. With the reform of East European economies and the reorganization of relations in the Council for Economic Mutual Assistance, new patterns of foreign trade and economic cooperation among the countries of Eastern Europe will emerge. The economically advanced Soviet republics have a good chance to play a major role in this sub-regional integration. Yet joint ventures, foreign trade, and the possible creation of special economic zones are bound to pull each region's economic interests in different directions and increase the cleavages among the republics.

Even though the exact international status of the semi-autonomous republics remains ill-defined, they will nevertheless play an increasingly visible, though limited, role in East-West relations. The Soviet leadership is unlikely to give up its control over international affairs; it will try to avoid the emergence of an uncoordinated "parallel" foreign policy at the republic level or the uncontrolled revival of old ethnic or political ties across borders. As international reactions to events in Lithuania demonstrate, most Western states prefer to avoid confrontation and place the improvement of overall relations with Moscow ahead of the promotion of direct ties with the republics. Ultimately, they perceive a close linkage between the promotion of détente on the one hand, and the success of *perestroyka* and achievement of more autonomy for the republics on the other.

Military Affairs

A heated dispute has also arisen over the role of republics in military affairs. Politicians in most parts of the USSR call for the organization of territorial armed forces under the command of the republics, something comparable to the US National Guard.[75] Minister of Defense Dmitriy Yazov and other military leaders have categorically rejected these demands as incompatible with the "internationalist structure" of the armed forces, with the military's need to maintain all-Union forces such as the air force or the navy and to deploy them according to the exigencies of the strategic situation. However, as a concession to local demands, Chief of Staff Mikhail Moiseyev has announced that 25 percent of all non-Russian draftees will be allowed to serve in their home districts.[76]

Yet the issue at stake is not the future shape of the federation, but the question of power. In many places, the Soviet Army is viewed as an "occupation force," which forms a state within the state and gives the central authorities the option to intervene with military force. This view has been reinforced by the events in Tbilisi, Baku, and Vilnius. Although rumors about resistance organizations, arms hoarding, and people's militias abound, the tug of war between the center and the periphery is so far limited to predominantly political means. The central leadership has therefore little interest in arming the contending ethnic and political factions by creating territorial, i.e., national, military units.

Draft dodging has become a political act supported by local parliaments, governments, and pro-independence movements. The legislatures in Vilnius and Riga have passed resolutions saying that their citizens have the right to serve exclusively in their republics, and Latvia has introduced an alternative service.[77] These acts of insubordination are posing an unprecedented challenge to the very foundations of the Soviet Army, which is already defensive about unilateral Soviet troop cuts, withdrawals of Soviet troops from Eastern Europe, internal social and disciplinary problems, attacks on it by the press and politicians, and accusations of corruption. The spring draft will be a major test of strength for the military authorities.

REPRESENTATION AND PARTICIPATION
IN CENTRAL INSTITUTIONS

Delegates from the Baltic republics, Armenia, Azerbaijan, and Georgia have repeatedly criticized the new USSR parliamentary system for denying them the opportunity to defend their republics' interests. Some deputies call for a new voting rule under which the delegation of each republic would have an equal vote on essential laws concerning the sovereignty of the republics. Others resort to such measures as walkouts and boycotts of entire legislative sessions. In February 1990, pro-independence delegates from the Baltic republics notified the USSR Supreme Soviet that they would not participate in preparing the "internal legislation" of the USSR, but would attend as "observers" charged with preparing negotiations on the independence of their republics.[78] That the absence or non-participation of entire republic delegations has had no impact on the functioning of the legislature contributes to the growing alienation of these dissidents from the existing parliamentary structures. The marginalization of the representation of the republics and the breakdown of parliamentary channels of communication have resulted in further polarization between the center and the periphery. Conflicts are transferred to the extraparliamentary sphere.

Like John Calhoun's theory of concurrent majorities,[79] the Soviet system attempts to combine parliamentarism with federalism. The dualist form of government is realized in the bicameral Supreme Soviet consisting of a Council of the Union and a Council of Nationalities in line with the newly amended Article 111 of the USSR Constitution. The latter is elected under a complicated system that assigns each union republic 11, each autonomous republic 4, each autonomous region 2 seats, and each autonomous area 1 seat, respectively. The constitution gives both chambers equal legislative rights. Both debate legislation. In case of disagreement between the two chambers, the matter at issue is referred for settlement to a conciliation commission made up of representatives from both chambers. In case of continued dispute, a joint session of the two chambers convenes. If agreement is still not reached, the President can submit an acceptable compromise or ask for the election of a new Supreme Soviet (Article 117).

With Gorbachev's emphasis on the soviets, the Council of Nationalities has been upgraded from rubber-stamp parliament to genuine legislature. In recent months, it has performed important legislative work focusing in particular on matters pertaining to republic and minority affairs. As in the case of the Land Law or the Law on Secession, national-territorial deputies have pushed through significant amendments. In comparison with other executive and legislative bodies, however, the Council of Nationalities continues to play only a marginal role. In practice, bicameral procedures are not strictly applied. Important legislation, such as the Law on the Presidency, was not submitted to the Council of Nationalities at all. The Presidium of the Supreme Soviet, the Council of the Union, and the numerous commissions and committees dominate the legislative work. The Supreme Soviet and the commissions frequently meet in joint sessions. With 35 percent of the seats (95 of 271) in the Council of Nationalities and 58 percent (156 of 271) in the Council of the Union, the Russian Soviet Federated Socialist Republic (RSFSR) has a predominant position in both chambers of the parliament.[80] Thirty-eight percent of deputies and a majority of commission and committee chairmen are Russian.[81] In order to initiate or overrule legislation, the other republics and nationalities have to form broad coalitions. Thus, the relative weight of republic delegations is diluted, the rule of the majority strengthened, and the balancing role of the Council of the Nationalities neutralized. During the ethnic clashes and center-periphery conflicts in the Transcaucasus, Uzbekistan, and Lithuania, the Council of Nationalities did not become a parliamentary platform for crisis management.

The creation of the two-tier Soviet parliamentary system has further weakened the principle of equal representation of the republics and undermined the notion of a union of sovereign member-states. The Supreme Soviet has been demoted from supreme legislature to a secondary authority subordinated to the new Congress of People's Deputies, which is a unicameral body. As Andrey Mishin, professor of law at Moscow State University, concludes:

> The Supreme Soviet is not in fact a parliament, but rather a grand committee of the Congress. It lacks two organic qualities of a parliament. First, it does not possess sovereign legislative power, for all its decisions can be rescinded by the Congress. Second, it is not directly elected by the people.[82]

The deputies representing national-territorial units, which make up one-third of the Congress, are elected according to a similar formula as the Council of

Nationalities. Yet the 50 or so parliamentarians representing each of the smaller republics are easily lost in the total of 2250 deputies.[83] The provision that the Supreme Soviet is not elected directly by popular vote but appointed by the Congress of People's Deputies violates another principle of federalism. The republic delegations in the Council of Nationalities thus consist of indirectly elected deputies and appointed functionaries of political and social organizations that function or reside in the respective republics. The new parliamentary system thus reflects the combination of mutually contradictory principles: those of federalism and those of a unitary state. The advantages of democracy and parliamentarism are outweighed by tendencies toward centralization and majority rule and a negation of direct, equal representation of the constituent states.

A similar conclusion applies to the representation of republics and regions in other central organs, namely, in the Council of Ministers, the Presidium of the Supreme Soviet, the Supreme Court, the Procuracy, etc. Ex officio representation guarantees a minimal degree of proportionality. Beyond this measure, the center has taken no additional steps to secure greater representation on the part of non-Russian officials in these bodies. A related problem is the representation of the republics in the non-federated structures, namely, the party, the armed forces, the KGB, the central planning bodies, or the USSR Academy of Sciences. Initially, Gorbachev's personnel policy led to a remarkable decline of non-Russian functionaries in these organs, but the trend has been somewhat reversed by recent appointments. At the moment, only one republic party chief—Volodymyr Ivashko from Ukraine—is represented on the Politburo, instead of the usual four to six.

The draft Party Statute envisages the creation of a Central Committee Presidium in which all republic party leaders would be represented. A radical improvement of the representation of the republics in the federal legislative and executive bodies, especially the upgrading of the role of the Council of Nationalities, is thus an important prerequisite for revitalization of the Soviet federation.

The reinforcement of the RSFSR's independent organizational political status and the creation of appropriate state organs form an important part in improving federal structures. In recent months, functions previously performed by all-Union ministries have been transferred to the RSFSR Council of Ministers, and a Russian Communist Youth League and Academy of Sciences have been created. In order to reinforce the RSFSR's status within the party, a new Russian Bureau has been set up in the CPSU Central Committee.[84] Gorbachev seems also to have dropped objections against the formation of a Russian Communist Party. Russian politicians will continue closely to scrutinize every privilege granted to the Baltic states and other republics and compare it with the treatment afforded to the RSFSR.

The Presidency

The creation of an executive presidency has a profound, yet ambivalent impact on the federal relationship. In the words of Academician Vladimir Kudryavtsev, the president will stand "above Party, institutional, and national divisions." Boris Lazarev of the Institute of State and Law sees the presidency as a "coordinating element," a "bracket for the union," a "guarantor of the federation."[85] In his acceptance speech, Gorbachev asserted that a democratic presidency will provide for "dialogue and cooperation with the representatives of different tendencies of society."[86] The proponents of a strong presidency seem to be influenced by the negative example of Yugoslavia, where the weakness of central authorities contributed to the progressive paralysis and disintegration of the central government. In a joint statement, 26 Baltic deputies, some of whom proposed the creation of a presidency in early 1989, welcomed the creation of a presidency as a step "conducive to the process of democratization." They seem to favor a consolidated central authority as *interlocuteur valable* in their negotiations for independence.[87]

Yet the creation of a strong presidency seems to reverse trends toward the sharing, decentralization, and democratization of power. It reflects the barely concealed frustration of the leadership with the slow pace of legislation and the time-consuming process of consensus-building. Prime Minister Ryzhkov has complained about the repeated readings of laws in the committees and chambers of the Supreme Soviet and concluded that the legislature takes "an extraordinarily long time reaching decisions."[88] Political scientist Andrey Kortunov asserts that "you cannot have a revolution at consensus speed."[89] Yet consensus forms the working basis of federalism.

The presidency also removes the representation of the republics in what is nominally the highest office in the USSR, since it replaces the collegial state leadership of the Presidium of the Supreme Soviet, in which each of the republics had a seat. The new Council of the Federation, which consists of the supreme soviet chairmen or presidents from the republics and is supposed to advise the president in the solution of interethnic disputes and related issues, will supposedly fill this gap. The competencies of the Council are, however, not clearly demarcated from those of the Council of Nationalities and the Presidium of the Supreme Soviet, in which 15 republics are also represented. In its first meeting, for instance, the Council of the Federation started to debate such legislative matters as the draft treaty on the federation. The Council is limited to consultative functions, its members have no voting right, and it is unclear what the procedures are for accommodating differences—say between Gorbachev and the representative of Georgia.[90]

Finally, the president can issue presidential decrees (*ukazy*) and has other powers that weaken those of the federal legislature as well as the sovereign rights of the republics. Gorbachev can declare martial law or a state of emergency in a particular region of the USSR, although this is subject to consultation with local authorities and oversight by the Supreme Soviet. New emergency legislation empowers the president to ban disturbances of the public order—strikes, demonstrations, assemblies, publications, or organizations and movements "pursuing militant and anti-constitutional goals."[91] He can introduce "temporary presidential rule," a form of direct rule over particular regions or republics, suspend the authority of their government, revoke their legislation, remove their governments, and dissolve their parliaments.[92] Sergey Stankevich refers to an "imperial presidency," while Anatoliy Sobchak calls the Soviet presidency an "all-Union gendarme." Konstantin Lubenchenko observed that "the traditional French model has been adopted with the old Soviet filling."[93] Even if exerted in a "democratic spirit," as Gorbachev promises, these extensive presidential powers seem to contradict the process of federalizing the government, create a broad array of overlapping competencies, and contribute to "confusion of authority" in the USSR.

The CPSU and Federalism

Despite the alteration of Article 6, which had previously secured the leading role of the party in the Soviet polity, the CPSU remains a highly centralized, unitary party that has so far formed a major obstacle to the implementation of federalism. An essential problem regarding the reform of the Soviet state structure pertains thus to the future role of the CPSU.[94]

In the draft Party Statute prepared for examination at the 28th Party Congress in June 1990, the CPSU has introduced provisions improving the representation of the republic parties in the central apparatus and granting them a degree of autonomy, including the right to draw up their own programs and statutes.[95] The Central Committee has, however, fiercely resisted attempts at federalizing the party and defended the organizational principle of "democratic centralism." Gorbachev warns that otherwise the party would "turn into an amorphous federalist club consisting of individual independent party groups."[96] These limited reforms are, however, unlikely to provide a timely and adequate answer to the more fundamental challenges to the CPSU, namely, the loss of power of the local and republic party organizations (the so-called "Polish challenge"), the erosion of Marxist-Leninist orthodoxy (the "Hungarian challenge"), and separatist tendencies within the party (the "Lithuanian challenge"). These trends toward political pluralism, de-ideologization, and decentralization are likely to put enormous pressure on the CPSU to rethink its role in society and to propose more fundamental reforms than discussed so far. Thus far, however, the transition to a multiparty system has not yet produced a political movement at the all-Union level that could compete with or replace the CPSU as an integrating and unifying force.

BARGAINING AND CONFLICT MANAGEMENT

The Soviet republics have few options for initiating, amending, or challenging legislation at the all-Union level or for seeking political or judicial adjudication in cases of conflict with the central authorities. Legislative initiative gives them the right to propose or amend legislation in the Congress of People's Deputies and the Supreme Soviet, a right qualified by the power of these bodies to decide whether or not to take up the proposal. The deputies from the Baltic republics have put forward alternative drafts and amendments on virtually every law and constitutional amendment on the agenda of the USSR legislature in recent months—to little avail.

The revised constitution also establishes a sort of referendum giving the republics the right to ask the Supreme Soviet for a country-wide discussion of draft laws and "other important issues of state life."[97] Soviet republics have no right to ratify—that is, to validate—legislation of the Congress of People's Deputies, the Supreme Soviet, and its Presidium, or to veto legislative acts of central bodies.[98] Union legislation thus enters automatically into force on the territory of a republic without the consent of its highest legislative body. There is also no formal mechanism to determine whether a republic agrees, for example, to having a nuclear power plant set up on its territory, a military installation expanded, or its natural resources exploited.

Federal systems are characterized by frequent disputes between the central authorities and the member-states over the interpretation of constitutional provisions, the division of powers, and related issues. Unlike other federations, the USSR does not have an independent judiciary, a constitutional court that could provide a legally binding ruling, arbitration, or an advisory opinion. The predominance of the Union is codified in the provision that union law prevails over republic law (Article 74). The Congress of People's Deputies is the highest constitutional authority. Together with the president and the Supreme Soviet, the Congress has a variety of powers for revoking the legislation of the republics, if it is not in line with the USSR Constitution and laws. There are thus no enforceable guarantees that the newly extended constitutional rights and freedoms of the republics will be safeguarded. A proper system of horizontal and vertical checks and balances does not exist in the USSR.[99]

Gorbachev seems to have recognized the critical lack of a constitutional judiciary. In November 1989, the Congress decided to create a Constitutional Oversight Committee. The body, which is to begin functioning in April 1990, consists of 27 "specialists in the field of politics and the law" with one representative from each republic, and is elected by the Congress of People's Deputies for a term of 10 years. It examines draft USSR laws, constitutions and laws of the union republics, resolutions of the USSR and republic councils of ministers, and normative acts of other state organs and public organizations—including the communist party.[100]

When a legislative act is found to contravene the USSR Constitution or laws, the Constitutional Oversight Committee is to communicate its findings to the organ that issued the act with the understanding that the violation will be eliminated. Communication of such a finding is to suspend the execution of the challenged legislation. In case a constitutional conflict cannot be solved in this way, the Committee is to refer the matter at issue to the higher authority of the body concerned. If, for instance, a republic parliament refuses to accept a finding of the Committee, the dispute would be submitted to the USSR Congress of People's Deputies, which in turn could force the republican parliament to bring its legislation in line with the USSR Constitution and legislation, even if the issue fell within the exclusive jurisdiction of the republic concerned.

The Committee's competencies are thus limited. It is not the highest constitutional authority. It has, for instance, no power to overrule executive or legislative acts by the central authorities or to provide independent, final, binding arbitration in constitutional conflicts. Enforcement depends on the cooperation of the organs to which the Committee communicates its findings. The right to submit "findings" and "advisory opinions" can be compared with a legislative initiative through which a review of a decision can be sought. Moreover, the Congress can overrule any decision of the Committee by a two-thirds majority. It remains to be seen how effective the Committee will be in challenging decrees passed by the Supreme Soviet or decisions of the Congress of People's Deputies, should they prove to contravene constitutional provisions. In the words of deputy Vladimir Denisov, "no judge in this country would dream of ruling against him [Gorbachev] in his worst nightmare."[101]

The Committee is thus basically a political organ. It is accountable to the Congress of People's Deputies and does not form part of an independent, professional judiciary.[102] Nor does it significantly shift the political and judicial center of gravity in favor of the republics. In the words of a Baltic delegate, the Committee will "not only fail to serve the restoration of the sovereign rights of the union republics, but restrict event their restricted rights."[103] Its main objective seems to be the enforcement of the legislation of the central authorities. Its creation can be considered as a semi-concession that is unlikely to contribute to the solution of the emerging constitutional crisis.

In federations, informal bargaining processes are much more important than formal procedures prescribed by law. Little is known about informal processes of consultation and consensus-building in the USSR. The highly centralized, authoritarian state structure is not conducive to internal bargaining and compromise. Nevertheless, Gorbachev has clearly departed from the administrative-command methods of his predecessors. He frequently consults with subordinate leaders, goes to great lengths to hear various points on an issue, and dispatches fact-finding or mediation missions to trouble spots. In the event of disagreement, he postpones decision or refers the disagreement to a commission. He thus attempts to be a consensus-building politician trying to reconcile opposing views.[104]   In many instances, Gorbachev's mixture of dialogue, persuasion, appeals, and open threats has, however, not produced a resolution of differences.   It is thus questionable how effective Gorbachev's remarkable bargaining attempts are as long as there is little room for compromise. It remains to be seen how far Gorbachev, the supreme ruler and proclaimed teacher of his people, can go in tolerating dissent and abdicating the old methods of diktat and the use, or threat of use, of force.

In the context of the growing self-assertiveness of the republics and the proposed decentralization, the absence of formal and informal mechanisms for the peaceful resolution of conflicts has become a decisive weakness of the Soviet federal structure. In recent months, the number of unresolved center-periphery disputes has proliferated. Some republics have resorted to unilateral measures in asserting their sovereign rights and interests.[105] Republic supreme soviets have taken legislation into their own hands, amending their constitutions and passing laws without much consideration for union legislation. Declaring their insubordination, the dissident republics thus challenge the very essence of the Union. They openly question the constitutionality of the Soviet system, point at the chronic and systematic violation of their constitutional rights and freedoms by the central authorities, refer to the absence of proper procedures in passing constitutional amendments in the USSR, and complain about the lack of an independent constitutional judiciary to protect their legally guaranteed rights and freedoms.   In their eyes, the supremacy of all-Union legislation is thus an instrument for ensuring the hegemony of the center and usurping the powers of the member-states.

The problem for the USSR is not too little, but too much, legislation. The vast number of normative decrees passed by central bodies has produced a kind of legislative inflation, with various bureaucracies claiming the same prerogatives without a legal basis to do so. The difference between a law as juridical act and as a political declaration has been lost. The result is atrophy of law, insecurity, and chronic confusion of responsibilities. At issue is the political and legal basis of the federation. The constitution drafted in 1977 under Brezhnev's leadership is in many respects outdated; lags behind political, economic, social, and psychological changes in Soviet society; and serves to protect the status quo. Deputy Konstantin Lubenchenko, chairman of the Supreme Soviet Committee on Legislation, Legality, Law and Order, asserts that it is untenable to check new laws for conformity with an outdated, delegitimized constitution.[106] Dissident legislators justify their insubordination as bargaining tactics, as acts of resistance aimed at changing the Soviet constitutional framework from below through political means.

CONCLUSIONS

While it is difficult to isolate specific deficiencies in the Soviet federal system or to suggest optimal solutions for center-periphery relations and the building of a "Soviet style" federation, the study of the Soviet problems from a comparative perspective allows one to draw some general conclusions. Soviet and foreign commentators contend that the transformation of the Soviet state structure into a "true federation" requires only modest adjustments in the existing constitutional framework and thus call it a relatively moderate approach toward resolving the concerns of minorities. All things considered, however, the renewal of the Soviet federation implies a revolutionary institutional reform and—most important—a radical departure from existing political practices in the USSR. It requires: (1) a substantial redistribution of powers, conceding exclusive jurisdiction and autonomous status to the republics; (2) improved representation and participation of the republics at the all-Union level; (3) federalization of the highly centralized party, administrative, and legal structures; and (4) the creation of mechanisms for the peaceful resolution of political and constitutional conflicts, that is, the formation of an independent constitutional court.

So far, the Soviet leadership has taken an administrative approach. It continues to deal with minority questions on a case-by-case basis. It extends special treatment to the most troublesome areas in an attempt to ease problems rather than solve them. The Soviet President has yet to define the objectives, essence, and design of a renewed federation. In order to accommodate the increasingly divergent aspirations and expectations of all of the Soviet Union's constituent republics, Gorbachev will have to set in motion a broad, bold, and focused policy process based on consultation and compromise with all the parties concerned, including the constituent republics.

In federal systems, however, processes can be as important as, or more important than, institutions; the spirit prevails over the letter of federal arrangements. In this respect, Gorbachev faces a more formidable task than just a constitutional reform. Soviet political culture is not hospitable to the federal idea; it lacks a tradition of seeking federal solutions. Notions of tolerance, mutual respect, power-sharing, consensus, fairness, and compromise are not (yet) the characteristic traits of the Soviet polity. Exceptionally great communication barriers caused by social, ethnic, political, or ideological polarization continue to exist. Soviet society has to learn to accept that social, ethnic, political, and ideological diversity is a source of strength rather than weakness.

Control and timing are two major determinants in this process of federation-building. The question is whether the federalization of the USSR can be managed and stabilized at a certain level or whether the concurrent processes of democratization and decentralization are simply reinforcing the centrifugal tendencies. In many respects, federalism goes against the logic of the system it is supposed to save. The implementation of the idea of a Soviet federation may simply aggravate the systemic crisis it is intended to alleviate. As the example of Yugoslavia demonstrates, giving more power to the periphery may only help to tear a divided state further apart. A thin line divides federalism, i.e., freedom in alliance, from separatism, i.e., freedom from alliance. In the view of Baltic and other popular fronts, a federation or confederation is but a transitional stage to secession and independence. For them, the question is not whether independence from the Soviet Union should be sought or not, but when and how it should be achieved. Federalism thus becomes a hidden form of separatism. Soviet politicians at all levels thus face the difficult task of dismantling the old system without sacrificing the stability and integrity of the Union.

In light of the growing dissatisfaction with the status quo and the increasing self-assertiveness at the local and republic levels, federalization is running out of time. Politicians in the Baltic republics and other regions have already rejected the CPSU Platform on Nationalities as too little, too late. They perceive Gorbachev's wavering agenda as part of the problem, not of the solution. In their view, *perestroyka* and the solution of the national question have become antinomies. With the elections of new republic and local parliaments, the quest for systemic change is likely to increase. Pressure from below may overtake the managed reforms from above as revolutionary upheaval replaces evolutionary change. The diktat from the street may follow the diktat from the center. Gorbachev's commitment not to use force in settling domestic conflicts will then be put to a test.

Yet such developments are also likely to increase the pressure for more radical—and more adequate—reform of the federal system, whatever the Soviet leadership's intentions. The Soviet Union is thus unlikely to see a uniform, linear, gradual, orderly, and controlled process of federalization. Nor is it clear what the final outcome of the process, the "true federation," will look like, whether it will result in "diversity within a single whole, or in single entities in diversity" as Karl Marx put it. If the 1990's turn out to be the decade for rebuilding the Soviet federation, it promises to be a long and difficult decade rich in domestic conflicts and disputes.

It behooves me to finish on a note of caution. Federalization solves some, but not all ethnic problems. Political reforms and economic improvements that succeed in reducing some manifestations of nationalism may exacerbate others. A Soviet Union in a new and more open political environment with a less rigid system of center-periphery relations will likely be characterized by an increase, rather than a decrease, of nationalism, particularism, and localism, i.e., it is likely to be less manageable and prone to greater ethnic conflict and competition. Yet in a federation, conflict situations are to be expected, and there is no reason to dramatize them as long as appropriate mechanisms exist to solve the conflicts peacefully and equitably.

Notes

1. For an elaboration of this argument, see Alexander J. Motyl, "The Sobering of Gorbachev: Nationality, Restructuring, and the West," in Seweryn Bialer, Ed., *Inside Gorbachev's Russia*, Boulder, CO, Westview, 1989, pp. 83-98.

2. The term "federation" is derived from the Latin word *"foedus"* (covenant, contract, treaty) and describes a voluntary association of sovereign states for some common purpose with limited delegation of powers to a central authority. The main characteristics of a federal state include: (1) the supremacy of the constitution defining rules of the federative relationship and providing legal guarantees for all parties involved; (2) the clear demarcation of powers between the federal government and the member states guaranteeing a certain degree of sovereignty for the constituent states (principle of non-centralization); (3) bargaining and arbitration mechanisms for resolving constitutional conflicts; and (4) a bicameral parliamentary system ensuring direct representation of the constituent states at the federal level. See Klaus von Beyme, "Federalism," in C. D. Kernig, *Marxism, Communism and Western Society—A Comparative Encyclopedia*, Vol. III, New York, Herder and Herder, 1972, pp. 314-28; R.R. Bowie and C.J. Friedrich, *Studies in Federalism*, Boston, MA, Little, Brown, and Co., 1954; C.J. Friedrich, *Trends of Federalism in Theory and Practice*, New York, Praeger, 1968; *Comparative Federalism—Conference Proceedings*, Philadelphia, Center for the Study of Federalism, 1985; M. Usteri, *Theorie des Bundesstaates* (Theory of the Federal State), Zürich, Schulthess, 1954.

3. Article 70 of the Constitution (Fundamental Law) of the Union of Soviet Socialist Republics, Moscow, Progress, 1985, with the subsequent amendments on Dec. 1, 1988, Dec. 22, 1989, Dec. 23, 1989, and Mar. 15, 1990.

4. Some Soviet experts continue to claim that the USSR is uniquely superior because Soviet republics enjoy broader rights than the member states of any other federation. See N. Michaleva, "The Fate of Our Federation," *Pravda* (Moscow), Oct. 18, 1989.

5. "Draft Nationalities Policy of the Party Under Present Conditions, adopted by the CPSU Central Committee Plenum, Sept. 20, 1989" (hereafter, *CPSU Nationalities Platform*), ibid., Sept. 24, 1989.

6. Mikhail Gorbachev, "The Fate of *Perestroyka* Is in the Unity of the Party—Report at the CPSU Central Committee Plenum on December 25, 1989" (hereafter, *Fate*), ibid., Dec. 26, 1989. For a discussion of Lenin's original conception of national sovereignty and self-determination and its subsequent "deformation," see V.D. Zotov, "The Nationalities Issue: Deformities of the Past," *Kommunist* (Moscow), No. 3, February 1989, pp. 79-89.; A. Zharnikov, "National Self-Determination: Concept and Implementation," ibid., No. 9, June 1989, pp. 58-63.

7. In *Sovetskaya Molodezh'* (Riga), July 7, 1989.

8. See the report on the Georgian Supreme Soviet's debate on the events leading to the "de facto annexation of Georgia" in *Izvestiya* (Moscow), Nov. 21, 1989.

9. In addition to Estonia, Latvia, and Lithuania in their boundaries of 1939, the two secret protocols to the Soviet-German Nonaggression Pact, which included maps delineating Soviet and German spheres of control, cover the Romanian territory of Bessarabia (Moldavia), Finnish Karelia, and the western parts of Belorussia and Ukraine (formerly under Polish control).

10. *CPSU Nationalities Platform*, loc. cit.

11. See N. Mikhaleva and Sh. Panidze, "Federal Union," *Pravda*, July 12, 1989. Their positions were disputed by R. Gudaitis and B. Genzelis, "So Who Does Know the Formula?" ibid., July 26, 1989, and I. Gryazin, "Is It a Question of Federalism?" ibid., July 26, 1989. N. Mikhaleva replied in "The Fate of Our Federation," loc. cit. See also V. Koroteyeva, L. Perepelkin, and O. Shkaratan, "From Bureaucratic Centralism toward the Economic Integration of Sovereign Republics," *Kommunist*, No. 15, October 1988, pp. 22-33; E. Tavosyan, "Soviet Federalism: Chains Against Progress," ibid., No. 13, August 1989, pp. 48-49; Yu. Bromley, director of the USSR Academy of Sciences Ethnography Institute, "Not a Return to Confederation but Development of the Federation," in *Sovetskaya Latviya* (Riga), Oct. 21, 1989.

12. The most important ones are the "Resolution on Interethnic Relations" passed by the 19th Party Conference on July 1, 1988 (hereafter, *CPSU Resolution*) in *Materials of the 19th All-Union Conference of the CPSU*, Politzdat, 1988, pp. 146-51; the "Draft General Principles for Restructuring the Leadership of the Economy and the Social Sphere in the Union Republics on the Basis of Broadening Their Sovereign Rights, Self-Management, and Self-Financing" submitted by the Council of Ministers on March 14, 1989, *Pravda*, Mar. 14, 1989; *CPSU Nationalities Platform*, loc. cit.; and the section on the nationalities question in the Platform for the 28th CPSU Congress, adopted on Feb. 11, 1990, *Pravda*, Feb 13, 1990.

13. *CPSU Resolution*.

14. Some Soviet commentators suggest that Gorbachev's philosophy of rebuilding the Soviet federation can be closely related to his "new thinking" in international affairs. The Soviet leadership's declared commitment to a balance of interests, a peaceful resolution of conflicts, and the supreme rule of law is also relevant for Moscow's relationship with its own periphery. The vision of a "common European home" can be equated with that of a "common Soviet home." See O. Redzhepova, "In Search of Balance," *Sovetskaya Kul'tura* (Moscow), Sept. 16, 1989. Politicians in the Baltic republics and elsewhere have, in turn, made a virtue out of justifying their demands with postulates of Gorbachev's foreign policy.

15. "Speech by M.S. Gorbachev to the Congress of People's Deputies," *Pravda*, Dec. 13, 1989.

16. Gorbachev, *Fate*.

17. The Central Committee Secretariat, the Supreme Soviet, and a series of commissions and working groups were charged with "studying the problem" and working out a program of concrete actions." *Pravda*, Oct. 6, 1989. A new Department of National Relations under A. N. Girenko was created in the Central Committee apparatus. See his interview in ibid., Nov. 30, 1989.

18. Ibid., Dec. 12, 1989. In Gorbachev's words, limits "beyond which one must not go must be clearly outlined, for going beyond them means a pre-programmed disruption of efforts to build a federation: if you like, a disruption of *perestroyka* as a whole." There seems to be a clear, yet constantly shifting, line between orthodoxy and heresy on the issue of federalism. See Gorbachev, *Fate*.

19. Quoted in *The New York Times*, Jan. 14, 1990.

20. "Speech by V. Väljas, first secretary of the Communist Party of Estonia, at the CPSU Central Committee Plenum, September 19, 1989," *Sovetskaya Estoniya* (Tallinn), Sept, 22, 1989.

21. See David Marples, "The Ukrainian Election Campaign: The Opposition," Radio Free Europe-Radio Liberty (hereafter, RFE-RL), *Report on the USSR* (Munich), Mar. 9, 1990, pp. 17-18. Economic autonomy is particularly important for Ukraine, since 95 percent of its industrial enterprises remain under Union control.

22. In January, Ukrainian separatists met in Jürmala, Latvia, to discuss "Problems of Ukrainian State Independence and Ways to Achieve It." See *Atmoda* (Riga), Feb. 12, 1990, p. 7.

23. *Neue Zürcher Zeitung* (Zürich), Mar. 25-26, 1990.

24. See *Pravda Ukrainy* (Kiev), Dec. 3, 1989.

25. See Jury Sienkowski and Kathleen Mihalisko, "Demonstrators Call for Free Belorussia," RFE-RL, *Report on the USSR*, Mar. 9, 1990, pp. 18-19.

26. TASS, Mar. 3, 1990.

27. *Pravda*, Feb. 1, 1990.

28. *The New York Times*, Mar. 10, 1990.

29. TASS, Feb. 27, 1990.

30. Annette Bohr, "Turkmenistan under Perestroika: An Overview," RFE-RL, *Report on the USSR*, Mar. 23, 1990. pp. 20-30.

31. In 1988 and 1989, the Baltic states offered a safe haven, political advice, and logistical support to movements from other republics still harassed and persecuted by their authorities. In 1990, the Baltic Council, a coordinating body of the popular fronts from Estonia, Latvia, and Lithuania, acted as mediator in the attempt to negotiate the conflict over Nagorno-Karabakh between the popular fronts of Armenia and Azerbaijan. After initial talks broke down, the Georgian popular front stepped in as go-between. The Tbilisi talks continue; they have produced various ceasefires and exchanges of prisoners and hostages. These diplomatic efforts have demonstrated that the popular fronts are capable of organizing and communicating outside the traditional channels of the Soviet system.

32. Published in English in *The New York Review of Books* (New York), Mar. 29, 1990, p. 27. Sakharov advocated a constitutional restructuring based on the principles of full equality, independence, and voluntary association (interview in *Komsomolskaya Pravda* [Moscow], Dec. 16, 1989). Yel'tsin favors a loose federation, with those republics that remain in the union having maximum independence and with the center retaining only some functions of strategic planning (interview in *Sovetskaya Estoniya*, Feb. 20, 1990). Yet, federalism is but an aspect of the democratization advocated by these reform groups. Their calls for a better division of powers, checks and balances, pluralism, democratic parliamentarism, decentralization, and self-government coincide with many demands of pro-independence forces in the republics. Many of their chief proponents belong to the Interregional Group of Deputies and other democratic alliances.

33. *The Boston Sunday Globe*, Jan. 28, 1990.

34. "The New Russia in a Changing World," *Literaturnaya Rossiya* (Moscow), Jan. 26, 1990, pp. 3-4, quoted in John Dunlop, "Ethnic Russians on Possible Breakup of the USSR," RFE-RL, *Report on the USSR*, Mar. 2, 1990, pp. 16-17.

35. Party members from the Baltic republics, Belorussia, and the RSFSR have created a "Renewed Federation" council. Georgiy Komarov, a Russian deputy from Kirgizia, has set up a "Soyuz" group in the Supreme Soviet whose aim is to resist "the breakup of the Soviet Union." Except for advocating a strong center and denouncing local pro-independence activists, these conservative organizations offer few ideas about how to revive the federation. See *Sovetskaya Latviya*, Jan. 24, 1990; TASS, Feb. 24, 1990.

36. *Pravda*, Mar. 16, 1990. Gorbachev has previously rejected the idea of drawing up a new treaty of union, since this would be tantamount to acknowledging that the USSR is not a voluntary union of sovereign republics. At the February 1990 CPSU Central Committee plenum, various leaders of republic parties, Foreign Minister Eduard Shevardnadze, and his deputy A. Kovalev came out in support of the idea. See Ann Sheehy, "Is Moscow Considering a New Treaty of Union?" RFE-FL, *Report on the USSR*, Feb. 16, 1990, pp. 9-11.

37. See the discussion in W. H. Riker, *Federalism: Origin, Operation, Significance*, Boston, Little, Brown & Co., 1964, pp. 5ff.

38. Gorbachev, *Fate*.

39. Ibid.

40. Quoted in *The New York Times*, July 2, 1989.

41. Speech to the Communist Party of Lithuania, January 13, 1990, quoted in ibid., Jan. 14, 1990.

42. Ibid., Mar. 8, 1990. Politicians, legal experts, and historians in the Baltics challenge these secession procedures on moral and legal grounds. Since their occupied territories had been annexed by force and their membership in the Union is null and void, their dissociation from the USSR is considered an act of international law, not subject to Soviet legislation on secession.

43. "Speech by M. S. Gorbachev, First Secretary of the CPSU, at the CPSU Central Committee Special Plenary Session on December 26, 1989," *Pravda*, Dec. 27, 1989.

44. Ibid., Mar. 16, 1990. See the Platform for the 28th CPSU Congress, ibid., Feb. 13, 1990.

45. Gorbachev, *Fate*.

46. See Zotov, loc. cit., pp. 79-39; Zharnikov, loc. cit., pp. 58-67. The respective terms in German, *Bundesstaat* (federation, literally federation of states) and *Staatenbund* (confederation, states in federation), illustrate the gradational differences. In the former, the emphasis is on the center, the federal level; in the latter, it is on the member states.

47. The relationship between the USA and Puerto Rico, Denmark and the Faroe Islands, Switzerland and Liechtenstein, or 19th-century Russia and the Duchy of Finland can be described as federacy or associated state federalism. See the discussion of various models of federal association in the field of politics, economy, and churches in I. Duchacek, *Comparative Federalism: The Territorial Dimension of Politics*, Lanham, MD, University Press of America, 1987, pp. 18ff.

48. Krasnoyarsk territory alone is vaster than the Baltic states, the Transcaucasus, and Central Asia put together. In terms of population and economic potential, some autonomous republics (the Tatar and Bashkir ASSR's) are larger than some union republics (Estonia, Latvia, Moldavia). And some oblasts (Moscow, Leningrad, Sverdlovsk) and territories (Krasnodar, Krasnoyarsk) are comparable to entire regions.

49. "Not a Return to Confederation But Development of the Federation," *Sovetskaya Latviya*, Oct. 21, 1989. In his election platform, Boris Yel'tsin suggested the creation of four economic regions in the RSFSR.

50. "Democracy and Borders," *Literaturnaya Gazeta* (Moscow), Aug. 2, 1989.

51. K. Lagutin, quoted in *Pravda*, Nov. 9, 1989.

52. *CPSU Nationalities Platform*, loc.cit., Yu. Maslyukov, candidate member of the CPSU Politburo and chairman of the USSR Gosplan, "Strong Center--Strong Republics," ibid., Mar. 23, 1989.

53. *CPSU Nationalities Platform*, loc. cit. See the extensive discussion of the notion of national self-determination in Zharnikov, loc. cit., pp. 63-67.

54. "Report by M. S. Gorbachev on the Party's Nationalities Policy at the CPSU Central Committee Plenum, September 19, 1989" (hereafter, *Report*), *Pravda*, Sept. 20, 1989.

55. See Article 14 of the "Fundamental Legislation of the USSR and the Union Republics on Land," *Izvestiya*, Mar. 7, 1990.

56. On January 1, 1990, Estonia, Latvia, and Lithuania introduced republic cost-accounting. The Tatar Autonomous Soviet Socialist Republic, Moscow, and Sverdlovsk oblast have similar arrangements. Limited economic autonomy allows these regions to race ahead, denationalizing assets and freeing locally-set prices more rapidly than other regions. The Supreme Soviet of the Lithuanian SSR, for instance, has adopted laws that allow unrestricted private ownership and free enterprise. In Latvia and Estonia, the number of independent peasants is surpassing the number employed by state farms. And in Estonia, some prices have been deregulated, creating the conditions for marketization.

57. *Ekonomicheskaya Gazeta* (Moscow), No. 43, 1989, pp. 4-7.

58. *Pravda*, Jan. 17, 1990.

59. Deutsche Presse Agentur, Mar. 1, 1990. The Bank of Estonia, for instance, has announced that it will issue its own currency in December 1990. The gold-backed, freely convertible Esti kroon is supposed to jumpstart economic reform and to protect domestic markets against excessive purchasing by consumers from other republics. Such republic currencies stand for the second currency advocated by some economists. Properly managed, they could contribute to monetization and accelerate, rather than impede, economic reforms.

60. *Izvestiya*, Feb. 21, 1990.

61. Speech to the USSR Supreme Soviet, Feb. 27, 1990, in Foreign Broadcast Information Service, *Daily Report: Soviet Union* (Washington, DC—hereafter, *FBIS-SOV*), Mar. 1, 1990, p. 58.

62. For a discussion of politically and economically motivated disruptions of trade with the Baltic states, see Bill Keller, "Baltics Say Kremlin Blocks Economic Shifts," *The New York Times*, Feb. 11, 1990.

63. See the discussion by S. Cheshko, "Economic Sovereignty and the National Question," *Kommunist*, No. 2, January 1989, pp. 97-105; also A. Maslov, "On the Legal Foundations of Economic Sovereignty, ibid., No. 7, May 1989, pp. 57-60.

64. "Our Own Common Market is an Alternative," *Izvestiya*, Feb. 21, 1990.

65. See *Sovetskaya Estoniya*, Oct. 15, 1989; and the debates at the CPSU Central Committee Plenum on the nationalities question, *Pravda*, Sept. 22 and 23, 1989.

66. See the Estonian Gosplan's "Document on Economic Accountability," *Sovetskaya Estoniya*, Sept. 19, 22, 23, and 24, 1989; the "Program" of the Armenian National Movement, *Komsomolets* (Yerevan), Nov. 4, 1989; the "Manifesto" of the Georgian National Accord Group, *Molodezh' Gruzii* (Tbilisi), Nov. 14, 1989; or the Moldavian Council of Ministers' "Concept for Socio-Economic Independence," quoted in *Izvestiya*, Dec. 11, 1989.

67. *Sovetskaya Litva* (Vilnius), Feb. 21, 1990. See the discussion by Kazimiera Prunskiene, "On Property Relations Between the Lithuanian SSR and the USSR," ibid., Nov. 8, 1989. Lithuania's Supreme Soviet, for instance, has submitted an alternative draft for the new USSR Law on Property containing these provisions (*Sovetskaya Rossiya* [Moscow], Nov. 21, 1989).

68. The main objective was to claim a permanent seat for Belorussia and Ukraine in the United Nations; otherwise this article existed on paper only. Contacts between republics and foreign states were almost always made through Moscow, and the role of the republics' foreign ministries was minimal. Lithuanian authorities, for instance, are still not supposed to negotiate regional and local issues directly with the Polish government.

69. Given the close links between Finland and Estonia, Väljas, First Secretary of the Communist Party of Estonia, accompanied General Secretary Gorbachev on his visit to Finland in October 1989. Soviet delegations to the United Nations have also started to include representatives from the republic foreign ministries and other republic officials.

70. See the interview with Yu. Kuplyakov, chief of the USSR Foreign Ministry Union Republics Department in *Izvestiya*, Nov. 21, 1989.

71. *Sovetskaya Moldaviya* (Kishinev), Jan. 30, 1990.

72. The Baltic republics can rely on the services of their legations in the United States and in other Western capitals where they continued to function since the 1940's. Thus, after the Malta meeting, in the highest-level contact in decades, US Assistant Secretary of State Raymond Seitz personally briefed semi-official Baltic representatives on the outcome of the summit. Baltic leaders have suggested that Estonia, Latvia, and Lithuania might follow the example of Switzerland and some Third World national-liberation movements and seek observer status at the Untied Nations. According to a report in *The New York Times*, Dec. 10, 1989, aides to UN Secretary General Javier Pérez de Cuéllar and leaders of the three Baltic popular fronts have had several encounters. After this press report, the United Nations announced that the contacts will not be continued, allegedly because Moscow protested.

73. Presently, foreign consulates operate in Leningrad, Kiev, and Minsk.

74. See the discussion on the republics' foreign policy interests in: "Listening to One Another—*Kommunist, Kommunist Sovetskoy Latvii, Kommunist Estonii,* and *Kommunist* (Lithuania) Roundtable," *Kommunist* (Moscow), No. 6, April 1989, pp. 76ff.

75. See Boris Yel'tsin in *Sovetskaya Molodezh'*, Feb. 6, 1990.

76. See Yazov in *Izvestiya,* Mar. 12, 1990; Moiseyev, in *Trud* (Moscow), Mar. 13, 1990.

77. In the Baltic republics, organizations such as Geneva-49, Cross of Fire, or the Women's League assist draft dodgers and deserters. In Ukraine, the Union of Independent Ukrainian Youth, the Helsinki Union, and other opposition groups demand the creation of a Ukrainian defense ministry and national forces. In Kishinev, the

National Guard group is encouraging Moldavians not to serve in the Soviet army. In Georgia, the Supreme Soviet has decided to bring up as a legislative initiative the question of restoring Georgian national military formations. Many of the opposition groups are urging a boycott of the "Soviet occupation army." Radical wings in the Armenian Liberation Movement and the Azerbaijani People's Front have organized their own militias.

78. Moscow Television Service in Russian, Feb. 27, 1990, translated in *FBIS-SOV,* Feb. 28, 1990, pp. 47-48. In an angry reaction, Gorbachev suggested excluding the Baltic deputies from the voting quorum.

79. John C. Calhoun, *Disquisition on Government and Selections from the Discourse*, Gordon D. Post, ed., New York, Bobbs-Merrill, 1953.

80. The RSFSR has 11 representatives for the republic, 64 for 16 autonomous republics, 10 for 5 autonomous regions, and 10 for 10 autonomous areas. In the old composition, with each chamber having 750 seats, the RSFSR occupied 33 and 56 percent of the seats respectively. The predominance of the RSFSR has thus been reinforced in the new, smaller Supreme Soviet.

81. For a breakdown of the ethnic composition of the Congress of People's Deputies and the Supreme Soviet, see V. Tishkov, "Assembly of Nations or Union Parliament?" *Soyuz* (Moscow), No. 1, January 1990, pp. 3-4. With the first of the annual rotations coming up in May 1990, the ethnic composition of the Supreme Soviet is likely to shift further in favor of the Russians, since they are underrepresented relative to their 45.6 percent share of seats in the Congress.

82. *Izvestiya*, Feb. 5, 1990.

83. Tishkov, loc. cit.

84. In 1956, Khrushchev set up a Russian Bureau in the Central Committee, but it was abolished by the 23rd Party Congress in 1966. The other departments dealt directly with RSFSR affairs; a parallel body covering the Russian federation thus became superfluous.

85. *Pravda*, Mar. 10, 1990.

86. Ibid., Mar. 16, 1990.

87. Moscow Television Service in Russian, Feb. 27, 1990, trans. in *FBIS-SOV*, Feb. 28, 1990, pp. 47-48. The Supreme Soviet of Georgia, in turn, issued a resolution instructing their deputies to abstain from voting on the Law on the Presidency, and declaring
"null and void" the provisions limiting the sovereign rights of the republic. TASS, Mar. 9, 1990.

88. In the CPSU Platform, the introduction of the presidency is justified with the argument that parliamentarism is still in its "formative stage," and that therefore a "reliable and effective mechanism" for the implementation of legislation is needed. *Pravda*, Feb. 13, 1990. Ryzhkov specifically refers to the draft law on land which was submitted to parliament in September 1989 and accepted at its third reading in February 1990. TASS, Feb. 27, 1990.

89. Moscow Television Service in Russian, Mar. 2, 1990, trans. in *FBIS-SOV*, Mar. 5, 1990, p. 60.

90. See Article 127, Para. 4 of the revised constitution, *Izvestiy*a, Mar. 16, 1990.

91. See the drafts of the Law on the State of Emergency and the Law on Accountability for the Infringement of Citizen's Rights and the Violation of the Territorial Integrity of the USSR. The strengthening of the troops of the Ministry of the Interior, the creation of military task forces, and the transformation of the KGB's Fifth Directorate into a Department for Constitutional Compliance provide the president with the material basis

for enforcing emergency provisions. See "Moscow TV Carries 26 Feb. Supreme Soviet Session," *FBIS-SOV*, Feb. 27, 1990, pp. 40-43.

92. "USSR Law on Instituting the Post of President of the USSR," *Izvestiya*, Mar. 16, 1990.

93. *The New York Times*, Mar. 14, 1990.

94. The Soviet press shows great interest in the events in Yugoslavia; see, for example, Y. Vostrukhov in *Izvestiya*, Sept. 23 and 28, 1989. The Party Statute of the League of Communists of Yugoslavia guarantees that no decision is taken without the consent of the parties of the major republics, i.e., Croatia, Serbia, and Slovenia. Each of them has a de facto veto right. Without their votes, the central bodies cannot reach the required quorum.

95. See the CPSU Platform for the 28th Party Congress, loc. cit.; and the Draft CPSU Statutes, *Pravda*, Mar. 28, 1990.

96. Gorbachev, *Fate*. See the proceedings of the CPSU Central Committee Special Plenary Session on December 25 and 26, 1989, ibid., Dec. 26 and 27, 1989. Gorbachev has presented the most detailed critique of a decentralized party in his "Appeal to the Communists of Lithuania," delivered to the LCP Central Committee Plenum by V.A. Medvedev, member of the Politburo, on December 1, 1989, ibid., Dec. 3, 1989.

97. Article 115 and Article 119, Para. 5. The procedures and results of such a nation-wide discussion remain somewhat unclear. In the 1935 constitution, the republics had the right to propose a country-wide referendum. While this provision has never been put into effect, it provided the republics at least with an option to challenge legislation of the central authorities. The right to initiate a referendum is now reserved to the president and the Congress of People's Deputies.

98. See the proposal to introduce ratification of Union legislation by the republics' legislatures in Andrey Sakharov, "Speech to the Congress," *The New York Review of Books*, August 17, 1989, pp. 25-26. The 1924 constitution had stipulated the right of the republics to object to laws passed by central authorities. The right was dropped in the 1936 constitution.

99. See the critique of the Soviet constitution in Andrey Sakharov, "On the Constitution," *Komsomolskaya Pravda*, Oct. 8, 1989.

100. Article 125 according to "USSR Law on Amendments and Additions to Article 125 of the USSR Constitution," *Izvestiya*, Dec. 26, 1989. (In the newest constitutional revision, the numeration has changed to Art. 124). A Law on Constitutional Compliance specifying the competencies and procedures of the Committee is in preparation. *Pravda*, Dec. 22, 1989.

101. *The New York Times*, Feb. 28, 1990.

102. In a symbolically important step toward an independent judiciary, the Congress has amended the Law on the Presidency so that the Constitutional Oversight Committee is not appointed by the president, as originally proposed, but by the Congress.

103. I. Gryazin, quoted in TASS (English Service), Dec. 21, 1989. The Baltic Parliamentary Group issued a statement criticizing the draft and abstained from voting on the amendment; the Group does not feel bound by the Committee's finding. See the speech by K. V. Motieka at the Second Session of the Congress of People's Deputies, Moscow Television Service in Russian, Dec. 22, 1989, trans. in *FBIS-SOV*, Dec. 27, 1989, pp. 65-66. See also the statement by Yuriy Afanas'yev in the name of the Interregional Group of Deputies, ibid., Dec. 22, 1989, pp. 40-42. Boris Yel'tsin subsequently suggested the creation of a constitutional court for the RSFSR.

104. The best example of Gorbachev's informal bargaining approach is his handling of Lithuania up to the declaration of independence on March 11, 1990. On several occasions, Gorbachev summoned the leadership of the Communist Party of Lithuania to Moscow in an attempt to reconcile the actions by the Lithuanian parliament and party with his own agenda. He also met regularly with the Lithuanian delegates to the USSR People's Congress, dispatched several high-ranking party leaders to Lithuania in a last-ditch attempt to prevent the secession of the republic's communist party from the CPSU.

105. In November 1988, the Supreme Soviet of Estonia amended Article 70 of its constitution to empower the republic parliament to suspend the application of USSR laws and ordinances in Estonia if it deems them to infringe on the republic's sovereignty, to violate the republic's constitution and laws, or to conflict with the republic's best interests in general. The Supreme Soviets of Azerbaijan, Georgia, Moldavia, Latvia, and Lithuania also decreed the supremacy of the legislation of the republic over that of the Union. See *Pravda,*, Nov. 19, 1989, for Azerbaijan's action; *Izvestiya*, Nov. 21, 1989, for Georgia; and *Pravda*, Nov. 24, 1989, for Moldavia. While the details of the constitutional amendments vary, they share the same view on the precedence of republic over Union legislation.

106. "A Fourth Constitution: Pros and Cons," *New Times* (Moscow), No. 41, October 1989, pp. 34-37. But Lubchenko rejects the drafting of a new constitution, on the grounds that there would be no consensus on its provisions.

ABOUT THE BOOK
AND EDITOR

Setting the context for the crisis that has fragmented the former USSR, this reader presents key essays by notable Western scholars who have shaped the debates within the field of Soviet nationality studies. Focusing first on the historical development of the Soviet multiethnic state, the discussions then turn to specific problem areas, including federalism, elites, economy, language policy, and nationalism. An introductory essay by the editor discusses how the works in the book contribute to our understanding of the current disintegration and analyzes opposing perspectives in the debates. Intended for use as a textbook in undergraduate or graduate courses on Soviet nationality problems or Soviet and post-Soviet domestic politics, this anthology will be valuable for students and professors alike.

Rachel Denber is a member of the W. Averell Harriman Institute for Advanced Study of the Soviet Union and a Ph.D. candidate at Columbia University. She is currently a research associate at Helsinki Watch.

ABOUT THE CONTRIBUTORS

Barbara A. Anderson is professor of sociology at the University of Michigan.

John A. Armstrong is professor emeritus in political science at the University of Wisconsin.

Donna Bahry is professor of political science at the University of California at Davis.

Mark Beissinger is associate professor of political science at the University of Wisconsin at Madison.

Walker Connor is professor of political science at Trinity College.

John Dunlop is senior fellow at the Hoover Institution.

Hélène Carrère d'Encausse is professor of political science at the Institute of Political Sciences in Paris.

Gregory Gleason is assistant professor of political science at the University of New Mexico.

Paul Goble is senior associate at the Carnegie Endowment.

Grey Hodnett is senior political analyst in the office of Slavic and Eurasian Analysis, Central Intelligence Agency.

Stephan Kux is lecturer at the University of Zurich.

Gail Warshofsky Lapidus is professor of political science at the University of California at Berkeley.

John H. Miller is senior lecturer in politics at La Trobe University in Melbourne, Australia.

Alexander J. Motyl is associate professor of political science at Columbia University and director of the Program on Soviet Nationality and Siberian Studies at the W. Averell Harriman Institute for Advanced Study of the Soviet Union.

Carol Nechemias is associate professor at the Division of Public Affairs at Pennsylvania State University.

Richard Pipes is professor of history at Harvard University.

Jonathan Pool is associate professor of political science at the University of Washington.

Teresa Rakowska-Harmstone is professor of political science at Carleton University.

Philip G. Roeder is assistant professor of political science at the University of California at San Diego.

Gertrude E. Schroeder is professor of economics at the University of Virginia.

Brian D. Silver is professor of political science at Michigan State University.

Ronald Grigor Suny is professor of history at the University of Michigan.

Roman Szporluk is professor of history at Harvard University.

V. Stanley Vardys is professor of political science at the University of Oklahoma.